THE SECRET ARMY

DEDICATION

This book is for three men who at different times tried to give me some insight into the subtle mysteries of history. I should like to think that their patience and their training if not completely successful in my case has, nevertheless, not gone for nothing.

William A. Jenks
Eber Malcolm Carroll
Harold T. Parker

THE SECRET ARMY
THE IRA
1916-1979

J. Bowyer Bell

POOLBEG

First published 1970
Revised edition published 1974
Revised and updated edition published 1979
This edition published 1989 by
Poolbeg Press Ltd
Knocksedan House,
Swords, Co Dublin, Ireland
Reprinted 1990

© J. Bowyer Bell 1970, 1979, 1989, 1990

ISBN 1 85371 027 X

Cover design by Pomphrey Associates
Printed by The Guernsey Press Ltd
Vale, Guernsey, Channel Islands.

CONTENTS

FOREWORD TO 1979 EDITION

Some months ago, while lecturing before a Provisional Sinn Féin seminar on the British response to colonial insurgencies, Richard Behal rose with a question he had previously asked me inordinately long years ago where my odyssey through the Republican movement began. While the question had remained the same — the Irish have long and exacting memories — I suspect my answer had not. In any case, having come full circle, it seemed time to bring the *Secret Army* up to date. In so doing I have not altered the text of any of the previous editions, except in one place and with apologies to Charlie McGlade, but merely added new material chronologically. This means that there still remain odds and ends that might well have been rewritten for greater accuracy or with keener hindsight. I have also kept to the basic scheme of giving each decade approximately the same space which clearly means that the last ten years of violence, turmoil, schism and change receive less than justice in terms of pages. As always, the sources have been people rather than the printed word and, of course, people with good reason not to be exceedingly forthcoming. It remains, however, impressive and heartening how many have been willing to talk into an alien ear. Of course, with the secret army back in the army business, many of the involved were actively engaged in shooting and being shot at. Thus, my in the first place not very academic research became less so, in that over the years, I have been shot at, gassed and bombed, questioned and followed — even had my phone tapped, that most elegant of status symbols. It has often been field work too close to the centre of the field. Finally, again, there are all those in Ireland whom I should like to thank for their time, their efforts and their friendship and who with few exceptions are undoubtedly delighted that they will not be singled out by name. The one exception I make is for Oliver Snoddy — who still sits at the centre of his vast web of contacts and sources, still always on call.

So here is the new model *Secret Army* up to date — perhaps engaged in an end game, perhaps not — but still beyond the reach of a final chapter.

New York City
Pembroke Lane, Dublin.

Beir Bua
J.B.B.

FOREWORD

My odyssey across the troubled waters, past and present, of Irish Republican politics began several years ago in Kilkenny. I drove over the River Barrow at Graiguenamanagh up the saddle of Coppanagh and down to Inistioge, the most attractive village in Leinster, to meet Paddy Murphy, then unknown to me, near the Spotted Dog. In the fullness of Celtic time and through various intermediaries, the Army Council of the IRA relayed to me in the regal Horse-Protestant atmosphere of the Russell Hotel on St. Stephen's Green their "utmost co-operation" in my projected history. Although this agreement was hardly binding on former volunteers and immediately assured that I would be regarded with deep suspicion in some quarters—in and out of the Republican Movement—nothing would have been possible without the tolerance and at times encouragement of the anonymous Army Council. As a result of the meeting in the Russell's upstairs lounge, I have spent more time on the IRA than a good many volunteers have spent in it.

I have travelled through all thirty-two counties, stood in a blinding snowstorm to hear Tomás MacGiolla's Easter Oration at Carrickmore in the hills of Tyrone, sat in the front room of Liam Ryan's on a summer's evening in the village of Doon in the hills of East Limerick to talk of the lost glory days, and listened to the young men in the Tomás Ashe Memorial Hall in Cork to dissect the new Sinn Féin. I have for several hours—vicariously—been on the run in Belfast when the Royal Ulster Constabulary after a banned meeting arrested several prominent Republicans, including my travelling companion Tom Mitchell, and then several months later had the opportunity to talk it over with the Northern Ireland Home Minister William Craig and Chief Inspector Sir Arthur Kennedy of the RUC. I have been to more Republican commemorations in the stretch of a year or two than anyone in Ireland but Joe Clarke, 1916 veteran, who two crutches or not, appears inevitably like the Spirit of Fenians Past. I have talked politics with Catholic students at Trinity College, failed monks, Senators, Aran Islanders, and Anglican clerics. I have listened to the daily tea seminars at the offices of the *United Irishman*, to the chatter in the pubs, and to the unsolicited wisdom of Celtic strangers on matters of personality and policy. I have fully enjoyed if not profited from it all.

I should perhaps have remained safely in the newspaper room of the National Library on Kildare Street, a high, draughty chamber filled with rustlings and coughs, which I grew to loathe. But there is no better introduction to the intricate world of Irish politics than the Irish—and no more charming, perverse, delightful, and mysterious people exist. And this book could not have existed without the quiet co-operation of well over a hundred individuals who gave me their time and told their story: this in a country where the battle of books is carried on into the pubs and lanes, and alien authors are anathema. I am not Irish, have no Irish connections to leave as hostage, and can remain off the island until any controversy that might arise dies down in ten or twenty years; but those who helped me are left, unprotected, to the all but inevitable howls of outraged indignation, to be savaged at the parish pump and hooted over the Guinness. Partly to minimize the anguish and spread out the guilt, I have squirrelled away the names of those to whom I am indebted (even those who read sections of the manuscript) deep in the bibliographical note and here leave them without the individual thanks they so richly deserve.

To the initiated the book that has resulted will seem curiously constructed: apparently as the present comes closer more and more is written about fewer and fewer. The glorious years from 1916–1921 are skimped and the narrow ones of the last decades delineated in detail. Essentially this is a study of an organization, a secret army, not of Irish political history or the impact or importance of the IRA. Obviously the IRA was the central force in Ireland in 1921, a significant factor in the 'thirties, and of much less importance in the 'fifties; nevertheless, generally speaking, each decade receives equal treatment. Still, the secret army in the service of the invisible Republic has had a greater effect on Irish events than might be assumed and it is essentially these hidden corridors of power after 1923 that have interested me. To write of the invisible has, as noted, required the aid of those who were there, within or without the Army; but I have often had to choose between conflicting stories, discard some evidence, and stitch together the narrative as I saw fit. Thus I remain wholly responsible for my text, and all errors of omission and commission are mine and can not be shuffled off onto my sources.

As for specific acknowledgements, the following have been of help in easing my way in unofficial channels, in the pursuit of the right contact, in the collection of material or in the weighing of evidence: Colonel H. Connor (Military Attaché, United States Embassy, Dublin), Seán Cooney (Dublin), Desmond Fitzgerald (Dublin), Senator Garrett Fitzgerald (Dublin), Richard Geffhert (Political Attaché, United States Embassy, Dublin), Richard Griffin (New York Institute of Technology Library, New York City), Dr. Hayes (National Library, Dublin), Patrick Henchy (National Library, Dublin), J. G. Hill (Ministry of Home Affairs, Stormont, Northern Ireland), Brigadier F. G. MacMullen (Military Attaché, British Embassy, Dublin), Brian Murphy (Dublin), Liam Murphy (Irvington, N.Y.), T. P. O'Neill (Dublin), Desmond Roche (Institute of Public Administration, Dublin), George Thayer (New York City). Several of the younger scholars working in the same general area have been kind enough to talk to me about their work: Maurice Manning ("The Blueshirts", M.A., Trinity College, Dublin), Peter Pyne ("Sinn Féin", M.A., University College, Dublin), Sister Bernard Mary ("Joseph McGarrity", Ph.D. Thesis, St. Johns, New York City), and Art Mitchell ("Irish Labour Party", Ph.D. Thesis, Trinity College, Dublin).

Three men have a special place in this book and at risk of contamination must accept my special thanks. Tony Meade, editor of the *United Irishman*, 1965–1967, and now with the *Kerryman*, gave of his time and energy and unsparingly of his enthusiasm. Charlie Murphy perhaps unwisely accepted responsibility for my first long, incredibly detailed briefings on the IRA in the 'fifties and yet remained cheerful, patient, and always on call. Oliver Snoddy, a brilliant scholar in his own right, sitting amid dusty swords and piled tomes in his office in the National Museum at the centre of a vast intelligence net stretching through Ireland, inevitably could put me onto the right man or the proper lead.

Finally while I was out under the hedgerows or in the back rooms of pubs, there were those who stayed behind in Pembroke Lane in Dublin or the Glebe House in St. Mullins. My eldest daughter learned to wear a tie to school, my next to speak, we think, in Irish, and my then youngest to walk in Ireland. There is now a fourth and "Irish" daughter, additional evidence of the charms of an Irish academic adventure. For my wife beset by my daughters, by my Irish Republican friends, who bore little resemblance to her Philadelphia variety, and in New York by my endless not-to-be-interrupted typing, the slow unfolding of the adventures of the invisible army has, I fear, been all too visible and much too slow—but as always she has coped.

Beir Bua

J.B.B.

St. Mullins, Co. Carlow
Ballsbridge, Dublin
New York City
Knightsbridge, London

1. Londonderry	7. Donegal	16. Meath	25. Wexford
2. Antrim	8. Leitrim	17. Westmeath	26. Waterford
3. Tyrone	9. Sligo	18. Offaly	27. Tipperary
4. Fermanagh	10. Mayo	19. Kildare	28. Galway
5. Armagh	11. Roscommon	20. Dublin	29. Clare
6. Down	12. Longford	21. Wicklow	30. Limerick
	13. Cavan	22. Carlow	31. Cork
	14. Monaghan	23. Laoighis	32. Kerry
	15. Louth	24. Kilkenny	

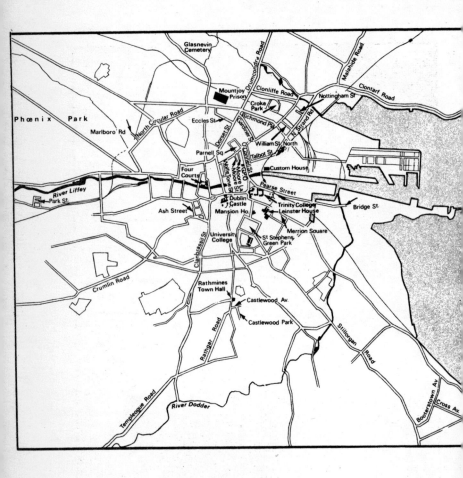

DUBLIN

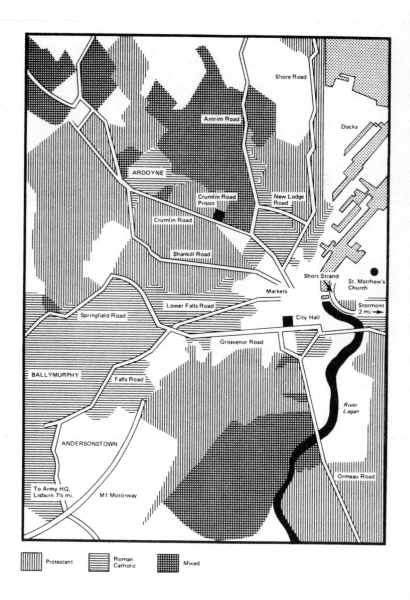

BELFAST

To subvert the tyranny of our execrable government, to break the connection with England, the never-failing source of all our political evils, and to assert the independence of my country—these were my objects. To unite the whole people of Ireland, to abolish the memory of all past dissensions, and to substitute the common name of Irishmen in place of the denomination of Protestant, Catholic, and Dissenter—these were my means.

WOLFE TONE

Life springs from death: and from the graves of patriot men and women spring living nations. The Defenders of this Realm have worked in secret and in the open. They think that they have pacified Ireland. They think that they have purchased half of us and intimidated the other half. They think that they have foreseen everything, think that they have provided against everything; but the fools, the fools, the fools!—they have left us our Fenian dead, and while Ireland holds these graves, Ireland unfree shall never be at peace.

PÁDRAIC PEARSE

It is not those who can inflict the most, but those that can suffer the most who will conquer . . .

TERENCE MACSWINEY

PART I

The Glorious Years: 1916–1927

CHAPTER 1

The Rising: The Republic Proclaimed, The Army Committed, April–September 1916

At a few minutes past noon on Monday, April 24, a glorious spring day, Pádriac Pearse came out between the Ionic columns of the General Post Office on Sackville Street in the heart of Dublin and began reading from a large, hastily printed Proclamation. In front of him was a scant crowd of the curious; behind him, inside the GPO, the forces of the Irish Republic which he was proclaiming were securing the building. Pearse finished. There was the odd cheer, mostly from his own men, and then more waiting. On the roof of the GPO, several volunteers ran up first a green flag, emblazoned Irish Republic, and then the green-white-and-orange tricolour. There were a few more scattered cheers. The very curious read the Proclamations stuck up on the walls, addressed by the Provisional Government of the Irish Republic to the people of Ireland. There were seven signatures to the Proclamation: Thomas J. Clarke, Seán MacDiarmada, P. H. Pearse, James Connolly, Thomas MacDonagh, Eamon Ceannt, and Joseph Plunkett. Some were well-known eccentrics: Tom Clarke, the old Fenian felon with a tobacco shop, Pearse with his Irish-Irish School out in Rathfarnham, and James Connolly, Ireland's most distinguished Labour radical and professional agitator. Apart from these, none of the other men were known except to the British police and a narrow circle of extreme nationalists. The Proclamation of the Republic was to change all that; but to the few who watched events from outside on Sackville Street or as temporary prisoners inside the GPO the whole affair reeked of farce. And yet as a young volunteer called Michael Collins began breaking the windows in the GPO to prepare for the defence of the headquarters of the new Republic, the onlookers realized that the mad men in their grey-green uniforms and slouched hats were serious. Across the Liffey an Irish Citizen Army group, Connolly's two-hundred-man force, shot the sentry at the Castle gate, broke in the yard, but then retired to the City Hall and the newspaper offices across the street from the main gate without realizing that the Castle had been stripped clean of British soldiers and lay open for the taking. Elsewhere Citizen Army men took over St. Stephen's Green and began digging trenches. A thousand Irish Volunteers occupied positions in an erratic arc around the rim of Dublin proper: Boland's Bakery and some houses commanding the approaches from Kingstown (Dun Laoghaire), Jacob's

Factory, a vast workhouse (the South Dublin Union), the Four Courts on the Liffey, positions near the railway stations, and on the North Wall. As at the GPO, there was little opposition. As at the Castle, there was almost total surprise. Despite ample evidence to the contrary, few in a position of power had in their wildest dreams imagined that the Irish would "rise again". A close watch had been kept on radicals like Connolly and extreme nationalists like Pearse, their newspapers had been shut down, their speeches monitored, and their names inscribed high on the list of the potentially dangerous; but no one had really expected open rebellion, if that was what was actually unfolding in Dublin early on Monday afternoon.

With the British caught entirely by surprise, the nerve centre at the Castle in jeopardy, the allocated positions occupied as intended by the forces of the Irish Republic, and the populace dumbfounded at the audacity of the rebels, the seven-man provisional Government might have been expected to feel well-pleased. The Republic had been proclaimed, and the tricolour flew over Dublin; but any joy was tempered by the cold knowledge that short of a miracle the Republic was doomed to a short and violent life.

The original decision to rise against the British had been taken at a meeting of the Irish Republican Brotherhood (IRB) soon after the European war began in August 1914. Then on September 9, in the rooms of the Gaelic League at 25 Parnell Square, the formal decision to revolt at some point during the war was accepted. An Advisory Committee was established but by the end of November the leaders of the IRB felt it was too large and too loose and allowed it to lapse. Instead, detailed planning of the insurrection was taken over in the summer of 1915 by a Military Council of three men, Pearse, Joseph Plunkett and Eamon Ceannt, reporting directly to the Executive of the IRB. In the autumn MacDiarmada and Clarke were brought on the Council, then Connolly in January 1916, and MacDonagh at the last minute in April. The forces for the rising would be drawn from units of the Irish Volunteers. These had been formed in 1913 at least partly in response to the creation by the Unionist Orange establishment of the Ulster Volunteer Force, whose object was to discourage the Liberal Government in London from proclaiming Home Rule for Ireland. The Irish Volunteers had mushroomed in size and by the summer of 1914 numbered 180,000. Few were armed despite the arrival of two "illegal" arms shipments in July/August 1914 and few were dedicated separatists. When the European war began, the leading constitutional Irish politician John Redmond, who had forced his way into the booming organization, pledged Ireland to the British war effort and split the Volunteers. The overwhelming number followed Redmond's lead and many enlisted in the British army. A hard core of eleven or twelve thousand stayed with Eoin MacNéill, the Chief of Staff. This was the base the IRB planned to use for the Rising, augmented by Connolly's Irish Citizens' Army and the tiny Hibernian Rifles financed by the Ancient Order of Hibernians (AOH).

To give the insurrection a better chance the Clan na Gael, the IRB in America, had early on approached the Germans as potential allies. Sir Roger Casement, knighted by the British Government for his consular services, had gone first to New York and then to Germany to attempt to create an Irish Brigade and negotiate an arms shipment for the IRB. By January 1916, the IRB was fully committed to the rising and anticipated the arrival of German aid. Casement in Germany might doubt Germany's good intentions, but the Clan in New York and the IRB in Dublin were willing to take what they could get even if it did not include a German expeditionary force or modern arms in quantity. As soon as the arms arrived, the IRB was ready to go. Connolly, who had often seemed on the verge of setting off a mini-revolt with his tiny Citizen Army, was co-opted onto the Military Council in January and the final plans were drawn up. All this was behind the back of MacNéill who felt that a Rising during the war was out of the question unless the British tried to introduce conscription into Ireland. After the war he was willing to threaten the use of guerrillas to achieve extensive Home Rule but clearly he felt a coup would be foolhardy. The IRB, however, had so penetrated the Volunteers that MacNéill's prudence would not be a serious consideration. When the German arms landed in Kerry, the Volunteers would receive the word to rise without MacNéill's consent.

This was largely the situation at the beginning of April. The arms were expected around Easter. They would be distributed in Kerry, Cork, and up to Limerick. There the country units would hold a great crescent in the south and west. Elsewhere units would rise, drawing off British reinforcements and confusing the pattern. The main key, however, was Dublin where Joseph Plunkett had drawn up an elaborate war plan. Central Dublin would be seized in a *coup de main* while the country rose. The British would be unable to control the country without pouring in massive reinforcements revealing to all that the Crown's control was dependent on British troops not Irish acquiescence. Perhaps if the people, reminded of their revolutionary heritage, came out—even with knives and forks—the British sorely pressed in the Great War might be unwilling, even unable, to pacify Ireland. This was a faint hope at best; the IRB accepted that the Rising would probably be a military failure, but a great and significant moral victory would have been won. Then within a few days of the hour chosen to strike, the whole intricate plot began to fall apart as had so many Irish plots in the past.

MacNéill and his staff suddenly discovered the plans for a rising. The deceit of his colleagues and the foolishness of the plan appalled him. MacNéill was adamantly opposed to an Easter Rising without a real hope of success. On Spy Wednesday, April 19, a document purporting to show the British plans for a swoop on all nationalist centres in Dublin was shown to MacNéill. This, coupled with the revelation that a German arms ship was already on the way, left MacNéill by Friday, April 21, with no alternative but to bow to the inevitability of the Rising. This was the last good news. The arms ship, the *Aud*, had left Lubeck on April 9 without a wireless transmitter and never received word of a change in landing dates. As MacNéill was agreeing to the Rising in Dublin, the *Aud* was being escorted by the British navy to Cobh harbour where Captain Karl Spindler scuttled her. Casement had equally bad luck. After landing from the German U-19, his two companions slipped away to make contact but he was arrested almost at once. The British had known something was up as early as April 18, as a result of a raid on the German Consulate in New York City. With the *Aud* and Casement in their hands by Friday evening, all hope of surprise appeared gone.

On Saturday, with no arms in prospect and the Castle almost certainly aware of the threat, MacNéill was adamant that no rising must take place. On the next morning the *Sunday Independent* carried a notice that the Irish Volunteer manœuvres announced on April 8 in the *Irish Volunteer* would not take place. MacNéill sent messengers to assure that the local units would carry out his last orders and not follow the IRB instructions. For the Military Council Sunday was a deeply depressing day. The loss of the *Aud* meant not only a military fiasco but almost certainly the swift destruction of much of the separatist movement. In fact on Sunday, Ivor Churchill, Baron Wimborne, Lord Lieutenant of Ireland, was unsuccessfully urging swift and extensive arrests. If MacNéill's order was let stand, the movement would be destroyed in any case by routine police measures. Most important the dream of a great blow for Ireland, a new generation's contribution to an Irish Ireland free of the Saxon would be gone; without such a gesture the slow absorption of Ireland into Great Britain would continue unimpeded and with every chance of success. The Military Council decided to strike. The Rising would be a failure, the Volunteers slaughtered and the Military Council shot, but Ireland desperately needed a glorious failure to awake the latent revolutionary tradition.

What to the Military Council and to a great many Irishmen was a glorious tradition, the annual of the delirium of the brave, was to the British the habitual and irrational outbreak of native Irish irresponsibility. During the previous twenty years, despite the persistence of a separatist fringe, the British had come to feel the Irish were at last accepting their rational place within the United Kingdom. Redmond, leader of the Irish Party in the

House of Commons, had pledged Ireland to the war effort. Two hundred thousand Irishmen had volunteered for service. Once the details of Home Rule, held in abeyance until after the war as a result of Orange manœuvres, could be worked out, the Irish problem would be finally resolved. Every sign pointed this way and had for years.

And yet, when on April 23 the Military Council decided on the Rising, the seven men were acting within a tradition and to a large extent as an organization which could trace its antecedents back into the eighteenth century. It was in the eighteenth century that Republicanism had been linked to the long-standing Irish revolutionary tradition. Wolfe Tone, an Irish Republican and Protestant, sought to unite the men of little property into the United Irishmen to break the connection with Great Britain with the help of France and set up an independent Irish Republic. Tone failed twice and the last time in 1798 was arrested and committed suicide in prison. He became not only another martyr but also the founder of Irish Republicanism, his written word the basis for future doctrine and his grave at Bodenstown in County Kildare the centre and shrine for generations of Irish revolutionaries. His contention that the connection with Britain must be broken by physical force became the foundation stone of Irish Republicanism. Robert Emmet tried and failed in 1803. Again in 1848 there was a new movement, Young Ireland, a new leader, John Mitchel, a new rising, and the same old failure, giving rise to new ballads, and new Wild Geese fleeing British persecution. Increasingly after the famine years of the 1840s, Irishmen poured into America, scraped themselves out a place often at great cost, and then many turned their attention to Ireland. Some of the men who had been out in '48 and some of a new generation in 1858 banded together into a new organization,[1] which in time in the United States became known as Clan na Gael. Ireland was organized on American money often by men with military experience gained in the American Civil War. By the mid-'sixties, the IRB—the Fenians—had honey-combed the British Army in Ireland and to some extent in Britain and a successful rising seemed assured. A typical Gaelic combination of bad luck, poor judgement, and informers turned a certainty into a miserable failure and from the years 1865 and 1867 came not an Irish revolution but another defeat, three new martyrs convicted of murder during a prison break, and another broken generation. In 1882 the "Invincibles" assassinated the new Chief Secretary, Lord Frederick Cavendish, and Under-Secretary, T. H. Burke, in Phoenix Park in Dublin. This flurry of violence in the 'eighties coupled with dynamite attacks in Britain seemed to be the last breath of Fenianism for Parnell and Parliamentarianism rode high.

When Parnell came to grief in 1890, shattering the Irish Party, little seemed to stand in the way of the eventual absorption of Ireland into Great

Britain. Even Gladstone's Home Rule had little chance in view of the adamant dissent of the House of Lords. Fenianism and the IRB, like the Young Irelanders and the United Irishmen, appeared more a subject of ballads than a living philosophy. Over 'he past generations Irish national-ism had been killed with kindness, the restrictions against Catholics slowly removed, the inequities of the land system slowly corrected. The old ways seemed to be going: the Irish language a burden not a joy replaced by English, Irish history forgotten in schools teaching the Victorian world view, Irish traditions fading away to be replaced by those of the Empire. There was a place for commercial success, professional recognition, amal-gamation, absorption into the United Kingdom—and many took the route as solicitors and soldiers, estate agents, policemen, and civil servants. Apparently Irish Ireland and Irish Republicanism, attractive to a few romantics or a few malcontents, kept alive more by exiled Americans than common sense, had seen its day.

Yet in the bleak years after Parnell, there were new if not yet powerful forces at work within and without the tradition of Irish Republicanism. In 1884 the Gaelic Athletic Association was formed to urge the old games, hurling and Irish football, on the young men. In 1893 the Gaelic League was founded in Dublin to salvage the dying Irish language and almost immediately was tremendously popular as the classrooms became jammed with eager scholars and young men stalked the West to hear the living language.[2] At the centenary of the 1798 rising, Wolfe Tone clubs were formed, attracting more onto the Republican path. In that year several Fenian prisoners were released, including Tom Clarke, and were greeted all over Ireland with bonfires on the hills. In 1902 a National Council with separatist aims was founded and in 1905 the Dungannon Clubs were begun in Belfast where Bulmer Hobson edited *The Republic*. The next year the Dungannon Clubs and Cumann na nGaedheal united to form the Sinn Féin League which absorbed the National Council in September 1908 and became Sinn Féin. Almost entirely a creation of Arthur Griffith, Sinn Féin was separatist but not Republican, proposing a dual monarchy like Austria–Hungary, to be achieved by a passive policy of abstention rather than by physical force. There was even an Irish literary revival; in April 1902, Maude Gonne appeared in the title role of *Kathleen Ni Houlihan*, a play by an Anglo-Irishman called William Butler Yeats. All this new nationalism, tentative separatism, and interest in Irish-Ireland had little real political impact. In 1908 Sinn Féin lost the Leitrim by-election and its membership declined to one Dublin club. Neither Irish speakers nor hurley players nor even poets were going to break the connection with England. Increasingly after the Liberal victory in 1906, the new leader of the Irish Party in Parliament, John Redmond, had seemed capable of working out effective compromises and continued to hold out hope that in time Home Rule could be achieved.

The 1910 elections again gave the balance of power to the Irish Party, and it appeared that Home Rule would follow close on the heels of the British Parliament Act, passed in August, which restricted the powers of the House of Lords. Just at this moment, however, as attention focused on events at Westminster, Irish Republicanism was again emerging as a political force of some significance. In 1907 Tom Clarke had returned from New York to begin reorganizing the organization, by then largely fraternal and futile. He had attracted several most interesting young men and edged out their tired elders. In 1909, under the auspices of the Countess Markievicz (Constance Gore-Booth), an avowedly Republican boy scout movement, Fianna Éireann, had been launched. On November 15, 1910, the little newspaper *Irish Freedom* appeared in Dublin—another IRB project. As membership of the IRB grew, Republicans shifted into positions of prominence or influence in all the separatist organizations. When the Orangemen had determined to prevent Home Rule by intimidation and had formed the Ulster Volunteers, the IRB had manœuvred MacNéill into heading an Irish Volunteer unit and remained close to the sources of control over the next years.

When Pearse read out the Proclamation in front of the GPO, he drew into the light of day not a single strain of Irish Republicanism but the entire tapestry of Irish traditions: social radicalism in the person of Connolly; the conspiratorial dedication to physical force personified in the old Fenian Tom Clarke; the romantic Ireland, supposedly dead and gone, glowing not only from Pearse's poems and his Irish-Ireland school, but from the poetry of Plunkett and MacDonagh. There was John MacBride who had taken the opportunity of the Boer War to fight the English so that the Irish sword would not grow cold. There was the Countess Markievicz with her slouched hat and wild, new ideas. An odd lot they were, few and fanatic; but what the British failed to realize during April week was that in one voice or another they called to all that remained Irish in Ireland. If the rose tree of Irish freedom had to be watered each generation with the blood of patriots, then they were willing, sure that their sacrifice would in time bring blooms to what seemed in the spring of 1916 to be a dry and shattered trunk.

That the British did not understand this clearly illogical, almost mystical commitment to the Irish revolutionary tradition is hardly surprising. The separatists, usually lumped together as Sinn Féiners, had of course attracted attention. The detectives in Dublin and the Royal Irish Constabulary in the country had reported regularly. The Castle had been concerned. But that men would revolt without the support of the country, without hope of success, was simply beyond the realm of orthodox thought. So despite the warning of the *Aud* and Casement, the British were caught badly off guard. The Chief Secretary, Augustine Birrell, was as usual in England, as was Major-General L. B. Friend, the Commander-in-Chief. On Monday, April 24, 1916, there were only 111 officers and 2,316 other ranks in Dublin, although there were troops close by at the Curragh and the country was tied together by nearly ten thousand armed RIC men. During Monday afternoon the Irish largely managed to achieve what they had intended. The Castle was missed, the Phoenix Park Fort raid bungled, and Trinity College ignored; but there was such a frightful shortage of Volunteers that everything and every place could not be covered. While the British were hurriedly calling up reinforcements and moving in artillery, the 3rd Royal Irish Regulars ran into an ambush and a little later a British lancer sortie down Sackville Street was broken up. By Monday night the British had a clearer idea of the Irish positions, of the extent of the Rising, and of the prospects for the immediate future.

On Tuesday the number of British troops in Dublin had risen to about five thousand and artillery had been moved in town. The Volunteers from the first had assumed static defensive positions which because of the shortage of men could not be tied into an all-around defence. Communications with GHQ at the GPO were poor at best and patrolling rare. As a result the British troops were able to move into Trinity College and into the Shelbourne Hotel overlooking St. Stephen's Green. This meant that the Irish grip on Dublin was split in half and the isolation and reduction of the various strongholds could take place at leisure. This was the pattern the British would follow over the next few days: artillery to smash the buildings, a very heavy covering fire from rifles and machine guns, and then a cautious advance. On Wednesday, the supposed seat of revolution, Liberty Hall, was blasted by artillery sited in Trinity College and by fire from the gunboat *Helga*. Although deserted, the ruin of Liberty Hall, the fires and destruction caused by British over-fires landing in the slums, and the weight of British fire-power notified even the optimistic Irish Volunteer that prospects for survival were not great. Still the Irish were holding: bitter house-to-house fighting was going on in the South Dublin Union, the Irish Citizen Army had withdrawn from the Green under fire from the Shelbourne Hotel and were solidly dug into the College of Surgeons; elsewhere only the odd outpost had fallen by Wednesday evening and in one area a substantial defensive victory had been won.

Two columns of Sherwood Foresters had marched away from the boat at Kingstown and into Dublin. One by way of the Stillorgan Road had reached the Royal Hospital without incident. One by way of the Ballsbridge Road walked directly into a series of cleverly sited Irish outposts overlooking the Lower Mount Street Bridge. In an action which would probably have led to a court-martial in other armies, the raw British troops were repeatedly ordered into the Irish cross-fire. The fighting lasted for five hours as time after time the Foresters charged in successive and futile waves. At eight p.m. the position was finally breached. The Irish had six casualties but the British had lost four officers killed, fourteen wounded, and 216 other ranks killed and wounded. The general situation of the Irish forces was not as bright. A great boiling cloud of black smoke hung over Dublin. Throughout the Sackville Street area fires were spreading under the British artillery fire. Firemen still held the conflagration in check but under artillery and rifle fire much of the time they could not work effectively. The GPO was on fire and by Thursday the fires in the area were out of control. By then the British had the Rising in firm control. MacDonagh in Jacob's factory was cut off and Ceannt at the South Dublin Union was besieged and holding with difficulty. Four Courts were solid as was de Valera's reduced perimeter at Boland's Bakery. The GPO was being reduced by fire and shot. All unity of command had been lost, each position fought its own corner, hoping to hold on as long as possible. Perhaps a few still thought the country might rise but most were content to have a go at the Saxon before the end came.

By Friday morning things were very bad. Connolly had been wounded twice. The upper storey of the GPO was still on fire. The neighbourhood was a mass of flames criss-crossed with fields of British fire. The roar of the fires and the artillery almost muffled the small-arms and machine gun fire. During the afternoon with the GPO blazing wildly over their heads, the garrison prepared to evacuate across Henry Street up Moore Street and into a factory on Parnell Street where contact with the garrison at Four Courts could be made. O'Rahilly, who had carried MacNéill's orders not to rise and then returned to join the GPO garrison, was sent out to scout the route. He was shot and mortally wounded in Moore Lane. The route out was under constant British fire. At dusk the last of the garrison did manage to get out of the flaming hulk of the GPO and into a house on Moore Street. Huddled in the temporary refuge in the middle of a blazing city Pearse and Connolly realized that the end had come.

At noon on Saturday, April 29, Pearse sent a Cumann na mBan girl, Elizabeth O'Farrell, out with a white flag and a surrender message:

> The Commandant General of the Irish Republican Army wishes to treat with the Commandant General of the British forces in Ireland.[3]

The British demanded unconditional surrender and at half-past three Pearse complied. Orders to surrender were sent to the other Republican garrisons where reluctantly the Volunteers gave in. The last to quit were de Valera's men in Boland's Bakery, not yet hard-pressed. Once de Valera was in hand the Rising was over. The country had not come out. Volunteers under Tomás Ashe and Richard Mulcahy had fought an engagement at Ashbourne in County Meath. The Belfast–Dublin railroad had been disrupted. Some of the North Country Dublin men had reached the city. In Enniscorthy Robert Brennan's brief Rising had aborted as had Liam Mellows' in Galway. The series of contradictory orders and lack of Dublin news or guidance had undone most of the units. Terence MacSwiney and Tomás MacCurtain in Cork were horrified that they could not come out since the British learned of the Dublin situation first and were totally prepared. Elsewhere the situation was much the same. It had been a Dublin coup and a Dublin disaster. While the Volunteers lost only fifty-six killed to the 130 of the British, no accurate estimate of the far more severe civilian casualties could be made. In property loss estimates ran to £2,500,000 with the lower Sackville Street area entirely gutted. On Saturday afternoon, April 29, Dublin still burned, the raggle-taggle rebels were led off to prison, and the hospitals filled with the bleeding. And no one knew why, nor what madness had possessed the rebels.

Everyone was shocked. Redmond and the Irish Party were shocked. The newspapers expressed shock and horror. The man in the street was shocked. Some of the women of the slums, the shawlies, had hooted the Volunteers as they had been marched away under guard, perhaps in fear that their British Army allotments would be cut off, perhaps in anger at the destruction brought on their own innocent heads by the Rising, perhaps in the simple tradition of Dublin rancour. There had been a few cheers, too, and even some feeling of pride in some quarters that the lads had fought a clean fight. But mostly there was shock and uncertainty.

On Friday, April 28, General Sir John Maxwell had arrived to take over supreme command in Ireland. Acutely aware of the dangers of allowing the Irish situation to fester while the European war teetered in the balance, Maxwell intended to crush the Irish "Republic" in the egg. British security had been endangered; British lives lost; British property destroyed. The rebels had risked all, now they must suffer all. This was hardly a novel British approach to the Irish situation. On May 3, the executions began, secretly, after brief trials, and swiftly. Word soon leaked out that the British were shooting their way through the leaders of the rebellion. Those who had been horrified at the Rising a week before were now horrified at the summary executions. Protests began to appear. George Bernard Shaw and Redmond urged clemency. On May 10, Prime Minister Asquith told the Commons that there had been fourteen executions, seventy-three sentences of penal servitude, six of hard labour, and 1,706 men deported from Ireland. Ultimately there were ninety death sentences and approximately 3,500 men and seventy-nine women under arrest or sentence. James Connolly was taken out, too damaged by British bullets to stand, tied to a chair and shot. Sir Roger Casement, tried under an obscure Norman statute, was allowed on June 26 to speak in his defence—a scathing indictment of British justice soon memorized by every Irish nationalist—and then was hanged in Pentonville Prison on August 3. By then the sixteen men executed had by that strange alchemy of Irish politics been transmuted into martyrs. No grass would grow over the grave of Connolly, Pearse, and Casement. The British had, again, misread the Irish.

If Pearse and Connolly and the rest had been correct about the ultimate meaning of the Rising for Ireland, then nothing that the British could have done would have mattered. The torch, British brutality or no, would have been passed; but almost every observer in retrospect has agreed that this time luck was on their side. The destruction of Dublin was being blamed on the British by the end of May. It had been British artillery shells and British fire on civilians that had caused the damage. Innocent men had been killed, even that strange and lovable Dublin character Francis Sheehy Skeffington, advocate of foolish causes, had been shot down in cold blood for no good reason and then the affair had been hushed up. The executions had been hasty, vindictive, and cruel. Pearse's brother who most assuredly was not a rebel leader had been shot because of his name. Connolly shot in his chair appalled many. The wild arrests throughout Ireland of men like Griffith, who disapproved of physical force and of Republicanism, grated. The British rode with the storm, certain that as in the past Ireland would settle down.

Asquith informed the House of Commons that an attempt would be made to settle the "Irish problem". David Lloyd George was put in charge of the new "settlement" and embarked on a series of involved and cloudy discussions with the Orange Unionists, Redmond's Irish Party, and various representative figures. From afar, particularly from America, there seemed to be progress; but the Lloyd George proposals were largely sham. If Redmond had accepted Lloyd George's final offer, which he refused to do on July 24, Ireland would have been partitioned and even real Home Rule in doubt. By then, however, with the Dublin executions well in the past, the Irish settling down under the eyes of the RIC and the detectives, with Maxwell and forty thousand troops in place, with 1,800 rebels safely interned or imprisoned, the Cabinet in London felt well out of the Irish crisis and more concerned with the results of Brusilov's offensive in Russia, the battle of Verdun, and the great sea battle at Jutland. The Irish had subsided and if the past were any guide, they would stay quiet for another generation at least.

The Cabinet was, of course, wrong. Even Pearse and Connolly were wrong, for their blood sacrifice had not watered another generation but their own. The rebels had been taken off to Dublin prisons, where the leaders were winnowed out for special attention and the average Volunteer sent off to be interned. From the very first they had felt April 29 was not the end. They were going to have another go of some sort. In the internment camps like Frongoch in Wales some 1,800 Irishmen turned themselves into a centre of separatism. New men were recruited to the IRB, particularly by Michael Collins; old tactics and strategies were discussed; long seminars in Republican philosophy were held; and morale was maintained by agitating the British. The Republican prisoners demanded political treatment, wrought havoc with the carefully regulated prison system, and prepared for another day. The Rising had been planned as a coup, a single great and daring blow, an all-or-nothing affair; but slowly, spontaneously, often without leaders, the Volunteers began to prepare for the next round when the Irish Republican Army would strike.

In Ireland the shift from shock and horror to admiration had begun early in May. Songs on Easter Week were heard. Poems were written. All the rites which turn a dead rebel into an eternal Irish martyr were performed. By-passed Volunteer units paraded with a new determination out of sight of the RIC. Mrs. Tom Clarke formed an Irish National Aid Association and an Irish Volunteers Dependents' Fund. There was a rush to contribute or to volunteer services. By mid-summer there were still six hundred prisoners in camps despite British efforts to get rid of the truculent Irishmen who would not be disciplined. As more and more were released and returned to Ireland the excitement rose. They came home not as fools or knaves but as heroes. They came back to find new Fenian dead, new hope for an Irish Ireland even among the timid. Maxwell had become the Butcher. His forty thousand troops made Ireland a garrison state. Dissent in public was impossible but it was agreed in private that there must be more to the Rising than sixteen graves. In September 1916, the National League called a meeting in Phoenix Park to oppose Lloyd George's partition plan. No one listened to the speakers but a vast hosting came to the Park, some in the uniform of the Irish Volunteers. The old songs and the new were sung. It was a tidy and proper meeting but it was an ill omen for the British. The latent forces of revolutionary Ireland had been tapped and the people were awakening. They had not come out in April even with knives and forks, and in September they were uncertain of their direction; but the great crowd in Phoenix Park felt deeply that they were living on the eve of glorious years for Ireland.

NOTES

1. In the United States the fragmented Fenian Brotherhood was ultimately united under the name Clan na Gael. The IRB was the term generally used for the Irish organization, although some were never sure if the "R" stood for Revolutionary or Republican: in any event, the Organization was by no means doctrinaire Republican.

2. At the 1915 Ard Fheis of the Gaelic League, the IRB saw to it that a separatist Executive was elected.

3. There has been in certain mandarin circles some concern as to when the expression IRA became identified with the Irish Volunteers. As early as the abortive Fenian invasion of Canada in 1866, a green flag was used with the letters IRA. Pearse in *Irish War News* on April 25 refers to himself as commander of the Forces of the Irish Republic and in a manifesto the next day as Commander-in-Chief the Army of the Irish Republic. The words IRA were found on a blackboard in the College of Surgeons and began to appear after the names of prisoners in their letters home. In theory, the Army of the Irish Republic existed from five minutes after noon on April 24—whatever it was called.

CHAPTER II

The Tan War: The IRA Triumphant, September 1916–July 1921

Irish separatism in 1917 was still an amorphous and inchoate movement. The military command structure in Dublin had been destroyed in the Rising, leaving many country areas still organized, still with a minimal supply of arms, but without any contact with a centre. Neither the IRB nor the Volunteers had done much to re-establish the links in the chain, and many of the important or knowledgeable survivors were in prison. At the end of November a small convention was held at Fleming's Hotel in Dublin. Cathal Brugha, who had been released in September because of his multiple wounds, was present on crutches. In this way various existing units were enabled to resume contact. Just before Christmas there was a meeting of the new Executive at Barry's Hotel in Dublin. It was attended by two delegates from each of the provinces and two from Dublin.[1] Discussion was confined to reorganization; until there was an army, there was no purpose in considering tactics and strategy.

As the British released the internees from Frongoch, the reorganization accelerated although there were often disputes within the leadership. Men like Brugha and de Valera saw no further use for the IRB, while others like Michael Collins felt such an organization would have a vital role to play in the days ahead. By 1917 both the IRB and the Volunteers had been reorganized, with Collins prominent in the latter.

On the political front there was the same vacuum and lack of direction at the centre. Although the Rising had been labelled Sinn Féin by the ignorant, the small orthodox Sinn Féin group had not in fact been involved nor was it clear how Sinn Féin might be made a part of a new revolutionary Republican movement. Fianna Éireann and Cumann na mBan, the Republican youth and woman's movements, would be useful as reservoirs of potential supporters but could scarcely be counted on for more. Arthur Griffith's journal, *Nationality*, was another positive factor: it urged independence and Irish participation in any postwar peace conference, opposed partition, and attracted support to separatism if not republicanism.

It was decided to run Count Plunkett, father of the executed 1916 leader, as a candidate in the North Roscommon by-election. Running on Griffith's abstentionist platform and with Father Michael O'Flanagan campaigning passionately on his behalf, Plunkett won the election with

,022 votes to 1,708 for his principal opponent, the Redmondite candidate, and 687 for an independent. Plunkett's victory was described as a triumph for Sinn Féin, now more an idea than an organization.[2]

In December 1916, Lloyd George succeeded Asquith as Prime Minister. His government's policy, although ostensibly one of appeasement, failed to take account of the changed atmosphere in Ireland. The creation of an Irish Convention, intended to involve all groups, made no headway against the intransigence of the Orangemen and in the absence of "Sinn Féin". Meetings began on July 25, 1917, and continued sporadically until April 5, 1918. Side by side with "negotiation" went a firm Castle policy aimed at the most visible of the militants. There were police raids. MacSwiney, MacCurtain, Seán T. O'Kelly, and twenty-three others ended up in British prisons. Yet nothing seemed to work. In South Longford Joseph McGuinness, who was in a British jail, won in a by-election; in East Clare de Valera won an overwhelming victory; and in Kilkenny William Cosgrave was elected.

These were the outward signs of reorganization. The IRB drew up a new constitution. The Volunteers were preparing for a national convention to be held simultaneously with the Sinn Féin Ard Fheis at the Mansion House in October. The Castle announced that no weapons were to be carried in public. There were police raids throughout the country. Men were arrested for seditious speeches. And in August Tomás Ashe died after forced feeding during a hunger strike. The British had bungled again. Collins' brief reference to the volley fired over his grave as the only proper tribute for a dead Fenian was an ominous note. On October 25, two thousand delegates met at the Sinn Féin Ard Fheis where a political form of separatism was created. Incredibly there had been a certain amount of scrambling to jettison the old "dual monarchy" formula in favour of republicanism. Elected President, de Valera, as usual, found the answer; as he noted, he was not a doctrinaire Republican. Under cover of the meeting, 250 delegates met in an Army Convention in the GAA[3] grounds Croke Park. De Valera was elected President, and Brugha Chief of Staff, but the IRB was prominently represented in the Staff: Collins was Director of Organization, Diarmuid Lynch Director of Communication, and Seán McGarry General Secretary. With the formalities concluded, the Volunteers returned to the countryside to continue the routine of training for the next round, while the Sinn Féin delegates prepared for the next by-election, hopeful that abstentionism would obviate the necessity for military solutions.

Then the tide seemed to turn, as Lloyd George had assumed it would. There were three quick by-election losses: South Armagh, Waterford, and East Tyrone. America's entry into the war as a British ally in April 1917 foreclosed the possibility of effective support for the Irish cause from that direction; and the Casement fiasco had exhausted Germany's interest in Ireland. And yet the work had gone on. In March an IRA GHQ had been organized.[4] And in April, despite the Anglo-American alliance, Lloyd George was obliged to contemplate conscripting the Irish. On April 9, after a series of cloudy and complicated manœuvres, whose purpose was to link conscription to the Home Rule Bill and to give Lloyd George discretionary powers in applying conscription to Ireland, the conscription bill was passed, 301 to 103, with the Irish Party abstaining. From a constitutional point of view Lloyd George was behaving with perfect propriety, but politically speaking it was an act of pure folly. In one stroke the bill united every Irish faction. The bishops at Maynooth were appalled; a general strike was called for April 23; young men flocked to the IRA in droves; and sedition was spoken on every street corner.

The British in response took a hard line. Firmer men moved into the Castle on May 17/18 in a giant sweep, the result of invisible evidence of a "German Plot"; over seventy prominent members of Sinn Féin were arrested, including de Valera, Griffith and Count Plunkett. In June at the East Cavan by-election, Griffith won a victory for Sinn Féin from his prison cell. The British banned Sinn Féin, the Irish Volunteers, Cumann na mBan, and the Gaelic League. Everyone went underground. The raids continued. During 1918 there were over one thousand arrests yet the level of sedition rose month by month. On August 15, 1918, the first edition of the IRA paper *an tOglágh* appeared with Piaras Béaslaí as editor. One of the most startling of the early articles, "Ruthless Warfare", written by Ernest Blythe, urged among other things that "all . . . having assisted the enemy must be shot or otherwise destroyed with the least possible delay".[5] But the leadership of the IRA was a long way from this kind of thinking. Brugha was concentrating on the anti-conscription campaign. Collins as Adjutant General was not only organizing the Volunteers but putting together an intricate intelligence web of Post Office workers, prison wardens, nicely placed clerks, and even detectives in the G Division of the Dublin Metropolitan Police:[6] Collins foresaw that his best weapons would be subversion and counter-intelligence. The Volunteers on their route marches murmuring of pike charges and open battle were romantic but obsolete. Operations would have to be swift, silent, and secret. For example, there were plans for retaliatory raids in England if conscription were enforced, tactics far more effective than any wild rising of the West without arms or prospects.

Then on November 11, 1918, the war ended and with it the threat of conscription. The almost immediate call for a general election to be held on December 14 gave Sinn Féin a new goal and the opportunity to ry out abstentionism on a mass scale. All seats would be contested, except our assigned to Irish Party men in the North to prevent Unionist victories; nd all Sinn Féin winners would eschew Westminster and meet in Dublin s the National Assembly of Ireland, Dáil Éireann. When the results were nnounced on December 28, there was no doubt about the magnitude of inn Féin's victory: seventy-three seats, a clean sweep in twenty-four ounties. The Irish Party won only six seats, four as a result of the deal vith Sinn Féin. The only anti-separatist bloc was the Unionists, the party f the Orange Protestants in the North-East and they had won twenty-six eats. The rest of the country had repudiated Britain and chosen Sinn éin, although for most Irishmen this choice represented a leap in the dark.

On January 21, 1919, in Dublin, the Dáil, or those members not in rison or on missions for the Republic, met.[7] Those present voted a Consti-ution, a Declaration of Independence, and a Programme of Social and Democratic Rights. After two hours, the legal government of the *de jure* Republic, which had been declared on April 24, 1916, adjourned. From ,ondon the whole enterprise appeared farcical: twenty-seven men in a rovincial capital declaring the independence of a non-existent Republic the presence of overwhelming British power and position. The govern-ent of the new Republic were men on the run or in prison cells. The rmy was invisible, clumsy peasants and clerks with few weapons and no aining. Continued subversion and sedition was likely, even probable; but he Dáil Declaration would have little real effect. The police had even elaxed their sweeps and searches during the winter and intelligence reports aggested that Volunteer morale was not good.

It was an assessment with which some of the local commanders would ave agreed. Separatism had been a political movement since the autumn of 316 and Sinn Féin's successes, while heartening, convinced the advocates f physical force that they were wrong. GHQ in Dublin seemed overly autious. With the threat of conscription gone, the new mass IRA had apidly dissolved. Nothing was being done. In Tipperary Seán Treacy, an Breen, and Seamus Robinson had watched their brigade all but isappear. By the end of 1918, Treacy was furious: "If this goes on, we'll ave to kill someone, and make the bloody enemy organize us."[8] On anuary 21, the day the Dáil first met, he, Breen, Robinson, and eight others ruck. An attack near the Soloheadbeg quarry in Tipperary on a cart of xplosives protected by two Royal Irish Constabulary constables produced e first British dead since Easter week.[9] Both constables were shot and lled when they attempted to resist. The conventional and conservative, ish and British, were horrified at murder from the safety of a ditch. The oliticians" of Sinn Féin were deeply uneasy. GHQ was hardly enthusi-tic but *an tOglágh* on January 31 gave limited support to the action.

C/Os elsewhere took matters into their own hands and began raiding for arms, intimidating the RIC with the odd shot, keeping the Volunteers eager for real action. From May until December 1919, eighteen RIC men were killed. The pressure of the attacks on tiny, isolated posts, a boycott by the population which extended even to a donkey carrying turf for the police, and the threat of more serious IRA attacks forced the RIC to evacuate their more vulnerable posts.

Meanwhile, the Dáil and the British government searched for less violent solutions. The Dáil, following Griffith's theories, was attempting to set up a Republican infrastructure throughout Ireland: courts, local government bodies, police, tax officials. In theory, the "legal" British administration would decay, and British control would be broken. During 1919 this policy was tremendously effective: in large areas only Republican courts sat, the stream of local government requests into the Custom House dwindled as Cosgrave's department took over, taxes were not paid, land annuity payments fell into arrears. In December Lloyd George responded by laying before Parliament the Better Government of Ireland Bill. Known in Ireland as the Partition Bill, it proposed dividing Ireland into two autonomous units, North and South, and giving each Home Rule. The only people it was likely to please were the Ulster Unionists, and in the South the Republicans were determined not to have it.

By the autumn of 1919, the IRA had found a task: neutralize the RIC. Scattered through the country were over nine thousand armed Irish policemen, familiar with their area and loyal to the Crown. If the RIC could be broken, Britain would have to depend on raw military power, which would arouse public opinion and might prove ineffectual in practice. The IRA had limited resources for this task, few arms despite the raids, less ammunition, too few trained men, no heavy weapons, and the tolerance but not yet the support of the country. By necessity the weapons used would be those of the weak: stealth, ambush, assassination, intimidation. To the British men who shot policemen from behind walls were murderers and the IRA a murder gang. This attitude was understandable, but the British made the mistake of supposing that the Irish public shared it. In fact, in Tipperary and Limerick no one cared very much what the British thought, as long as the lads were getting their own back. The more the British howled the more delighted the Irish were. The British were self-righteous: if the Irish would not listen to British reason then they would have to recognize British force—nine thousand RIC and thirty thousand soldiers could—or at least should—bring village murder to a halt.

The fact was that by the end of 1919 the RIC was intimidated, not the IRA. Barracks had to be abandoned. Recruitment had plummeted. Far too many men were retiring. The whole force was uneasy. The local army was o happier. It was almost impossible to pinpoint the guilt for a single ssault—no one would testify, no one would even talk, no one ever saw nything. All the Irish "natives" looked alike; the quiet and loyal were ndistinguishable from the terrorists. Much as they would have preferred o use minimal force to avoid mass retaliation, general internment, sum- nary executions, and all the coercive apparatus of a garrison state, the British found that anything less was ineffectual. Slyly, without formal ecognition, the British chose to permit unofficial counter-terror. In eptember, a column of Cork No. 2 under Liam Lynch ambushed a detach- nent of the King's Shropshire Light Infantry near the Wesleyan Church t Fermoy. An infantryman was killed, but the coroner's jury refused to eturn a verdict of murder, finding only that death had resulted only from ne bullet wound. Two hundred British soldiers rushed into Fermoy and wrecked the houses of several jurymen, doing three thousand pounds' worth f damage. No effort was made by the RIC or the Shropshire officers to op the unofficial raid. It was the first indication of a pattern that was to evelop during the next two years: assassination, indignation, retaliation.

The British came down harder on the Sinn Féiners. The Dáil was declared llegal, and, of course, kept meeting secretly. Sinn Féin headquarters were aided, but most important people had long been on the run. The news- apers were banned, but word of mouth spread the news nearly as fast the little papers had. The number of raids and sweeps multiplied. IRA ttacks continued. On November 17, 1919, Cork No. 3 Brigade achieved splendid coup by cleaning out the arms and ammunition from a British oop in Bantry Bay. A month later, Lord French, Lord Lieutenant of eland, only just missed being assassinated near his official residence in hoenix Park. The British were still convinced that force was the only nswer. In the new year a vigorous campaign was launched in England raise volunteers for the RIC, and by March the first new recruits ere being shipped to Ireland. These differed in one particularly obvious spect from the men of the old RIC, whom they at first reinforced and en, as resignations from the regular force continued, all but replaced: eir uniform. The situation had apparently been thought so urgent that o time was left to provide the men with proper uniforms and so they rived wearing hybrid outfits of black leather and khaki, and were romptly christened by the Irish, the Black and Tans—a name by which ey were known thereafter, even though sufficient supplies of the regular niform eventually became available and the distinction between the old d the new RIC was no longer so clear. However, there were other, more ndamental dissimilarities: the Black and Tans had been poorly and too pidly trained; few were native Irishmen or had any knowledge of the untry. They were likely to prove a blunt and brutal instrument. There

was further evidence of British determination in July, when the Auxiliaries
an élite force 1,500 strong under General Crozier, began to arrive. With
this new strength, the British hoped they might be able to make some
progress.

Instead the violence simply escalated. There were more raids, swoops
and searches. The Tans set up blocks on the roads, or sealed off streets
in Dublin, or went through small towns in the country. Every separatist
organization was proscribed, every paper banned, every prominent Republican a wanted man. The G Division of the Dublin police sought any tip,
any hint which would enable them to break the Dublin IRA centre.
The British army co-operated in the searches. In Ulster the Orangemen
ran amok in a series of medieval pogroms. Belfast became a city under
siege as sectarian violence erupted despite the presence of British troops.
And in the South the IRA attacks still continued. Order could not be
restored. Increasingly, the British turned to counter-terror. On March 20
a group of unknown "civilians" entered the home of Tomás MacCurtain,
Lord Mayor of Cork and C/O of Cork No. 1 Brigade, and shot him dead
in front of his family. IRA GHQ was satisfied that the RIC had been responsible, and in time Collins had several of the culprits shot, including
Detective Inspector Swanzy, who had been transferred to the relative safety
of Lisburn, County Antrim. The line between combatant and non-com-
batant was becoming more and more difficult to draw. The British could
claim that MacCurtain—even if the RIC had killed him in his home—was
a combatant. Similarly, when Collins' gunmen took Alan Bell, an elderly
Dublin magistrate, off a Dun Laoghaire train and shot him, the killing
might have been justified by pointing to the work Bell had done for the
British in tracing Sinn Féin funds in Dublin.

Throughout the year, small IRA columns hit RIC barracks in the South
and West; there were shootings in the cities, swoops and raids and retaliation. Part of Balbriggan was burned down by the irate Tans. Castle detectives were shot on the street before the eyes of seemingly blind witnesses.

In the spring General Sir Nevil Macready took over as Commander-
in-Chief of British forces, and Major-General H. H. Tudor succeeded
Sir Joseph Byrne, who was thought too mild, as Inspector General of
the RIC and the Dublin police. Their harder line had no effect. On
Easter Sunday, a hundred Inland Revenue offices and 350 deserted RIC
barracks were burned out, a major operation. More British troops were
brought in early in the summer, but the scattered barracks attacks continued. In June a British general was kidnapped while fishing. In July
a Restoration of Order Bill was passed and the first Auxiliaries arrived.
Train crews would not carry soldiers. Tan reprisals grew more harsh.
Belfast was in chaos. A Special Ulster Constabulary was set up to the

nguish of the Northern Republicans, who rightly saw it as a Protestant
Army enforcing partition. In Dublin Colonel Ormonde Winter, Chief
of British Combined Intelligence Service in Ireland, had brought in experienced Secret Service agents from abroad to counter Collins' invisible intelligence net. On October 14, Seán Treacy, the man who had set the machine
in motion, was shot dead in Talbot Street in Dublin. On October 25, after
a hunger strike of seventy-four days, Terence MacSwiney, MacCurtain's
successor, died in a blaze of anti-British publicity at Brixton Jail. On
November 1, Kevin Barry, an eighteen-year-old medical student and Irish
Republican soldier, was hanged for his part in a raid in Dublin. The Irish
public was particularly dismayed at this execution because there had been
rumours of torture and little evidence had been produced in court. Ireland
was suddenly full of heroes and martyrs. The poems and the ballads began.
In London they remained murderers.

On November 9, Lloyd George announced that the British had murder
by the throat. He was quite wrong. Every effort to coerce Ireland had
required greater force and produced only stronger resistance. On the
morning of November 21, Bloody Sunday, Collins' squad descended on
the safe houses of Ormonde Winter's undercover agents. Fourteen were
killed along with two RIC men. One IRA man was wounded and captured.
British intelligence had been dealt a crippling blow and British indignation produced the traditional reaction. Dick McKee, C/O of Dublin, and
two other men were picked up and shot the same evening "while attempting
to escape". At Croke Park during a football game the Tans fired into the
crowd, killing twelve spectators and wounding sixty.

During most of 1920, the IRA tactics—assassination in the cities and
ambush in the country—had been remarkably successful.[10] Outside the
Protestant North-East, the IRA had men in practically every parish and
township of Ireland—men, not arms, for the IRA was almost without arms.
Under ideal conditions there were weapons, of various calibres and obscure
makes, for about three thousand men. Even then the various regional
brigades could only keep a certain number of men in the field. Although
much of Ireland was wild and bleak, and there were few good roads,
it was not really guerrilla country, for the terrain was too open and the
wild areas were without food or farms. Under the best circumstances it
would have been difficult to keep more than one thousand to 1,500 men
on the move in flying columns. Much of the time, of course, "on the
move" meant hiding out in the hope that the Tans and the soldiers stayed
at the other end of the country. With only small arms and poor explosives, these columns even when concentrated could not stand up to the
British nor even manage at times to break into isolated RIC barracks.
What they could and did do was to keep the country in an uproar, drain

off a substantial portion of the British forces at great cost in time, nerves and gold, and through a series of pinpricks, delight the Irish and enrage the British. Since the enraged British now took their vengeance openly and violently, every IRA action almost guaranteed that there would be a further instance of British misconduct to be retailed to the world and to an increasingly uneasy public in Britain. And each example of Tan terror renewed the determination of the Irish people to resist Saxon arrogance and brutality.

A typical round occurred at the end of November when Tom Barry C/O Cork No. 3 Brigade, carried out a most successful ambush at Kilmichael. Eighteen Auxiliaries were killed, two armoured lorries burned and the British arms and ammunition captured for a loss of three IRA men. This was followed by another ambush, on December 11, in which one Auxiliary was killed. On the night of December 11, the Auxiliaries took their revenge: running through the streets of Cork, they literally burned the city down. Vast areas were gutted as the firemen, their hoses cut by the Auxiliaries, stood idly by. The damage was estimated at £3,000,000. In the House of Commons, when first questioned, Sir Hamar Greenwood chief architect of the hard line, at first denied that British troops or police had been involved, insisting that the citizens of Cork had burned their own city. Even the British public fed on a steady diet of Irish gunmen and murder gangs could not swallow that. Clearly the situation in Ireland had got out of hand. De Valera on tour in the United States decided the time had come to return to Ireland.

For over a year he had been collecting funds for the Irish Republic and seeking American assistance. He had gone to the United States in June, 1919, after Harry Boland and Collins had managed his escape from Lincoln Jail. Griffith had been left as Acting-President, to be succeeded in November, 1920, after his arrest by Collins. In de Valera's absence the political side of the Republican Movement, so prominent until 1919, had become less visible. The whole structure of dual government, so carefully constructed and so successful initially, had collapsed in the face of British arms. As a myth the Republican government was valuable, but except in certain departments and a few areas Ireland had become a garrison state. Irish diplomacy had failed at the Paris Peace Conference; failed despite de Valera's efforts to induce either the United States government or the major American parties to commit themselves to Irish independence and failed to secure recognition for the Irish Republic from any country of consequence.[11] The entire burden of Republican action rested on the IRA. GHQ, too, had failed to find foreign arms for the Volunteers in any quantity; failed to effect a real campaign of retaliation in England, despite a rather impressive Liverpool dock fire; and failed to clear any part of Ireland. To GHQ's credit, however, the IRA had been kept in action and it had continued to exploit the still little understood tactics of urban terror and rural disorder. The country had remained solid if exhausted. The North-East was bad but that was predictable. For a year GHQ had been forced to concentrate on tactical operations, without knowing where these tactics were to lead. De Valera's return on December 24, in the midst of rumours of peace proposals, indicated that there was at last a hope that Lloyd George might be ready to try a different approach.

If this were the case, there was little evidence in Ireland. The new year began as the old one had ended, with fresh raids, new murders in the street, and the same Tans drunk on stolen whiskey and daily danger. Somehow both sides found a way to increase the pressure in a search for the jugular. The Tans burnt creameries and Sinn Féin homes; the IRA burnt Unionist big houses, two for one in Tom Barry's area. The British hanged IRA volunteers as murderers. The IRA kidnapped British soldiers and officers as hostages and shot them. The British sought to break the united front with appeals to former loyalties, to avarice, and to fear. The IRA replied: between January and April 1921 seventy-three bodies were found with a placard announcing the removal of a spy and informer. The old RIC continued to resign. The new Tans, now for the most part in normal uniforms, continued to arrive. In Britain no responsible figure condoned the IRA murderers; but increasingly, prominent figures were expressing doubts about the use of terror tactics by the police and military, particularly if such a policy was ineffective. Statements to the effect that the situation had been brought under control were the prelude to more dis- order and more murder.

On April 21, during Lord Derby's visit to Ireland, A. W. Cope approached de Valera in an effort to promote private negotiations; but no common ground could be found between James Craig, the Orange leader, and the President of the Irish Republic. At least the attempt had been made and various other channels existed, if one side or the other decided that the time had come for compromise. In May a general election was held with Sinn Féin, a proscribed organization, using the British electoral machinery to vote for a second Dáil, also a proscribed organization. In the six counties of Northern Ireland, the Unionists were successful, winning forty seats to twelve for the Nationalists but Sinn Féin swept everything else but the four independent Trinity College seats. According to the British the provisions of the Better Government for Ireland Bill would now come into force, creating two Home-Rule statelets. If there were more than fifty per cent abstentions in either parliament, that part of Ireland would be ruled as Crown Colony. According to the Irish, however, another Dáil had been elected and would continue to meet to govern all thirty-two counties of the Republic. Neither position was quite practical; and in any case, no one seemed capable of governing Ireland.

On May 25, the Dublin Brigade under C/O Oscar Traynor carried out the greatest urban operation of the war, destroying the Custom House, the seat of nine British administrative departments including two taxing departments and the Local Government Board. Traynor's 120 Volunteers took over the building, piled up furniture and, using paraffin, got several major fires going. When the word to withdraw came, the British had already been alerted and were surrounding the Custom House. Several IRA men were hit trying to break through the cordon and about eighty members of the Dublin Brigade were captured. The Custom House was a flaming pillar by the time the British cleared the area. The fire roared on all night and by morning with the dome collapsed into the gutted centre only the blackened walls remained. In the ruins were the seared heaps of paper which had made possible the smooth control of Ireland. The British administration would be virtually impotent. In the meantime the IRA attacks, large and small, continued. Trains were ambushed coming into Dublin. RIC barracks were hit in the country. The swoops and searches went on. Peace, much less effective government, seemed a will-o'-the-wisp. The IRA GHQ, short of ammunition and without heavy arms, was reconciled to the long war. Clan na Gael was sending over a new sub-machine gun developed by a Colonel Thompson.[12] Buyers in Europe might find what was needed. In the meantime the brigades would have to hold on. In fact, the IRA had been reorganized into divisions in the spring, but these had so far proved ineffectual and the burden of the war remained on the strained and underarmed active-service brigades. The British, too, could see no light in the corridor and began to talk about 100,000 more troops, block-houses, and mass relocation of the rebel population.

By June, Britain had between 35,000 and 40,000 troops in Ireland, 12,500 RIC, over half the new Tans, 1,500 Auxiliaries, the new Ulster Constabulary, and a variety of agents and observers. The Castle pessimistically assumed that the IRA had between 100,000 and 200,000 Volunteers, but the military were still certain they could break the murder gang with additional reinforcements. Lloyd George, the century's wiliest politician, would have loved to believe the generals but he had made that mistake before. The time had come to talk.

After several ploys aborted, Lloyd George on June 22 suddenly found that de Valera had fallen into his hands. He was "inexplicably" released twenty-four hours later. On June 25, he received a letter from Lloyd George proposing a peace conference. De Valera replied on June 28 that he was calling a conference with the Ulster Unionists. The political leaders of Sinn Féin, the Dáil, and the Republic came out into the open. On July 8,

General Macready arrived at the Mansion House with his truce proposals. It was agreed that a general truce should come into effect at noon on July 11. The IRA in the field, admittedly often from the ditch and behind the wall, had frustrated the awesome power of the British Empire. Lloyd George had been driven to come to de Valera, since Britain was unable to crush the IRA and unwilling to massacre the Irish. To the jubilant IRA men their new guerrilla tactics

> had prevented British authority from functioning in Ireland, laid its administration in ruins, driven out or under cover the British minions, necessitated a large and costly army of occupation, humiliated British military power, caused the name of Britain to stink in the nostrils of all decent peoples, and inflicted sufficient casualties on their soldiers to seriously disturb a government finding it difficult to supply reinforcements.[13]

The IRA tactics, those of weakness, had not beaten the British, nor won the war, they had only prevented defeat. Yet this in itself was triumph. After noon on Monday, July 11, the days of fear and terror, of lives lived on nerves, of swift executions, and brutality, would be gone and the time of diplomats and deliberate negotiations would have arrived—or so it seemed.

NOTES

1. There are several excellent articles on the various reorganizations during 1916–1917 in *The Capuchin Annual* (Dublin) 1967. Tomás Malone recalls that the Executive formed in December 1916 did not meet again and that, in fact, he did not recognize some of the men, many of whom had still been in prison in April, attending the conference. It would appear that the December meeting was largely dominated by surviving IRB members, which may explain Brugha's absence; but in any case, the deliberations merely maintained continuity rather than decided policy.
2. On April 19, in Dublin, a meeting called by Count Plunkett sought to weld all nationalist organizations into one. A temporary compromise was reached but not until the Sinn Féin Ard Fheis in October was "Sinn Féin" as a post-Rising party defined and organized.
3. Men like Brugha and Rory O'Connor most certainly were doctrinaire Republicans while Griffith did not want to be bound to a Republic he did not understand. De Valera's formula: "Sinn Féin aims at securing the international recognition of Ireland as an independent Irish Republic" (Dorothy Macardle, *The Irish Republic*, New York, 1965,

p. 232) was obviously more Republican than not, but did not insist that the Republic was the final form for Ireland.

4. During all this period, there were complicated "legal" questions as to which body or official owed allegiance to whom or what. The Volunteer Executive decayed to be replaced by the GHQ staff which largely ran the war although nominally under the control of the Minister of Defence in the Republican government to which all Volunteers had taken an oath of loyalty at Brugha's insistence. More "civilian" control might have existed if de Valera had not felt it necessary to go to America; but as is usual, war was made by warriors and many of these warriors had ideological doubts about politics and politicians.

5. Edgar Holt, *Protest in Arms, The Irish Troubles 1916–1923*, New York, 1961, p. 164. Blythe took a similar stance in 1922–1923.

6. Two of Collins' agents, David Neligan and Eamon Broy, were to become official policemen in the Castle, facing the IRA as an enemy.

7. Although marked as present at this meeting, Michael Collins and Harry Boland were in England arranging de Valera's escape from Lincoln Jail.

8. Desmond Ryan, *Seán Treacy and the Third Tipperary Brigade I.R.A.*, Tralee, 1945, p. 53.

9. Several RIC men had been wounded in minor incidents. Two volunteers had been killed in a raid in Kerry and several wounded in other incidents. One man had been killed by the police in Clare during the dispersal of an illegal meeting.

10. Although all the romance is on the side of Barry, Breen, O'Malley, Seán McKeon, and the lads on the hillside, the core of Irish resistance was Dublin. The administrative GHQ was staffed by extremely capable men with, perhaps, less dash but vast amounts of disciplined drive. In addition the long campaign of street shootings may have done as much as anything to convince the British that Ireland could not be controlled solely by force. When it was no longer possible for a British officer to walk from his tea at the Shelbourne Hotel to an office at the Castle without risking a bullet in the back, then times were indeed black.

11. The only result of the diplomatic campaign was recognition by Soviet Russia, felt to be a mixed blessing by many of the more pious members of Sinn Féin.

12. Only about fifty arrived in Ireland before July 1921. The rest were seized in New York on June 16. See J. Bowyer Bell, "The Thompson Submachine Gun in Ireland, 1921", *The Irish Sword*, vol. viii, no. 31, pp. 98–108.

13. Tom Barry, *Guerilla Days in Ireland*, Tralee, 1955, pp. 189–190.

CHAPTER III

The Irregular Years: Schism, Terror, and Despair, June 1921–August 1923

For an army heretofore invisible the process of coming, slowly at first, from the underground world of sweeps, raids, and ambushes was a disconcerting experience. Overnight the IRA volunteers became heroes, feted in public, welcomed with bonfires on the hills and dances in the square. To the cynical there seemed to be more heroes of recent vintage than proper but in the general euphoria no one was too particular. The more dedicated volunteers were horrified to see GHQ men pointed out on the street, to be identified by all, including the still-present British. A few of the IRA leaders warned that the truce did not automatically mean the end of the campaign. A few men had their doubts about any discussions and anticipated renewed fighting by the end of the summer. The overwhelming proportion of the Irish people, within and without the IRA, felt that the fighting was ended for good, that the British would not dare to begin again, and while reasonable precautions might be necessary, military confrontation was a thing of the past. The celebrations continued, everywhere but in the North.

The North as always was different and for the IRA most depressing. Not until the Northern Ireland Government had begun to function in June had Lloyd George asked for a truce and to the Northern Republicans the reason seemed obvious: Ulster, or six counties of it, was to remain British no matter what happened to the rest of the island. The North was crammed with British troops, with RIC soon to become the Royal Ulster Constabulary, with Special Constables, with all the paraphernalia of British power. In Belfast the truce, a sell-out in Orange eyes, was celebrated not by bonfires on the hills, but arson in the Catholic districts. On July 10, Belfast's Bloody Sunday, 161 Catholic homes were burned, fifteen persons killed and at least sixty-eight wounded. It was only a taste of what was to come. The Orangemen, fearful of absorption into a Green, Catholic Ireland where past Protestant arrogance would not be forgotten, suspicious of betrayal by the British, and blindly angered by the presence of heresy and treason in their midst, struck again and again during the next year at the Catholic community. Men were hounded out of their jobs, then their homes, and finally their country. Mobs, unrestrained by the police or army, ran loose firing and beating. Homes were burned. Men, women, and children were shot down in the streets. Vengeful Catholics struck back with counter-terror. Ulster was barely under control; but the Orange leaders were determined that nothing would shake them—as Craig said in October, Ulster was "a rock of granite". The old UVF had been revived and 100,000 men enlisted. Ulster would stay British.

It was not only Ulster and *de facto* partition that the Irish diplomats had to face, but the very fate of the Republic. A thirty-two-county Republic, free and Gaelic, was a dream; the demands of British security and British imperial interests imposed a grim reality. Some men still dreamed the dream, still insisted, on point of principle, that Irish patriots must defend the Republic to the death. Most, however, were willing to compromise, within reason of course. The intricate web of proposal and counter-proposal, trips to and from London, public protest and private agreement, gradually defined the issues and edged the Irish delegation, dominated by Collins and Griffith, closer to Lloyd George. In 1919 de Valera had felt that his first duty was to be out of Ireland in America; now he felt it essential to stay in Ireland, even during the final crucial meetings at the end of November and the beginning of December. By this time all hope of a real Republic had disappeared; agreement had been reached on the question of control, with the Irish winning all but complete autonomy. A Boundary Commission established for Ulster would surely reduce Northern Ireland to an unviable statelet that would have to come into a united Ireland. But Irish insistence on some form of external association had been unable to budge Lloyd George very far from his demand that allegiance to the Crown was essential. If a break came, de Valera and the Irish delegation had wanted to break over Ulster, but Griffith had been finessed on that. In December he and the delegation were manœuvred into signing the Treaty. In many ways it represented a magnificent achievement beside Irish aspirations of a decade ago, but there were three things that were bound to disappoint: the Treaty did not recognize the Republic, it did not guarantee a free united Ireland, and it stipulated an oath of allegiance.

When the Irish delegates returned to Dublin, the word was already out that there was to be no Republic. Some members of the IRA wanted to arrest Collins and Griffith for treason but Brugha put a stop to that. For the orthodox Republicans like Brugha and Austin Stack anything less than a Republic meant a return to war. For those somewhat less doctrinaire, like de Valera, a compromise was possible, but this particular compromise went too far. Some of the delegation tended to agree with de Valera: under threat of war they had signed a Treaty they disliked, but at least the freedom to gain freedom had been achieved. Collins felt the Treaty with all its faults was an excellent stepping stone to the Republic. Griffith felt that Ireland had gained more, for at least twenty-six counties, than in the past seven hundred years: the removal of British troops and equality with England. The country at large divided along similar lines, doctrinaire Republicans, de Valera moderates, the men of the stepping stone, and solid Treaty men. Everything indicated that most Irishmen belonged to the last two categories, as did the newspapers, the business community, the hierarchy of the Catholic Church, the southern Unionists and the men of substance. However, the largest and most powerful of the "institutions" of the Republic, the IRA, over 100,000 strong, was assuredly not happy with the Treaty.

During the six months following the July Truce, the IRA above ground had maintained its structure. The full-time leadership continued to organize and train. Weapons had been smuggled into Ireland, particularly from Germany. Summer camps were opened. Although prospects for another round faded, the army kept at alert. Only in the six counties of Northern Ireland was there action and that mostly for the protection of the harassed Catholic population. Some on GHQ felt that the IRA had been fortunate that the Truce came when it had. Others felt equally sincerely that the IRA could have fought on indefinitely and could return to battle with equal prospects of success at any time. The Treaty had come as a shock because it fell so far short of what had been promised. Just as the Dáil Cabinet had divided four in favour of (Griffith, Collins, William Cosgrave, and Robert Barton) and three against (de Valera, Brugha, and Stack), the GHQ divided very nearly down the middle. Within the IRA no one liked the Treaty but on the GHQ many, like Richard Mulcahy, Eoin O'Duffy, and Gearóid O'Sullivan, accepted Collins' stepping stone theory. Others most assuredly did not and their distaste for half-measures was shared by a substantial portion of the rank and file and field commanders, particularly in the major Southern divisions. If the unrepentant Republicans were in the majority in the IRA, Collins had the support of the tremendously influential IRB, which did not formally support the Treaty but permitted Collins to secure substantial backing for his position.

During December the debate continued, leading to a final vote in the Dáil on January 4, 1922. By sixty-four votes to fifty-seven, the Treaty was accepted. De Valera's leadership and his efforts to find a reasonable alternative had been rejected. The Dáil was committed to the Treaty and to forming a provisional Treaty Government to carry out its terms. De Valera was replaced by Griffith. The guard had changed. For the Republicans the idea that the Dáil could vote away the Republic was ludicrous—the deputies had no right to do wrong. The work of the glorious years since 1916 could not be destroyed by a vote of sixty-four to fifty-seven. Some in the IRA had long suspected Griffith of unorthodox leanings, just as some had distrusted Collins' involvement with the IRB, or feared a sell-out to the politicians.[1]

Thus the orthodox sought to preserve the doctrinal purity of Irish Republicanism by casting out the devils or absorbing them. Reciprocally, the Treatyites hoped that negative criticism might give way to tolerance, that the IRA could remain a "Republican" army, that all the mixed bag of Treaty opponents could be held at bay while the inevitable work of establishing the new Irish Free State continued—until violent opposition would no longer be practical. The astute and the cynical doubted that the Republicans could wait that long; once de Valera had polarized opposition to the Treaty an open confrontation was all but inevitable. There could be no compromise with the narrow orthodoxy of a Brugha, but with de Valera such a possibility existed, and had now gone. Increasingly men like Griffith and Ernest Blythe felt that the vote in the Dáil would have to be enforced by arms. They were not alone.

Within the IRA during the next months, the strains grew unbearable as successive attempts to compromise the differences between the Free State men and the Republicans failed. The new provisional government, unrecognized by Republicans, set up a Ministry of Defence under Mulcahy, with J. J. O'Connell as Commander-in-Chief and Eoin O'Duffy as Chief of Staff. GHQ was at Beggar's Bush Barracks. Bit by bit, as men were recruited to this new uniformed, paid "branch" of the IRA, the split grew wider. On January 11, a large section of the army demanded a General Army Convention within two months. The Republicans, men like Rory O'Connor, Liam Mellows, Liam Lynch, Ernie O'Malley, and Oscar Traynor, wanted to wrest the IRA from the control of the Dáil and, it was obvious, prepare to defend the Republic. In the next two months the situation deteriorated further: militancy was growing on both sides and neither seemed inclined to compromise. To the disgust and alarm of the IRA, the Free State was building up an alternative army and police, while the Free State Cabinet was deeply concerned at indications that the radical wing of the IRA was one step from declaring for a military dictatorship. By February the bitterness had reached a point where an open break might come accidentally. The IRA was raiding barracks to collect arms for any showdown, just as the Free State army was attempting to occupy as much as possible while there was still an opportunity. In Limerick, between February 23 and March 10, IRA men under Tomás Malone (Seán Forde) and the local Free State commanders barely avoided open war. On March 15, the Cabinet prohibited the Army Convention. Mulcahy announced that any officer attending would be dismissed from the army. The division was thus acknowledged formally, but the ideological one had widened for months.

The General Army Convention met on March 26 in Dublin. It was attended by 223 delegates representing sixteen divisions with a listed strength of 112,650. Many felt the time for talk had passed, and resolutions calling for a military dictatorship or immediate war barely failed of a majority. A new Executive was chosen; a new constitution was to be written; and a new course independent of the Dáil considered. An IRA GHQ was set up at Barry's Hotel with Liam Lynch as C/S. After April there were two armies, one loyal to the Free State provisional government and the other only to the IRA Executive. During April and May as restraint between the two dissolved, the close ties of the Tan War snapped one by one and the shooting began. By May 6, eight men had been killed and forty-nine wounded in armed clashes. The IRA grew increasingly bold, seizing buildings in Dublin and raiding banks for funds—a swoop on the Bank of Ireland netted £50,000. For their part the members of the Free State Cabinet felt that the activities of the IRA were illegal, immoral, and undemocratic. The Dáil had spoken. Everyone admitted the people favoured the Treaty. The Republicans offered nothing but renewed war as a programme. Yet, despite the mutterings of traitor and rebel, no one in the army wanted a real split, a real war, if there was any way of avoiding it. All spring, various combinations of officers met under various auspices to seek a compromise. Nothing substantial occurred until May 20 when Collins and de Valera signed a pact concerning the coming general election, alloting each faction of Sinn Féin a proportion of deputies that would more or less preserve the *status quo ante*. Sinn Féin might yet avoid an irrevocable schism. As for the army, the only hope seemed to lie in making common cause against the common enemy. In both GHQs plans were drawn up for action in Ulster.

Arms were exchanged and rearranged so that the British could not blame the Free State government for renewing the war in the North. Units were moved up from the South towards the new border. On the other side, behind the patrols of RUC and Special Constables, the situation had deteriorated. On May 31, there had been another serious incident, bringing the death toll to eighty-seven Protestants and 150 Catholics killed. Over £2,000,000 worth of damage had been done to Catholic property in Belfast. There seemed no end to the pogroms. On June 7, British troops backed by artillery drove out IRA units occupying Belleck and Pettigo on the Northern Ireland side of the border. War in the North seemed the only way out of the IRA–Free State impasse. In Dublin the IRA Executive had no intention of making any further compromises with Collins and Mulcahy. Entrenched in the Four Courts, they had agreed to the Ulster campaign and had evacuated some of the more prominent IRA positions in the city to relieve British pressure on Collins; but on June 14, they rejected a more comprehensive unity plan. On June 16, Ireland went to the polls in the Pact Election, a pact which many claimed Collins had already broken. The results were grim for the Republicans. Only thirty-six of de Valera's men were elected against fifty-eight for Griffith, and thirty-four others.

On June 18, the IRA met in an Extraordinary General Army Convention. The fire-eaters wanted action instead of appeasement. Griffith and Collins seemed to be whittling away the Republic day by day. The Free State was established: there was a new army, called Republican, a new police force, and a new Dáil, elected by swindle and dominated by Treatyites. Lynch was criticized for failing to take strong action. Tom Barry moved a resolution that the IRA at once attack the British and renew the war. Lynch felt that this would be irresponsible and urged moderation. He was backed by Brugha. Both were impeccable Republicans arguing tactics not principles. They won by 118 to 103. The losers would not accept the continued delay. They withdrew from the Convention. Twelve members of the Executive had voted with Barry and now chose Joseph McKelvey as the new C/S. Lynch felt he could no longer go on as C/S. Although he remained in Dublin, the recognized centre of the IRA was the Four Courts where McKelvey, Rory O'Connor, Liam Mellows, Dick Barrett, and the other dissidents met to decide what the next step should be.

Then on June 22, Field Marshal Sir Henry Wilson, Chief of the Imperial General Staff and a bitter foe of the Irish Republic, was assassinated in London. The British government unjustly blamed the militant IRA leaders in the Four Courts and urged the Free State government to take appropriate steps. The Griffith–Blythe bloc had long been advocating to Collins the need for firm action; and with the IRA split after the June 18 Convention, the time seemed ideal. Also on June 22, in retaliation for the arrest of one of their officers, the IRA seized J. J. O'Connell and held him in Four Courts. This provocative action relieved the Free State of the burden of acting solely as a result of British pressure. However, the IRA leadership, once more almost united as a result of discussions with Lynch, did not believe with the joint campaign in Ulster in the wind that the Free State would actually attack. All day June 27, Dublin was filled with rumours. The IRA C/O for Dublin, Oscar Traynor, began to make preparations. Lynch stayed in conference at Four Courts from ten in the evening until one in the morning of June 28. At 3.40 a.m. the Free State demanded the surrender of Four Courts by 4.00. The request was refused and the IRA waited for the Free State to fire the first shot. It came at 4.30 from a British artillery piece.

From Wednesday morning until Friday, Free State artillery pounded the Four Courts reducing it to a flaming wreck. The IRA volunteers and most of the Executive were forced to surrender. Elsewhere in Dublin Oscar Traynor had alerted IRA positions, largely concentrated in a great triangle from the GPO down Talbot Street to Moran's Hotel and to an apex on Parnell Square. Once the Four Courts had gone up in flames and at the last minute spectacularly exploded, the Free State troops closed in on the

IRA. Put on the defensive at once, cut off from reinforcements, without artillery or armoured cars, the IRA re-ran the reel of 1916. Cathal Brugha held out at the Hamman Hotel until there was nothing left but a flaming ruin. Twice he refused orders sent in by Traynor to surrender and when he finally came out, he still carried a revolver. He was shot, as he might have expected, and died two days later. Overt IRA resistance in Dublin had ended.

Neither side knew exactly what to expect next. Both Lynch and Liam Deasy had been picked up during the fighting, interviewed by Eoin O'Duffy in Wellington Barracks, and let go apparently on a misunderstanding. Released they moved South to prepare resistance to the attack on the army of the Republic by the pawns of Britain. At this point the IRA outnumbered the Free State army by four or five to one. Mulcahy did, however, have artillery supplied by the British and the promise of more equipment and funds. Equally important the Free State had a firm, dynamic government installed in Dublin and recognized abroad as the legitimate government, whereas the Republicans were dominated by the IRA and had apparently determined on a military dictatorship. What Republican political talent that did exist was ignored by the IRA: for example, de Valera's official position was an assistant to Seán Moylan, Director of Operations. Still the Free State, fully exploiting its political talent, its "legitimacy", and its British connection, would have collapsed if the IRA had struck hard and fast at the Dublin centre. The IRA did not.

The closest drive was a bumbling operation up from the South through Blessington toward Dublin. Slow, uncertain of aim, the IRA columns were blunted and turned back. There was no other attempt. Apparently GHQ felt it sufficient to defend the line running from Waterford in the east to Limerick in the west and maintain contact with IRA units elsewhere. No overall war-plan appeared nor did the IRA show any indication of pushing hard against the Free State forces. Instead GHQ waited. The martial reticence on both sides was the result of a commendable reluctance to pursue civil war to its inevitable and bloody conclusion. Every few weeks there was some variety of peace feeler, secret conference, or neutral offer. None succeeded. Instead the Free State began moving on both flanks of the Republic of Munster, striking at Waterford and Limerick. Instead of the aggressive, belligerent Republicans, who had been crying war for weeks, it was the Free State men who seized the initiative and discarded any scruples over Irish blood. The Dublin IRA had given the Free State license to isolate and destroy the garrisons—admirable ethically but tactical madness. Once the Free State realized that the Dublin operation had not finished the "war" but merely begun it, the move to the South began. New men were brought into the army at the rate of three hundred a day until the total reached sixty thousand. Artillery and armoured cars were imported from the British. The offensive continued.

By the end of July, the Republican defensive line was badly strained. Without artillery, and thin on the ground, the IRA had been forced to give up Waterford and Limerick and, on July 30, Tipperary. On August 2, Carrick-on-Suir fell and the IRA position became precarious. The Free State had made few mistakes. IRA pools of strength in the rest of the country had been contained or eliminated. On the "front" in the South the initiative had been maintained and the IRA driven from one stronghold after another. Only in the managing of the 4th Northern Division had there been an excess of enthusiasm which drove the C/O, Frank Aiken, into the Republican camp; but Ulster was a special case and no great threat to the Free State. Essentially the success had come because of a tough-minded Free State GHQ in Dublin, the use of British artillery, and the failure of the IRA to master the small but conventional battles which made up the civil war. By August 11, the first phase of the war ended with Republican disaster. A seaborne landing had secured Tralee by August 6. Similar landings were repeated around Cork City on August 9/10. On August 10, the IRA pulled out of Cork. To the north Lynch withdrew from Clonmel, the last urban GHQ of the IRA. The Free State had won the conventional war of little battles and brief barrages. On August 11, Lynch was in the mountains, on the run again and forced to turn to the old familiar guerrilla tactics.

Neither GHQ nor the IRA commanders felt the war was lost. The Kerry C/Os felt they could hold off the Free State army indefinitely. The Volunteers were familiar with the country, with the tactics, and were certain that the Free State army would crumble when faced with a return to the Tan War strategy. So there was no swift end to the war. The cost to the nation began to mount. Brugha was dead. Harry Boland had been shot and mortally wounded in a hotel in Skerries on July 31. Michael Collins followed his best friend on August 22, shot dead in an ambush in County Cork. Griffith had died of a heart attack ten days before. The Free State had suffered approximately six hundred casualties and the IRA probably more. The material cost to both sides and ultimately to Ireland rose as houses were burned, bridges destroyed, and railways sabotaged. The IRA continued the guerrilla tactics all through the autumn forcing the Free State to increase the size of the army, import arms, and wage war instead of building the nation. A dreadful blow to Republican morale came when the Catholic hierarchy in an October Pastoral condemned the IRA volunteers for resisting and withdrew the right of the sacraments from them. The war of sniping, raids, and arson continued without the bishops' permission. The bitterness grew on both sides. The Free State to force the end of guerrilla tactics resorted to harsh measures. A Bill passed the Dáil authorizing military courts for a variety of offences. On November 17, 1922, four IRA volunteers were executed—essentially for waging war against the government. To demonstrate that no one, however exalted, would escape the government's campaign of legalized terror, Erskine Childers was shot on November 23, having been found in possession of a small pistol once given him by Collins, even while an application for an *habeas corpus* order was pending. The Cabinet had decided that in the long run a campaign of counter-terror would save lives and bring the war of attrition to a swifter end. The executions went on. The IRA replied by shooting two of the deputies responsible for the Murder Bill, one of whom subsequently died. Before the already uneasy Third Dáil could collapse in panic the Cabinet ordered the executions, without any pretence of legality, of Rory O'Connor, Liam Mellows, Joseph McKelvey, and Richard Barrett. They were taken out and shot on December 8.

The war dragged on through the winter. The executions continued. The casualties continued at the rate of three hundred a month. More houses were burned, more railway bridges sabotaged, more atrocities, particularly in Kerry, against IRA volunteers occurred. There were over ten thousand Republican prisoners. No county was really secure and particularly in Munster the Free State maintained only a tenuous order outside the cities. To the new Free State Cabinet under William Cosgrave the total eliminations of the "irregulars" was but a matter of time. The Free State army was now overpoweringly stronger, the executions had largely shattered IRA morale, and the people had lost sympathy with the IRA for dragging out the agony. From their safe houses in Dublin or the hideouts in the hills, the IRA was no longer united in optimism or faith in ultimate victory. As early as January Liam Deasy, after his capture, had called for negotiations. Some like Lynch continued to believe military victory was possible. Many others hoped that the Republican government, recognized by the IRA Executive in October 1922 but allowed to languish during the course of military operations, might find a compromise solution. Even by March, few could believe that the war was unconditionally lost. Admittedly there were twelve thousand Republican prisoners, little hope of heavy arms being smuggled to the IRA columns, and declining capacity to evade the endless searches and swoops, but with the IRA in the field some terms might be made. From March 23 to 26, the IRA Executive met to discuss the future. They were split almost down the middle on the prospects of the future. Tom Barry's motion that resistance would not further the cause of independence lost, five votes to six. The Executive decided to meet again in April.

On April 6, Maurice Twomey and Tom Derrig were captured. On April 10, on the way to the meeting, Lynch was shot and mortally wounded in the Knockmealdown mountains. The bad news began to pile up. Austin Stack was captured on April 14, Dan Breen was captured, as were Frank Barrett, C/O 1st Western Division, and Seán Gaynor, C/O 3rd Southern Division. On April 20, the Executive met again with Aiken as C/S. The will to resist had gone with Lynch. The hope was that de Valera and the "government" might be able to make some sort of terms. On April 27, de Valera issued a Proclamation suspending IRA aggressive action at least by April 30. Contact was made with Free State Senators Andrew Jameson and James Douglas but Cosgrave refused to negotiate. The Free State government knew they had won even if the IRA could not accept their defeat. There were no terms to offer, merely an unconditional surrender to accept. De Valera found no basis for a compromise and in the meanwhile the Free State army had continued operations ignoring the April 27 proclamation. The executions went on. There was, as Cosgrave recognized, no Republican alternative, "they are prepared to accept peace only if they are guaranteed a lease of political life. We are not going to guarantee them a lease of political life."[2] On May 13 and 14, the Republic government and Executive met again. The last gesture that anyone could find was a refusal to surrender or to give up arms. On May 24, Eamon de Valera sent the Volunteers still in the field a stirring message beginning, "Soldiers of the Republic, Legion of the Rearguard".

> The Republic can no longer be defended successfully by your arms. Further sacrifice of life would now be vain and continuance of the struggle in arms unwise in the national interest and prejudicial to the future of our case. Military victory must be allowed to rest for the moment with those who have destroyed the Republic. Other means must be sought to safeguard the nation's right.[3]

With the prisons jammed, the Volunteers defeated, the moral capital of the Republic squandered in the long, futile campaign of attrition, with Cosgrave and his men secure and comfortable in power, proud of their record of seventy-seven executions[4] and determined to rule within the narrow terms of the Treaty, no one could see what other means might bring the Republic, no one believed that the Free State's military victory was a matter of the moment. The glorious dream of Easter 1916 had gone. There was to be no Republic. There was only to be a mean, bitter Ireland, partitioned by the Crown, governed by murderers imposed by the British. There was nothing to be done. With de Valera's message came the order from the Aiken camp to dump arms and disperse.

NOTES

1. Oddly enough in 1919 Collins had opposed Brugha's insistence that the Volunteers take an oath to the Dáil on the grounds that some day the Dáil might compromise the Republic.
2. Dorothy Macardle, *The Irish Republic*, New York, 1965, p. 855.
3. *Ibid.*, p. 858.
4. Certainly some in the Cabinet were not particularly proud of what all agreed had been a necessary—and successful—act of state; but the executions were strongly defended in public, particularly by Kevin O'Higgins, and Richard Mulcahy said in the Dáil that "the pride we have is deep in our hearts, pride that we are shouldering responsibilities that are very heavy and great", after the shooting on December 8.

CHAPTER IV

The Legion of the Rearguard: The Response to Defeat, May 1923–August 1927

Despite the dump arms order on May 24, the war did not so much end as dribble away in brief clashes, private violence, continued arrests, and repeated Free State sweeps through "irregular" territory. Some of the IRA local commanders, particularly in Kerry and Mayo, either did not react to the cease fire immediately or were unwilling to accept the end; but it was obvious to most that all hope was long gone. By June 16, the Free State army could report that despite land trouble in Waterford and odd pockets of unrest, the "irregulars" were no longer of serious concern.

> A little improvement shows itself every week and if the present "peace atmosphere" lasts the country will not be long in getting back to normal conditions.[1]

The government, however, showed no sudden burst of magnanimity. The army was not demobilized and the swollen intelligence section working with police detectives continued to track down Republicans on the run. Not only were there no releases from the prisons but the arrests regularly added to the number scattered in the camps and jails. The number of prisoners had in fact been so great as early as autumn 1922 that the government had briefly considered borrowing the island of St. Helena from the British to use as an internment camp. This scheme was dropped in favour of a prison ship, an idea discarded in its turn. Meanwhile the existing prisons and jerry-built camps filled to overflowing. By July 1, there were 11,316 prisoners on the rolls, some the equivalent of prisoners of war, others members of dubious organizations, and still others detained on suspicion. Even the terror and violence did not end immediately. On July 3, Noel Lemass was "detained" and disappeared. Not until October 12 was his body found near the Hell Fire Club in the Dublin Mountains. For all intents and purposes the Cabinet showed not the slightest inclination to recognize even the legitimacy of defeat—and for good reason.

The Cabinet in Dublin continued the uninterrupted policy of coercion in the name of order at least in part because the Republicans had steadfastly refused to recognize the legitimacy, even in some cases the existence, of the victorious "order". There had been no surrender, sullen or unconditional, only a dumping of arms and a creeping away to wait for a better day. There had been no diminution of moral righteousness even in the face of majority opinion, no recognition that the terror burnings and sabotage had cost the Irish people—not just the Free State government—a fortune; in fact, there had been no sign of remorse, which after a bitter civil conflict might be reasonable. Even more ominous, not a word was heard, not a hint, that defeated in the field and the voting booth the cause of the Republic as defined by de Valera and defended by Lynch had floundered. Until the Republicans could accept the finality of defeat, recognize the new government, and live as repentant citizens or leave as wild geese, the Free State Cabinet could not afford to be magnanimous in victory without risking that very victory.

The prisons stayed closed. On July 26 the Public Safety Act was passed by the Dáil and sent to the Seanad. During June all *habeas corpus* writs had been denied on the grounds that "the Irish Republican Army did not state that a state of war had ceased to exist".[2] With the passage of time it was clear that this argument would be insufficient and that without additional legislation all internees would have to be released. The Public Safety Act corrected this situation by giving the government extensive emergency powers. It came into effect on August 1, barely in time. The release of Mrs. Connolly O'Brien had been ordered by the Court of Appeals on the previous day, the apparent harbinger of the end of detention of internees. In a burst of complex constitutional problems, a newer more efficient Public Safety Act was rushed through both Houses on August 3 assuring the government that there would not be a sudden flood of unrepentant Republicans released on the devastated countryside. Opinion was mixed as to the seriousness of any immediate Republican threat. Several members of the government felt little but contempt for the pretensions of "President" de Valera and the convoluted arguments of the second Dáil's *de jure* power. Although it was generally agreed that the IRA was, for the time being, a spent force, captured correspondence from Frank Aiken, C/S, indicated that a second round was envisioned by GHQ at least. With nearly sixty thousand men under arms, a monopoly on heavy equipment, nearly complete control of the countryside, the financial and military support of Great Britain, and the record of the last year, the Free State government hardly faced the prospect of a "second round" with trepidation; but the time to forgive and forget—and to release—had not come.

The prime concern of the government was not the remote possibility of renewed fighting but the arduous and highly technical challenge of creating a government, outlining a budget, devising an economic policy: in sum to give the Irish Free State institutions, directions, and policies in an atmosphere less hectic than that of the war months. One of the first steps to normal conditions was to be the general election in August.

Although there would be a wealth of independent candidates and representatives of Labour and the Farmers in the field, the government party of Cumann na nGaedheal which had been founded in the spring, would apparently have little serious difficulty. The Republicans, however, still organized legally as Sinn Féin, decided to contest the elections. Under Eamon Donnelly as Director of Elections, the party put forward eighty-seven candidates, including men in prison or still on the run. While the Sinn Féin people by no means had an easy time—workers were beaten or threatened, posters destroyed, meetings interrupted—the government did not stuff out the "legitimate" Republican opposition. Cumann na nGaedheal had little to lose since Sinn Féin was running on an abstentionist platform and could hardly threaten the government majority in the Dáil even if the Republicans did far better than most observers assumed. Opposed by the entire press and the Catholic hierarchy, crippled by arrests and the loss of ten thousand men in prison, the campaign seemed to many of the more pro-government men as a last effort to salvage something from the debacle. Whatever that "something" might be, the government knew that it was not going to be power.

All during August the Sinn Féin campaign continued gathering a certain momentum almost to the surprise of the Republicans. On August 15, de Valera, who had been nominated for his old seat in Clare, appeared as promised on the platform at Ennis in the midst of a huge crowd in the market square. Free State soldiers immediately approached the platform in two files with fixed bayonets protected by an armoured car with machine gun. Several volleys were fired over the crowd and in the mêlée de Valera was led away, as he must have anticipated. He was soon in solitary confinement in Arbour Hill Barracks. On August 18, the Dublin Sinn Féin headquarters was raided. Despite, or perhaps because of, the handicaps, Sinn Féin on August 27 did far better than anticipated even by the optimistic. Forty-four candidates were elected including a score of household names. De Valera, Frank Aiken, P. J. Ruttledge (Acting-President while de Valera was in jail), Mrs. Cathal Brugha, Mary MacSwiney, Austin Stack, Constance Markievicz. In Wexford Sinn Féin polled sixty per cent of the vote. In Kerry seventy-six, and in Clare eighty per cent. Overall, Cumann na nGaedheal had received 415,000 first preference votes to 286,000 for Sinn Féin and sixty-three seats to forty-four. The Irish press hailed the results as a vindication of the Free State and the Cosgrave government. As usual the Republicans were listening to a different drum: to them the forty-four seats heralded the first step back, proving that all the people had not turned from 1916 or swallowed whole the Treaty-line.

For most Republicans in the autumn of 1923 the road back appeared rather rocky. The IRA had gone underground. In Dublin Aiken kept a GHQ operating and maintained liaison with the Republican government's Minister of Defence Seán Lemass. Although, as usual, GHQ did not have money, there was sufficient to maintain the staff-men on the run and to keep organizers in touch with the men in the country. The IRA had always been organized from the parish up, so once the Volunteers returned home and assuming the Free State showed no interest, local units could be maintained. There was, however, no clear idea of what could be done. The reorganization of the IRA was as much a habitual reaction to disaster as a coherent preparation for the future. To some, even those involved, the day-to-day military activities seemed unreal—the Republic had been defeated militarily and ten thousand men were in prison, the Free State was operating normally, passing laws, and running the country, while the IRA GHQ in secret meetings under threat of arrest mulled over vague war plans.

The only virile, practical Republican activity was the prisoners' release campaign headed by Maud Gonne MacBride making use not only of the law and the scandal of conditions in the camps and jails but of the long-lived Irish distaste for political imprisonment. Life in the prisons was occasionally brutal, often unpleasant, the food was poor and monotonous, heating limited, sanitation scanty, and the guards prone to shoot at random to maintain discipline. The campaign contended that the prisoners were being held illegally, that conditions were appalling, and the repeated shooting incidents little more than criminal. The new Cosgrave government turned a deaf ear, stone deaf. Not only were the Republicans unrepentant but they continued to take no notice of the will of the people, as expressed in the August election, they continued to maintain a *de jure* "government" and they continued to rebuild the IRA for the next round. Army intelligence reported on October 15 that the Republicans had prepared during September a three-pronged assault on the Free State government.

(1) Secure release of prisoners.
(2) Strengthen and develop political machine to capture local bodies.
(3) Reconstruct and build up an invisible machine that may be used more on terrorist lines amongst the civil population than as a fighting force in the field.[3]

The Minister of Justice Kevin O'Higgins responded:

We will not have two governments in this country, and we will not have two armies in this country. If people have a creed to preach, a message to expound, they can go before their fellow-citizens and preach and expound it. But let the appeal be to the mind, to reason rather than to physical fear. They cannot have it both ways. They cannot have the platform and the bomb.[4]

To the government during the autumn there was no argument however humanitarian that could justify turning loose thousands of men still dedicated to destroying, with campaign speech or bomb, the still fragile Free State.

Inside the prisons the men were inclined to increase the pressure. Short of riot, which was used from time to time as much in boredom as a result of higher strategy, the traditional means of exerting pressure was the hunger strike. In Mountjoy most of the prison leadership was eager to undertake a strike and sent out word to Aiken at GHQ for permission.[5] Aiken was less than enthusiastic but allowed the Prison Council to determine the course of action. The problem with a hunger strike is that only certain men are temperamentally suited to maintain a fast—apparently it is not a matter of courage, moral or physical, but a lack of a certain kind of self-discipline whose absence is not easily recognized until too late. A *mass* hunger strike greatly increases the chances that some men will have to give up, thus weakening the morale of all. Even if all the men persist, a determined government can simply wait it out, throwing on the strikers and their leaders the onus of subsequent deaths, not an easy burden for weakened and pious men. Despite the problems, in October the leadership in Mountjoy voted for a strike. Soon there were 425 strikers including ten TDs. The strike spread to Kilmainham and then to the other prisons and camps. On October 23, the *Republican Bulletin* claimed that there were eight thousand men on strike. The number began to decline immediately. Outside the camps and prisons, Maud McBride intensified her campaign. There were parades, protests, pickets. Inside there were massive defections. On November 18, Cardinal Logue expressed the hope that before Christmas all prisoners not guilty of a crime would be released. The government did not respond. By this time only a few hundred men were holding out. Peadar O'Donnell, who had been transferred from Mountjoy to Kilmainham, felt that with the defections the point was gone.

> There were now some few hundreds of men still on strike, and any moment some of these must be due to die. Such deaths would, in time, shine out as terrible indictments of the jailers but in the immediate present they would only spread confusion among the mass of the people. Had it been possible for thousands to hold solidly to the hunger-strike we should have torn down the walls of the prisons and the abuse and misrepresentations of the new garrison would have been set aside. But once the solidarity broke . . .[6]

O'Donnell, like the others still striking, refused to quit. On November 20, Commandant Denis Barry died in Newbridge camp. On November 22, Captain Andrew Sullivan died in Mountjoy. With the deaths on one side and the defections on the other all hope had been lost. On November 23, the strike was called off in Kilmainham.

With the men split, sullen and embittered at the collapse of the great strike, the Free State government began releasing batches of prisoners. At first the Volunteers were asked to sign a form accepting the Free State. When most refused, the rule was changed, but by then it was too late; the schisms of the strike were largely closed by a renewed prison fellowship, easier since it was obviously the eve of release. By the time most of the camps and prisons were cleared of the average Volunteers during the winter of 1923–1924, all that had been lost during the strike had been regained. Inside the more prominent prisoners had begun again to plot and plan for the future. The lines into GHQ were clogged with proposals and prospects. The ex-internees returned to reactivate local units. The remaining internees contacted cousins, younger brothers, and old friends on the loose to get things moving. Again in just what direction the IRA and the Republicans would move remained unclear, but at GHQ the dominant feeling was that the first task was to reorganize the army and then see how the land lay. In 1923–1924, this "reorganization" was covert—the organizers slipping about the country in second-hand automobiles and on old bicycles. In Dublin GHQ had been beefed up by the arrival of Séan MacBride, Michael Price, and Dáithí O'Donoghue who had escaped in October from an ambulance moving them from Mountjoy to Kilmainham. Beyond the full-time staff men on the run a great many locals, now grudgingly tolerated by the police and army, were spending the nights and week-ends putting the pieces together again. No serious effort was being made at recruitment or training but rather an effort to get the old loyal men shaken down into proper units and an accurate check-list of both men and armament put together. Under the eyes of Free State intelligence, with many of the connecting links broken by death or continued imprisonment, this was not an easy task, nor one that showed ready returns.

The Free State had accepted that the country was going to have to live with unreconstructed Republicans. On January 16, 1924, the Public Safety Act was re-enacted giving the government emergency powers, including the suspension of *habeas corpus*, until January 31, 1925. This shoring up the state against the potential danger of the IRA ignored a long festering threat from within the Free State army itself. Many of those who had taken the Treaty side had done so in loyalty to Collins or in hopes that the Free State would be a stepping stone to a Republic. Collins was dead and the Cabinet seemed wedded to a narrow interpretation of the Treaty. More irritating, the army had kept former British professional soldiers and demobilized the old IRA men. Shot through the whole frustrating patch-work of policy disagreements, personal antagonisms, and temperamental clashes was the reluctance of a segment of the army to settle into the limited, humdrum garrison life of a tiny peace-time army. The glory days had gone to be replaced by busy ministers in three-piece suits quibbling over pension plans and licensing laws. The discontented army clique was bound together by shared sacrifices and a distaste for the Irish Republican Brotherhood, which had been revived to give a greater coherence to the army. Thus by March 1924, the self-nominated Old IRA felt in a position to challenge the direction of the Cosgrave cabinet and the position of strength enjoyed by the IRB.

On March 6, President Liam Cosgrave received an ultimatum from the "IRA Organization" signed by Major-General Liam Tobin and Colonel C. F. Dalton. What became known as the Army Mutiny was under way.[7] The mutineers made no move to leap to the barricades. Joseph McGrath, Minister for Industry and Commerce, was the only member of the cabinet to support the demands and he resigned on March 7. Later in the month eight other deputies followed his example. A few officers absconded with arms. Eoin O'Duffy, the Commissioner of Police, was brought in as Commander-in-Chief and Inspector-General of the Forces to deal with the emergency. O'Higgins, who had come to share the mutineers' dislike of the revived IRB, wanted O'Duffy to root out the organization, discipline the mutineers, and turn the army from politics to professionalism. On March 11, the Old IRA withdrew their demands following Cosgrave's Dáil speech on the Mutiny. Negotiations began, apparently with some prospect of success. The wrangling dragged on in vague backstairs plots and shifting conferences until March 16 when an unauthorized raid on Devlin's pub in Parnell Street collected ten of the "mutineers" at the price of an open gun fight. The members of the Army Council directly responsible, including the Chief of Staff, Adjutant General, and Quartermaster General, were dismissed by the Cabinet. On March 19, General Mulcahy resigned as Minister of Defence. O'Higgins was convinced that Mulcahy was too deeply involved in the IRB reorganization and the two men had often clashed on army policy. Despite the Cabinet's early intelligence reports on the discontent and the inept, undirected manœuvres of the Old IRA, the affair had not been handled with dispatch. In fact the policy of muddling through had taken so long that real rather than artificial disaster nearly struck.

The reorganization which had begun in 1923 resulted in a "new" IRB rather than a revival of the old IRB. The latter had been in an advanced state of decay by the time of the Tan War and was all but moribund after Collins' death. Seán McKeon had taken over as Chairman, Lieutenant-General Ó Muirthile was Secretary, and Eoin O'Duffy Treasurer (a fact that had escaped O'Higgins' attention).[8] The Old IRA malcontents, on the other hand, had renewed their allegiance to an earlier form of the IRB. Using links formed in the old days, they attempted to make contact with their late opponents, some of whom were still in Free State prisons. For most Republicans the IRB was dead and discredited. Although the IRB had split on the Treaty issue, two provinces for and two against, and thus no directions to members had been given, Collins had used the IRB for his own purposes whenever possible. When these purposes wandered from those of the IRA, the IRB became a Treaty-front. There may, however, have been a few old IRB–IRA members who were willing to listen to the propositions of the agents of the new IRB. Who the agents were, who they represented, what they said, remains mysterious; but the indications are that some hoped a new IRB–IRA attack on the British would heal the splits of the last years, provoke the British to retaliate, and provide a foundation for an Ireland united once again. On March 21, a four-man Republican attack-team dressed in Free State uniforms waited in a long, yellow limousine opposite the landing dock in Cobh where the boat from the British base on Spike Island unloaded passengers. When the launch drew up, the four men waited until the soldiers had disembarked and then thrusting two Thompsons out of the windows fired both magazines into the crowd on the landing-stage. Five civilians, two of them women, were wounded, as were an officer and eighteen soldiers, a private mortally. Despite intensive police work and a £10,000 reward, the four men were never found, although in time their names became well-known in IRA circles. As a pretext for war the shooting failed. The Free State government apologized and paid the British compensation. The British accepted. The last bloody act of the great Army Mutiny was over with the Cabinet stronger than ever and the possibility of an Army–IRA alliance, faint at best, snuffed out.

Except for the few men involved in the murky IRB contact, most Republicans in the spring of 1924 were interested in getting out of prison, or staying out, and finding a job. The number still held declined gradually: On April 2, 1,914 men, including 314 of those sentenced, were still held; on May 21, the total was down to 616. At this point the Republicans on the outside began to threaten to disrupt the planned Tailteann Games in protest. There was no comment from the Free State government; but on July 1 only 209 men were still being held. On July 16, de Valera was released. The dangerous and the notorious were freed during the remainder of the year in dribs and drabs. By then many of the "dangerous" were on the outside in any case, for at one time or another nearly every prominent IRA man had managed to escape: Barry, who walked in the front gate of a camp and out the back, Peadar O'Donnell, for whom the gates of the Curragh Camp "flew open" in March 1924, Price and MacBride, who recovered sufficiently to take over their ambulance during a prison transfer. Once the Army Mutiny was over, the Cabinet did not care much one way or the other whether the Republicans were plotting in prison or out. The Free State was now well and truly launched, significant legislation had been passed, the civil service, the police and under O'Duffy's eye the army, all were efficient and effective, order had been restored, war damage repaired, and plans prepared for the future.

One problem that persisted for the Free State was the negotiations concerning the North. As expected, the six counties had opted out of the Irish Free State at the first opportunity, but according to Article 12 of the Treaty the eventual North–South border was to be decided by a Boundary Commission. The government of Northern Ireland, well aware that two counties (Tyrone and Fermanagh) had Nationalist, i.e. Catholic, majorities as did South Armagh, South Down, and large parts of Derry, showed no interest in being whittled into an Orange enclave. On April 26, Cosgrave had to inform the British government that no progress could be made. Over the next few months a British Bill was drafted that unilaterally amended the Treaty to allow London to appoint a representative for Northern Ireland on the Boundary Commission. Cosgrave accepted this and did not seem alarmed at the "interpretations" of Article 12 coming out of London which suggested that the Treaty signers had intended no more than the exchange of a few parishes. In the South de Valera, once released, entered the fray to challenge Lloyd George's public "interpretations" that the boundary problem "was only a minor sectarian quarrel in a corner of Ireland".[9] In the North the Catholic population was increasingly uneasy at the prospect of being deserted by Dublin and left to the Orangemen. There was not much that could be done. The Unionists had a firm grip on the government at Belfast, the police were mostly Protestant, the British Army was on call, the prisons still held Irish rebels, the remains of the IRA were deep underground and the other Irish army in the South, wracked by mutiny, seemed a weak reed.[10] On October 7, at the opening of the Northern Ireland Parliament, Sir James Craig made it clear that he would not accept an unfavourable report from the Boundary Commission, a possibility that grew increasingly remote. During the Westminster elections at the end of the month, de Valera personally intervened in the North on behalf of Republican candidates. At Newry he was arrested, detained until next day, and escorted back to the border. He moved on to Derry where he was arrested, tried on November 1 at Belfast, and imprisoned for a month. Nothing came of his intervention for the power of protest was feeble indeed in the face of the Unionist determination to give not an inch.

If Republican political intervention in the North had been sterile, there were at least heartening signs of revival in the South. Gradually, at times reluctantly, the Free State government was returning the country to normal conditions. Civil persecution for military acts ended and the prisoners were almost all free. The police and army intelligence was still hyperactive in tracking down IRA men but Sinn Féin, the political wing, was allowed to function freely if under constant surveillance. On November 4, the Ard Fheis was held in Dublin with 1,300 delegates present. On November 19, there were five by-elections, two of which were won by Sinn Féin. More important in all five constituencies the Republican vote went up—most impressively in South Dublin (from 9,749 to 17,297), where Seán Lemass was elected. All these seats, however, remained symbolic; Sinn Féin TDs continued to shun membership in a usurping legislature set up by the British government. According to Republican dictum the only *de jure* government remained the Second Dáil, although of course Sinn Féin deputies to other Dáils had been elected in 1923 and 1924.

Excluded by dogma from Leinster House, the Sinn Féin TDs organized the Cómhairle, which included all TDs elected by Sinn Féin since 1921. There were those who anticipated the day when Sinn Féin TDs receiving a majority in the country could meet outside Leinster House and re-establish the Republic. In the meantime the Cómhairle na d Teachtaí, with only the second Dáil members voting, was the *de jure* government of Ireland.

For those who believed, the tide seemed to be turning, the current swifter. On March 11, there were nine by-elections, a little general election, and once again in every constituency the Republican vote increased and two Sinn Féin candidates won non-seats at Leinster House bringing the party total to forty-eight. On April 3, in the North Ireland elections, two Sinn Féin candidates won on abstentionist tickets and ten Nationalists were successful. More telling, Joseph Devlin, the key Nationalist in the north, took his seat in the Northern Parliament underlining by his acceptance of Northern Ireland institutions the hopelessness of the Free State efforts to undo partition. In April there was what appeared further evidence of the bankruptcy of Cosgrave's government. O'Higgins had brought in a Treasonable Offences Act, replacing the expiring temporary Public Safety Act; the new Act would impose the death penalty for levying war against the State and make the usurpation of executive authority or of parliamentary function and the formation of a pretended military force misdemeanours. The terms were severe and aimed as much at the current pretentions of Republican ideology as the future protection of the state. The Bill was popular in no quarter and O'Higgins only managed to steer the "Murder Bill" through the Dáil with the help of massive abstentions. On April 3, the Bill passed, securing only thirty votes. Could the government sink lower? The North abandoned, the Dáil ignored, the economy in ruins, emigration rising, the people turning to Sinn Féin, the Treaty discredited. Not all

Republicans, however, were so sanguine about the eventual triumph of justice and the cause of 1916.

These more practical men accepted, if reluctantly, that the growing enthusiasm for abstentionist Sinn Féin TDs was a transient phase. It was unlikely that substantial portions of the electorate would persist in fruitless symbolic votes against the Treaty. In time voters would turn to men who were in a position to pass desirable legislation, to guide citizens through the labyrinths of the bureaucracy, to look after the interests of a constituency. To depend on the unswerving loyalty of the average Republican voter was to build on sand. There were already signs of pressure. Almost from the moment the results of the March general election were posted, agents of the Free State government began to pick up garbled reports that some Republican TDs favoured entry into the Dáil.[11] Month after month Republican spokesmen publicly denied that any such move was contemplated. In private cautious probing and prodding went on in an atmosphere thick with the smell of heresy and apostasy.

Practical men argued the impracticability of a military second round; a continuing policy of abstentionism would surely but certainly isolate Sinn Féin from the main stream of Irish life and turn the party into a huddle of the bitter and by-passed capable only of criticism not construction, faithful to the ideal Republic but incapable of taking a step to achieve it; the only practical alternative was to achieve the Republic in stages by moving back into political life leaving behind the arcane theories of Second Dáil's *de jure* existence and the hedgehog soldier mentality of the IRA. As 1925 slipped by, there was accumulating evidence that a new direction could not wait forever. The Free State was determined to impose their legitimacy on the nation. Those who dissented could leave or withdraw into a corner of the stage. All government positions required an oath of allegiance to the government. Even local government grants were handed out with an eye to the ultimate receiver—the loyal ditch-digger. Jobs in any case were hard to find and the flight of the wild geese began again during the spring. Solid Republic parishes saw the young men in twos and threes leave for America or England until a firm Sinn Féin area had drained away.

There were other problems. There was not enough money and the golden tide from Clan na Gael had ebbed. During 1925 the lack of sufficient American funds meant a cut-back in all Republican activity. There was no hope of establishing a daily newspaper to balance the Treatyite press. The make-do *Daily Bulletin* had ended publication on August 13 to be replaced by *Sinn Féin* (vol. I, no. 1, August 7, 1923) which became the only Republican publication when *Éire* (Glasgow) ended publication on October 25, 1924. There could be no great flood of Republican publications to educate the masses. There were problems paying salaries, problems paying for meeting rooms. And all the while those content with their purity ran over the old wrongs like rosary beads and talked as if the Republican government existed in fact as well as fantasy. There is little doubt that the Free State ministers, when they had time away from the serious business of running the country, were constantly amused at Sinn Féin's dilemma. Flourishing a brush dipped in high moral principles, de Valera had carefully, speech by speech, anathema by anathema, painted himself into a sterile corner. De Valera, in fact, almost from the moment the Treaty had been signed had been forced to react to events: the hurried Document No. 2, the Treaty majority in the Dáil, and the independence of the IRA. Only when all else seemed lost had he been brought back into the councils of the IRA and then there was little to be done but give up the fight as gracefully as possible. After that had come prison and the gradual revival of Sinn Féin's fortunes but with no place for de Valera to go but into a self-imposed political exile. De Valera was not alone in looking for an exit between the immorality of the Free State Dáil and overwhelming Republican obligation to continue the struggle in whatever manner practical.

Within the IRA the soundings were subtle. No open indication was given. Minister of Defence Seán Lemass, accompanied by his ultra-Republican Secretary George Gilmore, and by Frank Aiken, met regularly with the uncorruptibles of the Army Council, but all three men kept their opinions to themselves and refused to discuss any options before they occurred. President de Valera was, as always, excruciatingly articulate and precisely vague. Still, the body of the Army grew uneasy. Although the IRA had faced the same problems as Sinn Féin—the decline of funds, the cuts of emigration, the strains of illegality, the frustration of inaction—few in positions of authority had been disheartened. In May the resources of the Army declined from £557 13s. 6d. to £250 13s. 6d. with no American income at all;[12] but on June 20, the first issue of the IRA weekly newspaper *An Phoblacht*, edited by O'Donnell, hit the streets. In May the Army Executive had met and agreed to call a General Army Convention in November.[13] Reorganization had continued despite the threats of arrest. In the North David Fitzgerald had managed to revive the local units; in the Midlands, Jim Killeen, C/O Midlands Division, had brought the strength of the IRA in Longford, Westmeath, and Meath up from three to four thousand. Elsewhere the story was the same—reasonable success, little money, spotty areas, few recruits, and occasional interruptions. Both Killeen and Fitzgerald were arrested in the late spring and imprisoned in Mountjoy, and most distressingly both army intelligence and Neligan's police had followed the IRA Director of Intelligence to the safe houses of MacBride, Aiken, and

Lemass, which subsequently led to further arrests. Yet there had been noticeable progress toward the day when the IRA could recapture the country.

Men like Lemass and Aiken had ever so gradually come to the conclusion that such a day was not going to come and, in fact, should not come since one civil war a generation was sufficient. Outside the IRA the arguments became sufficiently open, within Republican circles, that Killeen's replacement in the Midlands on July 6 ordered all his C/Os to withdraw support from Sinn Féin.[14] By September the suspicious had sniffed the rot in the army. George Plunkett was on the edge of decking Andy Cooney on his release from prison on the assumption that Cooney had been contaminated by the "new direction". The two of them went to see Aiken, who under their quizzing refused to give a straight answer, although he agreed to make a statement at the General Army Convention in November. There the matter seemed to rest. There was little indication that the average IRA volunteer was willing to accept the Treaty Dáil or a turn to politics. Ever since the "dump arms" order all efforts had been bent towards a second round. Those who for one reason or another disagreed with such a policy quietly returned to their private lives. Men like Seán Russell, Jim Killeen, Dave Fitzpatrick, Mick Price (who had been selected C/O of Dublin at the Brigade Convention on July 14), Maurice (Moss) Twomey, Seán MacBride, Tom Barry, Cooney, Plunkett, and the rest were hardly about to turn to politics. While many of the members of the Executive did, in fact, have deep political convictions, often of the Connolly–Mellows variety, the 1925 IRA remained largely apolitical.

On the evening of November 14, the General Army Convention opened in Dalkey. Aiken had arranged the agenda saving to the last those resolutions that might split the army over the still inchoate "new direction". A new Constitution was accepted, largely Aiken's work: it reduced the Executive to twelve members, who as usual would elect the seven-man Army Council, which would appoint the Chief of Staff.[15] The Convention moved on to the resolutions, from litanies of complaints—"failure of training . . . resignation of officers . . . reduction of the army to a shadow through emigration"—to proposals for reform—"That a powerful Secret Military Organization shall be built up in England . . . with the intention of waging active military operations there in the event of England waging war against us . . ." There was what was to become almost traditional in subsequent Conventions a demand for action: "A definite time be laid down within which a revolution shall be attempted, say five years."[16] The most startling, although in some quarters not completely unexpected, result came near the end of the evening during the discussion of a Tirconail Battalion resolution:

That in view of the fact that the Government has developed into a mere political party and has apparently lost sight of the fact that all our energies should be devoted to the all-important work of making the Army efficient so that the renegades who, through a *coup d'état,* assumed governmental powers in this country be dealt with at the earliest possible opportunity, the Army of the Republic sever its connection with the Dáil, and act under an independent Executive, such Executive be given the power to declare war when, in its opinion, a suitable opportunity arises to rid the Republic of its enemies and maintain it in accordance with the proclamation of 1916.[17]

The resolution had been written by O'Donnell who felt that unencumbered by the "theorists" of the Second Dáil, the IRA could play a greater part in Irish life. O'Donnell was well-known within the IRA as a man of the Left. He was already using the new Army newspaper in support of a Donegal campaign to withhold the land annuities.[18] All this was a little vague and "pink" for the average Volunteer and no one seemed to know what O'Donnell was up to, but George Plunkett snatched the chance to demand the statement Aiken had promised. Aiken noted that there had been talk about entering the Dáil and the stampede was on. Mick Noel Murphy, C/O Cork No. 1, emotionally urged a positive vote on O'Donnell's motion to save the IRA from the jaws of Leinster House. The motion carried. Discussion grew acrimonious: men like Plunkett felt Aiken was selling them out, while Aiken resented the charge. When the voting for the Executive occurred, the new departure men trailed far behind, their careers in the Army obviously over. The new Army Council elected Andy Cooney as Chief of Staff, with an implicit mandate to lead the IRA back from the stoop of Leinster House to the field of battle.

As had so often been the case, the first action, in the works since October 25, was a prison break. Several important IRA men had ended up in Mountjoy: Russell, who was picked up just before the Convention his pockets stuffed with documents and resolutions; Michael Carolan, Director of Intelligence, lifted in the midst of planning the break-outs; Jim Killeen, arrested in Mullingar during the spring; Fitzgerald, and fifteen others. On the outside Mick Price had been put in charge of the rescue operations.[19] GHQ had a line in to Killeen, senior man until Russell's arrest, and he had been informed that at a certain hour a door would be opened and a master key handed in. On the evening of November 25, a sergeant and two gardai appeared at the gate of Mountjoy with three prisoners. The sergeant announced to the warders that the lads would be serving three months' sentences in lieu of fines for poaching. In a bit of flurry, the prisoners were moved past the administration area, where they should have gone, and into the prison area. There was another little flurry and the sergeant, who now appeared to be George Gilmore, had control of the circle courtyard in the centre of the prison. An obliging warden did not throw away the master key in time and at the proper moment Killeen felt it drop in his hand. Within minutes all nineteen IRA prisoners, the poachers, the two gardai, and Sergeant Gilmore had bulled their way past the confused warders and military sentries into the street. Although only one of the promised cars was waiting, Mountjoy is right in North Dublin and there was no trouble disappearing down the side streets and out of sight.[20] Hurried Free State searches produced nothing. It was a nice coup for the new GHQ but the old political question had not been answered by the IRA's decision to split off from the "government" and in November 1925 the IRA was in no condition to begin any second round.

Pressure to take a step away from abstentionism had increased when on November 7 the *Morning Post* published a report purporting to reveal findings of the Boundary Commission. Although no one knew how the leak had occurred, the details were far too likely to be false. Not only was Northern Ireland scarcely touched, but one of the richest areas of east Donegal was to be taken away from the Free State. Irish opinion, totally unprepared for such a blatant violation of the intent of Article 12 of the Treaty, was appalled. The Nationalists in the North on the eve of perpetual domination by the Orange Unionists were more than distraught, they were desperate. The government in Dublin was equally desperate: the Irish representative on the Commission, Eoin MacNéill, revealed the worst and on November 21 resigned. On the same day the RUC arrested fifty in Belfast and moved B-Specials into Derry City. The Cabinet in Dublin was left helpless, unable to admit that the Treaty had been warped to British advantage while they had napped, unable to risk open defiance in the face of British power. The Republicans had little but scorn for the government men's dilemma; the feeling was that something "practical" had to be done. On December 7, a joint Sinn Féin-Labour Party meeting on the border question was held in the Shelbourne Hotel in Dublin but all hope of united action broke on the stone of abstentionism. In any case, on December 3, untroubled by an effective parliamentary opposition, the government had signed an agreement amending and supplementing the Treaty. The Six Counties were gone and Dublin had agreed to various financial settlements in what Cosgrave felt was "a damn good bargain".[21] The world moved on, in the wrong direction, and Sinn Féin watched from the sidelines.

On December 18, the Cómhairle na dTeachtaí met once again. De Valera seemed to find it difficult to tell whether he was addressing the Second Dáil or the Cómhairle or what. Mixed through the fairy tale world of *de jure* privileges, tightly reasoned, judicial arguments, and make-belief was the very real question of American money. Sinn Féin had run out of money and as far as the group behind de Valera was concerned, there was no likelihood of further funds appearing in the foreseeable future. In order to bypass the distaste of most Republicans for the usurping legislature at Leinster House, de Valera had devised a formula that would allow many to reach a sensible accommodation with reality. Sinn Féin would enter the Dáil once the oath had been removed. Its programme would be to achieve the Republic as rapidly as possible by constitutional means. De Valera felt that the oath—which he judged could be unilaterally removed by Cosgrave or by the Dáil—would provide Republicans with an emotional issue. Once the oath had been removed as a result of Republican pressure, Sinn Féin could enter Leinster House with a clean conscience, banners held high, principles intact. From December on, in public and private, de Valera hammered on the oath. Once it went, he knew what he wanted and how he could get it, but first must come Sinn Féin's acceptance of the new departure.

Not surprisingly, as the IRA General Army Convention had shown, many Republicans felt that the entire structure of the Free State was immoral, the result of an evil coup, and that to enter the Dáil, oath or no oath, would violate their principles, tarnish the cause for which so many had died, and dishonour the ideal Republic of 1916. In January the Sinn Féin Executive called for an extraordinary Ard Fheis on March 9 to consider the proposals put forward by the President of the Republic. For two months the issue was fought over again and again. The de Valera people were perfectly aware that there would be die-hards who could be persuaded neither by logic nor by history, but there was uncertainty about the numbers. The most visible core of intransigents was Cumann na mBan, the Republican Women's organization, which had voted 416 to 63 against the Treaty. On March 10, at the Ard Fheis, Father O'Flanagan amended a de Valera resolution in such a way as to bar Sinn Féin from the Dáil. As an amendment, the O'Flanagan resolution passed 223 to 218. Then O'Flanagan moved a policy resolution:

> That it is incompatible with the fundamental principle of Sinn Féin to send representatives into any usurping legislature set up by English law in Ireland.[22]

Everyone had the time to think over the consequences of the vote. A majority had been willing to prohibit the new departure by a hampering amendment but an affirmative and substantive resolution in direct opposition to the wishes of the President of the Republic was a serious matter. On the vote, the O'Flanagan resolution failed 179 votes to 177, with eighty-five abstentions. A majority of Sinn Féin wanted no part of the departure. On March 11, de Valera resigned as President, withdrew from Sinn Féin, and set about organizing his followers into a new Republican party prepared to enter the Dáil once the impossible oath to the British Crown had been removed.

The abrupt departure of de Valera and his men left the Republican Movement in considerable disarray. The Army split had alienated men like Aiken, Derrig, Traynor, and Breen who had found de Valera's proposals sensible. The vote at the Ard Fheis had produced self-exile from Sinn Féin for men like Lemass, P. J. Ruttledge, Seán T. O'Kelly, Seán McEntee, and Dr. J. Ryan. In fact as the rump Sinn Féin and the IRA still admitted, de Valera's men were as good a collection of Republicans as those who refused the new departure. The split was peculiar because it had come on an issue where the dispute was between tactics and principle not between opposing political ideas, economic philosophies, or contrasting social ideals. In all Republican organizations could be found men of the Left or women of the Right or, particularly in the IRA, soldiers without political ideas. Everyone seemed to have so much in common and so little in dispute—simply the means to get what all wanted—that there seemed no reason why the split could not with right reason, a little patience, and someone's good offices be healed. O'Donnell put a stop to the ubiquitous letters to the editor in *An Phoblacht* that would widen the gulf: "The columns of the paper are not for the present open for discussion of the issues raised at the Ard Fheis."[23] On April 2, there was an editorial on "The Deep Down Spirit of Unity" and on April 16 on "One Movement—Two Groups".

The Second Group had been officially founded on April 12 as Fianna Fáil and was introduced to the public at a meeting in La Scala theatre on April 16. The first Ard Fheis was announced for November 24, 1926; in the meantime, organizing went on apace and branches were set up throughout Ireland, forcing Republicans to choose between the old and the new. On the whole the split was effected peacefully enough with little bitterness. In the Army, the ordinary volunteer attracted to de Valera did not necessarily feel any strain of dual loyalties, though the officers favouring Fianna Fáil tended to withdraw formally after handing over their units. As time passed and Irish politics changed, the distance between the IRA and Fianna Fáil would widen, but at the start the two organizations operated as much in tandem as in conflict. In one area, however, competition was immediate and inevitable: fund-raising. Sinn Féin was as hard up as ever, and although those who had stood firm—Austin Stack, J. J. (Sceilg) O'Kelly, Brian O'Higgins, Count Plunkett, Professor Stockley, Thomas Maguire, and the unyeilding ranks of Cumann na mBan—comprised over half of the original leadership, they lacked the inestimable advantage of de Valera's name and his new programme. Moreover, Frank Aiken's trip to the United States in December 1925–January 1926 had given Fianna Fáil a headstart in cornering the movement's most important source of funds.

To blunt the effect of Aiken's trip and de Valera's epistles, the Army Council decided that the new Chief of Staff, Andy Cooney, would have to go in person to explain the new situation to the Clan. While he was out of the country, Moss Twomey would take over as acting-C/S with Tom Daly as A/G. Twomey although not as visible as some other more publicized Republicans—Tom Barry, Dan Breen, or Ernie O'Malley—was proving a tower of strength, in the grand Fenian tradition, an excellent organizer, a man trusted by all, with an almost faultless intuition. Cooney felt he could not do better than leave Twomey in charge. In June 1926, he entered England under an assumed name. From there he sailed to New York and began the appearances, conferences, explanations which were vital for the Army's future. The Clan had by and large remained loyal to the IRA, and there was little sympathy for de Valera's new policy. On the other hand, many Irish organizations and individuals whose original loyalties had been to Sinn Féin had transferred their allegiance to Fianna Fáil. The Clan was quite different and Cooney had no trouble explaining the need to maintain the Army to men like Luke Dillon,[24] with whom he stayed in Philadelphia, a man who had carried out a bombing attack on the House of Commons and spent fourteen years in a British jail for an attempt on the Welland Canal in Canada during the Boer War. For the IRA the most important man in the Clan had become Joe McGarrity whose loyalty and support never wavered. Yet by 1926 the Clan as a mass movement was slowly decaying, membership slipped away, branches broke off and were not replaced, and second-generation Irishmen were attracted in fewer numbers. Despite this, Clan money continued to come into Ireland, Clan-purchased weapons arrived, and Clan contacts were available.

With his mission complete, Cooney left the United States and returned to Dublin in October 1926. As expected he found the Army under Twomey considerably improved. An effort to reconstruct the units in Britain had met with some success. In Ireland although emigration remained a drain, the worst of the erosion had stopped, and despite Free State pressure core strength had been maintained. Parade strength was difficult to determine and not necessarily a true indication of the vitality of the IRA, but a fair estimate would have been twenty to twenty-five thousand members. Twomey had felt that with the growing confidence and efficiency of the Army some action other than the ceaseless routine of training should be undertaken. He informed Cooney that mainly for intelligence purposes but also to acquire new weapons he had prepared a series of raids on the gardai barracks throughout the country. Cooney favoured the raids and during October and November the final plans were drawn up. Each of the raids was to be left largely to the discretion of the local C/O, who would have a general outline of what GHQ wanted. The attacks came on November 14, but not all the units reached their objectives. Some local

C/Os felt they could not get in and out with ease or did not have enough
of their men in the right place at the right time or there was simply some
unforeseen hitch. Twelve barracks were hit but not with the desired result.
Little information was acquired and worse, two unarmed policemen were
killed, Garda Ward, Hollyford Barracks, and Sergeant Fitzsimons, Cork.
There were immediate police swoops, that picked up a substantial number of the GHQ staff and forced the Army in Dublin and the country to
reduce activity to a minimum.

Despite practically everyone's desire for a second round, GHQ realized
that immediate prospects were slight. The difficulties of reorganization had
been overcome but it proved necessary to keep full-time organizers going
the rounds to revitalize the bored or despondent, to discover the impact of
emigration, to see that the intentions of GHQ were not ignored. Police
pressure, particularly in the Six Counties, made this a slow, often frustrating routine. One member of the Army Council, Peadar O'Donnell,
working on his own and without authorization from GHQ, had been helping in the non-payment of annuities campaign, largely in the West. The
ultimate intention was to rally the people around resistance to the bailiff,
hardly a popular Irish figure, and thus unite the everyday people and the
IRA in an irresistible movement to topple the Leinster House regime and
replace the West Briton economic and social system with one modelled on
the ideals of Connolly and Mellows.[25] In 1927 the annuities campaign had
gained momentum, spreading through the West, and had attracted the
support of individual IRA units as well as a hard police counter-attack;
but O'Donnell had by no means converted the Army Council to his ideas.
He could use the columns of *An Phoblacht* with impunity and whip
through the West on speaking tours, haranguing and agitating, but a
substantial portion of the IRA remained apolitical.

Apolitical or not, the Army Council felt it essential to make some effort
to heal the growing difference between Sinn Féin and Fianna Fáil, who
were competing for the same votes, the same support, and the same contributions. A general election was scheduled for 1927 and the Army Council
felt that conflicting Republican voices would confuse the Volunteers.
Although Fianna Fáil wanted the IRA votes, their Executive was much
more concerned with the anti-oath campaign. As long as the oath barred
the way into Leinster House, Fianna Fáil was nothing more than another
abstentionist Republican party but without the purity of soul of Sinn Féin.
In one way or another most of the Fianna Fáil people felt that the oath
could be swept away by pressure, by law, by negotiations, or by judicial
interpretations. If not, the next step was obvious. In January Dan Breen
took the oath and his seat in the Dáil. Although on April 6, he introduced
a Bill to remove the oath and did not seem particularly concerned about

the formality necessary to take his seat, strict Republican opinion was shocked that a man like Breen would go so far.

> Irishmen will regret that he should have overshadowed his other days by this crime.[26]

This was the orthodox view but the wise or callous in Fianna Fáil knew that he might be the first of many and intensified the anti-oath campaign. Cosgrave had no intention of backing down on the oath or letting in de Valera or Fianna Fáil through a backdoor with their moral righteousness intact. He rejected Breen's bill, pointing out that the oath was an integral part of the Treaty—a Treaty which Fianna Fáil would have to swallow sooner or later since Cosgrave and the Cabinet would not tolerate an alternative Republican "Government" and "Army". Kevin O'Higgins, always the one with the hard word, had little time for de Valera's principles.

> . . . the man who did his damnedest to cut his country's throat now invited it to commit political hara-kiri in order to save his face.[27]

Whatever the ultimate fate of the oath, Fianna Fáil was running a strong race. Sinn Féin, with next to no money, had been able to nominate only fifteen candidates for the June elections. The Army Council arranged a series of conferences between Sinn Féin and Fianna Fáil, hoping to halt the drift apart and reduce the level of mutual abuse, but a united front election policy was completely beyond the Council's persuasive powers. On April 9, the Army Council, GHQ staff, and all major C/Os met in Dublin to hear the Council's formula for repairing the political split. The formula was accepted and referred to the Executives of Fianna Fáil and Sinn Féin. The Army wanted a tripartite conference on the bases of the restoration of the Republic, the repudiation of all agreements with Britain —the Treaty, the boundary *et al.*—the transformation of the IRA into the only army, a single panel of candidates approved by a board which was to select the future Cabinet before the election. Despite the hard work of many of the IRA people, particularly O'Donnell who had urged the proposals on the IRA at meetings in his house, 39 Marlborough Road, the response of the two political wings was negative. Sinn Féin was reluctantly willing to be convinced that after meeting outside Leinster House the Republican TDs with a majority could move into the Dáil and take over the reins of power. Fianna Fáil, however, once the oath was removed, intended to go into the Dáil even as a minority. With no agreement, the two positions hardened into the old ruts. The Sinn Féin Executive agreed to the conference on the condition that Fianna Fáil would "not enter any foreign controlled Parliament as a minority or majority, with or without

an Oath or other formal declaration".[28] Fianna Fáil's reply was equally
sterile:

> The memo on suggested basis for co-operation between the Republican parties
> for the General Election was placed before the National Executive at its meet-
> ing yesterday. It was unanimously decided that the proposals were not accept-
> able as the basis of discussion.[29]

When the Army Council asked what part of the proposals were un-
acceptable, the reply came that "We have to inform you that the proposals
were not discussed in detail."[30] Once the oath was gone, Fianna Fáil was
going into the Dáil. All the pretensions of Sinn Féin had been discarded
and a last-minute alliance would do more harm than good. The army was
left with the task of "organizing, training, and equipping the manhood
of Ireland as an effective military force".[31] In the meantime Republicans
were urged to vote and assured that the collapse of the unity negotiations
"have not really succeeded in really splitting the country".[32]

On June 9, Ireland went to the polls. Fianna Fáil had run a campaign
critical of the failures of the government and favouring the imposition
of protective tariffs; the party had borrowed from O'Donnell's programme the withholding of the land annuities and economics in the public
services.[33] Cumann na nGaedheal ran on their record, a mixture of highly
successful policies and several extremely unpopular ones, in particular the
Intoxicating Liquor Bill and the Boundary fiasco. Although there were a
covey of other parties—Clan Éireann, similar to the Fianna Fáil, the
National League, organized by Captain Redmond, the Farmers, Labour,
and the independents—the main interest was the prospects of de Valera's
new party. When the results were in, the results were revealingly incon-
clusive; Cumann na nGaedheal had elected forty-seven members, a loss of
eleven but still greater than de Valera's forty-four successes. In a Dáil of
153 members, neither major party had managed to collect a third of the
members and either would have trouble organizing a government. The key
question, of course, was whether the Dáil would have 153 sitting members;
for the oath had not been abolished.

On June 21, de Valera obtained an opinion from three members of the
Irish Bar that members of the Dáil could not be excluded before the Chairman was elected, hence a Chairman could be elected who had not taken
the oath, and to exclude a validly elected member from the vote on the
Chairman was unconstitutional. This opinion was made public on June 23
as de Valera was leading his forty-four elected members into Leinster House
but not past the Clerk of the Dáil who, legal opinion or no, insisted on
administering the oath. The doors to the Dáil were locked and de Valera
and the Fianna Fáil members had to withdraw frustrated. Back at Fianna
Fáil headquarters, de Valera explained the position to the party faithful.

They pledged themselves to the people that as long as they were the representatives of the people they would never take an oath of allegiance to a foreign king. They had been prevented because they would neither take a false oath nor prove recreant to the aspirations of the Irish people and renounce their principles.[34]

De Valera had other arrows in his quiver. Under Article 47 of the Irish Free State Constitution, a member of the Dáil could demand a referendum to amend the Constitution. De Valera felt that a referendum campaign against an oath to a foreign king could be won over the quibbling, legalistic opposition of the government and would revitalize Ireland. The contention that the Irish people could not alter the treaty except by agreement with Great Britain was denied and a referendum urged.

On July 10, the whole political balance was changed radically. Just before noon on Sunday morning, Kevin O'Higgins, Cosgrave's Minister for Justice and External Affairs and Vice President of the Executive Council, was walking alone to Mass from his home in Blackrock, a suburb south of Dublin. As O'Higgins approached the junction of Booterstown and Cross Avenues, a man stepped out of a parked motor car and fired at point-blank range. O'Higgins staggered, turned and began to run, followed by the man firing. O'Higgins collapsed on the other side of the road and two more men came from the rear of the motor car and fired down at O'Higgins as he lay on the ground. The men then leaped in the car and drove off. The first person to reach O'Higgins was Eoin MacNéill who found that despite the multiple wounds he was still alive. He had been hit seven times and was obviously mortally wounded. Moved to his house he lingered for five hours, dying a few minutes before five in the afternoon.

For the government there was not the slightest doubt why O'Higgins had been shot. Of all the Treaty leaders he was the most disliked; articulate with a rasping tongue, capable of the most slashing platform utterances, he was given credit as the man responsible for the seventy-seven martyrs and for shooting the four hostages on December 8, 1922, one of whom, Rory O'Connor, had been the best man at his wedding. Actually he was not as dominant a figure within the Cosgrave government as was generally supposed, nor had he accepted the need for the executions without argument.[35] But for a great many Republicans all this was beside the point. In 1927 there were still many Republicans who had sworn vengeance in the prisons and camps in 1923 and 1924, and had still not forgiven or forgotten. And so the Cabinet assumed that Republicans were to blame and probably the IRA as well. The police rushed through Dublin picking up known GHQ men—George Plunkett, Owen Donnelly, Michael Fitzpatrick, Frank Kerlin, Brendan O'Carroll, Kevin O'Carroll, Henry and Aubrey Hunt, Joseph Reynolds. On Monday the IRA issued a public denial. The police continued to be active picking up a few more men but they had no evidence connecting the IRA men to O'Higgins' murderers. Not only did the IRA deny any involvement but also many on GHQ suspected that the men after O'Higgins were some of the 1924 Mutiny group.[36] The most intensive Free State investigation produced almost nothing. The government then, and most observers since, accepted that it was an independent Republican attack for motives of revenge. At no time, however, did the identity of the assassins become known. Everyone in Ireland had their own candidates, put forward with great assurance and backed by claims of detailed inside knowledge, but there was never an arrest.

Beyond the reflexive police sweeps, the government responded, on July 20, by introducing three Bills in the Dáil: the first was a stringent Public Safety Bill which was swiftly passed and became law on August 11. The Bill clearly infringed on the guarantees of the liberty of the individual and trial by jury, but the Cabinet felt that desperate measures to curb the IRA were necessary.[37] The second measure provided that every candidate for election to the Dáil must on nomination swear to take the oath. This was passed on August 10, but formal enactment was later suspended. The third Bill proposed to amend the Constitution so as to restrict the call for a referendum to members of the Dáil who had taken the oath. There was no longer going to be any room for de Valera to manoeuvre. One Fianna Fáil TD, Patrick Belton, had already taken his seat on July 26. On August 10, the Fianna Fáil TDs met to consider the new Free State legislation. The meeting dragged on and on into the early hours of August 11, but the decision could not be postponed too long or the two Bills would become law.

On the following day, de Valera led the Fianna Fáil members to Leinster House. There de Valera announced that he was not taking an oath, pushed the Bible to one side, signed the book as directed by the Clerk of the Dáil, and passed through the portals towards power. He was followed by the members of his party and a billowing cloud of controversy over this perhaps not unexpected *volte face*. De Valera, however, insisted that there had been no about-face, no loss of consistency, no jettisoning of principle. He had simply, as he had told the Clerk, not taken an oath.

> I am not prepared to take an oath. I am not going to take an oath. I am prepared to put my name down in this book in order to get permission to go into the Dáil, but it has no other significance.[38]

Whatever the "significance" of his signature[39] "I signed it in the same way as I would sign an autograph in a newspaper"—there can be no doubt as de Valera has contended that there was never an "oath" under the eyes of God but merely a rather humiliating formality which the Free State government had the decency to make as easy as possible. However, the contention that the oath was nothing more than "a formality" lay uneasy on tongues that had spent months stressing its importance. On August 13, the Fianna Fáil newspaper, *The Nation*, sent to press just before the August 10–11 decision, put the Fianna Fáil case clearly:

> If all the Fianna Fáil deputies published tomorrow a signed declaration that in their opinion the oath in the Free State Constitution is an unsworn undertaking, the oath would still remain an oath and to swear it falsely would still continue to be perjury.[40]

Some members of the Fianna Fáil would have gone straight in after O'Higgins' death and the new Bills without worrying about casuistical niceties, as had Belton and Breen. But de Valera would not climb all the way down and insisted that a loop-hole did exist. Since this satisfied him and those members who had qualms about deserting what they had thought were their principles, the party was more than content. One especial reason for satisfaction was the possibility that Cosgrave and the Treatyites might be voted out immediately by an anti-government coalition.

While Cosgrave's Cabinet had recognized this possibility before August 11, the danger was less serious than might appear. Although the self-righteous de Valera and his unreformed Republicans were anathema, the Government recognized that the Irish Free State could not be secure until the real opposition was brought into the Dáil, thereby accepting the Treaty settlement and giving up the "alternative government" ploy. Cosgrave had watched the horse back up to the water and the August 11 legislation was calculated to force the first swallow of legitimate parliamentary opposition down its throat. If de Valera would not drink, there was not much doubt that many in his party would, which was nearly as good. If he did take the first sip, any subsequent election campaign could be run on a not entirely inaccurate attack on Dev's loyalty to his principles. Even if Fianna Fáil stitched together an anti-government coalition in the Dáil, the majority would be so small and Fianna Fáil so inexperienced in parliamentary manœuvre that a new general election within a few months would put Cumann na nGaedheal back in. There was an outside danger that the new institutions of state, particularly the Army, might be so fearful of Fianna Fáil vengeance that a foolish resort to force might be proposed by some. The Cosgrave people, however, felt reasonably sure that the growing professionalism of the Army, coupled with the hope of reasonable moderation, would make the obviously temporary transition easy.[41]

On August 16, after five days of wild lobbying and nose counting, the vote was taken in the Dáil. By the evening before de Valera had put together a majority of one, but then one of his votes, Alderman John Jinks of Sligo, decided, reputedly after some serious drinking, that whatever his party (the National League) might think, he knew his constituents would not want him voting for de Valera. So he did not appear.[42] The vote was seventy-one to seventy-one and the Speaker voted for the government. Obviously, Cosgrave could not run the country on the Speaker's vote. On August 25, he dissolved the Dáil, setting September 15 as the date for the next general election. That de Valera's "new direction" was highly practical, however impure his principles, was quite clear when Sinn Féin failed to nominate a single candidate—there was no money, the IRA had even prohibited Volunteers (or any rank) from running in the election, and the membership had deserted wholesale to Fianna Fáil. Although unwilling to accept the "Republican government" or co-operate with either Sinn Féin or Fianna Fáil, the Army Council through an editorial in *An Phoblacht* suggested a vote against Cumann na nGaedheal.

By September the IRA was feeling the pressure of the Free State security campaign under the provisions of the new Public Safety Act. The police had been very active in their attempts to stamp out O'Donnell's Land Annuity agitation, making regular arrests and harassing the Republicans as well as the ordinary people involved. To the more conservative members of Cosgrave's cabinets, the resistance to the bailiff that the IRA was sponsoring had a dangerous ring, and O'Donnell never pretended that he was anything but the man three steps to the Left of everyone else. The priests were worried about the taint of Communism and the solid people at the threat to property. O'Higgins' assassination had provided additional impetus for a serious effort to break the IRA, an effort that had accelerated during the first half of 1927, before O'Higgins' death, and by the time of the autumn elections had put a good many IRA men behind bars. At one time or another O'Donnell, Killeen, T. J. Ryan (a really hard, very active Left Republican from Clare), Twomey, Price, and Madden (from North Mayo) had been picked up and released. For men on the run a brief spell in jail was no trouble, but for the average Volunteer the cat-and-mouse arrests made it difficult to hold a position. At the same time events within the Army had made another re-organization essential. Andy Cooney, who had really not wanted the position of Chief of Staff, had resigned and appointed Twomey to replace him. Cooney was returning to finish his medical education, which had been interrupted by the Troubles, and felt that the C/S must be full-time and that Twomey was the man for the job. Finally, some political decision had to be made on the future relations with Fianna Fáil, now that the Oath had been taken.

On September 15, the election returns gave Cosgrave sixty-two seats and de Valera fifty-seven. This was a sufficient victory for Cumann na nGaedheal and on October 11, Cosgrave after a vote of seventy-six to seventy in the new Dáil could organize another government. Fianna Fáil was faced with the prospect of five years in opposition, five years in which to learn the ropes of parliament and the nature of government. For the IRA it meant that there would be no friendly Republican government sacking Neligan's detectives and disbanding the Free State army.

Still unwilling to give up hope that something could be salvaged out of the 1927 political splits, O'Donnell suggested that perhaps Sinn Féin should be reorganized, a proposal which did not go down too well. The Sinn Féin people felt the army had abandoned them, prohibiting Volunteers to work for the party or run as candidates. O'Donnell proposed the formation of a League of Republican Workers, to unite non-Fianna Fáil Republicans. That suggestion also fell through, and when the Army Convention finally met in the Little Theatre on Williams Street, Dublin, in November, there were still more problems than solutions.

As anticipated, Twomey took over as Chief of Staff, the overwhelming favourite and clearly the man for the job. Most of the efforts to devise a formula which would unify Republicans came to naught but it was now clear that whatever ties of sentiment might still exist Fianna Fáil was following a course that diverged from the ideals of the army and the faithful of Sinn Féin.

One interesting resolution was the decision of the eighty delegates that in the event of a war between Great Britain—then in the midst of a Red Scare—and the Soviet Union, the IRA would support Russia. There was a deep suspicion on the British Left that London was seriously considering renewed intervention against Russia. The new IRA policy, based on surmise about a distant and alien country, had little impact on the average delegate. There had been ties between Russia and Ireland during the Troubles and in 1923 Seán Russell and Gerald Boland, who in 1926 had gone Fianna Fáil, travelled to Russia to try and buy arms; but outside the few articulate men of the Left, the major factor was that any enemy of Britain's was a friend of Ireland. The only practical result was to accelerate IRA reorganization in Britain. Other than this the Convention was rather unproductive: the new staff had been anticipated, the new proposals to unite the non-Fianna Fáil Republicans were not novel, and the prospects for action seemed as distant as before. Thus when the delegates trailed off towards their homes early Sunday morning, they could hardly have felt wildly optimistic.

Yet in the over four years since the dump-arms order, the IRA had done much: reorganized, maintained the structure, and kept up the line to Clan na Gael in America. In fact, due to the administrative and organizational talents of the Army Council and GHQ, the scattered remains of the defeated army had been integrated into a large, covert, revolutionary, underground force still dedicated to a second round. If the IRA were not yet strong enough for that second round, if the Republican political movement had splintered, if the Army had found therefore neither a military nor a political role, nevertheless the IRA still exercised its most vital role—it was a power in the land, a threat to those who would deny the Republic. Within the leadership of the Army, that most impressive collection of men who had chosen service in an invisible army for an invisible republic over a more conventional career, there were those who wanted to be something more than handmaidens to history, who wanted to act, to involve the IRA in life, in action, in the mainstream of Ireland. The Army Council meetings and GHQ conferences seethed with ideas, dispute, options, and suggestions; despite the attrition of time and politics, there remained within the leadership as much talent as could be found within one group in Ireland—Twomey, MacBride, O'Donnell, Killeen, Tom Daly, Gilmore, Price, Russell, Dave Fitzpatrick, Barry, Tom Malone—the list ran on and on. All agreed that the achievements of the past must hold the key to the future. De Valera seemed willing to wait five years on the opposition benches, but the IRA knew too well that Cosgrave was not going to let them wait five quiet years preparing a second round. The next years would be violent ones and crucial: either Cosgrave would smash the Army or the Army would at last find the high road to the Republic and brush Cosgrave aside during the final charge.

NOTES

1. Irish Free State. Department of Defence, "General Report, No. 4", June 16, 1923.
2. Donal O'Sullivan, *The Irish Free State and its Senate; a Study in Contemporary Politics*, London, 1940, p. 126.
3. Irish Free State, from Department C of General Staff to Minister of Defence, GHQ Parkgate, Dublin, October 15, 1923.
4. Irish Free State, *Dáil Debates*, vol. X, col. 280.
5. On August 12, GHQ had sent in word to all IRA prisoners that all decisions about hunger strikes would be left to local C/Os and stressed the difficulties that would arise. Oglaigh na h-Éireann, from Director of Intelligence to O/Cs Jails and Camps, GHQ, Dublin, August 12, 1923.
6. Peadar O'Donnell, *The Gates Flew Open*, Cork, 1965, p. 96.
7. The Army Mutiny remains one of Ireland's latter-day mysteries. The government appointed an investigating committee, which held forty-

one meetings and examined twenty-seven witnesses. The Cabinet "decided not to publish the evidence . . ." and the end result was a brief *Report of the Army Enquiry Committee, Dublin 1924*. See *The Truth About the Army Crisis (Official) With a Foreword by Major-General Liam Tobin* (issued by the Irish Republican Army Organization), Dublin, n.d., as well as Ernest Blythe's appreciation of Joseph McGrath in the *Irish Times* (March 28, 1966) and a former Free State officer's reply "Army Mutiny—1924" by Black Raven (*Irish Times*, April 20, 1966).

. Eoin O'Duffy's sudden appointment made it necessary for him to resign as IRB Treasurer, leaving approximately £11,000 to £12,000 in the treasury. Martin Collins, the new Secretary, was mainly concerned with the disposal of the funds—part of which went eventually to the Wolfe Tone Monument. After O'Duffy's departure the IRB of Collins–McKeon–Ó Muirthile (who was removed as Free State QMG after the Devlin Pub Raid) Mulcahy–O'Duffy *et al.* apparently disappears from the Irish scene. The same seems to be the case for the Old IRA/IRB. Conspiracy being what it is from the spring of 1924 until the present the continued existence of the IRB has been muted but of visible evidence there is none—which would be quite proper no matter what the case. IRB-ties or no, O'Duffy did a first-rate job in clearing up the army, shifting out the mutineer types and keeping an eye on the potential IRB contamination. The government was sufficiently grateful later to overlook his irritating conduct as Commissioner of the Garda Síochána.

. Dorothy Macardle, *The Irish Republic*, New York, 1965, p. 873.

. To fill the gap a secret Ulster Federal Army had been formed in December 1923 and on February 19, 1924, taken limited military action against B-Specials. The organization was in touch with de Valera and Austin Stack but apparently faded away sometime in 1926.

. Irish Free State, "Minute Sheet: Sinn Féin Policy Summary of Reports Received March 1925" (Ref. S12022). The reports trickling in from agents, police information, and army intelligence gave the government a mixed, often contradictory, "inside" picture of the Republican policy. As late as October 30, Agent "70" revealed—as gospel—the following insight into Sinn Féin attitudes (*ibid.*, "Summary of Reports Received October 1925," Ref. S12022):

> A number of leaders in the Sinn Féin Organization, headed by Eamon Donnelly, want a change in policy and entry into the Dáil. De Valera, supported by Lemass and a majority of the military section, opposes this and the opposition are endeavouring to remove him from office on this account.

The army intelligence proved no more astute (Irish Free State, Department of Defence, "Monthly Summary Eastern Command, January 1926").

> The extreme element of the political group, headed by Seán Lemass and Miss MacSwiney, are opposed to entry into the Dáil.

Free State intelligence was not always so far off the mark, particularly on the rare occasions a man could be put inside the IRA, but depended largely on hearsay, gossip, and sound police work. From 1923 to 1926 there was some competition and jealousy between the army intelligence sections and the police detectives. Increasingly after 1926 Superintendent Neligan—Collins' man on the inside during the Tan War—dominated anti-Republican intelligence; but given his obvious talent, the firm backing of the government, the size of Ireland, and the inherent difficulties of secrecy in a Celtic atmosphere, the substantial collection of Republican data accumulated over the years produced a very limited picture of the nature, intentions, and composition of the IRA. Lots of details were filed but there was simply no real "feel" for the IRA as the years passed; however, the police became far more skilled—many doing little more than concentrating on a few important IRA men—in more normal police activities such as overt surveillance.

12. Oglaigh na h-Éireann, Financial Statement of the Cash Accounts of the IRA Army for the month ending 31 May 1925.
13. *Ibid.*, From A/G to C/Os, GHQ, Dublin, 2 May 1925.
14. "Volunteers will immediately withdraw all cooperation and support from the Sinn Féin Movement." *Ibid.*, From O/C Midlands Battalion HQ, July 6, 1925.
15. Since the IRA had been condemned—by the clergy among others—as an oath-bound society, a new form of "undertaking" was introduced and henceforth the IRA would no longer be oath-bound, popular and priestly illusion to the contrary.

> I . . . promise that I will promote the objects of Oglaigh na h-Éireann to the best of my knowledge and ability and that I will obey all orders and regulations issued to me by the Army Authorities and by my superior officers.

Ibid., Statement by Army Council to O/C All Units, GHQ, Dublin, November 20, 1925.
16. *Ibid.*, Draft Agenda for Convention.
17. *Ibid.*
18. See Peadar O'Donnell, *There Will Be Another Day*, Dublin 1963.

9. George Gilmore had apparently suggested the idea to Seán Russell who turned it over to the Director of Intelligence Carolan who brought in the C/O of Dublin, Price. See "Inner History of 'Sensational Jail Rescue'," *Irish People*, March 21, 1936.

0. One of Gilmore's escape team, Gerald O'Reilly, was arrested not long afterwards and discovered first-hand that prisoners were no longer brought directly to Mountjoy, thereby eliminating the possibility of a repeat performance for his benefit.

1. Macardle, *Irish Republic*, p. 892.

2. This is one of the few specific references in *An Phoblacht* to the events of the Ard Fheis (March 12, 19, 26, April 2, 9, 16, 1926).

3. *An Phoblacht*, March 19, 1926.

4. Dillon must have been one of the most curious of all the major Fenians in that he had never been in Ireland. Born in Leeds, the closest he came was on the trip to the United States when from the ship he could see the distant shoreline.

5. Officially the social and economic policy of the IRA was based on the relevant sections of the 1916 Proclamation and the Democratic Programme of Dáil Éireann of 1919, both sufficiently vague to be accepted by all wings. Mellows' brief notes from jail, seized and published by the Free State, could hardly form a basis for the Movement although his personality and potential transformed him, not unfairly, into one of the giants of the Left Republicanism. Connolly, of course, remained one of the giants, more honoured within the Republican Movement than the Labour Movement, which in an era of creeping conservatism apparently felt uneasy with the wild phrases of revolutionary socialism.

6. *An Phoblacht*, February 4, 1927.

7. O'Sullivan, *Senate*, p. 192.

8. *An Phoblacht*, June 3, 1927, reprinted the Army Council statement on IRA efforts to secure unity.

9. *Ibid.*

0. *Ibid.*

1. *Ibid.*

2. *Ibid.*

3. Despite the efforts of the police, O'Donnell's campaign had gained sufficient momentum to attract the cautious attention of the Left of Fianna Fáil. The Party's decision to include it in the 1927 election campaign was based more on the ultimate recipient of the payments —the British—and the legality of them than on O'Donnell's more radical ideas.

4. *Irish Times*, June 23, 1927. *Irish Independent*, June 23, 1927.

35. According to Ernest Blythe, when Cosgrave presented the request of the Free State Army for summary executions and asked for a vote, O'Higgins had in fact sought a way out: Desmond Fitzgerald, "Shoot them," Blythe, "Shoot them," O'Higgins, "Is there no other way?" Once the possibilities had been eliminated, however, it was O'Higgins who used the hard words on the second vote: "Shoot them." "Shoot them." "Take them out and shoot them."

36. GHQ Intelligence supplied their evidence to Fianna Fáil who in turn felt it was wiser to let well enough alone. The Free State police kept the O'Higgins file open until 1932 but no solution was forthcoming and not even any new evidence.

37. On August 12, the Army Council issued a statement on the Coercion Bill urging the volunteers to follow a policy of passive resistance (*An Phoblacht*, August 12, 1927). The IRA contended that the O'Higgins assassination was only an excuse to bring in a long-planned Coercion Bill.

38. Irish Free State, *Dáil Debates*, vol. xli, cols. 1101–1102.

39. *Ibid.*

40. *The Nation*, August 13, 1927.

41. There was sufficient uneasiness about the Army that Blythe took it on himself to visit senior officers to urge calm.

42. By so doing Alderman Jinks went down in Irish legend and racing history, for at Cosgrave's suggestion a horse was named after him and went on to win the Two Thousand Guineas in England in 1929.

PART II

The Cosgrave Years: 1927–1932

CHAPTER V

The IRA Goes to Ground:
Perseverance on the Road to the Republic,
September 1927–February 1932

As 1926 drew to a close, Cosgrave's new government settled comfortably
into power, a power which they contended only they were sufficiently
responsible, sufficiently capable to wield. With vast confidence, if not
outright arrogance, the government continued to build their vision of
Ireland, primarily agricultural, careful, conventional, conservative, sound
in money and proper in principle, and tied, of course, to the Crown. Once
attention shifted from the tempest in the Dáil, it was clear that the government had in fact achieved much: the huge Shannon hydro-electric and
redevelopment scheme had been instituted, the standards of Irish agricultural produce had been improved and farm exports had begun to bring
up prices in the highly competitive British market. Even industrial
employment was on the rise while emigration declined.[1] Ireland belonged
to the League of Nations, participated in the Imperial Conferences,
accredited diplomats, and stepping stone by stepping stone was taking a
proper place in the outside world. Naturally to Fianna Fáil, all this "progress" was invisible; through Republican glasses the Irish Free State
remained a West Briton puppet festooned with Imperial symbols and run
by successful murderers and traitors. In this the IRA agreed: Ireland would
not be a nation once again as a result of butter sales to the Saxon or a
place at an Imperial conference table.

What in the months after the September 1927 elections was so disturbing
to many in the IRA was the lack of a clear alternative to Fianna Fáil's path
to the Republic through the usurping Dáil. A few like O'Donnell wanted
a move from the Left but the pure in Sinn Féin felt he would lead them
down the slippery path of politics to disgrace and some in the Army felt
Peadar should spend more time on Army business and less on writing
and radical causes. Some like Seán Russell saw the IRA as purely military,
with no mission beyond preparation for a rising. The middle of the Army
like Twomey and Killeen were not without radical ideas but felt their
first task was to maintain and improve the IRA as an organization. These
organization men were open to suggestions; but in 1927 and 1928 despite
the calibre of the leadership, little practical was forthcoming. Thus almost

all effort went simply to holding the Army together. The Clan money mad
a full-time staff possible although with only marginal wages. The declin
of emigration and the efforts of the organizers kept strength stable an
gradually a new generation was attracted, although the majority of volun
teers were from the Civil War period. The arms situation remained spott
although more Thompsons began arriving from America. Outside th
Army, Cumann na mBan had lost few to Fianna Fáil[2] and the Fiann
although weaker still attracted some of Ireland's youth to the movemen
The most virile new organizations were the Republican Clubs founded i
the universities in 1924. All of these organizations attracted the regula
attention of the police. Thus without a specific direction, the IRA increas
ingly found that the only action readily available and ideologically desir
able was a hard response to police pressure.

On January 28, 1928, Seán Harling, a man later described as a Fre
State police agent, was fired on by two men as he entered his home, Woo
Park Lodge, on Dartry Road in Dublin. Harling returned the fire and sh
and killed Timothy Coughlan, a member of Fianna Fáil and (it wa
assumed) the IRA. The rather elaborate subsequent investigation reveale
for the interested that Harling had for some time been secretly accumula
ing information for the police. Clearly he had not been as discreet as he ha
assumed, and as soon as he had been exonerated by the Tribunal of Inquiry
he was paid a sum sufficient for him to leave the country.[4] Despite th
attempt on Harling, the government felt that the worst was over with d
Valera tamed and in the Dáil and repealed the 1927 Public Safety Bil
The police, however, continued their harassment of Republicans. Survei
lance was uninterrupted. Co-operation with the British was such that, f
example, when Killeen was arrested in London in 1926, the Deput
Governor of Mountjoy, Seán Kavanagh, and Detective-Sergeant Scully can
over to identify him; in return the British released him to the Irish poli
for removal to Dublin, where he was charged with the prison escape i
November 1925. The clashes and vendettas with the police were, howeve
no substitute for military action. So the months dragged by with raid
arrests, swoops, threats, and frustration. The Volunteers paraded secret
but without purpose. Arms were acquired and dumped. War plans we
discussed at all levels but the second round seemed no nearer.

There was going to be no help from Fianna Fáil. Seán Lemass mig
stand in the Dáil and speak like a revolutionary but the IRA knew Fian
Fáil had put aside physical force.

Fianna Fáil is a slightly constitutional party. We are perhaps open to t
definition of a constitutional party, but before anything we are a Republic
party. We have adopted the method of political agitation to achieve our e
because we believe, in the present circumstances, that method is best in t

interests of the nation and of the Republican movement, and for no other reason. Five years ago the methods we adopted were not the methods we have adopted now. Five years ago we were on the defensive, and perhaps in time we may recoup our strength sufficiently to go on the offensive. Our object is to establish a Republican Government in Ireland. If that can be done by the present methods we have, we will be very pleased, but, if not, we would not confine ourselves to them.[5]

One of the more effective alternative methods to harass the Treaty government came from Cumann na mBan, whose members were not satisfied with the more tranquil tasks ordinarily assigned to women. There had been all sorts of suggestions—boycotts and petitions, arms classes and publicity. What Cumann na mBan developed during 1928 largely under the direction of Sheila Humphries was a highly efficient series of pamphlets written by "Ghosts" attempting to subvert the loyalty of the police and army to the Treaty government.

Soldiers of the Free State Army, Members of the Free State Police. Where do you stand now? . . . Remember England with all her might and money cannot uphold her Governments in this country without the assistance of Irish Police and Soldiers. Are you willing to do her Infamous work for her? We cannot believe you are, be men, resign while there is yet time, show your masters that they have not bought your souls. If you want to fight, for God's sake fight on Ireland's side.[6]

In August a typical Republican stunt led Cumann na mBan to extend this appeal of conscience to private citizens. The less patient were soon underlining the Cumann na mBan's appeal with violence, which led to a series of clashes with the police. As IRA pressure increased and as the slogans and ideas of the Left began to take hold, the more nervous and conservative members of the government worried that the Republicans might at last have found an effective alternative to the mystical second round and the Fianna Fáil's waiting game.

A harmless but provocative expedient chosen by those who opposed Irish nationalism as a means to demonstrate their loyalty was a fervent display of British symbols. When appropriate "God Save the King" was sung with a feverish depth of feeling, when possible red-white-and-blue bunting was displayed along with massed Union Jacks, when available patriotic British films were attended *en masse*, and on every royal British occasion intense interest was publicly expressed by the West Briton community. In August, the Republicans took it upon themselves to tear down and destroy the "alien" decorations on some of Dublin's business buildings. The police managed to arrest four young men making away with a Union Jack. The four were charged with larceny, found guilty, but released immediately. Within Cumann na mBan a direct mailing campaign had begun, appealing to the national conscience of potential jurors on similar

cases.[7] Then on December 3, Con Healy was convicted on two counts of
shooting at members of the Garda Síochána and sentenced to five years'
penal servitude. The names of the jurors were circulated and some Republicans decided to make a stronger case than Cumann na mBan. On January
23, 1929, a group of armed men arrived at the Terenure home of Mr. John
White, the foreman of the jury in the Healy case, and shot him in the
stomach. Although gravely wounded, he survived. On February 20, Mr.
Albert Henry Armstrong who had given evidence against the four young
men who stole the Union Jack in August was killed outside his house.
On February 23, *An Phoblacht* made no secret of Republican sentiment,
"the slave-minded jurors . . . are responsible, and are paying for their
treachery, one lying in a Dublin hospital . . ."[8] Even the organ of Fianna
Fáil, the *Nation,* had little sympathy for the jurors cowardly or misguided
enough to convict Healy. As the *Nation* explained a month later, Fianna
Fáil did not condone brutality but "they did not wish to associate themselves with the equally brutal, inefficient, useless methods of repression
adopted by the Free State Government".[9]

The usual repression had, indeed, followed the shooting of Armstrong
—a rash of arrests—and had proven ineffectual. The government was
aware of the vast repercussions the shootings would have with potential
jurors and even a swift arrest and conviction would not reassure the
average man who was interested in present security not future vengeance.
On May 1, the government introduced a Juries Protection Bill which
called for secret empanelling, imprisonment for refusal to recognize the
court, and protection of jurors. In his attack on the Bill, de Valera defended
those who had not—like Cosgrave and company—turned their backs on
their principles. In fact, regularly through 1928 and 1929, de Valera
stressed the validity of the ideals of the men outside the Dáil:

> My proposition that the representatives of the people should come in here
> and unify control so that we would have one Government and one Army was
> defeated, and for that reason I resigned. Those who continued on in that
> organization which we have left can claim exactly the same continuity that we
> claimed up to 1925.[10]

This kind of reasoning coupled with the faint disapproval of violence
only infuriated the government who felt that de Valera was giving moral
support to murder. There was every evidence that the "murderers" had
not finished. In April, known Republicans had been implicated in a bank
raid in Tipperary. On May 20, a man suspected of being a police agent
vanished in T. J. Ryan's territory in County Clare. Despite the most
intensive police surveillance of Ryan and local Republicans, he stayed
vanished. On June 11, in the midst of the Clare investigation, four gardai
were lured to a "secret dump". Garda Tadhg O'Sullivan opened the large

box and was killed in a booby-trap explosion. While the threat to public order was not as yet critical, reports that the IRA was moving into a more active phase and disquieting rumours of more radical political involvement began to filter into police reports.

In January 1929, the General Army Convention had met and found itself with much the same problems that had faced the previous Convention. There was no real change in the leadership—the same ten or fifteen men continued to carry the Army on their backs. Some of the younger men like Frank Ryan, who had been active in the direction of na Fianna Éireann and the organization of the university Republican Clubs, might from now on from time to time be included on the Executive. There might be shifts of formal positions: Twomey's first A/G, Tom Daly, had to resign because of ill health and was replaced after his departure for the United States by Donal O'Donoghue and then Jim Killeen. By and large, however, the inner circle stayed the same. Much of the discussion at the Convention centred on political questions since Twomey stressed that the Army was still not in a position to accomplish its military goals. O'Donnell, still pushing his Annuities campaign, had begun to gather a small group of Left IRA men behind his proposals to form a radical political organization—tentatively named Saor Éire. Some of the delegates, Michael Fitzpatrick of Dublin, Frank Ryan, and Dave Fitzgerald, were quite enthusiastic. Some of the organizational men had their doubts. And, of course, the pure militarists disapproved of diluting the Army's prime mission. Thus, in 1929, Saor Éire was too radical, too much another O'Donnell stunt, and too alien for most delegates, and the Convention put the idea away for another day. The Convention did, however, permit volunteers to become involved in new organizations to give some coherence to non-Fianna Fáil Republicans.

The new venture into politics was called Cómhairle na Poblachta. In April 1929 a long meeting was held to bring together members of Sinn Féin, various Republican TDs and representatives of Cumann na mBan. Thus in one body were included Maud Gonne MacBride; solid IRA men like George Plunkett and Seán MacBride; Mary MacSwiney, J. J. O'Kelly and the *de jure* Republicans; the Republican Left like Frank Ryan and Mick Fitzpatrick; firm Sinn Féin people like Joe Clarke, and new IRA hopefuls like Michael Kelly, C/O 3rd Battalion, Dublin. This impressive grouping could hardly remain a secret for long and the Free State police took a dim view of the new unity move. They reported that the sole purpose of Cómhairle na Poblachta was "the overthrow of the State by force of arms".[11] Although the police noted it was filled with the most virulent and active extremists, they did not immediately note that its members had little in common. Cómhairle na Poblachta was a paper tiger, which after a promising start decayed leaving the individual organizations to go their appointed ways.

By 1929 the faithful of Sinn Féin were finding the way narrow and rocky. The abstentionist TDs had remained faithful but lacking sufficient funds to put forward candidates their number remained static. The irreversible decline began in 1929 with the death of Austin Stack, perhaps the most talented man in the party. By then even the police had given up worrying much about Sinn Féin.

> This organization does not appear to be in a flourishing financial position, as the balance sheet submitted at the last Ard Fheis shows the amount on hand as being £3/3/3.[12]

Although there were still seventy-one branches and some good as well as obstinate people, Sinn Féin was clearly a spent force. The government of the Republic still functioned but on such a high plane of moral righteousness that few could see the point. To the cynical it seemed only to provide a platform for the shrill lecturing of Mary MacSwiney and the disgruntled rumbling of J. J. O'Kelly; in any case, the "government" continued to meet under the jaundiced eyes of the police. The major governmental project during 1929 was a new Constitution. The first reading before the Republican Dáil was given on January 22, 1929, and much of the year was given to discussion and publication of the details of the ideal Republican government.[13] With the decline of orthodox Republicanism into romantic idealism and the drift of Fianna Fáil into legitimacy, the IRA was faced, reluctantly, with the task of giving Republicans a coherent form.

The refusal of the Army Convention to accept Saor Éire, and its preference for the more traditional Cómhairle na Poblachta ploy, by no means meant an end to radical agitation. In fact the opposite was true, for the men of the Left had been encouraged by the degree of support in the Convention and more important by the growing tolerance of the organization men, on the Executive and Army Council, those in the middle with the balance of power. In June 1929, a new organization surfaced; it was initially called the Worker's Defence Corps and its members were drawn from the trade unions and the IRA. On Sunday, July 7, the first national convention was held and prominent members of the IRA Left—Price, Fitzpatrick, Ryan, Geoffrey Coulter, and Thomas Merrigan—appeared. Renamed the Irish Labour Defence League this was the first Dublin–IRA venture in radical politics. By 1929 O'Donnell had passed back and forth through the West strewing the parishes with rural revolutionary groups—Irish Working Farmers' Committee, Irish Tribune League—which often included interested local IRA people. Despite the slow drift to the Left, Irish radical politics still had a long way to go but within six months much had changed.

With the onset of the Depression in 1929, Ireland's flimsy prosperity vanished. Ireland became again little more than an exploited agricultural province of Britain governed by men who had been grounded in the verities of nineteenth-century economics and were unable to understand the chaotic collapse of world capitalism, incapable of imagining alternatives for Ireland paralysed in the face of the crisis. In this they were hardly novel nor was the rapid demand from the poor, the exploited, the hungry and unemployed for radical solutions. Ireland in the best of times had always had too many poor, too many men for the poorest acres, too many old living near the margin of life, and too many children with no hope but exile. Even a modest fall in agricultural exports or a decline in the need for Irish labour in New York or Liverpool could cause severe economic pangs in Ireland. Thus even by the end of 1929 times were not what they had been, and except for the big farmer they had not been good. When the orthodox Cómhairle na Poblacht met on November 2, 1929, in Wynn's Hotel in Dublin, there were far more resolutions on unemployment and working-class problems than there were on military action or *de jure* privileges. The drift was becoming a tide.

The IRA had never been isolated from the currents of radical or even revolutionary thought. Either as trade union delegates or as official IRA couriers men had travelled to Russia several times during the 1920s. George Gilmore and Dave Fitzgerald attempted to negotiate an agreement with the Russians to assist in the training of selected IRA officers for command of larger units, since training under the eye of the Free State government was difficult to manage. O'Donnell with his rural agitation had long been in touch with comparable groups scattered about Europe. Any anti-imperial revolutionary sooner or later drifted into the IRA orbit. O'Donnell and MacBride attended a conference at Frankfurt-on-Main. Donal O'Donoghue and Frank Ryan went to Paris and the Land Annuity Committee sent delegates to Berlin. Neither personal contact nor the literature of revolution had converted the IRA to any "alien" philosophies. Even self-professed socialists or communists within the IRA—and there were not many—had sculpted the original theory with a green Irish hand. In any case most Irishmen assumed that a heritage beginning with Tone's radical Republicanism extending through Lalor's demand for the land and including the example of Larkin's great strike in 1913 and the works and deeds of Connolly needed no foreign importation. Thus there was in many volunteers a latent radicalism under invisible military uniform. By 1930 the stress of the times goaded the volunteers to the Left and the IRA to devise a form for the new direction.

On March 13, 1930, the Workers Revolutionary Party was organized as an avowedly communist group. Deeply involved was Peadar O'Donnell, who, it was assumed, would be the voice of the new party's paper, *The Workers' Voice*; several other IRA men were members, Fitzpatrick, O'Donoghue, and Donal O'Connor. The new party was simply the first out of the wings. Within months a whole galaxy of new radical characters tumbled onto the political stage: The Friends of Soviet Russia, the Irish National Unemployed Movement, the Women's International League for Peace and Freedom, the International Anti-Imperialist League, the Irish Workers' and Farmers' Republican Party[14] and even the Irish Communist Party. The forces of law and order were horrified. The conventional subversion of the IRA had fitted the police mind, and after the shootings in early 1929 incidents had declined and official anxiety lessened. Then without proper warning Ireland was filled with a different variety of wild-eyed radicals.

> The number of these revolutionary organizations all of which have something in common, is bewildering and each week so to speak gives birth to the new ones ... It is also of interest to note that much the same people appear to be behind several organizations, Mrs. Maud MacBride being as ubiquitous as it is possible to be.[15]

Some of the new radicals were old friends of the police: Mick Fitzpatrick —"this man has always been prominently identified with revolutionary organizations"; and Peadar O'Donnell—"considered a very dangerous individual"; others were new faces, like Geoffrey Coulter, an Assistant Editor of *An Phoblacht*—"only within recent years prominent".[16] But new or old, shipped in from England with Russian gold or home-grown in Donegal, the new wave forced the police to learn new tricks, to worry their immediate superiors and ultimately the Cabinet with rumours of revolution.

During 1930 at least there was still more red smoke than fire. The IRA had as yet not formally ventured into the world of radical politics. Some like MacBride had doubts and many of the militarists like Russell and George Plunkett were opposed; but the leverage of the Left was growing, spurred by the public agitation of O'Donnell and Ryan and the quiet persuasion of Dave Fitzgerald. Increasingly on their own hook from Belfast to Galway, IRA men were taking an active role in strikes and land agitation. The mass of the Volunteers, however, had not been given any clear direction. Many of the older men had begun to have doubts about the second round which had been just about the next corner for so long. As Volunteers in a military organization that could not or would not fight, they still did not see too clearly the ultimate purpose of the Saor Éire idea; but with worsening economic conditions and the patent futility of an inactive military course, they were willing to be convinced. Once the Army was committed to a truly radical course, the men of the Left expected not only the Treaty government with all its British ties and symbols to be swept away but the exploitive system of crude capitalism, big ranches, and Ascendency control to go as well.

The new radicalism was not limited to Ireland for the members of Clan na Gael in America were also deeply involved in revolutionary ideas and parties. When Price came to New York in 1930, Gerald O'Reilly, and Charles Harkin, both the very latest of wild geese, took him on a "Red tour" largely convincing him of the need for deeper IRA involvement in the struggle for a workers' Republic. In November 1930, Twomey arrived at the invitation of the Clan to address a series of meetings. Twomey's prime task was to see that the money kept coming in to Dublin GHQ and consequently he had less time for Irish-American radicalism. On his return to Dublin after his successful tour, his sensitive ear must have picked up the making of a Left Army majority. The men of the Left had done their job well and convinced a substantial number of substantial people that the time for Saor Éire had come at last. The Army Council approved the Saor Éire project. The IRA was going to take a giant step to the Left.

On February 15, 1931, the General Army Convention met in the house of Róisín Walsh, Chief Librarian of Dublin City Library, at Templeogue. This time the IRA commitment to Saor Éire was to consolidate the Republic, secure the leadership of the workers and farmers in order to overthrow British imperialism and Irish capitalism. Many in the IRA were enthusiastic about the prospects, for at last it appeared to them the Army had found a vehicle which could bull its way through the rigid Cosgrave regime. With rapidly deteriorating economic conditions, the IRA would be able to grasp and hold the masses in the country as both a socialist and Republican organization. Fianna Fáil, only as radical as de Valera's limited "national" Republicanism, would be outflanked on the Left but more important the general militancy of the country would be harnessed in an effort to smash Cosgrave.

The two men most responsible for outlining the still vague form Saor Éire should take were Peadar O'Donnell, always the one with a quick pen and a ready semi-colon, and Dave Fitzgerald, one of the quiet, conscientious ones with a deep involvement in the problems of the people—"He had more brains than any of us, but like Mellows, Gilmore, and Murray, he was a self-effacing man whose real quality was not recognized. He was deeply cultured with a passionate interest in social problems."[17] Together, O'Donnell as usual doing the writing, they put together the basic tenets to be presented to the first national convention. In the meantime throughout the country the purpose of Saor Éire was being explained to the units. It appeared that the enthusiasm of the Left and the Army Council was duplicated in most of the country; but all was not swift and easy; for the conservatives, Saor Éire was a radical departure using radical language.

As a contemporary observer was later to point out, the vote in the Army Convention was insufficient to transform the Army overnight.

> It should not be inferred that after the victory of the progressives within the IRA that the Right Wing were democratic enough to accept the findings of a majority. Quite the contrary, they were openly hostile to the whole project and never missed an opportunity to sabotage the young growth. For instance, the vast majority of the Battalion O.C.s could be classified as Right Wing and availed themselves of the authority to call parades, courses or classes on the nights or days when he knew that members of his Battalion were wanted for work within their areas with Saor Éire.[18]

The increasing radicalization of the IRA was only one aspect of what the Free State government saw as a serious threat to Irish stability. Apart from all the wild Left talk, which was lumped by the government, the press, and the police under the handy communist label, there was the naked gun. On January 30, 1931, just before the General Army Convention at Templeogue, the IRA carried out an official, authorized execution. At 8.25 that evening the Crumlin Garda barracks received a telephone call that a man was lying on the roadway near Stanaway House, Captain's Lane. The man, thirty-year-old Patrick J. Carroll (O/C 3rd Company, 3rd Battalion, Dublin IRA), had been shot twice in the head and then a grenade had been detonated under his head. He was quite dead. At first there was no announcement by either the police or the IRA of the motive for the killing; in fact, some of his colleagues in the Dublin Brigade had to be advised not to attend the funeral. Eventually the police indicated that he had been an agent[19] and on February 14 *An Phoblacht* printed an editorial entitled "Executed by the IRA". Although the execution cut off a most useful stream of information the police were not unduly alarmed since such a political murder was in the Irish tradition. On February 6, a week later, Superintendent Curtin in Tipperary initiated a treason case against suspected IRA men. The official Army response to the pressure of Curtin escalated the police–IRA clash to open warfare.

Despite Curtin's best efforts to eliminate IRA drilling in the South Riding of Tipperary, the prospective jurors with White and Armstrong in mind had no intention of bringing in a guilty verdict. On March 20, 1931, Curtin wrote to the Commissioner of the Special Branch that the situation was desperate.

> On the whole it is useless to have anything in the nature of a political case ever again tried in this South Riding of Tipperary. The result of this case should, I respectfully suggest, give rise for serious thought to abolish the Jury system in cases of political nature. As far as the Garda were concerned in this case all possible was done at every stage of the case to make it successful and no pains were spared.[20]

The IRA in Tipperary felt that Curtin had made too much of an effort and taken too many pains. They asked GHQ for permission to eliminate him. Two hours after he had finished his report, at 10.15 in the evening, he was shot outside the gate leading to his home. A very unpleasant shock went through the Garda Síochána for now each member was a potential victim of men who could strike and be reasonably assured of mute witnesses, highly sympathetic juries, and armed colleagues.

For their part the IRA felt that the shooting of Curtin, who was considered no more than a representative of an occupying army whatever the grim politicians might blather about a poor policeman, had had a highly desirable effect. The anti-jurors campaign needed only the most occasional light touch, a pub rumour or a brief unsigned note, to cripple the Free State courts. In the west the annuity campaign had by no means ended despite the increasing number of arrests. The appeals, instituted by Cumann na mBan, to the Free State Army to desert the British cause and come over to the Republic had not been a visible success although certain members of the government were concerned as much about the possibility of invisible contacts as public handbills. The campaign to cripple the police was extended to prison wardens, again never a highly respected Irish profession. Those men accused of abusing Republican prisoners were seized and manacled to posts, their chests decorated with signs. As the days passed and the "incidents" piled up—jurors complaining of intimidating posters, attacks on warders, open drilling, provocative insults to gardai, malicious damage—IRA confidence grew. Cumann na mBan opened a campaign to boycott English-manufactured candy—first, as usual, depending on right reason to end the sales, but, as usual, the impatient preferred intimidation. Police reaction to this kind of activity had in the past been a rash of paper arrests, rarely pursued so far as court appearances but intended to cool off the avid. After Curtin the IRA had an answer.

In suddenly sympathetic courts IRA men began a series of civil proceedings against the gardai for assault and false arrest. These and Mr. Justice Hanna's opinion, handed down at the trial of Seán MacBride, arrested at an IRA meeting, that the police could not arrest on suspicion alone, nor depend on "documents" as sufficient proof of guilt, drove the police to distraction. As Commissioner O'Duffy pointed out to the Cabinet, there is no magic weapon to eradicate political crime and the only one available to the police was being removed.

All one can do is to hamper and hinder the movement of the criminal as much as humanly possible: make them suffer, make their lives a burden, apply unremitting surveillance to their every movement and generally make their connection with conspiracy and murder a non-paying proposition. This harassing programme has been carried out effectively. Rigorously applied, it has been found to be a useful weapon.

We have no guarantee, however, that the Judiciary will support the police view that it is legal . . .

Can we as a Police Force exist and function through the tolerance of the State's enemies![21]

The IRA seemed progressively less hampered about police pressure. There were of course arrests and of significant individuals; for example, George Gilmore seemed to be more often inside prison than out. He had been arrested during an Armistice Day demonstration in 1926 and soon recognized as the "sergeant" of the 1925 escape. Since then he had been repeatedly detained, arrested, and occasionally charged. On April 24, 1931 he was arrested once more for having resisted arrest twelve months before, an odd charge but sufficient; despite his quiet, diffident manner George Gilmore was considered by the police to be a most dangerous man. These arrests, however, did little to lessen the IRA level of militancy since there were no mass sweeps or internments and a rapidly declining willingness by the police to arrest on suspicion. With or without the radical ideas of Saor Éire, an increasing number of volunteers felt the Free State had begun to crumble.

On June 21, Sunday, there was a great hosting for Wolfe Tone at Bodenstown, an opportunity to display the extent of IRA strength and the new depth of IRA ideas. The Easter commemorations had already been sufficiently impressive to give many of the more conservative, particularly among the clergy, indigestible food for thought. The Lenten Pastorals had warned the Irish flock of the dangers of radicalism and in the parishes the priest was increasingly identifying militant Republicanism with Godless communism. While disturbing to some of the more pious and certainly to their less political wives and parents, clerical condemnation of "Cut Throat Tone" or "Emmet's rabble" and their "Irregular" descendents only stiffened the determination of the average Volunteer to appear at Bodenstown on Sunday afternoon, June 21.

On Saturday evening a message was broadcast that the government had banned the procession to Tone's grave. All bus and train services were cancelled and units of the Free State army alerted to seal off the graveyard and road into the area. Meanwhile the police swooped through Dublin managing to pick up Seán Russell and Mick Price but not to disrupt the plans for the following day. On Sunday morning, after Mass, the Dublin IRA unit assembled at Parnell Square, marched openly to Kingsbridge Station and boarded buses for Sallins, the rallying point for the march to the graveyard. From all over Ireland convoys had been on the move, often since Saturday evening. Bicycles popping out of country lanes joined cars and farm trucks jammed with Republican families. As the crowd grew in Sallins, the gardai, brought in to prevent a symbolic demonstration, found in the face of first five thousand, then ten thousand then more and still more cheerful men determined to march, that it would be they who would be offering "symbolic" resistance to the banned procession. They gave way at a touch. The Free State soldiers at the graveside, surrounded by thousands of spectators even before the procession came into sight, could not have acted if they had wanted to, which apparently they did not. The procession arrived and the oration was given by Peadar O'Donnell, substituting for Russell, who was sitting out the ceremony in jail.

O'Donnell, the greatest agitator of his generation, gave them what they wanted to hear. To those who listened, Cosgrave and the Treatyites seemed to have entered the twilight, for the dawn of radical Republicanism was at hand. The country could take no more of the safe men—unemployment had soared, wages were low, emigration was no longer a solution, and somehow, in some way, the walk from Sallins to Bodenstown would be continued on up the high road to the Republic. Off to one side, listening to the soaring words of O'Donnell and testing the seething enthusiasm of the crowd, stood de Valera and the Fianna Fáil delegation, "waiting in the wings".[22]

After Bodenstown the Free State government, uneasy at the increasing radicalism of the countryside, unable to understand why conventional economic policies did not solve, much less ameliorate, the effects of the world depression, was well aware that de Valera was waiting for his opening. Although an election was not required until October 1932, it was clear that unless the decay of Cumann na nGaedheal could be reversed the party would be tossed out on a wave of protest votes by men who in the emotion of the moment would not realize the foolishness of de Valera's ideas and the irresponsibility of Fianna Fáil. This firm, unshakeable conviction in their own unique capacity to rule, despite considerable evidence to the contrary, had been increasingly buttressed during the first half of 1931 by the actions and words of their most militant opponents—the IRA. Within the government there were those sincerely concerned with the new wild men of the Left; others more cynical had little fear of a Red Ireland but saw the spin-off benefits of a Red Scare. Everyone in the government abhorred the new wave of violence and understood Eoin O'Duffy's anguish with the erosion of civil order as a result of murder, intimidation, and subversion. Regardless of the political situation, the potential chaos and the propagation of alien ideas must be controlled; but as O'Duffy pointed out this was difficult within the existing judicial and democratic system. He wanted a new

stringent public safety act. The government, beset with problems, begar
to swing into the new hard line.

On July 18, warders from Mountjoy prison were seized and one wa
handcuffed to an iron railing. On July 20, the Tipperary situation blev
up again. Two men posing as detectives called at the home of John
Ryan, one of the witnesses in the drilling case brought in by Superinten
dent Curtin. Ryan went off with the two men and his dead body wa
found together with a notice, "Spies and informers, beware!—I.R.A."
Again GHQ on request from the local men had felt that another
Tipperary execution was needed and co-operated in the elimination of a
man who in Dublin Frank Ryan for the benefit of British reporters called
nothing else than a traitor. Although some in the IRA and many out
side might have viewed the series of incidents during 1931 as an all-out
assault on the Cosgrave regime, this essentially was not the case. Most of
the IRA's violent responses were either accidental or a reaction to what
GHQ felt to be clear provocation.

To allow the Curtins, the Ryans and the others to have their way
would riddle the army with informers, dishearten the country units, and
lead swiftly to the decay of the organization. In point of fact, the idea
even of a second round or a military revolution had been slipping away
as the prospects grew of Saor Éire developing into a mass movement.
If the masses rallied under the banner of Saor Éire, there would be no
Ireland left for the Cosgrave people to rule, for their army was made up
of Irishmen who knew the fearful state of the country.

The Army Council decided that the time had arrived for Saor Éire
to make an official and public debut. By September, of course, the IRA's
new direction was a matter of public knowledge and government spokesmen were already at work. In Castlebar on September 13, the Minister
of Justice Fitzgerald-Kenny slashed the IRA and Saor Éire with delighted
abandon.

> Their avowed aim and object is to force, by means of threats and crimes
> of violence, a republic of Soviet nature, on this country. They are a minority,
> but they want to ensure their Soviet views by brute force, and we say we
> will not allow them.[23]

And the pressure against the IRA was stepped up. An Phoblacht was
regularly censored and often more policemen were in the offices than
writers. Known Republicans were closely watched and Seán MacBride,
organizing for Saor Éire in Kerry, claimed the police had threatened his
life. The government pointed out that already during September there
had been attacks on J. Lynch, a State Solicitor, and William McInerney
in Clare—both according to Bishop Fogarty "Bolshevik attacks". As yet,
no one could tell how "Bolshevik" Saor Éire might be, for there had been

no national meeting, there was no constitution, and the unpublished directives of the General Convention were none too explicit.

At a meeting in the Ellis Hotel, Twomey had assigned MacBride and Fitzpatrick to arrange for the first national convention.[24] In a period of tightening surveillance and increasing detentions this was easier said than done. Many hall owners wanted no part of the Reds. The first meeting in Abbey Street was cancelled by the police. A prospective room was found on Parnell Square but was soon discovered for some reason to have no floor. On September 28, the morning of the meeting, the manager of the Peacock Hall changed his mind. Finally at double rental they secured a ballroom—Iona Hall—on North Great George Street. The delegates managed to slip in before the circling police realized what had happened and so the detectives had to wait until the meeting was over to collect their head count. There were 120 delegates and twenty-odd observers from all thirty-two counties under the Temporary Chairman Fitzpatrick. Seán Hayes of the Irish Working Farmers was chosen chairman and David Fitzpatrick Secretary. A series of resolutions were quickly passed favouring public ownership of transport and co-operative control of land. MacBride moved and Price seconded the acceptance of the Saor Éire Constitution as drafted. This resolution passed and the delegates moved into a Committee-of-the-Whole and passed six additional resolutions touching familiar topics—political prisoners, the Indian masses, the Soviet Union, land annuities, and Free State terrorism. A National Executive was named including IRA, Cumann na mBan, radical labour and and-annuity people. Saor Éire was to be an organization of workers and working farmers based on the 1916 Proclamation but it was not at all clear what was to follow. Ireland had a dearth of industrial workers and those few were organized into a remarkably conservative trade union movement several times removed from Larkin and Connolly. Saor Éire called on the militant workers to take the leadership of the struggle against the capitalist class "out of the hands of labour officials who no longer fight the workers' battles".[25] Given the desperate reality of the weekly pay packet during the dark depression days it was unlikely that any such action would be undertaken. The working farmer, particularly the grossly exploited hired worker, was the most difficult of all to organize. Many marginal farmers were too old to change, too conservative to co-operate with others, and too tied to their own land. As O'Donnell had showed, something could be done, but the number of Seán Hayeses and Peadar O'Donnells was limited. In fact, in a desperately poor country, exploited by a lumpen bourgeoisie and the City of London, filled with men of no property weened on a revolutionary tradition, radicalism in the terms of Saor Éire instead of being rampant was hardly visible. The people were uneasy and despairing but socialist language and ideas did not speak clearly to the countryside where the horror of the parish priest at the audacity of the Reds and the traditional Republicanism of de Valera seemed more relevant. For Saor Éire to succeed in mobilizing the people would be more educational than revolutionary activity, more organizational than insurrectional. For this there was to be no time. When the delegates filed out of the Iona Hall, a dozen detectives were waiting. Two motor cars were drawn up with their headlights on the door illuminating for the Special Branch the faces of Ireland's largest collection of revolutionaries. No one was detained—but that was a matter of timing.

The government was advancing on two fronts. One was a wide-scale attack on radicalism, revolution, and the contamination of Irish Catholic souls of pagan communism. Backed by the press, applauded by the comfortable and successful, and propagated by the Church, the Doctrine of the Red Menace was spread from Leinster House to the most distant parish. A great help in this campaign was the acquisition by the police of a collection of O'Donnell's draft resolutions and unfinished notes for Saor Éire. These were carefully arranged and rushed to the seat of clerical power in Ireland, Maynooth. As anticipated the Bishops were suitably horrified at the "constitution" of Saor Éire. On Sunday, October 18, the Irish bishops and archbishops meeting at Maynooth issued a joint Pastoral which condemned Saor Éire by name and the IRA by implication: "the two organizations . . . whether separate or in alliance, are sinful and irreligious, and that no Catholic can lawfully be a member of them".[26] By then the successful culmination of the Red Scare had been accompanied by a more judicial ally—the Constitution (Amendment No. 17) Bill.

For months O'Duffy had been pressing for an extension of police powers predicting dire consequences if the situation in the country continued to deteriorate under the IRA campaign of violence and blackmail.

> . . . It is essential that I should be given sufficient legal powers to enable me to deal with the problem effectively and to put the position definitely before my officers.
>
> In conclusion I respectfully submit to the Government that the safety of the State demands the immediate enaction of a Bill suitable and adequate to deal with the position with which we are confronted.[27]

Although as usual O'Duffy tended to exaggerate the situation, the Cabinet was quite receptive. Most of the pages of suggestions were incorporated in the new bill, which was extensive, having thirty-four sections and an appendix. The most controversial provision was the establishment of a Military Tribunal to replace the normal courts. Provisions were made to declare associations illegal along with the anticipated extensive powers of search, arrest, and detention. O'Duffy was delighted and the Cabinet hopeful. As soon as the Dáil reassembled on October 14 after the summer recess, the bill which inserted Article 2A (a public safety bill) into the Constitution was introduced. The outraged opposition of Fianna Fáil was barely tolerated. De Valera's criticisms were not particularly relevant and his insistence that removal of the oath would eliminate the conditions the bill sought to end was a strained argument. Further steeling the government's determination to rush the bill through were several unsuccessful and unexplained threats against TDs. The IRA claimed that "no threats were made, nor was violence used"[28] by Volunteers, but at this date the government was delighted to use the threats as grist to the mill. The bill became law on October 17. The Executive Council promulgated the operation of "2A" bringing the act into force and the police were away and running.

Everyone had anticipated that the more notorious Republican and radical groups would be proscribed, but the government went full out and banned twelve: Saor Éire, IRA, Fianna Éireann, Cumann na mBan, Friends of Soviet Russia, Irish Labour Defence League, Workers' Defence Corps, Women's Prisoners Defence League, Workers' Revolutionary Party, Irish Tribute League, Irish Working Farmers' Committee, and the Workers' Research Board. Throughout the month there were irregular police raids all over Dublin on IRA homes, on radical offices, and on suspected "communist fronts" like the Russian Oil Products, Ltd. offices. The raids spread through the country although many of those arrested were quickly released. Issues of *An Phoblacht* and the *Workers' Voice* were banned. About the only "radical" organization left was Sinn Féin, which had not condemned Saor Éire but "deprecated any attempt to promote class distinctions and class warfare".[29] This sound approach to economics and Sinn Féin's limited membership and negligible funds kept it off O'Duffy's list. Sinn Féin did hold a rally but this was about the only open response from the Republicans who went to ground when they could and sought to roll with the punch.

That just such a Republican witch hunt had been in the works had been obvious during the spring and summer months. The Army Council had begun to doubt the IRA's ability to remain passive and intact under the provocative pressure. GHQ still contended that any military response—a second round or second rising—would be foolhardy; on the other hand, the leadership could not simply sit by and watch the Free State dismantle the Army. The decision was made by the Army Council after consultation with those men available that some sort of active response would have to be considered. There was no chance to call an Army Convention and in any case no desire to let word of what might be an unnecessary option

leak out. If action were necessary, the Council agreed that it would probably be guerrilla operations rather than a coup or a formal, set-piece
second round. Secondly, the Clan leadership was asked to ship as much
equipment as quickly as possible. In New York fund-raising increased, as
did the acquisition of weapons, particularly additional Thompson guns;
and some of the most recent wild geese made preparations to return for
the fight. In Ireland few of the Volunteers knew of any specific plans
but all could see that conditions were very bad. There was talk that something should be done. The police had for some time picked up rumours
of a new rising which, enshrined in reports as intelligence, had helped
to make the case for Article 2A,[30] but the actual Army Council plans
had been kept very quiet and very vague.

The only public response to the bill was a vast anti-Imperialist Rally
held on Armistice Day. These November 11, IRA-sponsored riots had become traditional, with baton charges, Union Jack burnings, bloody heads
and filled jail cells. The one in 1931 was pushed to show that, coercion
or no, there was life left in the radicals yet. Vast crowds showed up on
the eve of Armistice Day and on the next day the Anti-Imperialist
League, previously overlooked, was banned and raids took place all over
Dublin and in Cork and Kerry. This did not stop all concerned—police,
speakers, and crowd—from following the traditional programme. British
Legion HQ was attacked and generally it was clear that Article 2A had
not yet done the job. Police tactics were to harry the average Volunteer,
to arrest the leadership and the hard men, and to frighten off those on the
periphery. The IRA's policy, incorporated by the A/G in a message to the
Army, was not to react to provocation with sporadic violence, not to drill
openly, and to meet the hierarchy's misrepresentation by rational argument.[31] Except for the November 10–11 splurge, this remained the policy.
The immediate result was that the number of men in prison began to rise,
the number of Volunteers fired for police-enforced absenteeism increased,
and the flow of recruits dried up.

At the end of November, the Military Tribunal began sitting. Not all
the men accused were famous since the usual charge was illegal drilling,
but rumour had it that George and Charlie Gilmore, both arrested before
the enactment of Article 2A, would be tried by the Tribunal. George
had been in prison since April. The day before his arrest two Trinity
College students had been slightly wounded in the Dublin Mountains
when they ran in to an IRA unit drilling near the Hell Fire Club. The
police had kept men in the area and on June 10 discovered a large dump
of arms near the Gilmore home in the same area.[32] In July Charlie Gilmore
had been arrested and joined George in Mountjoy. Neither had wanted to
stay longer than necessary and October 10 with the use of two "pistols"—

ittled out of wood and covered with silver paper—had almost bluffed
eir way out. For twenty minutes, pistols levelled at the military sentries
ider the outer wall, they had waited for the expected ladder to appear.
hen it was clear that the escape had miscarried, they surrendered and
lowed themselves to be "disarmed". This kind of activity had done little
recommend the Gilmores to the government and on December 7, the
o were tried before the Military Tribunal charged with being members
an illegal organization and in possession of arms. George Gilmore
fused to plead.

I do not wish to be taken as making any defence at all, because I don't want
anybody to think I excuse myself for such a charge as having arms. I have
never tried to conceal the fact that I am admittedly hostile to British Imperialism and international capitalism.[33]

As expected the two received substantial sentences, George five years
id Charlie three, and were taken off to Arbour Hill prison where both
ain campaigned—naked except for blanket wrappings—for political
eatment.

On December 9, Frank Ryan of *An Phoblacht* and editor of the *Repub-
an File* was charged with seditious libel. By mid-December some of the
dice's most persistent tormentors were behind bars—Seán O'Farrell of
eitrim, T. J. Ryan of Clare, Sheila Humphries of Dublin and "Ghosts"—
it the total number was as yet very small. It was the day-to-day pressure
the average Volunteer that hurt, not the prominent staff officer or
lucky C/O who ended up in Arbour Hill. The first real victim was
imes Vaugh arrested in Leitrim on December 5 and interrogated by the
lice until Christmas Eve when he was released. He died the following
orning of obvious causes which the inquest overlooked to the outrage
Leitrim Republicans. Unless the Army Council was willing to resort to
rce of arms, there was nothing, however, that could be done. Cosgrave
as not required to call the election until October 1932, a date which
emed a very long way off to many Volunteers.

By January 1932, several factors were working to produce a "political"
lution to the confrontation between the IRA and the Free State govern-
ent. On June 20, 1932, the Eucharistic Congress was to be held in Dublin
multaneously with the celebration of the arrival of St. Patrick in Ireland
432, fifteen hundred years before. There was a feeling that what was
pected to be a bitter and perhaps violent electoral campaign should not
ar these proceedings. Equally important, the Imperial Economic Con-
rence was to open in Ottawa on July 21, 1932, and last a month. Attend-
ice, which was vital for Irish interests, would be pointless without a
roper mandate from the voters. Then, too, the relative success of the Red
are, the smooth operation of Article 2A, and the subsequent decline in

violence created a more promising atmosphere for an early election. Th Dáil was dissolved on January 29 and the general election set for Februar 16.

In early January, on release of the news of the election, and withou waiting for an Army Council directive, O'Donnell ran a banner headlin in *An Phoblacht*, "Put Cosgrave Out". Although IRA–Fianna Fái relations had cooled in the wake of Saor Éire (too far to the Left for man of de Valera's troops) and the various shootings (too brutal for de Valera[34] Fianna Fáil was the only Republican alternative to the Cosgrave govern ment. While not as pure as Sinn Féin about the usurping Dáil, man Volunteers were not particularly eager to vote in a Free State election fo slightly compromised Republicans. On the other hand, to abstain migh perpetuate Cosgrave's terror regime. Although tactically the ideal electio results would be so narrow a Cosgrave victory that the whole Free Stat structure might be toppled, most IRA men accepted the need for a Fiann Fáil success. Almost no consideration was given to using the electio campaign as cover for a rising or a coup. Without clearly recognizing it the leadership had largely put aside the war plans for a second round i part in favour of organizing the masses within Saor Éire or of simpl waiting. The talk of a 1931–1932 rising had been only the first desperat reaction to coercion. Whatever the Clan in America might think of th fire-breathing activists in the country, the Army Council felt that th attempt should be made to remove Cosgrave through the existing demo cratic means. An Army Council meeting was hurriedly called in Dundrun to consider Cosgrave's announcement that there would be an early election It was decided to rescind the General Army Order passed by the Arm Convention in November 1927, prohibiting Volunteers from voting o working in Free State or Northern Ireland elections. No IRA policy woul be put forward but Volunteers might co-operate in putting Cosgrave out although this was only a small step on the way to the Republic. To g the whole way would take other means than those of de Valera.

> . . . The Army Council would, however, emphasize to Volunteers that whil advocating voting at these elections, our objects cannot be achieved by th methods of politics of the parties seeking election.
> This fact should be borne in mind by Volunteers throughout the elections.[35]

IRA assistance to Fianna Fáil varied from area to area, as did the desir of de Valera's people to become involved with a "banned organization" Whatever the Army Council said, some units frowned on voting, althougl Volunteers might protect the polling booth or bring in voters. Elsewhere IRA assistance was not visible, while in other places the most intimat co-operation existed. Basically, the IRA could offer Fianna Fáil thei votes, which would never have gone to Cosgrave, and some extra-legal aid

Both were comforting but many of the votes would have come anyway and Fianna Fáil did not mind if the IRA performed all those little election chores so vital for success in Ireland until recently and so embarrassing to recall. The count in Irish elections has customarily been above reproach; however, multiple voting of emigrants, corpses, and the poor man who is slow to reach the booth is also a time-honoured custom. The idealist may take comfort by reflecting that since all the parties practised this form of ultra-democracy where even the dead might vote, all the manœuvring should have cancelled out. In any case, in Dublin for example, Fitzpatrick set up liaison with Fianna Fáil through Seán Lemass, one of de Valera's most promising lieutenants. The IRA got the appropriate lists of the absent and voted them for Fianna Fáil. Some active Volunteers tripped from booth to booth judiciously casting fifty ballots.

Whether such *sub rosa* help turned the tide, given the equally dubious activities of the men of Cumann na nGaedheal is problematical; but most observers agree that the Cosgrave people ran one of the most appallingly inefficient campaigns in living memory. Many of the "programmes" of Cumann na nGaedheal during 1930–1931 may have been actuated by the highest motives, but they were incredible political blunders—the reduction of pensions, the reduction of police salaries, the reduction of teachers' pay and the prohibition of married women teachers. With no new direction or programme, Cumann na nGaedheal stood on their record—a record which had produced 100,000 unemployed, beggared the country, and driven the poor to desperation and the rich to fear revolution. Brief as the actual campaign was, the government managed to bungle once more by having a suit brought against de Valera's new daily newspaper *The Irish Press* for libel. To compound matters the case came before the Military Tribunal. The country might tolerate stringent measures against a self-confessed revolutionary army but this was suspiciously like suppression of free speech. For eleven days before polling the trial dragged on, generating more doubts about the political sanity of the Cosgrave government. Cosgrave's attacks on de Valera might have amused his supporters but brought him no new votes. The Red Scare had petered out when the horrible communists could either not be found or turned out to be the Murphy lad down the lane. The suppression of the IRA had created as many problems as it solved, with Fianna Fáil running about the country howling to free the political prisoners. The country was in foul economic shape and the old war cries of 1923 sounded sour to the hungry. Even without the blunders and lunacy, the country wanted a change and a change was what Fianna Fáil offered.

Actually, Fianna Fáil's radical Republicanism had grown less radical and less Republican. The party platform included a commitment to abolish the old oath, but there was no mention of the Republic and there was even a promise not to seek constitutional changes without an additional mandate. Fianna Fáil offered an end to the land annuities. A new economic policy was to be followed which would encourage the development of Irish industry. De Valera also favoured self-sufficiency in agriculture through the encouragement of tillage at the expense of pasturage. It was a sound enough programme with attractive features—particularly the end of the annuities—but by no stretch of the imagination was it radical in a world filled with coloured shirts, flaming banners, and crumbling governments. Be that as it may, the platform and de Valera, the desire for a change and the tight organization of Fianna Fáil, the help of the IRA and the blunders of Cosgrave, all combined to put Cumann na nGaedheal out.

The results were a substantial but by no means overwhelming triumph for Fianna Fáil. De Valera had seventy-two elected members to Cosgrave's fifty-seven, a gain of sixteen to a loss of nine. Although he would be obliged to depend on the support of the seven Labour Party members, de Valera was going to be able to form a government and institute his policies. Just what this would mean to the IRA was as yet unclear, but expectations were high; the prisons would be cleared; the Free State villains, Neligan and O'Duffy and the rest, cast out; and the neo-British Imperial trappings discarded. But no one, not even his old friends from the years before the splits and odd new directions, really knew what de Valera would do next. Nothing could be as bad as Cosgrave, the devil the IRA knew all too well; but de Valera in power in the Free State Dáil was a devil that the Army Council did not yet know. All might go well but for the moment the IRA held itself in readiness and waited for the new Dáil to assemble on March 9.

NOTES

1. Employment in industry crept up from 103,000 in 1926 to 111,000 in 1931, but the basic ingredient of the brief Cosgrave prosperity was agricultural exports—the volume reached in 1929 was not equalled until 1960. The recipients of this brief prosperity were not, of course, the small farmers of the west and south, who gave de Valera and Fianna Fáil their votes.

2. Cumann na mBan, besides voting overwhelmingly against the Treaty, gave the most active support to the IRA in 1922–1923 and had never shown any interest in de Valera's new direction. There were several women on Fianna Fáil's first Executive—Mrs. Pearse, Madame Markievicz, Mrs. Tom Clarke, Miss Dorothy Macardle, Mrs.

Sheehy-Skeffington, and Miss L. Kearns—but the vast majority of the Republican women would have no part of the Treaty Dáil. Cumann na mBan, in fact, remained far closer to the IRA than to the posturing of the "Republican Government" or Sinn Féin.

3. Irish Free State, *Coughlan Shooting Inquiry, Report of the Tribunal of Inquiry*, Dublin, 1928.

4. Irish Free State, Department of Justice, Confidential Report by Commissioner, Garda Síochána, for the period January 1, 1931 to May 31, 1931. Dublin, July 27, 1931, p. 32.

5. Irish Free State, *Dáil Debates*, vol. xxii, cols. 1615–1616.

6. Ghosts, *"Soldiers of the . . ."* (broadsheet, n.p., n.d.)

7. Apparently at Maire Comerford's suggestion Cumann na mBan had begun a campaign to persuade jurors not to convict Republicans. Jurors' names were acquired through a contact at the Green Street Courthouse in Dublin and persuasive letters sent off.

8. *An Phoblacht*, February 23, 1929.

9. *The Nation*, March 23, 1929.

10. Irish Free State, *Dáil Debates*, vol. xxviii, cols. 1398–1405.

11. Irish Free State, Department of Justice, Garda Síochána, Report on Organizations Inimical to the State, October 16, 1931.

12. *Ibid.*, Memorandum on Revolutionary Organizations (S 5864), April 5, 1930.

13. Government of the Republic of Ireland, *A Bill for the Constitution of the Republic of Ireland*, New York, 1930.

14. Even the most highly structured and hopefully initiated of these organizations had brief life spans, often disappearing without a trace or merging without public notice. The Republican influence can be seen in the Irish Workers' and Farmers' Republican Party which lists as the first of its twelve objectives "to break the connection with England" and the last "to bring about the closest co-operation between workers in . . . rural districts and . . . in cities . . . all victims of the same exploiting agencies". Irish Workers' and Farmers' Republican Party, *Constitution and Rules* (typed copy, n.p., n.d.).

15. Irish Free State, Department of Justice, Memorandum on Revolutionary Organizations (S 5864), April 5, 1930.

16. *Ibid.*

17. Michael McInerney, "Peadar O'Donnell–6," *Irish Times*, April 6, 1968.

18. Leonard Larkin (untitled typed manuscript, n.d.).

19. The police handling of their agent was badly bungled; for instead of limiting his activities to the passage of information (he belonged to every radical–IRA organization in the city), he was used to finger

George Mooney, who knew who had set him up. Two IRA men Sweeny and McGuiness were allowed, while prisoners, to talk with Mooney and after their short sentences brought out sufficient information to confirm the suspicions that already existed in Dublin HQ. After that no IRA action was taken for months until the appropriate time occurred. Although from time to time the police managed to keep a low-level line into the Dublin Brigade this was the only serious leak; and because of the rigid compartmentalization with the Army, the police got relatively little.

20. Irish Free State, Department of Justice, From Superintendent Curtin to Commissioner "C", Tipperary, March 20, 1931 (typed copy).

21. Confidential Report by Commissioner (July 27, 1931), pp. 4, 46.

22. O'Donnell, *There Will Be Another Day*, p. 126.

23. *Irish Press*, September 14, 1931.

24. Some of the men of the Left later felt that MacBride had been assigned to Saor Éire as a counterweight and was not actually too enthusiastic. Regardless of what MacBride might actually have felt, the Left always suspected that GHQ and the Executive were not really radical and had to be regularly wooed or prodded.

25. *Irish Press*, September 28, 1931.

26. *Irish Independent*, October 19, 1931.

27. Confidential Report by Commissioner (July 27, 1931), p. 46.

28. *Irish Press*, October 19, 1931.

29. *Ibid.*, October 4, 1931.

30. Irish Free State, Department of Justice, from Superintendent's Office, Listowel, to HQ, July 30, 1931; *ibid.*, from Superintendent's Office, Tralee, to Commissioner, July 31, 1931; *ibid.*, from Chief Superintendent's Office, Thurles, September 1, 1931.

31. Oglaigh na h-Éireann, Adjutant-General to C/Os of each Independent Unit, GHQ, Dublin, October 22, 1931.

32. This dump, which had been in use for over a decade, revealed why GHQ felt that another round was foolhardy; out of fifteen revolvers there were eleven types including one "45 rusty" and the only uniform armament was twenty 303 Lee Enfield rifles.

33. See *The Story of Arbour Hill*, December 1931, p. 8.

34. "They have done terrible things recently I admit, if they are responsible for them, and I suppose they are. Let us appeal to them and ask them in God's name not to do them." Irish Free State, *Dáil Debates*, vol. xl, col. 298.

35. Oglaigh na h-Éireann, Adjutant-General to C/Os of each Independent Unit, GHQ Dublin, January 12, 1932.

PART III

The De Valera Years: 1932–1938

CHAPTER VI

De Valera in Power: The Devil We Don't Know, March 1932–June 1936

On March 9, when the Dáil reassembled, Eamon de Valera was elected, as expected, President of the Executive Council by eighty-one to sixty-eight votes. His selection was approved by the Governor-General and the Dáil assented without a vote to the new Executive Council.[1] The moment the formalities had finished, the new Minister for Justice, James Geoghegan, and the new Minister for Defence, Frank Aiken, went directly to Arbour Hill Military prison where the men sentenced by the Military Tribunal were held.

> The Minister for Defence spent some time in the cell of Mr. George Gilmore, who was serving a sentence of five years' penal servitude. The two men saluted each other warmly on parting, and Mr. Gilmore, who called the Minister by his Christian name, said he need not tell him that he had been glad to see him. All these prisoners were released on the following day.[2]

On March 18, the government suspended operation of the notorious Article 2A. These gestures to the IRA, fellow-members of the Legion of the Rearguard, were comforting to the militant in Fianna Fáil, and honoured the promises made during the election campaign; although they were irritating to the "Treatyites", they were not sufficiently radical to cause serious concern. De Valera had to tread warily between the boundless expectations of his own supporters and the sullen toleration of his political opponents, the Church, and perhaps the professional institutions of state—after all the army over which Frank Aiken now exerted control as Minister of Defence was largely the same army he had fought against only a decade before. While recognizing de Valera's difficulties, the average IRA Volunteer had somehow expected a more impressive change of direction in government.

Until the final moments in Leinster House some in Fianna Fáil feared that the Free State people might balk at an orderly transfer of power; however, the Cumann na nGaedheal leaders were determined that the democratic norms should be observed, that the uneasy and vulnerable in the army and police should act with excessive propriety.[3] All this had been done and so smoothly that the oddity of a secure government yielding power to bitter enemies with reasonable grace was largely overlooked.[4]

Forced to sit in the same chamber, on the same committees, the men of Fianna Fáil had been, as Cosgrave had hoped, "constitutionalized" during the five years of opposition. The other Republicans, the IRA, had not. They were uninterested in the slow unrolling of a legislative programme or the delicate position of de Valera in relation to the civil service, to the Treaty Army, to O'Duffy's Garda Síochána. The IRA wanted as a minimum wholesale dismissal of the "guilty", swift recognition of the peculiar position of the IRA, and a rush down the road to secure the Republic. This is what the Volunteers wanted but the expectations of GHQ and the Army Council were rather different.

One of the first contacts with de Valera was made by Seán Russell and George Gilmore. Russell, a simple and overwhelmingly honest man, had maintained through the years personal friendships with men who abhorred his "politics" and admired his character. Gilmore possessed, as all knew, quiet determination, a man absolutely without fear or interest in his own advancement. Representative of the two wings of the IRA, they were ideal men to discover what de Valera had in mind. The results of the conversation were difficult to interpret. De Valera talked about securing the provisions of Document No. 2, that hasty flawed alternative to the Treaty. About the IRA he was vague but managed to imply that with Fianna Fáil in power there was no real need for the Army.[5] This was by no means the last contact between GHQ and de Valera but the informal soundings by Russell during the next year did little to change the impression that de Valera intended to go no further than his stated programme; the removal of the oath, the reduction of the trappings of Empire, the end of land annuity payments, the encouragement of manufacture. There was to be no Declaration of the Republic, no crusade to break the connection, no vengeance on the Treatyites, nor recognition of the IRA. Thus, since the Free State was not going to be transformed into a Republic with the IRA as the formal army, the Army Council could hardly see any reason to disband.

The IRA was growing by leaps and bounds. Almost immediately open drilling had begun. The local police, uncertain of the future, looked elsewhere. Recruits rushed to join up, some under the impression that membership in the IRA would be the first step on the road to position and pension now that de Valera was in power, others eager to take the final step to the Republic now that the façade of the Free State had been pierced by Fianna Fáil. An Army that had literally been carried on the backs of the Army Council and GHQ, within a few months was filled to overflowing with the eager. The Dublin Brigade swelled to two thousand members. The Easter commemorations were well attended and the march to Bodenstown in June included a Fianna Fáil delegation—this time no longer in the wings but in the centre of the stage.[6] All this action and freedom of movement was exhilarating but GHQ was also aware that O'Duffy was still Commissioner of Police and Neligan at Special Branch had not yet been sacked. The same Special Branch detectives were still about. Fianna Fáil continued to move very cautiously. The Army Council requested "the Fianna Fáil government will provide payment out of public funds, of the legitimate debt contracted by the Irish Republican Army in the prosecution of the war in defence of the Republic since the 'Treaty'."[7] But this request was received without comment by the new government. On the other hand, the new atmosphere of toleration eliminated the need to continue the anti-juror or anti-police campaigns. On July 14, a jury found Gerald Dempsey not guilty; but the judge sentenced him to three months for contempt. On July 26, the new Minister of Justice released Dempsey unconditionally. On August 14, George Gilmore and T. J. Ryan were shot and wounded by detective officers near Kilrush, County Clare. On September 15, a Tribunal of Inquiry reported that their allegations against the police had largely been substantiated.[8] The IRA was free to act but how and for what purpose seemed no clearer than it had the year before in totally different circumstances.

First, the great experiment, Saor Éire, was quietly dying, a tenuous memory for all but the dedicated Left. Largely a response to the Cosgrave regime, it did not appear appropriate with de Valera in power, nor promising after the violent and vitriolic attacks of the clergy. Not all the Volunteers had grown accustomed to the thud of croziers on their backs and some felt as a practical matter the Army had enough trouble without going in for heresy. With Saor Éire out of the way—and the first Army Convention after de Valera's election took care of the last formalities—GHQ was stalled, since there could hardly be a second round against de Valera—at least in 1932 few could imagine the possibility. Thus with an Army bursting at the seams, with arms and even recruits arriving from the United States, and with morale at an all-time high, GHQ had to wait out the new government. In the meantime, independently in Belfast, the IRA had become involved in several serious and ultimately violent labour disputes. For the first and only time during the bitter depression days of 1930–1932 the rigid, sectarian separation in Belfast had crumbled at the edges under the mutual misery of unemployment and a joint interest in radical solutions. To the amazement and horror of Unionists in the north, delegations of Belfast workers even appeared at Bodenstown. The problems of the IRA in the North, however, were quite different from those of the IRA as a whole and the only real direction given by GHQ was a new boycott effort.

Although Cumann na mBan's Anti-British-Candy Campaign continued, a more extensive boycott was announced against British-made Bass Ale.

Pub owners were asked not to stock Bass nor patrons order it nor trucks carry it. Such a demand clashed with both the profit motive and long-established taste, so there followed a series of raids on Bass pubs and Bass trucks, then the traditional round of threats, arrests, and scuffles. Coupled with Union Jack burning, vocal assaults on Cumann na nGaedheal speakers, and the usual drills and parades, there was a tremendous sense of action and excitement that obscured the lack of direction. The Left, of course, was already mulling over a new approach to de Valera. The Right, as usual, was determined to maintain the Army as an Army for Armageddon. The Centre intended to wait and see.

What Right, Centre, and Left saw developing was a counter-attack by the forces which de Valera had defeated at the polls in February. To a large extent the growing militancy and intolerance of the IRA was responsible for the new opposition. On May 1, Cosgrave was prevented from speaking in Cork by the howls of the IRA men in the audience. This was not the first such incident but in the past campaign tactics had been more genteel. There were further disruptions at meetings in Cork and Kerry later in the month. In the spring of 1931, a group of Free State ex-army officers had formed the Army Comrades Association (ACA). The founder Dr. T. F. O'Higgins, the brother of the assassinated Minister of Justice, in August 1932 decided to transform the largely fraternal organization into a public movement partly in reaction to the IRA and partly in reaction to what seemed to be a rapid drift to the Left in Ireland. At the same time the IRA, sensing that they had the Cumann na nGaedheal people on the run, stepped up the harrassment of speakers. In October *An Phoblacht* published a battle-cry "No Free Speech to Traitors" which was taken up across the country by IRA speakers, notably Frank Ryan in the last great mob scene on Armistice Day Eve.

> No matter what anyone says to the contrary, while we have fists, hands and boots to use, and guns if necessary, we will not allow free speech to traitors.[9]

The Army Comrades Association were determined that the IRA should not force Cumann na nGaedheal off the platform nor would the Volunteers be allowed under the apparently tolerant eyes of the government to continue their boycotts, campaigns of intimidation, and public threats of violence. On December 14, the IRA held a Dublin Ale Party, dumping and destroying a glorious amount of alien ale. The ACA immediately announced that special units would henceforth guard the Bass shipments. The year drew to a close to the sound of scuffles over ale kegs.

While the IRA seemed to slip into stunts and street fights, de Valera with great caution and very considerable skill was broadening his base, chipping away at his enemies, securing his first-round aims, and edging the IRA further off the stage. After a relatively brief exchange of views with the appropriate British officials, de Valera had introduced a bill in the Dáil to abolish the oath, which wound its way eventually into operation to the horror of the opposition, who felt Ireland had repudiated a sacred agreement. On July 1, the Irish Free State defaulted on the payment of the land annuities. The British retaliated with duties levied on Irish imports. De Valera in turn introduced special duties on British goods. Most Republicans were delighted that de Valera was once again leading them against the Saxon, this time in an Economic War. Those hardest hit by British tariffs, the large agricultural exporters, were almost to a man Cosgrave supporters and their howls at the madness of Fianna Fáil's policy were heard with amused tolerance. The "war" against the British was carried out on many fronts: the Governor-General was slighted, ignored, and (so many felt) insulted; by October he had been replaced by an unsuccessful Fianna Fáil candidate, Daniel Buckley, who lived in a Dublin suburb and signed the required documents.[10] The lion's tail had once again been tweaked at no cost. Yet, there was no purge. The IRA's *bête noir*, Neligan of the Special Branch, was removed, although not immediately, and shifted to a pleasant and well-paying job in the Department of Lands. A group of old IRA officers went into the Free State Army but none did well. For most Republicans, however, the programme of Fianna Fáil was most attractive.

If the IRA felt that de Valera's pace was too slow, the Left in particular nursed growing suspicions that his radicalism was a dated, narrow distaste for the symbols of political oppression without any understanding of the nature of British capitalist exploitation. While he had, as promised, stopped the payment of land annuities to Britain, he insisted that he was not going to abolish them outright, but merely stop the illegal payment to Britain. The call of *An Phoblacht* for the division of the big ranches and the nationalization of the banks seemed as far to the Left of Fianna Fáil as it had of Cumann na nGaedheal. The uneasiness of the Left was not of paramount importance within the Army where the prime concern was the renewed vigour of the Treaty-forces. In November the National Farmers' and Ratepayers' League had united into the National Centre Party, an organization opposed to "radicalism". The ACA obviously had a growing attraction for the conservatives, for the old Treaty crowd and for those hit by the Economic War. De Valera, recognizing that the opposition was as yet neither fully organized nor prepared with a positive programme, suddenly called an election. The Dáil was dissolved on January 2 and a general election set for January 24. Once again the IRA would have to decide whether to play politics, this time to keep in de Valera, the Devil that even after a year in office they still did not know.

On the evening of January 7, the General Army Convention met to consider the political situation. Among the leadership there were only one or two new faces, in particular Tom McGill who had returned from America at the prospect of a rising against Cosgrave. There was no question of a change of leadership but of the direction of the IRA in general. O'Donnell, supported by Ryan, Price, and Gilmore, wanted to form a new organization to capture the high ground of the Republic from de Valera who was busy wrapping himself in the tricolour as Fianna Fáil fought the Economic War for what increasingly looked like the benefit of a new class of capitalist entrepreneurs springing up behind the tarriff wall. All this was a little much for the solid men and the average Volunteer who could see the danger in the Treatyite ACA or the need to keep Cosgrave out but not the urgency of still another organization to draw the outraged sermons of the clergy. Although the IRA was supposed to be committed to a radical policy much of the leadership had serious doubts about the continuing Leftward drift. Resolutions were carried which forbade Volunteers to write or speak on social, political, or economic questions, which meant oddly that the pages of the IRA newspaper *An Phoblacht* were for a time closed to Volunteers and open to Sinn Féin purists, funny-money currency reformers and the political fringe of Republicanism. The big issue, however, remained the January 24 elections.

The IRA accepted that Fianna Fáil's success the previous year was an important step, eliminating the need for a rising and smoothing the way to the real Republic.

> The overthrow of the Cosgrave regime last year was carried through in the face of frightful terrorism. That great achievement removed from our land the immediate dangers of Civil War, the foulest of all the evils British rule ever forced on our people.[11]

The delegates therefore passed a resolution that the IRA would continue to work and vote against Cosgrave. Why the resolution was worded negatively was obvious only two days later when de Valera spoke at Navan.

> No section of the community will be allowed to arm. All arms shall be completely at the disposal of the majority of the elected representatives of the people.[12]

He was relatively sure of the IRA vote in any case and could take the opportunity to reassure the timid and the orderly. Once again the IRA despite qualms voted for de Valera, but this time their help was not as necessary as it had seemed the year before, for he had used his year in power shrewdly. He had not proved incapable of ruling as his opponents had suggested. He had led the country into a "successful" confrontation with Britain, whittled away the imperial symbols, and given the nation a sense of excitement and motion. If economic conditions were no better (in fact worse), this could be ignored or blamed on British tariffs or brushed aside as a passing phase in the country's transition to wheat and manufacturing. In opposition Cosgrave proved no more subtle than he had in 1932. He offered to do no more than undo what de Valera had so far done.

The results of the election were a solid success for Fianna Fáil, a gain of five seats to a loss of nine for Cumann na nGaedheal. De Valera's seventy-seven seats in a house of 153 gave him an uncomfortable lead of one. A small majority, but a majority none the less, and one cushioned by the Labour support he continued to enjoy for about the next four years. He was now sufficiently solidly in control to begin a more extensive dismantling of the Treaty Free State. In this he had the whole-hearted support of the IRA and the desperate opposition of those defeated at the polls. Cumann na nGaedheal had lost two elections in two years and Cosgrave had seen his popular vote slashed both times. The new National Centre Party with eleven seats had done quite well but probably at the expense of Cumann na nGaedheal. De Valera clearly had the momentum to lead the Free State out of the Commonwealth, to ruin the fragile basis for Irish economic prosperity, and to force his opponents into a perpetual minority by giving free rein to the IRA while mouthing pious disclaimers. The reaction of the losers during 1933 was most unexpected.

On February 22, de Valera dismissed O'Duffy as Commissioner of the Garda Síochána. No explanation was ever forthcoming; but it was noted that Colonel Michael Hogan, brother of the former Cumann na nGaedheal Minister of Agriculture, and Inspector E. M. O'Connell had been arrested under the Official Secrets Act. The assumption was that O'Duffy had by-passed Nelligan's replacement, Colonel Eamon Broy, or allowed information to leak out to the wrong people. Almost immediately O'Duffy entered into negotiations with the ACA, who had read the election returns as a sentence of perpetual and futile opposition unless a new direction could be found. In this the more conventional politicians agreed and O'Duffy's decision to accept the leadership of the ACA was received with great interest.

In April the ACA adopted the Blueshirt as a uniform and a shudder went through Irish politics. The exploits of the Blackshirts and the Brown were all too well known by 1933. Elsewhere in the world there were Silver-shirts and Purpleshirts and all the eager proponents of the new wave of Fascism, which had so far not lapped on Irish shores. For three years the ideas and organizations of the Left had seethed, bubbled and frothed in Dublin to the consternation of the conservatives but without evoking any corresponding radicalism of the Right. But on July 20, by order of

Director-General O'Duffy, the ACA became the National Guard. O'Duffy's programme of physical fitness by drill and the protection of national honour, interests, and culture, hardly seemed a page out of Mussolini's book. Yet, the new organization created severe anxiety. Advocates pointed out that the ACA was ultra-Irish, not interested in aping alien ideologies, unarmed while the IRA was armed, and solely concerned with the protection of the rights of free speech and property. Defended by members of the clergy who suspected de Valera and despised the IRA, praised by the business community and the solid politicians, the Blueshirts blossomed. O'Duffy announced that on August 13 the new National Guard, clad in their Blueshirts, would march in memory of Griffith, Collins, and O'Higgins through Dublin to Glasnevin. With the memory of the march on Rome still fresh, many awaited the outcome apprehensively.

While an ultra-Right opposition was coalescing around O'Duffy after February, the Irish Left had not been inactive. Once Cosgrave departed, the revolutionary organization resurfaced. In June the Irish Communist Party was reorganized and the old *Workers' Voice* retitled *Irish Workers' Voice* instated as the official organ of the Party. This time the IRA wanted no part of it; previous efforts to establish an orthodox communist beachhead in Ireland had not been particularly successful because of a most appalling ignorance of Irish conditions.

> . . . the confused radicalism of the revolutionary Republican group like the IRA . . . IRA trying to retain the tradition of the national revolutionary struggle and is now eeking to link hostility to British Imperialism with social grievances of the toiling masses . . . is a decidedly petty bourgeois character and reveals the thoroughly petty bourgeois ideology of the leaders of the IRA . . . only Communism can liberate the toiling masses.[13]

In fact the "communists" had been largely dominated by their IRA members, and once these drifted out in 1932 the Irish Communist Party was left as a small, futile rump with one or two good men,[14] a few imported Englishmen, and the distant sympathy of the Left-IRA. Although IRA people were involved in several new radical organizations, the Army frequently disapproved of their activities. During an ill-contained outbreak of violence against Connolly House in March 1933 all the Dublin Battalions were moved out of the city for exercises, thereby eliminating the possibility of a decisive intervention by the IRA in its defence. When the police finally intervened, Charlie Gilmore was charged with possession of a revolver. In court he claimed he had the permission of the IRA. In a letter to the press the Army Council denied this claim, but in a subsequent letter the C/O 4th Battalion announced that he had given Gilmore permission because the Communist Party of Ireland recognized the IRA as the only authority competent to permit the carrying of arms in Ireland.

When there appeared to be a chance of a similar attack on the new Workers' College in Madame Despard's house in Eccles Street, several well-known IRA people suddenly appeared, but there was no announcement if this was an "official" intervention.

The apparent decline of IRA involvement with the radical Left[15] was largely an illusion. Within the Army a quiet "plot" was underway to secure a vote for a new Saor Eire at the next General Army Convention. Ryan, Gilmore, Price, and O'Donnell, among others, slipped around the country talking to key men, urging a vote for a Republican Front organization. If the dangers of fascism were not as apparent to the country Volunteer as to Ryan or O'Donnell, he knew full well that he faced his old Treaty enemy in a new coloured shirt and that the Treatyites, having failed twice at the polls, were going to try and have their way with muscle. This the IRA would not allow. De Valera's contingency plans apart, the IRA would see that there was no March on Dublin. The government had to depend on the Free State army and the Free State police to squash the old Inspector-General of the former and old Commissioner of the latter. The Army Council was not all that sure (supposing O'Duffy moved in for a coup), whether these "disinterested" arms of the state would respond to de Valera's orders.

De Valera had already taken steps to minimize the threat. On July 29/30, using the 1925 Firearms Act, the police confiscated all formerly licensed revolvers, including those of former Cumann na nGaedheal ministers. This apparently crude manœuvre may have been intended as much to underline to Fianna Fáil's political opponents just how seriously the menace of a Blueshirt coup was being taken. There was other evidence. O'Duffy's successor, Colonel Broy, was hurriedly recruiting a new "S-Branch" in the police. Made up of former IRA men, fully armed but with no police training, the new S-Branch, known almost immediately as Broy's Harriers, were already patrolling Leinster House by August 4. The government still had not announced any policy in relation to O'Duffy's grand parade. By Saturday, August 12, Dublin was crowded with police, including several hundreds of the new Broy Harriers. All government buildings, the railway stations, and the key routes in and out of the city were guarded. On August 13, at 12.45 a.m., the parade was banned using the provisions of the notorious and heretofore suspended Article 2A. The next move was up to O'Duffy.

By dawn Sunday morning, three hundred gardai surrounded Leinster House, the route of march was lined by seven hundred more, and the goal of the march, Glasnevin Cemetery, was under heavy guard. Not quite as visible, the IRA had acted as well, without more than a few hints to the government. The Dublin Brigade, which in two years had grown to over three thousand men, was fully activated. Preparations had been completed to attack the Blueshirt column in Westmoreland Street. All stations leading into Dublin were partly occupied by IRA units and a special armed unit had infiltrated the precincts of the government building in case a *coup d'état* was in the works. Early Sunday morning, O'Duffy cancelled the March on Dublin, insisting, probably truthfully, that nothing more than a parade was intended. Cosgrave concurred, insisting that all such rumours were fantastic nonsense. Be that as it might, the IRA had at last found an opponent worthy of their spleen, for O'Duffy was by no means finished. Under Article 2A, O'Duffy's National Guard was declared an unlawful association; but on September 8, the Blueshirt–Treaty forces merged. The new organization, United Ireland (Fine Gael), consisted of the old Cosgrave party, Cumann na nGaedheal, the new conservative National Centre Party, and O'Duffy's Blueshirts, now called the Young Ireland Association. O'Duffy was the new leader, with three Vice-Presidents, Cosgrave and James Dillon, and Frank MacDermot of the National Centre.

Nothing could have done more to unite the IRA and give it a sense of purpose, a relevant mission, than the amalgamation of the hated Treatyites with a movement permeated with the smell of fascism and clothed in the Blueshirts of the European Right. Although the detailed policy statement issued on November 11 by the United Ireland Party sounded more like Cumann na nGaedheal than Mussolini, the new paper, *United Ireland*, began to stress those too familiar words of the European Right—discipline, efficiency, order, authority—and criticize individualism and liberalism and always, always communism, which apparently included everything and everyone to the Left of Maynooth. Even the new November programme made use of "corporate" ideas, if of a somewhat watered-down variety. In *United Ireland* Professor James Hogan and Professor Michael Tierney began expounding fascist theory and its probable relation to the Irish situation. Perhaps the most important articles were those by Hogan entitled "Could Ireland Go Communist?" Hogan's conclusion was that only the United Ireland Party held any hope—the Blueshirts standing on the Green Sod holding back the Red Tide let in with malice or in ignorance by de Valera. Although Tierney insisted that the corporate state must come to Ireland, the old-line politicians were much more cautious in their involvement with fascism; however, on the platform O'Duffy and many of the activist Blueshirts were violent in their demands for action, their threats against the IRA and the Fianna Fáil dupes, and their plans for Ireland. They offered a heavy piety in place of alien communism, a sound business order of decent property owners over socialism; and, at first at least, a reasonable place within the Commonwealth without lunatic Economic Wars or stupid anti-Imperial rhetoric. It was the same as waving an expensive blue flag in front of the IRA bull.

Despite O'Duffy's loss of face when his show parade collapsed, the new United Ireland Party still seemed a great threat to a Republican Ireland and as a result the struggle between the IRA and the Blueshirts grew more bitter and more violent through the autumn and winter of 1933–1934. During much of the period, it seemed as if the government stood back allowing only on unusual occasions the Military Tribunal or the police to play the part of referee. This attitude of a curse on both your houses, particularly de Valera's speaking of the Blueshirts on the same plane as the IRA, deeply annoyed the Army Council.[16] It seemed incredible to them that de Valera could really feel that once the oath was gone the IRA could disband in peace—even while the Blueshirt Imperialists gained in strength; that he could announce that "there was no excuse whatever for the possession of arms" at the very moment when the forces of the Treatyites were rallying around fascism.[17] Hence the IRA pushed the Bass boycott again, guaranteeing clashes with the Blueshirts. On September 12, an IRA writ descended on The Dead Man pub in County Dublin and twelve men were arrested. One IRA man was actually convicted. *An Phoblacht* was outraged that Republicans should be sentenced for defending their country, particularly since the agents of Imperialism, the Blueshirts, always seemed to receive shorter sentences. On their part the movers and shakers of United Ireland pointed to the lengthening series of outrageous IRA attacks on the innocent and all but defenceless Blueshirts.

On September 21, an IRA squad shot and wounded a member of the United Ireland Party in Dingle, County Kerry. Two days later an attempt to break up a United Ireland meeting in Limerick resulted in a serious riot. On September 30, the riot was repeated in Cork. In the country the week-end meetings of the Blueshirts had to be of considerable size or the IRA would descend upon them, and the delegates and members had to be convoyed in guarded trucks. Fights broke out *en route* or were initiated by Blueshirts when they seemed to have a clear superiority. Trees were dropped on roads. Shots were fired. On October 6, at Tralee, a crowd of Republicans attacked O'Duffy and his Blueshirt lieutenants as they walked down the narrow Bridge Street. A couple of men got close enough to get to O'Duffy himself with several hard smashes—the last with a hammer. The Blueshirts, pummelled and buffeted, managed to reach the meeting hall which resounded to a hail of stones and even one grenade, which failed to explode. On October 16, five Blueshirts were wounded when shots were fired into a dance in Woodford, County Galway. On October 29, Hugh O'Reilly and O'Leary, prominent Blueshirts in Brandon, were attacked and beaten. O'Leary, although shot, recovered but O'Reilly died on December 28. However pleased the government was with the pounding the Blueshirts were getting, the country could not be allowed to fall into the hands of fighting gangs, even if one were made up of old comrades. Twelve IRA men were arrested after the Tralee riot, sentenced on December 1 from four to six months by the Military Tribunal, and moved to Arbour Hill military prison. In a speech in Tralee, de Valera urged the people not to surrender their right to run the country through the ballot box and criticized the outrages. There was no apparent effect and Fianna Fáil moved against the Blueshirts.

On December 8, the Young Ireland Association was banned. On December 17, General O'Duffy was arrested in Westport, County Mayo, on suspicion of being a member of an illegal organization but was released on December 21. He was immediately summoned to appear before the Military Tribunal, but his lawyers fought off the demand. The IRA was not impressed. The police had continued to arrest Republicans, and IRA men appeared before the Military Tribunal. On December 23, *An Phoblacht* pointed out that one Jerry Ryan, a Tipperary Blueshirt, had only been fined three pounds for possession of a revolver and had not been sent before a Military Tribunal. Underlining IRA complaints, the same issue of *An Phoblacht* was suppressed. By the end of the year, many in the IRA, some in private and some in print, were identifying de Valera with Cosgrave.

The new year brought no lessening of Blueshirt–IRA clashes—rather the reverse. On January 4, a publican from Dunmanway, County Cork, died after injuries received on Christmas Eve in a melee.[18] On January 9, two Blueshirts were robbed in Dundalk. On February 8, one of them, McGrory, identified the Republicans concerned. At 8 p.m. the following Sunday, February 11, a bomb detonated in the McGrory house, demolishing the structure, shattering windows all down the street, injuring two boys, and mortally wounding McGrory's mother. On the same day a serious riot occurred in Drogheda when Blueshirts were attacked by Republicans. On February 23, a bill was introduced banning the wearing of uniforms. Although the bill passed the Dáil amid cries of outraged indignation from the opposition in their new Blueshirts, the Senate on March 21 rejected the bill. On the following day de Valera introduced a bill to abolish the Senate.

While attention was focussed on de Valera's attacks on the Blueshirts and his lessening toleration of the IRA, little notice had been taken of Fianna Fáil's quiet and increasingly effective programme of legislation and Cabinet decrees which, partly intentionally, occasionally fortuitously, eroded the attractions of the IRA. The creation of the new S-Branch, Broy's Harriers, had presented several hundred sound Republicans with an opportunity to serve the Republican Party, to smash the Blueshirts, and to earn a decent salary with the prospect of promotion and pension. As a result several hundred good men were lost to the IRA. More specifically intended to cut away potential recruits was the organizing of a volunteer militia force; this was to have been called the National Guard, before O'Duffy absconded with the name. Recruits for the new volunteer force would wear grey-green uniforms and receive some compensation. The idea attracted those who wanted a bit of excitement, a new uniform, and didn't care to risk paternal or priestly disapproval of the more militant IRA. In the Dáil, several bills were passed, compensating Republican supporters for property losses suffered during the Civil War and providing pensions for the wounded. It was even rumoured that a military service pension for old IRA men would be introduced later in 1934. All these measures gathered Republicans more firmly into the Fianna Fáil fold. The end of the oath, the reduction of the Governor-General to a strawman, the promise of more Republican manoeuvres in the days ahead, and the Economic War under de Valera's generalship convinced many that Fianna Fáil was on the high road to the Republic. The IRA contention that Fianna Fáil was really not Republican simply was not very impressive.

That ever so gradually Fianna Fáil was outflanking the IRA, draining on their recruits, tranquillizing their old supporters, securing the confidence of the mass of the people was vividly clear to one sector of the Army who had for four years contended that without a revolutionary party to give a real Republican, anti-Imperialist structure to the entire Movement the end was in sight—futile terrorism or absorption by Fianna Fáil. The quiet canvassing for a revolutionary party had led to the idea of a Republican Congress. Many of the men who had been attracted by Saor Éire supported the Congress idea, but this time the members of the Army Executive and Army Council were less enthusiastic about a Leftward diversion from the military road.

> Within the I.R.A. Executive this situation was outlined to make the case for an uprising of Republican opinion, expressed in a Republican Congress, to rally the disrupted Republican masses on the high ground of the Republic, and to restate the terms of the national struggle so as to lay down the basis for active participation in working-class and small-farmer struggles through which the allies of Imperialism in Ireland could be isolated and exposed. In arguing for the Congress the case was made that Irish Capitalism was prepared to make terms with Imperialism and would become the leading formation in the subjugation of the nation and the exploitation of the people. The thing to do, therefore, was to confront the forces of Capitalism and Imperialism with a Congress of the Ireland of the poor, so easily mobilizable if the I.R.A. organization and tradition could be brought to bear on the task.
> Unfortunately the leaders of the Republican Army found themselves halted before the Fianna Fáil position, unable and willing to attempt to get on a higher plane of struggle. The idea that it would be possible to urge Fianna Fáil on to the Republic was not entirely absent. They failed to realize that the

interests on which Fianna Fáil rests had entrenched themselves across the road to the Republic. The need for gaining the leadership of the masses of the people was, therefore, very imperfectly understood, and it was possible for responsible members of the Army Council to make statements as "The masses of the people always let down the Republic," and "I dare say we *could* get a big following *but what would we do with it?*"[19]

Men like MacBride, who could not envisage a mass following, at least in O'Donnell's and Ryan's terms, were hardly rare within the Army; even during the Saor Éire days the IRA had remained the IRA, not a transmuted Congress of Left forces. The militarists, the traditionalists, the organization men, all suspected with some justification that the Republican Congress would turn a secret army into a mass revolutionary movement, slipping down the slope of parliamentary politics to end like Fianna Fáil, albeit further to the Left, one more Treaty party. Far better keep the comfortable military organization intact, ready to strike out for the Republic when and if Fianna Fáil faltered. The Republican Congress people were not unduly put off, because they anticipated that their secret campaign would secure them a majority vote in the General Army Convention in any case.

The Army Convention met on March 17, 1934, in a ballet school on St. Stephen's Green and proved not quite as packed as the Republican Congress people had hoped. The secret campaign had been a little too secret, some local C/Os had not been reached at all, and many of the delegates, some of whom would have been sympathetic, heard of the Republican Congress for the first time at the Convention. It was obvious that men like Twomey and MacBride were unenthusiastic. By this time O'Donnell's ideas were often discounted; and this sounded like one more high call for another step to the Left, steps that had led nowhere. The anticipated opposition of the hierarchy discouraged others—particularly after the Saor Éire experience. More than anything else the volunteers had joined an army to secure the Republic by means of physical force and it was not clear just how the Republican Congress fitted their normal frame of reference. On the first substantive resolution from the Left, Price wanted a return to the radical policy of an earlier day and IRA allegiance to the Republic as visualized by Connolly.

That we, authorized delegates from all units of the Army in Ireland and Britain, assembled at the General Army Convention of the I.R.A., redeclare our allegiance to the Republic of Ireland, based upon production and distribution for use and not for profit in which exploitation of the labour of human beings with all its attendant miseries and insecurities shall not be tolerated as shown in the pamphlet "Government Policy and Constitution of Oglaigh na h-Éireann" issued by the supreme authority of Oglaigh na h-Éireann; and

We again declare, in reply to the demands of and coercion by the Governments of "Northern Ireland" and the "Irish Free State" that the Republican Army shall not be disbanded (sic) until such time as the Government of the Irish Republic, based on the political and social principles in the pamphlet referred to, is functioning.[20]

The powers-that-be were harshly critical of Price's resolution and he withdrew it and stalked out of the Convention. O'Donnell now proposed the Republican Congress idea and was strongly supported by Ryan and Gilmore. As usual the discussions went on and on until well into Sunday before the vote was taken. The Congress group, limited preparations and secrecy notwithstanding, carried a small majority of the delegates but the almost solid Executive and Council negative vote decided the issue—by one vote. As far as the Convention was concerned, the Republican Congress was a dead issue for at least a year. The IRA Left, aware of de Valera's creeping success, felt that a year would be much too late. To some extent the leadership's negative vote had unmade a really representative majority from the country delegates and with a majority of the IRA behind the Congress, leadership or no, there was still a chance.

With half the delegates voting in favour O'Donnell, Ryan, and Gilmore felt that the Army Council would not risk a disastrous split if they went ahead and organized the Republican Congress. The Congress people toured the country in a whirlwind campaign to drum up support for a meeting to be held at Athlone. The determination of the Left to go it alone without the sanction of the Army Council caused a considerable flurry in the GHQ offices in Dublin. No one could tell quite how far they intended to go, or worse who might go along. No one wanted a split but the Athlone Conference smelled like gross indiscipline. Twomey, who more than anyone wanted to keep the organization intact, was sorely tried. O'Donnell seemed to imply that the Army which had voted against them was devoid of ideas and prospects.

If you get rid of us, you know, you will soon follow. We have a social policy and theory for keeping the military men and the terrorists in check. You have not.[21]

The Army Council felt that they did have a social policy and that the military men so scorned by O'Donnell were a solid and important part of the Army. The Republican Congress met in Athlone on April 8 and issued a radical manifesto calling a united front of Republican forces.

We believe that a Republic of a united Ireland will never be achieved except through a struggle which uproots capitalism on its way. We cannot conceive of a free Ireland with a subject working class, we cannot conceive of a subject Ireland with a free working class. This teaching of Connolly represented the deepest instinct of the oppressed Irish nation.[22]

This kind of beginning had become traditional, but the public criticism not only of Fianna Fáil but of the IRA for failure to react properly to events since 1932 seriously reduced the chances of healing the split.

> This retreat from the Republic was not, unfortunately, resisted by those organizations which would have rallied the people on the high ground of the Republic. Had the IRA leadership understood that the economic war was not being fought to free Ireland but to serve Irish capitalism they would have carried out this mobilization first before giving any support to that war. On account of their failure the Republican issue has been pushed further into the background. This mistake must now be remedied.[23]

The Army Council did not admit to any mistake, felt there was no need of remedies, and regretted that good Republicans lent their names to attacks on the IRA.

The number of good Republicans that had gone to Athlone was considerably less than might have been anticipated either from the results of the Army Convention vote or the known political orientation of certain IRA people: for example, Fitzpatrick, the first chairman of Saor Éire, did not break with the Army; nor did Donal O'Donoghue, although his wife Sheila Humphries signed the manifesto. Some areas, particularly George Gilmore's South Dublin, were badly eroded, but there seemed to be nearly as many Congress leaders as followers. The IRA was badly hit by the loss of talent and of the ideas of men like O'Donnell, Ryan, Price, and Gilmore; but it was far from destitute—even in men of the Left. On April 11, a court martial, chaired by Seán Russell, dismissed O'Donnell and Price with ignominy.[24] Other courts martial followed, unattended by the men who were now preparing for the all-Ireland Republican Congress meeting in the autumn and the publication, with O'Donnell as editor, of a new weekly newspaper, *Republican Congress*. George Gilmore soon left for the United States to explain all. To the IRA there was nothing to explain.

> Shorn of all the fine phrases in which the call for a congress issued from Athlone was dressed up, the congress means nothing more than an attempt to form a political party.[25]

After this the IRA and the Republican Congress went their own ways. Price organized a new Citizen Army, including Ryan, Gilmore, Roddy Connolly, and Seamus McGowan, which at first had about three hundred members entirely from County Dublin but was hardly serious competition to the orthodox IRA. The next informal contact was on June 17 at Bodenstown, when a scuffle developed between certain IRA battalions and the Republican Congress people over "unauthorized banners".

The ideological in-fighting within the Army had not damped down the continuing Blueshirt–IRA clashes. O'Duffy seemed to be leading his troops down a more radical road. Unofficially he was pushing a campaign of no-rates and no-annuities to bring pressure on the government to ameliorate the Economic War. British tariffs had excluded Irish goods and reduced the price for cattle and sheep to unheard-of lows. De Valera's "war" was well on the way to bankrupting the entire grazing farmer class. To secure the money owed the State, the bailiffs seized the cattle for forced sale. Blueshirts felled poles over the roads, cut telephone wires, harried the bailiffs, hid the cattle, broke up sales. The IRA in turn broke up Blueshirt meetings, fought against the no-annuities campaign, intimidated the big farmers, and slugged it out with Blueshirt heavies. In Dublin the Blueshirts sponsored an animal gang—an apolitical collection of north Dublin toughs—to run amok during Republican meetings. The Military Tribunal was still handing out sentences without noticeable effect. In fact after his loss of face over the August parade, O'Duffy seemed well on his way to recouping his losses. The IRA had split. Fianna Fáil seemed unable or unwilling to stop the decay of order.

This was a surface appearance. On June 26, local elections were held throughout the Free State. The United Ireland Party showed no significant gains. Politically the Blueshirts had added only sound and fury, not votes. There was no fascist tide and there was not going to be any. Essentially the Blueshirt movement had two routes to power—the coup and the ballot box. In the first case the only real chance to succeed would have been to persuade the Army to tolerate a March on Dublin to save Ireland from communism, a fate worse than O'Duffy. Unfortunately Cosgrave had already played the Red Card, frightening those who were so inclined but exposing the paucity of communist menace. The smooth turnover to de Valera, the relative conservatism of Fianna Fáil, the known distaste of the Cumann na nGaedheal people for illegality and violence, all meant that O'Duffy would have to go it alone, risking military or police opposition. This he would not do. The second route—a mass unarmed Blueshirt movement gathering momentum from month to month with O'Duffy in the van sweeping to electoral victory – had haunted Irish politics for nearly a year. But all that had been done by June 1934 was to identify by colour the anti-de Valera segment of Irish society. The Blueshirts did not convert any section of society, the small shopkeepers or the school teachers, nor did they radicalize the Right, transforming big farmers into big revolutionaries. From a distance Ireland might have looked ripe for fascism: a new and uncertain government of radical old gunmen, a massively influential Church which seemed more sympathetic to Italian fascism than Irish Republicanism, a body of proper and propertied supporters of the new wave, and a good cause. But by June it was clear, perhaps even to O'Duffy, that the Blueshirts did not have a good cause; all they had was the Cumann na nGaedheal programme wrapped up in vague corporate language. Pudgy middle-aged businessmen in blue shirts howling about cattle prices were not the stuff out of which revolution—even within a ballot box—was made. The stepped-up no-rates campaign was a sharp turn to radicalizing the entire United Ireland Movement.

As the timid had feared, it led nowhere but to violence. On Monday, August 13, at Marsh's Yard in Cork there was a cattle auction to pay for land annuities in arrears. The anonymous buyers were protected by a squad of Broy Harriers in expectation of Blueshirt intervention. A lorry did crash the gate and as the men piled out into the Yard the "S" men apparently panicked and began a wild fusillade. A boy, Michael Lynch, was killed and seven other people wounded. This is just what the conservatives had predicted if the no-tax campaign continued. To compound matters on August 18–19 at the annual congress of the League of Youth, a resolution was passed calling on farmers to refuse to pay their land annuities and labourers their rates until the government suspended the demand for payment or established a tribunal. This was a desperate step as far as the men of property were concerned. Before this O'Duffy had been vitriolic, his hotheads too violent, his pronouncements irresponsible and his fascist pretensions often embarrassing. The more radical he became—and what could be more radical than failure to pay taxes?—the more uneasy became the sound, solid men, their Donegal tweeds nearly hiding their blue shirts.

On August 31, the United Ireland Executive met in Dublin and O'Duffy was persuaded to back water a bit. This was not sufficient for Professor James Hogan, who resigned as a protest "against the general destructive and hysterical leadership of its President, General O'Duffy".[26] Not only had O'Duffy become involved in the no-rates campaign but he had begun to make wild speeches about renewing the war against Britain. It was all too much for the conventional. On September 21, O'Duffy's resignation was announced.[27] Commandant E. J. Cronin took control of the League of Youth—but the days of Blueshirts and street fights were clearly on the way out. O'Duffy after a futile effort to hold on to the League went his own way and established the Corporate State Party, which his isolation from the Right, his administrative ineptitudes, and his public blunders soon reduced to a small group of malcontents without power or prospects. After a thorough house-cleaning, the United Ireland Party put away their blue shirts, eased out Cronin, and settled down in the Dáil as a conventional, if somewhat discredited, parliamentary opposition. The great experiment had ended. With the Blueshirts in moth-balls on the Right and the IRA split into two groups on the Left, de Valera had the stage to himself.

During the late summer and early fall, the precipitous decline of the Blueshirts had not been so visible. When the IRA met in an Extraordinary General Army Convention on August 18/19, the main concerns were still how to regroup after the April split and how to respond to Blueshirt pressure. It was clear that the attractions of the Republican Congress were going to be less than the Left had anticipated. The attitude of watchful waiting with an occasional bitter word in *An Phoblacht* proved sufficient. The Republican Congress—supposedly a force for unity—destroyed itself almost at once. It met in Rathmines on September 29, ignored by the IRA. The orthodox Labour Party and most of the conventional trade unions felt that any united front should come together under their banners. Cathal O'Shannon of the Labour Party simply did not see the "united front" people had much to offer.

> Was it suggested that they should exchange views with, say, Peadar O'Donnell? He had no views and never had any. The Irish Workers' Party and the United Front Movement were already split from top to bottom, nevertheless they want to unite and to exchange views with the Labour Party . . . If anyone wanted to exchange views let them come into the Labour Movement.[28]

When 186 delegates arrived at Rathmines Town Hall, they seized almost at once on the question of political direction. When the elaborate radical rhetoric, the arcane language of the Left, was peeled aside, one resolution, supported by Price, Nora Connolly O'Brien, and R. J. Connolly, called for a drive for a Workers' Republic and the other, supported by O'Donnell, Ryan, and Gilmore, demanded a front which would detach the nationalists from de Valera to be grouped under the banner of Left Republicanism. The latter won ninety-nine to eighty-four and many of the former went their own way immediately. The Congress was shattered before it had begun.

The orthodox IRA could not but have felt a twinge of satisfaction. The Army Council's predictions had, to some degree at least, been fulfilled. There was no mass movement—only a quarrel about the meaning of the Workers' Republic. Price and his Irish Citizen Army remained in one corner. O'Donnell, Ryan, and Gilmore, with the newspaper *Republican Congress* and the fragments of the Left, in another. The IRA, on the other hand, had made good most of its losses, held on to those tempted by the call for a popular front, and continued pounding the Blueshirts. As O'Duffy clattered from one clumsy defeat to another, the IRA slowly noticed that they were running out of Blueshirts. The no-rates campaign tapered off. The animal gang was clubbed back into north Dublin. The action was slackened. The result was that once more the IRA had no clear direction. The membership, particularly in Dublin, remained quite radical and even the supposedly "conservative" Twomey insisted that imperialist capitalism was the prime enemy. Just how to get at such an enemy with an invisible army remained a difficult problem. Smashing the Blueshirts had been satisfying, apparently successful by the end of 1934, but there was no new target on the horizon. Action relapsed into stunts—disrupting the showing of "imperial" films or running wild during the Armistice Day riot—but there was no obvious next step. A few more analytically minded had been reflecting that to maintain the IRA purely as a military force was, as the Left had repeatedly suggested, insufficient, that the Army Council should consider sponsoring something better than the Republican Congress. Such "political" ideas found little response in the wake of the Congress schism, even though the IRA faced a growing challenge from Fianna Fáil, apparently securely holding the Republican heights.

The attractiveness of de Valera's Republicanism had its effect even among the supposedly hard-core IRA men in the years after 1932. In Leitrim, Seán O'Farrell went Fianna Fáil; in Dublin after the 1934 Army Convention, Michael Hilliard, long on the GHQ staff, resigned, went into Fianna Fáil and ultimately became Minister for Defence in the Cabinets of Lemass and Lynch; and in 1935 Seán Buckley, one of the fathers of Cork Republicanism, switched over and was elected to the Dáil. Further down in the ranks a similar drain occurred; once the Blueshirts threat had abated, there was a drift away from drilling, from arms classes, and tactical lectures that seemed to have no relevance to de Valera's progress or the country's need. The Army Council after 1934 was increasingly aware of the glitter and temptations of Fianna Fáil. Manifestoes were issued condemning the introduction of the Military Service Pensions Bill in August 1934 as outright bribery,[29] condemning the new Volunteer Force as an undesirable alternative to the true Army of the Republic.[30] *An Phoblacht* repeatedly criticized Fianna Fáil's "imperialist" policies. MacBride suggested that de Valera's lot would merge with the United Ireland people. Recruits to the Broy Harriers or the Volunteer Force were manhandled. Yet, nothing seemed to work very well and the Army's overall strength began to decline bit by bit from a high of approximately thirty thousand in 1932–1933. The howls from the IRA-Left that de Valera was selling out to capitalism or the bitter complaints of the IRA-Right that he was not on the high road to the Republic sounded shrill and querulous to the men who read every day in the *Irish Press* of "The Chief's" coups in the Economic War, of the dismantling of the Treaty-State, of the plain, blunt benefits of jobs and pensions and the promise of more to the loyal.

And yet, despite de Valera's efforts, the nation had not been transformed —either into a Republic or an economic paradise. Ireland in 1935 remained a bleak and brutal land after the worst year in living memory. The wildly heralded Fianna Fáil scheme for self-sufficiency, whatever that might have meant when explained beside the parish pump, had produced no remarkable changes in Irish life. Exports had fallen from £36,000,000 in 1931 to £18,000,000. The changeover from pasture to tillage had been slow and without impact, and the attempt to reduce the cattle herds in 1934 by slaughter had so shocked the public that the government had drawn back. Industrial employment had risen but not sufficiently to absorb the growing pool of unemployed. With the safety valve of emigration closed, in fact with more returning from the United States than going, the young men had to wait out the months and years on farms too small to support them or in shops without trade. There was no mass industrial unemployment since the mass had never worked in industry, but there were tens of thousands of semi-idle, living marginal lives in the country, always hopeful of work and always disappointed. That fat farmers, fathers of families, and pillars of the Church, could put on blue shirts, pay no rates, and fight in the lanes, revealed the depth of desperation and despair. The very poor, of course, could not afford a blue shirt and generations of exploitation had exhausted their energies so that they could seldom strike out at the system. In many of the country areas, the IRA, making a bridge between the radical ideas of Dublin and the old Fenian traditions of the countryside, sensed a mission. In the cities, particularly Dublin, the IRA looked with favour on the workers' efforts to strike for reasonable wages and decent conditions. This continuing IRA concern—although unstructured by a Saor Éire or a Republican Congress—led to intervention in a variety of disputes and in time to increasing conflict with the Fianna Fáil government over possession of the high ground.

On November 5, 1934, the Town Tenants' Association in Edgeworthstown, County Longford, passed a resolution requesting the intervention of the IRA in their dispute with the Sanderson Estate. On November 20, a second resolution invited the IRA to hold a public meeting in Edgeworthstown on December 2. The invitation was accepted and some violent speeches were made, threatening in particular the agent on the property, Gerald More O'Ferrall. Supposedly 121 tenants were to be evicted and no countryman, IRA or no, liked the sound of that. In effect, the Tenants' Association were using the IRA as a pressure group, a stick to hold over the Sanderson Estate, and the IRA units involved were delighted to be used. In an effort to step up the pressure, a decision was made to rough up Gerald More O'Ferrall so as to underline the IRA's seriousness of purpose. On February 9, a squad of a half-dozen men in a lifted car wearing disguises made out of caps stolen from a bandman's house arrived outside the More O'Ferrall house at Lisard, Edgeworthstown. At nine in the evening, four men forced their way into the house to get Gerald More O'Ferrall. His son Richard would not be intimidated and wrestled the gun out of one of the men's hands. Fearful that the whole attack would come apart in a gun-fight, one of the IRA men shot him. His father was also hit, in the chest, but a gold cigarette case deflected the bullet. Richard, with a bullet lodged near his spine, died twelve days later on February 21. Long before then, the tyres from the IRA car had been buried in a creamery yard, the car driven to an old house in Fermanagh and abandoned, and the "disguises" destroyed. All the same, the police felt they knew who had been involved and arrested four men on March 31. The first jury deadlocked on July 12[31] and the second in December found them not guilty. In the meantime three other men had been arrested: Mick Kelly, who had made some fiery speeches to the tenants, was charged with conspiracy; and Mick Ferguson and Hughie Devine were charged with murder. The arrests, trials, and revelations kept the case before the public for the better part of the year. The murder was used as a high card in the quiet discussions within the centre of Fianna Fáil about the dangers of tolerating the IRA much longer. No one held much of a brief for estate agents, but an innocent young man had been killed mainly because some men felt that they had a moral right to carry arms.

For the moment the government held back. The IRA, however, was becoming less tolerant of the police, more swift to identify the Fianna Fáil man with the Treatyites. The rapidly cooling entente between the IRA and Fianna Fáil brought, for a change, the Church in on the side of the government. In January the Rev. Dr. Kinane, Bishop of Waterford, gave Frank Edwards three months' notice in dismissing him from his position in a Christian Brothers School for attending the Republican Congress and noted that if the IRA's aims for Ireland were successful then the country would face "woes greater than any she experienced even in the darkest days of persecution".[32] The IRA replied and an exchange of letters was published in the daily press—the IRA was quite taken aback that the good Bishop had them confused with the Republican Congress. Letters to editors did little good and the clergy elsewhere took up the hue and cry. On January 12, Monsignor Byrne insisted that the IRA as an organization was "the most anti-patriotic and anti-religious that was ever attempted to be foisted on this country".[33] Some of the difficulty of rallying the Irish Left was revealed when the Waterford branch of the Amalgamated Transport and General Workers Union rushed to line up behind the Bishop, ". . . conscious of their duty as Catholics they accepted and would loyally obey his authoritative teaching given in the Cathedral on the 6th inst."[34] Fianna Fáil men could stand piously aside and watch the Church, once more, hack at militant Republicanism. By January 27, the bishop felt that even attendance at a meeting called by the IRA to protest his pronouncements would be "gravely sinful".

However, eight hundred men including Twomey, Barry, Patrick McLogan, and the Cumann na mBan women appeared at the meeting, proof that it would take more than one bishop to bury the IRA. As though renewed trouble with the Church were not sufficient, relations with Fianna Fáil deteriorated still further. In Kerry the IRA and a Fianna Fáil TD quarrelled openly in print. The Kerry Fianna Fáil claimed the IRA had fired at the homes of their supporters and attacked the new members of the Volunteer Force. Not all the old ties of friendship had been broken, but many had frayed. Fianna Fáil had given up the trek to Bodenstown—Aiken now appeared only at the Free State army ceremony earlier in the day— and no longer attended even the most innocuous IRA protest meetings. In April Fianna Fáil would give up the sale of "Easter Lilies", the symbol of "an organization of whose methods they disapprove",[35] and replace the old symbol with a new "Torch". The first really serious break came not over the More O'Ferrall shooting or the Church's increasing condemnation, which culminated in the Lenten Pastoral on March 3 forbidding membership of the IRA, but over the Army's continuing involvement in labour disputes.

On March 2, the tram and bus workers in Dublin had gone on strike, a bitter do-or-die effort which would last seventy-six days. Without public transport, Dublin was paralysed; and on March 20, the government intervened by sending in Free State Army lorries to replace some of the struck transportation. To the strikers and to the Army Council, the government was using soldiers as scabs. It looked as if Fianna Fáil had been creeping away to the Right under the lengthening shadow of Maynooth, first using the IRA to club down the Blueshirts and then using Blueshirt methods to crush the strike. During the General Army Convention early in March, there had been a growing militancy, a demand for an end to "politics" and a beginning of action. MacBride's proposal for a Republican political party had been overwhelmingly defeated and a resolution demanding that action be taken within six months had only been prevented by the intervention of Twomey who listed the pitiful resources available to the Army. Even so the final decision was to allow the Army to make such a war decision. The mood of the Convention had been clear. Thus the strike was a first-rate opportunity to involve at least the Dublin Brigade in action on the social issue. As soon as the army lorries appeared, sniping at the tyres began. On March 23, at midnight, two gardai patrolling Grafton Street were shot and wounded by mysterious men on bicycles. At the same time another garda was shot at near the offices of the *Irish Press*. On March 25, an Army Council public statement was issued announcing IRA "willingness to assist the workers in their struggle".[36]

What the IRA saw as an effort to end governmental strike-breaking, the government on the other side of the fence viewed as a dangerous and wholly illegal intervention on a gangster level. On March 26, the police swooped through Dublin, rounding up forty-three IRA and Republican Congress men—O'Donnell, his replacement at *An Phoblacht* O'Donoghue,

Mick Kelly, Tom Barry, Con Lehane, Tom Merrigan, Claude McLoughlin —many of the same men who had so worried the Special Branch of Neligan. On March 29, speaking to the Fianna Fáil Executive, de Valera explained that he had been patient for three years but the intervention in the trades dispute was the last straw. "There was only one thing the government could do."[37] Many of those arrested were quickly released, but the government's point had been made and to underline it the Military Tribunal began to hand out sentences. On April 24, Con Lehane received eighteen months, and Donal O'Donoghue, Claude McLoughlin, and four others got six months each. On April 25, five more received the same sentence, as did Tom Barry, who was charged with sedition, unlawful association, refusal to answer questions, and contempt.

After March the arrests, trials, and sentences continued in spurts and bursts. The Edgeworthstown accused were arrested. On March 17, when the Free State Army staged parades, the IRA organized a counter-demonstration. By April 20, 104 Republicans were in prison. Those accused of the Dundalk bomb explosion were tried and freed. Garda John Egan was shot by four young men on May 12 when he interrupted them painting "Join the IRA" on a footpath. *An Phoblacht* was censored. There was a raid on May 31 on the IRA Sweeps office in Dame Street. On June 24, Barry was acquitted on a new charge. On June 24, nine thousand heard MacBride speak at Bodenstown, but the loyal IRA unable to attend the hosting would not be able to read the oration: the June 15 and June 22 issues of *An Phoblacht* had been suppressed. The last typed issue entitled *The Republic* came out on July 6. There was no room for anything but one last snarl of defiance:

> Coercion is being used against Republicans today because they are an embarrassment to the conspiracy for another betrayal of the Republic, based on Mr. de Valera's "external association" plan ... Mr. de Valera can no more succeed in intimidating Republicans from defence of the Republic than Churchill or Greenwood, Collins or Cosgrave succeeded. The Republican Army will continue in its training and organization, preparing for its task of overthrowing British imperialism and native treason. That is our answer to Mr. de Valera.[38]

Then in July a series of not unexpected events overshadowed the worsening feud of the IRA and Fianna Fáil. In June the Dublin newspapers had published reports of rioting and sectarian violence in Belfast. Religious violence in the North was not new but there had been hope that the depression might unite men in their misery. There had been few treks down to Bodenstown by Protestant workers; and in October 1932 unemployed Protestants and Catholics in Belfast jointly protested the lowering of relief payments. Side by side with these hints of better relations between the two communities had been minor outbreaks of sectarian violence in Armagh,

Lisburn, Portadown, and Belfast in 1931, attacks on Catholics travelling to the Eucharistic Congress in 1932, and more minor incidents in 1933. The pause in 1934 proved ominous. The report of trouble in June 1935 became the reality of July as Belfast plunged into the worst riots of a generation without even the rationale that the Tan War had given. On July 3, the newspapers reported three men shot down in Belfast streets and with the occasional exception of a quiet day the remainder of the month was one long orgy of murder, arson, looting, assault, sniping, and terror. On the great Orange Holiday on July 12, two men were killed and fifty wounded. The RUC began blocking off the Catholic and Protestant areas with barricades cutting across the middle of blocks and sealing off the besieged enclaves. On July 15, the death toll had reached five and seventy were in hospitals. By the end there would be eleven murdered, two attempted murders which reached court, 574 injured, 133 cases of arson and 367 of serious property damage. The gossamer-thin ties of the mutually poor had broken at the first call to the old sectarian loyalties. In Belfast the ideas of the Reformation were more relevant, more matters of life and death—eleven deaths in fact—than the plea for class unity or the call for reason and tolerance.

That Belfast was unlike Dublin, capital of the Irish Free State and ninety per cent Catholic, had always meant that the IRA in Northern Ireland, particularly Belfast, was quite different. As far as the RUC was concerned, the IRA was a dangerous, violent conspiracy of subversives. There was never a moment of toleration, such as the IRA enjoyed under Fianna Fáil, nor a relaxation of surveillance and harassment: the IRA in the North was always at war. Although in dogma Leinster House to the South was an usurping legislature, the IRA in the North did not feel that it was quite as usurping as the vast new marble Parliament House at Stormont, built to last until the final pope died—some usurpers are more Saxon than others. In Dublin the tricolour flew, and the "Soldier's Song" was sung, and Dev could not be all that bad. Thus the Northern IRA tended to look back to the Tan War, see Britain as the first enemy and, despite Protestant ideological ancestors, be exceptionally pious in their Catholicism. In the South the bishops flayed the IRA but in the North the local priest was glad enough to have the lads about when trouble began. In the South the Army Council had talked about Cosgrave and a rising but in the North the enemy was Craigavon and the British.

All of this had led to occasional strain within the IRA and uncertain loyalties in the Nationalist population at large. Some conservative, pessimistic Nationalists were willing to make their peace with the Unionist regime, wait out on the years, and hope for the best. Others insisted on non-co-operation, abstentionism in politics, subversion at every opportunity, and unremitting loyalty to the concept of a united Ireland. Many of these were vicarious backers of Fianna Fáil but others were Sinn Féin or IRA; however, since the entire Nationalist population and even a few odd Protestants favoured a thirty-two-county Ireland, the compromisers—organized in the Nationalist Party—were often forced to withdraw from elections when faced by a radical challenge from the Republicans. From time to time Republicans had run in Northern Ireland elections, usually ensuring a reduced Nationalist representation in Westminster or Stormont. These abstentionist ventures into politics had kept the Northern pot seething, enforced the Orange dogma that all Catholics were disloyal and brought a united Ireland no nearer. The IRA, under surveillance and short of money, could hardly hope for a new "Rising" particularly since the bulk of the Army in the South had different priorities. The alternative strategy had been to act as a local protection society—a militia in times of Orange violence. Thus July was a vindication of the Northern approach.

After July, both tactics were followed. In the November Westminster elections the IRA, under the Republican banner, contested six seats. For the Army Council, secure with an orthodox abstentionist ticket, it was a good change to creep back into politics sideways after the Republican Congress affair. When the Nationalist Party convention met in Omagh, delegates could hear Moss Twomey speaking to cheering crowds outside the door. They withdrew. The Republican candidates with no hope in four areas insisted that this was to be a plebiscite against British rule. As expected, two abstentionists won, but this was the end of plebiscite. Resort to military tactics, the other achieved even less. In December the Belfast IRA, rather pleased with their showing as a homeguard during July, carefully planned a large arms raid on the armoury of Campbell College. On December 27, the apparently well-prepared raid for arms came apart in a violent gun battle with the police. Four men were arrested. Edward Mac-Cartney was not defended and received ten years. With IRA permission the other three men, totally innocent Volunteers, were defended and acquitted. The matter did not, however, rest there. All the evidence indicated that the Campbell College raid had aborted because of inside police information and the three Volunteers arrested to cover this fact. While Belfast HQ was carefully going over security checks to find their man, Dublin GHQ was most concerned at the violation of Army Orders by the C/O, Anthony Lavery, in allowing Volunteers to be defended.

Even while recognizing the special circumstances surrounding the trial, GHQ felt that Lavery would have to face a court martial although it was assumed that the penalty would be mild. On April 25, 1936, Jim Killeen, A/G, and Mick Kelly from GHQ arrived to chair the court martial which was held in the room of the Craobh Ruadh Club at No. 10 Crown

Entry. While Liam Rice guarded the room on the outside, Killeen began discussion with the ten Northerners present, who included most of the Ulster leadership: Seán McCool, John McAdams, James Steele, Charles McGlade, Anthony Lavery, and the others. At 3.25 p.m., the RUC suddenly descended, scooping up at one go the A/G of the IRA and the Northern leadership—a severe loss. The men were charged on May 29 with Treason-Felony in the archaic but appropriate language of a century before.

> Taken in the presence and hearing of the Defendants who stand charged that they at Belfast on the twenty-fifth day of April 1936, as well before as after that day together with divers other evil disposed persons feloniously and wickedly did compass, imagine, invent, devise and intend to deprive and depose Our Lord the King from the style, honour and royal name of the Imperial Crown of Great Britain, Ireland, and of the British Dominions beyond the Seas, and the said felonious compassing, imagination, invention, device and intention then feloniously did express, utter and declare by divers overt acts and deed and who further stand charged that they at Belfast aforesaid on the twenty fifth day of April 1936, and on divers other days as well before as after that day together with divers other evil disposed persons, feloniously and wickedly did compass, imagine, invent, devise and intend to levy war against our Lord the King in Northern Ireland by force and constraint to compel him to change his measures and counsels; and the said last mentioned felonious compassing, imagination, invention, device and intent feloniously and wickedly did express, utter, and declare by divers overt acts and deeds; contrary to the Treason Felony Act, 1848.[39]

The men received a total of forty-eight years' penal servitude: Killeen seven years, McCool and Michael Gallagher six years, McAdams, Steele, Kelly (alias O'Boyle) five years, and the rest two. By the time these sentences were handed down, the IRA was in even more serious trouble in the South, trouble that had begun with the increasing resort to violence first visible in the March 1935 transit strike.

In the Army the demand for action instead of talk had grown as more Volunteers lost faith in de Valera and challenged the continued police surveillance. At the same time GHQ and the Army Council felt acutely the need for a "political" initiative of some sort to counter the Republican Congress idea. In August 1935, another Army Convention had been called and the idea of an overt IRA abstentionist party had been approved—the ultra-militarists from the country couldn't afford to come up to oppose "politics". Almost at once rumours seeped out that the IRA was to organize a new party, but the November Westminster elections in Northern Ireland postponed the formal launching until 1936. The finished political vessel, Cumann Poblachta na h-Éireann, was largely the work of MacBride, the National Secretary, although McLogan was Chairman. Few had kind words for the result—another Sinn Féin, "no political realism in this vision of Twomey's"[40]—particularly the average Volunteer who had had his fill of "politics". To the cynical it looked as if every Republican who touched "politics", even abstentionist politics, was ruined. De Valera had sold out and was filling the prisons with the IRA; the Republican Congress group had collapsed; Sinn Féin and the second Dáil were pretentious jokes, one had split again in 1933 and the other was dying out; even Cumann na mBan had hived off an even purer Mná na Poblachta; and all the wild experiments of the Left, from Saor Éire to the Workers' College,had proven non-starters. Consequently, enthusiasm for the new, new look in IRA politics—Cumann Poblachta na h-Éireann—was severely limited: it was Sinn Féin writ small. The Volunteers preferred action, the sympathetic C/Os gave it to them, and disaster struck.

On March 24, 1936, at 9.30 p.m., an IRA action squad arrived at Castle-townshend, the home of Vice-Admiral Henry Boyle Somerville, in Skib-bereen, County Cork. The old Admiral, seventy-two, was well known in the area for giving references to any of the local lads who wanted to enlist in the British Navy—for the IRA a treasonous practice. The IRA squad had come to "get" the Admiral, as ordered by the C/O of Cork, Tom Barry, and sanctioned by GHQ in Dublin; but the leader of the IRA squad, not the most stable of men, apparently was carried away, interpreted his orders quite literally, and shot the Admiral dead. A small card was left by the body lying over the threshold, "This English Agent sent fifty-two Irishmen to the British Army in the last seven weeks." On April 26, less than a month later, and before the hue and cry had died down, an IRA squad once again with GHQ permission arrived in Dungarvan, County Waterford, in a car commandeered in Tipperary to execute John Egan, judged a traitor by the local IRA unit. The young man was shot down in the street at eleven that evening and died a few minutes later in a nearby priest's house. Once more the country was shocked. This was more than Fianna Fáil, patience long exhausted and fraternal ties snapped, could stomach. Plans were prepared to put an end to the IRA's repeated dis-ruptions of national life.

On May 21, 1936, Twomey was arrested at Home Farm Road, Glasnevin, under Article 2A of the Constitution and moved to Bridewell. On June 19, he was tried and sentenced to three years and three months. There was no indication that the government planned an early release for their old comrade. By 1936 the military guards at Arbour Hill made use of solitary and the quiet system to see that the IRA did not have a vacation on the state's expense. On June 18, the day before Twomey's trial, an Order was made by the Executive Council declaring the IRA an unlawful association under Article 2A. On June 19, the parade to Bodenstown, scheduled for the next Sunday, June 21, was banned. On Sunday one thousand troops with an armoured car and five hundred gardai were out in force all along the route and inside the cemetery. Some members of Sinn Féin and Cumann na mBan tried unsuccessfully to force their way through but in the end Mrs. Sheehy-Skeffington was forced to read Mary Mac-Swiney's address by the roadside to the little group of the faithful.

With the imprisonment of Twomey and Killeen, two of the IRA's strongest pillars had been removed for the foreseeable future. The formal banning of the IRA marked an end to toleration, although de Valera still showed a reluctance to say the final hard word. With the abortive introduction of Cumann Poblachta na h-Éireann, the last political avenue had narrowed remarkably. The Army in Ulster was in disarray after the Crown Entry arrests and in the South the strength and vitality had been dribbling away long before Twomey's arrest. If there was to be a future for the IRA— and clearly de Valera did not think there was—then there would have to be a regrouping at the Dublin centre and a clear realization of the means needed to achieve what all wanted—a free Ireland. In the turmoil of rumour and arrest, with GHQ on the run, the remaining leadership faced an awesome job. At least—small comfort–the devil de Valera had revealed his horns, reluctantly but unmistakably.

NOTES

1. As a result of Michael McInerney's articles on Peadar O'Donnell in the *Irish Times* (April 1968) a typical and extensive correspondence developed in the Letters to the Editor columns of the *Irish Times* during April and May over the exact formalities of de Valera's take-over—that he did, no one denied.
2. Donal O'Sullivan, *The Irish Free State and Its Senate*, London, 1940, p. 295.
3. Ernest Blythe went to the Free State army GHQ and insisted on the utmost respect for the new Minister of Defence Aiken, stressing that the army's first task had been to capture the Four Courts and now the army's task was to capture the Minister of Defence.
4. An excellent, balanced and highly detailed analysis of the implications of the easy transfer of power can be found in Frank Munger's "The Legitimacy of Opposition: the Change of Government in Ireland in 1932" (prepared for delivery at the American Political Science Association's 1966 Annual Meeting, New York, 1966—mimeographed).
5. Somewhat more bluntly Gerald Boland, Parliamentary Secretary to the President and to the Minister for Defence in the first Fianna Fáil

government, told Andy Cooney and Moss Twomey that all the government wanted was that they obey the law.

6. This is, of course, the Irish political stage, for at Bodenstown the Fianna Fáil delegation was seventh ahead of the Peoples' Rights Association and the Revolutionary Workers' Party.

7. Oglaigh na h-Éireann, from A/G to Editor *The Daily Mail*, GHQ, Dublin, May 19, 1932.

8. Irish Free State, *Report of the Sworn Inquiry held at Kilrush, County Clare*, Dublin, 1932.

9. *Irish Press*, November 11, 1932; *Irish Independent*, November 11, 1932.

10. The correspondence between the Governor-General, James MacNeill, who demanded an apology for specific slights, and de Valera, President of the Executive Council, was first published in the *Irish Times* on July 12, 1932, and re-published on May 9, 1968, as a result of various references in the Letters to the Editor section (*vide supra* note 1).

11. Oglaigh na h-Éireann, Manifesto Issued by General Army Convention, January 8, 1933.

12. *Irish Press*, January 11, 1933.

13. Draft Letter to the Comrades in Ireland from the Executive Council of the Communist International (1930).

14. One of the few was Seán Murray from Antrim, who was first secretary when the party was reorganized.

15. This switch in emphasis could be seen regularly in *An Phoblacht* despite its continuing Left politics; for example on June 17 along with an editorial attacking the communist smear of the IRA appeared the Army Council's reply to the charge that the IRA favoured seizing all the land: "This should allay any anxiety, due to Imperialist propaganda, that the Army aims at the confiscation of 'all lands', and the bringing of occupiers under a tyranny."

16. Oglaigh na h-Éireann, Statement of the Army Council, Dublin, August 2, 1933; *ibid.*, Statement of Army Council, Dublin, August 30, 1933.

17. *An Phoblacht*, August 5, 1933, quoting—with scorn—from de Valera's speech in the Dáil.

18. The five IRA men involved in the fight were questioned regularly and ultimately arrested in March partly as a result of "evidence" accumulated by local Blueshirts, who included an uncle, a cattle dealer, and a cousin of one of the accused. The case fell through but the question of fascist philosophy in the townlands was less significant than the feuds of the 'Troubles', the heritage of spite and narrow snobbery, and bitter, bleak abrasions of depression Ireland.

19. George Gilmore, *The Irish Republican Congress*, New York, 1935, p. 14.

20. *The Republican Congress*, May 5, 1934. The pamphlet, which was publicly distributed, was actually a slight step away from Saor Éire, but still too radical for the leadership a year later. See Oglaigh na h-Éireann, *Government Policy and Constitution of Oglaigh na h-Éireann Accepted by General Army Convention, March 1933*, Dublin, 1934.

21. Michael McInerney, "Peadar O'Donnell", *Irish Times*, April 6, 1968.

22. Republican Congress, "Manifesto", Athlone, April 1934.

23. *Ibid.*

24. "We were sentenced in our absence and hoped we would also be executed in our absence. We were expelled—but only after we had left." *Irish Times*, April 6, 1968.

25. *An Phoblacht*, April 21, 1934.

26. O'Sullivan, *Irish Senate*, p. 408.

27. The contention of the Republican Left at the time was that O'Duffy had been advised by his less conventional Italian and German ideological friends that the only hope for Irish fascism was to seize the leadership of the anti-Imperialism struggle—which may have been sound advice but resulted in a rapid peeling off of support and no noticeable conversions of Republicans, safely in possession of the anti-Imperial bloc.

28. Irish Communist Organization, *The Irish Republican Congress*, London, n.d., p. 16.

29. Oglaigh na h-Éireann, Army Council Statement, Dublin, September 10, 1934.

30. Oglaigh na h-Éireann, Statement by the Army Council, Dublin, November 7, 1933.

31. It was the later contention of the men on trial that in a jury made up of nine Protestants and three Catholics they had been saved by one of the Catholics who held out to the last.

32. *Irish Press*, January 7, 1935.

33. *Ibid.*, January 15, 1935.

34. *Ibid.*, January 16, 1935.

35. *Ibid.*, April 15, 1935.

36. *Ibid.*, March 24, 1935.

37. *Ibid.*, March 30, 1935.

38. *The Republic*, July 6, 1935.

39. This quotation is taken from the County of the City of Belfast, Commission of 21st July 1936. Charge: Treason Felon, The King Against James Grace or Killeen, Seán McCool *et al.* (Clerk of the Crown and Peace, Counties of Antrim and Belfast, 16 June 1936.)

40. *Irish People*, March 28, 1936.

CHAPTER VII

De Valera Pre-empts the Stage: The IRA without Direction, June 1936–March 1938

The double loss of Twomey and Killeen meant a transformation in GHQ. Seán MacBride was co-opted by the Army Council as C/S until the General Army Convention could meet and select a successor by normal constitutional means. Although he had a very sound man as A/G, Donal O'Donoghue, there was some reticence in various IRA quarters about MacBride, who was a quite different man from Twomey. Despite his 1916 name the average Volunteer felt MacBride was a strange Irishman: he had a peculiar accent, too much education, and was very, very clever. More than his politics within the Army or his plans for the future, it was his "differentness" which apparently grated, making him unpopular for a variety of often contradictory reasons. This was hardly a universal judgement since most Volunteers knew MacBride by little more than name and most men of the Army Council or GHQ were deeply impressed with his commitment and capacity. Any replacement for Twomey would have a hard time; but MacBride's apparent conversion to "politics" in his work for Cumann Poblachta na h-Éireann made him a subject of suspicion to the military activists. This delicate strain within the Army was intensified when MacBride and Russell came into open conflict.

Russell had regarded all the creeping steps to the Left with disdain and the IRA's involvement in politics as a detour. For him the only way to break the connection with England was by force and the only task of the IRA was to supply that force. Ever since the "dump arms" order Russell as Director of Munitions had dedicated his life to accumulating and storing sufficient weapons for the IRA, to urging more thorough training, and to preparing the Volunteers to fight. The philosophical minutiae of radical politics, which engrossed the Army Council, played little part in Russell's life and he gave them little time or thought. He knew his business—arms— and there he did not want advice or interference. MacBride, who had a lawyer's predilection for detail and precision, found Russell first difficult and then impossible. Russell simply ignored MacBride, not a new habit of his and not limited in its application to MacBride. Russell had increasingly urged action on the IRA, suggesting attacks on England from an Irish base, just as the Army Council had decided to back the political opening of Cumann Poblachta na h-Éireann. Yet, the breaking point came not over a matter of policy but a point of detail.

In certain areas Russell was a minor genius; but in matters of routine, dy book-keeping, precise records, he was at best careless. MacBride, gather-ng the strings of control into his hands, insisted on exact records, and ussell as usual ignored the new regulations. MacBride proceeded to collect case against Russell, revealing his failure to account properly for funds, cluding those for a car. A court martial was called. MacBride, the bar-ster, proved his complaints against Russell and forced a decision of mis-ppropriation of funds, although everyone knew Russell had never kept a enny for himself but spent it for the IRA. In any case, Russell was forced ut of the centre of the circle.

Many of those who disliked MacBride and suspected a quickening of political" activity rallied around Russell, among them Tom McGill and eadar O'Flaherty; but there was not for the moment an open split. stead a quiet campaign began in favour of Russell's idea of attacking ritain from Ireland, a prospect the more practical thought mad, but hich had a certain attraction for the bored Volunteers. The Army Coun-l's failure to risk a second round before 1932 and the long years of neasy truce with Fianna Fáil had sapped the patience of most Volunteers: ne conventional had gone into Fianna Fáil, the pessimistic had emigrated, ne radicals had hived off, and the militarists grown truculent. Little of nis latent rebellion appeared in Dublin GHQ where work was concen-ated on reorganization, preparation for greater political involvement, nd the next Army Convention.

In the midst of this quiet GHQ activity, a distant and unlikely event nce more stirred the Irish political pot. On July 18, 1936, Irish newspapers ublished reports of serious disturbances in Spain. The three-year Spanish ivil War had begun.[1] In 1936 few countries outside Spain had as broad representation of political parties—anarchists and fascists, communists nd monarchists, two kinds—something for everyone. Hardly a European ction or creed was without representation, so that when the rebellion egan in July, much of Europe was almost at once emotionally involved. he same was true of Ireland. On July 22, the *Irish Independent*, friend of ine Gael, sounded the call for the Right:

All who stand for the ancient faith and the traditions of Spain are behind the present revolt against the Marxist regime in Madrid.

The Spanish Nationalists were fighting for God and the Republic for ommunism. The balanced views of the *Irish Times* deploring the possi-ility of escalation into a general war and playing down a communist–atholic interpretation represented few Irishmen except perhaps in the nionist areas of the Six Counties. The Irish "Left" was in a poor position publicize its views on Spain during the summer of 1936; the *Republican*

Congress had died in February and *The Worker* had only a minuscule circulation. Even so, making use of the platform, letters to the editor, and word of mouth, men like Ryan and Gilmore explained that Spain was a battleground between the black forces of fascism, which threatened to sweep through Europe, and those of democracy represented by the Republic. This thesis had few public takers and most Irishmen outside Fine Gael tended to accept the views of the *Irish Press* that Ireland should remain neutral in deed and word if not thought. When in September an all-European non-intervention committee was formed, Fianna Fáil' advocacy of neutrality received the sanction of general international agreement.

Neither the anguished and troubled men who read daily of the violent persecution of the Spanish Church by the Reds nor the desperate and frustrated young men who read of "secret" fascist and Nazi intervention against the democratic Republic at Madrid could in good faith accept neutrality. The *Irish Independent* insisted that Ireland break relations with Madrid and this call was taken up. Various local government bodies debated and often passed the Clonmel resolution advising such action. Avidly supporting this manœuvre was the new Irish Christian Front under Patrick Belton. The Christian Front was supposedly a broad, non-party movement to turn back the threat of international communism. Seizing on the Spanish war, Belton's Christian Front was soon deeply involved in pushing the Clonmel resolution, gathering funds for the Nationalists, and holding monster rallies. All of this activity had the highly vocal support of the hierarchy of the Church. Against this the Left had at first little to offer. The Republican Congress telegraphed support to the Spanish Republic, to the horror of the bishops. Peadar O'Donnell who had been in Catalonia when the war began[2] returned to Dublin to urge practical aid for the Republic and George Gilmore left for the Basque country to see what could be done. One Republican then in Europe, Bill Scott, did not wait for a formal programme. He volunteered his services to the Republic. He was only the first of those from the Left and the Right who went to Spain to fight for their ideals, defying the policy of non-intervention.

News from Spain made little impact on the IRA. GHQ had for the time being turned away from international adventures. During August there had been two by-elections in Galway and Wexford with Republican candidates. Although the Army did not expect miracles, there was hope that Plunkett in Galway and Stephen Hayes in Wexford, both standing as abstentionists, would attract Republican voters tired of Fianna Fáil's halting progress toward the Republic. At times, in fact, it sounded as if de Valera were running against Mary MacSwiney, who slashed and cut at the chief apostate from one platform after another. De Valera, however, ad the last word: Hayes received only 1,301 votes out of a total poll of 5,574 and Plunkett did no better with only 2,696. By the time the IRA recovered from this cruel venture into politics, the question of volunteers for Spain had become more serious. In Dublin Frank Ryan had begun organizing Republican Congress people and anyone else interested in going to Spain. Many of the old IRA-Left were involved, although a few hesitated to support wild geese. The attraction to the bored Dublin Volunteer was considerable. This was particularly true since the old Blueshirt bogey, Eoin O'Duffy, had announced that he was organizing an Irish Brigade to carry the crusade against communism to the Spanish battlefront.[3] With Belton's Treatyite Fine Gael types in the Christian Front and O'Duffy's faded Blueshirts in the new Irish Brigade, eager to crush the Spanish Republic, many IRA Volunteers clearly felt that Madrid's cause must indeed be worthy of any aid.

On the eve of the Army Convention, the IRA felt then the tug of two calls for action, Russell's English campaign and Ryan's Volunteers for the Spanish Republic. The Army Council, faced with the by-election results and reports of feet-dragging in the parishes, could hardly hold up the prospects of Cumann Poblachta na h-Éireann as a viable alternative. When the Convention met, the frustration and delay was summed up by the C/O of Cork, Tom Barry, who in a fiery speech insisted that the Army leadership must act and act soon. Barry wanted immediate and terrible war on the British in six months and not in England but in Northern Ireland. The Convention, swept away in enthusiasm, carried the resolution by acclamation. When the Army Executive met during the Convention, there was unspoken acceptance that the resolution was unwise but an accurate expression of IRA sentiment. To tranquillize the wild men the new Army Council offered the post of C/S to Barry, who had been on the run since the spring. It seemed a political choice; the Army would not take McBride, however clever and dedicated, and no one wanted to be C/S with Barry's resolution hanging over the Army's head. If Barry wanted to invade the north within six months, he could now do so as the head of the Army. Less cynically, Barry was a good choice. He was well-known and popular in the IRA and out, one of the outstanding soldiers of the Tan War and, as the Army Executive knew, far shrewder than his simple soldier image and far too practical to involve the IRA in any wild Northern campaign of the scope proposed for England by Russell's advocates.

As for the lure of Ryan and the Spanish Republic, Barry insisted that there would be no wild geese—the Volunteers were forbidden to volunteer. Nevertheless, some found the temptation irresistible and with the compliance of various C/Os, especially Dublin, the men resigned and signed up with Ryan.[4] During the autumn they began drifting across to the continent

and into Spain to form the James Connolly Battalion of the Abraham
Lincoln Brigade. Eighty left with Ryan on December 11. Within two weeks
reports of Irish casualties began to appear in the Dublin newspapers. Ultimately some four hundred Irishmen, most of them old IRA men, would
make their way to Spain and the International Brigades. Many never came
back: forty-two were killed, twelve captured, including Frank Ryan, and
114 were wounded. This record was in stark contrast to O'Duffy's Brigade
which fought only two brief actions: the first with a Nationalist unit from
the Canary Islands resulted in the only battle deaths—two; and after the
second O'Duffy refused orders to attack again under Republican artillery
fire. Most of the time was spent on a quiet sector of the line where the men
lost any enthusiasm for the crusade, formed cliques, muttered mutiny and
sick, tired, and homesick, voted to return to Ireland when given the opportunity.[5] The war dragged on; de Valera's policy of non-intervention was
generally accepted; neither the Right nor the Left could generate continued
enthusiasm.

Belton's Christian Front collected a substantial sum of money for medical
supplies, held some monster rallies which recalled the piety and arrogance
of the Blueshirts, and then dribbled away without an Irish cause. O'Duffy's
Brigade, wrangling and feuding, came home in disgust. On the Left, the
resources were scraped together to replace the *Republican Congress* with the
Irish Democrat, largely written by O'Donnell. But with no advertising,
poor distribution, and minimal circulation, the paper managed to hang
on only until the end of the year and then collapsed. The *Worker* went
under as well, leaving the Left dependent on pamphlets, one-shot papers,
and the letter columns of the daily press. The efforts during 1936 and 1937
to generate enthusiasm for the Spanish Republic, even to importing a
Basque priest Father Ramon Lamboda, enlivened the Irish political atmosphere, enraged the Church—"it is a scandal and an outrage that an Irish
Catholic body should be guilty of pledging support to such a campaign"[6]
—but did nothing to convince the majority of Irishmen that their interests
were involved in Spain. In the July 1937 general elections for the Dáil,
instead of moving onward and upward from his Christian Front base
Belton lost his seat to G. L. McGowan of the Labour Party, and instead
of Frank Ryan, an authentic and articulate war hero, sweeping to victory
in Dublin City South as the candidate of a United Front Against Fascism,
he polled only 875 votes.

In the meantime the IRA had turned its attention to Barry's Northern
campaign. At GHQ preparations were made, not for a sustained series of
strikes from the South, nor a low-level guerrilla war based within the Six
Counties, but rather a *coup d'état*, which might or might not lead to a
general campaign. Other than staff work for the first blow, little time or

effort was spent on the future. The IRA in the North was highly enthusiastic that at last there was to be action against the prime enemy instead of the endless discussions about de Valera's treachery. Barry, however, turned to his own Cork for all the men involved in the first strike. The plan was for a raid on the Armagh Military Barracks with the IRA 26-man Active Service Unit. Word had already gone out to Cork for the Volunteers to move to starting point. The men had been to confession and were ready to move off as civilians to take the train to Dundalk. Then GHQ cancelled the entire operation. At the last minute a representative from Cumann na mBan had arrived at GHQ and announced that a resolution had just been passed requesting the IRA to allow their members to participate in the operation. GHQ had assumed that outside of headquarters only a few people in Cork and in the North knew of the raid. They discovered that word of the attack had been seeping through Army circles for weeks and was even common gossip in Belfast HQ and now was openly debated in Dublin at Cumann na mBan meetings. The Armagh raid was instantly cancelled. The great Northern campaign was over without a shot having been fired.

In the North, however, shots had been fired on and off for years and the RUC never ended their "campaign". Despite the size and enthusiasm of the IRA in the Six Counties, the North had played only a minimal part in the leadership of the IRA. Rarely had a Northerner served on GHQ much less the Army Council and rarely had the leadership in Dublin given great consideration to peculiar problems of the North. The failure of the Armagh raid, the most impressive sign of GHQ interest so far, was thus a cruel blow for the Northerners. It was particularly so since the pressure on the Army had grown slowly but surely since the Crown Entry arrests. To some degree the IRA had brought on the swoops, arrests, and sentences by two provocative executions. A former C/O of Belfast had been court martialled and sent to exile in Galsow after he had "exchanged" too much information with a supposedly friendly police agent in Belfast. More dupe than traitor, he had returned to Belfast disregarding the death sentence that hung over his head. In December 1936 he was duly executed. Within six weeks the former I/O of Belfast, who had given away both the Campbell College raid and the Crown Entry meeting, was shot four times on his way to church. The following morning, January 27, he died in hospital. The RUC estimated that there had been eighteen unsolved "political" murders in Belfast since the Tan War. Although the IRA had not been responsible for all of them, the figure explains the RUC distaste for any IRA activity and their determination to close down the IRA. As far as the more activist Northern members could see, the Dublin GHQ, after the Armagh fiasco, was willing to leave the North to the mercies of the RUC.

Russell, understandably bitter with MacBride and his colleagues in

Dublin, had determined not to accept the results of the court martial
decision without fighting back. Without permission he had left for America
to whip up support for his English campaign. Clan na Gael had been
further disrupted by the Republican Congress split, since many of the
radicals had supported the idea; unlike the IRA the Clan had not expelled
the heretics. The arrival of Russell—now "a dismissed volunteer"—once
more threw a spanner in the works. Men like McGarrity, dyed-in-the-wool
Fenians, could well understand Russell's call for action and sympathize
with his distaste for MacBride's "politics". Many of the most radical members of the Clan were old friends of Russell, who felt he was politically
naïve but still a great Irishman and a great soldier. If Russell wanted to
fight the English in England, then the Clan would do their best for the IRA.
Russell's problem was that he was no longer in the IRA. This could, however, be rectified if his supporters triumphed at the next Convention.

Barry had already run into trouble with Russell people at GHQ. He had,
hopefully, appointed Peadar O'Flaherty A/G, MacBride I/O, and Michael
Fitzpatrick of Dublin QMG. O'Flaherty despised MacBride, personally and
politically, and refused to obey orders from the Army Council. Barry had
to get rid of him and rely more on his Cork unit, particularly MacCurtain
and Tadhg Lynch. Once off the GHQ, O'Flaherty had linked up with Tom
McGill, and the two of them began shifting through the country sounding
out support for Russell. Perhaps O'Flaherty's most successful manœuvre
was to capture control of the IRA in Britain without anyone noticing. Telling neither the C/S nor the Army Council, he had arrived in London, fired
the C/O of Great Britain, and replaced him with Jimmy Joe Reynolds, a
devout convert to the English campaign, who brought Pearse McLaughlin,
Mick Ferguson, and Mick Welsh, all Russell men, onto his staff. Dublin
remained blissfully unaware of the change, although MacCurtain, back
after delivering an oration, did remark that the atmosphere in England
was peculiar. But before the pro-Russell men could bring their plans to
fruition, the next General Army Convention was called.

Barry, who had been unable to implement his previous resolution for
immediate and terrible war on Britain within six months, felt that his
tenure had been sufficiently lengthy. In mid-1937 he told the Army Council
in a meeting at Banba Hall that he intended to resign. A Corkman, he did
not really want to remain in Dublin, even on the run. With Twomey and
Killeen still in prison there was no obvious candidate. MacBride seemed
to be fading out with Cumann Poblachta na h-Éireann, which had held the
first Ard Fheis in Wynn's Hotel in Dublin in November 1936 and then had
disappeared from sight. The Russell people hoped that someone could be
found sympathetic to the English campaign to hold the C/S seat warm.
The anti-Russell people wanted to keep the Army out of the hands of the

mad bombers. The result was that the Army Council, still largely the same faces, selected Fitzpatrick, who had been on the Army Council for years if not in the centre of the circle. As a Dublin man, he could hold the Army together without arousing excessive jealousies or wild hopes. Fitzpatrick took over and appointed several new younger men to the GHQ: Seán Keating, who had been on Barry's staff as A/G, James Hannegan as QMG, Seán O'Brien as I/O; he also retained Barry's men, Lynch and MacCurtain. The Army Council and the new GHQ was obviously a holding operation against the return of Twomey and/or Killeen, not a beach-head, as some suspected, for Russell.

Fitzpatrick had the new GHQ staff experiment with some of the explosive devices proposed for use in the English campaign. Hannegan, the new QMG, tried out one of the most ingenious ideas, a balloon bomb containing chemicals which would ignite when exposed to the air, and acid to eat away the rubber. When Hanaghan tried out the bomb, the acid found a weak spot and the balloon went up in his hand. Like the whole Russell plan, the balloon bomb impressed Fitzpatrick as looking simple but in reality being terribly dangerous. Soon after this, word finally trickled through of the coup in London. Fitzpatrick went over, got rid of Reynolds and his staff, and reinstated the old staff with Jack Lynch, who had assumed the name Buckley, as C/O Great Britain. The difficulty with all this quite reasonable and practical GHQ works was, of course, that the activists were not satisfied. With the words of their local C/O ringing in their ears, many had come to the Bodenstown commemoration in June 1938 expecting not to return. Instead the commemoration was held as planned under the eyes of the bored detectives and Barry instead of calling for a crusade suggested only that those Republicans who voted in the July election not vote Fine Gael. For many it was the end of the road. They resigned or emigrated or agitated for Russell's return.

The Army Council was aware of the erosion but equally conscious of the frightful risks in Russell's idea. With the aid of Harry Fitzsimons, Fitzpatrick did investigate the possibility of raiding the armoury at the Magazine Fort in Dublin's Phoenix Park. GHQ decided that with a man inside there would be no trouble in clearing out a great deal of arms and ammunition in a short time but little hope of getting the stuff into dumps before the search began. The idea was dropped. In fact, the Army Council had seemingly exhausted most ideas—MacBride's political alternative had petered out; Russell's bomb campaign had attracted only the young, violent, and foolish; Barry's Northern alternative was a non-starter, and Fitzpatrick had offered nothing more than a willingness to mark time. The thoughtful began to wonder if the IRA had lost purpose and place in Irish life.

The decline of the IRA from the glory days with a unit in every parish and twenty thousand Volunteers waiting for the call, from the high drama of the Blueshirt confrontation, and the ferment of radical ideas had been precipitous and, so some thought, irreversible. Almost from the moment of Twomey's arrest, Fianna Fáil had relaxed with an audible sigh. The IRA was a spent force, potentially dangerous if captured by the wrong men but no threat to anyone as long as a rational and ineffectual Army Council held on to waning power, waiting for better days that would not come. Fianna Fáil now felt on the high road to the Republic, the promises of 1932 and 1933 had by 1937 turned into reality. The seat of Treatyite opposition, the Senate, had been eliminated on May 29, 1936. On the abdication of Edward VIII de Valera had seized the opportunity to speed through the Dáil the Constitution (Amendment No. 27) Bill eliminating the Crown from the Irish constitution: the Governor-General, long a cipher, no longer existed. In fact, de Valera was prepared to take the next step and abolish the Free State. A new Constitution had been introduced into the Dáil on March 10, 1937. Although the new state would not be labelled "a Republic", a step which might cut off the Six Counties for good, even the sceptical would have to recognize that the stepping stone technique, with de Valera doing the stepping, had brought the Twenty-six Counties close to the culmination of Republican dreams. Even the militant would have to recognize that the final steps would depend on peaceful negotiations not futile bellicose displays in the shadow of the awesome power of the British Empire. The militant, of course, did not and organized a monster protest rally with the usual collapse into riot and violence, and the usual victims: Major Frank Ryan, home from Spain, got a bloody nose and Tadhg Lynch a bloody head. In fact, neither logic nor results swayed the dedicated; but by the time for the general election and plebiscite on the Constitution on July 1, Fianna Fáil no longer felt IRA objections were of great interest. The commemoration at Bodenstown had been permitted, as much an act of harmless charity to an old friend as a devious ploy to get votes. The IRA was finished and Fianna Fáil had more important preoccupations, like winning the election and getting on with running the country.

As it turned out, Fianna Fáil could have used the votes in July. In the new Dáil, de Valera would be dependent on Labour for a majority. The new Constitution was accepted only by a simple majority of those voting. Thirty-one per cent did not vote at all and thirty per cent voted against it. Even so, Fianna Fáil had a majority in the Dáil and a new Constitution. On December 29, 1937, the Irish Free State, spawn of the Treaty, was gone at last, replaced by Eire/Ireland. With each year de Valera's stature had grown, his uncanny skill become more obvious, and his grip on Nationalist sentiment more secure. Operating from a narrow base he had crippled the Right, isolated his parliamentary opponents, waited for the collapse of radical rhetoric, and watched the pure Republicans contaminate themselves with violence. Absorbing into Fianna Fáil all those who saw the Economic War, the dismantling of the Free State, the new "Republican" institutions of the S-Branch and the Volunteer Militia as receptacles for their idealism or ambitions, he had watched the IRA erode, bent on sterile acts of violence. To the anger of the militant, he watched the savage decline with some pity for the past glory; for he still found it difficult in public to condemn out of hand the old friends of the glory years.

However de Valera might regret the continuing blindness of the IRA wedded to the gun, the police had taken the position that the IRA, banned in June 1936 and without friends in the Cabinet, were fair game. The Broy Harriers, former IRA men all, were no exception and in some ways seemed more determined than the long-time career detectives to prove their hostility to the recalcitrant Republicans. Regardless of their origins, the detectives, armed and dangerous, kept a cold, hard eye on the IRA. The politicians might feel the danger had gone but the old "Specials" of Neligan had often made a career out of the IRA and the new Broy Harriers followed in their steps. On June 15, 1937, in what later gave every evidence of being an unprovoked killing, the police in panic as much as malice shot down and killed Peter McCarthy in Clanbrassil Street, Dublin. No reasonable government explanation was forthcoming and whatever ties with the old comrades in the Broy Harriers had existed were snapped. The men who had served time in Arbour Hill came out to report on the grim conditions imposed by the military guards. During the Blueshirt fight, in the old heyday of the Military Tribunal, a few months in prison had been a vacation, no work, handball, and adequate food. After June 1936, there was no handball; the men were kept in solitary, forbidden to speak, living in a silent tomb where even the guards wore rubber-soled shoes. The culminative impact of the silent world drove Seán Glynn of Limerick first mad and then on September 13, 1936, to take his own life. After that, somewhat more humane, but by no means pleasant, conditions prevailed. But it was too late. Within the IRA a deep bitterness began to spread – de Valera was not like Cosgrave, he was far worse.

As the year 1937 closed, there was little sense of accomplishment within the IRA. There had been action of a sort and plans of a kind but the first had led nowhere and the second had aborted. The Armagh raid had failed. The wild and exciting Dublin anti-Coronation demonstrations on May 12 and 13 had led to baton charges and Barry's bloody head. Fitzpatrick's take-over had kept Russell's friends out but little more. Outside the IRA, the Republican movement, Left, Right, and Centre, had dried up, leaving small stains and spots: the tiny Sinn Féin and Second Dáil group, the

Republican Congress without funds or newspaper, and the embarrassing Cumann Poblachta na h-Éireann was being packed away. There were only two hopeful signs. First, Brian O'Higgins, helped by Joe Clarke, managed to publish and largely to write a new weekly newspaper the *Wolfe Tone Weekly*. Secondly, on December 14, eleven Republicans, among them Twomey, were released from the Glasshouse in Curragh Military Camp. Neither was an unmixed blessing. O'Higgins, a devout man of conventional ideas, used the *Wolfe Tone Weekly* to relive the past, not shape the future; and GHQ and the Army Council soon knew, as Twomey's notes out on the secret line had indicated, the former C/S did not want the seat Fitzpatrick had kept warm.

The first startling news of 1938 was that the train of de Valera's successes was far from over. On January 11, he informed the Dáil that he would meet with the British government's representatives in London on January 19. The culmination of various talks between Prime Minister Neville Chamberlain and de Valera led to the Anglo-Irish Agreement on April 25, 1938, which ended the Economic War and granted Ireland possession of the British Treaty ports. If, as seemed likely, a general European war developed, Ireland could remain neutral. De Valera, who had already made a considerable international reputation with his interventions at the League of Nations, now felt that Ireland was a fully independent state, a Republic in all but name. Only partition remained, and in this case a solution by force would obviously be counterproductive, Chamberlain having already indicated his own dissatisfaction with the Ulster situation. In a few months, the Irish people would give de Valera ample evidence that they approved of the progress he had made. On June 17, the election results gave him a substantial majority and seventy-seven seats in the Dáil. The IRA was obsolete as far as Fianna Fáil was concerned. By the spring of 1938, even the ubiquitous police, ever cynical, had eased up on surveillance and low-grade harassment.

This quiet confidence on the part of Fianna Fáil and the police was to some degree misplaced. Even though the IRA had been outmanœuvred by de Valera since 1932, weakened by schism and resignation, and unable to find a clear direction or a worthy strategy, the organization remained intact. It stretched through all thirty-two counties, into Scotland and England, and across to the United States. As the time for the General Army Convention approached, the IRA might appear feeble to its enemies, but its leadership knew that there were still plenty of enthusiastic young members, still a vast network of loyalty and shared sacrifice, still an unyielding belief in Tone's goal and in his means, still money from America and arms in dumps, still an absolute determination to hold out for the whole Republic, not de Valera's stunted copy, still a burning sense of njustice that six Irish counties were occupied by a British army. There vas also on the Army Executive and in the Army Council a bone-weary cceptance that the IRA lacked a feasible task—no coup in prospect, no esire for civil war, and certainly no enthusiasm for a "mad bomber" ampaign. The only men who claimed to know the answers supported Russell, and the solid men in the centre of the circle assumed the IRA had oo much sense to be led down that sterile by-way.

NOTES

. See J. Bowyer Bell, "Ireland and the Spanish Civil War," *Studia Hibernica*, 1969.

. Peadar O'Donnell, *Salud, An Irishman in Spain*, London, 1937.

. Early in August El Conde de Ramirez de Arellano wrote to Joseph Cardinal MacRory, Primate of Ireland, requesting Irish help. The Cardinal suggested O'Duffy, who accepted the task. Captain Liam Walsh, "General Eoin O'Duffy, His Life and Battles", typed manuscript.

. Very few Republicans of any persuasion supported the Spanish Nationalists—'Sceilg' being the notable exception.

. Several of the Irish Brigade had been recruited by O'Donnell and Gilmore and sent to Spain to stir up a mutiny; however, the orthodox members on the Brigade needed no encouragement.

. *Belfast Telegraph*, September 21, 1936.

PART IV

The War Years: 1938–1945

CHAPTER VIII

The English Campaign: Bombs for Britain, April 1938–September 1939

When the General Army Convention met on Abbey Street in April 1938, the long ground-work by Seán Russell's advocates readily became apparent.[1] While the Convention was not actually packed, sufficient units throughout the country had been impressed with the call for action to send men to Dublin sympathetic to a British campaign. These delegates, often unknown to the inner circle of the GHQ and Army Councils, had lost patience with the long holding action. An army which limits itself to violent speeches and passive parades was far too tranquil for many of the new generation and not a few of their elders. During the previous year all the old, patched-over schisms had begun to re-open. Many distrusted or disliked MacBride. Barry had talked too much and done too little. Mick Fitzpatrick was simply holding the chair for other men. Killeen or Twomey might have headed off the Russell people, but even when Twomey came out of Mountjoy in December 1937, he was reluctant to become deeply involved in Army politics. The old leadership, often out of touch with sentiment in the country, drifted into the Convention hopeful that the sure impracticability of Russell's proposal would sway an open Convention. They found that the delegates had arrived with closed minds and a determination to have a go at the British whether it was practical or not—after all Pearse had scarcely been "practical" on Easter Monday.

Opposition to the campaign coalesced around Tom Barry, who thought the whole thing was a damn fool idea, doomed to as signal a failure as the dynamiters of the 1880s. He claimed, as he had before, that there were sufficient British in the Six Counties for the IRA. He insisted that setting off a few bombs in London would be a fruitless gesture. If the Army really wanted a British action, he was willing to take a squad into the House of Commons or Lords and strike at the real culprits. No one was moved. Barry's previous efforts in the Six Counties had been abortive and the delegates were convinced that the time for a one-shot operation had passed. Like Barry, almost all the leadership of the 'thirties who were still in the Army violently opposed not only the campaign but also Russell's candidature.

Russell had always been considered a highly dedicated competent man as QMG but difficult to work with and impossible to sway. He was a fine soldier but had severe limitations at best and at worst might be tainted with a single-minded ambition to lead the IRA into a real war. The split with MacBride had been very bitter. The canvassing for Convention votes the secret change in the London command structure, the intervention of McGarrity, all had left a sour taste. Yet no one had made a supreme effort to prevent a packed Convention. After twenty years many had grown weary of splits, of the corrosive effect of covert politics, of the round of responsibilities which led nowhere. They did not want a campaign because it was foolish and probably immoral. They did not want Russell because they doubted him. But they had no alternative but patience, no candidate but a stop gap.

But prudence could not sway the delegates who voted in a new Executive with a majority committed to Russell and the campaign. The new Army Council was composed of firm campaign men: Russell; George Plunkett with his 1916 name; Stephen Hayes, the Wexford C/O; Peadar O'Flaherty, Russell's campaign manager; Larry Grogan, a solid, taciturn man from Drogheda; Maírtín Ó Cadhain, an Irish-speaking school teacher from Galway, the C/O of Dublin; and Patrick Fleming from but not of the Kerry IRA establishment. Russell became C/S and in order to ease the pangs of transition, Moss Twomey, who had acted as Convention Chairman, undertook one more task for what had for so long been his Army and agreed to remain as A/G for six months.

Few shared his feeling of responsibility. Since Russell and his men had captured the Army for dubious purposes, let them run it on their own, sharing the responsibility and any glory. Five members of the new Executive, Barry, MacCurtain, John Joe Sheehy, Seán Keating, and Johnny ("Machine-gun") O'Connor resigned, contending that the Army Council was unrepresentative of the IRA as a whole and had appointed a "dismissed Volunteer" as C/S in defiance of the decision of the out-going Council upheld by a General Army Convention. Mick Fitzpatrick and the GHQ Staff resigned from the IRA within a week and only the Director of Intelligence Seán O'Brien of Kerry relented and rejoined to help out. Barry left and MacBride and Con Lehane and Tomás Malone. Some did not resign formally but drifted away and out. Others stayed on out of habit disapproving of the new course but reluctant to discard decades of work. At last Russell dominated the IRA but it was very different from the organization to which he had given a quarter century of his life. Many anti-campaign men like T. Lynch, McLogan, Donoghue, Hannegan, and Frank Fitzgerald were asked to resign from GHQ; and unknown men had to be jumped into positions of responsibility. Rapid promotions became the order of the day. New members of the Executive were co-opted. In Dublin Willie McGuinness became C/O of the depleted, reorganized

nit. Only in the North was rank shuffling unnecessary for, by-and-large, it
as in the North that the Volunteers and their officers had called the loudest
or action. Russell's IRA was by no means a rump organization nor were
ll his officers either untrained or new to leadership[2] but the famous names
ad gone, the level of competence had been lowered, and the intellectual
esources of the Army depleted.

In May the Army Council adopted the campaign plan without specific
etails. Many units would not swallow it. Cork No. 1 (Cork City), Cork
Jorth-East, and Cork North—all Barry territory—held a meeting and
efused to give the campaign or the new GHQ backing. Similar meetings
vere held in the South, particularly Kerry. In Dublin, the 3rd Battalion
eld a Council and asked GHQ to explain how the Army Council was
amed in light of the resignations from the Executive and requested a
ieneral Army Convention in light of the indiscipline and tactics of the
ew Army Council. Russell and his men would not be swayed. For them
 was their opponents who refused to accept the democratic decision of
he IRA, not the Army Council. The split was not healed and grew
ery bitter indeed. The men formerly in the centre saw the IRA taken
own a road they abhorred, while the new Army Council felt betrayed
y men who would not serve the new direction. In any case, the Army
Council had no intention of temporizing or backing water. Plans went
head.

Faced with the vast and urgent demands for talent, money, and skill
hich the campaign would require, Russell turned to several old but long
nactive friends from the Tan War. Patrick McGrath, who had been out
n Easter Week and still carried a British bullet in his chest, agreed to
elp out. Most important, later in August Russell went to the Merrion
treet ESB office of Seamus O'Donovan, former Director of Chemicals for
he IRA GHQ, and pleaded for help. O'Donovan, who had seldom seen
Russell and taken no part in politics since his release from prison in July
924, felt that since the die was cast he would lend a hand. His acquisition
vas particularly valuable for he was not only a skilled explosives expert
ut he had a far broader vision of both military and political realities in
Europe than did any of the men surrounding Russell.[3] With his staff in
lace, the new additions incorporated into the leadership, and funds
uaranteed from Clan na Gael, Russell was ready to get down to the
asics.

Despite literally years of discussion, there was no master plan for the
ampaign, only the conviction that bombs exploding in Britain would
orce the Cabinet at Westminster to open negotiations. Russell believed
hat even if de Valera would not or could not openly support the cam-
aign, he would at least tolerate the IRA's activities in order to reap the

benefits—the end of partition. But little thought had been given to broad military planning and none to the political implications of an undeclared war. At Russell's request O'Donovan drafted a campaign plan as a basis for discussion. Russell accepted the document, read it through, and informed O'Donovan it was magnificent. He suggested no changes. He initiated no discussions. O'Donovan's draft, soon to be well-known as the S-Plan, was broad in scale, far beyond the IRA's capacities, and suggested certain sophisticated targets and tactics which were to be ignored. The S-Plan was a totem, admired but most assuredly not the strategic foundation of the campaign. In point of fact, the Russell campaign had no strategic basis. From April 1938 until January 1939, extensive technical and tactical preparations were undertaken, but no one thought to examine the actual "strategy" of a bombing campaign. The prospect of action was enough.

The "bombing campaign" had been a tactical weapon in the armoury of various revolutionary organizations seeking to force negotiations over the question of sovereignty. In brief there are two broad categories: sabotage or terror, and in either case operations may be directed against material or personnel.

In a sabotage campaign the targets can be quite specific. Obviously in 1939 the most vulnerable sites in Britain were key war industries. Even two or three successful strikes could have badly hampered if not crippled the British aircraft industry. On a broader scale, regular minor attacks on a single essential complex—the London underground or the railways or power transmission—could more visibly disrupt British economic life. The S-Plan had envisaged just such attacks, but in actuality target selection was left in the hands of local commanders without any firm overall direction. The IRA was not concerned with the material damage done to Britain, but the effect created by random explosions.

A terror campaign can be symbolic, striking at monuments of oppression, Buckingham Palace, or at individuals, from the king to policemen. A technical operation is also possible where individuals, or less likely material, are attacked to hamper coercive efforts to end the campaign. Thus Michael Collins' Bloody Sunday assassinations on November 21, 1920, were intended to wipe out the British intelligence network in Dublin and intimidate future operators. On the other hand, the assassination of Field Marshal Sir Henry Wilson on June 22, 1922, was a symbolic, punitive operation. There are campaigns of generalized terror where arbitrary explosions intimidate the population at large, a process which can easily be intensified by carrying out attacks on individuals. This, hopefully, for the revolutionary, creates an atmosphere of terror so intense that the population seeks respite rather than tolerate further abuse. From time to time, organizations have tried one or more of the terror options, usually with considerable prior calcula-

on. In Ireland during the Tan War at one time or another all were
used and there was even consideration of instituting retaliation into
Britain.[4] Later in the 1940s, the Irgun Zvei Leumi and the Stern Group in
Palestine, learning from the Irish experience in the Tan War, waged a
similar campaign against the British.[5] In time the British would seek to
bargain a way out of Palestine as they had in Ireland in 1921, and as they
would later in Cyprus and Aden. The obvious difference was that Russell
sought to inflict an atmosphere of terror, not on the British Army stationed
abroad, nor on a British colonial apparatus, nor even on the British police
in Britain, but on the entire British public.

Such a manoeuvre is apt, as it had in the dynamite campaign of the
1880s, to create an atmosphere of vengeance rather than a demand for
compromise. To shatter the normal ties of British life, to transform millions
of men into frightened ciphers, to overawe an entire people was a fantastic
undertaking. Even to disrupt British order through sabotage as outlined
in the S-Plan was a massive operation. Nothing reveals more clearly the
problem Russell faced, no matter which option he chose, than the response
of the British people two years later in 1940–1941 to the Luftwaffe's assault
during the Blitz. The unexpected and random IRA bombs had a greater
impact than was admitted at the time, but the incidents were too diffuse
to maintain any real anxiety in any one quarter. For sabotage the IRA
simply lacked the weight of metal, the access to vulnerable targets, and
efficient skills. For terror the IRA lacked, perhaps commendably, the
instinct for the jugular. That the IRA did not want to murder in the
streets and could not cut the economic sinews of order meant the campaign
was doomed to futility—spluttering on until hope and haven had been lost
and the men interned, imprisoned, or expelled. Prudent men, even with
ten times the personnel and equipment, would have thought the prospects
dim, but with the scanty resources available even the optimistic should have
drawn back.

Difficulties, however, have never deterred the determined. Revolutions
are made by the fanatic not the prudent. GHQ pushed ahead. The impressive S-Plan remained wishful thinking, an adornment to GHQ staff work
but not an outline of the future. GHQ's actual intentions were to carry
out synchronized but sporadic sabotage operations within the major
English cities. (Scotland and Wales were exempted as Celtic countries.)
Attacks on individuals were eschewed.[6] There was to be no real effort to
damage the British industrial or transportation structure but rather to
maintain the momentum of incidents. In theory the explosions would
erode British patience and security resources to such an extent that negotiations would ensue. There might be some "symbolic" targets chosen by
local commanders just as, inevitably, there would be loss of life; but the

idea was that serial explosions of whatever intensity and on whatever target
would in time have their effect.

To mount such an operation GHQ had to overcome several technical
problems. First, the quality of personnel left much to be desired. Several
men attached to GHQ had experience with explosives, but only O'Donovan
could be classified as really qualified. Many of the volunteers who attended
bomb-classes were being exposed for the first time to sabotage work; few
had technical training and many lacked any formal education beyond
primary school. A number of the devices, such as balloon bombs, were
simple to make and to use but potentially quite tricky.[7] Hasty, covert classes
over a period of a few weeks turned the volunteers into explosive placers
but hardly sabotage experts. Some of these classes (one for the London IRA
was held on the grass in Hyde Park) were very sketchy; but in Dublin a
concerted effort was made to create at least a core of good men in the
limited time available. Moreover, the quality of explosives, home-made or
stolen, was not the best. Sophisticated devices were out of the question.
Many chemicals were not available to GHQ, some ingredients could only
be acquired by theft.[8] Gelignite could always be lifted but it was bulky,
not too powerful, and decayed rapidly. Thus the campaign would have
to depend on poorly trained men using doubtful material of limited
efficiency.

Once the men had been trained and supplied, they would have to maintain themselves in an increasingly hostile city where Irishmen, betrayed
by their speech if nothing more, would be easily recognized. All the Irish
clubs and halls would be watched as would the trains and particularly the
boats to and from Ireland.

The British CID undoubtedly had long lists of people and places, but
the number of Irishmen in the industrial cities was so large and the flow
of immigrants into the country so great that the prospects were by no
means hopeless. Movement into Britain despite police precautions never
proved a serious problem and all the normal nationalist centres were
avoided. Most of the IRA staffs in Britain had been changed by bringing
in new men unknown to the police and to their new Irish neighbours. In
some cases secret C/Os were sent over—men known only to the very few.
New safe houses were found, often with old friends; but for the most part
the IRA planned to use "innocent" houses, hopeful that the wary landlady
would remain ignorant of the fact that the lad upstairs in the rear was
making bombs under the bed.[9] One difficult point, largely ignored, was
that the active-service people sent over from Ireland would be most
suspicious of all since they would have no regular employment. If they
moved regularly, kept proper papers, and did not spend the day lying in
bed, they might move unnoticed, but the risks were higher than GHQ

oresaw. Hence the problems of safe haven and freedom of movement for he most important people could not be solved.

Finally, the cost of the campaign would far exceed the very limited esources of the IRA. Men would have to travel, rent rooms, eat, and their quipment, however sparse, would have to be replaced. The greatest poten- ial drain would be the support of the volunteers' dependents. McGarrity's Clan na Gael had all but underwritten the campaign, but American money ad always looked more impressive in theory than in fact. The Clan had ong since dwindled into warring factions but McGarrity insisted that ufficient money for necessities would be forthcoming. Once the bombs tarted going off, there was every chance that the flow of American money vould increase as the donors vicariously followed the campaign. If for ny reason the American pipeline broke, the IRA would be in disastrous traits; but Russell was not a man to be intimidated by an occasional if".

If the technical obstacles looked awesome, the political ramification of campaign of raw violence on British and Irish politics should have ppeared awesome. In Ireland in 1938 and 1939, de Valera was running campaign to end partition. During the conversations with Chamberlain vhich led to the Anglo-Irish Agreement of 1938, de Valera came to the onclusion that progress might be possible. The return of the British bases o Ireland had made it clear that Chamberlain's policy of appeasement xtended across the Irish Sea. While many doubted the Unionists would udge an inch, there was growing optimism in Irish politics, an expectation hat the thaw was on hand. But Russell, completely out of touch with his 1en and with the time, still felt de Valera would not oppose the campaign. s for a purely diplomatic solution, Russell and the IRA were convinced hat the only means to break the connection was physical force and that ven de Valera, however he had strayed from Wolfe Tone's tenets, would 1ot have forgotten that. There was no understanding that in Dublin the Cabinet felt on the lip of success and in any case had forsaken force as a olution to a not too pressing problem.

As for British politics, Russell simply did not understand the system or he men. To imagine that any British government might be willing to ede part of the British Isles at the threat or display of violence was fanciful n the extreme. Perhaps *in extremis* the British government might have hosen such an unsavoury alternative; but later, on the brink of defeat, Churchill's first thought was not to bribe Ireland with the Six Counties in rder to get back the naval bases but to seize the country. In any case, Russell did not give British reaction serious thought beyond what he hoped night happen. As for the Unionists, they were simply ignored as misguided British dupes and their intimate ties with the Establishment discounted.

All speculation on the impact of the campaign was simply put to one side until the bombs started going off.

The Army Council, deep at work in the isolation of Dublin, gave no real thought to a foreign alliance, other than the Clan. Where Pearse and Casement had sought German aid, Russell was content with American money. That a European war was in the offing was hardly the conclusion of a seer in 1938. That once Britain was involved in such a war a campaign would have far greater impact seemed equally obvious. Action co-ordinated with Britain's enemies would have appeared a traditional snatching of opportunity. Again, no serious thought was given to relating the campaign to the European situation or seeking additional help in appropriate quarters. The IRA would strike alone and in its own time.

From the first, the whole campaign was the product of pressures and its direction was warped with personal ambitions and old feuds. For years the Army had drifted along in the wake of events, pulling small stunts and talking of a future Armageddon. The young and the active had been alienated. Russell had come back from America determined to strike and no one high or low had produced a decent alternative. Whether or not the campaign was technically feasible, it was emotionally desirable. Russell and the Army Council were far from mad but they were angry. Despair, drift, and delay had at last been put aside. If the odds were steep, so had they always been. For centuries in the marrow of their bones Irishmen had felt that in each generation someone, somewhere has to strike the first blow. Russell had offered his fist and the Army voted to follow him.[10]

During the late spring and summer of 1938, GHQ was gripped in a frenzy of activity; organizing bomb classes, vetting volunteers for duty in England, collecting chemicals, arranging secure houses and dumps in the major British cities, and building up a courier and intelligence net unknown to the British CID. The important staff officers were constantly on the move, visiting training camps, inspecting British units, and meeting endlessly to discuss details. American money and GHQ funds permitted a fair number of paid organizers to operate freely in Britain. Some of the chemicals for the various bombs had been acquired legally or stolen without raising suspicions. There was a steady supply of gelignite from the Wexford unit and bits and dabs from elsewhere. Considering the amount of movement and the Irish fondness for rumour, all the IRA preparations should have attracted official notice but the police seemed blind in both eyes. Mansfield, chief of Special Branch, had never seen the IRA as a major threat and was well aware of the series of splits. The government felt that after the rash of resignations in the spring of 1938 the IRA was at last a spent force. In the North the RUC was never too complacent and never completely off guard, but no significant activity had been noticed for some time. Even the provocative speeches and demonstrations at Bodenstown in June alerted neither the Irish nor British police despite a wealth of clues including the place of honour given the IRA-British detachments.[11] To a large degree the incredible audacity of the campaign protected the IRA from unusual scrutiny. Complacency was the order of the day. Minimal surveillance in Ireland and Britain missed the new course, overlooked the new men and the hidden network they were weaving. Opportunities which would be difficult to regain once the IRA went underground completely were let slip day by day.

By early autumn training had reached the point that several classes had graduated from sabotage schools, explosives were positioned in Britain, targets had been selected, and operations outlined. GHQ at the request of the Northern units was willing to run a try-out in the Six Counties. The operation, the destruction of British customs posts, would involve various local units under staff direction. Most of the men involved would not be able to participate in the British campaign and thus such an operation would simultaneously satisfy their need for action and reveal to GHQ the existing state of readiness. In late November the mines were put together in the South and moved to the border in suitcases. The time for the attacks was set for the evening of November 28–29 but, as would become almost traditional with IRA operations, things did not go as planned.

The border operations instead of producing a satisfactory field exercise collapsed in disaster. On November 28, Jimmy Joe Reynolds, attached to GHQ, and two local men, John James Kelly of Donegal and Charles McCafferty of Tyrone, had slipped into a cottage at Castlefin, Co. Donegal, near the border to activate the three mines smuggled in that day from Sligo. Their targets were the Customs huts at Clady and Strabane. One of the mines proved faulty and detonated prematurely. The explosion inside the closed room killed Reynolds and McCafferty outright and threw Kelly through the collapsing wall of the cottage into the yard outside where the disintegrating chimney toppled onto him. He lingered on for several days deliriously repeating Reynolds' final words inside the cottage, "Stand back John James—there's a wee mistake!"[12] A subsequent GHQ investigation revealed that one of the three mines had been marked faulty by a chalked "X" on the outside of the suitcase but neither this information nor the chalked "X" reached Castlefin. Reynolds had innocently opened the case and the entire charge had gone off almost immediately. The loss of three men was bad enough; worse still, the RUC–Special Branch stepped up intelligence operations in the wake of the accident and the successful demolition of the customs posts over the next two nights.

Many of the men involved in the North were well-known to the police.

As noted, unlike the IRA people in the South, the Six County IRA had supported Russell, often most enthusiastically, and stayed in place without a shift in leadership. Thus the RUC had fewer new men to discover and a great many more old trails and former spoors to sniff over. In the next few weeks, a great many hints and guesses were patched together by the RUC. While the outlines remained vague, day by day the RUC intelligence indicated that the IRA was far from moribund and planning some major operation.

In the meantime Russell had returned from an inspection trip of the British units with Stephen Hayes, his choice to succeed Twomey whose six months had run out. Hayes was a stocky, round-faced cheerful man, who worked for the Wexford County Council. He was popular throughout his area because, among other reasons, he was very active in the GAA, sports often being the high road to financial or political success in Ireland. During the campaign preparations, Hayes and his contacts had been most useful in the accumulation of explosives and their transfer to England on the boats out of Rosslare even though Hayes had not always run a very tidy ship in Wexford.[13] Russell, however, had always run a one-man show and his A/G while No. 2 at GHQ would, as was the case with most of the Staff, be dominated by Russell.

With the Army wound up and ready to go, Russell decided on two moves to strengthen his hand. He had for some weeks been in touch with the surviving members of the Second Dáil, seeking their authorization for the IRA declaration of war against Great Britain. The negotiations culminated in a public announcement in Brian O'Higgins' *Wolfe Tone Weekly* on December 8 that the Second Dáil had transferred the right to establish a Republican government to the Army Council of the IRA. With the possible exception of Tom Maguire, who went along, the Dáil members felt that the IRA request gave them the moral recognition so long denied by all factions and that their conditional devolution of power would in turn give the IRA the moral basis for the impending campaign. The IRA–Dáil Treaty,[14] unlike the S-Plan, was not simply a totem but was taken very seriously in some quarters both as a moral basis for violence and also a real step toward the Republic.[15] Russell's second move was an Extraordinary General Army Convention to generate the last necessary impetus. The Convention met in a tiny hall in the back of a shop near the Green Cinema, St. Stephen's Green. The only substantive issue before the fifty delegates, brought in from all over Ireland, was the reaffirmation of their support of Russell and the campaign. There were no longer many doubters in the Army. The last prudent man, Twomey, had retired after his emergency service as A/G. The Army Council remained as it had in April although Peadar O'Flaherty had suffered a period of disgrace for suggesting

e destruction of Nelson's Pillar while the entire resources of the IRA were
rained preparing for the campaign. During the course of the brief meet-
g, Russell told the men that never again would Irishmen die on Irish
il. The delegates then dispersed to continue final preparations.

The Army Council, after December 1938 simultaneously the *de jure*
overnment of Ireland, met for the formal declaration of war against Great
ritain. The vote, even at this late date, was not unanimous for Máirtín
Cadhain felt the IRA was not ready to take the last step. Ó Cadhain,
d he was not alone, had reservations about Russell's total lack of interest
an economic and social programme and argued that since the IRA was
lely a military organization a Third Dáil should be elected to meet the
eed. The other six members of the Council had no second thoughts
though during December they had been given fresh evidence of the
fficulties the Army would face when the warning buzzer was finally
ipped in Belfast. On December 22, the RUC pulled a surprise sweep and
rested known Republicans under the Special Powers Act.[16]

The men arrested were not simply given nominal sentences—for there
as no real charge against them other than being a potential danger to
e state—but were interned in Crumlin Road Prison. The RUC, still
ncertain of the aims of the IRA, apparently hoped that the sweep would,
mporarily at least, disorganize the Belfast Brigade and the Northern
nits. Then, too, the men under indefinite sentences would be hostages,
eir release dependent on the good behaviour of the IRA. The IRA bore
e arrests remarkably well. Many "prominent" Republicans played a
sser role in the IRA than the RUC assumed and several key men were
issed. Charles McGlade, for example, had returned from organizing in
ritain and was in an upstairs room when the RUC took away his brother
rank. Some of the men on the way up, like Seán McCaughey, Liam Rice,
d Pearse Kelly, had not reached sufficient prominence to attract attention
d others were in Dublin or Britain.

In any case by late December, Britain was already organized, the volun-
ers trained and most of them dispatched. Once operations began, all the
y moves would be made by GHQ in Dublin, limited by finances as much
by the loss of men. A bustling, active Northern IRA was not essential and
Belfast might be uselessly provocative. Other than supplying a few good
en, the Belfast Battalion could once more resume its role as a Home
uard to protect the Nationalist community in case the Orangemen ran
mok. This was a stance congenial to many of the Belfast IRA men and
ould have the advantage of keeping the Volunteers out of sight of the
UC. Thus the December arrests had little serious impact on the decision
go ahead with the campaign. As long as the Dublin GHQ centre
mained, the money kept trickling through, and the lines into Britain

remained open, the campaign could continue even if there were further and more extensive arrests on both sides of the border.

On January 12, 1939, the formal ultimatum signed by Fleming as Secretary of the Army Council was delivered to Lord Halifax, British Foreign Secretary, demanding the withdrawal of all British armed forces and civilian representatives from every part of Ireland. If the British government refused, then war was imminent for England.[17] It is doubtful if Halifax or Scotland Yard took the communication very seriously. As expected Halifax gave the Army Council no indication that he would act or even that he had received the ultimatum. On Sunday, January 15, on expiration of the time limit, an IRA Proclamation was posted throughout the country asking for support in the effort to complete the withdrawal of the British. It was signed by Russell, O'Flaherty, Hayes, Grogan, Fleming, and Plunkett, the Army Council and Government of the Republic. Russell was well known, the last of the uncorruptibles from the Tan War GHQ, and Plunkett's name was intertwined with Easter Week, but outside Republican circles the other signers were largely unknown. Their Proclamation attracted scant general interest.

On the following day, Monday, January 16, 1939, there were seven major explosions keyed on electrical lines and power stations: two in London, three in Manchester, one in Birmingham, and one in Alnwick. On the following day there were further explosions and it was recognized in official circles that the IRA Proclamation was something more than a bad joke. British security was immediately tightened. Police patrols at key points were reinforced. Plain-clothes men descended on the Irish districts of Britain's major cities. All the ships arriving at Liverpool, Holyhead, and Fishguard were gone over with considerable care and the passengers closely scrutinized. The British police discovered very little. In the next week thirty-three men were arrested on "suspicion". Then for the rest of the month, as GHQ had planned, nothing happened.[18]

The concern and anxiety lessened somewhat, for it was entirely possible that as in the past the IRA "campaign" was a one-shot affair designed more to appease the activists than intimidate the British government. Then early Saturday morning, February 4, two major bombs were detonated in the London underground stations in Tottenham Court Road and Leicester Square. The time-bombs, concealed in checked suitcases at the left luggage rooms, had unintentionally but inevitably resulted in two serious injuries. That there were not more casualties—or less—had been entirely a matter of luck. The British press was outraged at the pointless and wanton attacks. On the same day the public learned that the British government had been forewarned of the attacks. That night there were further explosions in London and fires in Coventry. On February 6, a bomb was detonated against the outside wall of Walton Jail in Liverpool. That these were not the haphazard actions of a few demented men became crystal clear when the government released an "operation plan" found on a suspect. The police had acquired a copy of Donovan's famous S-Plan, which was sufficiently coherent, detailed, and ambitious to cause serious misgivings. If the IRA were actually capable of activating the S-Plan, then the British were in for a bad time. While the Home Office, quite familiar with the Irish Republican organization in Great Britain, might have doubts as to the capacity of the IRA, the public and the press were more impressionable.

No one could understand what the Irish wanted or even who the "Government of Ireland" was; but the explosions were real, the S-Plan was real. If the ultimatum was ridiculous and the IRA Army Council beneath contempt, as *The Times* claimed, the government still had the responsibility of preventing a wild bombing spree. For police and public nothing is more unnerving than a mad bomber and suddenly Britain seemed filled with mad Celts carrying bombs. There was, in fact, every indication that despite stringent security measures the explosions would continue for some time. If the IRA bombs had not yet struck terror in the hearts of the British people or their government, there was little doubt that considerable anxiety had been generated in official quarters, in the press, and perhaps among private citizens.

In Dublin the explosions had come as a total surprise to the government and a most unwelcome one. Increasingly involved in the anti-partition campaign, de Valera and the Cabinet simply could not believe that any-one, even Seán Russell, would so foolishly sabotage their efforts. At first there was even the suggestion that the whole thing was an Orange plot to prevent a peaceful settlement of the border question. When the realization finally dawned that the IRA, so long discounted, had irresponsibly launched the violent venture, de Valera addressing the new Senate made clear his opposition to the use of force, to the pretensions of the unknown "Government of Ireland", and to the activities of the illegal IRA in Ireland. Although he passed over the bombing campaign, he informed the Senators that he would ask for repressive legislation designed to allow the government to uphold its position and authority.

As the bombs continued to detonate in England, the Army Council in Dublin suddenly were presented with a new and fruitful option just as the money situation was beginning to pinch. On February 1, a German agent, Oskar Pfaus, had passed through British customs and moved on to Dublin to make contact with the IRA.[19] As was often the case in the theoretically monolithic Nazi state, various factions had competed for years in a bitter jungle war waged with red tape and overlapping responsibilities to control German intelligence operations. For some time the more prudent

Foreign Ministry had prevented Admiral Canaris' Abwehr (Intelligence Organization) from operating in Ireland, where such activities might provoke the British, not to mention the Irish, thereby complicating the work of the Foreign Ministry. By January 1939, this deference to Anglo-Irish sensibilities seemed increasingly less necessary to Abwehr and the ban was ignored. Pfaus, who had spent several years in the United States, knew next to nothing about Ireland but was handy and eager. His briefing was little more than stale gossip and potted history retailed by men out of touch with Irish realities; for Abwehr had not as yet collected any Irish specialists but only an expert in Casement's life and Celtic literature.

When Pfaus arrived in Dublin, his only "name" was Eoin O'Duffy, well-known in Germany for his Blueshirt activities but hardly a sure entry into the counsels of his bitterest enemies in the IRA. Pfaus found O'Duffy horrified at the request for contact with the IRA and most unhelpful; however, O'Duffy's secretary, Captain Walsh, proved more pliable. Walsh was willing to put Pfaus in touch with the IRA though he knew even less than O'Duffy. He contacted Moss Twomey, whose politics were public knowledge. Twomey in turn arranged for Pfaus to meet some GHQ people in a house in Clontarf on February 3. There Russell, O'Donovan, and several GHQ officers listened to Pfaus' story. After some initial sparring, Pfaus made arrangements for the IRA to send a representative to Germany to explore the possibilities of co-operation. Russell, elated by the prospect of German arms, ammunition, and money to supplement the thin stream of Clan aid, decided to entrust the mission to Seamus O'Donovan. O'Donovan left almost immediately and got to Hamburg without difficulty. A brief but detailed discussion with the Abwehr men produced no firm agreement but represented an exchange of views. After promising to return after he had reported to GHQ, O'Donovan made his way back to Dublin. On April 26, O'Donovan returned to Hamburg for another short visit to discuss potential agents, the supply of arms in the event of war, radio sets, and courier communication. The only firm result was a courier route between Brussels and London using an exiled Breton. Everything else remained very tentative and a flood of Teutonic equipment remained very problematical.

In Britain the campaign moved along as planned. Although the explosions tapered off during the first weeks of March, the pause was tactical, not the result of the increasing British police activity. On March 29, there were two major explosions at Hammersmith Bridge in London. On the following day there were explosions in Birmingham, Liverpool, and Coventry, and the day after seven more in London. At GHQ in Dublin there was cautious satisfaction but increasing concern with the financial drain. The obvious solution, as in the past, was a whirlwind American fund-raising tour; however, the attrition in the leadership over the years had left the Army Council with only one big name, Russell himself. In the spring of 1939, the Army Council agreed that Russell, exhausted by the intensive activities of the past year, could best serve the IRA in America for the next several months. There was little dissent—the IRA needed the American money too badly. Russell suggested and the Council concurred that Hayes would take over as C/S while he was out of the country. At Easter, armed with the appropriate papers, Russell left for the United States.

During the following months the attacks in England continued. On May 5, fifteen persons were treated in hospital as a result of tear gas bombs in two Liverpool cinemas. On May 5, four explosions in Coventry and two in London were reported. On May 19, fires were started in eight English hotels by delayed-action incendiary devices. On May 29, four magnesium bombs detonated in the Paramount Cinema in Birmingham. Two days later, more cinemas in London were hit, forcing the police to search every cinema in London. In Belfast as a result of instructions given on the IRA secret radio transmitter, crowds in the Nationalist districts heaped up their gas masks in seven city streets and set them afire. On Friday, June 9, an extensive operation was carried out against English post offices. Letter bombs were exploded, twenty pillar boxes burst into flames, a mail van in Birmingham exploded, as did a sorting office in London. The series of post office attacks produced considerable British police activity. All leave in the twenty London Metropolitan police divisions was cancelled. Boarding houses all over Britain were raided. Special guards appeared at the Houses of Parliament, St. Paul's Cathedral, and Westminster Abbey. Every pillar box in London was searched.

Although doing little real damage the number of incidents in the post office operation after five months of police pressure immensely encouraged GHQ. At the same time good news arrived from the United States. Seán Russell had been detained in Detroit for making false statements on entering the country. To many Americans his detention was a step to prevent embarrassment when the British king and queen visited the country. What delighted GHQ was the refusal of some fifty members of the House of Representatives to attend the meeting of American legislators and the royal couple. Protests and petitions had barely begun when Russell was released, but the outcry revealed that the traditional Anglophobia of many American politicians had not been eroded by time. Hopefully Russell would be able to transform the emotion into dollars and cents. In the meantime the IRA was preparing its own celebration for the eve of the march to Bodenstown.

On Saturday evening, June 24, with Piccadilly Circus filled with the crowds from the cinemas and theatres, the IRA London unit set off a devastating series of explosions. The three main targets were the Midland Bank, Westminster Bank, and Lloyds Bank. The entire area was shaken by the detonations. The front of the Midland Bank was thrown out into the street. The area was filled with smoke and dashing crowds. Even Madame Tussaud's Wax Works was hit when a balloon bomb exploded in the chamber of horrors; Henry VIII was ruined and the Red Riding Hood Tableau saved only because the bomb in the Wolf's bed was a dud. The police dashing through the crowds haphazardly picked up thirty Irishmen. With no evidence against them except the possession of a brogue many had to be released, including several involved in the Piccadilly operation.[20]

In Ireland on the following day, the scheduled march to Bodenstown turned into a riot. The government had banned the commemoration but most Republicans decided to march anyway. At the Amiens Street Station two special trains from Belfast arrived and disorders began almost at once. The police eventually charged the crowd with batons. At the GPO there was a huge meeting and the Union Jack burned. The police and army had thrown a cordon around Bodenstown and fifty police and detectives waited in the cemetery in case the march materialized. In Fermoy protests were so violent that armed soldiers and two armoured cars were called in by local authorities. Strangely enough, the Irish Republican march in London went off without a hitch under the tolerant eyes of the police.

During the next week a series of fire-bomb explosions continued in the major target areas. Matters in Britain had clearly gone beyond the police. Even by stretching their constitutional powers, the police had been unable to break the back of the IRA.[21] The arrests and heavy sentences of ten to twenty years had been ineffectual. The close watch on the entry ports had not prevented the shipment of explosives out of Rosslare and eventually into the hands of the IRA bomb squads. The regular sweeps and raids picked up the odd man but the volunteers still had little serious difficulty slipping into the country and joining their units. The time for sterner measures had obviously arrived. On Monday, July 3, Miss Ellen Wilkinson, a Labour member, asked Prime Minister Chamberlain in the House if he was aware of the Irish grievances and would he consider any statement with a view to the removal of such injustices as might exist. The government, however, was not interested in concessions forced by violence but in coercion by broadening police powers.

On July 24, 1939, Sir Samuel Hoare, British Home Secretary, introduced the Prevention of Violence Bill authorizing tight control of immigration, the right of deportation, the registration of all Irish living in Britain, and the detention of suspects. He pointed out that since January there had been 127 "terrorist outrages" killing one person and injuring fifty-five, while sixty-six persons had been convicted of terrorist activity. The Labour Party agreed, reluctantly in some quarters, that stronger police powers were necessary and did not oppose the Bill. Even before the Bill could be rushed through Parliament, two more major explosions occurred, further alienating British opinion. On July 26, a bomb went off in the cloakroom of Victoria Station, injuring five people. At King's Cross Station a similar explosion tore off both legs of one man, who died the same afternoon, and seriously injured two luggage counter attendants. The following night there were three huge explosions in Liverpool, smashing a bridge and dropping it into a canal and completely wrecking the front of the post office in the centre of town. On July 29, the Prevention of Violence Bill received a third reading in the House of Lords.

On August 3, the first six deportees arrived in Dublin from London. The numbers continued to climb and they were often accompanied by "unofficial" deportees, skipping out just ahead of police detention. Throughout all the major Irish districts, intensive house-to-house searches continued. By August 5, forty-eight expulsion orders and five "prohibition of entry" orders had been issued, but far more were touched or intimidated by the pressure. The British were not alone. The Irish government banned a meeting for prisoners' dependents in Tipperary and prepared for more stringent steps. On Monday, August 14, there were police raids in the Dublin area. George Plunkett was lifted. So were Joe Clarke of the *Wolfe Tone Weekly* and several members of the Dublin unit, including Myles Heffernan who was caught with IRA documents in his house. On August 22, two proclamations were issued putting into force parts of the Offences Against the State Act, setting up special criminal courts and giving the government power to arrest, detain, and search suspects. On August 25, the Military Tribunal was set up in Dublin. On the same afternoon the bombing campaign which had continued despite the British arrests reached a new and grisly plateau of violence.

In Coventry an operation had been planned for mid-afternoon. As was the custom the bomb was made in one place, carried to another, and given to the last man in the chain. In this case the bomb ended in the basket of a carrier-bicycle. The bomb was pre-fused and the volunteer set out across Coventry. He had considerable difficulty finding his way and was increasingly delayed in traffic. Aware that the bomb was ticking away beneath him, his anxiety grew as his margin of safety slipped away.[22] Finally, with the time almost gone, he jumped off and left the bike leaning against a wall in the busy Broadgate. At two-thirty the bomb detonated, smashing in a shopfront, blowing out windows all along the street, and scattering debris ankle deep over a wide area. Five people were killed instantly and sixty more injured. Britain was horrified. The police went through every Irish home in Coventry. Inside Dartmoor Prison British convicts attacked IRA prisoners, badly injuring several. Although the carrier-bike man was in Ireland within the day, still badly shaken by the disaster, the British early in September did manage to pick up members of the Coventry IRA unit: Peter Barnes and James McCormack, who was using the name Richards, Joseph and Mary Hewitt, a married couple, and Mrs. Hewitt's mother, Brigid O'Hara. Barnes and McCormack were as horrified as anyone that the bomb had gone off in the wrong place making them even indirectly and at a distance involved in the massacre.[23] Although the IRA was still consciously attempting to avoid fatalities, the British were not interested in fine distinctions of intention or shared guilt but in a swift prosecution of the accused. All were charged with the murder of a young woman, the twenty-one-year-old Elsie Ansell.

By the end of the summer, the police pressure coupled with full public assistance had made life extremely difficult for the IRA men operating out of the Irish districts. All Irishmen were suspect. All suspicious Irish homes were watched. All boarding houses and inexpensive hotels were checked. Men without visible occupation or means of support were stopped and questioned. Anyone loitering was questioned. Active-service men had to keep on the move during the empty hours. Some men became so cautious that their contacts could never reach them in a crisis. Men in from Dublin often found their one link gone and were forced to fumble around to find someone or to return to Ireland. The steady pace of arrests cut into the strength of active units. Good trained replacements were hard to find despite the continuing bomb classes run in Dublin by GHQ. If the British police had not broken the net, they had torn out many of the threads and loosened the moorings.

At the Dublin centre, GHQ was living on borrowed time; the establishment of the Military Tribunals, so long the target of Fianna Fáil scorn, heralded new difficulties. Even GHQ realized that in the impending European war the government's determination to keep Ireland neutral would affect the British campaign. At last the IRA Army Council, collectively afflicted with political tunnel blindness, recognized that the war would create an entirely different situation in Dublin. From their point of view the difficulties and complexities far outweighed the opportunities. Russell was certain to be trapped in America. In July McGarrity, quietly visiting his ancestral home in Tyrone under the watchful eyes of the RUC, knew he would have to return to Philadelphia—which he did by way of Germany. The pipeline to America was cut and funds had to be found. O'Donovan went back to Hamburg once more.

Arriving in Hamburg on August 23, O'Donovan moved on to Berlin for the final conference with Abwehr. On his return German efficiency disappeared and Abwehr forgot to supply him with the key-code for radio traffic. On the eve of hostilities the Breton courier had to dash for the London drop with the code so that radio contact could be established. He got through and a new, long, thin thread had been spun out between Dublin GHQ and the Abwehr in Berlin. GHQ did not need a thread but a pipeline. By mid-morning on September 1, German panzers were deep inside Poland. On September 3, at eleven in the morning, Britain went to war, followed by France at five in the afternoon. On the previous day, de Valera had summoned an emergency session of the Dáil to announce that whatever the circumstances Ireland would remain neutral. The IRA's thread to Berlin was perhaps even more of a threat to that neutrality than the bomb squads in Coventry and London.

For the Irish government the practical problems of neutrality were immense. Ireland had a tiny army of 12,500, two small patrol boats, and a handful of obsolete aeroplanes. A formal military defence of neutrality against an armed attack would be little more than a symbolic gesture and a guerrilla struggle was likely to be hopeless. The only weapon de Valera could wield was the diplomatic rapier, parrying the British need for the bases returned in 1938 and the German interest in the inviting back door to Great Britain. To avoid provocation was vital, and the illicit coterie who called themselves the Irish Republican Army and the Government of Ireland, who sent misguided men to detonate bombs in Britain, was provocative in the extreme.

Despite assurances from the German Embassy that Berlin would refrain from every hostile action and respect Ireland's integrity, the possibility of an IRA–German contact, given the 1916 example, could not be discounted. That O'Donovan had already made three trips to Germany and secured just such a contact would have come as a cruel shock to de Valera but probably not a surprise; more than any other Irish politician of his generation he had always prepared for the improbable and planned for the contingent. Thus, to maintain the neutrality that every Irishman desired he would have to neutralize the IRA. At the same time he would have to guard against arousing the sentimental resentment of those still attracted to old slogans and the old examples. The IRA was obviously not the government's only problem or perhaps even the major one, but the time for tolerance had long passed. The IRA had the potential to do more damage more quickly than any other group in Irish politics. For their part, less subtle and less analytical, the IRA Army Council accepted that most of the pieces on the board had shifted. On the run, deeply preoccupied with the British campaign, the leadership could only wait out the days to see what the European war and Irish neutrality would mean to the Army.

NOTES

1. Russell was not present at the General Army Convention on Abbey Street since, as a result of the court martial, he was not a member of the IRA, a situation his advocates deplored.

2. Fleming had been on the Army Council for some years; Hayes on the Executive and a Republican candidate in a Dáil election; Ó Cadhain had attracted attention when his bishop removed him from his school post. Many of the other men like Jimmy Joe Reynolds (More O'Ferrall case) and Michael Conway (John Egan case) were at least notorious. Generally the men around Russell were younger than the old Tan War veterans but the charge that they were "unknown" and "new" was hardly fair.

3. Russell's GHQ was representative of the pure, nationalist strain in the IRA, distrustful of politics, unmoved by general causes, radical ideas, or European events. For many, physical force had become an end not a means.

4. The specific origin of the campaign is difficult to determine because in the long course of Republican tactics there are apparently endless antecedents for any action. During Russell's tenure as QMG in the Tan War preparations had been made to carry out extensive retaliatory attacks in Britain and discussion of the possibility recurred off and on for several years.

5. This interfertilization went full circle when the IRA in the 'fifties read, almost as a text, Menachem Begin's *The Revolt, Story of the Irgun* (New York, 1951).

6. At one point the Army Council reconsidered the decision not to take life when an elderly woman was tried for providing a safe house. The British were warned of this reconsideration but the Army Council took nc further steps.

7. Almost everyone who was active for any length of time in 1939 and 1940 had trouble with the bombs: trunks burst into flames, acid ate through clothes, chemicals decayed or detonated unexpectedly, and dumps exploded. In retrospect it is remarkable that more serious accidents did not occur.

8. In 1938 Denis O'Connell and Jimmy Joe Reynolds had been arrested in London in possession of considerable potassium chloride but were eventually released since the police did not make the connection between the chemical and its potential use.

9. In many cases operations officers literally made bombs in their rooms, not always successfully, and kept the result in the closet or under the

bed. Joseph Collins, for example, nearly lost his life as the result of a "minor" flaw in one of his bombs. "Because of impurity in the rubber container, the acid burned through in about half an hour instead of two hours. It was an explosive incendiary bomb. Along with the incendiary it contained a detonator and two ounces of gelignite. This was to burst the case and spread the incendiary material. Anyway it was enough to blow my head off if I hadn't answered the knock immediately. I was stooped over the open case on a chair when Volunteer Bernard McGuinness knocked on the door. I was expecting him, as he had already taken out two cases and given them to Volunteers in a public toilet to carry to their targets. I had just reached the door when it exploded. The light was blown out, also the glass in the window was broken and the bed and carpet were on fire. The room was full of black smoke from the incendiary. I got out as soon as I could find my coat and took the case of explosives with me." (Letter, June 6, 1968.)

10. Since the campaign was a disastrous failure in retrospect there were many who allotted the blame in generous proportions, usually to others. The fact is that most, if not all, of the IRA were desperate for action and went along with Russell. The only reasonable alternative would have been to give up the Army and turn to politics or retirement. Many simply would not face that alternative.

11. Russell had a tendency toward provocative public speeches, which were from time to time picked up by the newspapers. During the campaign preparations, IRA men in London were horrified to read in their tabloid that Russell was planning to bomb Britain—fortunately for them the correspondent assumed that the IRA had acquired an air force.

12. McCafferty Memorial Fund, *Comdt. Charles McCafferty* (pamphlet), n.p., 1966.

13. At one point it was rumoured that Russell was ready to court martial Hayes over the loss of some dumps but rumours and gossips about Hayes have multiplied over the years and any man in a position of authority within the IRA always has his critics—in any case, Russell chose Hayes to act for him on his departure to the United States.

14. The IRA–Dáil Treaty, formally signed and sealed in December 1938, is in all likelihood still in a sealed dump behind a fireplace at 16 Rathmines Grove where it was left after the police raid on September 9, 1939. Unfortunately the present occupant is unwilling to permit access.

15. For the next thirty years IRA men would quote the Dáil authorization as sufficient reason to carry arms no matter what the laws of the *de facto* government in Leinster House might say. In a practising Catholic milieu this moral right to bear and to use arms had, the IRA found,

a most salutary effect on volunteers. The "government" theory did not have as long a life although technically it is still valid, thus the only *de jure* government of Ireland is a General Army Convention in session.

16. The RUC contended that the raid was a result of information on an impending IRA action; but since none was planned, it is more likely that the RUC moved on the basis of the very limited information on hand rather than wait for the balloon to go up, or off.

17. "The Government of the Irish Republic believe that a period of four days is sufficient notice for your government to signify its intentions in the matter of the military evacuation and for the issue of your Declaration of Abdication in respect of our country. Our Government reserve the right of appropriate action without further notice if upon the expiration of this period of grace, these conditions remain unfulfilled." Oglaigh na h-Éireann (Irish Republican Army). General Headquarters, Dublin, January 12th, 1939, to His Excellency The Rt. Hon. Viscount Halifax, G.C.B.

18. Later, some of the most vehement criticism of the direction of the campaign centred on this very limited operation. Once surprise had been lost, all subsequent operations would be far more difficult. The only really coherent explanation is that GHQ did not really plan on effective sabotage, hoping to frighten not punish the British.

19. One of the very few serious studies of Irish history after 1923 is Enno Stephan's *Spies in Ireland*, London, 1963, which treats in detail and with basic accuracy the German espionage efforts in Ireland during World War II.

20. One of those who evaded the police, Terry McLaughlin of Leitrim, actually had his bomb go off in his hand leaving acid burns all over his clothes. He had discarded his coat before anyone noticed and was more concerned about how he could meet a girl Sunday morning without a coat than about being arrested.

21. Subsequently the IRA was extremely bitter about the conduct of the police in Manchester who they accused not only of brutality but also in one case at least of falsifying evidence against Jack Duggan, his sister-in-law and her brother. Duggan got twenty years on police evidence that there had been explosives in every room in the house. Although he was an IRA man and had actually been out the night before, Duggan claimed that no one would leave stuff in *every* room.

22. On July 6, 1969, the *Sunday Times* (London) published what appears to be an accurate interview with the still anonymous Volunteer responsible.

23. Barnes had been carrying material for the IRA but was never in any position of responsibility nor did he know where his explosives were

used. McCormack made the bomb and put it in the carrier-bike. The bike-man later suffered delusions partially as a result of treatment in an Irish prison and was transferred for a time to an asylum for the criminally insane.

CHAPTER IX

The Momentum Ebbs: Conspiracy, Coercion, and Desperate Men, September 1939–April 1941

The first indication that amid the multiplying problems of maintaining Irish neutrality de Valera had spared the time to consider the potential impact of continued IRA activity came with the appointment of his new Cabinet. Patrick Ruttledge, assumed by some to be too gentle to grasp the nettle of coercion, was moved from the Department of Justice to that of Local Government and Public Health. The Justice portfolio went to Gerald Boland, who had proved himself a suitably hard man when he took over briefly from Ruttledge three years before while Ruttledge was ill. Boland had revealed little sympathy for his "fellow Republicans" still outside the constitutional structure. One of his first acts was to have the Special Branch of the Garda Síochána at Dublin Castle quietly draw up a list of potential trouble-makers. The list, hastily compiled and often based on faulty or outdated information, included a mixed bag of IRA people, past and present, agitators of the Left, friends of fascism, and even the odd descendant of the Luddite machine-breakers. The list, however, remained just that, not a wanted poster, because even under the strict security acts a citizen could not be interned without cause but had to appear before the Military Tribunal. Internment remained a last resort, but in the meantime the first steps to tranquillize the IRA began, with a series of raids on the offices and homes of known or suspected members.

One of the first raids netted a major haul. On Saturday, September 9, the police descended on a small terraced house, 16 Rathmines Grove.[1] At one swoop Special Branch nearly decimated GHQ and tore the centre of the net apart. Inside were Stephen Hayes, Larry Grogan, Peadar O'Flaherty, Willie McGuinness, Patrick McGrath, and Matty Tuite. As the police came in the front door, the GHQ staff rushed for the rear exit. Grogan ignoring shouts to stop tore down the back alley putting as much distance in back of him as possible. Then, almost clear, he ducked down a side lane only to find himself in a cul de sac. Hayes and Tuite had better luck; the moment they were out of sight they heaved themselves over a wall into a neighbouring garden and disappeared. The others were rounded up. McGuinness still had nearly eight thousand dollars with him and there was more money and scattered documents in the house. The police had not only picked up most of GHQ but most of the IRA's liquid assets. Things could have been worse, for several men who had regularly used the house, Michael Traynor, Michael Conway, and other GHQ people, had not been present, and Hayes at least had got away;[2] but the message was clear, the partial toleration of the Irish government was over and the freedom of movement of the men still on the run would be narrowly restricted. About the country the police were picking up men under the Offences Against the State Acts. Some, like Twomey, were released—Dublin being what it was his retirement was generally known. Others like Con Lehane, whose association with MacBride's faction ought to have ensured his release, were kept in jail either through ignorance or because of the rush of arrests.[3] By the end of the month almost every IRA unit had losses to report. All the highly visible men were lifted; Máirtín Ó Cadhain, who had created a flurry in the press when he had been dismissed from his teaching position in Galway by a bishop unimpressed with his radical ideas; Seamus Dowling, who had been acquitted of the accidental shooting of Christopher Bird during a training class in May, and Myles Heffernan, who had taken a major part in re-organizing the Dublin unit after 1938. Despite the Rathmines raid and the September arrests, the IRA was by no means broken. Some of the cautious, like O'Donovan, were unknown to the police; others, like Traynor and Conway, had been lucky; and many men already on full-time service were not easy to root out. Everything had, however, become far more difficult.

In the North Stormont had stepped up sweeps and searches during 1939, as the campaign in Britain had intensified. Although the Six Counties was not intended as a centre of action, the new seven-county IRA Northern Command had been unwilling simply to mark time and send the occasional Volunteer down to Dublin for processing. Belfast had an IRA Freedom Radio, produced a Northern edition of *War News*, and from time to time an enthusiastic unit detonated a bomb. This continuing activity coupled with the reports of campaign incidents in Britain created a highly charged atmosphere. Nationalist crowds had burned gasmasks, violated black-out regulations, and generally indicated their distaste for the Unionist regime and the British war effort.[4] To most Orangemen, more British than the British, such displays were little more than treason. The government at Stormont was determined that civil order would be maintained despite the provocation. A hard policy against the IRA was both essential and congenial. The December 1938 raids had failed to break the IRA and continued arrests were no more effective. Once war came, the men interned were served imprisonment orders for the duration of the war, although the innocent were weeded out to reduce the number to sixty. There was never any great difficulty in determining the hard core, for Republican prisoners inevitably refused to sign a recognizance.

In Dublin during the autumn of 1939, the reorganized GHQ tried to maintain the momentum of the English campaign; but without American money and with the routes into Britain closely watched, operations tapered off. The heavy pressure after the passage of the Prevention of Violence Bill in July had curtailed IRA activity even before the declaration of war. Now that Britain was at war the police and the population regarded the IRA campaign as not only wanton violence but also a threat to the war effort. Safe houses became fewer. The major operation groups became smaller. Close contact with Dublin and with other units grew rarer. Despite the obstacles, GHQ was undismayed; furthermore, the German card was yet to be played. Hayes had brought in an American radio through his contact in Wexford; and on October 29, GHQ finally managed to establish contact with the Abwehr operator and requested arms and supplies. The Germans seemed more interested in urging the IRA to come to terms with de Valera than in making specific arrangements for arms. As in the case of the original "contact" through O'Duffy, the Germans were completely innocent of Irish politics. To imagine that the IRA with over one hundred men in de Valera's prisons, some on hunger strike, would ever seek an accommodation with the arch apostate was naïve. Such an agreement might have been advantageous to Germany but the IRA, like the Abwehr, operated on the principle of sacred egotism. The IRA wanted aid to fight the common British enemy not advice on how to deny its Republican principles. Thus the radio message brought no swift aid but only mutual confusion. On December 29, a raid in Dublin picked up the radio and cut the German thread.

Meanwhile, things had begun to settle down somewhat. Jack McNeela in charge of publicity was producing *War News* as well as operating the radio. New safe houses had been set up. Training classes in sabotage continued. Men slipped back and forth to England if at a reduced rate. In Dublin the Military Tribunal began to sit. On October 16, Myles Heffernan was the first to be sentenced—he received three months for possession of documents, his sentence to run from August 14, the day of his arrest. As the sentences continued, the IRA men in prison reacted violently. On October 22, the Republican prisoners inside Mountjoy tried to blow their way out; but the explosion failed to clear a way to the outside. Increasingly, the dedicated turned to the traditional hunger strike. Increasingly, a pattern was being established: coercion led to IRA resistance, in prison and on the outside, this in turn led to sterner governmental measures.

During the autumn of 1939, the most public IRA resistance was the hunger strike. While the limited hunger strike with an announced time span is effective as a means of protest, the real threat to authority is a strike to the end. Few men have the will-power to starve to death in the silence and isolation of a prison cell and few governments wanted to be faced with the unpalatable alternatives of concession through compassion or of collaboration in self-murder. To concede too quickly would soon empty the prisons and make a mockery of the law. To wait too long would engender the wrath of a people all too familiar with their heritage of heroes who had sacrificed themselves for their beliefs. For the government the most distressing hunger strike was that of McGrath who everyone knew had vowed to secure his unconditional release or die. McGrath had been out in Easter Week and still carried a British bullet near his heart. To allow him to die—and die he would, for though weak in body his spirit was implacable—would be scandalous. His "crime" was loyalty to ideals once held by the men imprisoning him and his means no different than theirs had been in the past. Times may have changed but McGrath had not. Yet his release would be a public sign of weakness and the first step toward the collapse of public security.

There were already those who felt the government had over-reacted to the IRA threat. In England the campaign seemed to be sputtering to an end in flaming pillar boxes and nuisance balloon bombs in buses. On November 7, the government nevertheless announced that there would be no release for the men on hunger strike; but there was no fresh wave of arrests. Seán MacBride had instituted *habeas corpus* proceedings on behalf of Seamus Burke, to force the release of the men arrested on grounds that the government had acted unconstitutionally. He won his point. On December 1, fifty-three men were released as were the other IRA men as they completed their sentences. Although the police were still active, the sentences on IRA men were mild. Finally on December 9, McGrath in the forty-third day of his strike and very weak was told that he was to be released and moved to a hospital. The strike was over. With the IRA threat declining, the government could appear to be magnanimous. McGrath, however, was not in fact released but had to escape from custody to make good his promise never to come before the Military Tribunal.[5]

In Britain, at the Birmingham Assizes, the trial of those accused of the Coventry explosion on August 25 opened on December 11. All five pleaded innocent. What particularly enraged not only the IRA but a great many apolitical Irishmen was that neither Peter Barnes nor James McCormack had been directly responsible for the explosion. As Volunteers of the IRA, engaged in what they considered a military campaign, they had indeed been involved in the early stages of an operation against a legitimate target, a power station. The premature detonation had horrified them as well. Through Irish eyes the British seemed determined to extract their pound of flesh from the unwitting accomplices because they could not find the man responsible. Whatever the subtle distinctions of British law might be, too many Irishmen had been exposed in the past to British justice to be overly impressed. They were impressed with the calm courage and dignity of Barnes and McCormack hopelessly trapped in a situation not of their own making. When the two men were sentenced to death on December 14, no one in Ireland was surprised at perfidious Albion. There were to be two more martyrs for Ireland.[6] In response, the IRA English units launched a broad series of attacks on the British mail service over the next several days. The IRA "problem" had not, as hoped, tapered off.

During November Hayes decided that with America cut off and the German contact problematical the IRA was soon going to feel the pinch. The basic and most effective weapon in the IRA arsenal for a decade had been the Thompson submachine gun. The Thompson had been smuggled into Ireland year in, year out, beginning in 1921. Occasionally they came in dribs and drabs but there had been several huge shipments. For IRA purposes the Thompson was an excellent gun, accurate, rapid-firing, and easy to hide. The great difficulty was that the Thompson used .45-calibre ammunition, rarely available in Europe in any quantity. The obvious source to renew the IRA's Thompson ammunition was the Irish Army, who were well supplied with Thompson and .45-calibre ammunition. In the course of discussions at GHQ it was decided to investigate a raid on the Magazine Fort in Phoenix Park or on the nearby Islandbridge barracks. As early as 1937 when Fitzpatrick had been C/S, the IRA had looked into the possibilities of the Magazine Fort. Fitzpatrick gave up on the project because he could see no way to store the booty securely, but times had changed. Hayes felt he must take the risk.

Since the September raid Hayes had slipped further into hiding, delegating more power to GHQ members and influencing events mainly through intermediaries. In this case, the intelligence work and preliminary planning were taken over by McNeela assisted by Traynor and Tom Doyle. It became clear almost immediately that there was every chance of success. GHQ soon had access to all the necessary information on procedures within the Magazine Fort. Security was negligible and with Christmas approaching even the limited security usually enforced would be relaxed. In fact it might be possible to bring off not a swift, snatch-and-grab raid but a major operation to clear out the Magazine Fort armoury and perhaps Islandbridge as well. Hayes was delighted and gave the word to go ahead. The Dublin unit was alerted. Drivers selected and paid. Lorries were organized. C/Os in the country were informed that safe dumps were going to be needed. All that remained was to wait for the holiday season.

The routine at the Magazine Fort had been almost unchanged for years; in fact, the C/O had been assigned to his position in 1924. The Fort was protected by a tiny guard of bored men who could be anticipated to perform their chores by rote. To slip through the gate by a rush, round up the guard, and seal off communications would not even require a major attack group or as it turned out extensive intelligence. The presence of sufficient men to load the ammunition on the lorries was more vital than gaining entry. The only organizational slip-up was that the men responsible for providing dumps were not informed of the scope of the raid or of the quantity of the material they would have to hide. Even the most conscientious QM was only prepared for a modest haul. By the middle of December, GHQ aspirations had gone beyond modest proportions.

Any raid on an Irish military installation would surely set the government fluttering but what GHQ had devised would obviously produce a major scandal. The goal was now a clean sweep of Islandbridge and the Magazine Fort or at least as much as a dozen heavy lorries could carry, which was nearly all the reserve ammunition available to the Irish Army. As always GHQ failed to consider the impact of the raid on others or on the future of the IRA. While there was speculation within GHQ on what might, once the ammunition had been acquired, be done both in the North and in Dublin,[7] supposedly the prime priority remained the English campaign, which required money and explosives but not cartridges. Just as practical considerations and strategic planning had not been of prime concern in 1938, the planning for the December raid concentrated on immediate tactics without much thought for the future.

At 8.35 on the evening of December 23, the bell on the outside gate of the Magazine Fort rang. The military policeman on duty saw a civilian standing on the other side of the grill holding a bicycle in one hand and a package in the other. When he opened the outer gate to collect the package, the delivery man shoved a gun into him and rushed him back through the inner gate. By then the other members of the attack squad were into the Fort and rounding up the other members of the guard. With their own man on the gate, the inside was cleared of the remaining guards. Since the Magazine Fort was surrounded by Phoenix Park, then always closed at night, there was little chance of interruption. When the C/O of the Fort, Captain Joseph Curran, returned from a visit into Dublin he was picked up by the IRA man on the gate and put in with the captured guards. In the meantime the lorries had been brought in and were being crammed with ammunition. Doyle was inside the magazine with his chart and light checking off the crates. The men worked so fast that within minutes some were gasping on the point of exhaustion. Since the Islandbridge attack had aborted, the lorries were sent up into the Magazine Fort. In little over an hour, the last one pulled away crammed to the top with the final crates. The rather peculiar traffic in and out of the Park and the odd men dashing about in the dark had finally come to the notice of the authorities when

an IRA patrol had fired on a military policeman at the gate of the Islandbridge barracks. By the time the alarm went up and the army sorted itself
out, all that patrols could find were a few slow IRA men slipping out of
the park. Five men were picked up. The IRA was free and clear with
thirteen lorries of ammunition, 1,084,000 rounds, the bulk of the Irish
Army's reserve supply.

Panic set in quickly. The Chief of Staff, Major-General M. Brennan, and
senior members of the Department of Defence met and spent most of the
night drawing up plans for an immediate mass search to get back the
ammunition. All police, military garrisons, and reserve units were notified.
By dawn the greatest combined search operation in the history of the Irish
army had begun. Nothing could move on the roads without attracting
attention. Spotter planes were used. Road blocks cluttered eastern Ireland.
Traffic crawled from one spot check to another. Everyone who might have
seen or heard something was contacted. Houses of known Republicans
were raided. The hills were patrolled, turf piles overturned, barns combed
out, and back rooms ransacked. For days all of Ireland watched fascinated
as the great December cartridge hunt continued.

If the raid had gone off beautifully for GHQ, the next days were a series
of cruel disappointments. The local units had simply been overwhelmed
at the quantity of ammunition. The good, safe dumps were intended for
a few rifles, a Thompson or two, and the odd box of ammunition. Asked to
dispose of 100,000 cartridges within a few hours, the men were desperate.
Cellars were stacked with Thompson ammunition. The old shed was full,
the car loaded, even the space under the piano filled and the lorry still sat
in the lane half-full. Seán Ashe, C/O of Kildare, had prepared more carefully than most, setting up a dozen dumps even though he was certain that
he would be ordered to drive his lorry straight to the border to participate
in a Northern campaign. Despite his efforts the searches uncovered over
three tons of ammunition in Kildare but he had managed to squirrel away
four tons.[8] No one else did as well. For men who had formerly scrambled
for fifty rounds the totals suddenly gained and lost boggled the imagination.
On January 1, the IRA had already lost 850,000 rounds. Many old dumps
around the country had come to light. The repeated raids swept up another
levee of IRA men. The American radio transmitter along with Jack
McNeela and three other men had been caught in Ashgrove House on
December 29. In Cork on January 2 Detective Officer John Roche had
been shot and killed during the arrest of Tomás MacCurtain, son of
the martyred Lord Mayor. In Dublin a general round-up brought in scores
of men who on refusing to answer questions were swiftly sentenced. All
the while reports of new finds continued: two-and-a-half tons in Dundalk,
eight tons in Swords, sixty-six cases of Thompson gun ammunition in

South Armagh returned by the RUC, one hundred crates containing 120,000 rounds at Straffan.

The success of the searches and seizures, which would eventually net more than had been lost, by no means calmed the fears of the government. On January 3, the Dáil met in an emergency session so that the Minister of Justice, Gerald Boland, could demand additional powers to crush the IRA. On the following day the Emergency Powers Act received a third reading but still had to battle its way through a thicket of legal challenges. It was clear that only a brief respite remained before the police with their lists in hand would be on their way to round up the suspects. In the meantime the Military Tribunal continued to hand out sentences to those already arrested. Once Boland was empowered to intern on suspicion hundreds of men would be swept up. At the Curragh military camp in Kildare, the first prisoners were locked in the large, bleak, bitterly cold Glasshouse while additional hardly more pleasant facilities were prepared at Tintown for the anticipated influx of internees.

Despite the police pressure many of the key IRA people evaded the big round-ups. Hayes went further out of sight and at times out of touch entirely. Many slipped into new rooms in Dublin. In the Six Counties the Northern Command HQ had long since battened down the hatches and despite regular attrition maintained their strength. The Western Command centred on Galway had to be reorganized. Cork had been badly hit by the arrests and never really regained momentum. The Kerry people seemed to grow increasingly concerned with Kerry and distant from the GHQ in Dublin although a few young Kerry men continued to supply some new blood. Control from the centre grew looser. Movement in and out of Dublin was dangerous. Hayes found fewer and fewer competent men to fill the gaps and in some cases did not try. No effort was made to co-opt men onto the decimated Army Council; in fact, with Russell still in America and Fleming in jail in Britain under the name Walker, only Hayes was left active. Still things were not hopeless. The Magazine Fort raid had raised morale if not ammunition supplies. A prison riot in Derry Jail on December 25 had again attracted wide attention to the plight of political prisoners. Most encouraging was the wave of sympathy for Barnes and McCormack scheduled to hang on February 7. As their appeals failed there was growing anger and on February 5 at the Mansion House in Dublin five thousand met to protest. Two days later both were executed at Winson Green Jail in Birmingham. On the following day Ireland went into national mourning, flags flew at half mast, theatres and cinemas closed, sports meets were cancelled, and masses were offered in the major churches for the repose of their souls. On February 21, at a public meeting, a new more radical Republican party, Córas na Poblachta, was formed by old

IRA men (Seán Dowling, Simon Donnelly,Séamus Gibbons, and Seán Fitzpatrick) angered by de Valera's policies.[9] For the IRA, however, there was no real return on the Irish emotional investment in the two martyrs. Indignation faded. Córas na Poblachta ran aground on the hard rocks of Fianna Fáil at the first by-election. GHQ was left with multiplying problems and dwindling solutions.

Even the unswerving realized that the English campaign had faltered if not failed. Most of the operation officers and unit commanders had been arrested or withdrawn. Even the nets and groups rebuilt under stress had come apart. Skilled men to repair the damage were no longer available; in fact, it appeared that even men were no longer available; a volunteer arrested turned out to be a sixteen-year-old Dublin boy, Brendan Behan.[10] The last real bomb incidents came on the eve of the execution of Barnes and McCormack. After that there were a few minor explosions, the odd fire, and then silence. Really more important than skilled men had been money. By 1940, with the American pipeline shut down and most of the activists on the run, spending not contributing money, the pressure was very, very tight. GHQ with barely enough funds for day-to-day operations could do little for the English units. Strapped for funds and limited in personnel, GHQ was forced to abandon the campaign. With the English venture gone, the IRA had to devise a new direction or as in the past wilt from boredom. The Magazine Fort raid had momentarily opened up wide vistas but all these new options had been lost with the ammunition.

After January 1940 much IRA staff activity throughout the country concentrated on little more than maintaining the organization. Recruiting was negligible. As the German threat became more apparent, many young men were attracted into the Local Defence Forces, which increased to a strength of 250,000 by the end of the war. The IRA men who had evaded the big sweep into the Curragh lay low and quietly tried to keep things going without attracting attention. With the campaign over, there was no longer any clear call from Dublin and no real demand in the South for new action. The clandestine *War News* was distributed, money for the prisoners' dependents collected, parades and camps held on rare occasions; but as they had in the past, most waited for word from the centre.

In the Six Counties, tempered by two years of RUC pressure and exposed to the reality of British occupation, the Northern Command was far more aggressive. In the summer of 1939 McGlade had reorganized on a seven-county basis, including Donegal at Dublin's request, and brought in younger men like Seán McCaughey, a metal worker who spent the summers teaching Irish in the Glens of Antrim. McGlade, very much the Belfast city man, shrewd and meticulous, felt that McCaughey was the best soldier in the country—a handsome, intense man, probing, analytical, completely dedicated to his religion and his Republican principles, he seemed to possess all the virtues of an ideal IRA man. When McCaughey returned in December 1939 after a short prison sentence in Dublin, McGlade made him C/O of the Northern Command and served as his Adjutant. One of the IRA's best finds was John Graham, a Protestant attracted to Republicanism by the Irish Union of Denis Ireland, which unwittingly supplied the IRA with some first-rate people. Elsewhere, despite the comings and goings during the campaign, the Northern Command built up a solid corps of good men. Eoin McNamee from Tyrone who had been in and out of England for three years as an operations officer was a solid man, though a bit to the Left of the usually apolitical Belfast people. Pearse Kelly, who on his own hook had reorganized Dungannon, looked promising. There were several other good hard men attached to headquarters although some of the best men had been shifted to Dublin or arrested in England. In 1938 Belfast alone had had a strength of nearly five hundred; by 1940 the arrests and resignations had cut the number to three or four hundred. To replace the losses the Northern Command created an auxiliary branch whose members were not required to follow the more rigid Army Orders. With their newly burnished organization, the make-work of putting out *War News* and collecting money did not seem enough.

Always keenly interested in intelligence, the Northern Command HQ had built up contacts with men in every British army camp in the North. One man had been asked to enlist in the British army solely to supply certain detailed information. Perhaps the most exotic of all auxiliary units was inside the Ballykinlar British army camp where five men and their IRA C/O reported into HQ regularly. To exploit the opening, a decision was made to carry out a snatch-and-grab raid for Sten guns at Ballykinlar. Liam McWilliams and Billy Graham organized the affair by lifting the longest, most elegant limousine readily available in Belfast. With their swanky transportation, the IRA men drove directly into the camp but missed the right hut and had to settle for rifles instead of Stens. The British sentry was bound, gagged, and popped in the back of the car while the men, working under the eyes of a crowd straggling back from the cinema, moved the rifles out one and two at a time. When the hut was cleared, they drove grandly out again, dumped the limousine, and put the sentry up overnight in a little club off Falls Road, where he got his fish and chips and an uneasy night's sleep on the billiard table before he was released the next morning. The next day for the first time the new Irish Republican Radio came on the air at three in the afternoon on the medium waveband to announce that a couple of hundred rifles had been seized, hoping to force the British to admit the raid. The radio broadcast again that evening at eight. After that, broadcasting continued once weekly after the programme had been distributed throughout Belfast on broadsheets. It was possible to walk through the side streets off Falls Road at the appropriate time and hear every radio tuned in to the IRA broadcast, to the dismay of the RUC who had failed to turn up a clue to the wandering transmitter.

In Dublin during February, GHQ more often reacted to events than determined them. In an effort to knit up the ravelled ends of the organization, meetings were held, but these often led only to more arrests. On February 17, the officers of the Western Command were meeting with GHQ Staff men in the Meath Hotel in Dublin when the police and army descended. Two hundred men surrounded the hotel and collected the whole lot. The IRA lost sixteen men including the C/O of the Western Command, Tony D'Arcy, and Michael Traynor of GHQ. Increasingly the scene of action shifted inside Irish prisons complicating the duties of the already hard-pressed GHQ. When the Meath Hotel men were put in Mountjoy, frustration and traditional Republican prison policy forced a crisis. As always, IRA prisoners were organized into a regular unit with an elected C/O; and as always, the unit insisted on political treatment. Not only was political treatment denied but both food and the conditions in Mountjoy were appalling. In an effort to force changes the six-man prison-staff, McNeela, D'Arcy, MacCurtain, Traynor, Thomas Grogan, and J. Plunkett, went on a hunger strike with the understanding that they would continue to the end and then be replaced by six more Volunteers. The Irish government ignored the strike and continued bringing prisoners before the Military Tribunal. When an effort was made to remove D'Arcy and McNeela, both weakened by the strike, the prisoners refused to allow them to be taken. The result was a wild and violent riot during which several IRA men were badly beaten. The hunger strike continued through March into April attracting growing concern as D'Arcy and McNeela weakened. The government would not back down. On April 16, Tony D'Arcy died; on April 19 McNeela followed him.[11] At this stage the prisoners were given to understand that political treatment would be given to IRA men. Simultaneously, Hayes, who had disapproved of the strike, sent in word from GHQ through Father O'Hare to call off the strike.

For most IRA men Mountjoy and Arbour Hill, the coldest prison in Europe, were way stations on the road to the Curragh Camp. Although the sentences handed out by the Military Tribunal were short—the "crime" was usually refusing to answer questions—the length of sentence was in fact immaterial. Boland's new powers ensured that men released from prison went directly into the Curragh Camp, and internment would last as long as the government felt an emergency existed.

The first C/O of prisoners at the Curragh was Billy Mulligan. Most of the better-known men were still in Arbour Hill or Mountjoy. The government, caught by surprise by the need for a concentration camp, had neither the time nor the inclination to set up an elaborate establishment but had cordoned off an area of bleak, wooden huts with a barbed-wire fence. Sanitary and kitchen facilities were primitive, the huts nearly derelict, and recreation possibilities remote. For discipline and the hardcore cases, there was always the Glasshouse, even more unattractive if possible. The food was monotonous; life was monotonous. Most of the men spent their days bored prey to schism, recrimination and dispute. One of the first serious divisions of opinion came with the transfer of Larry Grogan and O'Flaherty into the Curragh on the completion of their sentences at Arbour Hill. To the surprise of IRA staff in the camp, Grogan informed them that as a member of the Irish Government, courtesy of the Second Dáil, he was assuming the leadership of the camp. Normal IRA policy is that a man loses all rank in prison, and the internees had assumed that the Army Council outside was the government, not Grogan and O'Flaherty. Mulligan was unwilling to divide the camp over the issue or disobey the Army Council—Grogan was allowed to take over Almost at once Grogan decided that conditions were appalling and unlikely to get any better without IRA pressure.[12]

The plan was to burn down certain of the prison huts. On December 14, 1940, the fires were set and with the help of a brisk wind raced through the tinder-dry buildings.[13] The authorities reacted immediately and harshly. The camp was surrounded by fully armed soldiers backed by armoured cars. All the prisoners were rounded up by soldiers carrying small arms and locked into the remaining huts from Saturday evening to Monday morning without food. The suspected ring-leaders were taken out and forced to run through a double line of soldiers equipped with batons and revolvers. Most arrived at the other end of the gauntlet bruised and beaten. They were taken to the Glasshouse.[14] Some were beaten again and all kept in solitary confinement for ten weeks. On Monday morning, when the rest of the prisoners were finally released from their huts, the soldiers were waiting outside with arms at the ready. When the men, as was the custom, began to line up in hut order for breakfast, the soldiers suddenly opened fire without warning. Apparently they had been informed that the prisoners would not be allowed to line up, but whatever the explanation they continued firing into the stunned and milling crowd. Barney Casey fell to the ground shot in the back. A bullet grazed Martin Staunton's face and another struck Walter Mitchell's shoe bruising his heel. Bob Flanagan and Art Moynihan were hit. Then in the sudden silence Billy Mulligan walked directly to the gate and demanded a stretcher for Casey who was lying crumpled on the ground, his face and chest covered with a bloody froth. He died two hours later. To the prisoners then and later the massacre of December 16 was unprovoked and inexcusable, an exercise in brutality hushed up by the government. At the subsequent inquest Seán MacBride was allowed to ask a single question—"Why was Barney Casey shot in the back?" The inquest was adjourned at once. That the policy of hard protest had led directly to violence and brutality might have been anticipated.

With the removal of Grogan, Liam Leddy of Cork became C/O of prisoners and tried to hold the camp together. But as the futile months passed, and eventually the wasted years, schism, dissent, and dispute multiplied. One of the most unwelcome new internees was Neil Gould Verschoyle, a dedicated communist who had studied in Moscow and married a Russian girl. Gould soon surrounded himself with the IRA men who had either been in Spain with the International Brigade or were attracted by his Marxian ideas. Many devout IRA men were horrified at the presence of the Red Menace in their midst and demanded that he be ostracized. A communist bloc came into being. Soon there was another bloc formed by Tadhg Lynch, a prickly independent Corkman, who defied IRA policy over the minor matter of using coal—the prisoners had been ordered to refuse it. Several other men who either could not or would not accept camp policy drifted into Lynch's hut. The real break, however, occurred in December 1941 when Pearse Kelly, briefly C/S and representative of the Northern Command, challenged Leddy's leadership. Regional pride, old feuds, and the bile of boredom all played a part in Kelly's coup. Kelly was elected C/O by a group that in time comprised the vast majority, while Leddy held the loyalty of a smaller orthodox group. In 1942 several internees tried to remain neutral only to be ostracized by both sides. Kelly got rid of Gould by privately appealing to Cardinal MacRory underscoring the danger to the souls of IRA men exposed to ungodly communism. The other cliques and factions remained, the divisions festering in the isolation and loneliness of the Camp.

And as time crept by, the internees lost hope. Some signed out while on long parole. Others gave in and signed out. The rumours and reports of the divisions and decay of the IRA on the outside alienated others. Few gave up their principles; but most felt the years were slipping away uselessly while they rotted forgotten. Outside their families struggled without funds. Careers were aborted, fiancées found other men, children grew up into strangers, the world moved on leaving them behind. The usual activities of prison camps—the paper *Barbed Wire*, the classes in Russian by Gould, German by O'Donovan, and Irish by Máirtín Ó Cadhain, the endless seminars on policy and politics, the games and tournaments, the shows and dramas—only made life barely tolerable as the men waited for eventual release, never sure how long their dull agony would continue.[15]

If life in the Curragh were dull and futile, killing to the spirit, the fate of the IRA hard-core prisoners transferred to Portlaoise prison was a living death. Key men in the IRA were treated like common criminals. Among them were Tomás MacCurtain, whose death sentence had been commuted at the last minute with the gallows already erected and the hangman on call; Seán McCaughey, also with a commuted death sentence, and Liam Rice, wounded in a gun battle with Irish detectives. They were ordered to wear prison clothes, accept letters with prison numbers on the top, and obey conventional prison routine. The little group of men refused. Since they would not wear prison clothing, the authorities let them remain naked but for their blankets. They could not attend mass since they were not presentable. They would not accept letters with prison numbers, so they received none. They would not obey the routine, so they were locked in their cells. Sitting month after month, year after year, in the bleak solitary cells, they were taken out once a week for a bath, and for the rest of the week lived the life of an animal trapped in a burrow. Even in solitary confinement there was no privacy. The lights were turned on day and night at erratic intervals for security checks. There were no books, no contact with each other, no opportunity to talk with anyone. That they did not all go mad is a remarkable comment on man's capacity for survival. Some suffered from delusions, white horses standing in the cell, or collapsed physically under the strain; but most of the little handful persisted until their sentences were completed or release came.

In the North, Republican internees suffered the same agonies as the men in the Curragh but with even less hope of release and in more confining quarters. To rationalize the physical problems of internment, Stormont had taken many of the men out of the prisons in Belfast and Derry and locked them on the ancient steamer *Al Rawdah* in Lough Neagh. In time these internees were released or transferred back to conventional prisons; but no matter where they were, the tale of internment was the same. There were splits and disagreements. There were riots and attempted escapes. There was the same weight of frustration and boredom, for some resignation and for others defection.

In Britain, prison conditions for the men arrested during the bombing campaign were if possible as foul as those at Portlaoise. British prisons in the 'forties and even later were far closer to the nightmares of Dickens than to any dreams of modern penologists. Huge, grotesque, brooding buildings permeated with damp, bitterly cold winter and summer, the prisons were great draughty stone cages without recreational or reformational facilities where men were brutalized by a system calcified by routine and rote. The Anglo-Saxon mind is not attuned to the concept of political crime. The attempt by the IRA to alter the inviolate system outraged their captors much as their predecessors had been outraged in previous generations by the arrogance of the Fenians. In the best of circumstances, prison officials would have viewed the arrival of IRA men with a jaundiced eye since it heralded hunger strikes, riots, and escapes; but with crimes like the Coventry explosion on the books and bombs going off in luggage rooms and cinemas, requests for special treatment only antagonized the already intolerant. Wardens understood decent armed robbers and wife murderers; but Irish revolutionaries were beyond comprehension, beyond reform, and endless trouble. Nothing makes this more clear than the reports prepared in Parkhurst Prison by the Catholic Priest Father Lynch for the authorities. Their subject was Joe Collins, a West Cork man arrested in Manchester and sentenced to twenty years; "very little chance of becoming law-abiding . . . A very difficult case, and a confirmed Rebel,—both here and in Ireland . . . There's no change in this prisoner's political ideas . . . Is apparently unmoved by getting 20 years P.S. . . . It's most doubtful whether this man will ever lead a law-abiding life." Collins's sentiments were no doubt taken as ample evidence of the "perverse" nature of the Irish rebels but equally telling is that Collins managed to acquire his own record with the help of a professional, i.e. criminal, safecracker.

The most deliberate and direct assault on the British prison system came at Dartmoor where the IRA prisoners rioted and set fire to D block in 1940. The men refused to wear prison uniforms. For over two years they remained isolated in punishment cells, completely naked during the day since everything in the cell was removed at dawn but a Bible and a compressed paper pot. The only variation in the routine was the arrival once a week of the guards to dress, usually forcibly, the prisoners so that they could be brought before the governor to receive an additional week in the punishment cells for violating the rules on conventional dress. The rules did not change then or later; and in time, most of the long-term prisoners settled down to serve their sentences without, of course, changing their political ideas.

Outside of the prisons and camps, the IRA had not only to continue operations but maintain the prisoners' dependents, a double burden under heavy police pressure. While the Meath Hotel arrests in February 1940 threw the Western Command into disarray, GHQ still had several competent staff members, Michael Conway, McGrath, and a few others brought in from country units. The most important addition, however, remained a dead secret. Jim Crofton, who had worked on the docks in New York during the Free State years, had returned to join the Broy Harriers to help clean up the Blueshirts. He had grown disenchanted with the Special

Branch, since he was a rebel by nature not a policeman, and with his so-called Republican colleagues, who had been contaminated by the lures of the secret police. When the big searches and sweeps against the IRA men began he lost patience altogether. He had known Hayes in Wexford and in December before a raid on one of the IRA safe houses on Victoria Street in Donnybrook managed to find his way to the Chief of Staff to warn him. To have a sound man inside Dublin Castle was a fantastic coup and Hayes was delighted. Hayes and Crofton also made contact with a police clerk in the Castle; no one was ever certain how trustworthy he was, but every little nugget of information helped.

GHQ decided to use the inside information from the man in the Castle to strike at Special Branch headquarters. Joe Atkinson, who was known in Dublin as Dougherty, and Black Dan O'Toole from Belfast were the men chosen to take a small squad into the Castle and place a bomb in the radio storeroom. The idea was to destroy all Special Branch communication equipment and retaliate for the deaths of D'Arcy and McNeela. Using huge wire-clippers he had smuggled into the Castle by strapping them to his back, Crofton opened a way in for the bomb squad. But he was on the outskirts of Dublin, establishing an alibi, when the squad came in, and in his absence they missed the door and planted the bomb in the wrong room. When it detonated on April 25, five members of Special Branch were injured, adding one more grievance to the police litany of complaints against the IRA. On May 7, an IRA attempt to seize the dispatches of the British Representative, Sir John Maffey, developed into a wild gunfight on the Holles Street corner of Merrion Square near the centre of Dublin. The two Irish policemen carrying the dispatches in a motorcycle with sidecar were forced to the kerb by a car. The men inside opened fire with a Thompson and the two policemen answered with revolver fire even after they were repeatedly hit. The IRA men ran out of time and drove off leaving the two men, William McSweeney and William Shanahan, sprawled and bloody on the street, both severely wounded. The pattern of provocation, retaliation, and vengeance had been set. It was not to be altered for years.

Hayes and GHQ were well aware that the pressures building up against the IRA had to be reversed, but without money or men little could be done. Even a dozen more Croftons could not tip the balance. The one unexploited possibility left was the fragile German thread, broken with the loss of the transmitter in December. Actually, the Germans had sent a contact agent in February, but their vaunted Teutonic efficiency had completely evaporated. Repeatedly Abwehr's Irish adventures would be more ludicrous than profitable. Their agent, Ernst Weber-Drohl, who knew little of Ireland, landed from a submarine, lost his transmitter, and was arrested almost immediately. He did manage to deliver a message to O'Donovan before he attracted police attention but that was the limit of his activity. His strange, wandering story was so unlikely and his potential as a German agent so negligible that he was actually able to talk his way out of custody and turned, equally unsuccessfully, to an Irish stage career as a weight-lifter—Alex the Strong. Although O'Donovan had managed to get a message of sorts through Francis Stuart, an Irish professor married to Maud Gonne MacBride's daughter, there was still no real communication with Abwehr.

Hayes decided to send his own man across to Britain and then on to Belgium, still neutral, where he could slip across the border to Germany. As he was increasingly doing, Hayes went outside the ranks of the IRA for his man. Stephen Held, a forty-three-year-old Dublin businessman, accepted the mission. Hayes wanted Held to ask for assistance, hopefully against the British in the North, but most important to re-establish the link with Abwehr. The Germans were delighted with Held, although they found him a rather suspicious courier, nervous, inexperienced, and vague. The proposed joint attack on the North, still at best a hazy prospect from any point of view, was labelled the Artus Plan. Important for the IRA, Abwehr again viewed the Irish game with more enthusiasm. Unknown to GHQ Abwehr had received word on January 24 that Seán Russell in New York would be interested in coming to Germany. With Held's arrival and renewed contact with Dublin, Abwehr began to shuffle over the Irish possibilities.

German intelligence operations were still splintered by competing bureaux, overlapping authorities, and contradictory ambitions. Essentially in the case of Ireland the Foreign Office continued to feel that Dublin's neutrality was highly desirable and could best be maintained by non-interference. Great waves of German agents appearing in Ireland could only antagonize de Valera and provoke the British. While Ireland was far down on everyone's list of priorities, Abwehr felt that Russell's proposed trip held too many interesting possibilities to be discouraged. After further negotiations, Russell was slipped onto an American ship in New York through Clan na Gael contacts in the appropriate unions and arrived unnoticed in Genoa in April. He arrived in Berlin on May 1 just as the next Abwehr agent, ignorant of his arrival, was preparing to parachute into Ireland to establish firm contact with the IRA.

Of all the German agents sent into Ireland, the new man, Hermann Goertz, proved most successful, although on his previous record his selection was nearly as inept as the rest.[16] Goertz had already been arrested in Britain for espionage in 1935 as the result of a caper that the British regarded as hopelessly bungled. His four-year sentence, which he finished in 1939, may have reflected official opinion that Goertz was not worth the trouble. His background for the Irish game was not great, but at least he spoke English and had actually been to Ireland in 1927. His efforts in Germany to prepare himself for his mission had largely been futile, for even Francis Stuart knew little of the contemporary IRA. On May 5, Goertz's black Heinkel 111 took off for Ireland. He jumped into Meath far from his few contacts or his intended drop zone. His radio parachuted with him drifted away out of sight and disappeared. Left on his own, he stuffed his parachute under a hedge and began to make his way in uniform at night toward Stuart's home in Wicklow. His progress was so slow that he discarded his uniform and plodded on during the daylight hours. After four weary days he reached the Stuarts' house in Laragh. He was on the edge of exhaustion but the link was re-established.

Iseult Stuart contacted O'Donovan, who collected Goertz and took him to his own house in Shankill in South Dublin. From there Goertz at last reached Hayes, but from the first the IRA leader proved a disappointment to the German agent. Hayes was no charismatic leader. He had no real intellectual intensity, nor aura of power, nor, as Goertz soon discovered, any coherent plan of operations. When Goertz learned of the "ridiculous street shooting" in Dublin, he was stunned and dismayed. The IRA did not come up to his high expectations. Goertz, of course, had no real knowledge of the IRA and seemed to find it difficult to understand, as others had before him, why Hayes could not give up the internecine feud with de Valera and unite for German purposes. Goertz felt that the IRA should concentrate on the Six Counties, a proposition which Hayes seemed to accept. The truth of the matter, however, was that the IRA wanted arms and money, not advice on how best to serve German ends.

The clash of aspirations and personalities between Hayes and Goertz was interrupted by one more disaster on May 22 when Held's house on Templeogue Road, where Goertz had been hiding, was raided. Held was arrested. Most of Goertz's equipment, money, files, intelligence reports as well as his personal belongings were seized. The raid gave the Irish government solid proof that the IRA–German link existed, that a pipeline had been opened to IRA GHQ through which money had begun flowing: Goertz's safe held 18,500 dollars. Mrs. Stuart was picked up and the hunt was on for the mysterious "Mr. Brady" who had been Held's boarder. The German Ambassador, Dr. Eduard Hempel, eager to buttress Irish neutrality, was horrified and had to be soothed by an urgent explanation from the Foreign Office in Berlin that the agent meant no harm to Ireland. For Goertz the raid provided an escape from the protection of the IRA, which he suspected, and Hayes, who he felt was a weak and insecure reed. He went to ground in Dublin and although he maintained regular contact with Hayes and O'Donovan, in the main he kept very still, so still that Irish military intelligence assumed he had left the country.

While Goertz was deep in his Irish misadventures, the IRA again faced the problem of finance. The German money had come and gone and a second freshet of German dollars in the near future appeared unlikely. The Northern Command had in desperation suggested reverting to an old IRA tactic of the Tan War—bank raids. In Belfast after careful rehearsal the IRA hit three banks at the dot of eleven in the morning. The three squads, protected by a covering party, were in, out, and away within minutes; and the IRA was solvent. The funds so acquired were scrupulously accounted for, since the IRA was most reluctant to perform such near-criminal operations. Old debts were paid, dependants bankrolled, and HQ funded. In September the money had run out and once more the Belfast IRA raided two banks and several post offices. This time one Volunteer was caught and sentenced to ten years, but the Northern Command was again solvent. Force of circumstances drove the IRA to robbery in Dublin and Belfast several more times in the course of the next two years, but such operations were undertaken with great reluctance since only by a considerable stretch of the imagination could bank raids be considered military operations.[17] Other men on the fringe of the IRA, or outright criminals, followed their example and robbed for personal gain rather than political necessity and more items were added to the roster of the IRA "crimes".

The combination of the bank raids, the first since 1922, the gun fights in the streets, and the revelation of the German link resulted in intensive police activity in all thirty-two counties. In Dublin, the government felt that the crisis point of neutrality was at hand. The total German victories in May and June on the Western front had swept France out of the war and left Britain vulnerable to invasion. The British were desperate and might very well occupy the South to secure a safe flank and naval bases for the anti-submarine campaign. Despite the IRA, relations with London had remained cordial, although Irish neutrality was hardly popular.[18] During the previous winter close military contacts had been maintained and the British remained sympathetic to Ireland's military needs in case of a German invasion. During June and July, while the German Luftwaffe sought to smash the RAF over southern England, negotiations for a joint defence plan were undertaken. Although nothing came of this effort, the Irish government remained deeply concerned about the IRA–German contact. Irish intelligence was aware of the ebbing vitality of the IRA but there was no telling what wild adventure GHQ might launch in desperation.

During the tense and nervous summer of the Battle of Britain, Special

Branch chipped away at IRA strength. Key men were lost one by one. Patrick McNeela and Conway were shot and arrested. On August 17, the Special Branch raided 98a Rathgar Road in Dublin. The shop had been watched for some time; but in an effort to be first to sweep up the IRA, Sergeant Denny O'Brien decided to go in before his competitors in the Special Branch could get the credit and reward money from the slush fund. Inside McGrath, Tommy Harte, and Tom Hunt were determined not to give up without a fight. Bursting out of the door firing revolvers and a Thompson gun, they cut down three Special Branch men, killing Sergeant McKeown and Detective Hyland and wounding Detective Brady. The three IRA men rushed down the street away from the stunned detectives who had expected a swift coup and a fat reward. The police opened fire and hit Harte. When McGrath went back to help him, both were arrested. Hunt managed to elude the police until August 22 when he was arrested in a house on Gloucester Street. On the same day a raid on a safe house in 22 Lansdowne Road netted four more IRA men.

The Military Court met and sentenced McGrath, Hunt, and Harte to death. Despite appeals and McGrath's Easter Week record only Hunt's sentence was commuted. McGrath and Harte were executed in Mountjoy on September 6. Although police officers had been killed in the course of their duties there was considerable sympathy for the two men partly because Special Branch was acquiring a shoot-first-and-ask-questions-later reputation. On August 3, in Cork John J. Kavanagh had been shot down near an incomplete tunnel outside the Cork jail. There was every indication that the tunnel had been watched and that Kavanagh and two others had walked into an ambush. For their part the Special Branch remembered the bomb in the Castle, the men wounded on Merrion Street, and the two killed in front of 98a Rathgar Road. There seemed no way to end the street warfare that so distressed Goertz on tactical grounds and was increasingly disgusting all Irishmen on moral grounds.

One of the most unfortunate effects of the wave of August arrests and gun fights was long delayed but still deadly. The Special Branch had turned 22 Landsdowne Road into a trap-house, after the raid on August 22. Into it walked Michael Devereux, sometime QM of the Wexford Battalion. GHQ received two reports, one from Crofton and one from an IRA man in the next cell to Devereux, that under heavy pressure from Denny O'Brien he had talked and then been released. Hayes was not particularly inclined to take any action since Devereux had known very little to talk about; Crofton, however, despised informers and insisted that something had to be done. In time Hayes sent Joe O'Connor to George Plant with orders that Devereux should be taken care of by the people there. Tommy Cullimore, C/O of Wexford, was responsible for setting up Devereux so that he could be turned over to Plant who would settle with him. Cullimore felt it had been too long since Devereux's arrest to worry much about his lapse and in any case the man was just not that important for his "title" as QM was more a way for the IRA to gain access to his lorry than a symbol of authority. Still if GHQ wanted him beaten up or tarred-and-feathered, it was not a novel procedure. Devereux was asked to a meeting and when he appeared found Plant waiting for him. The weeks passed and no one heard from Devereux, and Plant was not a talker; in fact, Plant was another hard man in the Crofton tradition. A Protestant dissenter and a long-time Republican, he had been on the run off and on for years and at one time in exile in America. For him "to take care of an informer" could mean only one thing. Devereux had been executed.

The Devereux case was the least of GHQ's worries by the winter of 1940–1941. Although Hayes issued a wildly optimistic Christmas communiqué indicating that "victory is certain and a threatening prospect", the IRA in Dublin was little more than a truncated GHQ staff living from day to day. The Executive was defunct. No one had been co-opted onto the Army Council. The "Government of Ireland" had no programme or personnel. The Dublin unit had dribbled away in arrests and defections. A few men had been brought in from other units but nothing had reversed the decay. Hayes was depending on a silent net of non-IRA people or old-timers. Held and Crofton had been more help than his own staff. Hayes also valued the advice of his brother-in-law Larry de Lacy. De Lacy had been a Clan na Gael agent and conspirator during the Tan War and by 1940 had become a writer for the *Irish Times*; Hayes thought him sound though others, among them Goertz, did not. Most of this new net, which supplied identification papers, courier routes, houses, and dumps, remained unknown even to the GHQ staff; but known or unknown it was no substitute for the regular Dublin IRA.

If Dublin was bad, it was not hopeless. Hayes was still free and GHQ functioning. Goertz was safe and had been given a transmitter and an operator, Antony Deery, to maintain the link with Abwehr. Crofton was in the Castle. And outside Dublin the situation was brighter. The Northern Command had taken hold and was managing to survive quite well under RUC pressure. In May Seán Harrington, brought up from Kerry, had finally got the Western Command reorganized. With Pearse McGuinness as Adjutant and Andy Skelton as Training Officer, his units held their strength. His intelligence was good and extended into the officer corps of the Irish Army. His contact managed to have the *War News* printed in Galway City. His courier with Dublin, Jimmy Cullinane, who ran the dining-car on the Galway–Dublin section of the Great Western Railroad, was first-rate. Kerry remained solid Republican ground, even if the older generation was drifting away. Even those who had resigned from the Army in 1938 would help out. Cork had lost most of the top men, although Jack Lynch managed to evade arrest for some time. In some parts of the country, Kilkenny, Monaghan, and Louth, there were still whole units untouched. The IRA was not so much crippled as undirected. The centre had gone stale. Without a new course, a new campaign, a new initiative, the Army would remain static, vulnerable. The gun fights and arrests would continue until the police had broken the Army. Hayes realized some of this, but he was caught in a cruel dilemma. The IRA was too weak to risk a major operation; on the other hand if nothing happened, ultimate collapse was certain. He kept going day by day and hoped for an unexpected change—a German invasion, a British catastrophe, a shift in the political alignment.

Help was on the way. Without informing Goertz, the Germans had decided to send Seán Russell back to Ireland via submarine. After arriving in Berlin in May, Russell had spent his time taking a refresher course in sabotage and investigating the latest German work in chemical explosives. As often was the case with IRA men, Russell was a man without personal vices. He led a disciplined, routine existence, attended Mass regularly and expressed little interest in the charms of Berlin beyond his explosives classes. He was a pure Irish nationalist who had dedicated his life to achieving Tone's Republic and had no time for even the most attractive diversions of flesh or spirit. The Germans were impressed. For months Abwehr tried to decide how to use Russell. Everyone, including Russell, assumed that he should be sent to Ireland, but when and how, with whom and for what purpose, was uncertain. The discussions dragged on while Russell bided his time and occupied himself in the chemical laboratory.

In July, Abwehr pulled off one of the most curious operations in the Irish game. On July 14 or 15, Frank Ryan was handed over to Kurt Haller by two Spanish plain-clothes men under the watchful eyes of Señor Champourcin, his lawyer, and an observer for the Irish Ambassador in Madrid, Leopold Kerney, who wanted to make sure that the carefully planned "escape" did not end prematurely on the Spanish side of the border. Haller drove Ryan to Paris where he was accommodated in a country house. The next day Ryan still dazed by events ate dinner in the luxury of the Tour D'Argent, a guest of the Nazi state. He was free for the first time since his capture by Mussolini's fascist "volunteers" during the Battle of Ebro in 1938. The dinner in Paris had been long in the planning. One of Ryan's old German friends, Dr. Jupp Hoven, now in the Abwehr, had suggested the project, which soon became the basis for serious discussions. Admiral Canaris finally approached the head of the Spanish secret police, who was willing to allow Ryan to be handed over to the Germans. Ambassador Kerney was informed by Champourcin and de Valera agreed since this was Ryan's last chance. Ryan's first "escape" failed: he had not been informed of the German connection and by this time was too wary to "escape", having avoided a firing squad for two years. For the first nine months he had been locked in with eighteen prisoners; each morning nine were taken out and shot and nine new men sent in. All the efforts of the Save Frank Ryan Committee, personal intervention by de Valera, and the efforts of Champourcin, paid by the Irish government, had done no more than have the sentence reduced to thirty years' imprisonment. He seemed safely buried away in an obscure Spanish prison. Then, suddenly, in fragile health, gaunt and drawn, nearly deaf, and quite confused, he found himself an honoured visitor to Nazi Germany, the fountainhead of the fascist menace he had gone to Spain to fight.

In Berlin Abwehr was a bit uneasy about Ryan, the wild Irish Red, but despite his politics he charmed them as he had so many in Dublin. The Abwehr people, seldom devout Nazis in any case, were impressed with Ryan's rapid recovery from the nightmare world of the Spanish prisons and his insight into political problems. Of course, there remained the question of Russell, whose political views, what there were of them, were diametrically opposed to Ryan's. The Germans took the risk and without warning sprang Ryan on Russell, who was wildly delighted to see his old comrade—the ties of Irish Republicanism being beyond the scope of political logic. Russell immediately insisted that Ryan must go back to Ireland with him. Ryan totally out of touch with the world, with the war, with events in Ireland, was gratified for one more miracle—a trip home. On August 5, Russell met Admiral Canaris, Foreign Minister Ribbentrop, his Irish affairs adviser Dr. Veesenmayer, Kurt Haller and Lieutenant-Colonel Lahousen, to go over final plans. Ribbentrop, who had been brought in for the last briefing, managed as was his custom to irritate Russell by his pompous arrogance, but Abwehr's Irish group managed to get his permission for Operation Dove, the return to Ireland.

On August 8, Agent Richard I and Agent Richard II sailed for Ireland aboard Commander von Stockhausen's U-boat. The crew knew little of the mission and Ryan was largely ignorant of Russell's intentions or Abwehr's desires. Almost at once Russell became seriously ill. He had violent stomach cramps and was in severe pain. There was no doctor on the U-boat and the medical orderly could do little. On August 14, Russell died one hundred miles west of Galway Bay, apparently as a result of a burst gastric ulcer.[19] He was buried at sea. The operation was cancelled. It was intended that Ryan, once he had been briefed by Abwehr, would return. But the chance never came. He lived with Helmut Clissman, then in Abwehr, who had married Elizabeth Mulcahy of Sligo. He saw Francis Stuart and his German friends from time to time, but by no means became reconciled to the Nazi regime and refused to write or speak on Germany's behalf. His health destroyed by the years in prison, his life was a lonely one. Only the German invasion of Russia encouraged him, and he predicted that the Nazi defeat was now assured. In January 1943, he suffered a severe stroke and began to weaken. His strength ebbed gradually and on June 10, 1944, he died. He was buried in the cemetery at Dresden–Loschwitz under a wooden cross inscribed with his German cover-name, Francis Richard, and his own name in Irish.[20]

In Dublin both the IRA and Goertz remained ignorant of the existence of Operation Dove or the presence of Russell and Ryan in Berlin. Eventually in October or November word of Russell's death reached Hayes through Stuart and MacBride but no other information followed. In time garbled tales of Russell's death reached GHQ; it was said he had been killed by a British agent in Gibraltar, but there were other stories that contradicted this version. In the summer and autumn of 1940, no one in Dublin really knew what had happened and few had time for speculation at GHQ. In September the Battle of Britain entered a new phase with the mass air raids on London and invasion was anticipated daily. As the German threat grew more ominous, the Irish government was determined that the IRA should not be given the opportunity to endanger de Valera's neutrality policy. Police pressure intensified. Both Special Branch and Military Intelligence had swollen in size, in funds, and in efficiency. Under Colonel Dan Bryan, Military Intelligence concentrated on the German agents and their IRA contacts. Chief-Inspector Gantley's Special Branch had a new levee of detectives, few inhibited by Republican principles, and plenty of money to pay for information. Men like Michael Gill and Denny O'Brien had become experts on rooting out IRA men and in the process anathema to GHQ. All sorts of people were willing to keep their eyes open for a chance to protect Irish neutrality and turn a profit without earning the traditional informer's stigma. In the country the swollen Army and the local defence men were everywhere.

Times already bad grew worse. Safe houses grew fewer. Men on the run during daylight hours were constantly exposed to risk. For example, Tom Doyle, who was acting as Hayes' A/G during the winter of 1940–1941, was also working as a clerk in the Defence Department. He was known to Special Branch by sight as "Collins", an IRA man, but his true identity unaccountably had not yet been discovered despite, or perhaps because of, the fact that his brother James had originally been arrested under his name. In November he had been followed and then lost; but making use of a part-time agent, the Breadman, in February Special Branch picked up his trail again. This time they kept after him, following him from work to a shop off Queen Street Bridge, on to the Meath Hospital, then to a meeting with Seán Moore on Ash Street, next to Alice McNamara's home and finally with Joe O'Connor by foot and on a bus to a house in Mount Merrion. It was a nice clear trail and there could no longer be any doubt about Doyle's occupation. Special Branch kept a tight line on him, logging his movements and contacts. By then there were not too many new contacts for Doyle to make. GHQ consisted of a handful of the lucky like Hayes, Daniel Gleeson, Joe Dougherty, Joe O'Connor, and a few men, like Tommy Cullimore, who had been brought in briefly from the country. Gill decided not to drag out the game too long and decided to move in on the Mount Merrion house once Doyle's contacts had been noted. On the evening chosen, Hayes and Gleeson were out for a walk and returned just as the police arrived. Both kept going and whipped around a corner before Gill could make his move. Gleeson, however, stopped to tie his shoe lace just as the patrol car drove up and was picked up. He went into the Bridewell but Hayes had gone over the wall and disappeared. The next morning the man on Doyle reported he had not gone to work but to P. T. Martin's on the North Circular Road, where he was lifted. At the same time the house in Mount Merrion was raided Mick Welsh of Waterford, Conroy of Gorey, and Joe O'Connor were arrested. GHQ was once more decimated.

The only hope for the IRA, so it seemed, was to play the German card. Goertz, posing as the highly respectable Mr. Robertson, still had access to the IRA transmitter operated by Deery, but contact with Abwehr in Berlin was slow, halting, and dangerous. Conversations between Hayes and Goertz had continued around the same well-worn circle. Maps and diagrams of British military installations made by the Northern Command and passed on by Dublin GHQ were about the only solid return for Goertz's efforts. Meanwhile, he was secure enough. His landladies and supporters, a tight little band of Republic women, the hard core of the old Cumann na mBan, could, if he were quiet, keep him safe forever. He had rented his own safe house in Dun Laoghaire, where he arranged his meetings and met his few contacts, but he was largely neutralized. In November 1940, he had direct contact with Abwehr through an Irish courier, "Margarethe", actually a Mrs. Daly who had been willing to carry a few things from Spain to Galway on the Japanese ship *Fushimi Maru*. The Galway stop-over to evacuate Japanese citizens from the British Isles gave Abwehr an opportunity to smuggle in some odds and ends. Margarethe brought in more invisible ink, a new code hidden in an alarm clock, messages ironed into her lingerie, and a wad of five hundred dollar bills in her toothpaste tube. After this, the futile round of furtive meetings and wasted hours began again.

Goertz was convinced that he must return to Germany to report on the moves in the Irish game and prepare for future operations. Several escape arrangements were discussed with Hayes but all aborted. Finally in January arrangements were completed for still another try. Crofton, who had worked on the docks and boats much of his life, volunteered to sail Goertz to occupied France on a small fishing boat purchased with the declining German funds. While Hayes was more interested in getting Goertz out and some sort of practical German help back in, Crofton had little time for the Germans. He wanted to bring Frank Ryan, whose presence in Germany was known, back to Ireland. Crofton did not bother to inform Hayes of his intentions because by this time he had his doubts about IRA security. Hayes hated to lose his man in the Castle but went ahead with the final arrangements.

By this time Crofton's days at Special Branch were numbered. The first whimpers had begun after the bomb in the Castle the previous April. Security had been drastically tightened and information was now compartmentalized, but Crofton was still free. That he was still largely unsuspected was a damning indictment of Special Branch internal security, often as careless as the IRA's. Crofton and his uncertain associate in the Castle had regular meetings in a pub with Hayes and a few IRA staff officers. No one had spotted the C/S. By 1941, of course, Hayes was no longer the red-faced, ebullient footballer from Wexford but a prematurely aged, grey-faced, nervous man. He had been on the run for over two years, missed arrest by inches several times, and had lived on his nerves too long. Both Hayes and Crofton knew that Special Branch was closing in and the Goertz escape would free two birds with one boat.

In February Crofton arrived in Kerry, where he stayed with Denny O'Connell and John Joe Sheehy while local arrangements were completed. Then Goertz, camouflaged with a "wife" and "child", drove down to Fenit to meet them. The start was delayed, and by that time Kerry intelligence had spotted Crofton and his aide, Johnny O'Connor. Major Florence O'Donoghue, Director of Intelligence for the Irish Army's Southern Command, had put together a highly efficient operation; but in any case, Fenit was not big enough to allow strangers to move about for long without the wrong people taking notice. Crofton and O'Connor were arrested. Goertz got back to Dublin and went to ground again. Crofton's arrest—for refusing to answer questions about fifty pounds in his possession—was a body blow to Special Branch. Crofton was sentenced to five years and shifted on Gerald Boland's orders to Portlaoise Jail to share the long agony of the hard-core IRA men.[21] Inside the Castle, draconian security measures were instituted. At one shot Hayes had lost his man in the Castle and the chance for German aid.

The decay in Dublin had attracted the attention of the Northern Command, where Seán McCaughey, under similar pressure from the RUC, began to doubt the capacity and leadership of the Dublin centre. His admiration for GHQ efficiency had suffered a blow when along with several other northern men he had been arrested at a training camp in the Dublin Mountains. Because he had held a return ticket to Belfast, he had been released at the end of his sentence; but the arrest had soured him on Dublin security. During 1940, as the new C/O of the Northern Command, he had been operating almost independently of Dublin with little time to worry about GHQ. As the reports of gun battles and arrests continued to appear in the tightly censored press, McCaughey and McGlade grew uneasy. They felt the North was solid. Strength had been maintained in most units. New men had been brought on the staff. Parades were held. The Republican radio broadcast regularly. *War News* edited by Tarlach Ó hUid, who doubled as the radio announcer, came out regularly.[22] The Nationalist population remained sympathetic and even the rumour of conscription in Northern Ireland could ignite demonstrations. Admittedly the activity of the IRA was a holding action. The only positive step other than the swoop on the Ballykinlar base and the bank raids was the accumulation of information about British military installations for GHQ to turn over to Goertz. McCaughey felt it was time for renewed action, but there was no clear lead from Dublin.

He began to slip down to Dublin occasionally, to find out what the situation was. To the young men of the North, Dublin was the centre, the core of the movement, the base of the Russells, Twomeys, MacBrides, and Killeens, names to conjure with. McCaughey's unofficial poll of Republicans, old and new, revealed that Dublin had indeed decayed since Hayes, most assuredly not a name to conjure with, had replaced Russell. Every golden IRA opportunity had turned to ashes. The "Government of Ireland" had vanished. No one knew who was on the Executive or Army Council or if they even existed. Some of McCaughey's informers may have been motivated by jealousy of Hayes or by long-lived feuds or by distaste for the whole direction of IRA activity since 1938, but there was ample evidence to indicate that the hard core was soft to the touch.

McCaughey's questioning and probing never ceased, but at the same time he began to put out feelers of his own without notifying GHQ. In Armagh a known agent of the Fianna Fáil government approached the Northern Command with a remarkable suggestion. Apparently, the Irish government was interested in obtaining information about British military preparation and proposed a meeting, up to Cabinet level, to discuss the possibilities with the IRA. The Northern Command HQ decided to go ahead and see what developed. McCaughey slipped down to Dublin and met with Assistant Superintendent Carroll of the Special Branch and Seán O'Grady, a Clare TD close to de Valera. Nothing much did develop since both sides hedged. The Northern Command decided to let the whole matter drop. McCaughey tried another ploy in Dublin and approached the other side of the Irish political fence, General Eoin O'Duffy. McCaughey and McGlade met O'Duffy at his home in Mount Merrion, hoping to persuade him to work for IRA intelligence. O'Duffy, deep in political retirement, must have been astonished at the two intense young Northerners who sought to enlist him in the ranks of his most bitter opponents. That both had mutual enemies in Fianna Fáil and, perhaps, in Britain hardly seemed sufficient rationale. O'Duffy played the scene by ear, talked in generalities, and at one point remarked that the police thought the IRA were easily caught. On this point at least, McCaughey secretly agreed, but nothing else came of the O'Duffy meeting.

By early spring McCaughey was convinced that there must be a leak in Dublin, too many men were too easily caught, too much went wrong too regularly. On his return from another probing trip to Dublin he asked McGlade what he thought. "I think it's Hayes." "I do too," said McCaughey.

NOTES

1. The house at 16 Rathmines Park had been used for some time by the GHQ staff and the constant traffic on the short back street was bound to be noticed eventually, particularly since a detective lived a few doors away.

2. After the raid Hayes went directly to Maeve Phelan's shop at 5 Harcourt Street and used the telephone to warn everyone that the house had been raided.

3. Lehane went on an unsuccessful hunger and thirst strike to secure his release. He was freed with MacBride and spent much of his time over the next years defending IRA men charged with various crimes by the government.

4. Westminster recognized the special situation in Northern Ireland. Even during the war conscription was not imposed, much to the disgust of the Unionists.

5. Myles Heffernan, released on November 13, visited McGrath the night he was moved to Jervis Street Hospital and showed him the newspaper report that he would still appear before a Military Tribunal. McGrath asked Heffernan to get him out and GHQ arranged the escape.

6. See Letitia Fairfield, *The Trial of Peter Barnes*, London, 1953.

7. An article under Hayes' name, in *The People*, November 11, 1962,

indicated that there was an IRA plan to seize government buildings in Merrion Street and hold hostage Cabinet Ministers. Although such a remote possibility may well have received passing consideration, there were no firm plans.

8. Most of Ashe's ammunition was eventually lost when a lorry containing five thousand rounds of .303 ammunition was stopped in Swords on the way to Dundalk on July 19, 1940. Crofton relayed a report from the Castle that the driver had given the lorry away and on November 20 the suspected informer was shot and wounded outside Dundalk.

9. Seamus O'Donovan attended this meeting and proposed several of the basic resolutions. This was one of the rare times he had publicly dabbled in politics although if anything his association with the other old IRA men long out of politics may actually have diverted attention from him.

10. Out of Behan's brief participation in the British campaign came *Borstal Boy*, one of the few positive results of Russell's grand scheme.

11. Patrick Shannon has produced over thirty mimeographed memoir-articles mainly on the events of the 1939–1941 period. These are distributed to the interested, often at Bodenstown, occasionally printed in the *United Irishman*, but are as yet uncollected. The *United Irishman* has also printed articles on the period. The government's *Notes on the IRA* contain some relevant material but is still classified. Very little can be gleaned from the closely censored press of the period.

12. The IRA camp council had presented a list of demands, more or less in the form of an ultimatum. In retrospect the key demand is recalled as the return of the butter ration.

13. Under one of the first huts to be lit was the still hidden escape tunnel. Later this was to cause bitter recriminations. Grogan and the staff contended that they had not intended to burn down the camp but the fires got out of hand.

14. A few of the obvious leaders like Grogan received prison terms.

15. The Curragh seminars have gone down in Irish legend. The most famous were Ó Cadhain's classes in Irish which turned hundreds of men with little knowledge or interest in the language into Irish speakers. Ó Cadhain is presently Professor of Irish at Trinity College, Dublin, and an outstanding Irish author, although little of his work has been translated into English. He, Seamus O'Donovan, and Joseph Deegan also sought to identify all English base words in the standard Irish dictionary while waiting out the Curragh years (see O'Donovan, letter to Liam Grogan, National Museum, May 16, 1943).

16. Goertz made two official statements (Dublin, December 1941, and Athlone, October 1941) as well as writing his own story in the *Irish*

Times, August 1947. For obvious reasons all must be treated with scepticism for even after the war Goertz hoped to be able to stay in Ireland and had no intention of incriminating himself or endangering his German and Irish friends.

17. The Dublin bank raids were set back in the autumn of 1940 when Special Branch picked up three men near Eden Quay, one of whom they claimed was C/O of Dublin, with a set of plans. The raids did take place in the spring of 1941 and continued, officially and unofficially, during the next year.

18. Irish neutrality was weighted in favour of the British from the beginning; no British airmen were interned, overflights were permitted, contact was maintained with the British Army, and Irishmen enlisted in the British armed forces and worked in British war industry. The price the British paid, albeit, reluctantly, was the loss of the naval bases. The Germans seemed willing to tolerate this unequal neutrality and informed the Irish government that Berlin recognized Dublin's peculiar situation. The German Foreign Ministry continued to feel that any provocation would only be to Britain's advantage and eventually even turned over the Embassy transmitter in Dublin to the Irish government.

19. There are various theories on Russell's death other than the prosaic gastric ulcer. One is that he was poisoned—as apparently suggested by Colonel Lahousen during Ribbentrop's trial. While nothing is impossible, it appears unlikely that any German faction would have waited until Russell was under the Bay of Galway to act. Frank Ryan managed to smuggle a message to Gerald O'Reilly in New York, albeit by a German agent, which did not indicate foul play; but this is hardly conclusive.

20. The first written revelation of Ryan's German experience was Francis Stuart's "Frank Ryan in Germany", in *The Bell*, vol. XVI, no. 2, November 1950, and no. 3, December 1950. Michael McInerney in a series of articles on Peadar O'Donnell (no. 6, "The Rise of Fascism", *Irish Times*, April 6, 1968) gives further information on Ryan's continuing anti-Nazi stand during his German exile and indicates that Ryan wanted to land in Ireland rather than return to Germany on the U-boat.

21. If anything, Crofton's wife had as difficult a time as he did, for she and the family were completely without resources and often literally on the edge of starvation. After his release, close surveillance by the Castle and the difficulty of finding work while in police disfavour forced the Croftons to emigrate to London. His occasional visits to Ireland still attract official interest.

22. Tarlach Ó hUid has written one of the few books on this period (*Ar Thoir Mo Shealbha*, Baile Atha Cliath, 1960). His first book, a novel (*An Bealach Chun a'Bhearnais*) was written in Crumlin Road Prison and smuggled out in the bottom of a laundry box.

CHAPTER X

Turmoil at the Centre: The Stephen Hayes Affair, April 1941–September 1941

In the spring of 1941, Hayes had to fend off the emissaries from the Northern Command, who were demanding action and an accounting for past prudence, while at the same time attempting once more to reorganize the Army. He still hoped that there might be a chance for the one big blow; but no one, least of all Hayes, could imagine what might be the target or the outcome. Simply to keep GHQ operational was all but impossible. Down to the last few pounds, Hayes decided, as had the Northern Command, that his only remaining option was a renewal of bank raids. His acting A/G, Joe Dougherty, arranged for the raids. On May 5, the IRA hit the Northern Bank at Oldcastle and on June 9 the Hibernian Bank at Castlepollard. The grand total realized came to nearly £1,400 which was enough to remove the immediate threat of insolvency. These operations were the last to be authorized by Hayes, for by then Northern Command had intervened aggressively in Dublin affairs.

By April at the latest, McCaughey and McGlade had come to the conclusion that Hayes' conduct was treasonable.[1] In May they arrived in Dublin, demanding that GHQ be reorganized. There seemed to be no functioning Government of Ireland, no visible Army Council, and the GHQ staff consisted simply of Dougherty and a few errand boys. Hayes apparently gave more credence to Larry de Lacy's advice than to the counsel of orthodox IRA men. Hayes had little choice if he wanted to avoid a violent split but to appoint McCaughey A/G and McGlade GMG. He considered both men fanatics without a sense of the possible, but GHQ had enough dedicated enemies without alienating the entire Northern Command. By this time the Northern HQ was concentrating almost entirely on the Dublin situation. Liam Rice was brought down to Dublin to aid the investigation and Pearse Kelly assigned as C/O of Belfast. In their own minds the Northerners accepted Hayes' treachery as a fact. To them he had been not simply inefficient but an informer. Yet they had no hard proof. McCaughey sought not only previous examples of Hayes' guilt but tried to set up a trap which would prove to his satisfaction that Hayes was still selling them out. At one point he told Dougherty exactly where he was staying and, as he expected, his safe house was raided.[2] This, more than anything else, was the final straw. McCaughey decided to act before Hayes could weasel away or have the Northerners arrested.

More than anything else, McCaughey and McGlade had been disgusted by Hayes himself. He simply bore no resemblance to their image of an IRA Chief of Staff. Flabby, grey-faced, with a reputed weakness for the bottle and his fingers stained by chain-smoking, he was strained, vague, cautious, evasive. They had expected a dynamic, dedicated successor to Russell— another hard man without personal flaw or second thoughts. Instead they found a soft, uncertain temporizer whose character appeared weak, whose habits were indulgent, and whose purpose had been lost. Their investigations confirmed that Hayes' career in Wexford was spotted by gossip if not scandal. Under his leadership the IRA had descended from failure to failure. Most of the men of reputation were in prison. McGrath, D'Arcy, and McNeela were dead. So, if the story was true, was Russell. Dumps all over Ireland had been uncovered. The weapons and ammunition from the Magazine Fort had been lost in a week. The English campaign had floundered in toy explosions. The German contact had produced nothing and the resident agent Dr. Goertz clearly held Hayes in contempt and despised de Lacy. Old Republicans of consequence indicated that the Army was near collapse and all the evidence examined by McCaughey confirmed this unpleasant fact.

In Belfast, it was a reflex action to suspect treachery. Twice in recent years, informers and *agents provocateur* had been trusted men. The greatest RUC coup, the Crown Entry arrests in 1935, had been the direct result of information supplied by one of these men. Consequently the Belfast IRA was intensely security conscious, urging all new recruits to beware of the informer.

> Does it not sometimes arouse your curiosity when the police raid certain houses, when they come and arrest these men and boys and even girls, whom you know, or when they suddenly swoop on a collection of documents or arms' store? Surely there must be a missing link somewhere in the background that would explain all this apparent police activity, and the campaign of intimidation and midnight raiding.
>
> Yes, there is a reason for it all! For seven hundred and fifty years, in generation after generation, we have suffered from shameful and detestable depredations of the traitor, informer, and police tout . . .[3]

By June, McCaughey had no doubts that he had found his generation's greatest traitor, no less a man than the corrupt and devious Chief of Staff. Once sentiment had crystallized, Northern Command no longer felt that additional analysis of the decline of the IRA was necessary. If, as was apparent to McCaughey, Hayes was a bad one, then everything else was clear. All that remained to be done was cut out the rot once the extent of the betrayal was clear.

While Hayes was quite aware of McCaughey's distaste, he had no clue that for months his life and leadership had been inspected with the cold eye of a prosecutor. He was not, as were McCaughey's colleagues, impressed with the young man from the North. Slipping in and out of Dublin urging immediate and violent war, McCaughey seemed out of touch with reality, unaware of the unremitting pressure of hundreds of detectives, army intelligence agents, and paid informers clotting Dublin's streets. He seemed to want some great symbolic stroke, regardless of the consequences, demonstrating to Hayes not his ruthless dedication but his callow ignorance of the harsh facts of life. It was a classic confrontation. The fanatic revolutionary, his spirit burning with an inner light, untouched by mundane obstacles, faced across the ruins of the IRA the cautious, prudent sceptic, whose flame had gutted low under the long, cold winds of coercion. McCaughey could scarcely understand the exhausted practicalities of Hayes, who in turn did not completely hide his distaste for the arrogant fervour of McCaughey. Nor, of course, did Hayes ever understand that McCaughey's passion for an explanation of the shattered condition of the IRA would coalesce into a charge of treason. To Hayes this was unthinkable, while it was McCaughey's first reaction.

On June 30, 1941, Hayes and Dougherty met with McCaughey, McGlade, and Liam Rice, in a safe house in Coolock, County Dublin. McCaughey had decided to wait no longer but spring the trap. After several minutes of meandering conversation, Liam and four other men who had escaped from Belfast Jail in July 1940 walked slowly down the corridor into the room and stood with a revolver pointed at Hayes. The other three forced him against the wall, searched him, tied his wrists and arms with telephone wire. Dougherty was sent off. Hayes was bundled into a car and driven by way of Drogheda and Dundalk to a house in the Cooley Mountains where he was dumped in a small back room.[4] Very little had been said on the way up and Hayes was still confused and bewildered, but the utter contempt of McCaughey and McGlade was obvious.

His captors felt that they had the traitor, the man responsible for the unnecessary deaths of IRA men and the collapse of the Republican movement. They felt no twinge of sympathy. They were determined to discover just how far the rot had gone, for other men's lives might depend on the revelations made by Hayes. He was blindfolded and tied to a chair but refused to answer their first questions about the constant arrests and lost dumps. Losing patience, they began clubbing him around the head and later pounding him with revolvers. The beating had none of the cold cunning of torture but it was sufficiently painful to shock Hayes, still not fully aware of their intentions. However, he would say nothing. McCaughey warned him that if he persisted in remaining silent he would be shot. Hayes was in a desperate position: if he told McCaughey what he wanted to hear, he would be shot as an informer; if he did not, he would be shot in any case. The following night McCaughey arrived with a watch and a revolver and announced that Hayes had fifteen minutes to begin talking. However Hayes had misjudged his man, there was now no doubt of McCaughey's ruthless determination. Hayes began to give a few evasive answers to the questions. The rounds of interrogation and pummelling continued off and on for several days, but McCaughey was not getting a detailed confession, only vague, often incoherent replies that answered nothing.

By this time word had spread through GHQ circles that Hayes had been arrested. There was mixed reaction, but few knew very much about McCaughey's reasons. To make his case in the only court that mattered —the Republican Movement—McCaughey began to bring in people to explain the arrest. Seán Harrington, C/O Western Command, closed down a small training camp on Clonliffe Road in Dublin when word of the arrest arrived. Along with Dan O'Toole and Jack Lynch he met two former C/S's, Moss Twomey and Andy Cooney. The five men drove up to the Cooley Mountains, arriving well after dark. McCaughey revealed that Hayes had already made certain admissions. Harrington in the glimmer of the candle-light saw Hayes tied to a chair in the next room. Treason or no, he told McCaughey, he did not believe in rough treatment. Twomey and Cooney had little to say; in fact, no one was quite sure what was going on. McCaughey did tell Harrington that de Lacy had been implicated and he too was to be arrested. Nothing further came out of the meeting. The affair was, however, taking far too long. The house in the Cooley Mountains was isolated and the arrival of strangers was bound to attract unwelcome attention; Hayes was moved back to Dundalk and held for two days, while a safe house was readied elsewhere. Then he was moved down to Dublin and on July 8, out to a cottage in Glencree, County Wicklow, owned by Roger McHugh, who in the past had turned a blind eye on IRA men staying there.

The next step was to arrest de Lacy who increasingly loomed in the Northerners' eyes as the puppet master of the whole plot. He was picked up on a ruse. Dougherty went to his flat on Clare Street and asked him to bring out an IRA typewriter. When he emerged, McCaughey was under a tree with a Colt revolver under his mackintosh. Inside the car were Tadhg Lynch and Seán Harrington. When de Lacy reached the car he was covered back and front, forced into the rear seat, and driven off to Glencree to join Hayes. De Lacy at first assumed he was in the hands of the Special Branch and even at Glencree was confused because McCaughey seemed un-interested in asking questions. Soon, however, the three, McCaughey, McGlade, and Rice, were grilling both de Lacy and Hayes and comparing the answers. During his stay at Glencree, Hayes was questioned again and again by McCaughey and roughed up when his answers proved unsatisfactory. One night he was marched out, hands tied behind his back and blindfolded, to the bank of a stream. Assuming he was to be shot he asked permission to pray. Kneeling down, he wormed part way out of his ropes and tried to make a break. He fell and was beaten once more.[5] The round of questioning, cuffing, and threats continued the next day. McCaughey's hopes to play off Hayes's statements against de Lacy's came to nothing. With only three men in on the Hayes affair, there was no chance to collect evidence against Hayes, maintain contact with the rest of the IRA, and keep an around-the-clock guard at Glencree. De Lacy simply waited until the house was quiet and no one was in the yard outside. He then dropped from the window, disappeared out the back into the fields, and made his way to Dublin.

With de Lacy free, the Glencree House was useless. At midnight on July 12, McCaughey decided to move to the last safe house he knew, No. 20 Castlewood Park in Rathmines.[6] There was no car at Glencree and no telephone to arrange transportation, so the whole party would have to move to Dublin on foot. Hayes was poked out of bed and in carpet slippers and socks was hobbled with a lead rope on his left ankle. He was told that if he made a break or tried to signal anyone he would be shot immediately. With that, the strange little group moved off for Dublin twelve miles away. In the dead of the night on little used roads they met no one until they neared Rathfarnham. There a garda rode by on a bicycle but to Hayes' relief seemed oddly uninterested in the weird pre-dawn procession. Finally, at five in the morning they arrived at Castlewood Park.

De Lacy's escape and the rumours of Hayes' arrest precipitated a crisis in Republican circles.[7] Many of Hayes' associates disliked McCaughey's assumption that they had been duped and disagreed with the Northern Command's premise that the IRA in the South had been in ruins. All agreed that things were bad; nevertheless, many C/Os felt their areas were still solid. Harrington, who had reorganized the Western Command, knew that his men were sound. Staff officers in Cork and Kerry felt much the same. Other units elsewhere had been untouched. Everyone acknowledged that the survival of much of the IRA apparatus might simply be due to the conspirators' forebearance or Hayes' inefficiency as an informer; but given the supposed scope of the plot, the determination of the government to crush the IRA, and the string of Republican disasters at Hayes' door, it was strange that anything was left of the IRA. Still, no one felt he knew enough to judge and no one denied treachery was possible. There were some outside the IRA but in far more intimate contact with Hayes than his own officers who refused even to consider the charges. For over a year Hayes had been piecing together his own net of couriers, agents, and drops to replace the IRA men lost. Crofton was simply the most visible of a group known only to Hayes and a few others, who had compiled a photographic file of Special Branch, arranged through the Dublin Port Workers Union to get men on the ships, carried messages and money, and kept the Dublin centre operating. Highly vulnerable and seldom caught, they were certain that they would have known if Hayes had been bad.

It was not only some of Hayes' officers and associates who were uneasy or outraged at the charges but also other Republicans confused by the rumours and partial revelations. None of these "circles" would have been visible on an organizational chart; there had always been loose groups outside the IRA of retired militants, old friends, former Tan War comrades, relatives, and perhaps the most dedicated of all, the Republican women. Goertz, for example, had been most fortunate to have found refuge with Miss Coffey, Maisie O'Mahony, and Cáitlín Brugha, widow of Cathal Brugha. Under the suspicious eyes of Special Branch this uncompromising Republican sorority continued operating. One of the founder members, Maire Comerford, felt it would be disastrous to execute Hayes if he were not in fact guilty. Although no friend of Hayes, she discovered that some of the charges were unlikely and others clearly inaccurate. McCaughey was willing to listen to her evidence but after a long, three-hour meeting was unswayed. It was not only the women who had doubts, for dotted across the country were men who at some point had parted with the orthodox policy but not with their principles or their pride in the IRA. These men, too, felt they had a stake in the Army and its reputation. Few wanted the stigma of having dedicated the best years of their lives to an organization which could be led by a traitor.

Thus many Republicans, past and present, simply did not want to believe that the Chief of Staff could be an informer. A few may have believed in Hayes personally but most simply found the charge unlikely and the evidence insufficient. McCaughey was committed to his course but was equally eager to accumulate overwhelming evidence. Pearse Kelly was brought down to Dublin from Belfast to aid in the interrogation. The Northerners were absolutely convinced that the reluctant revelations made by Hayes at the Castlewood House were if not accurate in detail—after all an informer and traitor was doing the talking—substantially true. Day after day the intense grilling had elicited a tissue of deceit, a catalogue of agents, a calendar of subversion. That the revelations were a result of considerable physical force and great mental pressure did not in McCaughey's eyes invalidate them. Hayes had talked enough to prove his guilt and would have to face the consequences. He would be court martialled for treason. Any remaining Republican doubts would evaporate in the face of the evidence McCaughey had accumulated.

At nine on the evening of Wednesday, July 23, the three-man court met in a downstairs room at Castlewood Avenue. Jack Lynch had sent up a man named McCarthy from Cork and Tommy Farrell of Galway and Pearse Kelly were the other members. McCaughey acted as prosecutor. McGlade, Rice, Burke, and O'Toole, all from the North, were also present. The bulk of the evidence was Hayes' own revelations, written on quarto sheets under the pressure of the long, often day and night, grilling. In a highly charged atmosphere Hayes slumped mute in his chair unwilling to recognize the court or answer the accusations. Hour after hour, until dawn came, McCaughey outlined Hayes' treachery. The verdict was a foregone conclusion. Hayes was taken from the room and the court quickly voted a guilty sentence and ordered his execution. Provisionally it was decided that his body would be left in front of Leinster House. Later Liam Rice left the room and tossed Hayes a prayer book and told him to get himself ready. Actually it was McCaughey who was not yet ready for the final step. Although Hayes had written out, often at his interrogators' dictation, several confessions, he had as yet not signed one. McCaughey wanted not only a signed confession but also every last drop of information that could be squeezed out of Hayes.

Hayes eagerly grasped at the last straw and agreed to write out a full confession and sign the finished document.[8] He began to fill the quarto pages with long accounts of his machinations which he would later claim he invented and elaborated as he went along, confessing to acts so outrageous no one could believe them. Literally writing day by day to postpone the final day of execution, Hayes lived in a desperate, dream world. Sore and aching from his buffeting, constantly prodded and probed,[9] existing on tea and bread, tied to his bed at night and hobbled with a light chain during the day, he wrote on and on. The delay began to concern those around McCaughey who felt that the sentence should be carried out. This from the first had been the general reaction—that if Hayes were guilty he should be shot and the matter dropped. As early as the two-day stay in Dundalk, the local IRA men urged immediate execution. The body could be dropped into the fast riptides below the cliffs. Once the court martial had taken place further delay seemed pointless but McCaughey persisted and Kelly continued to accumulate his quarto sheets.

On August 28, Hayes signed his confession, which he has always claimed was a tissue of lies invented by a desperate man writing for his life.

I, Stephen Hayes, have made the following confession of facts concerning my complicity in the conspiracy with the Free State Government through their agents, Dr James Ryan, TD, Minister for Agriculture, Tomás Derrig, TD, Minister for Education, Senator Chris Byrne, and Laurence de Lacy, to wreck the Irish Republican Army. It has been made with the hope that it will undo some of the harm and injury I did to Oglaigh na h-Éireann (Irish Republican Army) through my cooperation with them.

I decided on making this Confession after I was made aware of the verdict of the Court martial.

I further affirm that this Confession of facts is the truth, the whole truth, and nothing but the truth, and has been made voluntarily by me.[10]

Kelly immediately began editing the confession for security reasons so that the basic revelations could be printed and distributed.[11] McCaughey was still not satisfied and insisted that Hayes reveal all his contacts and agents. Again the quarto sheets began to fill up as Hayes drew on names he recalled from his GAA days and the payroll in the Wicklow County Council. For him, however, time was about gone for he could hardly fill up another 160 pages with names alone; but when he was on his twentieth page, the whole picture changed.

GHQ had moved to a house in Whitehall on the north side of Dublin soon after Hayes had been brought to Castlewood Park. Usually the GHQ staff, Kelly, McGlade, and McCaughey, stayed there and took a tram over to Rathmines to question Hayes, who was guarded by Rice and Burke. One morning McCaughey was unlucky and a Special Branch man identified him on the tram. Instead of trailing his man, the detective picked him up when he got off the tram at Harcourt Street and Rathmines Road, a short distance from the house on Castlewood Park. As quickly as possible a meeting was held of the available men to appoint a successor to McCaughey. John Joe Sheehy was up from Kerry where he had been quietly on the run for some time and Patrick McLogan came in from Portlaoise.[12] Both had been opposed to the Russell take-over but were willing to lend their support in an emergency. All the Northern Command people, McGlade, Kelly and Rice were present as well as one or two other men, who happened to be in Dublin at the time. Sheehy nominated Kelly for C/S despite his relative youth. McGlade was to act as A/G and Rice was the third member of the honed-down GHQ staff. Eoin McNamee, who had taken over as C/O of the Northern Command when Kelly came to Dublin, would remain on in Belfast.[13]

With GHQ still in considerable disarray, Kelly was anxious to finish up the Hayes affair and unclog the centre for more effective action after the long internal crisis. Across Dublin in Rathmines, Rice and Burke remained around the clock guarding Hayes but they had settled back into a routine. Rice had taken a considerable interest in the daughter of the landlady and spent much of his free time chatting with her. Burke spent his time in a chair watching Hayes at work on his endless confession. Even at this late date the timing of the execution was still up in the air. McGlade and Kelly were still trying to put together the exact sequence of events. McGlade had brought in Tom Cullimore, Divisional C/O of Wexford, Wicklow, Carlow, and Kilkenny, who had been on Hayes' staff for several months to check over details. At the next staff meeting there was strong sentiment that the time had come to shoot Hayes instead of dragging out the affair any longer. The next Sunday was the All-Ireland Football Final at Croke Park and tens of thousands of strangers would throng Dublin, an ideal time for an execution. There was an argument as to whether Hayes should be shot in a public place or whether his body should be left in front of Leinster House. The little group of men, McGlade, Kelly, Cullimore, Harrington, Burke, and Michael Quill from Kerry, were still unable to reach a final decision.

On the morning of September 8, GHQ paid the penalty for its continued delays. With Rice off chatting, Burke was sitting in the drawing room before the fire writing a letter and keeping an eye on Hayes, who slumped in his chair, his legs hobbled and his mind wandering. When the landlady called him, Burke got up from his letter and, leaving his Webley service revolver, stepped out of the room.[14] Hayes' moment had come at last. He snatched up the gun and threw himself out of the window. Frantically he staggered down the street, still hobbled, grasping the Webley and searching for sanctuary. He found it in the Rathmines police station where the astonished gardai were confronted by a grey and shaken man, dangling chains and clutching a revolver, who announced that he was Stephen Hayes, Chief of Staff of the IRA.

At Castlewood Park the escape was discovered almost immediately when Burke stepped back in the room to find Hayes gone. Rice said he would stay in the neighbourhood to warn off Kelly who was on his way from Whitehall. Burke rushed across town to GHQ and burst in on McGlade, O'Toole, and Cullimore with the news. Almost as soon as Burke had gone, police patrol cars began to arrive. Inspector Gill leaped out of one of the squad cars and started for the house. Rice decided that the only hope for Kelly would be a distraction. He stepped forward and opened fire on the detectives. The police returned the fire immediately. Rice fell to the ground shot through both lungs. In the confusion over Rice's body, Kelly moving in from another direction arrived at the house unaware of the gun-fight down the street or Hayes' escape. As soon as the landlady told her story, he scooped up some documents and dashed out and away just before the police arrived. Rice was rushed to a hospital and eventually recovered sufficiently to be tried.

With Hayes gone, McCaughey in prison, and Rice desperately wounded under guard in the hospital, the whole Dublin situation was chaotic. At least Hayes' "Confession" had been salvaged but even over this there was a dispute. Cullimore was opposed to the whole idea of letting the public in on the affair by releasing the document, for once a chain of revelations had started there would be no end in sight. Kelly contended that the public reaction to Hayes' treachery and Fianna Fáil complicity could only be to the advantage of the IRA. Finally Cullimore and Kelly decided to get an outside opinion and went to see Seán MacBride. His advice was that publication would be a foolish move, dangerous to the Army and ineffectual as an attempt to damage Fianna Fáil. They listened and returned to GHQ where the decision was made to send out copies to specific individuals. Thus within days the infamous "Hayes Confession" dated September 10 became the source of the most violent private controversy.

The "Confession" purports to reveal in detail a long-lived, covert association between Hayes and various government agents to destroy the IRA. The collusion began in 1935 and continued up to June 1941 and largely determined the course of events relating to the IRA. In almost all ways, it is an embodiment of the devil theory of history: every disaster, every defeat, even the apparent successes had been planned long in advance by the conspirators. Apparently the IRA had for years been completely manipulated. Where there seemed to the participants to be an element of chance, a choice of options, an error in judgement, a brilliant coup, or the play of free will, there had only been the hidden and invariably successful tugs of the conspirators' strings. Everything had been foreseen, the contingent eliminated, and the IRA, a helpless puppet, blithely unaware of the secret strings, had fallen in, as planned, with the desires of the Irish government. The conspirators, for ulterior motives, arranged the timing of the English campaign, the December 1938 Belfast internments, the difficulties of the IRA in Britain, the departure of Russell, the Coventry explosion, the arrests in Dublin, the Magazine Fort raid and so on and on. In each case, the decision had been made, the wires pulled by Hayes, the IRA puppet activated, and the desired results achieved. The conspirators apparently never faltered, never failed. If the "Confession" reads like a fairy tale, there were other very specific peculiarities which as time passed and evidence accumulated attracted attention. Parts of the published "Confession" were obviously untrue and were not merely the results of contradictory evidence.[15] Of course, from the first those accused of conspiracy adamantly denied the validity of any part of the "Confession". All the individuals named as agents swore the "Confession" was a lie, as did all the members of the government in a position to know of any such plot, as did most of the individuals in the IRA listed as dupes or victims. In general, then, the "Confession" recounts the history of the IRA as a tapestry of fraud woven on an omnipotent loom by awesome and prophetic devils. In particular it is a maze of little errors and large assertions and assumptions, where every betrayal is denied by agent and victim.

Not that this worried those who were deeply and sincerely convinced of Hayes' guilt. After all, the "Confession" was written by a twister and, therefore, in detail or in tone, it too might be twisted, but in essence there must be fire where there is smoke, and there must be treason where there is a confessed traitor. In September 1941, most of those still active in the IRA accepted that Hayes was bad even if the "Confession" was confused. A few men even accepted the "Confession" as verbatim. Only a handful of men had really been involved in the Hayes affair and the dominating and determining figure, McCaughey, was silent in prison. For those still free the immediate task was not to pick over the evidence but to close down the Hayes affair and to reorganize the Army. It proved, however, easier to open the box of treachery than close it. On September 23, the police discovered the body of Michael Devereux in a cave in County Tipperary. He had been shot in the back of the head and covered with a pile of stones. Until the distribution of the "Confession", Devereux's fate had been a matter of quiet speculation in limited circles. After September 10, the police moved in with a vengeance.

Devereux's car had been found broken down in sections and scattered about Tipperary. Several local men had talked too freely and the police had put together what had happened. A few weeks after the finding of the body, George Plant and Joe O'Connor were brought to trial for the murder of Devereux. The two key prosecution witnesses, Michael Walsh and Patrick Davern, supposedly the accomplices of the accused, suddenly announced that they had been beaten into giving incriminating statements before the Special Criminal Court and refused to testify. The case collapsed. The prosecution entered *nolle prosequi* and the charges were dismissed. Plant was immediately rearrested in the courtroom and put in Arbour Hill. Meanwhile Boland transferred the case from the Tribunal to the Special Military Court, where the only sentence was death and from whose verdict there was no appeal. If the Military Court found the defendant guilty, the sentence had to be carried out within seventy-two hours. For cases before the Special Military Court the normal rules of judicial procedure were revoked. Thus Plant was tried the second time for the murder of Devereux and convicted on the statements of Walsh and Davern, which they had disclaimed, read to the court by a police officer. On February 26, 1942, Plant, Davern, and Walsh were sentenced to death; but only Plant's was carried out. On March 5, 1942, he was executed by a firing squad.[16]

Whether the publication of the "Confession" led directly to Plant's arrest was to become a bitterly disputed point in the rapidly developing controversy over the entire Hayes affair. For a generation Republicans would dispute the validity of the "Confession" in whole or in part, while remaining ignorant of either the charges or Hayes' subsequent defence. To many the damning evidence was Hayes' willingness to seek refuge in police station and, far worse, his testimony against McCaughey.[17] That by September Hayes was a dazed and broken man, who had lived in fear of death for ten weeks, was discounted. That Hayes might have sought revenge against McCaughey, the man who beat his body and tainted his honour, was discounted. That Hayes, who had spent his life in the IRA, might have been so repulsed by his ordeal that he no longer felt any loyalty for men who had almost been his executioners was discounted. For the stern and the pure, Hayes had sold out in court and in public and that was enough. Others who admired McCaughey, who in many ways was clearly a most admirable man, simply took his word against the confused apologists for Hayes. Some, however, remained loyal, if not to the man, at least to the Army and withheld judgement. Many felt that a long wrangle could only damage the Army and kept their peace; but once the spectre of treason was loose, neutrality became difficult. When Pearse Kelly came into the Curragh early in 1942, a decisive split developed over the issue of Northern Command's actions during 1941. In Crumlin Road news of the Hayes affair shattered morale as the long years had not; if Hayes were a traitor, then membership in the IRA had been a farce; if he were not, then the means to force his confession had contaminated the Army. Few signed out, but many in their hearts had finished with the Army. Men would say later that if a conspiracy to destroy the IRA had been planned, then no better means could have been found than the Hayes affair. In less hectic times the IRA might have held a formal inquiry, but after 1941 there was no time for disinterested investigation and no desire to open old wounds. After the war the IRA had too many problems to waste time raking over the glowing embers of dissension and no serious effort was made to open the case.[18] By then Hayes had disappeared into obscurity and McCaughey had become a martyr, dying on a hunger and thirst strike in Portlaoise Prison. The IRA left well enough alone.

Hardly anyone else in Ireland did. For a generation Hayes' guilt was a source of debate. Several individuals, notably Maire Comerford, Peter Mohan, and Richard Sherlock, had tried to track down the evidence. For a while at least, Hayes hoped for rehabilitation and prepared a case,[19] but other than an article by Peadar O'Donnell in *The Bell* no forum ever presented itself. On the other hand, the key for the prosecution was McCaughey, who could no longer testify. Although Kelly, McGlade, and Rice, who survived not only his wounds but a term in Portlaoise, were familiar with their evidence, they felt that the case had been closed with the court martial in July 1941. Thus the debate was carried on by men who knew only part of the evidence and depended more on their instincts than the available facts. For the sophisticated, the charges seemed so improbable and the "Confession" so weird that the whole affair was dismissed. For the ordinary people, Hayes-the-Informer was a figure from the past and they accepted his guilt. For Republicans, much of the evidence

f Hayes' innocence was discarded immediately as contaminated; the
enials of Ryan, Derrig, and Boland and the rest were meaningless, part
f the conspiracy. Even the doubts of those innocent IRA men involved
ith Hayes were ignored on the assumption that no dupe likes to admit
e fact.

In the spring of 1941, McCaughey's suspicions appeared quite justified:
e IRA had suffered a series of severe reverses and Hayes had been less
an impressive as Chief of Staff. Once an investigation of Hayes began,
nd all other options had been discarded, there was ample evidence that
HQ was far from perfect and Hayes no Seán Russell; but all the evidence
ying the blame on Hayes was circumstantial at best. Once Hayes was
rrested on June 30, all subsequent evidence extracted from a frightened
nd maltreated man was contaminated. The various confessions were
ictated to please, not volunteered in shame. The published "Confession",
ally the tip of the iceberg of revelations, reads like a malicious fantasy.
he strongest evidence available before June 30 is McCaughey's conten-
ion that Hayes gave away his safe houses when no one else knew of them.
Iayes subsequently denied knowledge of the houses; furthermore, the
Iorthern Command was known to have used houses, like Mrs. Rogers's
ooms over a fish shop on Dorset Street, which had been off-bounds for
he Dublin IRA, and no matter how innocent the house McCaughey's
ccent and his odd hours might well have attracted attention in any case
n a Dublin swarming with police and police informers. As Hayes was to
oint out later, he could hardly be blamed for McCaughey's arrest, or
hose of the subsequent Chiefs of Staff, or the loss of dumps, or the multitude
f IRA failures, all of which occurred while he was in Mountjoy. If Hayes
vere a traitor, why did the IRA decay even more rapidly once he was out
f power? It was a difficult question for men whose first instinct after a
lisaster was to smell treachery.

Over the years the belief in Hayes' guilt has persisted despite the weight
f contrary evidence and more rational analysis. Although the simplest
xplanation is always more elegant and generally more likely, one cannot
gnore the tortured arguments for Hayes' guilt. After all, one of the first
f Lenin's Bolsheviks to be elected to the Duma was a police spy, as was
ather Gapon, hero of the Revolution of 1905. History, particularly Irish
istory, is spotted with informers and traitors, as the men of the Northern
Command had good reason to know. Although it is most improbable that
he C/S of the IRA was a traitor, it is not impossible. However, the con-
inced have been quite unable to prove Hayes guilty, even to the satisfac-
ion of all Republicans. The prosecution's evidence was flawed and its
nterrogation self-defeating. In the face of so many disclaimers and errors,
he certainties of the convinced are insufficient for the dubious as is the

evidence of innocence which Hayes' apologists offer. No matter how high the facts are heaped, much went with McCaughey to the grave.

And so, the Hayes affair is likely always to remain a tangled web, with too many broken ends and lost strands to reweave. What remains of the prosecution's case can hardly convince the fair minded, but few of the convinced cared for judicial balance. They knew, in their heart of hearts, that Hayes was wrong. As a result Hayes was condemned in the minds of a generation as surely as he was by the court martial, his past service blackened, and his honour lost. His accuser died a hero and Hayes lived on in a suspended twilight world supported by a few friends and suspected by the multitude. It was a harsh and horrible fate for any man—particularly for one who on the weight of the evidence was in fact innocent.

NOTES

1. It is likely, given the uncertainty of the remaining participants' memory after twenty-five years, that the moment of decision came as early as January or February.

2. McCaughey would not even tell McGlade where he was staying and the assumption was that Dougherty had, as he said, told Hayes, although Hayes subsequently denied that he knew of the safe house.

3. This is from the series of Northern Command recruits' lectures and is dated June 1941 (i.e. before Hayes' arrest but probably after McCaughey was convinced of his "treachery"). However, similar admonitions were normal procedure in Belfast where HQ, perhaps justifiably, had an informer-complex.

4. Published accounts of Hayes' ordeal are to be found in the reports of his trial (June 1942) in the daily press and later in his own "articles" in the *Sunday Press*. There also exist "Notes" by Stephen Hayes (hand-written) dated March 18, 1949; and of course his own recollections (taped interview).

5. The same ploy was used against de Lacy whose response supposedly at the moment of execution was to tell McCaughey what he thought of him, which greatly impressed the latter.

6. McCaughey while in Belfast had been told of the house offhand by Pearse Kelly. With the possible exception of McCaughey none of the Northern Command staff was really familiar with Dublin.

7. Soon after de Lacy had returned to Clare Street to tell his wife that he was safe, Maire Comerford, a fellow journalist, arrived to find out what had happened.

8. To secure Hayes' co-operation McCaughey once more ill-treated him and threatened to hang him up in the kitchen without food, water, or sleep until he agreed. After twenty-four hours without sleep Hayes agreed to go ahead with the confession.

9. The last serious beating came soon after the court martial when Hayes' guard destroyed his farewell letter to his sister and struck him repeatedly on the arm with a revolver. However, after Glencree physical force was rare; the interrogators depended on non-stop grilling and Hayes' lack of sleep. The line between ill-treatment and torture is a vague one, but the report of the government doctor at the time of the trial indicated that Hayes had marks indicating serious ill-treatment. That his interrogators felt justified in the use of force to secure vital knowledge is obvious and hardly unique in comparable situations; that they did not resort to more unpleasant means to extract information is also clear; but the fact remains that Hayes was repeatedly beaten.

10. Oglaigh na h-Éireann, "Special Communiqué Issued by the Army Council", September 10, 1941.

11. The September 10 "Confession" is the basic document although other "Confessions" based on edited versions of it have been circulated. The vast pile of pages remained in an Army dump until the late 'forties when they were removed and are now, apparently, in the possession of a former C/S.

12. Both McLogan and Sheehy had been contacted earlier by McCaughey when he was investigating Hayes. Neither had been sympathetic to the English campaign and, as was the case with several of the retired Republicans McCaughey met, would have viewed Hayes with a cold eye; but very few were willing to buy McCaughey's plot theory. A prominent Republican had announced that he would eat his hat if Hayes were guilty, yet the responsibility lay with the active leadership and following the habits of a lifetime no one was willing to interfere.

13. Eoin McNamee had spent some time in Dublin during the spring of 1941 but had not seen Hayes and played only a peripheral part in the investigation.

14. Apparently Burke had removed his revolver in order to be at his ease in writing the letter. After ten weeks Hayes no longer seemed much of a threat.

15. Responsible people, for example, knew that Hayes was not where he was supposed to be according to the "Confession" or that certain decisions or acts had simply not been as described. Many of those involved, however, were interned or imprisoned in 1941 and Hayes in

Mountjoy could be of little help particularly since he did not read the printed "Confession" until his release.

16. The inability of the courts to function properly during a national emergency was most worrisome for the government. To let Plan escape punishment might have had far-reaching consequences and not for the first or last time the government chose order over law.

17. McCaughey was sentenced to death but his sentence was commuted some within the IRA feel because of the intervention of Cardinal McRory. He was shifted to Portlaoise. Hayes was sentenced to five years' penal servitude on June 19, 1942, and served nearly all of his sentence instead of the normal three years and nine months that time off for good behaviour would have indicated. At Mountjoy he was not allowed contact with any IRA prisoners, a fact many later held against him assuming that he was avoiding them.

18. Most of the men involved in organizing the Army after 1945 had been anti-Kelly in the Curragh. A brief investigation was begun. Liam Rice did write his recollections of the events of 1941. But GHQ wanted to let well enough alone and the matter dropped. Some of the convinced wanted to take matters into their hands and one of the hard men even appeared in Wexford in 1948 looking for Hayes. During 1948–1950 Hayes was occasionally mentioned in Army Conventions but by then as far as the Army was concerned the whole affair was an embarrassment, particularly when the subject came up in recruits' classes.

19. Hayes had written Maire Comerford on December 21, 1941, outlining his defence but without knowing the contents of the "Confession". This letter was seized and used during his trial in June 1942. During his time in Mountjoy he corresponded with several of his defenders; for example, a long letter to James Sherlock, March 26, 1944, stresses the continuation of arrests, lost dumps, and failures at an accelerated rate after his own arrest. Nothing came of all this since both the IRA and the Irish government had finished with the affair. As late as 1949 Hayes was corresponding with Eoin O'Mahony and together they went over the "Confession" building a defence but it was a defence that could never be presented to a court because no such court of last resort existed. There the matter rested!

CHAPTER XI

The Edge of Chaos: Twilight of the Gunmen, October 1941–December 1944

n Dublin in October, no one in the IRA had any more time to spare for he Hayes affair. Somehow the centre had to be restored, morale lifted, nd the Army given a new life and a new direction. While GHQ had been eized with the ramifications of the conspiracy, the forces acting on Irish politics had shifted. On June 22, the German army had launched Operation Barbarossa against Soviet Russia. Week after week reports of massive German victories appeared even in the closely censored Irish press. For many Irishmen these successes over the atheistic legions of communism were not unwelcome. For those who disliked the Nazi regime, opposed the German bombing raids on Northern Ireland, and favoured the Allies, the blitzkrieg into Russia added still more complications to the maintenance of Irish neutrality. Even with the belated entry of America into the war in all but name during the autumn of 1941, there was no blinking the fact that there seemed little in the way of a total German victory. American lend-lease and military aid could hardly maintain Britain once the Germans controlled Europe to the Urals and threatened the Suez Canal and India. Increasingly the evidence indicated that the ultimate decisions on the future of Europe would be made in Berlin. Yet Britain driven behind the last barricade might still in desperation strike out against Ireland for immediate strategic advantage.

For the IRA their largely neglected German contact had grown in importance. On his part Goertz had found his mission suddenly transformed after Barbarossa. So deep underground that Irish Army intelligence had given up looking for him, he almost overnight became the lodestone of those, many in positions of responsibility, who wanted to discover the intentions of the Germans.[1] The IRA was no less interested; but unlike some of the Irish politicians, GHQ placed little faith in Berlin: the Germans would act for German ends. While contact was maintained with Goertz, the major emphasis was on the reorganization of GHQ. Associations with Abwehr had brought only querulous complaints, undesired advice, and recriminations. Goertz while accepting the new GHQ obviously had lost faith in the IRA. If the IRA were to be revitalized out of the rubble of the Hayes affair, GHQ would have to rely on its own efforts not on the problematic shifts of German interests.

The IRA was not entirely finished with high policy, but as the Army's base narrowed, so did the aspirations of GHQ. Once a serious factor in the decisions of the Irish government, the IRA gutted by arrest and then splintered by the Hayes affair faded rapidly as a threat to neutrality or even to civil order. If anything the midsummer rush to Goertz's door was potentially a greater danger to Irish neutrality than any provocation the IRA could manage. In the autumn of 1941, the IRA no longer seemed a clear and present danger to the men of Leinster House. And in the North, with the lid screwed on tightly, the RUC had for some time felt that, bar the odd exploit, the IRA had been neutralized. Both Irish governments felt the worst was over, but the pressure was kept up to finish what the Hayes affair had begun—the elimination of the IRA from Irish politics.

The unrelenting process of attrition by arrest continued unabated; most policemen had personal interests in wiping out the IRA. In September, Tom Cullimore was picked up by Special Branch man, Tom Morris, on his way to the pictures with his girlfriend. In October McGlade was spotted walking down Wolfe Tone Street by a detective cruising by on a bicycle. McGlade grabbed the detective's gun over the hammer, but another detective appeared pedalling wildly and shouting. McGlade took off down the street. The police opened fire. The third shot brought him down, hit in the calf. Denny O'Brien, who had been in charge of the mobile bicycle squad, had scored another coup. The new C/S Kelly, using the name Paul Kelso, was now very much on his own in a city he still did not know well. He moved out of the house in Whitehall into the refuge of last resort, the Brughas' in Rathmines. There he began to organize what was left of Dublin.

While not too hopeful of the German contact, he did meet Goertz, who encouraged by his exciting summer discussions did not want regular contact with the IRA. Kelly in turn wanted Goertz out of his hair and other than warning the German that his safe house in Blackheath Park, Clontarf, was being watched let the German thread drop. Instead he began contacting the remaining units in the country and setting up liaison with an older generation. He persuaded Helena Moloney and Liam Lucas to form a group to evolve a social and economic programme—the ultimate aims of the Republican Movement. Since the Army Convention in April 1938, the strategy of the IRA had been narrow military tactics. Kelly wanted something more than a hit-and-hide IRA. Already by 1938 most of the men of ideas had left the Army. Kelly had to spend the autumn simply discovering who was left and where they were. Broad Republican programmes were dreams. The reality was that the days of a mass IRA had long gone and the time of fugitive gunmen had arrived.

On November 27, Kelly once more felt he must warn Goertz that he had been foolish to move back into the Clontarf house which was still being watched. He cycled out and walked directly into a trap-house filled with detectives who had arrested Goertz a half-hour previously. Kelly was violently angry with himself for walking up to a house blazing with lights in wartime and repeatedly rapping on doors and windows until the detectives finally consented to open up for him. Once more the arrest of the C/S left a vacuum in Dublin. Once more a hurried Army conference was called, bringing together the few men still left on the run. The meeting was held in the Longford Hotel in Upper Dominick Street. Eoin McNamee came down from Belfast, and Seán McCool, who had just been released from prison after completing his sentence for the Crown Entry affair, agreed to attend. Tommy Farrell, C/O of the Western Command, Andy Skelton, GHQ organizer, Johnny O'Connor, Jack Lynch, Steve Wren, Seán Harrington, J. J. Sheehy and several others, perhaps twelve in all, made up the Hotel Longford Conference. It was a far cry from the Army Conventions of the past. They spent the day in discussion of the prospects and arranging a legitimate GHQ staff.

McCool, the senior man, was by-passed in the leadership stakes, perhaps partly because of his reputed Left leanings and partly because of his long absence from the scene. Instead Harrington, who had supported McCool, was chosen as C/S. McNamee, also from the Left, became QMG, McCool A/G, Skelton Director of Training, and Jack Lynch of Cork GHQ organizer. For the first time in nearly a year, the IRA had an effective GHQ staff—on paper at least. Perhaps more important than the staff changes was the basic decision to concentrate exclusively on the North and abandon any military or offensive action in the Twenty-six Counties. For the first time since the English Campaign collapsed, the IRA would have a clear military purpose and with an end to shooting incidents in the South, it was hoped a more secure base. Everyone agreed that the gun fights in the streets had done little good. Both Rice and McGlade had been wounded in action against the police. Not only were the detectives, particularly O'Brien, apparently growing more vindictive but also the image of the IRA as an Army of the pure had been tarnished. Many decent people now felt they were little more than a Celtic branch of the Chicago gangsters. The bank robberies, however essential, had not helped and had led directly to the execution of Richard Goss at Portlaoise on August 9. Following what appeared to be the IRA example, men claiming to act for the Army robbed pawn shops, fired stray shots, indulged in petty crime, and carried out private vendettas. Hopefully with a Northern operation in the works and a passive policy in the South, all this would end.

Harrington, who had been Director of Training and GHQ organizer for nine months, was directed to open up the contacts throughout the country while everyone not directly involved with the reorganization lay low. Like Kelly, Harrington was pretty much on his own. He lost Skelton by arrest almost immediately and had to depend on Jimmy Wren from Leitrim to do the organizing in the country. McCool was still in Donegal visiting his relatives although he had promised to be back in Dublin within a few weeks. O'Connor, who was not wanted by the police, could not be too active without attracting attention. The other men still on the run had to stay in their own areas. With almost no money (the income from the bank raids had gone very swiftly), the IRA had little freedom of action. Harrington by necessity had to work very cautiously.[2] Even this was not enough. Special Branch had stayed on all the contacts they had discovered or had reason to suspect as a result of the various arrests during 1941. Two girls living in the Iveagh flats who had once met Tom Doyle when he was Hayes' A/G were watched off and on in case they led to someone worth while. By this time the combined strength of Special Branch and the Military Intelligence[3] grossly outnumbered the IRA men on the run in Dublin. What with the regular police, the army units stationed in the city, and private informers working on a commission basis, Dublin was all eyes. Nearly every house that had ever been used, even as a drop, was under surveillance. Agents drifted through the pubs listening for clues. Detectives rode the buses with their eyes on the crowds.

Finally, through the girls at the Iveagh flats, Special Branch picked up Harrington's trail and made the identification when he stopped at Russell's shop on Nottingham Street off the North Strand to pick up a message. He got out the back door and moved out of his safe house into the O'Mahoneys' on Gardner Place. Although the new safe house was under twenty-four-hour surveillance, there was access to the roof and a route across the roof to an exit-house four doors away. For four or five days he lay low; but when Wren came from Leitrim, he had to risk going to Russell's again to pick up some money. This time the Special Branch was better prepared. When he walked out, he was surrounded by ten men under Superintendent Gantley. Three squad cars had appeared and the detectives covered the arrest with Thompson guns. With Harrington on his way to the Bridewell, the only man left in Dublin was Stephen Wren waiting on the bridge on the North Strand for his money. McCool was not back from Fermanagh and Eoin McNamee who had been asked by Harrington to come to Dublin to help out had not left Belfast.

While Harrington had been trying to put a Dublin centre back together again, the Northern Command, particularly in Belfast, continued to operate with reasonable success. McNamee had been forced to resort once more to authorized robbery to fill the depleted treasury. This time, more fittingly, the Civil Defence Headquarters on Academy Street was raided by an IRA squad under Patsy Hicks. An ARP man was wounded and lost a leg and one of the IRA volunteers, Bob McMillan, was wounded by the same bullet; but the lifted payroll netted the IRA over £5,000. There were also problems of high policy. On January 26, Northern Command HQ was faced with what was felt to be a peculiarly delicate foreign policy decision when four thousand American troops disembarked in Northern Ireland, the first visible sign in Ireland of America's entry into the war in December 1941. As far as the IRA was concerned, and de Valera shared the Army's view, this was an "invasion" without prior notification of the appropriate *de jure* authorities. The delicate point was that America had always been the ally *par excellence*, a source of succour in times of want and the home of millions of emigrant fellow Irishmen now apparently dedicated to winning the war at the side of the Saxon. Not to protest might be craven but to protest too much would be foolish. The Americans were not unaware of the potential problem with the IRA and Major-General Harknett had a Catholic chaplain make contact with Northern Command. Harknett indicated he wanted no involvement in any IRA–British trouble and was willing to initiate discussions on the matter. HQ considered the problem; and although there was brief interest in a proposal to kidnap Harknett, the staff decided to ignore the feeler. John Graham and Hugh McAteer did write a "Manifesto", published in the *Belfast Telegraph*, advising the United States not to become an agent of the British; but after that the matter dropped—the first faint sign of political realism.

Beyond bank raids and manifestoes, the Northern Command, like Dublin, was faced with organizational problems since McNamee would have to move to Dublin to help out the centre. In February an Army Conference was held with nearly thirty men present. The chairman was Hugh McAteer, who had been released from prison in 1941, and had agreed to come back into the command structure. Present were Hugh Matthews, I/O of Belfast, his adjutant Seán Dolan, his very sly I/O Gerald O'Reilly, and selected men from the Belfast unit like Patsy Hicks, C/O of the ARP raid, Dan McAllister, and Tom Williams, acting-C/O of Belfast C Coy and a young man on his way up within the Northern Command. McAteer took over as C/O of the Northern Command with O'Reilly as Adjutant and John Graham as I/O and Director of Publicity. The Belfast staff stayed in place. The Conference opened up the entire programme and policy of the IRA for discussion and agreed that the first priority was a campaign in the North. Secondly, the Northern Command was to effect the democratic election of an Army Executive, since the 1938 members had disappeared in the welter of arrests and internments. The decision to elect a Executive to oversee the campaign seemed even more appropriate a few days later when word came from Dublin that Harrington had been lifted even before McNamee could make firm contact.[4]

The difference in the Dublin and Belfast situation could not have been more pronounced. That there was such a unit as C Coy for Williams to lead reveals how effectively the Belfast IRA had eluded the sweeps and comb-outs of the RUC. At the beginning of 1942, there were over three hundred Volunteers in four companies making up the Belfast unit with the small Northern Command staff integrated at the top. The strength of the auxiliaries, organized by McGlade and McCaughey, and Cumann na mBan had tapered off, but both still supplied considerable aid and assistance. One of the most interesting Belfast assets was the Special Operation Group, a special company under the direct control of Northern Command HQ, composed of Volunteers from Denis Ireland's Irish Union, a non violent group seeking to persuade the Protestants of the virtues of a united Ireland. Composed of trade union people, mild Republicans, and the odd Protestant, unwittingly the Irish Union became a way station on a pipeline into the IRA. Several Protestants had "graduated" from the Union and sought out the IRA, including John Graham, Gideon Close, William Smith, and Rex Thompson. Usually with far more formal education than the northern Volunteers possessed of an idealism without sectarian foundation, they were immensely valuable. John Graham became Director of Intelligence for the Northern Command and editor of the newly issued *Republican News,* the successor to the Belfast edition of *War News.* He supplied what the Belfast IRA had consistently lacked since the exit of the radicals and professional people in the 'thirties—a keen, urbane mind, and an acid pen. The relative success of the IRA in the North was not solely or even mainly the result of the skills of the Grahams and McNamees and McAteers but rather the transformation, out of necessity as much as choice, of the movement into a truly underground force. In the North, particularly in Belfast, most of the active men were on the run in areas where they could trust nearly everyone. In Dublin safe houses and safe people had grown rare. In Belfast, with rare exceptions, every Nationalist home was safe and every Nationalist mute. Many might disapprove of the IRA but few would turn on their own, however misguided and futile. Thus as long as an open confrontation with the RUC was avoided, the North could hold on.

In Dublin times had become so hard that GHQ was more a symbol than a reality. McCool, back from Donegal, took over as C/S and McNamee as A/G. The staff had been pared to the bone leaving only Charlie Kerins a young man brought up from Kerry to help out, another Kerryman, Mick Quill, and from time to time one or two others whom the detectives had overlooked. In and out of the city was Patrick Dermody of Cavan, who was C/O of the Eastern Command and the main contact man with the units to be assigned to preparing for the attack on the North. McCool and McNamee, both new to Dublin centre, had come into a situation cluttered with booby-traps and dead-ends. A great many contacts had simply disappeared with the rapid arrests of Kelly and Harrington not to mention the fall-out of ill feeling and suspicion after the Hayes affair. Even to move round Dublin was difficult and yet there had to be constant coming and going, endless little non-stop conferences with a handful of men hastily trying to make good the losses of a year. McCool occasionally travelled out of Dublin to keep in touch with local units. In March he slipped down to New Ross with Frank Driver of Kildare. But he did not call a general conference, since it would only attract attention. The only light at the end of the tunnel was the planned Northern campaign. The prospect of action inspired many who had lost heart after the failure of the English campaign and the ensuing years of quiet. McCool and McNamee were tireless and even took up the German thread again.

On February 28, 1942, German Sergeant Gunther Schuetz escaped from Mountjoy. He had been parachuted into Ireland in March 1941 but had been picked up under the name Hans Marschner by the Irish police, one more Abwehr failure. Once helped out of Mountjoy by the IRA he disappeared down the old Republican pipeline to appear, hardly unexpectedly, at Mrs. Cáitlín Brugha's house. Mrs. Brugha was still running her own private network based on the talents of her two daughters, Nóinín and Neassa. Nóinín had established a courier and intelligence service between Dublin and Belfast and word was sent to the Northern Command that a useful German was in hand. McCool established direct contact with the Brughas and plans were begun to get Schuetz out of the country on a fishing boat with a shopping list of IRA needs. Schuetz was delighted and quite willing to take along the request for weapons, ammunition, explosives, radio equipment and, of course, money. GHQ collected a crew and persuaded a well-known Irish adventurer, Charlie McGuinness, to captain the operation. McGuinness was cloaked in legends: he had been Harbour Master at Leningrad after the Revolution, served in the International Brigade in Spain, and even been president of a Latin American country. Legend aside, he knew boats, was a reserve officer in the Irish Navy, what there was of it, and best of all was of no interest to Irish intelligence. GHQ managed the boat, the crew, the debarkation point at Bray, south of Dublin, and was ready to move Schuetz as soon as the weather was better. All this was done on a frayed shoe string in the midst of the campaign preparations and despite the arrest of McCool in the midst of the project. On April 30, the police swooped on the Brugha house, picking up Schuetz only hours before he was to sail, and on Bray, seizing the boat. The crew and McGuinness were arrested. One of Nóinín's couriers had been picked up on the

Belfast–Dublin train in possession of the ubiquitous documents, without which no IRA agent seems capable of travelling. Coupled with their information, the Special Branch then managed to nip the entire operation at the last moment.

In the midst of all the preparations and plots in Dublin, the Northern Command had nothing more on hand than the Easter commemoration. As traditional as Bodenstown and as vital for morale purposes, these ceremonies, particularly in the North, often provoked the police to baton charges and arrests. With nothing but bad news out of Dublin, where McNamee was struggling along as C/S, McAteer in Belfast decided that an open symbolic display in response to RUC pressure was necessary. In order to minimize the risks of arrests, he planned a diversion. On Sunday April 5, Tom Williams would stage an "incident" in C Company area. The police would rush in reinforcements leaving the IRA a free field to hold a brief public ceremony elsewhere. What was intended as a pinprick to RUC confidence turned into another IRA disaster. Williams along with five volunteers and a girl, the "action squad", decided to fire a few shots over a patrol car and then disappear into the side streets while the RUC pulled back for aid. When the police car pulled up to the corner of Kashmir Road and Clonard Gardens, the squad opened fire. Understandably the RUC did not realize that they were merely part of a diversion and assumed that the IRA intended to hit where they aimed. The constables piled out of the car firing at the retreating IRA squad. The Volunteers were forced to withdraw into a house on Cawnpore Street and fight a real gun battle. Williams was hit twice in the left leg and once through the left arm. An RUC constable was killed outright. The squad was arrested, all six men were tried for murder, convicted, and condemned to death.

The accidental gun fight on Cawnpore Street was not the only violence over the Easter weekend. On Friday night in Dungannon, two IRA men, Jimmy Clarke and Seán Donnelly, had evaded a raid only by shooting two RUC men. They managed to contact help before the RUC net closed in and were whisked across the border. In Dublin on Sunday in Glasnevin Cemetery, the Special Branch tried to pick up three members of the Dublin unit still in circulation. One of them, Lasarian Mangan, drew a gun; but when he seemed to hesitate, Brendan Behan, recently released from Borstal in Britain, took matters into his own hands. He shouted, "Use it, use it. Give it to me and I will shoot the bastards." He snatched the revolver from Mangan and the police, waiting no longer, opened fire. Behan fired back and took off down the street and over the wall into the garden of the nearest house. After wandering around Dublin and Belfast on the run, hunted for varying reasons by Special Branch, the RUC, and the IRA, he was arrested in Dublin, tried, convicted, and sentenced to fourteen years. Whatever his other virtues, the IRA found that Behan's military talents were at best unorthodox and his capacity to accept discipline negligible.[5]

The last act of the Easter shootings came several days later when Frank Morris, who had helped get Clarke and Donnolly across the border, decided to act on one of Eoin McNamee's rules as C/O Northern Command—if stopped for identity check by the RUC, have a go if there is a clear exit. The hope was that one or two such "incidents" would result in a drastic decline in identity checks by the RUC.[6] At Strabane near the bridge across the Foyle to County Donegal, an RUC constable stopped Morris and began asking questions. Within a couple of hundred yards of the bridge to the other Ireland, Morris decided to have a go. He drew his revolver and fired twice. The constable crumpled to the road, badly wounded. Then everything went wrong for Morris. An unnoticed man standing two hundred yards off lifted a hunting rifle and began firing. Another man on a bicycle pedalled in front of him and cut off the route to the bridge. Dodging through the roadside bushes, Morris leaped into the river. Since he could not swim, all he could do was huddle under the bank for hours until the RUC patrols found him. He was sentenced to ten years and fifteen strokes of the cat for attempted murder.

On April 20, in the wake of the shooting, the new Army Executive met and elected an Army Council. The new IRA-centre immediately began steps to complete the reorganization of the IRA and to review the plans for the Northern campaign. To avoid confusion caused by the previous rapid turnover in GHQ personnel, Deputies were selected. Plans were prepared to organize the Twenty-six Counties on a battalion level. More important, the whole history of the German contact was reviewed by McNamee, who was hopeful that something positive might develop if Germany could be tied into the Northern campaign. At this time, Schuetz had not been arrested and prospects of a clean escape still looked good. Resolutions were passed outlining the policy to be followed while the German contact was being made.

> That as a prelude to any co-operation between Oglaigh na h-Éireann and the German Government, the German Government explicitly declare its intention of recognizing the Provisional Government of the Irish Republic as the Government of Ireland in all post-war negotiations affecting Ireland.[7]

Given the composition and resources of the IRA "government" in the spring of 1942, the resolution seemed straight out of cloud cuckooland; a handful of wanted men meeting furtively in back rooms directing a largely non-existent army in gun fights with the police hardly seemed competent to speak as the Provisional Government of Ireland. Yet the structure of

Europe had been so torn in the years since the war began that the IRA might perhaps be excused for hoping that the situation in Ireland might be transformed. Although Germany had not finished off the Russians, the panzers were again on the move in the East, the submarine campaign in the North Atlantic was fast eroding British maritime strength, and in Asia Japan seemed to go from strength to strength.

In practical terms, the Army Council agreed that GHQ should have the authority "to give military information to powers at war with England, which would not endanger civilian lives, even before any definite contacts have been established with these powers".[8] This potential exchange of intelligence for military material regardless of the course of the European war could only be to IRA advantage and while scarcely high politics was a giant step away from the narrow parochialism which had gripped the Army since June 1941. The step was never taken, for within ten days Schuetz was arrested. Even without the dim prospect of German aid, the Army Council was firmly committed to begin operations within the Six Counties. If Berlin would or could co-operate with the IRA, fine and good, but the Army Council accepted that a campaign would have to depend on the IRA's own efforts and resources.

These "resources" left much to be desired. Ireland was pocked with dumps, known only to the locals and one or two men. There were plenty of country units untouched but long out of contact with GHQ. There were good sound Republican areas, reservoirs of money and comfort, if the right word were spoken in the right ears. While the Army Council was not operating totally in the dark, most of the members were from the North or young men unfamiliar with the old faithfuls, the distant parishes, and the invisible networks in alien areas. McCool in a short while had done an impressive job in organizing for the campaign. He had been in the Army a long time, was well known in many places, and had avoided the contamination of the Hayes affair. His arrest had been particularly disconcerting because he had kept the location and contents of most of the local dumps in his head. With all this information out of reach behind the barbed wire of the Curragh where McCool was interned, the work would have to be done over again. McCool, however, had one last card up his sleeve. When he arrived in the Curragh, he found the feuding factions in full voice, Kelly on one side and Liam Leddy on the other, with a mixed bag of dissidents, independents, and odd men trying to stay neutral. One of the later-comers to the "neutralists" was Harry White, who had been an operations officer in England and an instructor in the training camps outside Dublin. A tough, hard man he had cast a cold eye on the camp squabbling and gone neutral. Since he was a known malcontent, the authorities might assume that he had grown tired of the rangling and lost the faith. For McCool's purposes he would make an ideal messenger.

McCool approached White and asked him to sign out with the information about the dumps. White refused, since signing out was a violation of General Army Orders, but McCool found a way round the inviolate rules. White resigned from the IRA, memorized the locations, and signed out. As expected he was released. By this time long paroles and quick releases were the order of the day. IRA morale in the Curragh seemed to go from bad to worse; and although there would be another long hunger strike the next year,[9] the government assumed, with some justice, that only pride stood in the way of mass resignations. White arrived in Dublin and made contact with Charlie Kerins. Once he had relayed the information, White waited around in Dublin for a week on the odd pound given him by McCool and Kerins until his reinstatement came through and he was once more back in the IRA attached to GHQ. As usual in Dublin, GHQ was more of a proving ground for the police than an effective centre. On May 23, McNamee was arrested, an average of one C/S lost every six weeks. This time, however, the link was not broken.

White's information was still in IRA hands and McNamee's Deputy, Hugh McAteer, took over as planned and was confirmed as C/S by the Army Council on July 19 with Kerins as the new Deputy C/S. For the first time the centre was shifted to Belfast. Kerins was left in the South with a skeleton crew but operations were to be run from the North. Dublin had lost any value as the centre of the net and turned into a bottomless trap for staff officers. With all the action to be in the North and along the border, McAteer as both C/O Northern Command and C/S intended to stay close to the action. While time was consumed in the defence of the six men arrested for the Cawnpore Street shooting and dithering about marginal matters like the Bodenstown commemoration or a by-election in Belfast, GHQ, now staffed by full-time men, spent most of the waking hours preparing for the Northern campaign. The basic plan was to collect the contents of the Twenty-six County dumps, move the stuff close to the border, and then just before operations were initiated, smuggle it over.

On August 15, the Army Council met to go over the final details and draw up the Campaign Proclamation. All preparations were far advanced. GHQ envisioned spearhead, commando-type units, forty or fifty men all told, striking up from the South across the border to open up operations. All the material that was needed was on the move. Farrell, C/O Western Command, and Dermody, C/O Eastern Command, had accumulated over twelve tons of arms, munitions, and explosives. There had been no leak. After the Army Council meeting, GHQ sent out word to move the stuff north. On the night of August 30, the major shipment of about three tons came over near Newry in two lorries despite the tight border security The lorries left the material in a barn on McCaffery's farm, near an unused quarry outside Hannastown. The Volunteer in charge, Jerry O'Callaghan, came on into Belfast to report to McAteer that the distribution could begin. He then returned directly to the dump. In the morning another IRA man, McDowell, was sent out to help O'Callaghan; but he was apparently spotted as he entered McCaffery's farmhouse. The RUC quickly called in reinforcements. When the patrol cars arrived, O'Callaghan and McDowell were inside the barn laying out the arms and ammunition for inspection. The RUC burst in the door. O'Callaghan had a Thompson in his hand and the police opened fire, killing him instantly. McDowell was so dazed by the raid that even afterward his recollections of the shooting were not clear. What was clear at GHQ was O'Callaghan's seemingly needless death and the loss of three tons of arms.

By September 1, the machinery for the first operation had already been activated. These attacks did not depend on the Hannastown dump. The Army Council had sent out a General Army Order that in the event of the execution of Tommy Williams, the only man whose sentence had not been commuted for the Cawnpore Street shooting, all C/Os were to take aggressive action.[10] The major thrust, intended to be the first of a series of sporadic attacks along the border from both the North and South, was an attack from County Monaghan across the border against Crossmaglen in County Armagh. The C/O was Dermody, who had found a lorry for the attack. With the exception of one or two Northerners who were attached to the Dublin staff,[11] his men were all from the South. The twenty or so men in the commandeered lorry and a trailing car had already decided that they would take reprisals when they moved out in broad daylight several hours after Williams had been hanged in Belfast.

Beyond the Twenty-six County side of the border, at Culloville, an RUC patrol car passed the lorry full of armed men. Then, suddenly, when the penny dropped, the driver braked to a halt and spun the car around. As the squad car neared the lorry, which had stopped as had the trailing car, a fire fight broke out. One IRA volunteer was hit and taken back to the hospital at Carrickmacross. One policeman was hit and the others, outnumbered and outgunned, surrendered. All were disarmed and released. There was no longer any point in trying to reach Crossmaglen since both sides of the border would soon be crawling with police and army units alerted by the long burst of gun fire. The lorry was driven back towards Dublin and the men dropped off along the way to find their way home. Abortive as the raid had been, Irish security forces were shocked. Their success in bagging Chiefs of Staff and Abwehr agents had persuaded them that the IRA could be discounted. That the Army was still capable, in September 1942, of putting on a full-scale raid from the South was disquieting. A week later the police's false sense of security was again rudely and violently shaken.

At 9.45 on the morning of September 9, Sergeant Denis O'Brien was standing beyond the gateway to his house at Ballyboden, Rathfarnham. Before he could reach his car, came a burst of fire, out of nowhere. O'Brien dropped dead in front of his gate. Three strange men had been seen in the neighbourhood, one with a bicycle, but no positive identification was forthcoming. Specific names aside, the Castle knew who had shot O'Brien and why. Of all the Special Branch men, O'Brien, a Broy Harrier, had achieved by far the greatest notoriety, not only for his successes but his brutality. He had entered into the great game of searching out and often shooting down the IRA men with far more dedication and satisfaction than any of his colleagues. He had sneered at Liam Rice lying in his hospital bed and at first refused to take the wounded Charlie McGlade to a hospital. He had led the raid which netted McGrath, Harte, and Hunt and led to the firing squad for two. For the IRA men, no friends of detectives on any occasion, O'Brien had pushed his luck and his investigations too long and too hard. While GHQ in Belfast had prohibited such operations, the desire for vengeance finally overcame Army policy. O'Brien was shot. Once more Dublin swarmed with police. A £5,000 reward was offered. A list of men wanted was circulated but the names indicated only that the Castle had lost touch with depleted Dublin centre. In Belfast GHQ was horrified: no matter how vicious O'Brien had been, the order had been to avoid provocation. But there was little that could be done, even though a court martial for Kerins, who must have ordered the shooting, was briefly considered. On October 2, Michael Quill, who had been Kerins' Adjutant in Dublin, was arrested in Belfast and taken to York Street RUC barracks. When he refused to talk, he was taken by the RUC to the border at Carrackaron, County Louth, and turned over to the Irish Special Branch. He was not tried until January 11, 1943. The Military Tribunal found him not guilty and he was interned in the Curragh.

In the meantime the gun fights continued in the South, Army Orders notwithstanding. On September 30, Patrick Dermody decided to go home to his sister's wedding in Cavan and invited a fellow GHQ man along for the party. The ubiquitous Special Branch had set a watch on the house and saw Dermody and his friend slip in. With the house cordoned off, the police burst in the door and rushed into the kitchen. Both sides opened fire simultaneously. The police outside were directing a withering but blind fire through the windows. The wedding guests were scattered on the floor. The IRA men were struggling to get to the back of the house. One of the officers chasing them stumbled in front of a window. He was shot dead by the police fire from outside. In a second Dermody fell dead. The remaining IRA man, hit twice through the leg, jumped out of a window firing as he ran. In the uproar he managed to get through the cordon into a nearby field where he went to ground. For two days he lay in the field barely out of sight of the Dermody house while police patrols circled and searched. Finally he was found by one of the soldiers who had been helping in the manhunt. Fortunately for the Volunteer, the soldier had little use for the police either and helped him into a barn and treated the wound. The anonymous soldier then made contact with the IRA in Dublin and the wounded Volunteer was shifted to a safe house, near the Malahide Road.

Then, on October 19, word arrived that an IRA refuge on Holly Road, Donnycarney, was no longer safe. The two IRA men inside, Maurice O'Neill and Harry White, wounded in a previous escapade, would have to move out immediately. As soon as it was dark enough, they collected their things and slipped out the back door to get their bicycles. Suddenly the night was filled with people shooting and shouting, "Put your hands up!" The two IRA men scrambled out of the back garden and into the lane, firing wildly behind them. With surprise lost the neat police ambush degenerated in a wild orgy of shots. In the confusion Detective Mordaunt was hit and fell dead in a garden on Oak Road.[12] White ran on down the lane firing in front of him to break out of the police ring. He turned into another garden and ran in the backdoor of a house, down the hall, and out the front. He hadn't a clue where he was, but the police were out of sight. He took refuge on a railway embankment out of sight of the patrols. The next night he slipped away to a house in Cabra and made contact with Kerins. He had nearly used up his allotted lives and kept very still in a safe house in Rathgar until he could slip up to Belfast and take over as C/O Northern Command. Maurice O'Neill was not as lucky. He was arrested and put on trial for the murder of Mordaunt. His counsel, Seán MacBride, pointed out the police had not identified themselves before firing and that without an autopsy there was no evidence that O'Neill's bullet had killed Mordaunt. The Military Tribunal was unmoved by quibbles. O'Neill was sentenced to be hanged. On November 10, 1942, the government endorsed the decision. At 8 a.m. on November 12 the imported British hangman, Mr. Pierpoint, performed the execution.

The renewed police pressure after the September 2 border raid and the gun fights was taking a toll in the North as well. McAteer had been picked up in October with his Director of Intelligence, O'Reilly. McAteer had believed a policeman from his old street in Derry who claimed he would supply the IRA with certain useful information. When McAteer and O'Reilly arrived at the man's house, a squad of the RUC-CID were waiting for them. McAteer got fifteen years for treason and was likely to be off the scene for some time to come. Kerins, as Deputy C/S, automatically took over; but the centre of any action remained Belfast. When White arrived, he found that Rory Maguire, C/O Belfast, had a full staff but a badly depleted unit. In less than a year, the same slow war of attrition had cut away the Belfast strength. Meetings were kept to five or six men to avoid arrest. After the September raid, the Army had lost momentum. The RUC allowed no freedom of movement. Dumps were uncovered. The men on the run kept running into the police. The RUC descended on the IRA publicity office and editorial room of the *Republican News* in Belfast and captured Graham after another violent gun battle. All told, there were still fifty or sixty men free; but most had to keep deep underground and very still. All the same, the Army managed sixty armed attacks in three months, Belfast had to be put under curfew, and the RUC moved in "cage" lorries and armoured cars. There were small units in Tyrone and Derry but many of the good, old Republican areas had been cleared out long before. Some of the solid units like Archie Agnew's in South Derry and Arty McAlinden's in South Armagh were simply unable to take any action in November whereas two months earlier GHQ could depend on them.

Across the border Cavan and Monaghan were in better shape than seemed possible given the level of police activity, but GHQ recognized that if the volunteers were activated for a single operation these areas would be cleared out as well. With no orders to send, without active couriers or staff organizers, the centre was losing touch with the units along the border, then with those in Munster and the Western Command. The local C/Os had no intention of risking arrest to keep up a good front. Even the relatively innocuous Republican "political" activity that had been tolerated in the past now might lead to the Curragh. Parades ended. Training ended. Often even meetings of the IRA people ended. The intricate and long-lived infrastructure of the IRA in the country began to fray and break. The leaders and the best men were in prison. The men from the glory years—Barry, MacBride, and Twomey—had left. The GHQ policy of recent years alienated many as had the German contact. The Hayes affair had confused everyone. With no clear call from an acknowledged centre, with no plan of action, with the police eyeing the suspicious and their neighbours committed to neutrality, the local men withdrew into silence. The units imperceptibly disintegrated.

During the winter of 1942–1943, the end seemed at hand. Kerins, disguised as a seminary student, was holed up in the home of Dr. Kathleen Farrell. He could not move far and was rarely in communication with Belfast. His "staff" had long since been whittled down to Archie Doyle and Liam Burke, who acted as his A/G; even his QMG, Harry White, was in Belfast. The situation might have been called a holding action, but no one wanted to consider what the truncated IRA was holding out for. More than anything else the refusal to give up was a result of pride and a lack of alternatives. Most of the men on the run faced long sentences or execution. Emigration to exile in war-time was unlikely even if they had been willing to admit that the end had come. So in Dublin and Belfast they waited.

What little action there was could be found inside Crumlin Road Prison, where McAteer was desperate to break out and redeem himself after his foolish capture. While still on detention, he began sawing through his cell bars, but even before one was half cut he was sentenced. In with the other Republican prisoners, McAteer suggested to the C/O of Prisoners, Pat Donnelly, that the weakest spot in the prison was the roof. Permission was given to break up instead of out. Ned Maguire, who was a slater, was brought into the attempt as a technical specialist, and Jimmy Steele, perhaps the best known Belfast IRA man, along with McAteer and Donnelly, would make up the team. Once through the roof, the four would drop forty feet on a twisted-sheet rope to the ground, move over to the twenty-foot outside wall, throw a grappling hook over the barbed-wire on top, climb up on an extension rod made from brush shafts and strips of leather from the prison shoe shop, and drop the twenty feet to the ground. After a careful study of the moon calendar, a day was selected when the moon set early and the sun rose late; in fact, with summer time still in effect as a war measure daylight did not come until nearly ten o'clock. The four could slip out during breakfast hour between half-eight and nine when the warders were eating. All the preliminary work on the bars, rafters, and slates went unnoticed and the variety of tools, ropes, hooks and rods were made without discovery. The line to GHQ was activated and White was ready for them when the final word was sent out. The word never came, the four men decided to have a go while the going was good without waiting for GHQ to prepare a proper reception.

On the morning of January 15, while the warders breakfasted, the four went to the toilet, then through the ceiling into the roof space, and out through the slates. It was a dark, frosty morning and as expected, no one on duty was interested in the roof. They slid down on the sheet rope, dashed to the wall, joined the pole, affixed the hook, wrapped it with cloth to prevent noise, and after some trouble hooked the barbed wire. Still no one had noticed them. The first three went up and over, but McAteer's arms were tired and just at the top he slipped and fell back into the prison yard twisting his ankle. Giving it one more try, he struggled back up the rope, dragged himself across the barbed wire, ripping open his hand, and fell to the ground, this time on the outside. They rushed out the main entrance, still unguarded, and walked as fast as they could into the dark streets of Belfast. In fifteen minutes all four had knocked on the door of the prearranged safe house. A doctor was found for McAteer's leg, and the local IRA man contacted. That evening Harry White and Liam Burke arrived to collect the four men and move them to another safe house.

As McAteer had anticipated, the break recouped considerable prestige for the IRA. The RUC clamped down even harder. A reward of £3,000 each was offered but there were no takers. Once the most immediate hue and cry had died down, GHQ staff met again, to integrate the escapees. There was no longer any pretence that a democratically elected Executive existed or even an Army Council. The GHQ staff acting for the Army had to create a provisional Council and new GHQ until such time, in the far distant future, as the normal procedures could be used. The continued decay of the "constitutional structure" was worrisome, since to maintain IRA continuity the traditional offices had to be filled—not to do so would have reduced the Army's claim to legitimacy, and without the right to resort to physical force there was no purpose in the existence of the IRA. Thus at a time when there often seemed more leaders than followers and certainly more pressing affairs than staff appointments, GHQ had to remain involved in ritual and regulation.

On Sunday, February 14, Kerins came up from Dublin for the Staff conference. McAteer returned as C/S with Kerins as Deputy C/S and Burke as A/G. The Northern Command Staff was enlarged with Steele brought in as Adjutant and Maguire as Q/M. Five provisional members of the Army Council were appointed pending sanction of the all but defunct Executive which had to be restocked at the same time. No matter how bad the times outside the small meeting room, the "institutions" existed once more, to convince the volunteers and even the staff that conditions were not as hopeless as they might appear, that the IRA was not really as weak as a head count would indicate, and that some high purpose could still be served by the Army. As long as there is an Army Council, even if the seventh man has to be dragged off the street, then there is hope. As long as the C/S, duly appointed, can send out orders under a GHQ letterhead, then there is hope. Since revolutionaries live on hope not on numbers or rational prospects or tidy analysis, the elaborate allotment of appointments, largely to extinct commands over a vanished army, was essential.

By February 1943, the long attrition had removed, even for the persistent, the hope for action. Resumption or suspension of the "campaign" was left to the Northern Command staff, which meant McAteer and White, and the order forbidding all operations of a military nature in the South was continued. It was hoped that Kerins would be able to deliver both war material and men to the North; but most of the February 14 meeting was spent on a discussion of prisoners, their feuds, dependants, and prospects. With much of the IRA in jail in one country or another, the prison issue now came far ahead of "foreign relations", which had shrunk to the possibility of re-establishing contact with Clan na Gael.[13] There was vague discussion of publicity and radio transmitters but no concrete conclusions. Even *in extremis* the delegates passed a resolution in the following grandiose terms:

> A political arm be formed representative of the whole country, whose constitution shall be based on the Constitution of the Republic proclaimed in arms in 1916 and ratified by the free vote of the Irish people in 1918.[14]

Then the meeting broke up. Kerins was on his way back to Dublin and the rest of the GHQ staff to their safe houses. McAteer felt the meeting had gone well and that with a solid little nucleus of Volunteers the IRA was far from moribund.

Almost at once GHQ had an opportunity to discover how effective the IRA still was. Word came into Belfast on the line out of the Derry Jail that preparations for a major break were nearly complete. The Derry prisoners wanted GHQ aid on the outside once the men were beyond the wall. By the time GHQ got the word, the break was well along. The IRA Prison Council had decided to try and tunnel out, always a risky proposition because of the problem of excavated dirt. In the time-honoured tradition of prison tunnels, the dirt was slipped out in pillow slips, sifted, and flushed down the toilets. Inexplicably, the repeated visits of plumbers to repair blocked sewers never alerted the warders. The tunnel, sighted on a chimney on Harding Street, inched forward day by day, buttressed by floor boards borrowed from inconspicuous floors. The dirt was flushed away, scattered in the yard, thrown to the wind. Really big rocks were buried. Finally, it was estimated that the tunnel was nearly under the wall. GHQ in Belfast were notified. McAteer and White mobilized about twenty-five men on both sides of the border. The C/O of Tyrone, Jim Toner, and his Adjutant, Joe Carant, were put in charge of moving the men out of Northern Ireland. GHQ would get them away from the vicinity of Derry Jail.

On Saturday morning, March 21, Joseph Logue and his daughter Mary were at breakfast in their house off Harding Street. Glancing out on the back garden, which abutted the prison wall, they were stunned to see part of the garden disappear into the ground leaving a gaping hole. Even more startling was the unexpected figure of a man popping out of the hole followed by another and another. Twenty-one men dashed into the kitchen, past the gaping Logues, down the hall, out the front door, and down Harding Street. As the last man was popping out of the Logues', the first of the line was disappearing into a large furniture van parked at the corner of Abercorn Place. In the cab were Steele and Burke. When the last man climbed in, the van moved off and disappeared leaving the Logues with a private tunnel into the Londonderry prison and the prison with a very embarrassing informal rear exit. The van drove toward the border and turned the escapees over to the next unit. The men got into Donegal without trouble but not before the Irish authorities had been alerted. Over the next twenty-four hours, the Irish Army and Special Branch picked up all but a few. Alfie White made his way back to Belfast and was attached to GHQ staff. The unlucky majority were shipped straight to the Curragh. Irish opinion was outraged. Always a sporting nation, it seemed to the country very unfair, unsporting, to pop the men who had tweeked the lion's tail into a concentration camp. Apparently, the government saw the point that the Derry break was a grand stunt and gradually in small lots the men were released. By the spring of 1943, few felt the IRA had any relevancy and most of the released men drifted away. One, Seamus "Rocky" Burns, had not given up hope and like Alfie White made his way to Belfast and joined up again.

In April the IRA pulled off another brief stunt by seizing the Broadway Cinema in Belfast for the Easter Commemoration. The *Republican News* in the April issue printed the Army Council's annual statement. Here and there could be found a touch of realism—"that cause had not yet triumphed"—but even in the spring of 1943 the Council found cause for optimism.

> Ireland is being held within the Empire by sheer force and by force alone can she free herself. Now with Britain engaged in a struggle for her very existence, we are presented with a glorious opportunity.

The glorious opportunity evaporated; in fact, the last husks of the IRA decayed swiftly. Belfast was soon no better than Dublin, a little huddle of men seeking refuge not action, holding on out of pride and habit, unable to act, barely able to keep in contact. The ties to the men on the run in Northern Ireland went one by one. The arrests clipped away at the GHQ staff. Steele was lost in May and then Burke and then McAteer in October leaving Kerins once more C/S.

In Dublin the shooting was still going on. On July 4, 1943, Jackie Griffith, who had escaped from jail and linked up with Kerins, was cycling down Holles Street past the hospital when a patrol car filled with detectives pulled in behind him. A police machine gun sputtered and Griffith collapsed into a tangle of bike wheels and blood. He was dead. His father, a compositor on the *Irish Press*, took up the telex of his son's death and fainted over his machine. The Castle was not beyond vengeance either.

Kerins was almost alone in Dublin, as was White in Belfast. Rocky Burns, who had come back to help out, was picked up on February 11, 1944. When he tried to break away from the detectives he was mortally wounded in a brief gunfight. In 1944 White decided to move out of Belfast. He went up to Derry where he took a job playing the banjo with the Magnet Dance Band. He kept up the line into the prisons and oversaw an occasional limited issue of *War News* but lost contact with Dublin. Apparently only Kerins was left, C/S of a one-man army.

Kerins eventually left his safe house at Dr. Kathleen Farrell's and returned to Kerry to let the heat cool. He felt the police were very close and knew of the house; nevertheless, he left some papers and guns behind to be picked up. The year 1944 was so bad that he could not find a single man left to go by the Farrells' and collect his dump. In June he came back to Dublin and hired a pony cart to move the things from the Farrell house. He called in a disguised message over the tapped phone that he would be over that evening, June 15. There was no sign of the police when he arrived at 50 Rathmines Road and he slipped in quietly. Late that night the trap finally closed. The police arrived with squad cars, ambulances, tin hats, coats of mail, and machine guns. They pried off the side door lock and went straight up six flights to the room where Kerins and Dr. Farrell's seventeen-year-old son were sleeping. The detectives burst through the door. Kerins had a Thompson under the bed but he never had a chance to use it for he was seized before he was fully awake. He was tried before the Military Tribunal in October. The government was quite sure that Kerins had given the order to kill Sergeant O'Brien, even if he had not fired the shot, so no one was too fussy about the details of his case. On October 9, as expected, Kerins was found guilty and sentenced to hang. On December 1, 1944, the imported English hangman carried out the sentence. Charlie Kerins, the Boy from Tralee, was dead and with him died the last fragile symbol of IRA continuity.

For the first time in generations the line had been broken. There no longer was a Chief of Staff or a GHQ or an Army Council or even an IRA. The prisons and the camps held those who would not quit but few of these men looked forward to more than their own freedom and the chance to lead quiet private lives. The bitter schism in the prisons, the turmoil of the Hayes affair, the gun fights in the streets had destroyed the purity of the Army. The hard men and the persistent had been shot down or arrested or died on hunger strike. Many still faced long years in prison. As late as 1947, there would still be twenty-five long-term men in English jails. Not until a change of government in Dublin in 1948 were the last few IRA men to be released from Portlaoise. Until 1950 twelve men remained in Crumlin Road, Belfast. By then the IRA had become an anachronism for most Irishmen. The time for physical force had passed: partition would be ended by political agitation not gunfire in the streets. The Irish Minister of Justice, Gerald Boland, announced in pride that the IRA was dead and that he had killed it. He had been helped by the RUC, the British police, the Irish Army, and of course by the IRA itself, but to all intents and purposes he spoke the truth. Once committed to a campaign of terror after 1938, the IRA was on a one-way road to victory or defeat, life or death. In 1945 the IRA had apparently died, defeated, another romantic cord in the pattern of Irish history frayed and broken.

NOTES

1. Professor Desmond Williams wrote twice on this midsummer madness ("A Study in Neutrality", *The Leader* (Dublin), January/April 1953, and "Neutrality", *Irish Press* (Dublin), June/July 1953), which led, among other things, to a lawsuit. The names of Goertz's contacts are still not publicly known—he never revealed them—but with the passing of the years a few men have privately admitted meeting him although they deny that they initiated the step.

2. Despite the bank robberies, the IRA was scraping bottom. Most men on the run had to depend on their families or their meagre savings or loans. GHQ could only find the odd pound and these were often borrowed from old friends.

3. One of the great assets of the Castle was the money available to pay "informers" although much of this kind of information was not from IRA people but from people who had noted something odd and hoped to pick up a few pounds. Military intelligence had two very good men who developed their ability to pick bits and pieces of information from suspected IRA men. With the rare, rare exception most of the "successes" against the IRA were the result of good, solid, often dull, police work—and a bit of luck.

4. With the decline of the IRA, the available documentation becomes very scanty. The total GHQ files for 1942–1943 number only a few dozen pages and reflecting the seriousness of the times all names are in code.

5. Behan has written (or taped) his memoirs for this period, *Confessions of an Irish Rebel* (London, 1965), but his colourful account bears only marginal relation to the activities of the IRA. During his time in Belfast he outraged his more puritanical IRA hosts by pressing while under the influence of drink his affections on his landlady, who though

middle-aged had the foresight to lock her door. Abroad Behan may
have seemed the typical Irish rebel but within the IRA he was the
antithesis of what a volunteer should be. No one could ever manage to
dislike him, but there must have been those who felt the IRA was
better off with him in prison out of harm's way.

6. It should not be forgotten that the IRA considered members of the
   RUC to be uniformed, armed enemies to be treated just as the French
   resistance would treat German soldiers.

7. IRA, "Minutes of the Army Council meeting held on Sunday, 20th
   April, 1942" (typed).

8. *Ibid.*

9. This strike lasted forty-nine days and like all mass strikes during the
   1939–1945 period ended in failure. By 1943 the internees were largely
   forgotten men. Their existence was never noted in the censored press;
   for example, sweeps winners' addresses were given so as to indicate
   they were in the Curragh Army camp and when Seán O Tuama was
   elected president of the Gaelic League his address was given as County
   Kildare.

10. Williams had not, in fact, shot the RUC constable but as C/O of the
    squad had taken the responsibility.

11. Dermody had picked most of the men, who were usually on the run.
    Harry White, Liam Burke and Rory Maguire, C/O Belfast, had been
    included.

12. Even the leader of the Castle, Chief-Superintendent Gantley, fell victim
    to his detectives' erratic aim and was shot dead during a chase after an
    escaping criminal.

13. Michael McInerney in "Gerry Boland's Story—10", *Irish Times*, October
    18, 1968, mentions an IRA contact with the Japanese Vice-Consul
    Kazuo Ichihashi during 1942 and 1943, but little apparently came of it.

14. IRA, "Report of General Headquarters Staff Council, held on Sunday
    14th February, in the Northern Command Area" (typed).

PART V

The Campaign Years: 1945–1969

CHAPTER XII

The IRA Endures: The Agonizing Reconstruction, 1945–1951

The IRA was not exactly dead but the signs of life were few and fragile. Out in the country isolated units, somehow overlooked in the years of sweeps, arrests, and internments, still existed, but most lived only in the hope of some far-distant better day. Out of touch with Dublin, with other units, with the times, the faithful became fewer and fewer. In a parish in County Monaghan, where there had not even been a house raid in over five years, a full unit remained; but there was nothing for the men to do and no one to tell them if there had been. GHQ had been shattered. Harry White, the last free member of the staff, sat on a bandstand in Derry, playing a banjo with the Magnet Dance Band while the Special Branch searched for him in darker corners. All White could manage was to stay free day by day and keep a line into Crumlin Road Prison. This line was the last and only thread left in the once vast IRA web. With no central direction, no purpose or programme, first parades had been given up, then discussion, and finally hope; all that was left was principle and a stubborn reluctance to concede defeat. As time passed men were being released, some late in 1943, a larger group of the irreconcilables from the Curragh in November 1944. They emerged to a cold and alien world that had long ago forgotten them.

Most of them had no further interest in the fortunes of the IRA. The years of bitterness, splits, frustrations, and scandal had sapped their commitment. Few had changed their minds but most could see no future in a new IRA—there was no point in carving rotten wood. The prospects of private life, a home, a job, a wife, just the chance to walk free after the caged years, attracted all and claimed most. A few, deeply dedicated to Republican ideals, felt a responsibility to maintain the organization no matter how bleak conditions appeared, no matter how low the Army had fallen. In Cork Mick McCarthy along with several solid men began to reorganize the city as soon as they arrived home from the Curragh. McCarthy became C/O. He soon found that his major problem was not his own unit, which, all considered, came along nicely if slowly, but a connection at the top. Cork existed in a vacuum. McCarthy's problem was a universal one. There was no top unless Harry White and his banjo counted—and they didn't. The country units existed in a void, unknown to anyone but themselves, unable to trust anyone but themselves, suspicious, uncertain, and futile.

In 1945 one of the first attempts was made to create a centre in Dublin. Seán Ashe came in from Kildare to meet with a handful of men, Micksy Conway, Tony Magan, Willie McGuinness, Bertie McCormack, and a couple of others. They did not know who else would help, in fact they were not even sure who had been in the Army.[1] The problems were obvious but no one had any ready answers. The disappearance of all the GHQ staff and their records or contacts had left Dublin as isolated from the country as the country was from Dublin. The obvious first step was to get some sort of unit going in Dublin. To organize Dublin twenty-five or thirty men met at O'Neill's pub in Pearse Street and set up a provisional staff which included Cathal Goulding, Dan and Jim McCarthy, Terry Sweeney, Seán Sheehy, and Gerry McCarthy. Willie McGuinness was appointed C/O and Dublin was organized, more or less. The next step was to resurrect the Army Executive and, through it, the legitimate structure of the IRA.

The last Executive to be elected had been the one chosen by the 1938 Army Convention at the time of the Russell take-over. In 1945 only five remained. Ned Carrigan (representing Clonmel and Tipperary), Ted Moore (for Mooncoin and Kilkenny), Charlie Dolan (for Sligo), Larry Grogan (for Drogheda), and Peadar O'Flaherty. These five, who viewed the reorganization efforts with varying degrees of enthusiasm, agreed to the co-option of new members to the Executive. If the men in Dublin wanted to have another go, the Executive was willing to give them constitutional legitimacy. The new Army Executive appointed an Army Council, which included Conway, McGuinness, Ashe, and McCarthy. The new Council appointed Paddy Fleming, who had been released from internment on the Isle of Man, as Chief of Staff. Fleming did not prove all that popular. Some had complaints concerning his conduct of the English campaign[2] and others doubted his organizational ability, but at least he had not been present in the Curragh during the bitter in-fighting and he had had no part in the Hayes affair. In any case, the main thing had been to get under way. One of Fleming's first acts, on March 10, was to order a ceasefire with Great Britain, thus cancelling the 1939 IRA declaration of war. The Dublin unit was organized and operating and a GHQ had been created. At about this time Gerry McCarthy did a grand mid-winter tour by bicycle to re-establish contacts. He went to Belfast, Derry, back down to Sligo and through the west and then home to Dublin. There had been a meeting in Phoenix Park in the late summer to consider the need of a new leadership. It was attended by O'Neill, Conway, Ashe, McGuinness, McCarthy, Sweeny, Pearse McLaughlin, and a few others, but Fleming was pointedly not invited. If there were already sentiment in favour of a coup, then real progress was being made.

In September the Dublin unit met and passed a resolution calling for a meeting of the Executive and representatives from each organized area—a little Army Convention. It was hoped such a meeting might find a more dynamic Chief of Staff. Without Fleming's knowledge, Cathal Goulding took to the road to persuade the local leaders to come up to Dublin and help straighten things out. Goulding was a small, intense, happy-go-lucky young man from an old Dublin revolutionary family. His father had been out in 1916 and his grandfather had been a Fenian. He, however, was associated in many minds with his old friend, Brendan Behan, hardly a glowing recommendation in Army circles, and looked twelve years old.[3] Still, there were not too many enthusiastic men, old or young, around in 1945 and Goulding probably did as well as could be expected. From the 1938 Executive only Larry Grogan showed any real interest. Long considered one of the soundest men in the Army, Grogan had been released in March 1945 and agreed as soon as contacted to do what he could. Some, like John Tobin of Dungarvin and John Joe McGirl of Leitrim, agreed to come in to Dublin but others refused point blank. Finally, early in 1946, a meeting was set up for the Ardee Bar.

By this time Goulding's activities in Dublin and the country had attracted the attention of the Special Branch. It is likely that the police did not take the various reorganization efforts very seriously but force of habit prevailed.[4] A man was put on Goulding. On the day of the meeting, Goulding was tailed from ten in the morning until six in the evening and then handed over to the next shift. The Special Branch had a good idea that some sort of meeting was coming off and that Goulding was involved. Goulding met McGirl and they waited on the corner of Park and Parade Street for Seán Ashe to come in from Kildare. He never came. Eventually Goulding and McGirl walked on to the Ardee Bar. As soon as they went inside, the Specials surrounded the place, moving so quickly that Micksy Conway and Tony Magan, who had arrived a little late, saw the ring form and tried to back off and give the police the slip. They did not make it in time. Only Tobin got back to Dungarvan safely. The other twelve were pulled in and received sentences from a year to three months. Until December 1946, Dublin was very quiet. The actives were in jail and the centre had again gone from the net. The Specials had apparently stepped on the egg before it could hatch.

Magan and Conway were the first important men out and immediately began picking up the loose ends. Conway was already considering giving up revolutionary politics for the Church. He seemed intent on building up the IRA before he withdrew into a monastery. Magan was willing to help but he was trying to put together a bakery business at the same time. As soon as enough prison sentences had run out, the new Executive met and appointed a new Army Council. Fleming was ignored and Willie

McGuinness moved from C/O of Dublin to Chief of Staff, Seán O'Neill became A/G and Conway stayed on the GHQ staff. Jack Finlay became a full-time organizer at a miniscule wage under orders to travel through the country appointing local C/Os and contacting sympathizers. Seán Sheehy took over as C/O of Dublin and once more the centre of the net was in place. On June 23, 1947, at Bodenstown, Frank Driver gave the traditional oration, signifying that the Republicans were back in business. Most important was the Army report, read to the crowd, the first public sign that the IRA still existed. Despite the obstacles, the cynicism, the residue of suspicion and doubt, despite the enforced recess after the Ardee Bar arrests, the IRA did exist. There was a legitimate Executive, an Army Council, a GHQ, and even a paid organizer to knit up the ravelled ends of the lost national network.

During the next eighteen months the IRA concentrated on rebuilding throughout the country, seeking out the men still willing to work. At first Dublin hoped that the entire country could in time be organized. Drogheda and Dundalk under Grogan came back very quickly. McCarthy already had Cork under way by the time GHQ made contact. In some formerly solid Republican areas, there was very slow progress. In some parishes the men had drifted away or emigrated. The Curragh splits still rankled. After the Hayes affair no one trusted Dublin too far. A few good men who had drifted away would take the area with them. In Meath there was a feud between the McKennas and Maguires. In Carlow no one seemed capable of creating a unit despite a good deal of time and effort. In the Six Counties GHQ decided not to stir the waters pointlessly and prolong the sentences of the men in prison. A few local units like Liam Kelly's men in Pomeroy, County Tyrone, met and organized but Dublin showed little initial interest. The Belfast unit still existed but was very quiet. Here and there, particularly in Derry, a few younger men showed an interest in activity; but the general feeling was to go slow in the North until the heat was off. As in the Twenty-six Counties the whole process of building up the contacts and renewing confidence proved excruciatingly slow.

While a handful of men in Dublin were covertly trying to glue the IRA's scattered pieces together, the majority of Irish Republicans were left without a programme or a platform. The one rallying cry on which all could agree was "Release the prisoners". In Belfast such a cry might have little effect on a government inured to Republican arguments but in Dublin de Valera might be more willing to listen to reason or public opinion. There were already grim rumours about the conditions in Portlaoise, where men had been kept in solitary for years. In the Six Counties and in Britain there were men with long sentences still to run for actions in a political war long over. At the end of 1945, a Republican Prisoners Release Association was formed in Dublin. In April 1946, the RPRA issued a constitution. The provisional National Executive included some of the most famous of the militant Republicans: Twomey and Killeen from the 'thirties, and Simon Donnelly, who had not been in the IRA since the Troubles. According to the Constitution

> The Association has no connection with any political party, and its appeal is directed to all freedom-loving men and women who believe in the right of Ireland to be free from foreign aggression in any form.[5]

The response throughout the country was far greater than had been anticipated and continued to mushroom.

On May 11, 1946, Seán McCaughey died after thirty-one days on hunger strike and the last twelve on thirst strike for his unconditional release. On the heels of what seemed the totally unnecessary death of a man who had long since expatiated his supposed crimes came revelations as to the exact conditions in the prison. The Ministry of Justice had refused to concede political treatment and Republicans had refused to compromise, preferring years in solitary, naked rather than wearing common criminals' clothes, cut off from the outside world rather than accept a prison number on correspondence.[6] These were men—like McCaughey, Liam Rice, Jim Crofton, Tomás MacCurtain—whom the de Valera government apparently wanted to break. Even to the disinterested this treatment seemed mean and vindictive. Then, in the same month that McCaughey died, the Stormont government unconditionally released David Fleming, a Kerryman, who had been on hunger strike. The contrast with Dublin hardly went unnoticed.

As the din of agitation rose for the release of the prisoners, it became clear that the country had grown tired of de Valera and Fianna Fáil, of the frugal comforts enjoyed by too few, of the drain of emigration, of the sated old revolutionaries in power. It looked as though a political party dedicated to throwing out de Valera and his crowd might be promising. Fianna Fáil had hardened into conservatism, giving up the ideals of the Republic for the rote work of power. Private talks between like-minded Republicans blossomed into tentative conferences. Seán MacBride began to draw the bits together. In July 1946, in Dublin, Clann na Poblachta was formed. Republicans now had a platform, a programme, and a party.

Not all Republicans wanted such a party. The Clann, like Fianna Fáil before it, had sold out Republicanism by recognizing the institutions of the Leinster House government. Good men like MacBride, Killeen, and Mick Fitzpatrick had organized the Clann. But good men had been codded before by the siren of politics and had lived to be corrupted on the altars of power. The *real* Republicans put their trust only in physical force and abstention from the puppet assemblies, waiting for the day that a real Republican Dáil for all-Ireland could function. Immediately there was a split in the Prisoners Committee, which many thought had been misused as the stepping stone to Clann na Poblachta. The IRA decided to expel the Clann members. Conway brought the word into the RPRA Executive meeting but failed to sway Fleming, the Chairman, who was now well out of step with the Army. The vote, however, went against the Clann members.[7] After this the orthodox IRA and their civilian allies regarded the Clan with distaste as Treaty Party Number Three.

The Clann had no time to spare for a few narrow-minded purists crying in the wilderness. During 1946 and 1947, the party was booming in the parishes. The crowds grew at the meetings. The most optimistic began to wonder if Seán MacBride might not take them all the way, if not by the next general election then by the one after. In the autumn of 1947, the Clan won two vital by-elections and its momentum accelerated—MacBride was already in Leinster House, soon he might be Taoiseach. Snatched up as if by a magnet were a great many of the dedicated and determined Republicans of past years and with them a whole new generation, avid for instant change. In the face of this enthusiasm and excitement the orthodox Republican organizations—Sinn Féin, Na Fianna Éireann, and Cumann na mBan—found the going hard. Reduced by the passage of time and the failure of slogans years out of date, their leaders could arouse none but the long committed. Without funds or members they held on to the faith.

In June 1946, during Wolfe Tone week, an independent group of Republicans, suspicious of the Clann men, out of sorts with the IRA because of old scores and new suspicions, had brought out their own newspaper, *Resurgence*. Essentially it was a reaction to the death of Seán McCaughey. While the editors offered little new, they had been determined not to go the way of the Clan. The committee joined Sinn Féin as a group and in August 1946 began publishing *Resurgence* as a monthly. The paper only lasted until the November–December issue. Then it published a scathing attack on the transfer of Harry White,[8] finally arrested, from the authority of Stormont to that of Leinster House. As a result it was banned. Plans for another paper began at once, but Sinn Féin's fortunes had showed no noticeable improvement. A handful of old timers, imbued with the Second Dáil mentality, and a few of the Curragh men drifting in, had kept things going, but the attractions of the Clann and later the Anti-Partition Movement left Sinn Féin a lonely, isolated movement cut off from the political Clan on one side and the militant IRA on the other.

Thus, in 1947, the orthodox channels of Republican action were hopelessly clogged. The old organizations were flotsam left on the barren shore when the tides of history moved out, empty shells, of interest only to antiquarians not politicians or policemen. The IRA at least was seeking desperately to fight off futility, but the country seemed weary of conspiracy. Even the young had heard of Stephen Hayes. Even the militant activist could not see the end of the tunnel. In Dublin Cathal Goulding had run training camps in the Wicklow Mountains in 1947 and 1948, but no one really knew for what they were training. Tobin kept to his long, dreary appointed rounds of organization. Here and there a few more local units held parades. Contact was established again in 1948 with Clan na Gael, no longer a great reservoir of strength but rather a handful of small clubs which could send little encouragement and less funds.[9] Still, by 1948 the Army was ready to assemble the first formal Convention.

Tobin's long journeys had borne some fruit. In a great many areas a nucleus had been re-formed and some units were solid, parading and recruiting. The North had been brought back into the net although everyone was still very quiet. The old faithful had been activated and it was hoped they would act as lodes to a new generation. But in many places the old were no longer faithful. Elsewhere the faithful were ineffectual.[10] Parishes and counties that had ten years before produced hundreds of militant Republicans now were populated with safe men uninterested in adventures or young men unaware of the Army's existence or bitter men all too familiar with the immediate past of the Army. Despite everything, GHQ estimated that there were two hundred real activists at work and hundreds more on the fringe.

Many of the delegates attending the Army Convention in September 1948 had come to elect an Executive that could be relied on to appoint Tony Magan Chief of Staff. Magan was a hard man, tightly disciplined, and utterly painstaking. He had very few close friends and some formidable enemies within the Army. Several capable men on McGuinness' staff, Dom Adams, McNeela, and O'Neill, were not particularly impressed with him, but at first at least, when his name came up, they were not violently opposed. The Dublin people in particular felt that the Army needed a steel core and that Magan could supply it. The fifty delegates included most of the active men, Conway, Grogan, O'Neill, McGuinness, McCarthy, Paddy McNeela, and Dom Adams. There were two men who were new to the postwar IRA but fine, old Republicans. Paddy McLogan had been in the Army since 1913. He was in Mountjoy with Ashe in 1917 and in 1921 was locked up in Belfast under an assumed name while the RUC hunted him for murder. A publican from Portlaoise, he was a traditional Irish conspirator, an heir of the Fenians and the IRB, quietly weaving involved nets, placid in temperament and ice cold in contention, but easy to trust. He had been a significant figure in the IRA since the 'twenties, a Republican abstentionist MP for South Armagh from 1933 to 1938, and to many of the young men seemed a second Tom Clarke, steeped in the Republican tradition, the Father of Republicanism, the austere plotter from a previous generation. Tomás MacCurtain was the second man. Son of the martyred Mayor of Cork, he had surely suffered as much for his ideals as any living Republican. Snatched from the gallows at the last minute, he had endured the long purgatory of solitary confinement in the cold cells of Portlaoise Prison. The tall calm McLogan, the great bearded giant MacCurtain, and Magan, the iron man, would form the triumvirate which was to dominate the IRA for the next decade.

The quiet lobbying for Magan paid off. An Executive was elected sympathetic to him. The new Army Council included Magan and MacCurtain, not McLogan who would never let his name go forward, Grogan, McCarthy, McNeela, Seán O'Neill, and Seán Fox of Armagh. Apparently Magan's health forced an interruption in his tenure as C/S and the IRA did not come fully under his direction until 1950. Magan's staff included Grogan QMG, and Gerry McCarthy A/G as well as several of the men who had worked for McGuinness. In spite of the new leadership, many in the Army had grave reservations for the immediate future. Cork proposed a resolution, presented by MacCurtain, that the IRA was not sufficiently representative to be called the government of the Republic and therefore did not have the right to take life. While this was obviously true, MacCurtain's resolution was a little too bleak for the more optimistic delegates. McLogan, Chairman of the Convention, tempered the proposal by suggesting the addition of the words—until such time as the IRA has been reorganized. The amended resolution passed and the major preoccupation of the Army continued to be reorganization. The purpose of the reorganization was at last clear since the Convention accepted two resolutions: first, support for a military campaign against the British in the North; second, no aggressive military action in the Twenty-Six Counties. This policy was then stated at Easter 1949 but the hope of action in the North was still distant.

Magan wanted to create a new Army, untarnished by the dissent and scandals of the previous decade. There was to be no shadow of a gangster gunman, no taint of communism, but a band of volunteers solely dedicated to reuniting Ireland by physical force. The volunteers were to lead exemplary lives; appearance in court even for minor matters meant instant dismissal. They were to train as soldiers not to meet as armed conspirators. The ideas of the radical Left, however mild, were anathema. The volunteers were prohibited from belonging to the Communist Party by General Army Order No. 4 (a policy dating back to 1933), which was as much a matter of tactics as of principle—the "Red Menace" had proved a deadly weapon in the hands of the IRA's enemies.[11] Already out in the parishes Clann na Poblachta politicians suffered under the "Bolshie" label, applied as always by men who had little idea of the nature of communism but an excellent grasp of political realities. Magan, a devout Catholic, had no intention of risking either a Red Smear or a Gangster Image—the IRA was to be a pure, bright weapon.

One of the more important developments for orthodo:: Republicans had come in May 1948 with the appearance of a small monthly, the *United Irishman*. In May and June of the previous year, two committees had met to see what could be done about a newspaper. Jim Doyle had sent out invitations to good Republicans in Dublin like Seamus G. O'Kelly, Micky Traynor, Gearóid Mangan, and others, but not until December could sufficient support be collected. With the first issue in January, Republicans had a newspaper for the first time since O'Higgins' *Wolfe Tone Weekly* was banned in 1939. The small blurred *United Irishman* was a long way from the violent, muckraking *An Phoblacht* edited by Ryan and O'Donnell; but it was a beginning, a sign that Sinn Féin was not dead. Men who would not find a home in Clann na Poblachta moved into Sinn Féin. Tom Doyle, the IRA A/G during the 'forties and active until his death in 1962, brought a little life to the often stale discussions, but progress was slow.

Although the IRA was to be apolitical, one of the most obvious mistakes of the British campaign in 1939 had been the failure to harness popular support. The endless Curragh seminars had concluded that the IRA had been politically naïve. In 1949 the Army Council accepted this view without question but at the same time could see no point in playing the political game. The very basis of the IRA was to deny the legitimacy of the existing British-imposed political institutions. Abstentionism had become an outward sign of the inward legitimacy of the IRA.[12] Sinn Féin, while not necessarily accepting the IRA's claims to act as the government of the Republic, had held firmly to abstentionism as a matter of principle. In the 1949 Army Convention, a resolution was passed allowing the IRA to infiltrate and control the Sinn Féin party so that the Army could have a political wing. Few in the Army, with the possible exception of McLogan, had any real interest in the issues with which the Sinn Féin members had been seized for years but there were no real principles at issue between the IRA and Sinn Féin. Thus the Army Council sent volunteers off to enlist in Sinn Féin. Tom Doyle, already a member, became Secretary in 1949; he was followed by Seán Kearney, who was to leave Republicanism for the Church in 1950; and he in turn was succeeded by Charles Murphy in 1951. Of course, Sinn Féin knew the reason for the sudden spurt of new members and in 1950 accepted the election of McLogan as the new president. They saw no contradiction between Sinn Féin and the IRA. Thus, after 1950

Sinn Féin was the civilian wing of the IRA. But as the Army Council discovered, the ideas of Sinn Féin had a peculiar power to permeate Army thinking, often converting the apolitical volunteers into dedicated Sinn Féin members. In the February 1950 election, Sinn Féin ran two of the IRA men, McAteer and Steele, both of whom were still in Crumlin Road. The alliance was sealed and Sinn Féin was again a factor in the Republican movement. And so the Trinity of Republicanism was created; the IRA, Sinn Féin, and the *United Irishman*, three in one and one in three.

As expected, Magan was a hard man, but he also proved rigid. As Chief of Staff he wanted to control the Army in detail and from the top down. He was uninterested in endless discussion, plausible alternatives, reasonable excuses, and argument in general. The result, hardly surprisingly, was considerable unhappiness in certain quarters. Very quickly Magan had found it difficult to get along with several members of McGuinness' staff. He was not interested in trying very hard and Leo Duignan, Paddy McNeela, and Dominic Adams soon felt frozen out. MacCurtain and Adams scuffled over the financing of a car, a minor matter but one more step to increase the tension. Magan simply dropped the three from the GHQ staff, disgusting several members of the Executive who saw him wasting talent in an organization desperately short of good men. Magan, however, would not tolerate endless wrangling, even with good men, and refused to reconsider. He wanted his own staff. Finally Seán O'Neill complained so long and so bitterly at an Executive meeting that an Extraordinary Army Convention was called in May 1951 to consider the situation. The Convention backed up Magan. The split became final as the dismissed men along with their supporters drifted away over the next year or so. Thus most of the early organizers had gone, Conway at last in 1950 into the Church, Fleming and McGuinness out of the Army, Adams, McNeela, Leo Duignan off the staff, and eventually in 1955 Ashe and O'Neill from the Executive. The three "Ms"—Magan, McLogan, and MacCurtain-froze out articulate opposition, believing that a wrangling Army could not grow.

Beyond the narrow world of the IRA, several factors had, by 1950, created a climate for a continued revival of Republican hopes.The Clann na Poblachta had, as predicted, done remarkably well in the general election of February 1948, polling 173,166 votes, electing ten men to the Dáil, and coming very close in several other districts. The campaign had generated immense excitement and, if nothing else, brought again into public view many of the issues of concern to Republicans. The day after the election any rational man would have considered the future of the irreconcilable Sinn Féiners, wedded to past mistakes, to be bleak indeed. The future obviously lay with MacBride and parliamentary politics. Then, almost immediately, as the unswerving Republicans had predicted, Clan na Poblachta "sold out" and formed a coalition government with the help of Fine Gael—the party of seventy-seven murders. Apparently desperate to get de Valera out and seize the chance to enact some of the Clan's programme, MacBride had convinced the waverers. The new Cabinet was formed and MacBride became Minister of External Affairs. This curious government, led by John Costello of Fine Gael, was unified only by a shared distaste for de Valera and the pursuit of power. Many of the young idealists, who had been attracted by the Clan's revolutionary slogans, were alienated by the cynicism of MacBride's manœuvre, as were many of the older Republicans who had adopted a wait-and-see attitude. All the same, with MacBride in the Cabinet there were specific advantages to the hard-core Republicans: as in 1932, so in March 1948 the last five Republican prisoners at Portlaoise were released; in September the bodies of the executed IRA men were released for Republican burial; and most important came the end to police harassment and intimidation. Still, the militant Republicans felt MacBride had sold out for a seat on the Cabinet, albeit a useful seat.

The impact of the Anti-Partition Association was much the same as the Clann: great initial enthusiasm, influential speeches and publications, high hopes and then no tangible results. In 1949 the contacts between the Anti-Partition Association and the Dublin government convinced many that a real campaign to end partition had begun. The only result of the Clann's entry into politics and the long campaign of the Anti-Partition forces was the proclamation of the Republic of Ireland in 1949 by Costello. The immediate reaction in Westminster was the passage of the Government of Ireland Bill, turning over the future of the Six Counties to the Stormont government. If anything a united Ireland seemed even further away as a result of all the agitation and excitement. By 1950, although both the Clann and the Anti-Partition Association remained active and apparently virile, the IRA and Sinn Féin had begun to pick up the disenchanted. There were not many but the IRA could not absorb many. More important was the slight rise in the temperature of Irish politics. MacBride and his reformed Republicans in Dublin, the politicians in the Anti-Partition Movement, and Eddie McAteer in Derry with his concept of Passive Resistance, had each excited hopes which could not be fulfilled. They had revealed the evils of a divided Ireland to many who had grown comfortable in the presence of the border. They had, however, devised no means to remove the border. Their methods—pacifism, propaganda, and politics had achieved nothing, no victory only words.

The victory envisaged by the IRA, a united Ireland achieved by physical force, seemed nearly as far away in 1950 as it had the day the Curragh closed. If the politicians had led the Irish people down the garden path of anti-partition to the locked door of British intransigence, the IRA assuredly did not have the key. The Dublin unit, strongest in the country, had a paper strength of no more than forty men, divided into two companies which could seldom parade more than a dozen men each. The traffic in and out of the Army continued year after year as the enthusiastic young recruits swiftly became bored by pointless parades and vague programmes. The situation was no better elsewhere. In the North organization had accelerated but units were often small, clotted around one or two strong men and subject to the same regular attrition through boredom. Throughout Ireland, large areas still remained unorganized. Some counties might have one or two men and little more. Others would have a unit of four or five, which never grew and never quite dissolved. Without action or the prospect of action, without a programme, the climate created by the politicians and the organization built up by five years of work would go to waste. The IRA was either going to decay into a bitter little group of ageing and unsuccessful fanatics, conspiring pointlessly in odd corners, or act even when unready. Thus 1951 would be the key year.

In May 1951 a Military Council consisting of three "Ms" was created and instructed to draw up in detail a Campaign Plan based on the resolutions passed by the September 1948 Army Convention. In time an overall plan was developed and circulated among the Military Council. After the finishing touches had been put to it, the plan was submitted to the Army Council who accepted the entire proposal. Later still, salient extracts were read to General Army Conventions. Regardless of the details of the plan every volunteer knew that the direction of Army policy was for a campaign in the North.[13]

To attack the British army in the North, the IRA clearly needed something more than the odds and ends of arms left over in old dumps. The first step should therefore be arms raids on British military installations within the Six Counties. But even after five years, the IRA was in no shape to swoop down on the British posts in open battle. Even so, in 1950 and 1951 serious consideration had been given to the whole arms question as well as to accelerated training.

The ideal alternative presented itself when the Derry unit, reorganized in 1947 and up to a solid twenty men by 1951, requested permission to raid the Ebrington Territorial Barracks inside the Joint Royal Navy–Royal Air Force Anti-Submarine School (HMS *Eagle*).[14] When Magan investigated, he found that the raid would actually be a silent theft without armed confrontation; furthermore, Derry's intelligence was excellent and chance of success good. The Army Council agreed, and in May Magan gave Derry formal permission. Magan and another staff man came up to join the Derry attack team. On June 3, the raid came off as scheduled and without a hitch. The IRA cleared out twenty Lee Enfield Mark IV, No. 1 Le rifles, twenty Sten guns, two Brens, six BESA 7·92 mm. machine guns and ·303 and 9 mm. ammunition. No one noticed a thing; in fact GHQ had to issue a statement to the press before the British army and the RUC were even aware of what had happened. In the *United Irishman* the purpose of the raid in relation to the new policy was implied.

> . . . the only effective protest that can be made to England's claim to rule in Ireland, viz.: the placing of guns in the hands of men who are willing and anxious to use them to drive the British Army out of Ireland.[15]

Most of Ireland may have been little interested in a single snatch-and-grab raid but within the Army it made a difference. Some sort of corner seemed to be turned. Volunteers were now using the Lee Enfields, better rifles than those of the Irish Army. The Military Council was at work. The first printed directives on Organization had been issued in May 1951, the first training notes had been printed in June, and in July the first re-issue of *an tOglágh*, the IRA monthly, came out.[16] When Magan spoke at Bodenstown on June 24, he might well feel the Army was truly under way.

While Magan might justifiably feel some satisfaction in June 1951, there was still a very long way to go. The life of an activist at this time was an endless and largely unproductive round of busy work. Sinn Féin cumanns were organized, attended by a faithful few, and maintained only by constant infusions of time and effort in hopes of a change in the political tides or the sudden conversion of the disinterested. Commemorations had to be organized; pipe bands hired, speakers brought in from Dublin, flags accumulated, Fianna scouts found, posters scattered and loudspeakers wrangled. The *United Irishman* had to be imported and thrust on reluctant and sceptical newsagents to go largely unsold and if sold unread. At election time for county council or urban district seats, personnel was drained off into the campaign, the tiny husbanded treasury was depleted, and the results were seldom cheerful. Always there were the long, long hours after work pedalling through the bleak, wet countryside to meetings sparsely attended or abruptly cancelled. There were the small outdoor rallies, too often held in a constant drizzle before an apathetic audience, and the smaller indoor protests, too often held in a cold, empty hall before the same, old faces. There was the wheedling of money and time, the long dark nights of doubt when the faithful gave it up and emigrated. When the IRA unit built up with excruciating effort dissolved over a trifle, when the returns on election day showed that even the candidate's cousins had voted against him, when the scorn and amusement of the safe, sound men began to gnaw, when girls smiled and mothers cried, when there just never was any visible sign of progress, however slight, at last all these became too much. Faith and the spirit would fail.

Away off, very, very far from the life in the country, the GHQ or the Sinn Féin Executive at the centre of the web in Dublin would note in passing that there was nothing much doing in Westmeath or Carlow. In time, too late to be very effective, someone would descend from Dublin: an IRA organizer filled with enthusiasm and new instructions, or a big name from Sinn Féin hopeful of gingering up the dulled by distributing the new programme. Sometimes it would work and the erosion of the Republican spirit would be reversed. More often nothing helped and Westmeath or Carlow had to be given up, the two or three good men left isolated on their hillside or in their chemist shop. Gradually it became clear that despite local pride there were no strong Republican areas but only a few men who attracted converts by their personality and maintained the faith by exhaustive investment of time.

To create a revolutionary base, a secret army, a band of brothers, no matter how deep have run the currents of nationalism and no matter how long has been the tradition of service, patience is more a virtue than daring, persistence than sparkle. The patient years, the long plodding routine, the scars of past failures add the steel and ruthless dedication to a movement centred on a faith that the future will not deny what the past already has. In 1951 the IRA was still a fragile structure, often maintained by inertia rather than action, totally incapable of the grand plan or the big coup, but each month a bit stronger, a bit harder, a bit more like the weapon Magan wanted.

NOTES

1. The situation was so bad that the IRA Intelligence got access to a copy of the secret government publication, *Notes on the IRA*, and used the names to make their early contacts under the assumption that if Special Branch thought a man was an IRA troublemaker he would be a good man.

2. On his arrest in England, Fleming using the name Walker swore he was not an Irishman and drew only eighteen months. He ended up interned for the remainder of the war in a camp on the Isle of Man. Many of his peers spent the war and then some in prison, a fact which they did not soon forget. Such complaints, however, were traditional within the IRA, where conspiracy often breeds contempt.

3. As previously noted, what was most irritating was that Behan's image

—irresponsible, hard-drinking, quick-fighting, gay boyo from the nether slums—oozed over and often for the British or American mass media became that of a typical IRA volunteer. There could be no greater contrast between the tightly disciplined, totally abstaining, Irish speaking, lay volunteers and the wild bear Behan.

4. Practically everyone concerned with politics in 1945–1946 agreed that the IRA was done. Boland as Justice Minister was no longer greatly concerned, but the Irish detectives, little occupied by major crime, kept to their appointed rounds: if the IRA did not exist they would invent it. Apparently they were close to the reorganization because O'Neill was warned off when he became A/G; later a "British" agent approached Tony Ruane to get him material. Not until the departure of de Valera did the police seem to lose interest, tolerating drilling and even advertisements in the *United Irishman* urging enlistment in the IRA.

5. Republican Prisoners Release Association, *Constitution*, Dublin, 1946, p. 2.

6. Generally, conditions at Maryborough (Portlaoise) became public only during the inquest on McCaughey and subsequent questions in the Dáil. Many with no Republican connections were appalled that a civilized government would allow men to go naked for four and a half years, prohibited from attending Mass because they "were not properly dressed," and keep men in solitary for seeking political treatment.

7. Actually the decisive vote was cast by Jack Sullivan who was not eligible to vote, a fact discovered too late to prevent the expulsion of the Clan members.

8. Harry White was arrested in Derry in October 1945 and the RUC Special Branch tried to discover the nature of the line into Crumlin Road. When White would accept neither their offers nor threats, the Northern Ireland authorities handed him over to the Irish government who wanted him for the murder of Mordaunt. Maurice O'Neill had already been executed for the crime and White's chances did not look too good. He was found guilty and sentenced to be hanged, but Seán MacBride and Con Lehane appealed to the Court of Criminal Appeal and the charge was reduced to manslaughter and the sentence to twelve years. If the Military Tribunal had still existed (it had been abandoned a few months before) there could have been no appeal. And so the time spent on the banjo in Derry was not wasted.

9. From 1938 on, the Clan's strength, influence, and cohesion declined rapidly. After 1945 while "Clan na Gael" assuredly existed, it was a faint shadow of the massive organization of the 'twenties. Usually only

a few clubs or branches would support the IRA (after 1948 collected under Joseph Stynes) and even then the members were apt to change their minds.

10. Some of the good old areas had grown too old to be good. Some villages simply had no young men, for the old ones held on to the farm and the young ones went to England.

11. Although some of the volunteers held radical political views, GHQ did not encourage their expression nor the emphasis on "bread and butter" over the National issue in public speeches. Even Sinn Féin concentrated on the National issue despite some work on economic and social programmes.

12. In a Catholic country the idea of a just war is important and IRA claims to be a government-in-waiting were necessary. To train a man to shoot, often a policeman, in cold blood is not an easy task; for he must be persuaded that he is committing not murder but a morally justifiable military act in a patriotic campaign. To shoot solely because power comes out of a gun would not do—at least in Ireland.

13. A campaign of some sort had a long and honourable history stretching back to efforts made after the 1921 Truce through Barry's Armagh Plan, the 1938 explosions, and the 1942 aborted raid. The real novelty of the Military Council's approach was the change towards the Dublin government—which in time would appear on paper as General Army Order No. 8.

14. Eamon Mac Tiománaí and Seamus Ramsaigh, "The Campaign of the Fifties. Notes and observations on the Campaign in the North with especial reference to Republican activities in Derry," Birmingham, 1967 (typed copy). *Cf. United Irishman*, June 1951.

15. *United Irishman*, June 1951.

16. Although in theory *an tOglágh* was a monthly addressed only to volunteers, issues came out sporadically because of the pressure of time or of the police. Most issues contained training hints and an editorial similar to those of the *United Irishman*.

CHAPTER XIII

The IRA on the Move: The Great Arms Raids, 1951–1954

Only slowly did the average volunteer realize just how GHQ intended to use the weapon that was being forged at nightly parades and occasional weekend camps. Little filtered down during the discussions and the 1951 Army statement did not really indicate how the new policy—for a campaign in the North—was likely to affect the Army. A great part of the Army's energy seemed to be concentrated on gathering intelligence, more often about Special Branch than potential military targets. In the Army Council, while comfort was drawn from the Army's growing strength, particularly in Dublin, it was also noted that schism and separatism, ever-present dangers, were threatening once more.

In October 1951, Liam Kelly of Pomeroy, County Tyrone, was dismissed for planning an operation in Derry city without GHQ consent. Kelly had his own power-base in eastern Tyrone and simply took the local IRA organization with him in a new direction. He founded Fianna Uladh, a political party which recognized the legitimacy of the Leinster House government. In 1953 he was elected to Stormont from Mid-Tyrone but immediately arrested, charged with sedition, convicted, and sentenced to twelve months' imprisonment. Seán MacBride, eager for a break in the log jam of partition, secured Kelly's election to the Senate in Dublin in June 1954.[1] On Kelly's release on August 19, 1954, he returned to a wild welcome in Pomeroy which included a bloody riot as the police and his constituents struggled over possession of the tricolour. Despite the baton charges the excitement, the broken heads, and the publicity, Kelly's Fianna Uladh faded away, contaminated by compromise in the eyes of the militants and too tinged with violence for the conservative Nationalists. Kelly turned his energies to his "military arm"—Saor Uladh. Although there were scattered units outside County Tyrone, Saor Uladh remained a local movement. The IRA kept a close watch on it, warned off orthodox Republicans, criticized Kelly for dividing the faithful, but because of Kelly's local popularity could do little but isolate him in one area of Tyrone.

Another thorn in the side of the orthodox was a wild splinter group called Laochra Uladh run by Brendan O'Boyle. O'Boyle had joined the IRA in the summer of 1940 and had been arrested and interned in Crumlin Road in Belfast in September 1941. Transferred to Derry, he was one of the twenty-one men who tunnelled out in March 1943. Once over the wall, he disappeared from sight for a while, emerging as a jewellery salesman in Dublin. Apparently he had been to the United States and made useful friends. In any case, the splintered "clan" was split again with Tadhg Brosnan backing O'Boyle, and later Kelly, while a group under Paddy Smith remained independent and Stynes' group continued to back the IRA. In any case he travelled regularly "on business" into the Six Counties. Considerable IRA intelligence work produced relatively little information on O'Boyle. He seemed to be using his American money to run a one-man bombing campaign. Then, in July 1955, he was killed in a premature explosion outside the telephone exchange at Stormont.[2] By this time the IRA had decided that he was a tolerable if dangerous crusader.

Even in Dublin several minor groups had appeared, purporting to be dedicated to a policy of physical force. Fearful of both rivals and amateurs, the IRA spent long hours and great effort on such groups only to discover in most cases that it had not been worth the trouble. By 1951 Goulding had broken one splinter, which called itself the IRB. Another group Arm na Saoirse led by Raymond O'Cíanáin seemed unaware of the existence of the IRA and once contact had been made was absorbed. A private and somewhat violent youth movement, the Irish National Brotherhood (later the Irish Volunteers) that had been organized by Gery Lawless was absorbed into na Fianna Éireann. While none of these Dublin groups was any real challenge to the IRA, the GHQ staff worried about them instead, perhaps, of reflecting that a commitment to physical force still existed barely submerged in Irish society. In any case intelligence operations continued to absorb as much energy as planning for the campaign. The Special Branch men were photographed and followed.[3] Dossiers began to pile up not only of targets in the North but the personal habits of detectives.

Early in 1953 word reached Dublin GHQ from a friendly Scot with no official connection with the IRA that an ideal target for a smash-and-grab raid would be the Officers Training Corps School at Felstead in Essex. In March, GHQ sent a man to check over the school. At the time the prospects looked hopeful and GHQ decided to go ahead but to keep the raiding party very small and skip contacts with known Irish Republicans in Britain. There were very few active IRA men in Britain in any case since GHQ had a healthy respect for the British Special Branch and a deep scepticism about the degree of security in Republican organizations in Britain. There was, however, one man, Seán Stephenson, who had been born in London and served in the RAF, who was considered sound and secure. He would go on the raid and with him Cathal Goulding from the GHQ staff and Manus Canning from the Derry unit. Magan went over first to make the London arrangements and round up the necessary arms. Things did not go well. Goulding bringing the ammunition was trailed onto the boat by a Special Branch man and had to dump the stuff. He lost his shadow in Liverpool and arrived in London to find that Magan had not been able to get the arms. Goulding, Stevenson, and Canning decided to have a go anyway.

On the evening of July 25, 1953, they set out from London in an old van. There was no trouble at Felstead. They simply put the van up close, cut open a window, and piled the arms in the back. In fact, they piled in so much that the elderly van settled down on its tyres and refused to move. Reluctantly, they unloaded half the booty and still overloaded set off for London. At Bishop Stortford at the main Cambridge–London road, they took a wrong turn. Heavily overloaded and rumbling down a steep hill they attracted the attention of two police patrol cars. The police evidently thought that an overloaded old van wandering around in the middle of the night should at least get a summons. The first patrol car pulled alongside. The van jammed past that car but could not manage the second. Five or six amazed policemen piled out and rushed up to the van, ordered all three men out, and began demanding rational explanations. Even so, it was not until one of the policemen opened the back of the van and looked in that it became clear why three Irishmen in a waddling old van should have been so interested in avoiding the police. Inside were ninety-nine rifles, eight Bren guns, ten Stens, one PIAT, a 2-inch mortar and a Browning machine-gun. The police were even more fortunate that the arsenal was in the back of the van not in the cab. Subsequently, all three IRA men were convicted and each sentenced to eight years' imprisonment. Magan was shattered. He sent over one of his new men, Charles Murphy, to see if there was a possibility of springing at least Goulding from prison. For the time being, Murphy reported, there was not much chance, but Goulding soon had a line out of prison, maintaining it even when he was shifted, so a break was not discarded.[4] In the meantime Magan had to turn his attention back to Ireland.

Murphy, Magan's messenger, was typical of the new Dublin IRA man —young, ruthlessly dedicated, single-minded and capable of sustaining both discipline and enthusiasm. There were others: Eamon Thomas, steeped in Irish history; Robert Russell, Seán Russell's nephew; Eamon Boyce, a small man with a cunning mind; Joe Christle, an undergraduate at University College Dublin and a well-known bicyclist; and still others— Tom Mitchell and Pat Murphy. Although all these men were eager for action of some kind, the Army only reluctantly undertook certain symbolic "displays" during the coronation of Elizabeth II in June. Attempts to repeat a Felstead operation aborted. The Army lost a man or two but

not in operations: Joe Campbell of Newry got five years for possession
of gelignite and Kevin O'Rourke of Banbridge, five years for possession
of a pistol and ammunition. Although the volunteers felt they were at
last ready for a big effort, nothing seemed to happen. The streak of bad
luck finally ended when Leo McCormack, a full-time organizer, returned
from a swing through the North mulling over an odd bit of information.

McCormack, a former British Commando, had by chance passed in
front of the main gate into Gough Barracks, the home of the Royal Irish
Fusiliers in Armagh. As might be expected, there was a guard armed with
a Sten gun in front of the gate; but what McCormack had not expected
and what intrigued him was the absence of a magazine in the Sten. In
effect Gough Barracks was guarded by an unarmed man. On his return
to Dublin, McCormack told Murphy, who was equally fascinated. The
long fuse had been lit by that chance glance. McCormack did not get to
see the end result. He was arrested at the border and received four years
for possession of "documents". In April Murphy decided that they might
have a go at Armagh. This would be no smash-and-grab effort but a major
raid into a British Army barracks requiring highly detailed planning,
excellent intelligence, discipline, and the best of Irish luck. Magan
approved Murphy's proposal and the wheels began to turn.

On the intelligence end Magan and Murphy asked Eamon Boyce, the
I/O of Dublin, to run up to Armagh on his day off and look over the land.
Boyce went up on a Thursday afternoon and checked over the barracks
that evening. After that he was up every Thursday but still Murphy was
not satisfied. All their information so far was from the outside and he
wanted more inside details. He came up with the idea of sending one of
the Dublin volunteers up to Armagh to enlist in the British Army. Then
the only problem would be setting up a communications link. The man
Murphy wanted for the job was Seán Garland, an ideal volunteer in the
IRA who should certainly pass muster as a British recruit. Garland, a
hard, red-headed Dublin lad, was willing and went up to Armagh and
enlisted without difficulty. Almost at once, information about the barracks
began to arrive in Dublin.

The flow of maps, documents, time schedules, training programmes, even
photographs taken with a mini-camera, flowed into GHQ for processing.
Murphy and Boyce continued to visit Armagh during May. Finally, a last
intelligence coup was arranged. Using Garland's information, the IRA got
inside the barracks to have a look around. On a Saturday night Boyce and
Murphy slipped into the barracks as "guests" at the weekly dance. They
even brought a girl, Mae Smith, on loan from Cumann na mBan. At the
last light Boyce managed to get a series of pictures with the Minix. Then
Garland cut in on Murphy and Mae Smith. After an appropriate whirl

ound the floor, Garland took her outside for what his fellow soldiers ssumed was a traditional hour of light passion but was in fact a detailed our of the entire barracks.

By early June GHQ was overflowing with intelligence. Training had ontinued as usual because for security reasons Murphy and Magan had old no one of the raid. Murphy, who had been named A/G after the 1954 rmy Convention, had taken over most of the planning and preparations. Ie anticipated using about twenty men, half of IRA strength in Dublin, o move into the barracks through the front gate after replacing the neffectual British guards without raising an alarm. A truck would drive a. The men would load it up with arms. The truck would drive out. Iurphy actually worried more about securing transportation than he did bout the raiding party. He could count on the volunteers but he wasn't o sure about the truck. Then about a week before Murphy's target date, ord came from Garland that all the arms were going to be concentrated t the armoury for a check. The raid could sweep the place clear but only the IRA went in during the day. Murphy came down on the side of a aylight raid despite the risks. The orders went out. The volunteers col- ected still unaware of their target. Dundalk was to provide transportation. arland was to stay put in Armagh.

Murphy, Magan, and Boyce moved up to Dundalk to pick up the trans- ortation only to find, as Murphy had feared, that no truck was available. y the time the men arrived from Dublin[5] a large red cattle truck had een lifted and the driver quietly tied up and left with two guards. When he men filed into the back of the truck, they learned for the first time he target of the raid. By then the truck was well on the way to Armagh. lespite the foul-up in Dundalk, the truck arrived outside the barracks orty-five minutes early. Rather than sit and wait, Murphy decided to go n ahead of schedule. He got out of the truck, walked over to Boyce sitting n a car and told him they would go in.

Paddy Ford got out of the car and moved off toward the British sentry. Vhen he reached him, he asked about enlisting in the British Army, a ourse of action the sentry did not advise. When Ford wouldn't go away, he bored sentry glanced down to find a large ·45-calibre Colt revolver a the prospective recruit's hand. He kept very still. Across the road, the RA lookout scratched his head. Three IRA men went past into the uardroom. The sentry was whipped in after them and while he was being ied up a new IRA sentry, complete with British uniform, white webbing elt, regimental cap, and Sten gun—with magazine—stepped out to stand uard as usual over Gough Barracks. Murphy had rushed through the uardroom to clear out any soldiers beyond the gate area. In the first oom two British soldiers looked up and demanded to know what the silly civilian wanted mucking around inside the barracks. Murphy reached in his coat pocket to pull out his revolver and found his hand was stuck.[6] He turned around, muttering that he would be with them in a moment, and finally tugged his revolver out. The two were still waiting patiently to find out what their demented visitor wanted when Murphy finally faced them the second time with revolver in hand. The two were bundled off to be tied up in the guardroom and stacked in the corner. As soon as the proper sentry had appeared, the truck had started up, driven through the gate, and come to a halt outside the arsenal door. After fumbling through two hundred keys, Boyce found the proper one and the raiding party popped out of the truck and into the armoury to begin loading weapons.[7]

As the truck filled up with arms, Boyce, guarding the prisoners, was growing concerned—not that everything was not going well. There had been no alarm. The barrack square was quiet and Garland, sitting quietly on the opposite side, was putting blanco on his equipment and explaining to his pal that the truck was probably a lot of territorials. Still, Boyce was worried about his prisoners. There were too many of them stacked up in rows, neatly tied. Boyce went to Murphy to complain he was running out of rope. Everyone who came in or out of the main gate was directed into the guardhouse to be tied and fitted on top of the crowd of old lags. One or two attempts by British soldiers to spread the alarm only added to the pile. A woman across the street suggested to a passing British officer that something was wrong. When he discovered that she was correct, it was too late. Muttering "I'm a British officer," he found himself at the end of the line of prisoners. Even a strange civilian in a green coat wandered in to find out what was going on and added to Boyce's worries. Eventually he had eighteen soldiers and one civilian when Murphy told him the cupboard had been bared. In a little less than half an hour, the job was done. The telephone was smashed. The barracks locked. The big red cattle lorry followed by the car drove out, picking up the "British" sentry at the gate on the way, turned right and rumbled through Armagh toward the border. Fifteen minutes later, at 3.25, the first alarm was given, but it was not until 5.00 that the general alarm was given and by that time the big red lorry was long gone.

When the truck crossed the border, Murphy knew he was clear. Any alarm in the Twenty-six Counties would be hours off. The next step was to get the truck to the dump, well to the south. When the truck arrived, Magan, who had been waiting anxiously, was crushed. Obviously if the truck was arriving two hours early, the raid had failed. Murphy opened the back of the lorry to reveal 250 rifles, thirty-seven Stens, nine Brens, and forty training rifles. Magan was ecstatic. This was the culmination of all the

ears of work, planning, and risk. This was the first big strike. The momen-
um had begun to accumulate.

 The arms were dumped and the raiders started back for Dublin. Through
misunderstanding Joe Christle directed the driver to keep on for Dublin
istead of abandoning the lorry near Athboy. Outside Blanchardstown
squad car signalled him to stop. The lorry kept going. Before the patrol
ar caught up, Christle and the men in the back dropped out. Even then
ie truck was not abandoned and two men, after their release, drove it
p to Dundalk, but were stopped at Swords, Co. Dublin, arrested, but
:leased for "lack of evidence". By then everyone and his brother knew the
istory of that particular big, red cattle lorry. At one swoop the British
rmy had been made to look the fool and the darlin' lads of the IRA had
one it again. Even the British had to admit that the raid was a neat job—
iey could hardly do anything else. In Dublin on Saturday night, June
ı, Magan and Murphy met McLogan who still could not absorb the news.
he next morning the Army Council met in a house off Clontarf Road in
ı atmosphere of guarded enthusiasm. Magan felt that they might have
»me difficulty keeping the arms. Few others shared his doubts. When the
.epublicans trooped to Bodenstown for the most enthusiastic Wolfe Tone
ommemoration in a generation, they heard Gearóid O Broin outline the
iture.

Let there be no doubt in the mind of any man or woman in Ireland on this
matter. These arms were captured by the Republican forces for use against
the British occupation forces still in Ireland and they will be used against
them, please God, in due course.[8]

The possibility of further raids on British barracks were almost the
rst order of business. Garland had remained in place in Armagh, un-
scovered despite lengthy questioning of all Twenty-six County soldiers
/ the CID and Army Intelligence. There was a chance of another Armagh
id or an ambush of the ammunition truck during training exercises. If
ot Armagh, there were other installations in the North. During the
immer GHQ considered various plans for a raid which would produce
nmunition for the Armagh guns. Requests came in from various local
RA units asking for a chance to participate in any future raids. The
rmy Council, particularly Magan and Murphy, preferred total control
om Dublin and had grave doubts about the Six County units, prey in
ie past to lax security and the skill of RUC intelligence reports. Nothing
as decided, however, and enthusiasm remained high. A large summer
aining camp was held in the Dublin mountains for fifty men on each
 two weeks. The one hundred men were trained with the Armagh arms.
 technical film was even made at the camp for use in America, where
ıe Armagh raid had at last sparked a little serious interest. Once the

training camp was over, Murphy and Magan went back to mulling over potential targets.

Their thoughts began to focus on the Royal Inniskilling Fusiliers' Barracks at Omagh in County Tyrone. The local Omagh contact, a tradesman with access to the barracks, insisted that the place could not be touched in view of all the new security measures taken after the Armagh raid. Murphy was not impressed. He felt that if British soldiers could get in and out quietly late at night to sample the dubious joys of Omagh, then the IRA could go in the same way. Magan agreed and the drill began again. This time it was Patrick Webster who enlisted at Omagh barracks and began sending out information. Webster did not have as orderly a mind nor as sensitive an eye for the lay of the land as Garland had. Murphy asked Garland, who had been transferred for final training to Ballykinlar at Dundrum, Newcastle, County Down, before being sent out to Cyprus, to drop into Omagh barracks and confirm Webster's reports. To Webster's horror Garland wandered into the barracks one day, checked out the information, and wandered out again. In Dublin with the usual Minix pictures, the detailed maps, and the daily schedules, Murphy worked out an operation far more complicated than Armagh and far more dangerous.

It was decided to send a sixteen-man raiding party in over the wall, the Late Date Route. The unit would then move up behind the barracks square. Two men would take care of the caretaker in the steam room. Another team would take out the key sentry at the breeze-way at the bottom of the barracks square. Once this man was gone, the raiding party could slip across the huge open square, past the motor transport pool, and into the main gate area from the rear. All told, four sentries would have to be taken quietly before the main gate could be opened to the large party of loaders outside. If all went well, the ammunition could be loaded into British Army lorries under the eyes of IRA sentries, while the barracks slept. Once loaded, the lorries in column could make for the border. The empty lorries would recross the border into County Armagh and be burned. MacCurtain would pick up the drivers in a car and bring them back across the border. Everyone recognized that the plan was tactically sound but dicey, depending on each step coming off quietly. Magan insisted that if there was a slip and the alarm was given, the job was to be abandoned. Finally, GHQ reluctantly accepted Cork men and Fermanagh transport. On the Sunday before the raid, all the in-and-out routes for the trucks were gone over several times. The target date was the next Saturday night, October 16.

On Saturday nothing went well. The weather was bad. The locals mobilized the men in a wet field without lights or fires and everyone was soon soaked. No transport showed up although Gearóid O Broin had seized a covered lorry as planned. Waiting, everyone got more nervous. At this point, Magan announced that Murphy would not be C/O; Boyce would lead the attack party and Tom Mitchell be the man outside the wall. Murphy's prestige was sky-high and although no one had anything against Boyce or Mitchell the change did not go down well. After some further delay Boyce decided that they had to start. The odds had already gone up with the waiting since the ideal time to move past the sentries, 3.00 a.m., could not be met. At 3.30 the men moved up in cars and the one truck. The attack party went quietly over the wall and thumped down inside the barracks. There was no alarm.

Eamon Thomas and Paddy King moved off to take the boilerman. A bit of a scuffle ensued when the man refused to come out of the toilet until his pants were in place. Struggling out he came face to face with two panting men in black face and boiler suits carrying guns. He refused to be overawed and kept on scuffling. Desperate to end the nonsense, Thomas stuck a gun in the back of his neck, "If you don't let go, I'll blow your hagging head off." Embarrassingly the answer was to go ahead and blow and everyone continued scuffling. Finally Thomas whacked him over the head just as Joe Christle poked his head in the door to find out why it had taken the lads so long to tie up a sitting duck. King and Thomas set off toward the square with the trussed-up boilerman in tow. When they were about ten yards into the square, a sudden roaring and howling echoed through the night. The key sentry, like the boilerman, had refused to play dead. As soon as he felt the knife against his throat, he had squealed at the top of his voice, whether in fear or defiance did not much matter. No one, awake or asleep, could have missed the noise. The raiding party started across the square heading for the main gate. Christle yelled "Follow me" and led the charge. In a wild hundred-yard dash, Christle outdistanced the rest of the party, some of whom were still in the centre of the square plodding along a little vaguely. Four British soldiers popped round the corner of the guard house. Christle fired. Pat Murphy opened up with the Thompson. A wild, confused fire-fight broke out. With the screams of the wounded sentry and clunking chatter of a Thompson, every British soldier in Omagh knew that the IRA had arrived.

Lights went on all over the barracks. A stand-by party on one side of the square opened up at the shadows. Thomas had found himself a comfortable spot under one of the lorries where he was joined by Jack McCabe. Neither had a clue what was going on or whom they were firing at but they banged away. Up at the gate Christle had dashed through the cone of fire from the guard house and was trying to push off the great bar and let in the outside party. Two IRA men on the way to help were pushing a British soldier along as a shield. He kept shrieking "Mummy, Mummy, Mummy."

The din was fierce and the confusion total. Christle was hit in the arm and fell back from the gate. Joe MacLiatháin was hit in the leg. Suddenly realizing that there was no chance for anyone else to get through to the main gate, the IRA men turned and along with the two casualties rushed off for the bottom end of the square. Thomas sitting under his lorry with his mind a muddle suddenly heard a great stampede from the direction of the gate. There was a pounding of boots as everyone tore past the centre of the square. A faint voice came trailing back to announce that "We're evacuating". Thomas took off like a big bird. The last he saw of McCabe he was popping over a hedge. Eventually everyone or almost everyone got to the proper spot at the wall. Boyce knew Paddy Kearney had not come along and no one could find McCabe. There was no chance of delaying too long inside the wall. The big fellows started helping the little ones over. Thomas, one of the little ones, was boosted up, over, missed the annex roof and sank down into muck three feet deep. When they started off Indian file most were soaked, all were shocked and confused.

Paddy Ford, who had broken his shoulder falling off the wall, rushed past the car parked on the road and told the lorry driver that everyone was over the wall. Malachy Ford said that was fine but he had to wait for Tom Mitchell who had taken four men up to the main gate when the firing started. Everyone agreed that by this time Mitchell's lads must have gotten into one of the cars. The lorry drove off. The same uncertainty as to who was where occurred in the cars. Most of the attack party piled into the last car. Eleven men crammed in shouting and swearing. Thomas was bleeding from a badly cut leg which had been torn going over the barbed wire. From what everyone had seen Christle's arm was very bad. Someone kept shouting, "I got the guy that shot you, Joe. I killed him." Someone was being sick. The driver started off. Behind, just out of shouting range, Eamon Boyce who had stayed to see if his other men could get out, ran after the car along the moonlit road.

In the chaos inside the car no one noticed him as he almost reached the rear fender before the driver snapped down on the accelerator and took off for the border. Boyce stood alone in the road feeling he was the only man left. As soon as there was a head count, he was certain the car would come back. He walked on down into Omagh town, passed a very quiet RUC station and trudged on down the road. After an hour or so he realized that no one was going to come back for him. It was five in the morning and he hadn't a prayer of making the border or hiding out. He moved south without hope. He was not, however, the only man left. Kearney and McCabe had managed to get over the wall but too late to find transport. Mitchell with his four-man squad, Seán O'Callaghan, Seán Hegarty, Liam Mulcahy from Cork, and Philip Clarke from Dublin, made

r the County Donegal border in their boiler suits and black faces. Against
ll odds Kearney and McCabe got to within a few hundred yards of the
order before an RUC sweep picked them up at seven o'clock Sunday
vening, well after Boyce and Mitchell's group had been arrested.

Inside the crammed car weaving south at high speed, the driver from
e North explained that he would have to be back before light and could
nly dump them over the border. As it was he had taken one wrong turn
nd almost ended up back in Omagh. Thomas desperately decided that
eir best hope was Belturbet, County Cavan, where he had set up an
RA unit and knew a couple of people. The driver got them through to
elturbet and turned back north, racing the dawn. Thomas ended up
oing to Brendan McDonnell, who had recently been dismissed from the
RA but reacted as if he had not. A doctor was found for Christle, break-
st and dry socks for the lads, and transport to Dublin organized.

At approximately the same time Boyce was picking his way through a
eld south of Omagh and McDonnell was producing eggs and socks for his
nexpected guests, GHQ was on the edge of panic. They had sent almost
irty men into the Six Counties and as far as they could tell the whole lot
ad disappeared without a trace. There had been no news of any sort.
ctually the lorry and car had crossed the border easily enough but missed
opping at the checkpoint where Magan, Murphy, and MacCurtain waited.
inally no one could stand it any longer. Murphy and MacCurtain reck-
ssly hired a taxi in Monaghan town and started north. Over the border the
untry was swarming with RUC and B-Specials and units of the King's
wn Scottish Borderers on patrol. There were blocks all along the road.
he army was out. Helicopters were overhead and dog tracer teams in the
ills. It was in fact a bad day for IRA men to taxi to Omagh but to their
mazement they arrived safely just before noon. They popped into twelve
clock mass to keep out of sight and contact their man in town. He whipped
p, said there had been a raid and shooting, and took off. Murphy and
acCurtain were little wiser. They got back in their taxi and started for
e border. Their chances of getting back were not much better than
itchell's or Boyce's. Sitting unshaven and crumpled in the back of a
wenty-six County car with noticeable Southern accents, they did look a bit
range for a Sunday morning. To cap matters Murphy even had five rounds
f ·45 ammunition rolled up in his handkerchief. Yet at each block along
e way, the RUC peered in the window and waved them on. At the last
lock before the border the RUC put them out on the road with hands in
e air and decided to search them, but at the last minute changed their
inds, believing that the taxi must have been gone over several times
efore. Once across the border MacCurtain and Murphy rushed down to
ublin to try and put together the pieces.

On the surface Omagh had been a shambles, the raid aborted and eigh
men captured. But success is not always the key to esteem in Ireland. Ther
was considerable public enthusiasm over the spirit and daring of th
Omagh raiders, their ability to spirit away the wounded—for most volun
teers soon knew that Christle had been inside Omagh—and their willing
ness to engage in open conflict with the British Army. Admittedly, thi
enthusiasm was particularly keen among militant Republicans and thei
friends and markedly absent in the headquarters of Fine Gael and Fianna
Fáil. For conventional politicians the Armagh and Omagh raids stirre
waters they preferred to leave undisturbed. The activities of the Specia
Branch on both sides of the border intensified, surveillance became mor
exacting, and efforts to penetrate to the IRA organization increased. Al
this public excitement, political indignation, and police interest booste
morale within the Army but also raised a variety of distracting politica
questions.

Before the Army Council could turn to politics, there were pressing ques
tions concerning the debacle at Omagh. An all day inquiry was held i
Russell's shop on the North Strand with McLogan as chairman and wit
Andy Nathan and Ned Gargan sitting as the other members of the court o
inquiry. In sum, the court was critical without blaming any individuals,
decision which did not altogether satisfy the group forming around Jo
Christle. Within the Army Council, discussion centred on the problem o
striking a balance between stagnation and activity that would antagoniz
the Dublin government. Out of the discussions came General Army Orde
No. 8, a logical corollary of the Army Convention policy of concentratin
on the Six Counties. The new policy specified that volunteers caught wit
arms in the Twenty-six Counties should dump or destroy them instead o
as had been the policy in the past, defending them. Even defensive actio
in the South was proscribed. Henceforth arms were to be used only agains
the British in the North.[9]

Outside the Army Council public interest in the Omagh raid remaine
high. The eight prisoners had been charged with Treason Felony, a
archaic charge originally devised for John Mitchel and used in th
1936 Crown Entry case, and in these circumstances were guaranteed wid
sympathy. The character and conduct of the men during the trial went fa
to disprove the smear of gunman and criminal and even farther in attract
ing funds, recruits, and friends. The Prisoners Dependants Fund, fo
example, had collected a few hundred pounds; but with the Treason Felon
trials, the arrival of Christmas, and adoption of Christle's church-gat
collection advertised in thousands of pamphlets, the total sum had reache
£30,000 by March 1955.[10]American money from the still disorganized an
feuding Clan na Gael clubs had been coming in dribbles and continue

out in slightly larger droplets. The Armagh keys carried away by Eamon Boyce were displayed and the training film brought in more money. In every phase of Republican activity there were spin-off benefits. Sinn Féin, increasing weekly in size, could now complete plans for the Westminster elections in the Six Counties with a roll of martyrs as candidates, more money in the coffers than there had been since the golden days of the Troubles, and the rare, sweet smell of success hanging in the air.

GHQ had every intention of keeping up the pressure. There were two aims: acquire British ammunition, which was in short supply, and maintain momentum even in an attack that did no more than shoot up a barracks. One plan was to hit Omagh again, a proposal which was not altogether welcome in some quarters where the first raid, whatever its spin-off benefits, was *still* considered a military debacle. For Omagh II the C/O who had been nominated was willing to go but not as C/O. Magan insisted on his dismissal from the IRA and in the meantime Omagh II was postponed. A second crisis developed when, after the usual chaos in acquiring trucks for Omagh II, Charlie Murphy found that several of the raiding party had not appeared for various "personal" reasons. The result was more dismissals. McLogan and Magan discussed the problem and decided on an elite striking force, the Active Service Unit. Magan and Murphy selected fifteen men from the Dublin unit to train together. Some of the best volunteers, among them Pat Murphy and John Lillis, were assigned to the Active Service Unit, and in the meanwhile GHQ stayed interested in an immediate attack.

Murphy had been working on Armagh II. Although both Garland and Webster had been withdrawn from the British Army, GHQ had men in Saint Patrick's Barracks in Ballymena and again in Gough Barracks. Armagh looked like the best bet since Liam Sutcliffe, the IRA man, was proving most able. Again the maps, photographs, and schedules arrived in Dublin. The final proposal was a night raid by fifty men from Dublin, Belfast, and various county units. After several false starts, now almost traditional, the raiding party assembled on the evening of March 5, 1955. The trucks would move into the Six Counties on an unapproved road. When the first truck reached the border, men from the Armagh unit, who were to act as guides, reported that mass mobilization was in process all along the border and that blocks were going up manned by RUC and B-Specials. Murphy had his doubts and sent his man back to check again. The raiders waited in the freezing cold under a full moon, with a strong party of Thompson gunners on guard. Finally, giving up on the Armagh unit, Murphy took a foot-patrol into the North. The Armagh people had not been exaggerating. The countryside was alive with RUC and B-Specials, fully armed and obviously up to something. There were not even any

British soldiers to offer a target of opportunity. The trucks were turned around and driven back. The next morning the newspapers reported that B-Specials had opened fire on a passing van and killed eighteen-year-old Arthur Leonard and seriously wounded his sixteen-year-old companion Clare Mallon. It was the first incident where B-Specials or RUC had shot civilians or themselves—a by-product of the growing border emergency which would continue for the next decade.

With the failure of Armagh II, attention shifted to England where the IRA had another good man. Frank Skuse of Cork had seen the *United Irishman* while on leave from the British Army and made contact. Magan passed his name to Murphy who had visited Skuse in England and discussed plans for a December raid. This project had been discarded because of the isolation of Skuse's camp on the Welsh border and the difficulty of finding a safe dump. Then Skuse was transferred to Arborfield in Berkshire outside Reading and close to the main roads into London. In the spring Murphy went over to visit Skuse and look around the camp. He returned to Dublin enthusiastic over the possibilities and the drill began once more as the sentry schedules, detailed War Department maps, and general information began to arrive in Dublin. To handle the London end, Murphy made contact with James Andrew Mary Murphy, a volunteer with no connections with any London Republican organization, and prepared general plans to set up transportation and a safe dump. Outside GHQ no one knew of the Arborfield operation and outside the IRA of Omagh II and Armagh II but despite the difficulties and postponements momentum was maintained.

Sinn Féin had thrown all its energies into the Westminster elections. The nominal opposition party in Northern Ireland, the Nationalists, were caught in a bind: running their candidates in opposition to Sinn Féin would guarantee Unionist success and might well leave the Nationalist party smeared with the taint of treason. Given the nature of Six County elections, the Nationalists did not have much of a chance but many took a dim view of the sudden Sinn Féin entry. The conservative Nationalists— Green Tories to many—could see only intensification of the bitter divisions within the Six Counties if Sinn Féin ran a successful campaign on an abstentionist platform. Previous trial runs, however, had shown that the Sinn Féin candidate could count on a substantial protest vote. So the Nationalists hesitated, uncertain of the political temperature or the practical prospects. In Dublin the Sinn Féin Executive went ahead with their plans, announced in 1952, of nominating candidates, mostly Omagh prisoners serving terms in Crumlin Road. Some Nationalists insisted that the Sinn Féin challenge should be turned back. In 1955 Eddie McAteer wanted to go ahead and Cahir Healy, MP for South Fermanagh, unsuccessfully fought the Nationalist endorsement of Philip Clarke. The

Sinn Féin people had put in a great deal of groundwork. Micky Traynor had come up to work full time as did several other men, and every week-end there was a considerable influx. Some of the activity was at cross purposes; Christle and two of his associates, William Fogarty and Seamus Sorahan, had arranged the nomination of their friend Clarke instead of Boyce as Sinn Féin had originally decided. Whatever the results of the in-fighting, Sinn Féin's momentum was obvious. The Nationalists would have been swamped not only in votes but in scorn. They nominated no one.

On May 26, 1955, Sinn Féin polled 152,310 votes and elected two candidates to parliament, Tom Mitchell for Mid-Ulster and Phil Clarke for Fermanagh and South Tyrone. It was impossible for anyone to deny the impact of the victory. Sinn Féin had swept almost the entire Nationalist vote on a platform stressing only the national issue. Pledged to take their seats only in an All-Ireland parliament, the candidates obviously favoured not only the ideals of Sinn Féin but the means of the IRA. Incredibly, the campaign victories led not to a post-election depression but to yet another campaign against British imperialism. Since both Mitchell and Clarke were convicted felons under British law, they were ineligible to hold their seats. Mitchell was deprived of his seat in Mid-Ulster, renominated and ran again in the August by-elections. In May he had defeated Charles Beattie by 29,737 to 29,477, but in August his margin tripled, 30,393 to 29,586. Once more Mitchell was disqualified but so was Beattie for holding an office of profit under the Crown. This meant another by-election with one more opportunity for Mitchell to run. This time an effort was made to finish off the long-lived "Mitchell Affair" by running a third man to siphon off enough votes to allow a Unionist victory. Michael O'Neill was induced to run as Nationalist and Anti-Partitionist candidate. The intensity of feeling was such that when O'Neill arrived in town, the people of Carrickmore, County Tyrone, cleared the streets, retreated into their houses, pulled down the shutters and shades, leaving the streets completely silent except for one lone dog. Realizing the boycott was incomplete, the dog was hustled inside as well. The point was made and taken. O'Neill gave up meetings. On May 8, 1956, Mitchell got 24,124 votes to the Unionist George Forrest's 28,605. O'Neill's 6,421 votes had done the trick and the "Mitchell Affair" was finally over, but in the process the alienation of the Northern Nationalist population had been starkly revealed.

Sinn Féin's Northern success, particularly the huge vote in May 1955, was variously interpreted depending on whose ox was gored. Some felt it was a straight sectarian protest vote. Others felt it was a patriotic gesture. Still others saw it as moral authority for the use of physical force. However interpreted, the huge vote, the wave of emotional enthusiasm, the heaped collection trays, the wild meetings could hardly be considered evidence of failure![1] In June 1955 the local elections in the Twenty-six Counties also provided evidence of substantial Sinn Féin strength. Within the Army Council and GHQ, all but a few had their thoughts on other matters, but after the long slow years the changed atmosphere was exhilarating. When the Army Convention met in a hall on Parnell Square, there was general enthusiasm. Despite Armagh II and Omagh II, the events of the previous year had transformed the IRA. The seventy delegates made no significant decisions and merely endorsed the leadership all but by acclaim. Ostensibly, the next big item on the agenda was the summer training camp, which it was hoped would be the largest since the 'thirties. Actually, the most important project was the Arborfield Raid, but the volunteers knew nothing of this. What they did know, what everyone felt, was that the momentum could not now be stopped. The Army was on the move. More raids, more volunteers, more of everything was merely a matter of time. The Military Council's plan for a campaign in the North which even a year ago had seemed distant and utopian now made sense. When Gearóid O Broin at Bodenstown in June 1954 had said that the Armagh arms would be used in "due course", no one doubted him but no one had really anticipated the pace of events. Now, a year later, the "campaign" was no longer an arcane dream, fuzzy in outline, distant in time, but the next and proper step toward the Republic.

NOTES

1. Seán MacBride had quickly seen the possibilities in Kelly's movement which while abstentionist expressed the aspirations of most of the Nationalists more accurately than did the uncompromising anti-Dublin stand of orthodox Republicans. Rumour, in fact, has it that MacBride wrote Kelly's speech from the dock.
2. His wife was with him at the time and was slightly injured. Neither the police nor the IRA ever discovered much more about O'Boyle and, of course, the sense of urgency had passed.
3. Within a year the IRA had built up a most creditable file, including close-up photography. At one point a group picture was lifted which greatly accelerated total coverage.
4. Eventually Goulding would be shifted nine times and everywhere he was watched closely as the "IRA man". The British prison authorities obviously recognized that very few prisoners would have as much help from the outside as Goulding could count on if he had escape in mind —and he did.

5. Joe Christle was a bit late getting to Dundalk since he had been given permission to take his UCD constitutional law examination that morning. The first question had been "What are the safeguards in the Constitution against armed insurrection and rebellion?"

6. While contemporary photographs of this coat indicate that it is a Troubles Trenchcoat, Murphy insists that it was a plain old gaberdine, albeit with small pockets.

7. Boyce still has one key, the rest are reported to have been sold in America. For the purpose of raising funds, several odd bits and pieces were taken away. The raid went so smoothly that later there was regret that a film hadn't been made as well.

8. *United Irishman,* July 1954.

9. The significant Army Orders were No. 4, barring communists, and No. 8; the others dealt with hunger strikes, unofficial operations, courts martial, membership of the Army, letters to the press, etc.

10. Much of the money came in half-crowns, five shillings and ten shilling notes, often from people who had no connection with the Republican Movement. Eamon Boyce's mates at CIE agreed to make up his salary so that Mrs. Boyce would not suffer. Few believed their enthusiasm would last long but when Boyce left Crumlin Road over eight years later the money was still being paid.

11. Tiománaí and Ramsaigh, "The Campaign", p. 6: "The interpretation of election results can be misleading as the 1955 experience proved in the North. Support for a revolutionary policy is measured not in the numbers of votes cast in an election, important though this may be, but rather in the numbers of those who are prepared to play an active role in the revolutionary movement."

CHAPTER XIV

The Campaign: The Build-up, 1954–1956

Even to those entrusted with planning the campaign, the specific nature of the proposed operations remained none too clear. By 1951 the Military Council had presented the Army Council with an overall plan, later read in part to the 1956 Army Convention. With the passage of time, however, there were those who had come to doubt if the IRA would ever "fight". Everyone agreed that before any campaign could be started the IRA needed more training, more arms and ammunition, more intelligence, more preparations in the North, and more time. Magan, never one for grandiose ideas, was inclined to take care of one thing at a time and let the future remain vague. No trained military man himself (few IRA men had been), reports from the large summer training camp indicated that his army was shaping up. Even if the volunteers had received no training the fact that one hundred men passed through the course each of the two weeks gave the whole IRA a boost. Then, too, by summer the Arborfield raid was definitely on.[1]

Murphy, increasingly optimistic about Northern operations, had received Army Council approval for a raid rather like a smaller, night Armagh. Despite the existence of the Active Service Unit, the seven members of the raiding party were selected individually from the Dublin unit, partly on their ability to drive a car. The C/O was to be Rory Brady, who while a student at University College Dublin had in his vacations kept together what there was of the Longford IRA. Brady, teaching for a year in Roscommon, had missed both Armagh and Omagh; but GHQ had kept an eye on him and at the Army Convention in the spring he had been elected to the Executive. At the end of July, Brady went to London and was first briefed by Magan and Murphy. Skuse, who had been transferred to Blandford in Dorset, then went over the details. Brady was enthusiastic. He had his men training together by the end of July but without revealing the objective. Skuse was somewhat sceptical after the first cancellation in December. However, once Brady and James Murphy had made arrangements for two Austin vans and a Vanguard car and set up a safe dump for the arms, Skuse cheered up. Brady continued casing Arborfield, accumulating final details from soldiers who accepted lifts in his car.

On Thursday, August 11, the rest of the raiding party arrived. Making their way separately from Ireland, they registered at the National Hotel

that evening.[2] At 6.30 the next evening, they arrived at a restaurant, the
Green Parrot, outside Reading on their way to Arborfield. They persuaded
the proprietor to give them an early dinner. To pass the time Jack Hicks
carried on a conversation with their host in German. Later the proprietor
remembered this clearly, even if he did identify James Murphy on oath
as the German-speaker, as well as the strange group driving off in a Standard
Vanguard.[3] The rendezvous with the two Austin vans was made near
Arborfield. At 2.00 a.m. on Saturday, August 13, the sentries changed. The
IRA now had two clear hours. The first four men walked past the sentry
box outside the camp and walked on through to the guardroom door. As
they went in, a second party picked up the sentry at the gate. Inside the
guardroom, the sergeant was writing bad verse to his girl friend. The rest
of the British soldiers were sound asleep. The IRA simply picked up the
poet and the sleepers, trussing them up and stacking them neatly in a row.
The IRA sentry was out and on duty at 2.12 a.m. Two minutes later the
first van drove through the gate, followed two minutes later by the second.
Fourteen soldiers and the guard commander were out of the way. The
soldier in the telephone exchange had been picked up to join the row. By
250 all the binding and gagging had been completed. The only hitch was
that keys No. 45 and 46 to the magazine and armoury doors could not be
found.[4]

The door locks were forced and the boxes of ammunition were loaded
into the vans. By 3.15 the first lorry with nearly fifty thousand rounds in the
back was on the way. Thirty minutes later the second with more ammunition and weapons drove off. The combined total was later reported as 28,123
rounds of ·303, 30,899 rounds of 9 mm., 1,332 rounds of ·38 and 1,300 rounds
of ·22 ammunition along with fifty-five 9 mm. Sten guns, ten ·303 Bren light
machine guns with spare barrels and ample magazines, one training rifle
and one pistol. With the booty on its way five of the IRA raiding party
stayed put, waiting for the next shift of sentries, who arrived ten minutes
late. When the last four were in the bag neatly lashed down, the IRA sentry
waved at the civilian boilerman who bicycled past him at four-thirty and
took off for London at ten minutes before five, Sunday morning.

The guard commander finally rubbed the blindfold off and scrunched
over to the fire alarm. All he could muster was a faint dong. He scuffled out
of the door and hopped across the road to the house of the regimental
sergeant. Curled up against the door he banged away with his body until
an appalled sergeant finally appeared. They hurriedly called the Woking-
ham Police and gave the alarm. By this time the Berkshire County police
were already aware that something was up. A Berkshire radio patrol car
manned by police constable George Kerr and his wireless operator Phillips
noticed a speeding Austin van from their patrol station at Frambank

Road. Deciding on a routine check, they noticed that the van had swung on to the main London road and was travelling at nearly seventy miles an hour. Kerr had to run his prowl car up to eighty before he could catch up and force the van to the side of the road. Vaguely suspicious at the driver's explanation of a load of batteries from Newbury, Kerr had him unlock the rear door. No expert on batteries, Kerr still had no trouble in recognizing the huge stack of crated ammunition as something out of the ordinary. He decided to take the two men, Donal Murphy, Charlie's brother, and Joe Doyle from Bray, into Ascot police station.

While policemen Kerr and Phillips were occupied with their van full of goodies, Brady in the second van sped past. Someone noticed an Austin van off to the side of the road but no one was certain if it was theirs. Even if the police had already nabbed it, Brady could do little. Magan had suggested that the main thing to do was get back, even if the ammunition had to be abandoned. Even so, Brady stopped to confer with Tom Fitzgerald in front and Skuse and Jack Hicks in the rear compartment. Aware of GHQ orders and the importance of his own load, he then drove on into London. Skuse was dropped off, appropriately enough, at the Union Jack Club near Waterloo Street, where he would spend the night before making his way back to his "official" position at Blandford. Brady and his last passenger Tom Fitzgerald, then faded out of the picture. The ammunition brought in the vans would go into a dump in the Caledonian Road. After a bit of a recess to let the public lose interest, the cases would be shipped on to Ireland as batteries.

When the police arrived at Ascot, they found they had two peculiar Irishmen, sixty-three cases of War Office ammunition, a brand new hacksaw with a used blade, two loaded revolvers, and an odd lot of fake documents, annotated ordnance maps, and a few receipts. By six the alarm from Arborfield had come in and the origin of the Austin van became clear. More important, among the odd bits was a receipt made out in favour of one James Murphy. At once the police were on their way. Murphy was picked up in his flat. On Monday the dump at 237 Caledonian Road, a derelict and war-damaged shop, was given away by the IRA's "landlord". The police set up a futile round-the-clock watch. On Wednesday Special Branch gave up as no IRA man seemed willing to walk into their trap. In front of television cameras they went in cautiously and collected the rest of the ammunition and the arms from the empty dump. As in the case of the Felstead raid in 1953, the curiosity of one policeman bored by late-night duty had negated all the planning and daring execution.

Donal Murphy, James Murphy, and Joe Doyle appeared at the Berkshire Assizes in October but refused to plead. Found guilty, Doyle replied for the three:

We're soldiers of the IRA. These arms and ammunition were to be used against the British Army of Occupation in Ireland. We have no regrets and do not apologize for our part in the raid on the camp. Our only regret is that it wasn't successful.[5]

All three received life sentences. The sentences created as much of a stir in Ireland as the Treason Felony charges for the Omagh raiders. It looked like an act of mean revenge against three young men who had made fools of the British Army. "Ah, why didn't they hang them?" was the reaction of the Irish public, long gone sour on the virtues of British justice.

The Dublin GHQ, continuing to prepare for the campaign, while keeping one eye on events in Berkshire, was suddenly outflanked. GHQ's difficulties with Liam Kelly came back to haunt the IRA in November 1955. According to IRA intelligence, Kelly's Saor Uladh was preparing to hit the RUC barracks at Rosslea, Co. Fermanagh, or the one at Castlederry, Co. Tyrone. At 5.00 one November morning, while four constables were peacefully sleeping upstairs and the orderly downstairs in the guardroom, Kelly struck Rosslea. The raiding party crept in and placed their mine by the downstairs guardroom window. They withdrew around the back of the barracks and detonated the mine blowing in the window. The building shook, the alarm bell went off, and the upstairs constables scrambled to their feet in confusion. The orderly downstairs was unconscious on the floor beneath the window, lucky to be alive. The raiders swept the ground floor with Thompson gun fire through the hole torn in the wall. Then they moved through the gap into a room swirling in plaster dust and billowing smoke. Upstairs Sergeant W. R. Morrow moved over from the married quarters and snatched up a Sten from the rack on the left of the staircase. He went to the top of the stairs and looked down into the clouds of dust and fumes dotted with flickering lights. There was movement at the bottom of the staircase and someone shouted for surrender. Morrow fired his Sten into the movement below. There was a scuffle and then silence. Creeping down Morrow found that Constable Knowles with his head almost next to the hole in the wall had been wounded by gunfire. There was a Thompson on the staircase, three surplus respirators, a stylographic pencil loaded with a teargas shell and outside a box of rather dubious hand-grenades.[6] A swift patrol along possible escape routes found nothing. The RUC had no idea who had attacked, if they had suffered any casualties, or what the future held. IRA GHQ in Dublin swiftly issued a denial.

It soon became clear to the public that Kelly's Saor Uladh had pulled off the raid. Some felt Kelly had been provoked by IRA sneers and others, even more cynical, by personal political considerations. The second piece of news was that Connie Green, probably Kelly's best man, had been killed and quietly buried. There were those who felt this would be the end of

Saor Uladh: a gesture, a strike against the British, was fine, but not at the
cost of a life. Kelly did not see it this way and maintained his organization.
His strength lay in East Tyrone, Pomeroy, and Carrickmore, with a few
friends and one or two small core units elsewhere. Saor Uladh could probably muster some fifty men and there were some arms, including the odd
bits Brendan O'Boyle had collected. Kelly was anathema to the orthodox
Republicans, not because of the raid, to their minds dangerous and
irresponsible, but because of his recognition of the Leinster House government. Politically he was a heretic, more dangerous than the pagan; militarily he was premature. In Dublin Prime Minister Costello at the end of
November made it clear that his government would take strong action if
the raid was repeated. The IRA was forced close to an all-or-nothing
position. If Kelly had been still, the question need not have come up as
soon or at least so GHQ felt.

In the autumn of 1955, the assets of the GHQ were increased unexpectedly. Magan had heard from Clan na Gael in New York that a
certain Seán Cronin, who had been an officer in the Irish Army, then a
journalist, had decided to return to Ireland and was interested in joining
the IRA. When Cronin arrived, Magan advised the C/O of the Dublin
unit, Eamon Thomas, that Cronin should go through recruits' classes like
any other volunteer despite his experience and age. Since one of the major
purposes of recruits' class was to discourage the romantic and bore the half-
hearted, this might not seem the best use of Cronin's talents, but GHQ felt
exceptions were unwise. The recruits' officer, George Dearle, a sincere and
pleasant young man, soon found to his horror that the new volunteer knew
more than he did. Cronin was very gentle but Dearle felt the regular
initiation rites were pointless in this one case. Thomas brought in Murphy,
reluctant at first to bother with a new volunteer. Magan and Murphy
moved Cronin out of Dearle's class and attached him to GHQ to draw up
a programme of training and instruction. Cronin, a dark intense man,
was not simply an "expert" on military affairs—something which the
IRA could certainly use at any level; far more important, he was a leader
capable of instilling unshakeable confidence and great loyalty in the
volunteers who could see that under his tutelage the IRA was becoming far
more professional. Some months later he was named Director of Operations.

In November Murphy, upset at his brother's sentence, finally ran afoul
of Magan over the firing, apparently in a fit of pique, of "Pasha" Michael
Donovan, the faithful if eccentric manager of the *United Irishman*. Murphy
protested and Magan, unemotional, would not budge. Murphy resigned
and returned to the Dublin unit as Training Officer and Robert Russell
took over as A/G. "Pasha" was reinstated and matters returned, despite the
different titles, to normal. Murphy and Cronin, still technically attached

o the staff without specific duties, concentrated in detail on operational
plans for the campaign, training schedules and techniques, and the theory
of guerrilla warfare. Some, particularly in the North, felt that Murphy and
Cronin were far too optimistic about Six County operations; that GHQ
should concentrate on the practicalities of the North and not a theoretical
campaign.[7] Cronin had not come to work on a long, slow build-up, a process
apparently acceptable to Magan, MacCurtain, and McLogan, who knew
first hand the long, long road the Army had come since 1945. Cronin wanted
action and could see no reason why a year should not be sufficient time:
". . . a plan of resistance did not require a long period of military preparation. Indeed long preparation would inevitably lead to destruction of the
movement before it ever got started, as has happened so often in Irish
history."[8] His obvious competence, ruthless dedication, and enthusiasm,
and Murphy's backing, all impressed even the cautious members of the
Army Council. In any case, as a result of Kelly's "stunt", time was running
out.

The Six County election results, particularly the returns in the three
Mid-Ulster elections, indicated to the politically minded within the Army
that a solid basis of support existed in the North, where practically the
entire Nationalist population had voted Sinn Féin. Cronin and Murphy
were less impressed, needing no further evidence than the courage of their
convictions. By May 1956 the operational plans of the old Military Council
required a detailed tactical plan. Cronin with Murphy's aid prepared a
series of operational schedules and attack procedures. The training of the
Dublin unit was transformed and preparations made to introduce the
principle of an attack party and a covering party in the July Battle School.
Cronin attended one Council meeting to detail the state of the Army's
progress. The Council had gradually become infected with his confidence.
In fact events had reached the stage of the Army Council formally deciding
in favour of a campaign against the British in the Six Counties. Magan,
Murphy, Larry Grogan, Brady, Paddy Doyle from Belfast, and Robert
Russell voted in favour and only MacCurtain against. The last had doubts
concerning the actual preparation outside Mid-Ulster but stated that of
course he would contribute his all to the campaign. It was the second time
Larry Grogan had voted for a campaign and the last one had been led by
Robert Russell's uncle. This time, however, Grogan, Russell, and the rest
were certain things were going to be different.

Magan still had his little problems in keeping a tight ship in Dublin
while the secret planning continued. For some time Magan had felt he
might have another Kelly-heretic on hand in the Dublin unit in the form
of Joe Christle. To many Christle would have appeared a major asset to
the IRA instead of a growing irritant to the GHQ staff. As a night student

at UCD in December 1954 he had organized the National Students Council, sympathetic to militant Republican views, and made Republicanism a force in the university organizations and politics. He had brought students in large numbers into the street to demonstrate for appropriate causes and involved members at times in stunts which produced publicity if not political gain.[9] His skill as a cyclist and his contacts all over the country in the Irish bike world gave him a name few normal volunteers had. His talents for organizing and his "independent" spirit were obvious in his work on the *United Irishman*, within Sinn Féin, and for the Prisoners Dependants Fund. His physical courage and daring at Omagh could not be doubted. He was shrewd, clever, very bright, very popular, very brave and to most of the IRA leadership totally unreliable, a man without inner discipline intent on flashy display and without concern for the Movement other than as a vehicle for his own ambitions. Since 1953 there had been a long series of incidents, some no more than minor "stunts", others more serious and in violation of IRA instructions, that had tried the patience of GHQ. There had also been rumours of more serious misdeeds. Magan wanted him out.

As Dublin C/O, Thomas had the job. In 1955 the GHQ organizer in Cavan and Monaghan, Joe MacLiatháin, had reported back to Dublin after one of his motorbike tours that Christle was building his own organization. Thomas himself had run across whispers that Christle was organizing some sort of coup within the Unit and assigned two men to watch him. More rumours of a Christle whispering campaign in the country seeped into Dublin. It was common knowledge that Christle had irritated Magan by diverting the truck into Dublin after Armagh and annoyed others by his egotistical conduct after Omagh. The people like William Fogarty and Seamus Sorahan associated in his various manœuvres did not—for very good reasons—seem likely to take orthodox discipline. On October 30, 1955, GHQ banned membership for volunteers in the National Students Council, a not too subtle slap at Christle, who "resigned" at once and continued his involvement in student politics as before. GHQ was not impressed. In April 1956, on his own hook, Christle organized the theft of a picture from the Lane Collection in the National Gallery in London to publicize Ireland's claim to the paintings. As a result an IRA safe house in London was raided, not the first time that a Christle stunt had had unwelcome side effects. Some place along the line Magan had enough. He could not trust Christle to accept discipline and such a man, Magan felt, should not be in the IRA. Thomas agreed with all this but from a different point of view, for he knew that getting rid of Christle was not going to be a straightforward matter.

The difficulty was that Christle was immensely popular with about half

he Dublin unit and through his cycle contacts with many in the country
as well. This would not have been fatal if there had not been a growing
uneasiness among the more aggressive volunteers that GHQ had no real
intention of undertaking a campaign. To some very solid men in the
Dublin Unit, it looked as if the leadership, particularly Magan, Mac-
Curtain, and McLogan, would be satisfied with an endless round of raids
and Sinn Féin elections, would be content to maintain the Army without
risking a real go at the North. There were other complaints: the failure
to use the Active Service Unit at Arborfield; the conduct of the Omagh
raid; the conservation of the GHQ, of the Sinn Féin Executive, of the
whole leadership; orthodoxy and discipline seemed more highly valued
than spirit and talent. None of these complaints, which given the nature
of conspiratorial organizations, even domestic ones, tended to grow and
fester in the dark would have mattered greatly if the momentum had been
greater or if no "issue" had appeared. Thomas knew that Christle was an
"issue" not just a troublesome volunteer. He hedged and kept Christle
under observation and relatively neutralized within the Dublin Unit.
Magan kept at Thomas and Thomas kept hedging. Finally, on the Friday
before the Wolfe Tone Commemoration at Bodenstown, Magan called
Thomas into the *United Irishman* office and removed him as C/O. Murphy
was put in as C/O and expelled Christle on a technicality, for speaking
at a Sinn Féin rally without specific GHQ permission.[10]

Christle did not take dismissal meekly. He called a meeting at the
Queen's Hotel in Dalkey and organized a separate Oglaigh na h-Éireann.
The IRA to heal the breach called a meeting at Orwell House in Rathgar
with both sides present and Murphy presiding. Some would not even come
to hear Murphy talk or Thomas plead for unity. Christle took about half
of the Dublin unit with him including much of the former Active Service
Unit and many of the best men like Pat Murphy, John Lillis, Liam Atkins,
and Liam McKay. The group of radicals led by Gery Lawless, a tough,
violent, undisciplined agitator, left the ultra-conservative Army they distrusted and went with Christle. Magan opposed any compromise and even
refused to allow the repentant Lillis to return. The drain continued over
several weeks and the bitterness grew. Even the Fianna Boy Scouts split.
The "Christle Group" met in a convention and decided on action within
three months and expansion throughout the country. Support was solicited
from units in Meath, Limerick, and elsewhere but without firm results.
The pace was too slow for some. Lawless and Seán Geraghty felt Christle
was hedging and "kidnapped" him to urge action. Refusing to talk under
duress, Christle later agreed to the three-month provision. Both groups
agreed that if they began action the IRA or Kelly would have to quit
stalling and begin fighting, which was just what the IRA did not want

to do prematurely. At GHQ it appeared as if Christle had destroyed the Dublin unit out of unbridled egotism. The charges and counter-charges continued to the point that Magan was even attacked and had his hand cut defending himself against a Christle man who tried to stab him.

In September to get things moving, eighteen Volunteers from the old B Company moved up to the border of Donegal and Fermanagh and sat, hoping to blackmail either Kelly or the IRA into action. Eventually this Lawless "column" withdrew and Christle agreed to amalgamate with Kelly, who had little Twenty-six County support outside the border areas. A joint border operation was planned for November against custom posts. Christle brought in Seán O'Neill, formerly on the Executive and a persistent critic of the IRA leadership, to whom Christle had voiced his doubts soon after Armagh, and Jim Killeen, one of the hard men of a previous generation who was another avid bike man. Two or three men with no past Republican ties became involved including a first-rate demolition expert. In the North, Kelly began picking up several old IRA men out of favour or out of contact with Dublin. Various disenchanted volunteers, who had been expelled or drifted out of the IRA, signed up with Saor Uladh. The whole organization, despite the Executive of elders and the Christle–Kelly union, remained very loose. There were irregular meetings, private plans, uneasy alliances and no real central direction but above all else the desire as well as the capacity to act existed.

While much of this was going on in the private world of Republicans, sufficient bits cleared the surface for the Special Branches, North and South, to know that a split had occurred. The raids on six custom posts on November 11, 1956, by Kelly, Christle, and Pat Murphy caused renewed concern about the gun in politics and violence on the border. In fact, from June to December, attention was diverted from the IRA's own campaign preparations. The loss of half the Dublin unit was, of course, far too high a price to pay for a distraction that might actually provoke retaliation against the "innocent" IRA; but at least it was some consolation. Since there was little more that Murphy and Cronin could do about the Christle affair by the end of June, they concentrated on the July battle school. There, Cronin taught his new field tactics while the training officers weeded through the men for future column commanders and liaison training officers. Some members of the Dublin unit might have had doubts about the reality of the campaign, but Cronin and Murphy had none.

GHQ planned that a group of trained men from the South would go into selected areas of the Six Counties to begin training the local units and collecting intelligence. Most of these men, once the campaign opened, would command local operations. Dublin would pick the major targets from their intelligence reports and control the major thrust of the action, but local units would use their option of targets or seize any unexpected opportunity to act. Although the general battle plan had been evolving for months by the end of August, Cronin was still busy filling in the details. The training officers were ordered to the North late in the month and by September all were in place. In County Derry, for example, five men were sent up to live for three months out of the public eye. In that time a competent man could train up to fifty men; but the pressure of an isolated, uncertain existence wore on some while one or two clashed with local C/Os. In South-East Derry some forty-five men passed through the training course, in South Derry fifty-two, and Derry North seventeen; but in Derry City the liaison officer caused a near mutiny. Still, a good many volunteers had been trained, although it was not expected that all would stick it when the shooting began, and a great deal of intelligence on targets piled up in Dublin. The Northern units, beefed up during the autumn of 1956, would form the basic web along which supplies, instructions, and reinforcements could be run in from the South. Flying-columns, at first solely from the Twenty-six Counties, would complement the local operations of the Northern units. It was hoped that as the campaign got under way and the excitement mounted, so too the number of active service men would increase. Originally the Army Council had planned that the campaign should begin some time in October, when the nights first became long enough for extended operations; but the impact of the Christle split and the strained resources of GHQ forced a postponement.

Then, unexpectedly, the increasingly hectic planning for the campaign was interrupted by one of the most daring operations ever conceived. Magan had always been determined to get Cathal Goulding out of prison but Goulding had been cursed with incredibly bad luck. From 1953 until 1956, a variety of plans had aborted. Perhaps the most frustrating occasion of all was when Goulding broke free into the prison yard assured that the escape drill would give him sufficient time to reach the wall and climb a rope over and out. Once outside there would be ample time to drive off before the local police were notified of the break. Goulding was in place on time in the fourteen-foot ditch below the thirty-foot wall. On schedule the rope came over but it was brand new and kinked so that it did not reach him. Time after time the two men on the other side hurled it over; but in the tiny two-foot alley on the other side of the wall they could only work slowly. Goulding stood in his ditch listening to the shouts of the two patrols circling the wall toward him and counted off the seconds left. Finally with his time almost gone, Goulding saw that he might just reach the rope by jumping across the ditch and grabbing the end on the fly. He scrambled up and as he crouched at the lip of the ditch for the leap, the rope was once more and for the last time pulled back over the wall. He had to run for some sheds in the far corner of the prison yard to hide his intentions and protect those outside.

Though his enthusiasm for a new attempt was scarcely shared by Cronin and Murphy, who were desperate to get their campaign under way, Magan nevertheless won the day: it was agreed that Goulding and the other three men in Wakefield prison—James Murphy, Seamus McCollum, and Joe Doyle—should be liberated. Once again Goulding was informed through his line to Magan that arrangements were being made on the outside and that this time, once over the wall, the method of escape would be by chartered aircraft direct to Dublin. The IRA was to have an air force. Murphy and Cronin went first to a Captain Kennedy at the Dublin airport hoping to lease a private plane. All Kennedy's planes proved too small for the rather grandiose escape team envisioned. They next tried Aer Lingus (Irish International Airlines) and found no difficulty in renting a DC-3 for The Skellig Players, a not too well known Irish Drama Group conceived on the spur of the moment. The Skellig Players were to fly over to Huddersfield, which was about fifteen miles west of Wakefield prison, and give a Sunday night Irish drama. Seán Garland and small Seán Cronin were already in England setting up the break. The Skellig Players, all fifteen of them, took off from Dublin on a fine Sunday morning. The five actresses carried broken-down Thompson guns in their rather lumpy costume bags and the actors all had odd bits and pieces of lethal equipment stowed away. The IRA DC-3 had no problems at Huddersfield. All the players piled out and into a rented bus. The actresses were dropped along the way in the care of Noel Kavanagh to take in a film while the actors moved on. The bus took a devious route to Wakefield. On arrival the whole complicated plot aborted when Goulding and the others could not get over the wall. The men at the wall reported an alarm. Everyone piled back in the bus and on the long devious ride back there was considerable anxiety that the IRA air force might have flown back to Dublin without them. Arriving late, they were delighted, at least momentarily, to find their pilot cheerfully drinking in the bar, set for the night. Once more The Skellig Players climbed aboard the plane and flew uneventfully back to Dublin where Magan and Larry Moran, who had picked them up that morning, had given up hope. It was not a very cheerful recapitulation when GHQ went over the operation. Goulding was still in Wakefield and the IRA had put up £800 for the DC-3 and another £200 for expenses. Magan told Murphy that the IRA was broke, which was no novelty.[11] The chance of bringing off a successful escape, sure to be generally popular in the Twenty-six Counties and a vital boost to IRA morale, had been lost. There was no thought, however, of abandoning the campaign. Magan had already formed certain Northerners in July that the campaign would open before the end of the year.

One of the ideal operational campaign plans devised by Cronin had been designated Operation Harvest. Somewhat ambitious, the scope of Harvest had to be reduced and the preparation time increased, but the outline was essentially if not specifically the IRA's battle plan.[12] After the period of training in the North, four mobile attack columns of twenty-five men each from the South would open the operation. The Dublin column ("Pearse") would move into South Armagh and on to Fermanagh; the Cork–Limerick ("Lynch") column into Fermanagh and then operate in Fermanagh–Tyrone; Connacht ("Teeling") was to move into Fermanagh; and another ("Clarke") to be ready to move in after the first three in the Monaghan–Fermanagh–Tyrone area. During the first three months of the campaign, these four columns would hit priority targets with the co-operation of local units who would also raise new flying columns. As the campaign intensified, the direction of operations would move from west to east as IRA control of the terrain grew.

The mission of each force in these areas was to cut all communications, telephone, road and rail; destroy all petrol stations, and enemy vehicles found, hit enemy strategic strongpoints where supplies could be found, or where administration of enemy could be disrupted . . . Our mission is to maintain and strengthen our resistance centres throughout the occupied areas and also to break down the enemy's administration in the occupied area until he is forced to withdraw his forces. Our method of doing this is use of guerrilla warfare within the occupied area, and propaganda directed at inhabitants. In time, as we build up our forces, we hope to be in a position to liberate large areas and tie these in with other liberated areas—that is areas where the enemy's writ no longer runs.[13]

It was an ambitious undertaking, obviously a little too ambitious for the IRA, even accepting the premise that in 1956 such a campaign had any chance at all of success, which few did outside the IRA. The size of the four columns had had to be reduced from twenty-five to fifteen or so, but their missions were much the same. Seán Garland, O/C, and Dave O'Connell of Cork, 2nd O/C, would take a column into Armagh on the first night and aid Seán Daly's column in an attack on Gough Barracks, Garland's old regiment. Afterward Daly would fall back on South Armagh and Garland would move into Fermanagh–South Tyrone. Noel Kavanagh would lead the South Fermanagh column and soon after the first attacks be reinforced with Rory Brady's Teeling column. While the attack groups would have ample light arms (usually one Bren, Thompsons and rifles, a few pistols and hand grenades), there were no bazookas, no mortars, no radios, and only gelignite and Molotov cocktails by way of explosives. In open attacks the men would have to depend on surprise and speed; and

if surprise was lost, explosives would have to be hand-placed under what
ever covering fire could be supplied. Dressed in ex-British, American and
Irish battledress, with shoulder flashes, wearing active service headgear—
and later black berets—to observe the Geneva Convention, these column
were to be the cutting edge of the weapon that the IRA leadership had
been forging for a decade.

On December 1, ten or twelve training officers still in the North were
brought back to Dublin for a final briefing. They were ordered to select
targets of opportunity in their areas within the capacity of their units. GHQ
wanted them if possible to avoid attacks on the RUC and especially the
B-Specials for the first forty-eight hours and only to fight if attacked.[14]
Cronin's Operation Harvest represented a new direction in that targets
other than British military installations had been selected. Although there
was in theory still some reluctance about shooting up the RUC and
B-Specials, it was recognized that in practice attacks directed only against
the British Army would be self-defeating. Thus the local units unable to
charge the gates of Gough Barracks would have to attack or destroy non-
military targets, more than likely opposed by the RUC and the B-Specials
not the British Army. The training officers were informed that all the last-
minute preparations had been made. Arms and ammunition were on the
way to border dumps, safe houses had been set up for men on the run,
medical supplies had been accumulated and a hospital in Monaghan ear-
marked for early casualties. The training officers, duly briefed, returned to
the North.

The four column leaders were ready to go. Brady had moved his men
into the mountains of North Mayo for last-minute training. Kavanagh
although delighted to go into action was appalled to find that the three
columns were composed of a mix of men from different units, breaking up
the cohesion of years of training in some cases. Cronin and Murphy had
chosen to whisk the cream off the Army rather than send in complete local
units.[15] Another grave difficulty for the three columns was that few of the
men were familiar with their assigned territory and would therefore have
to depend for some time on the locals for intelligence, guidance, and advice.
Again GHQ felt this was unavoidable; to wait for perfect conditions with
ideal men would be to wait for ever. The column leaders were in any case
enthusiastic about the campaign, about the prospect of action, and only in
retrospect noted the apparent flaws in planning.

The campaign's most obvious weakness lay in the simple fact that two-
thirds of the population were Unionists, dedicated and determined enemies
of Irish Republicanism. The IRA's columns were not going to swim in a
sea of green support but would be forced to avoid contact with the angry
Orange populace. Many areas were Nationalist but not necessarily sympa-

etic; without the support or toleration of a majority of the people, the IRA faced an almost insurmountable obstacle in Northern Ireland as a whole. In fact it was only in the border areas that the Army could count on wide popular support. Because Republican theory insisted that the division of the country was maintained by the British Army, this Orange hostility was played down or ignored even when it was evident that the disappearance of the entire British Army would have made little operational impact. Not only did the IRA have to contend with a hostile population in the North, they had little hope of official sympathy in the South.[16] Again, the theory was that the IRA's policy of quietism in the Twenty-six Counties would induce Dublin to tolerate the campaign. This expectation persisted in the face of specific warnings to the contrary and despite the evidence of the past. Volunteers, high and low, took comfort from the popular enthusiasm after Armagh and Omagh and from the action of the Twenty-six County police who on the very eve of the campaign freed a group of Northern Volunteers caught with weapons, which were confiscated. Thus no detailed plans had been made in case Dublin closed the border or opened at Curragh. GHQ and the Army Council knew that it would be necessary to go underground eventually, but despite MacCurtain's constant urging Magan even after the campaign counselled delay. Finally no one had thought about how, in the long run, to take political advantage of the campaign, if it went as well as the most optimistic hoped. To all the important thing was to get under way, not to brood on problems that could not be solved and conditions which could never be met.

The target date, December 10, had to be put back twenty-four hours because of logistic problems along the border. Some units in the country still did not know the campaign was about to begin. GHQ had doubts about security in the North, particularly in Belfast,[17] and preferred to reveal nothing. Derry City, for example, received only twelve hours' notice of commencement. The Army Council did not inform the Executive until their regular meeting in late November. Thus the initial operations came as a considerable surprise, and not always a pleasant one to many in the North. In a hard decision GHQ had decided this was preferable to a leak. With contact soon broken and the unit disorganized, there was to be no action in Belfast. One result was that Belfast remained quiet and the extreme Orangemen did not turn to riot and ruin, which the IRA would have been unable to prevent, and which the RUC might have preferred.

On December 11, Murphy moved into Monaghan to establish a field headquarters and wait for reports from the columns. Kavanagh drove up from Navan to Ballyconnell on the border. At dusk his men moved out to contact the locals bringing the explosives to his first objective, the Ladybrook and Carry Bridges around Lough Erne. Garland discovered that as

usual the transport had failed; there was nothing to be done but sit until the
local unit knocked off another lorry. By the time Garland was on his way to
his rendezvous with Daly—they were supposed to mount a joint attack
on Armagh—H-Hour had gone. Elsewhere, though, the campaign was
at long last under way in the roar of exploding gelignite and the chatter
of Thompson guns. Despite Kelly's raids in November, the RUC had been
caught by surprise, assuming that the IRA had been temporarily neutralized by the split. With reports of shooting and burning flooding the
switchboards, the word went out that the "balloon had again gone up".[1]

NOTES

1. An interesting British source for the Arborfield raid is Norman Lucas
   The C.I.D. (London, 1967), perhaps accurate for the British investigation but rather romantic for the IRA. Usually the account of a raid
   given in the *United Irishman* is substantially accurate; for example
   in the case of Arborfield, it was written by Brady and for Armagh
   by Christle.
2. Some of the "cover" names used by the IRA at the National Hotel and
   elsewhere included Magan, Garland, Robert Russell among other
   original choices forced by the need to use borrowed drivers' licences.
3. As usual for IRA Volunteers in court on less than a capital charge,
   there was no defence other than a statement. As a result James Andrew
   Mary Murphy's conviction, apparently largely as a result of eye-witness
   testimony, was, technically at least, a judicial blunder.
4. Lucas, *C.I.D.*, pp. 164–165, reports that the Irish police had tipped off
   Scotland Yard that the IRA was planning a raid. As a result the keys
   were never kept on the open board.
5. J. McGarrity (Seán Cronin *et al.*), *Resistance, The Story of the Struggle
   in British-Occupied Ireland*, Dublin, 1957, p. 74.
6. The RUC asked the British Army demolition squad to remove the
   hand grenades, which they did with some hesitation, hurriedly bury-
   ing them. Kelly and Christle later imported Japanese lighters set in
   grenades, removed the lighter, and inserted their own charge. Eventually customs noticed the high quantity of imported lighters that
   never appeared on the market and the supply was cut off.
7. Cronin produced a manual, *Notes on Guerrilla Warfare*, as well as a
   series of twelve battle lectures. It was generally agreed that the most
   important addition was Cronin's assault party–cover party technique.
8. Seán Cronin, "Notes and Correspondence, 1968" (unpublished).
9. Christle edited and had published, for example, a pamphlet entitled

The Writings of Phillip Clarke (Dublin, 1955) which ran through several editions, and some of the Sinn Féin people suspected that Christle was trying to create a new "Pádraic Pearse" for some diabolical personal motive—and in this they may have been right.

10. The only thing resembling a printed account of the Christle split except for a few criptic notes in the *United Irishman* is Gery Lawless' "Where Hillside Men Have Sown—40 Years of the I.R.A.", *The Workers Republic*, no. 17, Spring 1967, pp. 26-40. Lawless' article is vivid, highly coloured, and a bit hard on the IRA.

11. As every man on the street could tell you at the time, the IRA was getting money from the United States but never in the glorious vast amounts rumoured; in fact, things were very tight as a captured GHQ cash book read out in court in January 1959 later showed.

12. Cronin was picked up by the police on January 8, 1957, and Operation Harvest was later found during a raid on his flat. A fifteen-page IRA "master plan" was read during the trial. Actually Harvest was one of many such documents but close enough to reality to worry both GHQ and the units in the North.

13. *Irish Times*, January 18, 1957. Despite the publication, listing among prime targets the Dungannon Territorial Army Barracks, the Lurgan column directed by J. B. O'Hagan went ahead and blew it up that evening at 6.30 p.m.

14. Some of the Volunteers in the North felt they were not meant to fire at RUC or B-Specials at all; others were vague about deadlines and mixed patrols or had their own plans. In any case, it soon became clear that military targets were few and far between and that since the RUC and B-Specials patrolled together discrimination during an attack was impossible.

15. Brady had drained off all in the West who were suitable but others in the West were available. Even with the three other columns filled, there were volunteers in Dublin, Cork, and elsewhere eager to move North. In the first instance a few other men were added on the basis of personal recommendations.

6. *Cf.* Oglaigh na h-Eireann, "Letter", GHQ, December 12, 1955, to O/C each unit from C/S:

> In view of recent pronouncements by the leaders of the Twenty-six County government and his reminder to the press of the fact that certain Acts passed by the Leinster House regime in 1939, are still in force, it is not reasonable to assume that coercive measures against the Army are under consideration by the 26 County authorities.

7. The Belfast unit, like several other Six County units, had declined since 1954 to the point that it had to be totally reorganized into two

companies—the known Volunteers and the (hopefully) unknown ones. The arrest of the O/C Paddy Doyle, who had kept much to himself, a week before the campaign created chaos. Assigned the job of cutting the cable to Britain on December 11/12, the unit failed to reorganize in time. GHQ in Dublin felt the unit was no longer too reliable. Belfast felt this was hardly fair and that their security was not as bad as Dublin assumed, but at this stage the evidence was against them.

18. Wallace Clark, *Guns in Ulster*, Belfast, 1967, p. 99: "Balloon's gone up, Sir, Balloon's gone up!"

CHAPTER XV

The Campaign: The IRA on the Offensive, December 1956–July 1957

Despite the intensive IRA organizational activity during the autumn of 1956, the Northern Ireland authorities had been largely caught by surprise by the attacks on December 11/12. Many of the normal RUC warning barometers had not functioned properly. Belfast had been unusually quiet. There had not been a single whimper to reveal the presence of the IRA liaison and training officers in the Six Counties. The RUC had spotted Cronin and Murphy on a week-end inspection trip but had not acted. While the RUC could never be *totally* surprised by any IRA action, the strikes all over the North beginning at midnight on December 11 revealed that for once the ubiquitous RUC had nodded. Even the weather over most of the Six Counties was good to the IRA; for, however uncomfortable, rain, sleet, and snow can be guerrilla assets. Most important, the long December nights gave the columns that extra margin of time needed to fade back into the countryside. Still, as has often been the case with more complicated military operations, very little went as planned.

In the far north at Torr Head in County Antrim, a column under Anthony Cooney of Cork had the incredible bad luck to run directly into one of the few RUC patrols. There was a brief exchange of shots. The RUC, reacting quickly, closed in on the column and picked up Cooney and two other young Cork men, William Patrick Gough and James Joseph Linehan. The column's objective, the RAF radar installation at Torr Head, escaped unscathed. The Derry City unit operated effectively despite the only twelve hours' warning that operations were to begin and despite a most meagre shipment of explosives. A five-man raiding party destroyed the BBC Low-Powered Transmitting Station at Park Avenue, Rosemount, and slipped away unseen. At Magherafelt, County Derry, Seamus Costello's column had to settle for their secondary target, the courthouse. The caretaker and his family were moved out, the rooms saturated with a mixture of creosote, petrol, and paraffin, and the building lit. The IRA men were long gone before anyone noticed the blazing courthouse. At Newry a B-Special hut was burned down. In Enniskillen the Territorial Army building was badly damaged by a mine. Elsewhere there were other incidents, alarms, and shots.

The flying columns from the South had only limited success. Kavanagh took seven men into Fermanagh to link up with Pat McManus and the local people, and then drop three bridges around Lough Erne. Without use of the bridges, RUC patrols would have difficulty in moving through Fermanagh in reaction to future IRA operations. Two men were dropped off at Ladybrook Bridge with a thirty-five-pound mine and Kavanagh went on to Carry Bridge, Innismore Island, with another mine. Both charges were placed as planned and detonated almost simultaneously. In both cases the explosions cratered holes in the floor of the bridge but were not sufficiently powerful to do any permanent damage to the reinforced concrete bridges. After the charges went off, Kavanagh crossed Lough Erne in an open boat lashed by the rain, sleet, and a bitter wind. After a brief rest to dry off in a safe house, Kavanagh moved out and placed his third mine. This misfired, ending the first night's activities on a sour note.

The major effort of the evening, the joint Daly–Garland raid on Armagh Barracks, aborted as well. A hurriedly lifted cattle lorry finally showed up at the base camp but long after midnight. More frustrating, the lorry had seen far better days. Sometime in the distant past the exhaust had dropped off and no one had bothered to replace it. The column moved into the Six Counties trailing an almost visible cloud of engine noise. Finally the lorry clattered into Armagh near the top of the hill in back of the still quiet Gough Barracks. Directly over the lorry loomed a new watch-tower. A sentry peered over at the noise, fired his rifle into the air, and popped out of sight. Almost at once a klaxon went off. With surprise gone, there was not a hope of slipping the mine up to the front gate. Garland shoved it out of the rear and the lorry revved up. Spraying the barrack wall with a quick volley, the column withdrew banging and clattering. The sudden alarm, cruelly disappointing at the time, had saved the column from a grim surprise, for the C/O of Gough Barracks had made the most careful preparations for just such a repeat of the 1954 raid. Major Brian Clark, appointed in 1955, had been determined that his barracks would not be taken twice. He had his officers draw up contingency attack plans, checked out all access points, and put up the unexpected watch-tower in the major blind spot. Short of men, Clark kept a flying patrol moving around the wall day and night. A few minutes earlier or later and there might not have been a sentry in the tower and the mine might have been placed. As it was, the Armagh incident was typical of the first night, alerting the British without inflicting serious damage. Ineffectual or not, the scale of the attacks, the presence of Cork men at Torr Head, and the possibility of further action had a sobering effect on the authorities at Belfast.

On December 12, the IRA Campaign Proclamation indicated that the previous night's activities were not to be an isolated strike.

Spearheaded by Ireland's freedom fighters, our people in the Six Counties have carried the fight to the enemy . . .

Out of this national liberation struggle a new Ireland will emerge, upright and free. In that new Ireland we shall build a country fit for all our people to live in. That then is our aim: an independent, united, democratic Irish Republic. For this we shall fight until the invader is driven from our soil and victory is ours.[1]

On December 13, an additional communiqué pointed out that the RUC and B-Specials had cooperated in actions against the IRA despite the warning in the proclamation that if they did not stand aside "they will be adjudged renegades by the Irish people and treated accordingly by the Resistance Movement".[2] In Belfast all this sounded ominous, something beyond the usual smash-and-grab raid or border stunt; but as yet no one could really tell if the proclamation was simply Republican rhetoric or the start of one more emergency.

On Thursday night, December 13, the IRA as planned hit the Lisnaskea and Derrylin RUC barracks as well as blowing two bridges, putting in a diversionary attack on the RUC barracks at Roslea, and blocking roads and cutting communications.

Garland's column had moved through County Monaghan into Fermanagh for the Lisnaskea operation. He now had twenty-two men and new mines made from the gelignite that Dave O'Connell of Cork had lifted from a local armoury. Charlie Murphy, attached to the column as a GHQ observer, put the mine together just before the assault section went in. Unlike Armagh, there was no hitch. The RUC and B-Specials seemed to be keeping to the barracks and there was no alarm when the mine was placed at the front door. When the fifty pounds of gelignite went up with a roar, the whole front of the barracks seemed to come down into the street. Actually the mine had sheered off the entrance porch and dumped it in a huge pile in front of the barracks. The door was blown in, but the solid, old building remained intact under the volley of shots. The brick walls shed most of the bullets and the RUC with or without the entrance porch and door gave no indication of surrendering. Firing back from cover, they kept the IRA away from the door and waited for help. Outside one IRA Bren stopped firing after a few rounds and the other would not fire at all. The attack could not be pushed further without walking directly into the RUC field of fire. Murphy with no time to spare decided to pull out. The men moved out by truck up to the mountain's border and then crossed over into Monaghan by foot arriving at field headquarters after daylight.

Simultaneously, Kavanagh's column to the south hit the Derrylin Barracks. He assumed he had the advantage of surprise but the diversionary attack on Roslea had made sufficient noise that two Derrylin constables attending a dance a half-mile away felt that something might be up. The two hurried back, bringing RUC strength up to five men and a sergeant. Two constables, Ferguson and Oakes, decided to ambush the IRA and slipped outside. They first moved right past Kavanagh who was already in place only twenty yards from the end of the Barracks. Instead of cutting them down, Kavanagh decided to keep his surprise and let them walk by him. What troubled him was a wildly barking dog determined to rouse the countryside to the fact that the ground was littered with strange men. The RUC men did not come closer to investigate and Kavanagh assumed they had gone back into the barracks giving him the time needed to reach the door with the mine. Oakes had but Ferguson had slipped into an old coal house. Kavanagh snatched up his mine with its wire-lead and electric detonator and stooping over scrambled for the end of the barracks. The cover party opened up on the Barracks, raking the windows. Inside the coal house, Ferguson assumed that the dog had done the trick. Suddenly, when Kavanagh was nearly across the yard, Ferguson saw him. He waited a second or two until he angled up just opposite the coal house and fired. Kavanagh banged to the ground hit hard in the stomach. While he lay there searching for the source of the fire, Ferguson popped back into the barracks to get another magazine. Kavanagh, putting an angle to the flash of fire that hit him, got up and fired a burst into the coal house and then ran on to the window of the barracks. He shoved his Thompson through the window and emptied the magazine. Inside Wilson and Ferguson had been talking about going out again. Just as Kavanagh reached the window, Ferguson glanced up, in time to pull Wilson over backward so that the burst of Thompson fire missed them both although the shattered window slashed Wilson's cheek.

By this time Kavanagh's stomach had seized up and he was losing sensation in his legs. Time had about run out in any case and there was no hope of planting the mine. Kavanagh called off the attack and withdrew. The RUC Land-Rover patrols appeared almost at once but missed them in the dark. Even better when the column finally reached base, Kavanagh found that he had been shot not in the stomach but in the belt buckle. He had a massive bruise, a hard knot of muscles, and a mangled buckle, but nothing worse. Two days later the column moved out in a blinding snowstorm to withdraw into Cavan.

By this time the governments, north and south of the border, had accepted the fact that the balloon had, indeed, gone up. The IRA had obviously caught everyone off guard. At night in many areas of the Six Counties, the roads were deserted, left to the IRA if they wanted them. Some of the B-Specials wanted out and others wanted a fight. The RUC hastily mobilized on an emergency basis. Plans for additional patrols, more equipment, and more men were being drawn up in Belfast head-quarters. The Unionist population was outraged. The Prime Minister, Lord Brookeborough, left for London. Prime Minister Anthony Eden's Conservative government, harassed beyond measure by the fall-out of the Suez debacle, distracted by the Hungarian Revolution, slipping from disaster to disaster, had to take time off to reassure Brookeborough and to chide Dublin. The Irish government, another inter-party affair under John Costello, was as concerned as Brookeborough, albeit for different reasons. Costello's fragile coalition, supported by the remaining three members of Clann na Poblachta, had to tread warily, fearful that the campaign might set off a patriotic orgy in the Republic. On December 14, he had reinforced the police border patrols and sent in army units. On December 16/17, thirteen men were arrested in a farmhouse on the Monaghan–Fermanagh border. Although they had to be released because they carried neither arms nor documents, Costello had made his position clear.

The Unionist politicians, however, wanted action by the Republic. On December 18, the British Ambassador, Sir Alexander Clutterbuck, handed the Irish Minister for External Affairs a stiff note. It was understood that the wording might have been even harsher if Costello had not already made known his displeasure about the events in the North. Costello, who had once boasted he had taken the gun out of Irish politics, obviously abhorred the violent acts of an "illegal organization" but he did not necessarily want to arrest Irishmen at Britain's bidding or risk a popular outcry if he cut the lads down from behind. Like Brookeborough, he wanted the campaign to burn itself out as soon as possible before the Irish population could become committed and before the country was dragged into a confrontation with Great Britain.

On December 19, before the House of Commons, Eden made quite clear the determination of his government to maintain order in Northern Ireland.

In the Ireland Act, 1949, the Parliament of Westminster declared Northern Ireland to be an integral part of the United Kingdom. This is a Declaration which all parties in this House are pledged to support. The safety of Northern Ireland and its inhabitants is, therefore, a direct responsibility of Her Majesty's Government, which, they will, of course, discharge.[3]

Northern Ireland had substantial forces of its own to maintain its own safety. The RUC numbered 2,800 men, a first-rate police force, practised, dedicated, and quite prepared, in some cases eager, to take on the IRA. Backing up the RUC, the B-Specials had one thousand men full time and 11,600 part time. Standards between B-Special units and within certain units varied considerably. Many had more enthusiasm than training or more sectarian spirit than military discipline. On December 17, for example, a

B-Special patrol fired by error on a RUC jeep, seriously wounding a constable.[4] During the emergency, accidental shootings by the B-Specials continued to rack up an unfortunate total of innocent victims—an almost inevitable by-product of an inadequately trained civilian militia. The B-Specials, however, were a potent force, loyal, already armed, and capable of filling in at once all those chinks in a society's armour through which subversion may seep. While Eden had in effect promised the British Army, the Stormont government already had on hand the men to go out on the patrols, put up the road blocks, carry out the sweeps and house-searches, and flesh out the RUC detachments. There was no need of a violent dislocation of Six County life to meet the thrust of a marginal guerrilla-terror campaign.

In mid-December no one as yet knew what the scale of the IRA campaign would be. Much of the Orange–Unionist population entertained grave doubts about the loyalties of the Nationalist population. What Brookeborough and Eden and Costello were really frightened about was the possibility of insurrection involving the entire Nationalist population and triggering a violent Orange reaction. More than likely, the population and politicians in the South would not stand aside if things got out of hand in the Six Counties. The shadow, still faint, of the Black and Tans and the Belfast pogroms hung over the North during the long, cold December nights.

Although the flying columns had been pulled out of the North for a breather and the Christmas holidays, there was no real respite. The "incidents" continued. The RUC began cracking down. Sinn Féin was banned and the Belfast headquarters raided. The number of arrests under the Special Powers Act increased. On December 20, despite meticulous security procedures, the Derry City unit lost two men, who had been exposed the previous July by a GHQ slip. On the night of December 21/22, the RUC picked up thirty more men throughout the North. Some active service men walked into the bag, victims of sweeps or bad luck. On December 30, John Kelly's column was surprised near Dunamore in Tyrone. Kelly with J. O. Madden as his 2nd C/O had left the Pomeroy area after the failure of the planned attack on Dungannon and moved off for a go at Omagh instead. His column ran into the RUC and Kelly, Madden, and D. T. Lewsley of Lurgan ended up with eight-year sentences, while the local man, Peter Monaghan of Dunamore drew three years. There were not only arrests but casualties. While Seamus Costello's men were resting in their safe house after the opening round, there was near disaster. While they were sitting around a table, Costello looked up to see a grenade roll slowly off the edge of the table. Hitting the floor it detonated scattering shrapnel through the lower half of the room and setting off a Thompson gun.

Spinning in an arc on the floor, the Thompson fired an entire magazine. Miraculously no one was killed. Costello, peppered with shrapnel, had to be withdrawn to Dublin for medical treatment. Most of the others had minor wounds. Considering the number of men in action for the first time, however, it was the lack of casualties that was most impressive. Despite the accidents, the arrests, the confusion, GHQ Dublin felt they still had the initiative.

After Christmas the columns moved back into the North. This time the advantage of surprise was missing but some combat experience and the confidence that came with it more than compensated. Kavanagh was eager for another shot at Derrylin. He had begun training local intelligence agents in Cavan and Fermanagh and setting up a more effective system of communications. McManus, a natural guerrilla, was organizing South Fermanagh. Rather than wait until the infrastructure was neatly in place, Kavanagh decided to keep up the momentum with Derrylin II. GHQ agreed and Murphy attached himself to the column which was beefed up with Brady's smaller "Teeling" group. Although Kavanagh could not expect to catch the RUC at Derrylin off guard again, he could hardly have anticipated that Ferguson and some of the other constables had spent the last week of December laying preventive ambushes. No one walked into them. Kavanagh had, however, taken steps to stretch his margin of time for the second raid. The local Fermanagh unit had been assigned to cut the two most likely routes for RUC reinforcements. On one road they planned to create a block with fallen telephone poles and on the other with a dummy mine in the middle of a bridge.

On the night of December 31, Kavanagh got his men in place early and without detection. It was a night free from RUC ambushes. Kavanagh took the assault section slowly up toward the barracks but underestimated the time it would take to creep across the yard. Brady and the cover section opened fire exactly on time; but the assault section was still in the open. There was a brief scramble. The IRA called for surrender. There was no answer. Moving up with Pat McGirl, Kavanagh prepared to make the last dash. He had two haversacks filled with gelignite with a fire fuse instead of an electrical detonator. He dumped the mines and sprinted to the end of the barracks, shot out the front light with a short Thompson burst, and threw a grenade at an upper window. Dashing around the corner of the barracks, he could hear a radio working over the noise of the firing. The sound came from directly over his head. He leaned back and lofted a grenade through the window of the radio room and rushed back to collect his first mine. McGirl lit the fuse. Hugging his awkward Guy Fawkes contraption, he ran back up and shoved it against the front door. Almost immediately a thundering explosion smashed in the door and shattered the inside stairway. The inside of the ready room looked a shambles, covered with debris and thick with smoke and soot. The mine had caved in the door but if the RUC was not demoralized a frontal assault was risky. Despite his two road blocs, Kavanagh felt time was slipping away again. Brady, back in the ditch with the cover party, had been raking the windows with Bren and rifle fire; but he noted that the level of fire had dropped because of duds, jams, and inexperience. With the volume of fire off and seventeen minutes gone, there was no time to get up with another mine. Murphy urged Kavanagh to break off the action and get Brady's men disengaged before RUC relief arrived. Kavanagh agreed and the column merged and began to move off down the road. Almost immediately a Land-Rover without lights appeared behind them on the road barely inching along. In the roadside ditch Kavanagh felt the column had a chance to ambush the patrol but at the last minute let it creep by.

Inside the Derrylin barracks things had been hectic. There had been no indication that the IRA were outside. Constable John Scally had returned without any trouble just before the attack, changed his clothes upstairs, and come back down into the guardroom. Almost as soon as he sat down, the first burst of fire had torn through the window behind him. Scally leaped to his feet, his back arched, clawed the air, and collapsed mortally wounded on the floor. Heavy firing began. Bullets clipped into the windows and doors on the first floor. Ferguson looked out and thought he saw a Bren behind one tree, another to the left behind another tree and one more at the rear of the school at the back of the barracks. Although mistaken, there could be no doubt about the intensity of the IRA fire. Holes were appearing across the front door and bullets pocked up the stairs, splintering the wood in short little bursts. The fire tapered off for a moment and Ferguson rushed up the stairs. A new burst followed just behind him up the stairs. On the second he ran to the window and began firing blindly at the blinking muzzle flashes. Kavanagh's grenade hit the floor of the radio room and exploded. The explosion shattered the room, blowing bits out through the window. In the next room a constable flopped down on top of still another grenade and barely escaped in time. Ferguson fired at the shifting shadows outside a couple of more times with a shotgun and then asked the sergeant at the front where they were—"Running everywhere." The next thing he knew he was lying on his back with the ceiling piled on top of him. He never heard the mine go off, only voices crying from outside, "Surrender." Struggling up through the piled plaster, swirling dust and smoke, he sprayed the front stairs with his Sten gun. By this time the IRA column had withdrawn. The mobile relief patrol arrived, delayed only briefly at the telephone pole bloc. For Ferguson it had been a busy twenty minutes although he felt that the attack had gone on for hours.[5]

By the time the RUC had taken stock and run out the two Land-Rovers, the IRA column was moving up into the hills prepared to evade the patrols. Flares were going up and the men were still flustered. As the mist came down, they slipped through the gap in the mountains, through the hasty RUC cordons, and were relatively safe. Murphy wanted to hole up for a while, but Kavanagh pushed them on. Snow began to fall and the temperature plummeted. No one could see where they were going or where they had been. The column straggled out. Paddy Duffy stumbling along fell into a deep bog-hole and had to be dragged out wet and frozen. Conditions were so unpleasant that Brady, a total abstainer, was persuaded —for medical reasons—to take a drop of brandy. Finally, fagged out but not demoralized, the column circled back to the Derrylin staging base. Then almost exhausted the men moved back into Cavan. Kavanagh was too tired to move further and asked to be left in a house to recover. Twenty-six County police found him first. Brady ended up in the bag by taking his men down out of the mountains to another house. Murphy in a neighbouring house with the rest of Kavanagh's men sat it out until a secure contact had been made in Leitrim. Then they slipped down and away.

The news of the Derrylin attack reached Garland's column further north in Fermanagh. For days they had been laying ambushes along the roads with no luck. Their deadline for pulling out and refitting was January 4 and so far they had nothing to show. With considerable enthusiasm and very little recent intelligence, Garland decided to hit the Brookeborough RUC barracks. He had a town planner's map but no local man in what was largely an Orange town. Since most attacks had been late at night, he decided to surprise the RUC by moving in at dusk in a lifted lorry. There was no trouble arranging the transport, a quarry dump lorry. He had two mines, both ready, with a $4\frac{1}{2}$-volt battery which supplied sufficient current under optimum conditions. Garland and everyone else accepted that for guerrillas optimum conditions seldom occur. The plan was to drive the truck down the single main street past the barracks and park. Two lookouts would be dropped on the way in and the escape route was set, although some of the men were a little vague about the countryside. Once the truck was in place, the cover party using it as protection would fire into the barracks when the mine was laid. With twelve men in action and an unprepared RUC post, Garland felt he had a decent chance of forcing a quick surrender. There was no dissent. Everyone was eager after the long hours lying around futilely waiting for a RUC patrol to wander into their net.

Driving slowly into town, Vince Conlon soon had his problems. They were late and by seven the last light was long gone. Peering out of the window, he could not find the barracks, one low two-storied house in a line of low two-storied houses. He finally pulled up just past the barracks, too close in and almost directly under the corner of the building. The assault section piled out and ran toward the barracks with the mine. Inside Sergeant Kenneth Cordner was about to open the door into the street. The mine had just been placed when he swung open the door. A fusilade of shots splattered all over the front of the barracks. Cordner hastily slammed the door, which did not catch, shouted a tardy warning, and ran up the steps to the second floor. In the truck Seán South was firing the Bren with Paddy O'Regan feeding him the magazines. The cover fire over the tail board was splashing all over the first floor windows, sandbagged that morning; but because of the position of the truck, South could not get sufficient elevation to reach the second floor. Then the juice was turned on to detonate the mine. Nothing happened. With both the cover party and the assault party firing at the barracks, another mine was placed. The cable was straightened and the wires tipped. Nothing happened. Dave O'Connell, 2nd C/O, fired his Thompson into the two mines. Nothing happened.

By this time Cordner had reached the front room upstairs. He switched on the light to find the Sten. A long burst of fire smashed in the windows. Out went the light. He dropped down and sidled over to the Sten and then edged up for a quick look out the window. In a glance he saw the big red, quarry lorry and a mob of milling men directly below him. He emptied the magazine and slammed the shutter. Down below Garland and O'Connell fired back at him. Hand grenades tossed by the assault party hit right on the upstairs windows but the diamond-shaped casements were made of cast-iron and bounced the bombs back into the street. Inside Cordner fumbled around for another magazine. Bullets continued to splatter through the window showering him with glass. The second time he stuck his gun out he could see the truck more clearly, forty feet away and at a forty-five degree angle. He squeezed off a full twenty-five rounds in one long burst. At just that moment Garland, calling off the assault, had moved with his men up to the back of the lorry. Feargal O'Hanlon, who was carrying the Molotov cocktails, slumped badly hurt. Garland was hit in the leg. Both were dragged into the truck.

The back of the truck was a butcher shop. Seán South was sprawled over the Bren gun unconscious. O'Regan had been shot twice, once through the neck and down his back and again in the back by a ricochet which cutting down from above tore out a banana-shaped rut in the roadway and ploughed back up under the lorry into him. In the cab Conlon had been hit in the foot. Phillip O'Donoghue was grazed. The lorry was a sieve.

Two tyres had burst. The cab was riddled with holes. The tip-gear had been shot through and the whole rear kept tipping as Conlon started up. O'Hanlon, his femur broken and an artery cut, moaned and collapsed. On two cylinders the lorry ground through the main street of Brookeborough and stopped to pick up the lookouts, Mick Kelly and Mick O'Brien. Conlon got them under way again. Even in the shambles in the rear of the truck, there was no doubt that South was finished. O'Hanlon was almost gone. Somehow Conlon got the swaying truck five miles outside of town toward the mountains. The men stumbled out. South and O'Hanlon were left in a shed and the people up the road told to call the priest and the doctor. There was no time to wait. A RUC car had followed them. Two RUC patrols were moving in from both sides. One Land-Rover pulled in fifty yards away and raked the abandoned truck with machine-gun fire. Bloody and limping the men stumbled back into the hills.

They evaded immediate pursuit and got into the Slieve Beagh Mountains. Taking a compass bearing on the border, they set out. Flares went up all night. Some of the wounded had to be carried part of the way. Garland, who had asked to be left with a Thompson next to South and O'Hanlon, at last gave out with a gaping hole in his thigh. They kept on for five hours until at last a scout reported that they had crossed the border into Monaghan. They had avoided four hundred RUC, B-Specials, and the British army, who kept looking all the next morning with the help of two helicopters. They were not as lucky on the Twenty-six County side. The wounded, left in a house near the border, were picked up by the Irish police and army when O'Connell went for help. The whole border area seemed to be crawling with patrols, Special Branch, and Irish army units. Exhausted and staggering along, the survivors ran into a patrol and were arrested but not before the arms had been safely dumped. The wounded went into a hospital, to recover and await trial; and the others went into the Bridewell in Dublin. All twelve of the living got six months in prison under provisions of the Offences Against the State Act for refusing to answer questions.

The Brookeborough raid became a legend overnight, Seán South and Feargal O'Hanlon martyrs within a week. The military shambles of January 1 was to be the source of a hundred ballads sung through the years. In 1798 there had been Father Murphy of Booloavogue, in the Tan War Kevin Barry, in 1944 The Boy From Tralee, Charlie Kerins. Now, in 1957 there was Seán South of Garryowen.[6] No tradition runs deeper in Irish politics than to turn physical defeat into spiritual victory, the slain rebel into a patriot. When the bodies of South and O'Hanlon were carried across the border, their transmutation from young men to martyrs began. There began a week of all but national mourning. Crowds lined the route of

South's funeral cortege to Dublin. Larger crowds came to pay their respect. Mass cards piled up and overflowed. Town Councils and County Corporations passed votes of sympathy, in some cases not only for South and O'Hanlon, but also for their cause. Many were truly and deeply moved.[7]

While O'Hanlon was a fine young man who had played senior football for Monaghan, made a host of friends, and impressed his elders as a cheerful, solid lad, South was something very special. Deeply religious, dedicated to the Irish language, highly talented, he was well known to all shades of Gaelic opinion. He spoke only Irish if possible, wrote in Irish on the problems of the West, the fate of the language, and the future of the nation. He painted. He published his own magazine, *An Gath*. He drew cartoons. He played the violin. He loved deeply and well his country, his language, his church, and his peoples' traditions. Using any criteria he was all that Ireland needed and could sore afford to lose. In the last issue of *An Gath*, he had written "*Jacta Alea Est!* There is an end to foolishness; the time for talk has ended!"[8] and left Limerick to act. And he had died a gallant, brave death under the cold Northern skies in the street of an obscure little town in County Fermanagh so that Ireland might be free. The conscience of the complacent was bruised. The criticism of the practical politicians turned sour. Ireland, or much of it, had a hero again. Despite the petrol shortage after Suez, tens of thousands flocked into Limerick for his funeral. At midnight on January 4, twenty thousand including the city mayor were waiting for the hearse. The next day a great silent procession of fifty thousand followed the casket to the grave.[9]

As far as the Taoiseach John Costello was concerned the worst had happened. Ireland seemed to hover on the brink of a deep emotional commitment to a desperate crusade. On January 6, Sunday night, he spoke on Radio Éireann pointing out that within a week three young Irishmen, Scally at Derrylin and South and O'Hanlon at Brookeborough, had been killed. He insisted, as others had before him, that in Ireland there could be but one government, one parliament, one army. More specifically the word had gone out to the police to round up all known Republican activists under the provisions of the Offences Against the State Act. Relative toleration of the campaign during December had brought three deaths and dragged the country to the edge of a confrontation with Great Britain. The situation could not be allowed to deteriorate further. On the night of January 8, came the first arrests; Seán Cronin, Robert Russell, Noel Kavanagh, and Paddy Duffy, who had escaped from hospital, were picked up outside Belturbet. Later, when the police searched Cronin's flat, they came upon a fifteen-page document headed "General Directive for Guerrilla Campaign". At Cronin's trial, the prosecution read the directive out. Whether it was material evidence in the case in hand or not, it was vitally important to Leinster House as support for the government's contention that the IRA was a danger to the peace of the state. On January 12, at a massive Republican rally held in College Green, MacCurtain insisted that the IRA would not even return the fire of Irish soldiers, that there was no threat to the Irish government. The following day, MacCurtain, Murphy, Grogan, and Magan were all picked up in a raid on Charlie Murphy's house. Many days later the police picked up two dozen other prominent Republicans.

As a result of the January sweeps almost the entire Army Council and GHQ staff ended up first in the Bridewell, then in Mountjoy, with three- to six-month sentences. Control at the top, as the government had intended, was ended. Almost immediately Eamon Thomas, who had evaded arrest, got in touch with McLogan, who as President of Sinn Féin must have been considered a "political" Republican at this stage. McLogan and Micky Traynor, a member of the Sinn Féin Ard Comhairle, who had been re-activated in the Army since the previous summer, heard Thomas out and agreed to fit together a temporary Army Council. By the beginning of the week a Council—Traynor, Thomas, Brendan Sealy, Gearóid O Broin, Tom Doyle, and Dick Burke—had been organized. Burke, out of sight for some while because of illness, became Chief of Staff with Tom Fitzgerald, former liaison officer at Derry City, as his A/G. Between January and April, when the first of the leaders were released from Mountjoy, the new Council carried on. Arrangements, often abortive, were made with various local Northern units. Explosives were moved up to and across the border. The campaign, if muted and scarcely under Dublin control, was kept going by the energy of the local units in the North.

One of the most impressive incidents took place on January 18 at Dungannon. Even though Cronin's "Directive" had pinpointed the Dungannon Territorial Army Barracks as a prime target, the local IRA unit decided to go ahead with their attack. John Kelly, captured during December, had been replaced by Tommy Ferris, but for several weeks the column had been able to do little more than keep out of sight in Tyrone. On January 18, at 6.30 p.m., J. B. O'Hagan and five volunteers arrived at the barracks unnoticed. Two charges were planted, one in the engine room behind an iron door and one in the shooting range. Children playing in the area were removed. The locals faded away and the Active Service men moved out. The fifty pounds of gelignite placed in enclosed areas were detonated with a safety fuse on schedule and as intended, the barracks was gutted, nearly a total loss.

While the Dungannon job was one of the most successful sabotage operations during the campaign, Derry City had prepared an even more extensive and complicated action to knock out the railways in the Six Counties.

Since the Irish railway system is a different gauge than the standard
European system, there were only a limited number of breakdown cranes
in the country and some of those were in the South. If all the cranes could
be sabotaged, no derailment could be cleared until an Irish-gauge chassis
could be fitted to the replacements. The first step was to derail a train
thereby ensuring that the valuable breakdown crane would be brought out
into the open to clear the wreck.

> . . . early in the morning of Saturday 2nd March two volunteers, by means of
> emergency detonators, stopped a goods train shortly after it had left Strabane
> on the G.N.R. line for Derry. The crew were informed that charges had been
> placed on the line outside Derry and they were ordered to return to Strabane
> on foot. They were also warned not to carry police or military on trains, other-
> wise they could leave themselves open to attack without warning. With one
> man on the foot-place and the other in the guard's van the volunteers took
> over the train and drove it towards Derry. A few miles from Derry the train
> was slowed to a walking pace, the guard's van was evacuated, the regulator
> was then opened for maximum speed and the volunteer driver jumped from the
> foot-plate. It was arranged that explosive charges were to have been placed on
> the line outside Derry with a view to blowing the train into the river Foyle;
> it was further planned that the break-down train would likewise be destroyed
> and blown into the river, when it would arrive to clear the line. Unfortunately
> as a result of the IRA activities of a few hours earlier exceptionally heavy
> patrols of the road which ran parallel to the railway prevented the two volun-
> teers detailed to place the charges on the line from carrying out their part of
> the operation. The train wrecked itself on the buffers of the station in Derry.[10]

The RUC, of course, knew nothing of the long-range operation against
the breakdown cranes-only that the train from Strabane at full speed and
without a crew had ploughed straight into the Derry station. Even at that,
the result was a most expensive wreck.

Despite the ingenuity of the local units and the efforts of the Active
Service liaison men, the initiative in the North was gradually lost. The
RUC moved in armoured Land-Rovers, often in convoy. All barracks were
reinforced, sand-bagged, and tied into an early warning network. After
the wild shooting incidents, the B-Specials settled into a regular routine.
Along the 250-mile border only seventeen roads were left open to normal
traffic and these were well guarded. The maze of unapproved roads were
first patrolled, then cratered, and finally spiked, thus drastically reducing
the routes into the North. In December and January, the RUC rounded
up the most notorious Republicans under the Special Powers Act. The
men, uncharged, were interned in Crumlin Road Prison. Although many
of them, particularly the older men, were hardly Active Service material,[11]
the RUC, by isolating them in Crumlin Road, was hitting at the Republican underground, the fund raisers, and the sympathizers. In point of fact,
internments remained at a low level, peaking at 187 in 1958. During the

entire campaign, only 113 persons were imprisoned, although 204 were prosecuted.[12] Despite the small number of men imprisoned or interned, considering the scope and cost of the campaign, the IRA felt the pinch. On January 4, for example, seven men, including four from the South, were arrested in a British military comb out of the Mourne mountains in County Down. On January 15, two Dublin men, Pearse Doyle and Pat Hodgins, were picked up in a cottage near Glenshane Pass, County Derry. Until men like these could be replaced, their areas would be vacuums, their local contacts isolated. The pressure of these sweeps and house searches kept the Active Service men on the run, often forced to concentrate on evasion rather than attack. Many began to give up safe houses and take to dugouts. As the weeks went by, the longer days cut into the dark hours necessary for a fully active campaign.

In the South with most of the leadership in Mountjoy, attention shifted to the political front. On January 28, Seán MacBride, leader of the three-man Clann na Poblachta, in the Dáil, tabled a motion of No Confidence in Costello's Inter-Party Government. Although concerned with both partition and economic matters the No Confidence motion was the result of the determination of the rank-and-file to penalize Costello for his efforts to end the IRA campaign. MacBride, Con Lehane and others had advised against such a move, fearing the way would be opened for a Fianna Fáil victory. If de Valera came back to office, there could be little doubt on his past record that a new generation would taste the dubious joys of the Curragh. The rank and file, however, voted with their hearts and Costello was forced to call an election for March 5. Sinn Féin, if not on the crest of the wave at least on the up-sweep, nominated nineteen candidates, including, as usual, many of the prisoners. Seeking a symbolic mandate for the campaign, as well as support for the Movement, the Sinn Féin leadership was not overly concerned about the eventual composition of the Dáil but only in harnessing support and accumulating a solid protest vote. There were ample funds, high enthusiasm, and monster meetings. On the night before polling, fifteen thousand gathered in O'Connell Street before the GPO to hear predictions of victory.

Campaigning almost solely on the national issue, the result for Sinn Féin was impressive. The party received 65,640 first preference votes and elected Rory Brady (Longford–Westmeath), Feargal O'Hanlon's brother (Monaghan), John Joe McGirl (Sligo–Leitrim) and one of the grand old Kerry Republicans, John Joe Rice (South Kerry). As MacBride had predicted, however, Fianna Fáil in the greatest Irish electoral triumph swept back into the Dáil with seventy-eight seats, a solid majority.[13] De Valera was back. As had been feared, his tolerance for IRA activity was, if anything, lower than Costello's. His shadow Cabinet had already decided to take swift, punitive action if the IRA campaign resulted in additional loss of life. Sinn Féin, however, was satisfied with its showing; 65,640 out of 1,127,016 votes cast might not be a mandate for violence, but then the party had only run candidates in nineteen out of forty constituencies. The Republicans still felt they were on the move, the tide running their way. In March John Joe McGirl, TD, came home from Mountjoy to a tumultuous welcome. In Limerick there were eight new Sinn Féin Cumainn. In Tralee the influential *Kerryman* sympathized with their efforts. In the United States the Clan na Gael seemed revitalized. In Dublin in light of the declining incidents in the North, the new Fianna Fáil government had begun to release the Mountjoy prisoners. If all was not going right with the campaign, politically or militarily, there was still ample cause for optimism.

In April the temporary Army Council handed over to the old Council and the December GHQ—Magan C/S, Murphy A/G, Cronin Director of Operations, and Russell QMG—once more took control of the campaign. It took some while to re-establish contacts in the North, replace some of the lost active service men, and analyse the events of the previous three months. Some areas needed hard work. Just before the campaign Paddy Doyle, the C/O of Belfast, had been lifted, and other arrests had further disorganized the unit. The first steps were taken to create a strong and efficient underground courier, supply, and service system. One of the key agents would be a young woman whose brother was in Crumlin Road. In Derry City, the local unit had been nearly wiped out by April. The C/O, Eamon Timoney, had been arrested while on the run on March 30—but the unit carried out operations on April 9 and again later in the month. RUC pressure was very strong and by October the units' effectiveness had been destroyed. In some areas, particularly South Fermanagh where Pat McManus was C/O, the situation if anything improved. McManus, keeping to the hills and out of houses, was putting together a first-rate organization, not so far spectacular but most promising.[14] J. B. O'Hagan on the run was gradually tying together his area, although he remained out of contact with Dublin and was not tied back into the net until May.

Realizing that momentum could not really be regained until the campaign season of long nights began again in the autumn, GHQ still wanted to keep up continuity even over the summer. Word was sent up to some local units to try for an ambush of British troops even during the off season. In Armagh Tommy and Paul Smith and the O'Hagan brothers began to pick likely sites. The same process went on elsewhere but by this time RUC patrols had become both cautious and well protected. None of the units could manage an ambush or a big operation; but the small incidents continued; telephone poles were dropped, wires cut, fires started, small sabotage raids made. As the campaign sputtered on in the North,

GHQ in Dublin concentrated on planning for the 1957–1958 operations. Everyone was still enthusiastic. On May 11, there was a monster rally in Dublin and the ex-prisoners spoke to the cheering crowd. Apparently de Valera was going to tolerate Republican activity. The Special Branch remained just as inquisitive nor were the police and border patrols dismantled; but there were no arrests. No one went on the run. The meetings, the plotting and planning went on largely under the eye of the Specials. The government seemed to hope that as the number of incidents declined in the North, as the days lengthened, the "campaign" would peter out.

On Thursday, July 4, at 2.00 a.m., a RUC commando patrol travelling in a military tender ran into a waiting IRA battle-group at Carivegrove, County Armagh. The summer ambush had finally come off. IRA fire killed Constable Cecil Gregg and wounded another RUC man. The next day the newspapers were filled with the "Forkhill ambush" and the renewal of violence in the North. The IRA had obviously not learned its lesson. De Valera's cabinet had little need to discuss Forkhill. Their minds had long been made up. No matter how unpleasant internments might be, politically and personally, "murder" would not be tolerated. On Saturday, July 6, Dublin seemed to be teeming with Special Branch men, hovering on the edge of Republican vision. Murphy and Cronin slipped into the *United Irishman* office at No. 1 Gardiner Row and told Magan that the police were all over Dublin and a big sweep might be under way. Magan decided not to go on the run just yet. Cronin and Murphy slipped out and as they walked down O'Connell Street toward Trinity College decided that Magan was too sanguine. They agreed the time had come to fade out of sight.

That evening the police swooped on Sinn Féin headquarters at Wicklow Street and lifted twelve men, including seven male members of the Sinn Féin Ard Comhairle. Only Mrs. Buckley went untouched. Everyone in the *United Irishman* office was cleaned out. MacCurtain was picked up in Cork at 10.30 that evening when he got off the train from Dublin. By Sunday morning, sixty-three Republicans had been picked up around the country in simultaneous swoops. By some strange oversight only Limerick escaped, allowing the IRA people to get out of town into a hide-away in the hills of East Limerick at Doon. The swoops continued during the week cleaning up the loose ends. All the Sinn Féin Ard Comhairle, except Mrs. Buckley, most of the Army Council and GHQ staff, and many of the people in the country were in the Bridewell—only too aware that the next stop would probably be the Curragh. Only Murphy and Cronin had flown the coop and then only just. Murphy had left Cronin and gone home to pick up a few things. He had to go out the back way when a "van" suddenly appeared in front. He slipped through an alley and managed to get a lift from a safe driver. He stopped off to call Cronin from Clondalkin to arrange a pick-up. After collecting Cronin, he paused again, to have the word passed back to Magan that the hunt was on. By then time had run out. The Special Branch were handling all inquiries at the *United Irishman* office. That evening Cronin and Murphy moved into Tadhg Lynch's house in Santry to sit out the next week without any outside contacts. Lynch, long out of the IRA and no friend of Magan, provided an ideal safe house. Few other prominent IRA people had been as fortunate. More frustrating, the prisoners still in Mountjoy, with only days to go before release, were trapped. When their sentences expired, they faced internment not active service.[15]

To fail to foresee the July arrests and internments as almost inevitable was a blunder of major magnitude. At one go, for the second time in six months, the top had been clipped off the IRA and many of the activists swept from the scene. The reason that the IRA leadership failed to learn from the January lesson, itself a gross error, was not a simple oversight but a complex habit of action and thought. For ten years the leadership had put together a secret army for a specific task, but little time had been taken to consider the probable impact of their activities. Narrow-minded, deeply suspicious of "politics", limited in vision, the Republicans intuitively and inaccurately felt that their prejudices were verities, their aspirations analysis. Few understood the motives, pressures, principles, and personalities of Twenty-six County politics and fewer still were capable of predicting rationally the course of the complex chain-reaction an overt campaign would set off. Despite all the evidence, the leadership held fast to the illusion that their simple promise to remain quiescent in the South would be sufficient surety for the Irish government, a government whose legitimacy they publicly denied and whose actions they refused to recognize.

There existed a belief that because their goals were those of the Irish nation that their means would be tolerated by the "puppet" government in Leinster House. This conviction was not simply the result of gross optimism, which abounded, but simple political naïveté. They did not grasp the reality of political power. To imagine that the election of four men to the Dáil, none of whom would make use of his legal powers, and a vote of five per cent of the electorate gave them real leverage or even moral backing was a sterile exercise in wishful thinking. Because they were so deeply involved in the campaign, they imagined Ireland was as well. Because they were so vitally concerned with military victory, they assumed Ireland was as well. Ireland, however, had other problems and priorities, difficult to achieve during a futile exercise in violence. Most Irishmen, including many who followed Seán South's casket, thought the campaign madness and the IRA irresponsible. Without public opinion or political leverage, the IRA had only the gun.

The Irish government simply could not long tolerate a secret army which denied the validity of the state, which undermined the authority and prestige of the Cabinet and the Dáil, which involved the nation in a precarious adventure that could only lead to massive economic and political retaliation by Great Britain. The IRA leadership misjudged the aspirations of the Irish people and gave little serious thought to the potential decisions of other men—politicians who had been neatly catalogued as knaves or fools and then forgotten. This absolute inability to read anyone's mind but their own crippled the campaign in 1957 and would have, even in more favourable circumstances, prevented the IRA from exploiting any political advantage which might have accrued through military success.

While the arrests and the opening of the Curragh was a harsh blow, it was by no means fatal. With Cronin and Murphy still active, the centre of the net had not entirely disappeared. By autumn new Active Service men could be run into the North and a more efficient intelligence net would be established. Whatever happened in Dublin, the IRA infrastructure in the Six Counties, hardened by coercion, not only existed but functioned. In the autumn the slow grinding process of disorder, sabotage, sporadic ambush and subversion could begin. The chance for a swift victory or rapid escalation had gone, if it ever existed; but now, stripped of any early illusions, GHQ could settle in to the long campaign of attrition that almost all guerrillas must wage.

NOTES

1. The Proclamation was distributed throughout Ireland during December and printed in the *United Irishman* (January 1957).
2. McGarrity, *Resistance,* pp. 96–97.
3. *Parliamentary Debates, House of Commons,* 5th Series, vol. 562, col, 1266.
4. At the time this attack was reported to be an IRA action and was cited by Lord Brookeborough in a public speech as an example of the problems faced by the Northern Ireland government.
5. As anyone who has attempted to interview former combatants, even immediately after an action, can attest, there is no simple tale of what really happened but a collection of conflicting and contradictory evidence, uncertain time sequences, and total blanks. In this case even subsequent interviews did not bring full clarification. It is of some

interest that the IRA found, as others had before them, that the rate
of fire of inexperienced men is very low, that long training does not
necessarily produce automatic responses, and that men immediately
after combat are often dull and vague. Guerrillas, however, must learn
by doing and the penalty for failure is high.

6. 'Twas on a dreary New Year's day as the shades of night came down,
   A lorry load of volunteers approached a Border town;
   There were men from Dublin and from Cork, Fermanagh and Tyrone,
   But the leader was a Limerick man, Seán Sabhat of Garryowen.

   And as they moved along the street up to the Barrack door,
   They scorned the danger they would meet, the fate that lay in store.
   They were fighting for old Ireland's cause, to claim our very own.
   And the foremost of that gallant band was Sabhat of Garryowen.

   But the Sergeant foiled their daring plan, he spied them thro' the door;
   Then the Sten guns and the rifles, a hail of death did pour;
   And when that awful night was past, two men were cold as stone;
   There was one from near the Border and one from Garryowen.

   No more he'll hear the seagull cry o'er the murmuring Shannon tide,
   For he fell beneath the Northern sky, brave Hanlon at his side,
   He had gone to join that gallant band of Plunkett, Pearse and Tone,
   A martyr for old Ireland, Seán Sabhat of Garryowen.

   From *They Kept Faith*, Dublin, 1957. South's name is spelled Sabhat
   in revised Irish and Sabat in the previous system.

7. South's brother had arrived to meet the body at the border, cold and
   bitter to the waiting IRA men, whom he blamed for luring Seán into a
   reckless adventure. As he followed the funeral procession and realized
   what his brother's death meant to so many ordinary people, his mood
   and manner changed. After the funeral he became a convert to Irish
   Republicanism.
8. *An Gath*, vol. 2 (November 1956).
9. Commemorations are still held on January 1 beneath the great Celtic
   cross over South's grave but the crowds have dwindled to the faithful
   few, his old comrades and the loyal Republicans; but because of the
   ballads and the Irish folk memory, it is likely that he will be remembered long after the politicians are forgotten. This "memory" is vitally
   important in an army without pensions or medals.
10. Eamon Mac Tiománaí and Seamus Ramsaigh, *The Campaign of the*

Fifties. Notes and Observations of the Campaign in the North, with Especial Reference to Republican Activities in Derry (typed manuscript, Deire-Fomhair, 1967), p. 21.

11. Several of the Republicans such as Frank McGlade and Jimmy Steele had already served long years in jail. At present Steele holds the record, having spent seventeen Christmases in prison.

12. Royal Ulster Constabulary, *Summary for IRA Campaign: 12.12.1956 to 26.2.1962* (typed copy, August, 1965) and Ministry of Home Affairs, *Civil Authorities (Special Powers) Acts* (mimeographed copy).

13. In passing: the election all but wiped out Clan na Poblachta—MacBride lost his seat and the party vote dropped from 51,042 and 20,632, leaving but a lone Dáil member.

14. "Pat McManus operated in his own territory (South Fermanagh, N.I.) from the start of the campaign until his death in July 1958: as O/C South Fermanagh Active Service Unit from the summer of 1957 he carried out a number of daring actions. He went on the Army Council in the spring of 1958. He was the only active IRA leader to escape arrest during the period. An intrepid guerrilla fighter he preferred the mountains to the towns and disliked leaving his own area for meetings in strange places. Operating mostly from dugouts—a string of which he had built right across Fermanagh—he rarely slept in a house. His death was a major blow to the struggle. Born in Kinawley, Co. Fermanagh, he was 29 when killed. An uncle died fighting with the Republican forces during the civil war, 1922–23." Seán Cronin, "Notes" (typed manuscript, January 1968).

15. Not all the Mountjoy prisoners waited to be shipped to the Curragh. Twenty-four of the thirty-six or so prisoners decided to break out on July 20. All the IRA men were in on the plot under the direction of the prison C/O. A large scaling ladder twelve feet long was organized which would allow four men abreast to go over the wall; but when the first rank of heads popped over a guard outside saw them and the break had to be called off.

CHAPTER XVI

The Campaign: The IRA on the Defensive, August 1957–March 1962

The big July swoop had the unexpected side effect of increasing the efficiency of GHQ. While on the run Cronin and Murphy could give full time to the campaign without needing to maintain a cover occupation or to follow the involved command procedures of a peace-time GHQ. At the end of July, both Cronin and Murphy agreed that although preparation for the 1957–1958 campaign season was the prime consideration at the moment, there was a need to increase active political agitation. The arrest of all male members of the Sinn Féin Executive coupled with the government's denial that membership in Sinn Féin had been a consideration seemed to open up various political ploys. GHQ wanted a release-the-prisoners campaign with protests, parades, petitions, and public pressure. GHQ wanted wide publicity given to the errors and evasions in the various government statements. The Sinn Féin people still outside prison, Seán O'Mahoney and Mae Smith (Mrs. Robert Russell) cooperated at first, although soon GHQ sensed a certain coolness, perhaps as a result of instructions coming out of the Curragh from the Executive. Elsewhere cooperation was excellent.[1] To keep the American money flowing, a new book-keeping system was established with IRA receipts sent out directly from Dublin instead of through New York City to donors whether clubs, like the Red Branch Knights of San Francisco, or to individuals. The circulation of the *United Irishman* continued to climb, reaching 120,000 a month. Politically the high point came in October but not as a result of GHQ agitation, money or publicity or at least not directly. In the Dáil in Leinster House, Jack McQuillan, one of the founders of Clann na Poblachta, put forward a private member's motion calling for United Nations observers to be sent to Northern Ireland. The debate on October 23 showed that Fianna Fáil had no intention of being pressured. Outside of a few scattered independent-minded TDs, there was little support in the Dáil. On October 30, McQuillan's motion lost sixty-two to seventeen.

Although GHQ concentrated on winter plans summer action was not abandoned. A manifesto was posted throughout the North. Communications into the North were improved and gradually a highly effective intelligence, courier, and supply network was put together making use of full-time people and locals still unknown to the RUC. In the South Paul Smith,

Liam Gleeson, and Frank Driver set up training camps. At a camp in Tipperary experiments were made to produce a more effective mine. While all this activity went on out of sight, the attention of the press and police was attracted by the occasional violent IRA sortie in the North. The situation in Newry, the key town in South Armagh, reached the point that on August 13 the Minister of Home Affairs, Colonel W. W. B. Topping, felt it advisable to impose a curfew rather than risk the Nationalist population being converted to open defiance of the government. The situation in Newry seemed touch and go for a while, to the delight of the IRA GHQ. In East Tyrone a similar situation existed and the RUC carried out extensive sweeps. On August 17, RUC Sergeant A. J. Ovens opened a door of a deserted farmhouse near Coalisland and was killed in the explosion of a booby-trap mine. It was reported that the RUC patrol had been lured into the area by a telephone call. This assassination by remote control produced renewed indignation in the Unionist population and a demand for the culprits. Renewed sweeps and long interrogations produced no one until November, when two young men, Talbot and Mallon, were arrested and charged with the murder. Their trial soon became a *cause célèbre* since both men claimed to have been beaten and tortured by the RUC.[2]

GHQ, highly encouraged by the extensive popular support, planned a winter campaign which included a new approach: the concentration of control near the border instead of in Dublin. During the late summer and early autumn, arms, explosives, and ammunition were collected from various dumps in the South and stored in Dublin. An active service force was put together in September to operate along the Leitrim–Fermanagh border. Divided into three groups under Pat McManus, Liam Gleeson, and Seán Daly the men concentrated on training additional units. There were still some problems of liaison and communication with GHQ because of the pressure of the Irish army and police. The general plan for the coming season was to give up attacks on strong points and concentrate on ambushing British armoured patrols. When the season began, the planned ambushes did not prove too effective. The British were wary and their patrols well-armed. The ideal conditions of time, place, and strength seldom occurred. The IRA could never be stronger than the British in any one place and were generally weak every place. Service units shot up Roslea RUC barracks, triggering an ambush of a RUC commando patrol rushing after the raiders. On October 10, a Derry RUC patrol was shot up and on December 1 in Fermanagh a RUC armoured Land-Rover was damaged and two constables wounded. Except in rare instances, the IRA did not have the fire-power or the proper mines to take on armoured cars and protected vehicles. Increasingly, the IRA had to confine itself to sabotage operations, often on a low level. All this could easily change if GHQ could find effective heavier weapons. In the meantime the IRA tried to keep up the pressure.

Many of the active service men within the Six Counties were concentrating on creating an effective, covert infrastructure of dumps, communication nets, safe houses, and trained local men. It soon became obvious that RUC security techniques, based on first-rate local intelligence and constant searches, had just about done away with the safe house. The local RUC knew every house in their district, who lived in them, whether they were in the Gaelic Athletic Association or spoke Irish or belonged to the Legion of Mary. Over the years the police had forgotten nothing, accumulating a fantastic amount of hard data on people, places, and movements. Thus, when the IRA active service people went underground, it usually meant exactly that. It became necessary to dig into the hillsides in hidden dugouts. Some of these were miserable little holes covered with a few branches and good for a damp one-night-stand. Others were elaborate and carefully planned. One of the best examples was built in South Derry at Knockoneil near Maghera. A local man, something of a genius in the devising of dugouts and dumps, had dug a shaft into the side of a steep hill by a boundary ditch. Inside the shaft a small insulated shed had been built with room for two or three men. The entire excavation had been filled in and sodded over but a spy hole had been left so that the men could look out across the fields and watch the RUC patrols.[3]

Life for active service men in these dugouts was difficult and unpleasant, RUC searches aside. There were bugs, bad and unbalanced food, too little sleep, no heat, constant frustration, and always the anxiety of being on the run. The men in the South Derry dugout, for example, had been ordered in to reactivate the area, formerly one of the best Republican districts in the North. They soon discovered that the cream of volunteers had been swept away for active service elsewhere or had been lifted by the RUC. Training classes in weapons and explosives had to be set up and every meeting meticulously planned in order to evade the RUC. A new intelligence net had to be put together with each new contact increasing the risk. Weapons and explosives had to be accumulated. Alternative dugouts had to be constructed at great risk since everyone was exposed in the event of a snap search. None of these efforts were easy and some proved impossible. Nothing could be done about new dugouts. The best alternative to the hillside shaft had the roof kicked up by a transient cow. Nothing could be done about getting in explosives. The training classes improved the level of the local volunteers but not sufficiently to allow for ambitious operations. From late summer until mid-winter, visible activity was negligible. Finally in January operational plans were put into effect. Late in December the three IRA liaison men, aware that the operations would place them in jeopardy when the big comb-outs came, bailed out of South Derry across the border into Donegal. The dugout was not properly sealed by the local man and was discovered by the RUC almost immediately. The operations, however, came off as planned—an explosives job near the Derry–Antrim border and a second attack on Swatragh RUC barracks. After four months on the run in the North, the men were undernourished, exhausted, eaten by vermin and a bit nervy. They left behind a fair local unit, several empty dugouts, and a record of two small actions. The popular conception of a guerrilla flitting from hill to hill at one time everywhere and nowhere bears little relation to the hard, uncertain, miserable life of the IRA man in his filthy little dugout, seldom able to move, reacting to pressure rather than initiating action, never at ease, never comfortable, rarely able to see any return on his investment or savour a moment of glory.

There were worse things. On the night of November 11, just off the Dublin–Belfast road about one hundred yards inside the Twenty-six County border, a small Active Service unit of four men were preparing a mine for an operation. They were crowded into a small farm house on the side of a hill overlooking the border. The owner, Michael Watters, fifty-five, had been glad to help out the lads. Apparently the men were preparing for an operation on Armistice Day, an IRA non-holiday because of the extensive display of Union Jacks; but no one will ever be sure just what they had in mind.[4] Probably the timing mechanism on one mine short-circuited, always a danger unless exceptional care is taken; in any case the gelignite detonated prematurely. The cottage at Edentubber was literally blown apart and down across the hillside. All five men were killed instantly, the greatest single IRA loss since the Civil War.

On the day of the Edentubber tragedy, the first Army Convention since 1955 opened proceedings in a borrowed house in a Dublin suburb. The Convention had been called to regularize the new leadership, approve the progress of the campaign, and calm the doubts of the Cork unit over their losses. The loss of the four young men in the explosion did not so much cast a cloud of gloom over the Convention as it deepened the dedication and determination to make the deaths worth while and the campaign successful. The Convention produced little new. The new Executive elected an Army Council with the old names—Cronin, Murphy, O'Hagan, McGirl, McCarthy. Cronin remained C/S, Murphy A/G, and a new man Myles Shevlin, was brought on the GHQ staff. The doubts of Cork seemed to have been erased. Except for some discussion of the need for rocket launchers, particularly by some of the Active Service people brought down from the North for the Convention, almost no serious military questions were discussed. The delegates generally saw no need to ask questions or offer suggestions. The next day the Active Service men moved back to their area and the others either surfaced or returned to their safe houses.

The level of campaign actions continued about the same. Lots of sabotage but few big operations. A growing difficulty was the heavy Twenty-six County activity along the border. When IRA units withdrew after operations in the North, they found the Irish police and army in blocking positions. At times the Irish police were tied into RUC radio nets.[5] Thus one of the basic prerequisites for a guerrilla campaign, sanctuary, was being denied the IRA. On November 29, two of the three column leaders operating in the North, Seán Daly of Cork and Liam Gleeson, walked into an Irish border patrol and ended up in Mountjoy. Once through the border area the problem was less severe, although there was always the danger of arrest and internment if the Special Branch ran across the volunteer. While the border sweeps continued to net good men, by mid-winter this obstacle was taken as a matter of course, unfortunate but unavoidable.

In order to heat up the campaign, GHQ had several interrelated projects. In view of the real need for some sort of mobile artillery, Cronin proposed a raid on the British Army barracks at Blandford to take out rocket launchers and shells. Murphy, who had a brother serving a life sentence for the last raid, had personal misgivings and some practical doubts. The problem was not so much the raid which would jeopardize key men—particularly Cronin—but getting the stuff from England to Ireland. Cronin felt there was a good chance. Finally at a three-hour meeting of the Army Council on a Sunday morning early in January, it was decided to go ahead. Shevlin, now on the Council, and McGirl felt a coup was necessary. Cronin knew the rocket launchers were vital. Murphy's doubts were overcome.

Under Cronin the attack team of six was carefully selected: Mick Finnegan, Paddy Sullivan, Tom Nixon, S. Hennessy, Frank Skuse and Frank McCarry. All but one of the seven had guerrilla experience and all by previous example were aware of the risks. As usual with detailed intelligence, careful timing, and substantial gall, the attack team hit the Camp at Blandford in Dorset at 1.15 a.m. on February 16. Two IRA men remained in the car. Five men went into the guard area and bound and gagged ten British sentries right on schedule. The magazine was protected by a moving patrol of two sentries and both had become suspicious after listening to the scuffling sounds from the guard room. The IRA men could not surprise them. During the confused struggle, one British sentry was knocked unconscious with a gun-butt and the other shot when he tried to bayonet the IRA man. The two sentries were brought in the guard room and the wounded man treated. Two more unexpected British soldiers appeared and an IRA lookout had to fire over the heads of the two corporals to persuade them to come into the guard room. The neat, quiet operation seemed to be coming apart leaving the attack team of seven sitting in the midst of two thousand British troops with another 1,500 a half-mile away down the road. Then the main guard commander appeared, alerted by a telephone operator who had heard the shots. He, too, was bound and gagged; but the string had run out. When he failed to return the balloon would go up. Cronin ordered the raiders back into the car and withdrew just as the general alarm went off. Despite the police blocks along some highways and the sealing off of railroad stations, airports, and ferry terminals, the attack party got clean away—but barely. The British police either through Irish contacts, or information from Ryan's car-hire firm, or good police work had had an inkling that a raid was to take place. They arrived at the door of the safe house exactly one hour too late to collect Cronin. Once more despite the failure to get away with the arms, the fringe benefits of the raid for the IRA were considerable. Seven men holding a British military camp, garrisoned by two thousand troops, for nearly an hour and then evading the massive security cordon had a decided effect on morale.

A week after the seven Blandford raiders arrived in Waterford, an Army Executive meeting was held in Bagnalstown, County Carlow, well away from the eyes of the Dublin Special Branch. Cronin went over the raid in detail and the discussion turned on the campaign. Despite the lack of rocket-launchers, there remained certain possibilities. Nothing too complicated could be put together in the time left before the longer days began. Instead, during and after the meeting, attention turned to a shift of pace for the following season—a concentration of men rather than a dispersion, continuous action in one solid area instead of penny-packet sabotage. The most appealing area was South Fermanagh; McManus had built up a first-rate guerrilla operation and RUC reinforcements could be interdicted most easily. A battle plan began to develop. GHQ would move up near the border. McGirl in Leitrim would supply a solid sanctuary. The first step would be to start small in South-West Fermanagh, and lure the British into a mountain area pre-loaded with IRA men.

As the campaign season dwindled into the spring, GHQ settled into a safe house on Serpentine Avenue in Ballsbridge and began serious work on the Fermanagh operation. Mick McCarthy drove up from Cork with a Vickers heavy machine-gun to add to the arsenal. It was not a rocket-launcher but with the proper ammunition the Vickers would come as quite a shock to the RUC, armoured mainly against lighter-calibre weapons. There were one or two interruptions in operational planning. Frank Skuse had been picked up by the police under the name of Paul Murphy. GHQ wanted, if possible, to break him out before the police discovered his proper identity. His British army "service" obviously made him very vulnerable if the Irish government were to deport him. Between May 6–12, Skuse was in St. Brigit's Hospital where the IRA had made certain contacts with his guards. Frank McCarry, C/O of the Rescue Squad, was supposed to have the time to clear Skuse out while the right people looked the wrong way. It sounded too easy. At this point an "unofficial" escape try by non-IRA people almost came off but alerted the guards. All the IRA escapes seemed to go wrong that spring. On May 6, a mass breakout from Mountjoy had failed followed by a fifteen-day hunger strike and fourteen days in solitary. At the Curragh three men broke out, but all three were recaptured within ten days. That particular unofficial escape led to a vast police and army sweep through Kildare—much to Mick McCarthy's alarm, for he was on his way to Dublin with the Vickers in the boot of his car. Once the Vickers arrived, the last steps could be taken to acquire ammunition and parts. An Irish army officer, P. S. Dolan, had been discovered to have strong sympathies with the campaign. Regular contact was set up by Frank McCarry and plans were in the hopper for his eventual defection. Dolan, however, had been less than discreet, even lending his car to Sinn Féin during the election campaign. On May 31, McCarry could not make a meeting with Dolan, and Charlie Murphy, anxious to keep Dolan on the line, suggested that he and Frank McDonnell go instead. The two of them stepped into a police trap. Dolan had raised sufficient suspicion for the Special Branch to set up a stake-out. Murphy and McDonnell walked right into it. Dolan was sentenced to two years and did his time in Portlaoise Prison, isolated from all Republicans. Murphy and McDonnell after serving time in Mountjoy were transferred to the Curragh in September. At GHQ Murphy was replaced as A/G by Shevlin and on the Council by Patty Murphy. Planning for the autumn campaign went on as before.

During all the preparations for operations in the North, considerable attention had to be paid to the activities of the Kelly–Christle Saor Uladh group, which had by no means faded into the woodwork. There was still a central Executive, consisting of Kelly, Christle, Jim Killeen, Seán O'Neill, Frank Morris from Donegal, and one or two others, but the group remained loosely organized. The emphasis was more often on certain specific operations rather than on a continuing campaign. Kelly did on occasion put active service units into the field—at one point Joe Lyons had a small column operating out of Donegal and there was another under Pat Murphy out of Monaghan; but Saor Uladh's most successful operations were one-shot affairs. On May 12, 1957, Saor Uladh blew the locks on the Newry Canal causing immense damage at a minimal cost in stolen gelignite. Due mainly to the service of a first-rate demolition expert, a number of bridges were dropped—instead of cratered or cracked as was so often the case with IRA operations. Mostly, however, Kelly stuck close to his home territory in Tyrone, helping out the IRA when they needed a hand and venturing out on occasional sorties. Christle's lot in Dublin remained completely isolated from the IRA—he and his were heretics while Kelly was just politically misguided. Christle gave no indication that IRA distaste had any effect. His men went ahead carrying out raids in the South for explosives and using them from time to time in the North.[6]

Certainly the most spectacular exploit of Christle's branch of Saor Uladh was a successful prison break. Christle with his legal training had long been interested in the case of J. A. M. Murphy, convicted on mistaken eye-witness testimony for participation in the Arborfield raid. Christle decided to spring Murphy and Joe Doyle, both in Wakefield Prison, by putting his own man inside as a sleeper. Elaborate preparations, involving a great many of the members of Christle's loose organization, were necessary. Since funds from the American contacts did not arrive in time, Christle eventually secured a loan from a member of his Executive and went ahead. Pat Donovan got into Wakefield without the British being aware that their new prisoner was anything but a normal criminal offender. At this point Christle made contact in London with the Cypriot underground EOKA. The Cypriots were particularly anxious to get out their man, Nicos Samson. Christle agreed. Another prominent Wakefield resident Klaus Fuchs, one of Britain's premier atom spies, decided to turn down the offer to join the break; however, he did contribute a highly detailed plan so that a Dublin architect could create a scale model of Wakefield. Eventually, on February 19, 1959, after six months of work and at the cost of £500, Murphy was the only one to get over the wall. Doyle was too ill, Fuchs too cautious, and Samson was left standing in the prison yard when things went wrong.

Usually the key to a successful prison break, despite Goulding's long run of bad luck, is not getting over the wall but disappearing on the far side. Once he was over the wall Murphy vanished into a maze of carefully laid false scents, errant clues, and even a spurious interview given by his mother in Castledermot, Co. Kildare, on her son's appearance while Murphy was still hiding out in Manchester. Eventually he flew home from Glasgow via Aer Lingus without attracting undue attention. After considerable excitement Murphy drifted away, his conviction unexploited by Christle, into Left-wing politics, converted it was muttered by Fuchs, who remained in Wakefield coaching Donovan in mathematics for his GCE examination.

However praiseworthy Murphy's escape was, the IRA was angered by the anxiety Saor Uladh caused. The most unpleasant complication was the raids for gelignite within the Twenty-six Counties. These raids strengthened the hand of the Dublin government in contending that the campaign was a threat to the peace and security of the country. Disclaimers by the Republican Publicity Bureau published in the *United Irishman* and distributed to the newspapers enraged the Saor Uladh people without impressing the government. The only fringe benefit was that some of the gelignite occasionally sifted through to the IRA. Of more importance militarily, Christle had sent Pat Murphy to the United States rallying support, which he did. Kelly, who had even better American contacts, also spent some months in the United States during the campaign making more friends and influencing more people. Consignments of arms and ammunition slipped through to Saor Uladh. One large shipment contained two anti-tank guns. Others had Thompsons and ·45 calibre ammunition. Some of this material was given to the IRA, particularly Thompson ammunition and explosives; but when Kelly emigrated, Christle kept control of the bulk of the stuff. During the autumn of 1957 and on through 1958, military cooperation with Kelly in the North increased. There were occasional meetings between IRA GHQ people and Kelly, but politically he remained anathema. The IRA was more interested in the help Saor Uladh could give the IRA Active Service people in the North than in improving relations with Kelly. The IRA had to depend on Kelly in his area of Tyrone and did so with a minimum of friction. In general the result was close cooperation in the North and continued alienation in the South: at the same time that Kelly was turning over ammunition to IRA people in the Six Counties, the Saor Uladh men interned in the Curragh were ostracized by the orthodox IRA internees.

While Kelly's bits and pieces of ammunition and equipment were some help, GHQ was very concerned after a year of equipment attrition about weapons—or the lack of weapons. Because there were no anti-tank rockets or light artillery pieces or even bazookas, attacks on sandbagged barracks could not be pushed nor did ambushes of heavily armoured vehicles stand much of a chance. There was for a time a mortar, picked up in a snatch-and-grab raid in the North. This could be used in training, but would not fire in action. Not until the summer of 1959 were a couple of American bazookas smuggled in, but test firing proved that the projectiles travelled only a few feet. A vital section of the firing mechanism had been replaced with burnt cork—a sad commentary on the low moral calibre of illicit arms dealers. In time a curious British development, hopefully called the Boyes Anti-Tank Rifle, was tried on one operation. The Boyes, a strange shoulder rifle with attached tripod, intended, one assumes, to be fired by a giant from a prone position at a lightly armoured vehicle at very close range, had been given up eventually by the British as a bad job. Why it was introduced as a "standard" weapon in the first place is beyond even those with some insight into the British military mind. Although Cronin had test-fired it at four hundred yards without damage, he felt it was too cumbersome. In the case of the IRA, thieves could not be choosers, and the Boyes was fired at a RUC barracks. According to later reports, the recoil broke the gunner's shoulder. The Boyes swivelled in a great arc in the air and embedded itself in the ground behind the firing point. The projectile tore through the wall of the parish priest's house some distance from the RUC barracks. The Boyes, like the bazooka, had to be discarded.

The IRA continued with the weapons on hand. The most vulnerable as well as the most useful was the Thompson, which needed ·45-calibre ammunition generally available only in the United States. Through the efforts of the Clan and with an occasional assist from Kelly, the Thompsons were always supplied. GHQ never managed to acquire really effective explosives but gelignite remained plentiful and the mines became increasingly more effective. One difficulty absent during the Tan War was mine concealment. Since most of the roads of Northern Ireland had been paved, any mine, in fact any suspicious lump, on the road attracted the attention of the RUC. A variety of stratagems were devised to surmount this technical difficulty. One device was a milk can sawed in half, filled two-thirds full of gelignite, and implanted in the bank of a road. Detonated from a distance the explosion funnelled out into the road striking the patrol vehicle on the side. Apart from the Bren, the only heavy machine gun was the elderly Vickers brought up from Cork. As the campaign continued, the sweeps, searches, and arrests reduced the number of weapons in the country; but with a small dribble of outside material the losses never reached the point of prohibiting operations.

One of the obvious ways to cut the attrition rate of weapons and ammunition was to buy them, better yet have them given to the IRA. Unfortunately the IRA had great difficulty in discovering a sponsor other than the Clan. An approach from Germany by old friends of Frank Ryan failed to produce results. Several IRA initiatives were made elsewhere. In Dublin the old IRA man, Tadhg Lynch, suggested to Murphy and Cronin that the Spanish Republicans, exiles in Paris, had access to arms which might be donated or sold to the Irish Republican Movement, partly at least in remembrance of the Irish contribution to the International Brigades during the Spanish Civil War. Some of the Clan's labour leaders in New York produced a letter of introduction for Lynch. Cronin, however, decided to send the letter with a well-known Irish revolutionary who had been a firm advocate of the Spanish Republic. Unfortunately for the IRA, when he arrived in Paris, his contact proved to be a Spaniard who had known and disliked him in the old days. The arms agreement fell through. In London Brendan McConnell made contact to see if the Russians were interested in Irish revolutionaries. Donal Murphy, who was in prison with Gordon Lonsdale, a convicted Soviet spy, sent out word that Lonsdale was certain Russia would be interested in the IRA. But all that could be elicited from the

Soviet Embassy was that Moscow supported revolutionary governments not revolutionary movements. Kelly, too, had tried the Russians, spending three days in Lisbon in a conference that elicited much the same reply. The most promising of all contacts, however, was with the Cypriots, but in this case the matter under discussion was not arms.

EOKA, devoted to seeking union, *Enosis,* with Greece, had waged sporadic guerrilla and terror warfare against the British since April 1955. Word came out of Wormwood Scrubs Prison from the Cypriots that a contact with the IRA would be of mutual advantage. The EOKA people in London asked Dublin to send over someone. Tony Meade, attached to GHQ in Dublin, was sent to London. As appropriate to such an international contact, Meade found his man sitting in a certain Cypriot restaurant, at a particular table, smoking a special black cigar, and reading a predetermined newspaper. Meade's contact was Nico Ioannou, whose brother was in Wormwood Scrubs. At dinner in Nico's flat, Meade made arrangements for a second meeting at a specific hour in front of the lion house in Dublin's Phoenix Park Zoo. What evolved from this contact was a discussion of a mutual prison break.[7] The IRA would even make arrangements to train certain selected EOKA men in Ireland if need be. This particular arrangement fell through when all the Cypriots were transferred out of Wormwood Scrubs. Contact faded as the situation in Cyprus changed, thereby depriving the Gaelic denizens of some small parish of the sight of a score of small, dark men with black cigars and flowing moustaches gambolling about on the green hills.

Thus all ventures into foreign waters, except for the traditional one across the Western Sea to the Clan na Gael, aborted. The obvious reason was that very few governments or even revolutionary movements had much to gain from an association with the IRA, which if it had a long tradition of rebellion also had a rather disquieting record of failure. Even the support of the Clan was barely enough to keep the campaign afloat. The drain of supporting men on the run and their families and the prisoners' dependants cost an average of £400 a month, a not inconsiderable sum in Ireland; and this had to be found regularly, month after month, or the campaign would flounder to a halt. Various funds, drives, loans, public collections on flag-days, private lotteries and public sales, and the occasional American cheque kept the wolf from the door; but as time passed money became harder to find and the campaign costs no lower.

Nevertheless, the campaign ground on through the summer months, keeping up sufficient pressure to force expensive security operations but not enough to endanger civil order. Despite the long summer days, the local units in the North had planned a variety of operations which did not depend on the covering dark. The high point of the summer operations came during three days in July when the IRA struck in twelve different areas, cutting roads, cratering bridges, blasting custom posts, and ambushing a RUC patrol. One of these summer operations, ingenious in conception and potentially devastating in effect, missed coming off by the tug of a hand and another cost the IRA an almost irreplaceable man.

In the first case, Willie Reilly had come down from Armagh early in July with a quite simple plan to blow up the Irish Street RUC barracks. All he needed was a couple of men for a couple of days. Reilly had noted that for a few minutes around eight in the morning it was possible to walk directly by the unguarded but heavily sandbagged front door. It would be a matter of seconds to lean over and place a mine inside the sandbags, walk on to the corner with the cord, and detonate it before the guard came on duty. The force of the explosion driven inward by the sandbags would turn the old barracks into a heap of rubble. It was neat, feasible, and entailed no great investment of limited IRA resources. Cronin agreed to the plan and found two young volunteers to go along to Armagh. Tony Meade had left his dugout in South Derry exhausted and undernourished and spent the remainder of the winter resting up in Kerry. Denis Foley, who had despaired of being asked to go on active service, had on his own bat joined the British Army at Armagh and contacted GHQ. However he could not bring off the operation to smuggle in time-bombs. Both were attached to GHQ waiting for action.

Reilly returned to Armagh on July 12 and two days later Meade and Foley slipped across the border and contacted him. The first attempt on July 15 had to be called off. A delay in acquiring electrical cord had used up the brief time slot in the RUC routine and in any case the street had suddenly filled up with children. The next morning they tried again. The mine, eighty pounds of gelignite, was quite capable of pulverizing the barracks; but by that time the three men would be in a taxi on their way to a safe house. The three moved down the street and the mine was slipped into place without difficulty. Reilly began backing away, unreeling the detonating cord, but the process was much too slow. Time was running out and an aggressive dog had suddenly developed a keen and highly vocal interest in Meade's shins. Then almost at the corner the cord broke. There was no time to go back. Meade took one shot at the dog and the three rushed to the waiting and innocent taxi pre-ordered to pick up three customers. The taxi driver took them close to their safe house near St. Patrick's Cathedral but clearly suspected something odd about the three. By the time the three piled out of the taxi, their local contact had disappeared and the hue and cry over the eighty-pound mine had begun. The RUC were almost on their heels and the only way open was up the hill and into St. Patrick's.

The three were picked up hiding in the confessional booths, tried, convicted, and sentenced to fourteen years. Pat McManus had even worse luck. On July 15, at Derryrealt just over the border in Cavan, the mine he was preparing went off prematurely, killing him and injuring two others. McManus had developed into a natural guerrilla leader and his area in Fermanagh was to be the key to the 1958–1959 season. His loss could not easily be made good. The RUC also lost a man killed following an attack at Carrickbroad, County Armagh. This brought another British request that Dublin do something. The British Ambassador, Sir Alexander Clutterbuck, delivered a note to the Irish Minister of External Affairs, Frank Aiken, and the two discussed the situation. There was really little more that the Irish government could do without risking political backlash: the Curragh was open, the border patrols active, censorship in effect, and the police on the alert. The northern incident sputtered on through August. On August 23, a Sinn Féin organizer, James Crossan, was shot and killed by the RUC in what looked like an ambush inside the Twenty-six Counties.[8] In September the Republican Publicity Bureau issued a proclamation that there would be no cease-fire until Ireland was free.

By early Autumn the pressure in the South was beginning to pinch. Regularly the Army Council was forced to co-opt new members as Active Service men were arrested and the men on the run in the South ran into the Special Branch. Then late in September the Irish police finally staked out the house on Serpentine Avenue. The net picked up Cronin, Mick McCarthy, Seamus Graham, Seán Hennessy, and Hugh Heaney. Cronin's loss was catastrophic. Such had been the attrition rate for Army Council members and GHQ people that Cronin had been running much of the campaign from under his hat. Shevlin as A/G had only bits and pieces of the picture and few of Cronin's contacts. Things were so desperate that when the Army Council met on September 29 only three members were present, Shevlin, John Joe McGirl, and Paddy Murphy. All that could be done was to try and read Cronin's mind, to try and link up with the men in the North, and to appoint McGirl as C/S. The only firm IRA contact was Maurice Fitzgerald who had escaped the Serpentine Avenue coup. He was instructed to bring out some of the active service people so that GHQ could find out what was going on.

One hopeful note was that Rory Brady and Dave O'Connell had broken out of the Curragh on September 27. They might bring advice and comment from the Curragh leadership; more important, GHQ in a period of chaos would have the services of two good men. That was the first thought. The second thought was that it might be difficult to make contact with the two. It was a good thought. Brady and O'Connell disappeared, gone to ground where neither the IRA nor Special Branch could find them.

The confused Army Council had to struggle along on their own. At a meeting in Meath near Navan, the Council of three questioned some thirty active service people trying to find out what orders they had from Cronin. No clear picture emerged. He had sanctioned or ordered quite a few operations. Time was dribbling away and the interim Army Council knew that there was little hope that they could mesh all these operations into a coherent pattern. Control from the top had been lost and with it direction of the 1958–1959 season.

Finally, on October 24, Brady and O'Connell surfaced and a joint Army Council was created. Brady became C/S. There was little that could be done with the winter season. Local units in the North were left on their own to attack targets of opportunity or to wait out the winter. GHQ efforts to reorganize in the border areas seemed to dispel the good will of past years without improving a deteriorating situation. The number of operations dropped precipitously. In the South the decline in incidents raised hopes in the Cabinet that the campaign was finally finished. If this were the case, the Curragh internment camp could be closed down.

Inside the Curragh, conditions among the IRA prisoners were nearly as chaotic as for the men still on the run. As had so often been the case in the past, dissension, petty jealousy, sterile policy disputes and all the minor irritants of confined living had festered for months. The old leadership, Magan, MacCurtain, and McLogan, isolated from events, had sought to advise GHQ through their line to the outside. Not only had their advice been ignored but at Cronin's request Murphy had sent a message suggesting that the GHQ would have to deal with the situation as it saw fit. In prison an IRA man loses all rank and control, but the letter rankled. That GHQ wanted escapees to be young active service men and not the old Army Council members, rankled. These slights, real or imagined, were from the outside; but there was evidence within the Curragh that the prestige of the leadership was evaporated. MacCurtain had been elected Prison C/O and had instigated a soft policy toward the guards, having seen the futility of a hard policy during the internment of the 1940s. He explained to the young men that the Curragh had been the graveyard of Republicanism for his generation and this time he wanted no disastrous schisms or futile protests. However logical this might have been under the circumstances, the long useless hours led to fault finding. MacCurtain had entered the Curragh a hero to most of the volunteers, but no man remains a hero to his valet or his fellow prisoners. There was grumbling in some quarters and the Saor Uladh men made no secret of their distaste for MacCurtain's soft policies. Some volunteers had almost openly begun to criticize MacCurtain but most of their grievances, large and small, arose from frustration, boredom, and the anxiety of indefinite internment.

The only substantive issue was the failure of effective escape plans. There was, everyone knew, an escape committee. There was a tunnel under way. There were lots of plans but no authorization from the leadership. There had been the one brief unofficial escape in May 1958 which underlined that escape was possible despite the doubts of the official planners. MacCurtain and his staff did not want to risk a mass go at the wire because the military guards might fire on the men; nor did they want to risk a break which might require force. On September 27, when Brady and O'Connell broke out, their official variety of escape came to fruition. Under cover of a football game, Brady and O'Connell had slipped beyond the wire a few feet and covered themselves with a camouflage grass-blanket. By the time they were missed at the breakfast roll call the following morning at seven thirty, they were long gone, free and clear. MacCurtain's official escape had got two vital active service men away without risking violence and with a good chance of evading the first searches.

Instead of calming the critics the break simply whetted other appetites. When Charlie Murphy was transferred to the Curragh, he found to his surprise that he was a villain to the leadership and a hero to the discontented. MacCurtain and Magan blamed Murphy for most of the GHQ actions since July 1957 that had annoyed them. These grievances had festered month after month. Murphy did not understand the ingrown distaste; but did feel that particularly in the matter of escape the "Ms" had been too cautious. Murphy, wisely or unwisely, accepted the role of leader of the discontented. Isolated in their hut, "Little Rock", they began to prepare for their own escape without official permission. They selected a section of the wire which MacCurtain had already turned down, since the alarm would give too little time for the escapees to get away. Murphy's group, which was growing in size, decided to take the chance. Despite the fact that there had been a few releases and rumours that the Curragh would close by Easter, Murphy decided to go ahead with a mass break.[9] On December 2, the men rushed the wire with Frank McDonnell's cutters made from stool legs, snipped through and began dashing off across the countryside. The alarm did not go off in time but soldiers rushed in swiftly. Some gas grenades were dropped into the crowd milling at the cut wire. By then sixteen men were through the break where Frank Driver and Murphy were holding back the wire. Despite an extensive sweep through County Kildare, only two of the men were picked up. The "unofficial" escape was a spectacular success.

For MacCurtain and the camp leadership, it was the last straw. Murphy had wilfully disobeyed IRA camp policy—more frustrating he had successfully disobeyed the no-escape order. The division within the camp became irreconcilable. To the leadership the escape had been a pointless challenge and a violation of Army discipline. The escape-group felt their success simply underlined the mistakes and timidity of the leadership. On the outside, GHQ, well aware that the escape was "unofficial", had to decide what to do with fourteen good but disobedient men. Reluctantly, GHQ overlooked the infraction and reinstated the escapees, choosing practicality instead of principle and further alienating the Curragh leadership. As each side sought to justify their actions, the dialogue became very bitter indeed.

Although Murphy had good reason in December to believe that the Curragh would remain open, it soon became obvious that the Fianna Fáil government had decided to end internments. The major consideration was the sputtering out of the campaign in the North after the summer operations. There were other factors beyond, of course, liquidating a political liability. The Irish President, Seán T. O'Kelly, was about to visit the United States where demonstrations against internment would hardly create a favourable image of the new Ireland. There were also cases before the European Court of Human Rights. Gery Lawless's plea, entered in November 1957, was accepted as admissible on August 30, 1958.[10] In Dublin, Shevlin had secured a *habeus corpus* writ for a man arrested in his brother's name. All these international and domestic complications could be eliminated without much risk, since the Offences Against the State Act would still allow the police to pick up IRA people and the courts to sentence them for refusing to answer questions. Internees began to be released unconditionally in batches.

In the North there was no indication that Stormont felt the emergency was over or the internments unnecessary; in fact, the action of the Irish government in closing the Curragh and releasing the "terrorists" was deplored in print and in parliament. Stormont intended to keep their internees in Crumlin Road until all danger had passed—Republican internees of the Six Counties were a political asset not a liability. As for the other IRA prisoners in A Wing, they had been convicted of crimes and would have to serve their sentences. Even the few men in A Wing like Joe Campbell and Leo McCormack who had served out their sentences were not released but simply interned under the Special Powers Act.

Inside A Wing of Crumlin Road, unlike the Curragh, there was never a split. Tom Mitchell, regularly re-elected as Prison C/O, proved capable of getting along with everyone and smoothing down the rough edges of faction. The problem of escape was not as vital in Crumlin; for beneath the great walls, topped by watch-towers, and under the eyes of well-armed warders, a break seemed much more complicated than it did looking at the fields of Kildare through the strands of wire at the Curragh. Despairing of the official escape committee's lack of enthusiasm, most soon gave up hope. The old pre-campaign prisoners had accepted that they could not make

it by themselves and GHQ was not going to help, despite all the floor plans
and warder schedules smuggled out. A few did not give up so easily and
against the most unlikely odds two even made a break. John Kelly with
his Belfast contacts had managed to smuggle in the proper tools at Christmas
time 1960. Along with Dan Donnelly, who was not a member of the Crumlin
IRA unit at the time, Kelly got onto the wall but slipped and fell into the
yard below. Donnelly made it all the way, the only man to escape from
Crumlin Road during the entire campaign. Inside, the rest of the Republicans realized that this one break was it and that they would have to settle
down and serve out their sentences. Most of the others had long since
accepted their condition.

   The first campaign volunteers, who had been sentenced in December
1956, had arrived to find the old men, mostly from Omagh, easy and comfortable. All the eager new IRA volunteers anxious to go over the wall
quite upset their comfortable world. For them the campaign had been a
distant dream not a present reality. For them Cronin was a name and his
tactics strange. Mitchell proved to be capable of absorbing the new men
into the prison unit without serious disagreement. As the years passed
he proved to be an astute politician, considering that all his highly publicized political campaign in Mid-Ulster had gone on without his physical
presence. The penny finally dropped for most of the men as it had long
ago for Mitchell—no one was going to go over the wall. Some spent their
time in study, even in some cases for certificates, and nearly everyone
read voraciously. Others dissected often at great length the past, present,
and future of the Republican movement. These Crumlin seminars were
at first limited to repetition of the orthodox line but in time broadened
their scope to social and economic issues. Some got by without study or
discussion; bored, mute, cheerful or sour, waited out the years. How many
years there would be, no one knew; as long as the campaign ran, releases
were unlikely. When the campaign failed to regain the momentum lost,
during the 1958–1959 season, the Northern authorities waited a while and
in 1960 began releasing the internees. On April 25, 1961, the last internee
left; but the IRA men under sentence stayed in until they had finished
their allotted sentences.

   In the South, once the Curragh closed for good on March 15, 1959, the
IRA seemed preoccupied with the Curragh feuds, which had grown to
overpowering proportions in the hot-house atmosphere of the last months
of the camp. The first joint meeting of the Curragh men and the existing
Army Council took place on Spy-Wednesday before Easter. The Army
Council's idea was to co-opt the best men onto a new Council while the
interim Council resigned man by man, thus giving continuity of leadership
until the Army Convention could meet. The Curragh group was not willing

to give up their grievances. They had suffered too much abuse and too many insults. MacCurtain was bitter that Charlie Murphy was at the same table. They wanted justification. Frank McCarry drafted a resolution which if accepted would be read at all Army meetings. The wording left no doubt that the Curragh group had always been correct. The escapee-group was appalled, feeling that it was vital that their actions be accepted as proper. GHQ was caught in the middle. No one could step in and heal the breach. Positions hardened and things were said in private or public that were difficult to forgive. Manus Canning and Cathal Goulding came home at last to find the Army seized on issues they knew nothing about, quarrelling over reputations and rights instead of preparing for the future. It was a bad time.

The first victim was Murphy. Responsible for the Curragh escape, he had further weakened his position by coming out of Mountjoy with a message for GHQ. This had been given him by Chief Superintendent Philip McMahon and hinted that prisoners would be released if the IRA stopped the campaign. Cronin rejected the "offer" and Murphy returned to prison. Criticism of Murphy's actions was so harsh that he asked for a Court of Inquiry. Cronin suggested that the Curragh escape be considered a breach of discipline not an "unauthorized operation" which was a violation of Army Orders and that the Mountjoy message could be considered an error in judgement. Murphy's judges were more interested in getting him out of the Army than keeping him. The Court found against him. Others decided not to wait to be asked to leave by one side or the other. As the squabbling dragged on into the spring, meeting after meeting found no common ground. Seán Quinn had been brought down from the North by Brady only to hear long discussions of "the Curragh Problem". He went back and mailed Brady a letter saying he could no longer attend meetings. Liam Gleeson wanted no part of the feud, asked for active service, and drifted away. Others like Noel Kavanagh simply had enough and opted out. In April 1959, the Army Council decided to hold a Convention at the end of May or early in June, in the hope that the issue could be buried before it infected the entire IRA.

When the Convention met, most of the old and new leadership was present. On one side were two "Ms"—MacCurtain and Magan[11]—and the Curragh Group, all still determined that their resolution be accepted and their conduct vindicated. On the other side were a highly vocal group of active service men, sympathetic to the December escape, who insisted that the Curragh was past history and the IRA should get on with the campaign. In the middle were the interim Army Council, a few men like Goulding and Canning who had been too far away to be contaminated and men like Cronin who felt the campaign was more important than the Curragh issue.

The Convention produced a long wrangle devoted almost entirely to the problem of the Curragh. The "Ms" wanted the matter discussed and the majority did not. No compromise could be found. At last, well into the next day, Magan rose to speak in defence of the Curragh-group. He talked on and on, read document after document. Time slipped by as the exhausted delegates listened to him. Eventually, near dawn, the exhausted Convention voted not to discuss the Curragh further. The "Ms" did not get their resolution and refused to allow their names to be put forward for the Executive. MacCurtain insisted there would never be a MacCurtain-faction but it was obvious that a split had occurred.[12] After twenty years, MacCurtain and Magan had returned to the ranks, McLogan, who was still on the Executive, was no longer a key man, and Murphy had gone altogether. The new Army Council—Cronin, Brady, Goulding, McGirl, O'Hagan, McCarry, and O'Dowd—was dominated by the campaign people. The people in the centre of the circle during the previous three years had not greatly changed but the "Ms" had not been able to step inside with honour.

The Convention, though torn by the Curragh issue, had accepted the continuation of the campaign almost as a matter of course. With Cronin as C/S, Brady as A/G, and Goulding as QMG, the summer was spent preparing for the 1959–1960 season in the North. Control from the top had to be established, the guerrilla infrastructure reactivated, and operations co-ordinated. Despite the best efforts of GHQ the campaign simply failed to gather momentum. The loss of control during the period of chaos in the autumn of 1958 had done considerable damage. The infrastructure had largely rotted—the couriers retired, the informers mute, the dumps forgotten. All the tiresome drudgery of putting the net together had to be undertaken with limited personnel and under maximum RUC pressure. GHQ began to notice that some of the escapee-group so eager for active service had begun to fade from the scene for one reason or another. Within a few months Vincent Conlon, who had turned down a position on the Executive, left for England. Tommy Ferris stayed on for a year and then emigrated to the United States in 1960. Although some, like Don Donaghy, stayed to the end of the campaign, most had gone by November and December. The reason was not lack of courage or determination but the slow recognition that the campaign was hopelessly mired. The rot of defeatism in the face of waning support, unending obstacles, and negligible results had crept into the Army.

There was ample reason for pessimism. Very few operations could be mounted despite the number of active service people in the North. During all of 1959, there were only twenty-seven incidents. In 1960 there were twenty-six. In the first month of the campaign, December 1956, there had been twenty-five and in 1957 a total of 341. If all efforts to get things moving again produced such scant results, it was no wonder that some volunteers began to have doubts. In Dublin, GHQ seemed to get nothing but bad news: resignations, aborted operations, arrests, missed meetings, and declining resources. On November 4, word arrived that Garland had been arrested in Belfast. On the night of November 10/11, O'Hagan and O'Connell were on their appointed rounds in County Tyrone near Lough Neagh trying to reorganize. At Killycolpy near Arboe they were walking along the road when they came to a laundry van pulled up on the verge. Suddenly a group of men without uniforms leaped out. Almost simultaneously with the shout to halt they opened fire. O'Connell about four yards away received the full burst. He was hit six times, in each hand, in the shoulder, chest, stomach and groin. Yet somehow he stumbled on down the side of the road away from the ambush. With O'Hagan's help he managed to reach a farmhouse three miles away. There he collapsed. The RUC arrived almost immediately. O'Connell recovered to stand trial in March and received a sentence of eight years. The loss of O'Hagan was particularly damaging, for he had become one of the key links in the northern net.

The writing on the wall should have been visible by now to GHQ in Dublin. The Curragh-group and the escapee-group were going and with them some very good men. Replacements were hard to find for men like McManus, O'Hagan, O'Connell, and Gleeson. Momentum had been lost. The RUC was everywhere. The quality of northern units had fallen. In Tyrone, Kelly had given it up and decided to emigrate to New York, leaving what there was to Christle. Popular support in the North and along the border had been declining since 1958–1959. In fact every index of guerrilla success gave a negative reading. No one, however, seriously thought of abandoning the campaign. First, once a campaign of attrition has begun, there are bound to be periods of great frustration and failure, when support disappears and the faithful are reduced to the very few. It was vital to keep going, forcing the Stormont government to pay exorbitant sums for security, preventing an irrevocable return to normal conditions, and keeping alive the hope of a shift in the tide. Second, if because of temporary difficulties, the momentary failure of nerve, or too easy rationalizations, the campaign were called off, then all chance to unite Ireland might well be lost. If, admittedly a large if, proper weapons could be found, GHQ felt certain the situation would change drastically for the better. Cronin and the Army Council felt that they should persevere. A normal Army Convention was called for June to examine the campaign season of 1960–1961.

At the Convention in June 1960, renewed determination was expressed. The younger active service men refused to despair, despite the evidence.

The IRA had grown used to the obstacles which should have prohibited even a marginal sabotage campaign: the lack of sanctuary, limited popular support, lack of space for manœuvre, severely limited foreign aid, and a desperate inferiority to British security forces in numbers and equipment. In fact the government at Stormont had been able to maintain the normal flow of civilian life, ignore all but the most violent incidents, and relegate the "emergency" to a secondary position in the state's list of priorities. However, Cronin felt now that control had been re-established at the top, now that the infrastructure had been reactivated, now that the Army had more sophisticated weapons, the breakthrough could at last be made—if not this season then the next. He did not have the chance to direct even the coming guerrilla season, however, for on the way home from the Convention he was spotted at a traffic light by a Special Branch man with a photographic memory. One glance was enough—Cronin was arrested and out of the picture. For the next six months he was confined in Mountjoy for failing to account for his movements. Brady took over as C/S and the autumn operations began at a higher level than the previous year but without much more effect.

Then in November a letter arrived from one of the splintered off-shoots of Clan na Gael—the Irish Freedom Committee. It accused Cronin of a variety of offences—even implying he was a Free State Agent, not to mention a Communist. Neither Brady nor Goulding was prepared for this kind of smear nor saw the point of the Freedom Committee's wild charges. The Army Council met and agreed to a Court of Inquiry. The Committee would have to produce hard evidence. In December, Cronin was released and found himself the centre of an unexpected crisis. He was inclined to feel that the Committee should have been asked to substantiate the charges before the Army called a Court of Inquiry. In any case the step had been taken and the Court asked the Committee for sworn statements and other written evidence. There was no answer for two months. In early March the Court finally received a letter stating that to protect their sources no evidence would be forthcoming. The matter, however, did not end there. Cronin felt that the campaign was largely dependent on funds and equipment from America. The IRA needed the money, even if it were not very much, and the equipment, even if it rarely appeared. No matter how wild the charges and how vicious the unsubstantiated smear, the fact remained that good relations with America were essential. It hardly seemed likely that with Cronin in a position of leadership the Committee would continue to show enthusiasm for the campaign. Cronin insisted he was a liability. The Army Council did not, co-opted him to membership, and insisted on his remaining. He attended one meeting to explain that his presence would cripple the campaign and resigned.[13] He stopped running, surfaced, and took a job on the *Irish Independent*. Brady carried on as C/S and the campaign ground on into its fifth year.

On January 27, 1961, the campaign made the front pages once again when an IRA attack-team assassinated a RUC man near Roslea in County Fermanagh. The Republican Publicity release accused Constable Anderson of spying on the IRA inside the Twenty-six Counties. The local IRA units had reported to GHQ that the border was filled with police spies and had specifically singled out Anderson. The Army Council and GHQ had been deeply concerned that RUC intelligence might permit a major ambush of an IRA group along the border. Such a loss in a period of declining morale would put paid to any hopes of continuing operations. Consequently the Army Council gave its consent to the elimination of Anderson. The repercussions were immense, for there was general horror at what seemed a cold-blooded murder of a defenceless policeman. In both Belfast and Dublin, spokesmen for law and order condemned the act in the strongest terms. Rumour had it that Anderson only crossed the border to see a girl and the IRA killing was thus neither "military" nor "political" but criminal, sectarian vengeance. To a large extent the smear stuck, despite Republican efforts to point out the strange lack of sympathy when Crossan was shot inside the Twenty-six Counties or O'Connell wounded six times in a RUC ambush. Public outcry or not, the Army Council felt it had taken the only decision possible to maintain pressure on the border.

In March and April, things finally began to heat up as the northern units began to strike more effectively. Bridges were cratered, roads cut, transport destroyed, and customs posts levelled. On March 28, Glassdrumond bridge in South Derry was destroyed and a RUC patrol ambushed. On April 5, two bridges in West Fermanagh were hit. As the number of incidents mounted during April, the British Army mounted an extensive comb-out of South Fermanagh on April 17–18–19. On the last day of the British sweep, a bridge was cratered in West Fermanagh. On April 26, the Dublin–Belfast railway line was cut in County Armagh. As May came, the flurry of incidents ended. Although encouraging, the final spurt had still not reached a level much beyond nuisance value.

During the summer of 1961, the Army Council and GHQ searched for a new approach to regain lost ground. Hopes to cut off an exposed enclave from the rest of the Six Counties by blowing bridges in South Fermanagh had to be given up because of the intensive patrols south of the border. Big ambushes outside the border areas were almost impossible. Sweeps and searches made any movement very difficult. After five years local support in many areas had disappeared. The penny-packet battle teams had been driven back to the line of the border. Deeper inside Northern

Ireland, the active service people had almost no operational freedom and many of the local volunteers had shown an increasing distaste for major risks. As a result GHQ discussed single-man terrorist operations or a machine-gun attack on British soldiers in a dance hall or any kind of violent action to enliven the campaign. When the 1961–1962 season began none of the new tactics proved feasible.

As the days lengthened the number of incidents, mostly minor, climbed. Spike barriers on cross-border roads were blasted in Gortoral and a bridge blown, so as to cut if off from the rest of Fermanagh—thus re-uniting "thirty families with their natural hinterland and trading area". The momentary snipping off a bit of Fermanagh did not alter the military situation. The IRA simply could not gain sufficient momentum. The hard core of thirty or forty guerrillas remained but they were too few and still badly armed. Stormont could continue to release internees and men who had completed their sentences. The campaign had sunk to the level of vandalism. All the ambushes, big and small, failed to net a RUC patrol. Even the terrorist forays in the North could not find targets.

Then on October 4, the Twenty-six County elections revealed the extent of decay in Republican fortunes. The Sinn Féin first-preference vote for twenty-one candidates was only 36,393 out of a total poll of 688,691—three per cent. Fourteen candidates lost their deposit and only J. J. Rice in Kerry South polled over nine per cent of the votes in a constituency. It was such an obvious disaster that a special statement urging that the reverse be assessed in the proper perspective was issued on October 18 by Sinn Féin. The Army Council met soon after the election to assess the military situation. The all too public denial of support at the polls had badly damaged morale. There had been no spectacular operation in the North. Public and private pressure to call off the campaign was growing. The Army Council agreed that a big effort must be made to rectify the situation but that they might have to quit. They agreed that if the campaign was to be ended, a course no one liked to consider, then the IRA would announce the fact openly and not just pack it in quietly. In the meantime they would try to keep up the pressure and hope that some of the units could pull off one of the operations they had in the bag.

Finally, on November 12, 1961, at Flurry Bridge near Jonesboro, Co. Armagh, the long-sought-for ambush came off. A RUC patrol had set up a block to check out the Northern Republicans who were travelling south to attend commemoration services for the five men killed at Eden-tubber in 1958. The IRA attack team moved in on the block and got in several bursts of fire before the RUC could get out of range. Constable Hunter was mortally wounded and three others hit. The five-man IRA battle-team got away clean. Intense searches in the area revealed nothing.

The immediate reaction in Belfast and Dublin was that the death was the most useless of all since the "campaign" had obviously failed. Once more the press and politicians in the North demanded action, particularly action by the Taoiseach Seán Lemass. On his part Lemass had already condemned the Jonesboro ambush—"Some sinister influence which directs these outbreaks of violence and their timing, so as to do maximum damage to the nation's interest" seemed to him to be behind the affair.[14] The Unionist Cabinet was not interested in unnamed "sinister influences" only action. An appeal went to London and once more a British Ambassador in Dublin approached the Irish government. To crush the campaign once and for all, on November 23 the Irish government reintroduced the Military Tribunals, so effective in the 1940s. The Military Tribunals had been in limbo for twenty years, but the Cabinet simply announced that the Tribunals were again functioning—in some cases with the same if somewhat aged personnel. Three days later in South Armagh a jeep moving out from the RUC Whitecross Barracks hit an IRA mine. The jeep was blown off the road and three RUC men were injured. On November 28, at Stormont the Minister of Home Affairs Brian Faulkner threatened to impose the death penalty. In the South the Tribunals began to sentence Republicans. Where in 1959 Michael McEldowney had received a six months' sentence after a failed ambush near the border, in 1961 he was sentenced to eight years. By the end of December, twenty-five men had been sentenced.

Coercion alone would hardly have intimidated the Republicans nor would the expressions of horror by the press, the condemnation of politicians nor even the sermons of the priests. The Army Council had more important matters to consider—the campaign could continue with men in jail, hardly a novel situation, and with a bad press, a constant condition; but wars, even little marginal wars, cost money, the outward symbol of popular support. By the end of December, the money was about gone. The collections before Christmas for the prisoners had been dismal. In December word came there would be no more money from America. In the South, the Tribunals were turning out sentences, the government was harassing former prisoners, making re-employment difficult or impossible, the police were accelerating pressure on Republicans and Sinn Féin people. This could be endured. In the North the Nationalists were tired of the campaign and the IRA. Many good people had grown hostile and bitter. From enthusiasm they had passed through toleration and by 1961 would respond only to force. The green sea of support had largely dried up, leaving the few IRA fish gasping near the border.

On January 18, the Army Council met and agreed to consider ending the campaign. The seven members along with two of the GHQ staff strongly indicated informally that the time had come to quit. On February 3, the Army Council met again and formally and unanimously voted to end the campaign. The Army Executive concurred. A Special Army Order on February 5 directed all IRA units to dump arms and move back. At 19.40, February 26, the campaign was formally ended with a public statement largely drafted by Brady.

To the Irish People
   The leadership of the Resistance Movement has ordered the termination of the Campaign of Resistance to British Occupation launched on December 12, 1956. Instructions issued to Volunteers of the Active Service Units and of local Units in the occupied area have now been carried out. All arms and other material have been dumped and all full-time active service Volunteers have been withdrawn.
   The decision to end the Resistance Campaign has been taken in view of the general situation. Foremost among the factors motivating this course of action has been the attitude of the general public whose minds have been deliberately distracted from the supreme issue facing the Irish people—the unity and freedom of Ireland.

.   .   .

   The Irish Resistance Movement renews its pledge of eternal hostility to the British Forces of Occupation in Ireland. It calls on the Irish people for increased support and looks forward with confidence—in co-operation for the final and victorious phase of the struggle for the full freedom of Ireland.[15]

That was the end of sixteen years of work, planning, sacrifice, death, and hope. Eight IRA volunteers had been killed, two Republican civilians, and two Saor Uladh men. Six RUC had been killed and thirty-two of the British security forces injured. Hundreds of men had spent up to four years interned in prison without trial. Over two hundred others had been convicted and sentenced for their part in the campaign. In 1962 there were still Republicans in Mountjoy and in Crumlin Road; and in England Doyle and Murphy were still serving life sentences. In the South "there was no question" of releasing the prisoners and in the North "under no circumstances will there be an amnesty . . .". The campaign had cost the Northern Ireland government a small fortune—£700,000 in outright damages and approximately £500,000 a year since 1956 to maintain security forces. In the South the extra police and military expenses cost £350,000 a year. In blood, time, and gold, the campaign had exacted a considerable price; but for the IRA, dedicated to a united Ireland achieved by force, the failure had destroyed the hopes of a generation—the gun would go on the shelf, the volunteers back to the rounds of private life, and Ireland would remain divided and unfree.

NOTES

1. No IRA prisoners have ever had any great difficulty in establishing some sort of line out of prison. McLogan's dispatches, for example, came out typed on toilet paper and were addressed not only to GHQ but to Sinn Féin people who did not always reveal the contents to the IRA.

2. For the Republican view of the Talbot and Mallon case see Irish Republican Publicity Bureau, *British Torture in Ireland*, December 1957 (broadsheet).

3. Drawings of various stages of dismantling of the dugout are in Wallace Clark's *Guns in Ulster*, Belfast, 1967.

4. The Irish Republican Publicity Bureau issued a denial that the men were preparing for Armistice Day operations; however, mines are seldom prepared well in advance of an operation, rather the opposite is desirable.

5. The IRA felt they had ample evidence, circumstantial and actual, that there was extensive RUC–Special Branch co-operation—among other things photographs of Cronin and Murphy taken by the Irish police in Mountjoy appeared on wanted posters in Northern Ireland.

6. Saor Uladh in Dublin was run out of the offices of Angle Engineering Ltd. in Abbey Street but with declining interest in military affairs. Several members became converted to a variety of Trotskyism and later emigrated to London, where they are involved in publishing the *Irish Militant*. In Dublin they had become involved in the Unemployed Protest Movement and the curious career of John Murphy who was elected to the Dáil in March 1957 as the Unemployed Candidate and resigned in 1961.

7. On July 17, 1958, Nicolas Ioannou was killed in a road accident in England and papers relating to the Irish connection disappeared from the body, presumably into the hands of the British police.

8. United Irishman, *The Murder of James Crossan*, Dublin, n.d.

9. Murphy had got word from Seán MacBride that the International Court at Strasbourg probably would not find against the Irish government on the question of internment. It was also clear that a successful ambush in the North would keep the Curragh open and that waiting on the good offices of the Fianna Fáil government was something of a risk.

10. Registry of the Court, Council of Europe, *"Lawless" Case* (Publications of the European Court of Human Rights, Strasbourg, 1961).

11. McLogan had been released from the Curragh before the worst of the

quarrel and then in April had left for a visit to the United States missing still more of the squabble. Thus while he supported Magan and
MacCurtain he was less deeply committed to their position than he
might have been. He was elected to the Army Executive but resigned
in October 1959 without having attended any meetings.

12. MacCurtain returned to Cork and soon resigned from the Army
because the local C/O no longer had any use for his services. Magan
and McLogan remained active in Sinn Féin but relatively isolated from
the decisions of the Army Council.

13. Cronin withdrew his resignations when the Military Tribunals were
instituted in case his action might be misconstrued. He was tried and
sentenced by the Court and was in Mountjoy when the campaign
ended. He again resigned from the IRA on Good Friday 1962.

14. See *Irish Times, Irish Press, Irish Independent, et al.*, November 13,
14, 15 for general reaction—all bad.

15. *United Irishman*, March 1962.

CHAPTER XVII

The Gun on the Shelf: The IRA in the Doldrums, March 1962–July 1969

On the surface the Republican Movement shifted gear from one phase to the next with a minimum of anxiety. Immediately a traditional Republican battle cry was raised: Free the Prisoners. Committees were formed. Monster meetings were organized in England and Ireland. Fraternal organizations in the United States paraded and petitioned. In Dublin the government announced the release of the men held in Mountjoy. The Movement turned their attention to the North. Local government authorities were urged to vote in support of appropriate resolutions. Nationalist MPs in Northern Ireland urged compassion now that the violence had passed. Prisoners released on completion of their sentences were given enthusiastic receptions, in the course of which speakers took the opportunity to remind their audiences of the men left behind in Crumlin Road or England. The issue united all Republicans and secured considerable popular support. County Councils called for the release of prisoners. Cautious politicians said the proper things. County newspapers lent their support. As far as anyone could see the 1956–1962 campaign was dead and being buried. Nevertheless, according to Tomás MacGiolla at Bodenstown on June 17, 1962, it had not been a failure nor the decision to quit a mistake.

There should be no disappointment or defeatism about this decision. This was not a step backward but a step forward. It is an opportunity to conserve our resources, consolidate our position, and gird ourselves to move forward with enthusiasm and optimism to the next phase in the struggle for freedom.[1]

Once the prisoners had been released, Republicans might expect new ideas and new directions.

But beneath the smooth patina applied by MacGiolla, the Republican movement seethed with bitter faction and the advanced rot of despair. In February many of the active service people had been appalled at the order to dump arms. Others in the Movement immediately suspected that they would be made the scapegoats for the failure. By 1962 many others had long since faded away in despair, in disgrace, or in dudgeon. The Army was a husk—its strength eroded, its purpose lost, its future unclear. Sinn Féin lay shattered on the far shore of Irish politics, without power or prospects, still a captive of the principle of abstentionism. In America the remnants of the Clan had withdrawn into silence. In Dublin the *United Irishman* faced rising debts and declining circulation. All the Republican organizations had shrivelled except the National Graves Association, which when all else failed could still put on a good commemoration. Defeat and despondency were hardly new to Republicans, nor was schism; but in the spring of 1962, the greatest danger to the Movement was not despair but disintegration. After three dormant years, in deference to the demands of the campaign, the Curragh-group was still hellbent on the justification denied at the 1959 Army Convention. No matter how wizened the Movement, there were still those who cherished its blessing.

During the years after 1959, the bitter division between the IRA leadership and the Curragh-group in Sinn Féin had largely been ignored. After his visit to America in April 1959, McLogan had remained as President of Sinn Féin. Magan had remained on the Ard Comhairle, as had his advocates, Micky Traynor and Seán O'Mahoney. During the last years of the campaign, Sinn Féin gave all support possible to the IRA, despite the cankering grievances of the Curragh-group, isolated from control and ignored in counsel. After the electoral disaster of October 1961, McLogan and Magan feared, with some justification, that the IRA would contend that Sinn Féin had let the campaign down and forced the Army Council to give up because popular support had been squandered through the inefficiency of the Ard Comhairle. Unsympathetic to the IRA leadership, who were either new men they did not know or trust or the old leaders who had failed them in 1959, McLogan and Magan decided to act rather than tolerate further abuse. There was serious discussion of mass resignations. Although several members of the Ard Comhairle were sympathetic to the idea, others feared an irrevocable split would destroy the Republican Movement. Tom Doyle, for example, though he died on March 12 before the final confrontation came, felt that he could not resign as long as he was responsible for the dependants of the prisoners and the slain. Others like Robert and Mae Russell felt that the Movement could not honourably malign men like Magan and McLogan. Eventually the Curragh-group decided that Sinn Féin had to be captured from the IRA by an internal but legal coup. The 1949 take-over would be turned inside out and the IRA link broken.

A general statement was issued criticizing the conduct and end of the campaign. Even without specific charges, the conflict was now in the open within the Movement. In April, after forty-nine years of service, McLogan resigned from the IRA and Magan only retained a nominal attachment to the Dublin unit. The key move was a petition circulated to the Ard Comhairle calling for an Extraordinary Ard Fheis. In the final analysis, despite considerable lobbying and parliamentary manoeuvring, the Curragh-group acked sufficient votes on the Ard Comhairle to arrange matters to their satisfaction. Rumours of some sort of split had begun to appear in the Irish and British press when the July *United Irishman* briefly noted that McLogan, Traynor, Magan, and O'Mahoney had resigned from the Ard Comhairle. The split was long past healing and the Curragh-group drifted out of the Movement by the end of the year. Defying IRA policy, Magan seconded a pro-Curragh-group resolution at the 1962 Sinn Féin Ard Fheis and was expelled from the IRA. After three years, McLogan and Magan were forced to join MacCurtain on the sidelines, all links with the Movement broken and a lifetime of Republican service ended. They took with them some very good people, men who were unable to make their peace with the new leadership and unwilling to move forward "to the next phase in the struggle for freedom" with the men who had botched the past.

In September 1962, the Army Convention met to consider the problems arising from the split and the possibilities for the future. The Sinn Féin split was water over the dam and the attitudes and actions of the Curragh-group roused little sympathy even among those few of their old friends still present. As for the campaign, the unrepentant activists were by and large reconciled to the February orders and the prospect of peace. The Army Council's explanation of the factors that had forced the termination of the struggle was accepted without serious question. Only Packy Ryan of Limerick noted that the open guerrilla season on the British still had a couple of months to run; but everyone agreed that once the decision had been made, there was no point in delay. Once more the IRA was re-organized. Exhausted by two years on the run as C/S, Brady wanted to teach in Roscommon, too far from the centre of the circle to be effective. The only man left with sufficient experience and dedication was Cathal Goulding. Most reluctantly, he accepted the leadership of the shattered remains of the Army. There were still eager young men at the Convention, but it was all too clear that for many the IRA held no further charms. During the years in prison or on the run, they had discovered alternatives, political or personal, forsaken violence if not their beliefs, and withdrawn into private life or the blurred periphery of Republican activities. In September there were many familiar faces missing. It was not a happy Convention.

Some of the older generation stayed, particularly in Sinn Féin, because they were unable to face the prospect of private life after their Republican investment—years in prison, careers aborted, families denied. With rare exceptions these were not men of ideas but of persistence, whose vision focused only on the single issue of national unity. Their limitations were often magnified within Sinn Féin, the depository of retired revolutionaries clinging to the idols of their youth. The new ideas oozing out from the Dublin centre were rarely of interest unless there was prospect of physical force.[2] This dead weight of tradition, unimportant during a military campaign, made it difficult for the young men to chart an alternative course once the military option had aborted. Out in the country or in the North, the Movement seemed content with the rounds of commemorations and the threadbare speeches extolling patience, faith, and the Republican heritage. The old concept that they who endure the most will win the most rang hollow on young ears. The leadership of the IRA, forced to forego the gun, began to march to a different drum.

Even before the 1962 Convention many in the Movement had begun, some for the first time, to define the mystical Republic in everyday terms, to analyse the possible strategy and tactics for a real, multifaceted revolutionary movement, more akin to the ideas of Connolly than the poetry of Pearse. Even in the isolated orthodoxy of Crumlin Road Prison, walled in from the currents of exterior thought, the change came spontaneously. The secret prison paper *Saoirse* (Freedom)[3] published an article by Eamon Timoney, "Quo Vadis Hibernia", urging the Republican Movement to be concerned with day-to-day local government, with co-operatives, with economic and social issues. By the autumn of 1962, this was the new direction that attracted the Army and, perhaps to a lesser degree, Sinn Féin. There was after all a tradition of the Left, Connolly–Mellows–O'Donnell–Ryan–Gilmore, and more telling a desire to serve Ireland, to act rather than sit out the bleak years ahead turning the knife in old wounds.

Such a shift in emphasis and directions was not easy to achieve without sparking a rush to the Right by the traditionalists welded to the old ways and the old slogans. In Ireland, populated largely by men of no property, the poor have been remarkably reluctant to accept either the ideas of social revolution or the other doctrines of the Left. Many of the ambitious emigrate with their dreams, leaving the very young and the very old, neither of them fertile ground for change. The Irish river of ideas still flowed sluggishly past the crumbling ruins of orthodox institutions. In the early 'sixties even the Labour Party, deeply rutted to the right of centre, hid its socialist light under a bushel of piety and practicality. The Catholic hierarchy was ever alert to the long-standing communist threat —and the bishops were not the only watchdogs. MacBride's Clan na Poblachta had been attacked by outraged pious men, not all of them wealthy and well-placed, who feared revolution at best, heresy at worst. In Ireland there was no "government ownership of the means of production" but only euphorically entitled semi-state bodies dominating, nevertheless, much of the economy. In theory and in public, if not always in practice, Ireland remained Catholic and conservative, immune to the flash and glitter of European ideas and movements, a rural parish on the fringe of a throbbing, industrial continent. Self-proclaimed revolutionaries in any field walked a lonely road—as the Republicans were to find.

By 1963 the rigid conservatism had begun to soften. Within the Church, particularly after the pontificate of John, fresh ideas and new men could be found. There were young men in the Labour Party who did not flinch from "socialism". There were economic technicians in the government who were no longer bound by classical rules that had long been discarded elsewhere. In politics, if there was no great stampede to the Left, at least there was a growing flexibility, a freedom of option almost totally lacking a decade before. The old men, bedecked in medals of past wars, seemed increasingly out of place. The old evils cloaked in complacency masquerading as spiritual virtue seemed increasingly intolerable. The Republican Movement, like most Irish institutions, contained a solid ballast of the orthodox and a leavening of reactionaries. Their ways were set and their minds closed. Yet they could not be lightly discarded; for many had been the best men of their day, giving their years and their prospects for Republican ideals. In a Movement without pension or promotion, gratitude is vital. No matter what the Army Council or the Sinn Féin Ard Comhairle thought, new policies would meet stubborn, often conscious opposition, from men who still listened to a different drum, who did not feel the wind of change on their face, who wanted to husband the past not mould the future.

The IRA was particularly vulnerable, for its stated purpose was to unite the nation by military means. In point of fact, the IRA was incapable in the foreseeable future of performing a military function but, as always, was responsible for Republican policy. Without the IRA the Movement would be a fraternal society, a clan of the alienated, not a force for change. Without the IRA the Movement would wither and die. Thus the IRA was maintained; organizers travelled the hinterland, training camps were held, equipment was polished—and there was no action. With not even the distant prospect of action, the IRA was building with sand. Recruits drifted through a revolving door of idealism, boredom, and departure. Units dissolved or squabbled. Pressed for money, for time, for men, Dublin GHQ had to move ever faster on the treadmill even to shore up the Army much less to enlarge it. For many of the volunteers the new official interest in co-operatives and strikes and housing held little delight. They had joined an Army to fight not to agitate.

In Cork on March 17, 1963, two young men, both with service in the North, decided to prevent President de Valera from dedicating a monument to Republicans they felt he had later betrayed. In the attempt to destroy the monument, Desmond Swanton was killed and Gerard Madden badly maimed by a premature explosion. They were representative of the young IRA men who were not averse to political and social ideas, but wanted above all else a chance to fight, an opportunity for a go at the real enemy, the British. If that could not be, at least a symbolic operation could be partial compensation for idleness. In time a tiny schismatic group in Cork would publish a secret paper *An Phoblacht* violently critical of the IRA for refusing to take action in the North, for continuing the hands-off policy in the South, for concentration on lesser issues than the border.[4] There is little doubt that within the IRA many privately echoed these views while reluctantly accepting the practicality of the official policy.

The tension that this restraint caused in the local units was revealed following the first IRA action authorized in the Twenty-six Counties since the proclamation of Army Order No. 8. As a matter of policy, the Republican Movement opposed visits to Ireland, North or South, by the Royal Family, by the Royal Navy, by the Royal anything. There had often been protests or warning explosions or threats. In August 1964, protests prevented seventy British Army cadets and instructors from vacationing in uniform in County Mayo. Shortly thereafter an even more provocative visit to Ireland was announced. Princess Margaret and Lord Snowdon intended to visit near Abbeyleix in County Laois. A protest which included dropping trees with a chain saw escalated into wild demonstrations in January 1965 when the men involved were charged at Mountmellick. Many of those involved had no IRA connection but the temper of the local units was raised. Some of the IRA people in County Kilkenny were eager for the next step. At the end of the summer, their opportunity came when the Army Council decided to order an operation against the British Navy. A British torpedo boat, "Brave Borderer", was to visit Waterford and the Mayor would provide an official reception for the members of the crew. The IRA men fired on the boat before being rounded up by the police. On September 10, 1965, three men, Richard Behal, Edward Kelly, and Walter Dunphy of Kilkenny, were arrested for obstructing, resisting, and assaulting the police and for possession of an anti-tank rifle and a pistol. At their trial on November 23 in Waterford, Behal claimed that the attack on the torpedo boat was being reduced to a minor charge because of cowardice on the part of the state to face the issue. Be that as it might, Behal and Dunphy were sentenced to nine months and Kelly to six. A variety of protests, less violent than those at Mountmellick followed; again non-IRA people were involved. And there the matter rested for both the police and the IRA GHQ.

Behal was not a man for the easy life nor were his friends. On Februar o, word came that he had escaped from Limerick Prison. While the prison governor and his family celebrated the twenty-first birthday of his daughter, a non-IRA escape team broke into the prison from the outside. They went over the wall carrying their equipment with them. At Behal's cell they sawed through the bars from the outside. They all went out the way they had come leaving the impression Behal had made a one-man break. A very considerable manhunt produced nothing. Authorized or not, the Kilkenny people were delighted with the escape. GHQ, however, could find no use for Behal even during the approaching Easter celebrations. On their own hook some of the Kilkenny people arranged for Behal to appear unexpectedly at a dance hall and give a twenty-minute oration—to the gratification of the customers who were treated to the sight of Ireland's most wanted political criminal. Once independent action had been taken there was a feeling in the country that more protests should be made, whatever GHQ did or did not do. At the time Cathal Goulding and Seán Garland had been arrested on February 6 for possession of a revolver and ammunition. Goulding's case had been adjourned several times, the postponements amounting to imprisonment without trial—although, of course, perfectly legal. This time the unauthorized protest was made at Kilmacow in South Kilkenny. An automatic telephone exchange was blown up and shots fired down the main street. This display was a direct violation of long standing Army Orders and GHQ felt it compromised the Army in the entire area.

The Republican Publicity Bureau denied complicity—"the Republican Movement is directed solely against British Rule in Ireland and the Movement is prepared only to engage in actions against British Forces in Ireland". Behal had got out of hand. Some felt that he should be dealt with very severely indeed, but the IRA court simply dismissed him from the Army. Behal had gone further down the road seeking action than most other volunteers.[5] In this he had the support of his Republican friends who chafed at the restraints of GHQ policy. But the IRA was not interested in displays to appease the activists. The torpedo boat had been British and was a suitable target to underscore IRA views on Royal visits. Kilmacow, on the other hand, gained nothing, disturbed much, and encouraged indiscipline. Other splinter groups, and there were one or two loose organizations, were less restrained. The most publicized operation occurred on March 7 at 1.32 a.m. when a violent explosion toppled much of Nelson's Pillar into O'Connell Street. After years of frustrated attempts, legal and illicit, to remove Nelson, symbol of British Rule, the end had come in time for the fiftieth anniversary of the Easter Rising. Many were delighted for either political or aesthetic reasons. Others were appalled at violence in O'Connell Street. Yet the destruction of the Pillar was not a revelation of a new militancy but of a corroding frustration. British rule in the North had never seemed less vulnerable. The "extremists" were forced to turn on monuments. The IRA saw the explosion as sterile. "As a corollary to this attitude the Republican Movement has not concerned itself in the slightest way with the destruction of monuments of foreign origin, nor has the Movement aided implicitly or explicitly such demolitions."[6]

The Republican Movement might not be officially interested in the destruction of monuments but privately, in the quiet of the night, many volunteers surely wished that GHQ was interested in some form of operation. As time passed after the decision in 1962 to become involved in all phases of contemporary Ireland, there was little evidence that the typical member of Sinn Féin or the IRA had been converted to the new direction. The young men dedicated to force fretted and resigned. The old men shrugged off the detailed economic and social programmes, the manifestoes out of Dublin, the pamphlets and the programmes, and kept to their appointed rounds of commemorations, public collections, and set speeches. These solid men, the backbone of the Movement in most of the country, did not necessarily disapprove of the co-operative movement or the call for more housing; but they found the new activities largely irrelevant to their Movement, to their past, and to their vision of the future. What was worse, these new "political" involvements first threatened, then struck at the moral basis of Republicanism.

Just as the volunteer wanted action so did the new young members of Sinn Féin. To secure their ends they needed power—and political power rested in the Dáil at Leinster House. To the orthodox this was rank heresy. For them abstentionism was a principle, the Dublin government a corrupt puppet no better than Stormont or Westminster. To sell principle for power as de Valera had done in 1927 and MacBride in 1948 would bring the Republic no nearer, would only split the faithful. The insistence that a *de jure* Republic did or would exist, a Republic to which Irishmen owed allegiance, had for generations been the justification for the IRA's use of force, for the sacrifice of idealists unwilling to compromise, for the best years of many futile lives. To go into the Dáil, to seize power, was not only an invitation to corruption, a tainted tactic already proven sterile, but also and most important outrageous immorality. The orthodox dug in their heels. Many would not be soothed by reassurances that political involvement did not necessarily mean the end of abstentionism, and their alarm increased when the prospect began to be discussed in the Ard Fheis.[7]

As late as January 1966, the President of Sinn Féin, Tomás MacGiolla, admitted that it was not until 1965—over two years after the new direction was introduced—that the Sinn Féin organization began to take an interest in the everyday problems of the people. Dublin GHQ or the Ard Comhairle might introduce new concepts or argue new issues but they could not, yet, impose their new ideas on the suspicious. Many had already accepted the fact that the task was beyond the leadership. The campaign generation had emerged from the military phase in February 1962 disillusioned about the Movement and its prospects. The attrition rate after 1959 had been great: few had changed their ideals, but few retained any hope that they could be implemented. Many Republicans simply felt that the rotten wood of the Movement could not be carved into new shapes, that the orthodox form guarded by the hoary ranks of bitter old men was immutable. Most simply foreswore any activity. A few went into the Labour Party. Others emigrated. A few stayed on.

While some of the faithful were dedicated Army men, willing to serve out the barren years for the benefit of a new generation, others turned to the problems of Ireland. Denis Foley came home from Crumlin Road to edit a *United Irishman* increasingly concerned with the economic and social shortcomings of the country. The space given to old heroes and past injuries declined, the analytical articles became more contemporary, the layout and typography brighter. For the first time in nearly twenty years, the names of the old Republican Left, Peadar O'Donnell and George Gilmore, began to appear in the columns. In October 1964, the Wolfe Tone Society was founded. Its purpose was to judge the present so as to act on the future instead of responding to the past. Seminars began to meet under various auspices. O'Donnell and Gilmore began to speak to a new generation. In a country with no really radical party the new brand of Republicanism began to attract those who would have had little time for the old orthodoxies. Dr. Roy Johnston, who had been involved with the Irish Marxists in Britain, the Connolly Association, shifted allegiances and came into Sinn Féin. A young lecturer at Trinity College, Anthony Coughlan, deeply involved in social issues, joined the Wolfe Tone Society, as did others who felt the solutions to Ireland's problems needed a more radical approach than the conventional half-measures. At Trinity College, long considered a citadel of the Protestant Ascendancy, a Republican Club was founded, prospered, and became the largest club in the University. Gilmore, O'Donnell and Máirtín Ó Cadhain, Dean of the University of the Curragh in the 1940s, spoke on the challenges of the future. Republican Clubs followed in Queen's in Belfast and even University College, Dublin. Labour Party radicals talked seriously of a Republican alliance; and Republicans worked seriously, if independently, for Labour's new young men when they ran for the Dáil. Young men became involved in the exciting new co-operative experiment of Father James McDyer of Glencolumbkille. Some of the disheartened young Republicans drifted back into a Movement that was no longer so preoccupied with past errors.

Within a few years, in Dublin at least, the Movement seethed with new ideas, new approaches, and new directions.

Yet all of this ferment in Dublin had not converted the Movement as a whole. Many of the pious deeply distrusted the "atheistic Left". Many did not know nor understand the new men who had not always been visible during the campaign. Many feared the end of abstentionism or the radical reconstruction of their comfortable attachments to the old ways. Many, particularly in the North, felt the unity of the country was the first priority and all the talk in Dublin was not going to budge the British an inch. This continuing intransigence alienated many of the impatient. Seán Caughey of Belfast, a vice-president of Sinn Féin, resigned in June 1965 because the Movement refused to give *de facto* recognition to both governments of Ireland. In Dublin Denis Foley, who had resigned as editor of the *United Irishman* in 1965 to be replaced by his colleague in the Armagh Irish Street bomb affair, Tony Meade, finally left the Movement entirely in 1967 to return to Kerry. Despite defections, which were not limited to the "liberals", the drift toward the new ideas continued, just fast enough or slow enough to prevent a serious split. In Dublin contacts with Labour matured. In Belfast relations with Gerry Fitt, who as good as owned and operated the new Republican-Labour party, were good if not intimate. His tactic of using his seats in Stormont and Westminster to harass the Unionist machine was analysed if not emulated. Under Meade's, and after 1967, Seamus O Tuathail's editorship, the *United Irishman* became a first rate monthly agitating against the appalling housing situation, investigating ownership of Dublin ground rents, exposing hypocrisy and attracting new reviewers and correspondence.[8]

Yet the Movement remained stalled, trapped between the orthodox and the radical. Worse, there were only rare successes for either persuasion. Despite Sinn Féin's carefully wrought electoral programme, the results of the local elections in 1967 were almost unmitigated disaster. The rare victories came despite the Sinn Féin label not because of it. The voters when they thought about Sinn Féin at all considered the Republicans hopeless cranks and even formerly loyal voters saw no need to waste their franchise when there was no campaign to support.[9] Funds were sadly lacking. The *United Irishman* long hovered on the lip of insolvency. Clan na Gael had splintered so often that little could be expected from America, where allegiances were shifting and the ties of the old country loosening. The new Clann na h-Éireann in Britain was hardly a replacement. Within the IRA the strain of maintaining an inactive Army was as onerous as ever. Despite a variety of organizational alternatives suggested by committees and individuals, GHQ continued to depend on organizers rushing out from Dublin to patch up uncontrolled leaks. Within five years the IRA eemed composed mainly of the impatient young and the exhausted old. The effort was a tremendous drain on Republican energies and produced very little visible return on the investment beyond creating a disgruntled and impatient Army of rapidly shifting personnel. Astute and not necessarily unsympathetic observers gave the Movement only a few more years before it decayed into a bitter band of old malcontents husbanding their humiliations at annual ceremonies. The leadership seemed capable of making thought and recognizing the alternatives, but too tired to grasp the nettle of change.

Outside the inner circles of the Movement, life went on in Ireland. Except for a few exciting moments, such as the torpedo boat affair or the loss of Nelson's pillar, few cared about the "Sinn Féiners" except the police. In the South, Special Branch continued regular surveillance of known IRA people, of Sinn Féin meetings, of the offices of the *United Irishman*, even of the Trinity Republican Club. The cynics contended that if the IRA had not existed Special Branch would have had to invent it to explain their salaries.[10] During the mid-sixties the traditional confrontation came at Easter time when the Republican Movement sold Easter lily badges in the annual fund-raising drive. Refusing to recognize the "state" no one requested a permit, leaving the police free if so ordered or inclined to harass and arrest the sellers, who refusing to pay fines to a puppet court went off to jail. The consequences were public scuffles, brief baton charges, hunger strikes, and public anxiety about infringement of civil liberties. In 1967 police pressure tapered off, but surveillance continued. Too often in the past the IRA had suddenly reanimated itself after a long dormant period.

In Northern Ireland the problem for the Unionist government was rather different and potentially far more serious. With the retirement of Prime Minister Lord Brookeborough and the advent in March 1963 of his successor, Captain Terence O'Neill, there had been almost for the first time a concerted effort to ease the mutual animosity of the Nationalist and Unionist population. A few Unionist politicians began, hesitatingly at first, to discard the more unpleasant sectarian slogans. Protestants of good will spoke of bridge-building and community responsibility. This mini-thaw in the frozen North was regarded with suspicion. Hard Orange men saw intimations of treason to Protestant–British–Ulster principles. Jaundiced Nationalists saw window-dressing to fool Westminster critics of the unsavoury Unionist machine. Then on January 14, 1965, Seán Lemass travelled to Stormont to meet O'Neill—an almost incredible political event for Ulster—and a month later O'Neill paid a visit to Dublin. The skies did not fall. While many Orangemen were uneasy, the more moderate hoped that the exchange was a wise move and might help to ease sectarian

strife in the North and blunt the pointless animosity of Dublin. No Unionist was prepared to give an inch on the constitutional issue, but bigotry
had become increasingly distasteful, marring the image of a progressive
Ulster and damaging almost irreparably community relations. The more
militant Orange extremists, however, sensed a sell-out. For them the issues
of the Reformation were alive and O'Neill's dealings with a Papist tanta-
mount to treason. The most vocal of the extremists was the Reverend Ian
Paisley, who castigated O'Neill in the language of a seventeenth-century
Anabaptist. Less vocal was a newly organized convert Ulster Volunteer
Force, prepared to defend Ulster Protestantism with the gun against the
inroads of liberalism. This small, violent group of young men, captives of
a narrow vision of the world, carried their protest to the point of shooting
two young men in Belfast only because they were Catholics. The Malvern
Street murders brought the ugly danger of riot and pogrom to Belfast. Only
the swift apprehension, trial, and conviction of those involved dampened
down emotions. The UVF faded temporarily away—what O'Neill faced
was the danger that any Republican activity in the North, however innocuous, would trigger a disproportionate reaction by the extremist Orange
element, setting off a cycle of retaliation and violence.[11]

While Unionists, mild and stern, felt that Ulster would always be
plagued by some form of extreme Republicanism—the doldrums today
and the gun tomorrow just as it was the gun yesterday and the doldrums
before that—the contemporary problem was to move Northern Ireland
gradually away from the sectarian bitterness of the past without igniting
Orange passions. Few divided nations have so institutionalized provocative
displays of symbols abhorrent to the opposition and cherished by the faithful. The anniversary of the Protestant King's, William of Orange, victory
at the Battle of the Boyne on July 12, 1694, over his Catholic father-in-law,
James Stuart, is the opportunity for parades of tens of thousands of bowler-
hatted, black-suited men, waving Orange banners, beating huge Lambeg
drums, and bearing in serried ranks their Union Jacks. This is a calculated
affront to the Nationalists; just as is, in turn, the Nationalists' flaunting of
the banned tricolour, the singing of "The Soldier's Song"—the National
Anthem—or the Commemorations for Casement or Tone. Walls a few
doors apart are covered with "No Pope Here" and "Up the Republic". As
Easter 1966 approached, the Northern Ireland government was sincerely
fearful that Nationalist demonstrations on the fiftieth anniversary of the
Rising would be more than some uneasy Orangemen would tolerate. Any
"symbolic" action by the IRA might set off the powder train to disaster.
Elaborate security measures were taken but the month of parades and
orations passed without serious incident.

As Easter 1967 approached, the Minister of Home Affairs decided to prevent a repeat of the uncertainty by banning any demonstrations on the one hundredth anniversary of the Fenian rising. To the Orangemen the name Fenian is an insult, a sectarian smear separate from any historical context, and for the Nationalists or Republicans to honour the original rebels would, as usual, be a blatant provocation. The government decided that a ban would save money and trouble. At the same time, the newly organized Republican Clubs were banned on the grounds that they were front organizations for Sinn Féin and illicit recruiters for the IRA. The Republicans retaliated by holding a public "banned" meeting, which was attended by civil liberties representatives, Gerry Fitt, and one or two interested non-Republican figures, and the press and television people. Although the RUC were out in force, they did nothing except arrest and then release a few prominent Republicans, among which were Tom Mitchell, the old Omagh Raid man who was the Sinn Féin representative. The matter was allowed to fizzle out thereafter, the government insisting that the Republic Club at Queen's University could continue to exist if the members simply changed its name. Stormont was less interested in rooting out Republicanism than in keeping the peace.

In the North, the harassment of Republicans was partly a tactic to placate the Orange extremist, thereby reducing the chance of sectarian violence, partly a reasonable police precaution to contain avowed rebels. In the South, surveillance was, and is, a normal, if at times overzealous, security measure against a potentially troublesome minority. Since the campaign ended, the Republican Movement, whatever the new direction, had given little evidence that a clear and present military danger to either Dublin or Stormont existed. On both sides of the border, life went on normally, without anyone taking much notice of the desires and aspirations of the Republicans. The new Fianna Fáil Taoiseach, Jack Lynch, had in his turn met with Captain O'Neill. North–South co-operation on all levels had continued. Various advocates of Irish unity from time to time urged a labour alliance, or economic ties, or cultural exchanges, as the means to the desired end—not coercion. Physical force as a means to break the connection with Britain had never seemed more irrelevant; Ireland in the 'sixties seemed more concerned with the fruits of the good life than the bootless ambitions of the romantic past. All the wild dreams were dead and gone, the roads were clogged with traffic and the pubs with whiskey drinkers.

Then in 1968 came the first signs that the Army's doldrum days were nearly over. Gradually the radical Republican programmes had attracted more young idealists and more sympathetic publicity. The campaigns against ground rents in Dun Laoghaire, office buildings instead of workers' houses in Dublin and privately owned fishing rights in Irish waters began here and there to develop a momentum of their own. At the centre the decision was made to undertake direct military action in support of appropriate social causes. Operations were to be carried out that used the Army as an instrument of social justice. Buses carrying what many workers considered to be strike-breakers to an American-owned factory became legitimate targets—and were burned. At the beginning of August 1968 the IRA took part in a fishing dispute and destroyed the lobster boat *Mary Catherine*.

> The action was undertaken to protect the Irish shell-fishing industry against exploitation by foreign interests, to protect these natural resources, and to preserve them for our own native fishermen.[12]

Action of this kind was a long way from guerrilla warfare intended to end partition by physical force. Within the Army the operations were immensely popular, if for no other reason than they gave the volunteers some hope of action. While IRA intervention in social issues did not and would not always please all of those for whose benefit action was taken, some sympathy was generated in the country and considerably more among young radicals in Dublin who now saw the IRA as a Citizen Army protecting the workers' interests. Still, despite the enthusiasm within Republican circles, the new policy or policies had really made little impact on Ireland in general or the British-Unionist hold on the North.

The Fianna Fáil government went right on pushing for a constitutional amendment to discard proportional representation, thereby apparently ensuring their perpetual hold on office. Inside and outside the government the cute money was on the Common Market despite nationalist agitation. To the North there seemed to be no change as William Craig told an Orange meeting at Desertmartin in County Derry that the threat of the IRA was as great as ever—mainly because certain groups in Ulster were urging acts of civil disobedience: the very sort of activity IRA policy envisioned. Stormont Ministers were always telling Orange lodges about IRA subversion and sabotage—particularly when little activity was visible to the disinterested eye. In the summer of 1968, civil disobedience still seemed largely a matter of conversation and editorials in obscure monthly papers. The Northern Ireland Civil Rights Association had been formed the previous year and despite the odious conditions in the North, the glaring inequalities, and the sectarian establishment, little of substance had been accomplished. On August 24, three thousand people marched from Coalisland to Dungannon in the first large civil rights demonstration organized by NICRA. Although little noted at the time, the march was to be long remembered as the opening of the most dramatic year Ulster had known in at least a generation.

NOTES

1. *United Irishman*, July 1962.
2. Although Ireland is a small country the distance from Dublin to the far parishes can not be measured in miles but rather in generations. Then, too, the young emigrate to the cities or to Britain leaving the old men as stern rocks of the Republican Movement rarely eroded by the current arising far off in the councils and committees of Dublin.
3. *Saoirse* was typical of newspapers in high-security prisons in that there was a single copy of each issue, in this case four, and was hand-lettered. The editor Dave O'Connell managed to get one issue out and another prisoner smuggled out one so that against the odds fifty per cent of the issues still exist.
4. "The great question then is: What is Sinn Féin doing toward the seizure of State Power? Are its policies and actions determined by this primary issue? If not, why not?" *An Phoblacht*, no. 12, August 1967.
5. Behal's subsequent career was equally spectacular. He appeared in Paris and gave a widely published interview, drifted about for a while, and finally returned to Kilkenny in June 1967. Although rearrested his case was dropped on a technicality.
6. *United Irishman*, May 1966.
7. Almost from the beginning of the new direction in 1962, there was agitation to enter Leinster House. When to the horror of many the question actually came before the Ard Fheis, the vote in favour of abstention was overwhelming—as it was, for example, at the 1967 Ard Fheis; but for many Republicans a matter of principle is not subject to a majority vote. Worse there was a feeling—largely justified—that whatever the vote in the Ard Fheis a majority accepted or supported entry into Leinster House and had the backing of the Army Council.
8. Editorials based on the *United Irishman* investigation appeared in the *Irish Times* and the monthly *Hibernia* gave its Press Award to the paper for Best Investigative Reporting.
9. For example, the distribution of Sinn Féin votes under proportional representation in one Dublin district showed no obvious second choice. There is some tendency for Sinn Féin votes to go to Labour but the indication is that average candidates attract a friends-and-neighbours poll rather than a "radical" vote.
10. On May 7, 1966, the Twenty-six County police seized a Republican programme outline during an arrest. On May 13, Brian Lenihan, Minister of Justice, revealed sufficient selections of the document to show that the Republicans had done long and serious rethinking.

Instead of creating a Republican scare, the document actually attracted sympathetic attention in some quarters—including *TCD*, the magazine of Trinity College, "a well thought out plan of social reform and democratic ideals".

11. The Nationalist living in Belfast has retained a strong loyalty to his city, if not to Stormont, despite the raw edges of discrimination. In the years since the pogroms of the 'thirties, there had apparently grown a determination not to tolerate Orange assaults. To some degree the Belfast IRA thought of itself as a local defence force in case of trouble; but more important the average Catholic, unconcerned with extreme Republicanism, seemed unlikely to suffer any real outrage in silence —not because times were hard but because they had got so much better.

12. *United Irishman*, September 1968.

PART VI

CHAPTER XVIII

The North Explodes and the Army Divides

The next civil rights target was to be Derry with its Nationalist majority and Unionist government, with massive unemployment, with demonstrable inequalities in housing, with unequal representation in local elections—with, in fact, an abundance of targets which might well catch the eye of the British press if not the British government. The march was announced. With Pavlovian predictability Craig banned it, insisting that there would be no more Armaghs (a Republican march in Armagh had led to disturbances). No civil disobedience movement could have had a more co-operative Minister of Justice. The march went on. Leading the way were Gerry Fitt and Eddie McAteer, leader of the Nationalists. The march was ambushed by Orangemen right on schedule in Derry. Under the interested eyes of British politicians and British journalists, down came the batons of the RUC—first on Fitt—and up went the balloon.

The Unionist reaction to agitation in the streets had been honed on decades of practice in dealing in quiet isolation with "subversives". Come down hard with the RUC and, if need be, the B-Specials, blame the IRA and/or communist agitators, deplore the fact that demonstrations will lead to sectarian violence (i.e. Orange mobs and pogroms) which the RUC will be powerless to stop, and above all give not an inch—no surrender. What had worked in the past should have done so in October 1968—and Craig should have been the ideal man to apply the remedy—but for one or two new factors. First a Labour government sat in London. On July 11, Prime Minister Harold Wilson had told O'Neill that he could not wait forever and that Northern Ireland's house must be put in order. Even more important, British television brought the riots, marches, and demonstrations into every British home. English MPs could see for the first time—often in living colour—the excitement of RUC baton charges, the howl of an Orange mob, and could hear the long litany of Nationalist grievances. Viewers in Leeds and Coventry were stunned to learn that the police were armed in Ulster, that people could be detained without trial in Ulster, that people's religion determined their housing and their job in Ulster. English politicians were stunned at the mess at their own back door. And the Unionists were stunned to find themselves at stage centre under the eye of the television camera and the Mother of Parliaments.

Week-end after week-end, huge demonstrations in Derry kept up the pressure. As expected, the pure unbending Orange elements, certain that O'Neill would sell out Ulster, rushed into the streets led by the Reverend Ian Paisley and Major Ronald Bunting. Just as the NICRA had led to a proliferation of Civil Rights associations—the Derry Action Committee or the People's Democracy at Queen's University Belfast—so Paisley's intervention led to the formation of a covey of Loyalist groups, all determined to give not an inch. On October 30, the British government appointed a commission: years too late said the Civil Rights people. On November 4, O'Neill went to London. He left behind trouble in Belfast and in Derry; a Movement that regarded him as little more than a smiling mask for the Unionist machine; and growing uneasiness among his supporters, who sensed that his days were numbered. Nothing visible came out of the London meeting. The demonstrations continued. Craig banned those he could, sent in the RUC, blamed Republicans and agitators, and hoped he could hold Paisley's followers in check.

Neither he nor the RUC could. First Paisley seized the centre of Dungannon to prevent a Civil Rights demonstration. On November 30, his followers repeated their action at Armagh; and only the swift intervention of the RUC prevented a potentially deadly confrontation between Paisleyites and the Civil Rights marchers, who were determined to push on into town. Craig felt that only by the grace of God had a civil war been averted. As one unkind observer pointed out, Northern Ireland was in the curious position of being a police state without sufficient policemen. On December 5, the government announced that more RUC were to be recruited and B-Specials were called up. Craig and the hard-liners felt that with the proper application of force the agitators could be broken. O'Neill knew Northern Ireland could not risk going it alone and alienating London. Craig made disgruntled public speeches and on December 11 was sacked. Apparently the Unionists under O'Neill were going to try to muddle through with a more moderate approach. No one in the Civil Rights movement was impressed—for them a moderate Unionist was a contradiction in terms. In Belfast the Queen's University students of the People's Democracy decided on an extended march to Derry beginning December 31 and ending on January 4. By this time almost all non-Unionist opinion had solidified behind the Civil Rights movements. Some were Green Tories who saw the potential gain of One-Man-One-Vote, some were young Protestants disgusted with cant and religious hypocrisy, some were left-wing radicals excited by the prospect of revolution, and some were Republicans. All, however, intended to go as far down the road of civil disobedience as they could—and once more the road led to Derry.

The students' march was publicized, frequently televised, and produced one drama after another. Ambushed by an Orange mob while—apparently

—the RUC looked on, stoned *en route*, hounded and hooted, threatened again and again, they were finally batoned in Derry for good measure. To round off what strategically was an immensely successful confrontation, the frustrated RUC ran amok in the Catholic Bogside area of Derry breaking windows and intimidating the people. Police control of Derry disintegrated before the threat of open revolt—the days of quiet pogroms were over. The local citizens took over control of the Lecky Road area. A pirate radio station, Derry Free Radio, began to suggest in its broadcasts that independent local authorities should be set up. On March 11, at Newry the Civil Rights demonstrators disobeyed their marshals and rushed several RUC tenders. The final count was seven tenders burned, twenty people injured and twenty arrested. Four days later the Stormont government decided to appoint a commission to investigate conditions and urged improved riot-control legislation. This was clearly insufficient. The hard old ways had not worked. The movement could not be discredited by being smeared as communist, Republican, or Papist. The RUC could not beat it into the ground or Paisley intimidate it or O'Neill placate it—and given the nature of the Unionist machine, compromise was out of the question. Ulster was stuck tight on the lip of chaos. O'Neill's most formidable rival, Brian Faulkner, resigned from the cabinet and Unionist MPs began to desert what seemed to be a sinking ship.

O'Neill called what surely must be one of the strangest of general elections, an election solely to determine the leadership of the Unionist Party. He asked for the support of the citizens of Northern Ireland, Catholic or Protestant, for his announced policy of moderation and gradual change. The issue was complicated by the divisions within the Unionist party and the introduction of Civil Rights candidates in some constituencies and Protestant militants in others. However, the election did very briefly create a breathing space which after months of non-stop demonstrations was welcome.

By this time the Republican Movement, North and South, was deeply involved in the events in Ulster. From the beginning Sinn Féin people had played a prominent part within the NICRA—they at least knew at first hand how limited civil rights were in Ulster. The IRA felt there were two major considerations: the first, always a factor in the Ulster IRA, was to act as a protecting shield against sectarian assaults or police injustice; the second was to co-operate with the Civil Rights movement in dismantling the Unionist machine. In effect the IRA GHQ accepted, for strategic reasons, the tactics of civil disobedience. The result was that by 1969 the most militant members of the IRA in the North were often undertaking regular assignments to prevent attacks against the RUC or the Orange mobs, and to contain the demonstrators. It was obvious that many

Republicans were involved in the movement. The Inspector-General of the RUC, Anthony J. Peacocke, told the press that the police had evidence of IRA collaboration, but "I do not think they are organizing it, but it fits in with their long-term plans for uniting Ireland forcibly."[1] This was essentially the case. In fact once the demonstrations gained momentum, the Army could have had little hope of keeping their militant young radicals away from the action. In fact as time passed, the principals of non-violent confrontation, the validity of political action, the futility of "physical force" as strategy began to convert previously narrow-minded Army men. It would be fair to say that the Civil Rights movement had far more influence on the IRA than the reverse. The Movement had found a way to crack the Unionist grip on Ulster—and it worked. And the RUC knew it worked: "Most of the police understand that you cannot win. You might get a draw, but you are likely to lose."[2] This from the Chief Inspector of the RUC. Whatever the election results the Movement would push on.

The results were hardly encouraging to the moderate of mind and tranquil of disposition. Despite hopeful predictions of a Catholic switch to pro-Unionist candidates, the election results changed little—except for the worse. In O'Neill's own Bannside district, Ian Paisley polled 6,331 votes to the Prime Minister's 7,745 with another 2,310 votes for a Civil Rights candidate. It was a humiliating showing. In Derry McAteer, the leader of the Nationalists, went down before an independent Civil Rights candidate, John Hume—Green Tories had apparently outlived their day in Derry. Although O'Neill announced he intended to remain in office after the February 24 elections, many felt his days were numbered. Many local Unionists were bitter with the splits. There was a hard core of anti-O'Neill MPs. O'Neill had been unable to carry through significant reforms or to crush the demonstrators or to reassure the conservatives.

In the absence of an effective alternative to O'Neill and his policy of moderation the demonstrations began again. There was trouble in Derry. An explosion of unknown origin did £500,000 damage to the installation of the Electrical Board of Northern Ireland at Castlereigh south of Belfast. Paisley was sent off to prison briefly, cheered by his Orangemen. And there was a by-election for Westminster in Mid-Ulster.

A great many of the stresses and strains within the Republican Movement were revealed in the delicate shifts and swings behind the scene during the long by-election wrangle. Although Mid-Ulster had a non-Unionist majority, a Unionist usually sat in Westminster as a result of a split Nationalist vote. In the existing circumstances a non-abstentionist Republican was assured of a majority and an abstentionist Republican might under very special circumstances achieve a majority. This meant that with the death of the Unionist MP, the Republicans could leap into their "own" Mid-Ulster constituency, nominate someone appropriate, hopefully keep out competitors, and win a *succés d'estime*. On November 23, a Mid-Ulster Convention nominated Kevin Agnew, a member of the NICRA Executive, a well-known Republican, and if not as popular in the district as Tom Mitchell, still an excellent candidate. He would, naturally, run on an abstentionist ticket. And there came the crunch. There was every indication that the Civil Rights Movement wanted a front candidate, a winning candidate, and one who could carry the struggle to Westminster. There was also every indication that Austin Currie, the Nationalist MP at Stormont, sought the honour. With a Civil Rights candidate in the field, Agnew would not only lose but harm the Movement. If Agnew did not run, Currie might get a stranglehold on the seat. The solution was, of course, to discard abstentionism—but that would be a violation of Republican principle.

The agitation for an end to abstentionism had been making headway among Sinn Féin members, but no one knew exactly how successful the campaign had been; the only votes taken were those at the Ard Fheis, which were largely pro-forma affairs to demonstrate solidarity. The pressure increased. Seamus Costello, who had built up a first-rate machine in Wicklow, was pushing so hard that he had to be suspended to cool off. In 1968 the General Army Convention argued out all the various factors once again without any firm and final decision. Then at the Sinn Féin Ard Fheis on December 8 and 9, Motion 17 to end abstentionism was brought before the delegates to be amended by Seán Garland. The pre-arranged Garland Amendment suggested a Commission to investigate abstentionism. Costello's seconding speech, so enthusiastic for dumping abstentionism, gave many the impression that the die was cast. In point of fact it was not; the Commission began to meet and to meet again and—as usual— there was no decision as month followed month. This kind of thing was not what the Ulster Republicans wanted. They felt that Dublin did not understand the political situation in the North or appreciate the momentum of the Civil Rights movement. On January 28, six prominent Republicans from County Tyrone—Tomás O'Connor, Patsy McDonald, Paddy Coyle, Brian Quinn, Kevin Mallon, and A. Molloy—resigned. "We believe that the abstentionist policy bears no relevance to conditions in 1969 . . . an abstentionist candidate . . . ensures the return of the Unionist nominee. This would be a disaster for the Civil Rights movement . . ."[3] And these were no fair-weather Republicans—Tomás O'Connor was a member of the Ard Comhairle of Sinn Féin and the others held significant Republican offices.

In Dublin the leadership seized on the issue. There was no doubt that political logic dictated that either Agnew run on a non-abstentionist ticket—a violation of standing orders—or withdraw. On April 2, Agnew withdrew. The Republican Movement agreed, backstage, to support the candidacy of Bernadette Devlin, a young university student who had lost to Major Chichester-Clark in South Derry, 5,812 to 9,195, in the February election. Very young, very sincere, wildly out of touch with the tradition-encrusted electorate, she was accepted by the Republicans because she did not look like a stayer in Mid-Ulster politics, backed by the Civil Rights movement because she symbolized all the idealism of the young, and endorsed by Austin Currie because he had no choice. The old men in cloth caps and their pious, conventional wives came down off the bleak hills to vote for the wild-voiced little girl from the university who preached toleration and unity and progress toward a fairer Ulster. Whatever Bernadette Devlin was for, Mid-Ulster knew what to vote against—and the Unionists lost a seat. With Devlin at Westminster, the Republicans had scraped through.

The Civil Rights Movement was stronger than ever. The new MP made good copy. The demonstrations continued. O'Neill hung on. Then early on the morning of April 20, an explosion destroyed a pipe-line at the Silent Valley reservoir near Belfast. There was an explosion in Armagh. Seven post offices were set on fire in Belfast. The Northern Ireland government met hour after hour. There were Civil Rights demonstrations in Dungannon, Armagh, Newry, Lurgan, Toomebridge, Dungiven, Strabane, and Belfast. Riots in Derry led to a reported round hundred casualties. No one knew who was behind the explosions. The Unionists dearly wanted evidence that the IRA had entered in force; but the IRA denied the accusation and in turn accused the RUC and B-Specials. All too obviously the explosions were not in the interests of either the IRA or the Civil Rights Movement. More likely was the premise that militant Orangemen wanted to put pressures on O'Neill. All that the Cabinet could do was arrange for 550 British troops to help keep order.

For much of the Unionist Party, O'Neill had now lost all credibility. Major Chichester-Clark resigned on the grounds that O'Neill was pushing One-Man-One-Vote for local elections too quickly. The explosion in Silent Valley and Chichester-Clark's resignation proved too much. On April 25, British troops were on their way in and O'Neill was on his way out. He was replaced not by Craig and the No Surrender faction nor by his old rival Faulkner, but by Chichester-Clark, whose policies would be the same but who would not have to carry the weight of old grudges and past feuds. The basic situation had not changed but the level of passion dropped. There was a moratorium on demonstrations, giving the Civil Rights Movement time to squabble and split, and the Unionists space for reflection.

Although the peaceful weeks stretched into months the basic issue remained. Apparently no Unionist government could go far enough fast enough to satisfy the Civil Rights Movement without arousing the violent ire of militant Orangemen. In time a new round of march and counter-march appeared inevitable. Little had really changed in Northern Ireland —all that had happened was that grievances had surfaced and had thereby become intolerable.

In the South the IRA was pursuing the new policy of social action. With the example of Derry before them, the leadership was convinced that there was power in the streets, that a hard policy of direct action would yield appropriate dividends. At the various Easter ceremonies the IRA statement could have been written by a Ryan or a Gilmore.

> . . . we call on all Irishmen and women to support our programme of economic resistance, political action and military action in pursuance of our objective— a 32 County Workers' and Small Farmers' Republic.[4]

The leadership decided to take direct action to prevent "alien enterprises acquiring property in Ireland". No action could have so nearly suited the economic and social priorities of the new Republican Movement as some kind of demonstration against huge farms owned by alien landlords, particularly since such landlords were unpopular with the local people. This was overwhelmingly true of German farm owners, who seldom hid their distaste for Irish indolence and refused to tolerate old footpaths and rights of way on their new property. Disagreeable German landlords might be hard to find but rumour had it that Ireland was cluttered with greedy foreigners gobbling up the best land and insulting the locals. In truth there were sufficient alien land purchases scattered about in the rich farming areas to have created some concern even outside the Republican Movement. When the *United Irishman* published a threat to alien landowners, some serious notice was given to the statement. A great deal more attention was given when on June 11 buildings on three big farms in Meath and Louth were set afire.

The Taoiseach Jack Lynch condemned these silly subversive activities. The German Ambassador, Dr. Felicien Prill, appeared at the Ministry of External Affairs for an explanation. The Special Branch spread out over the Midlands. On June 12, the Republican Publicity Board issued a statement accepting responsibility for the burnings carried out by the units of the IRA "in accordance with our policy of resistance to foreign take-over of our land, fisheries, industries, and other assets that belong by right to the Irish people".[5] The strike at German-owned farms had a far greater impact than the previous destruction of property on a large estate in County Galway and the destruction of a house at Ferrans Lock

Estate in Meath, but there was little indication that Ireland hovered on a social revolution or that IRA direct action found much favour outside the councils of the Dublin centre. The new policy had produced foot-dragging and outright defiance among the more conservative Republicans but was welcomed by most militant members. Even with full support within the Movement the new hard line seemed unrealistic in an intensely conservative country.

Just how little had changed in Ireland became clear in June when the results of a surprise general election began to trickle in. For nearly a year Ireland had seemed to be on the move—and on the move away from Fianna Fáil. In October 1968 the referendum on the two amendments discarding proportional representation had been defeated overwhelmingly with neither amendment managing to pull forty per cent of the vote. Criticism of Fianna Fáil's arrogance had grown. Lynch seemed to be slipping. The Labour Party had thrown caution to the winds and trumpeted the slogans of socialism. So swift was the swing to the Left that one Dáil Labour member resigned rather than be associated with a lot of communist radicals. Thus when Lynch called for an election, the optimists foresaw gains for Labour and Fine Gael. Labour brought home Conor Cruise O'Brien and nominated two or three other outstanding intellectuals like Justin Keating and David Thornley. The young people rushed to the hustings and Fianna Fáil seemed to be hurting. For the first time in a generation, Fianna Fáil speakers found it necessary to smear Labour with the communist-brush.

At the end of the day Fianna Fáil, having made optimum use of new constituency lines, returned to the Dáil with an increased majority. Outside Dublin Labour was practically wiped out. Fine Gael as usual came in a distant second. Although the quality of the Dáil had improved, the balance had remained almost unchanged since the early days of de Valera. Except for the brief flash of the Clann, Irish politics had remained largely unchanged. Clarion calls for change and revolution had little effect on a slowly shifting, highly pious electorate who had under Fianna Fáil seen sufficient change to satisfy their frugal aspirations. To the North across the border, power could indeed be found in the streets, and in the ballot box, and in subversion and sabotage. In the South the burning of the odd German farm was not likely to convert the complacent masses, deeply concerned only about the odd penny on the milk or the price of a pint. There were plenty ready for a little vicarious excitement or a moment of national piety, but pub patriotism was short lived—as the Army had reason to know.

However discouraging the situation in the South might look, there could be no doubt that the Army was at last out of the doldrums. Violent social action was a policy and one which gave a direction and demanded the appropriate structure. Abstentionism was no longer as burning an issue now that there was ample opportunity for agitation and action. Since conventional military action was increasingly unlikely, the form of the IRA began to shift to accommodate the new direction. After the autumn 1968 Convention increasing stress was laid on large meetings to decide policy on particular problems or in a particular sphere that previously would have come before a Convention. Particularly with the fast moving events in Northern Ireland, the old structure would not do. Thus, soon after O'Neill resigned and was replaced by Chichester-Clark, a meeting of all Northern Commanders and organizers was held in Dublin to go over future policy. This was in tune with the decision to let the GHQ staff lapse—since their spheres of responsibility had little relation to their actual title—and depend on the IRA organizers to be, in effect, both GHQ and Army Council. This was far more satisfactory and far more effective than hanging onto the old system. In fact abstentionism, reconfirmed at the 1968 convention, was one of the few issues left from the old days. The IRA itself had practically given up maintaining the old military structure. Potential volunteers were turned away into more relevant organizations. Units were closed down. Parades and weapons training were reduced to a once-a-month routine and the volunteers spent their time elsewhere. At the same time pressure from the centre of the IRA to secure acceptance and support of the new hard policy increased. Just as before 1956, the leadership of the Army had created a Movement capable of carrying out limited guerrilla attacks in the North—the goal of that day—so in 1969 the leadership was transforming the Republican institutions, creating a revolutionary citizen army, dedicated to economic resistance and political action as well as military operations.

The leadership was also increasingly antagonizing many of the faithful who suspected that the end of abstentionism was a matter of timing, that the new breed of radicals had little in common with traditional Republicanism, and that both Sinn Féin and the IRA were being led down the garden path. To many it appeared that the GHQ was slicing away the heart of the Movement in the name of an alien revolutionary theory. In 1966 the entire North Kerry Comhairle Ceantair of Sinn Féin, thirteen Cumann and 250 members including venerable Republicans like John Joe Rice and John Joe Sheehy, had been expelled. Reluctant or conservative Cumann were closed down or ignored. Fine old pure Republicans like Jimmy Steele and Seán Keenan were discarded and radicals embraced. No one in Dublin GHQ had seemed worried. The military capacity of the Army was declining and GHQ intent on irrelevant and dubious political adventures, guided by suspected Marxists and

callow "revolutionaries". As long as GHQ avoided a show-down on abstentionism, most of the reluctant were willing to keep within the ranks.
Many doubtful of GHQ's new radicalism did not themselves feel reaction-
ary, did not oppose extensive social change but were concerned with the
new revolutionary language, when there were ample traditional Irish formulas to hand, and with the new men, when there were numerous solid,
dependable non-Marxian Republicans available. No one really wanted
a show-down on a split but no one could see how it could be avoided
forever. Then in August 1969 the North, as predicted, blew up again.

At a fair-housing demonstration on August 11 in Dungannon, the police
after months of relative peace showed little evidence of a new moderation.
On the following day in Derry, the Protestant Apprentice Boys parade
collapsed into an escalating riot that ripped apart the city. Catholic Bogside sealed itself off in a state of siege, defending Free Derry from both
the Orange mobs and the B-Specials. Tear gas, Molotov cocktails, and the
barricades turned Derry into a re-run of Budapest-1956 or Watts or any
city savaged by mobs and violence. Stormont mobilized the B-Specials,
and on August 14, they clashed with Catholics near Falls Road in Belfast.
Then the North slid rapidly into widespread violence, arson, and at last
the shooting in the streets that everyone had predicted, everyone had
feared, and yet no one seemed able to prevent. In the South Lynch called
for talks and set up Irish Army hospitals along the border. The British
government rejected Lynch's suggestion for a United Nations peacekeeping force. To the north Belfast had collapsed into anarchy. On the night
of August 14, six people were shot to death. Derry was quiet but Belfast
had gun battles raging on the Falls Road. By early morning 121 persons had
been treated at various hospitals, forty-two for gunshot wounds. The Protestant mobs seemed determined to break their way into the Catholic districts
alongside the RUC and B-Specials. On August 15, British troops moved
into the city. By August 16, 427 people had been treated in hospitals,
108 for gunshot wounds. The gun fights continued along Falls Road.
Belfast had passed the stage of a pogrom and moved on to civil war. The
Irish army called up two thousand reservists. More British troops moved
into the city. The Northern Ireland and British Cabinets were in constant
contact. And Belfast burned under the horrified eyes of the British television audience. It seemed almost incredible that a religious war was
being fought in the streets of a British city and that even the presence
of the British army could not impose peace. On August 19, the British
government assumed effective control of Northern Ireland, the British
GOC in the North, Lieut-General Sir Ian Freeland, became overlord of the
RUC and B-Specials, two British civil servants were posted to Stormont,
and the British Home Secretary promised a visit within ten days.

Slowly order was restored; but the barricades remained up, the hate and bitterness remained, the lack of faith remained. All during the autumn the North lived on the edge of the precipice. Only long weeks of patient negotiations brought down the barricades of Free Derry, and Free Belfast. There were repeated outbreaks of shooting, arson, and riot. For two months Belfast week-ends brought the mobs into the streets to savage each other. Children learned to make petrol bombs and their elders guerrilla patrols in a gutted and razed city. The UVF returned and struck at the Fenians even deep into Irish Ireland, bombing Wolfe Tone's grave at the end of October. The fires of August did not die down to white embers until late in the year. And the British army remained. And the bitterness and division over whether the B-Specials had rioted or the IRA intervened or Bernadette Devlin had instigated revolt could not be decided by courts or commissions. The promise of massive economic development and extensive political reforms could calm the Catholics and only drove the Protestants to despair. No one foresaw a lasting or just peace and few a return to the uneasy truce before the great marches of 1968.

Despite all the dire prophecies of imminent violence, everyone had been caught by surprise in August. The unleashed mob had ruled largely undirected by overt or covert organizations. The revived UVF, a collection of like-minded, and bloody-minded, extremists, had not been the point of the lance; rather the mobs had been led by simple if violent men, bred of hate, tutored in bigotry, rampaging in the streets for the bitter pleasure of maiming heretics even at the cost of gutting Belfast and with Belfast the Northern Ireland entity. Casualties would have been even higher if either side had prepared more carefully for insurrection, accumulated more arms, and acted under direction. The fact was that neither side had the capacity to slaughter the other. The Catholics could not even adequately defend their homes—and this became a serious issue within the IRA. GHQ had not wanted to play the "military" game in the North. Cathal Goulding as C/S at the height of the troubles had warned that IRA units were active in the North, which they were; but they were not sufficiently active for many of the militant. Living with the very real possibility that the Orange mobs would break through the barricades and massacre their families, many felt that IRA "political" approach to the possible pogrom unwise, to say the least. The IRA, on the other hand, during 1968–1969, had seen no profit in pogroms for anyone. Provocation would surely lead to violence on an appalling scale. Instead the IRA had built up a system of auxiliaries, often without arms, as a home guard. Beyond these thin ranks were the local Citizens Defence Committees, often acting under the assumption that the auxiliaries were, in fact, the IRA. The main purpose of the vague network was self-defence, not vengeance and not sectarian murder. The

IRA, like everyone else unprepared for the August outbreak, had too few
men on the ground, no real chance to bring in people from the South,
Goulding's statement to the contrary, and very few available arms in the
city. If the Belfast command had sought recourse in Thompson guns, the
slaughter on both sides would have been far greater. There is little doubt
that the well-armed B-Specials, certainly, and the RUC, perhaps, would
have run amok; and London simply did not have the troops on hand to
control the situation. As it was, the Rhine force had to be drained to make
possible a greater British army presence in the North. In any case, unwilling and largely unable to respond, the IRA had held off.

While Dublin backwatered, London undertook investigations and reforms, and Stormont suffered in less than silence as Northern Ireland was
reorganized, the IRA GHQ began an agonizing reappraisal. A Nine-
county Northern Command was established, on paper, partly in response
to efforts to establish a central Citizens Defence Committee and partly to
appease the IRA men in the North who felt the Army had let them down.
More than the specifics of reorganization, the GHQ felt that events had
largely passed the point of no return, that there could no longer be any
hedging on the issue of abstentionism, which barred Republicans from
effective political action and left the door open for future Bernadettes,
and that the Republicans must go all the way in their revolutionary philosophy and form a united, national liberation front with the like-minded,
Marxists included. In December 1969, the Army Convention met in
Dublin and voted, reportedly, thirty-nine to twelve to recognize—*de facto*
—the two Irish governments and Westminster. For the Army abstentionism had died in the flaming streets of Belfast. The Northern "political"
policy was approved and the decision for a liberation front accepted. The
Army had spoken. Not all the Army listened in silence. Revolutionary
rhetoric and political policies were one thing but the principle of abstentionism was another. Republicanism for many was valid only so long as
principled—and abstentionism was a moral principle not to be discarded
by a vote in the Army convention. The dissenters withdrew and formed
a Provisional Army Council:

> We declare our allegiance to the 32-County Irish Republic proclaimed at
> Easter 1916, established by the first Dáil Éireann in 1919, overthrown by force
> of arms in 1922 and suppressed to this day by the existing British-imposed
> Six-County and 26-County partition states.[6]

The other IRA's obsession with politics was scorned, the failure to maintain the basic military role of the Irish Republican Army was criticized,
and the inability of the Army to provide the maximum defence possible
for the people in Belfast was noted.

We call on the Irish people at home and in exile for increased support towards defending our people in the North and the eventual achievement of the full political, social, economic and cultural freedom of Ireland.[7]

The Provisional IRA immediately contacted the purists throughout Ireland. Many long inactive and often long suspicious of GHQ returned to the new fold, particularly many of the men of the campaign years and before. There was some support in Belfast, although less than claimed, little elsewhere in the North, and a reasonable response in the areas long dominated by the purists, particularly Leitrim, Roscommon and parts of the West and Kerry. A six-county Northern Command based in Belfast was established to rival the vague nine-county IRA Northern Command. The Provisional IRA did, however, indicate that their hard military policy was by no means a return to an open campaign or pointless provocation but rather a determination to defend the people of the North from "the forces of British imperialism". Simultaneously with the rapid organization of the Provisional IRA, the purists turned their attention to the January Ard Fheis of Sinn Féin where the case for abstentionism could be made again, hopefully to sway sufficient delegates so that the party after fifty years of fidelity to the Irish Republic "would not be diverted into the parliamentary blind alleys of Westminster, Leinster House, and Stormont".[8] The purists were not alone for GHQ hoped that the needed two-thirds vote at the Ard Fheis might be in hand and if not a majority resolution supporting the new IRA policy certainly could be found. The rush to get the maximum number of appropriately instructed delegates was well under way even before the December Army Convention.

By the time the Ard Fheis met at the Intercontinental Hotel in Ballsbridge on January 10, the split in the Republican Movement was irrevocable. Those opposed to the IRA policy realized that they could not secure control of the Ard Fheis and would not follow the leadership down an unprincipled road. Tom Maguire, the last Republican member of the Second Dáil, announced that the IRA "convention had neither the right nor the authority"[9] to pass a resolution ending abstentionism and the dissidents agreed wholeheartedly. If the IRA persisted, and there was every indication that they would, then the true, traditional Republicans would not follow. On Sunday night, January 11, the resolution ending abstentionism passed but nineteen votes shy of the needed two-thirds majority. The anti-abstentionists called for a resolution supporting IRA policy, which would need a simple majority.[10] In response approximately one-third of the 257 delegates walked out to meet immediately in a pre-hired hall in Parnell Square. There, in their own Ard Fheis, allegiance was given to the Provisional Army Council and a Caretaker Executive of Sinn Féin created dedicated to abstentionism.

The Caretaker Executive later released the specific reasons for the break other than the resolution on abstentionism: the leadership's support of extreme socialism leading to totalitarian dictatorship, the failure to protect the people of the North in August, the suggestion that Stormont should be abolished and the North come under direct Westminster rule, and finally the internal methods of operation within the Movement since 1964 which expelled the faithful and replaced them with people interested "in a more radical form of movement".[11] The Caretaker Executive completed plans for a new Republican paper, *An Phoblacht*, which appeared in February and sold twenty thousand copies of the first issue. Every effort was made to accumulate support, attract existing Cumann and bring back men long disappointed with the Republican leadership. Those who supported the new Executive, with very few exceptions, were largely predictable, men largely of the 'forties and 'fifties deeply dedicated to the traditions and ideals of the Easter Republic and, although not necessarily bedrock conservatives, certainly more concerned with the national issue than a socialist programme. Rory Brady became Chairman and with him on the Executive many prominent Republicans, his brother Seán, John Joe McGirl, Seán Stephenson, Eamon Thomas, P. Mulcahy of Limerick, Charlie McGlade, Joe Clarke, and Larry Grogan. Elsewhere in the country old familiar names rallied to the cause like Frank Morris and Dave O'Connell in Donegal. Regular reports of IRA units of Sinn Féin Cumann pledging support appeared. Where the old leadership held sway, as in Dublin, preorganization of the loyalists was necessary. But everywhere the Caretaker Executive and the Provisional Army Council could feel that vast progress had been made on short notice and with insufficient reparation so that the Republican Movement could no longer be carried into alien parliaments or down alien radical roads on the backs of the old leadership.

The reaction of many Republicans in Dublin less intimately involved with "principles" was that a great deal of dead weight had been stripped from the real core of the Republican Movement by the split, albeit at the cost of real personal bitterness and the loss of many honest and talented men. The Caretakers appeared very much that, custodians of an irrelevant past. However distinguished the Executive might be, there were no young men and few associated with the Movement since 1962 had joined the dissenters. Many of the distinguished names had been just that, "names", for a great many years. *An Phoblacht*, particularly the second issue, more closely resembled the *United Irishman* of the previous generation, filled with commemoration news, circulation figures, publicity funds, and Easter lily appeals. The new programme of social and economic reform was, as might be expected, a return to the ideas of Comhar na gComharsan

(Neighbours' Co-operation) developed in 1939, and afterward recalled whenever the traditionalists felt need of a philosophic position beyond partitition. No one seemed willing or able to explain what new "military" policy would be followed in the North differing from the discarded IRA policy or how different would be the new approach to the Civil Rights movement. None of the carefully reasoned explanations of the split nor the call for a Thirty-two county Democratic Socialist Republic could fully hide the fact that some would rather be few and faithful, perhaps futile and faithful, than move into the future on a different path. The feeling within the existing leadership was that the Caretakers were going to wither on the vine, unable to attract the young into a political dead end, that the roots had been cut off for love of the branch.

Behind these issues made public, commission, abstentionism, military policy, and constitutional niceties, another most important unmentionable factor existed. Many of the majority — the Official Republicans — suspected that the split, first in the Army and then in Sinn Féin, had occurred not so much as a result of irreconcilable differences within the movement but rather as a result of exterior manipulation. In the previous February with the prospects of serious violence to the more astute, an effort had been made to co-opt the IRA by some of the more nationalistic, or ambitious as the case might be, within Fianna Fáil. A meeting between emissaries of Fianna Fáil and those of the IRA revealed an interest in arming Active Service Units' in the North. Obviously the IRA had no argument with the proposal so that in subsequent meetings in Dublin the Army Council asked for £50,000 as a sign of earnestness. Although the Fianna Fáil agents were not that earnest, they did produce £2,300. And with the money came conditions. The IRA would have to give up "socialism" and political agitation in the South; Goulding, Costello, and Johnston would have to go; and action would be limited to the North. At that the "alliance" immediately collapsed. Subsequently, the Fianna Fáil people made contact with various Northern C/Os who with the knowledge and consent of the Army Executive in Dublin continued to discuss matters of mutual interest. At least one C/O managed to wrangle a car out of the discussions, but essentially the Dublin GHQ had no interest in acting as a proxy agent for Fianna Fáil politicians playing war games. The Army Council, however, knew that various members of the Northern Command — the core of the Provisional IRA — had had no such scruples.

The realization that during the August days Belfast was defenseless — local IRA units had a few dozen small arms — had been a harsh blow but nothing compared to Goulding's revelation in Dublin that GHQ had nothing to send North. The men from the North began to look elsewhere.

The IRA men of the 'forties like Joe Cahill, Seamus Twomey, or Jimmy Steele were physical force men and, like Seán Keenan of Derry, deeply suspicious of GHQ's politics. They wanted guns and were supported by the purists like Dave O'Connell, who even in the worst years after the campaign felt certain that "this thing wasn't finished yet," and the pragmatists like John Kelly. Kelly later summed up the Northerners attitude: "At the time we, to be quite honest, didn't much care whether there were strings attached to the guns or not."[12] For a time the Northern Command, the Official IRA, and Kelly's Citizens' Defense groups existed together in a twilight world where both sides still spoke. Then after the November Army Convention, the two sides went their own ways.

By then most detailed negotiations had been opened again by various Southern "representatives," in particular Captain James Kelly of Irish Military Intelligence, who had first unofficially contacted Northern Republicans even before the August 1969 violence. After the August events, it appeared that Jack Lynch's Fianna Fáil government intended to play an active role in defense of the Nationalist communities, would not stand idly by. Some within the Cabinet even proposed an invasion but were satisfied with the creation of a Northern Sub-Committee of the Cabinet that included Neil Blaney, who pushed a very hard line on the North, and Charles Haughey, who had even more extensive ambitions. John Kelly immediately appeared seeking arms in the name of the Citizens' Defense Committees. Intricate maneuvers with a variety of agents on both sides began and continued without a clear picture of just who the Southern agents represented—the Cabinet, Fianna Fáil, the Irish Army, individuals, or the Northern Sub-Committee. For the Northerners this was not a significant matter, for as Kelly noted "We did not ask for blankets or feeding bottles. We asked for guns—and no one from Lynch down refused the request or told us that this was contrary to Government policy".[13] By the time of the Dublin IRA Convention in November, money was already funneling through various bank accounts into the hands of the Northerners who thus no longer needed or wanted advice and assistance from Goulding. In Official eyes the "Provos" had been bought by Fianna Fáil for Fianna Fáil purposes—the IRA split for party gain.

Between August 1969 and the following April, the Dublin government appeared to be following a policy of a tacit alliance with the Provos for the defense of Northern Catholics and some suspected in hopes of a United Ireland. There was money for a variety of purposes, including the purchase of arms. There was official aid and comfort in arranging a £30,000 shipment of "untraceable" arms from Vienna into Dublin where it would be turned over to Kelly after clearing customs and moved on to a dump in Cavan. A propaganda paper *Voice of the North* appeared—financed from the same sources.[14] Training was offered to Northerners in a camp in Donegal just across from Derry. Rifles had been moved up to Dundalk near the border and plans were underway to create a covert Republican radio station. All of this activity apparently had the support of the Lynch government. Certainly Blaney and Haughey on the Sub-Committee appeared to be actively engaged in directing a policy clearly supported with enthusiasm by many within Fianna Fáil. This continued to be the case until April 20 when Lynch discovered the proposed arms shipment. On May 6, the arms case became public and Lynch fired Blaney and Haughey. Fianna Fáil was badly shaken—Kevin Boland resigned in protest. Lynch continued to deny any previous knowledge of the arms shipment, which had by then aborted. Blaney, Haughey, Captain Kelly, John Kelly, and a volunteer intermediary Albert Luykx were brought to trial the following autumn and were acquitted as expected.[15]

By the time of the arms trial, the Provisional IRA—the Provos—had become an established fact in Irish political life whether or not they had been, as the Officials claimed, created by Blaney and Co. And the Provos could not have cared less what the Officials claimed. The aid and patronage of Blaney and Co. had been accepted and freedom of action maintained. The Officials could claim them to be creatures of Fianna Fáil reactionaries or Northern Fascists or anything they chose; for increasingly the Provo Army Council felt that Goulding's lot was irrelevant to the real world in Belfast and Derry. The "National Liberation Front" dream of grasping power in the streets by organizing the people to agitate, by recourse to revolutionary rhetoric alien to Ireland, by Marxist-Leninist analysis better suited to a Trinity College debate appeared to the Provos to be just that, a dream. The Provos dependence on the gun only slightly hidden with a few wisps of a political program—a Catholic gunman for a Catholic ghetto—appalled the Officials, who while not adverse to the gun felt a single-minded dedication to physical force would lead to pogroms and sectarian war and would never unite the whole people of Ireland. And both lots tended to exaggerate their approach to Ireland's problems. Those outside Republican circles for good or ill tended to polarize the two postures even further: Communist Radical versus Catholic Gunman. The split, however, was not simply a disagreement over politics, abstentionism or communism, or military policy or even Blaney and Co. but rather was over very different Republican responses and attitudes toward the reality of Ireland in 1969. Both reactions were clearly within the Republican tradition. Neither IRA had foresworn physical force, neither had denied the need for revolutionary reform, neither failed to identify Britain as the major enemy, both continued despite the evidence to place hope in the Ulster Protestant working class. In the North, the Protestants, too, saw little difference in the two "non-sectarian" IRAs, both defenders of the Catholics, both opponents of the Crown-and-Stormont, both prone to identify the people—"our people"— as the Catholics, and both Fenian to the core.[16] Yet there were indeed very real differences between the Provos and the Officials. And if these differences had been no more than tactical, they still would have changed the course of events in Ireland. As it developed, the Provos' posture and potential coupled with a series of errors by British security forces led to one more IRA campaign—and this time the greatest challenge to the continuance of the British connection in fifty years.

NOTES

1. *Irish Times*, February 6, 1969.
2. *Ibid.*
3. *Ibid.*, January 29, 1969.
4. *United Irishman*, May 1969.
5. *Irish Times*, June 13, 1969.
6. *Ibid.*, December 29, 1969.
7. *Ibid.*
8. *Ibid.*
9. *Irish Press*, January 5, 1970.
10. Quite accurately the minority pointed out that a majority resolution would be unconstitutional. Those who so voted on January 11 thus gave their support to what "the Sinn Féin constitution stigmatized as 'an act of treachery' ". Rory Brady in *An Phoblacht*, March 1970.
11. *Ibid.*, February 1970.
12. Rosita Sweetman, *On Our Knees, Ireland 1972*. London, 1972, p. 202.
13. James Kelly, *Orders for the Captain?*, Dublin, 1971, p. 171.
14. Seamus Brady, editor of *Voice of the North*, has written his impression of events in *Arms and the Men, Ireland in Turmoil*, Bray (Co. Wicklow, Ireland), 1971.
15. Other than the Brady and Kelly book on the arms case there is T. MacIntyre, *To the Bridewell Gate*, London, 1971, and a mass of journalistic investigation; however, nothing reveals any more than the transcript of the trial—and that did not reveal enough for most.
16. Conor Cruise O'Brien in *States of Ireland*, New York, 1972, attacks Republican pretensions at length and with relish.

CHAPTER XIX

The Rise of the Provos: 1970–1972

By the end of February 1970, the Provos with Seán MacStiofáin as C/S[1] and Sinn Féin (Kevin Street) with Rory Brady as President had sorted themselves out in the midst of the demands from a variety of sources. Everything had to be done from scratch—restructuring Sinn Féin, recruiting and training the growing number of volunteers, putting together units in the North, particularly outside Derry and Belfast, collecting arms, dispatching agents to America and Britain to raise money and organize aid committees, calming the anxious, and patching up the inevitable quarrels. Already some money had begun to flow through a variety of pipelines, in some cases to independent defense groups in the North but increasingly through overt or covert conduits to Dublin GHQ or various Republican aid committees. The response from America was like nothing since the Troubles as all the old Irish-American loyalties and fears surfaced during 1969.[2] For the first months of the Provo's existence, the crucial issue remained arms—political organization, *An Phoblacht*, new recruits, Republican publicity, all were secondary factors—without arms there might well be no one to recruit, organize, and indoctrinate.

Until April, the Provos had hope of a very large shipment of arms brought in through John Kelly's efforts and the help of Blaney and Co. Even before that small amounts were shifted from the South and over from Britain. For some time it would also be relatively easy to bring in odd lots by various means from the United States. The most notorious of these were the civilian version of the military M-16—the AR 15 Armalite. Even with the spate of American money, there was no sudden change in the arms situation. The money was not that easy to spend. The GHQ lacked foreign contacts and foreign allies, had little knowledge of the nature and problems of illegal arms traffic nor the diplomatic resources to purchase "legally" what was needed. As a result a string of failures and abortive plots occurred—and in some cases received wide publicity.[3] By and large from beginning to end, British intelligence managed to keep on top of Provo efforts, but still a trickle reached the North. Even the well publicized sympathy of Colonel Qaddafi of Lybia could not surmount British experience and Irish naïveté. Very little, of course, was actually needed in the North in the Spring of 1970 simply because there were relatively few Provos active, although there were many men eager for arms if not Republican discipline. To a large degree the failure to arrange large shipments of arms—several thousand rifles or sub-machine guns—meant that desirable or no the Nationalist's defense would have to depend on a small armed elite, the IRA Active Service Units, rather than an armed militia, and there could not be a massive rising.

No one then or later thought much about a mass Rising, although the Officials still had hopes for the masses. Until well into 1970, the Provos remained thin on the ground—as did the Officials for that matter. They were quite incapable of harnessing or directing any spontaneous mass movement, in fact, hard put to maintain order in the presence of rioting school boys. In time, the Provo structure in Belfast was sorted out and expanded into a real Brigade for the first time in over a generation. The Upper Falls, Ballymurphy, and Andersontown became the First Battalion; Lower Falls and Clonard, Second Battalion; and North Belfast to the Markets along with East Belfast, the Third Battalion. For some while certain of these areas such as the isolated Short Strand across the Lagan River or the Arydone remained largely independent—many of the early Provos were self-selected. The Belfast staff under Billy McKee as C/O not only had to rush from one threatened dike to another but also to attempt to instill discipline from the center. These schismatic tendencies remained, particularly after the Brigade grew to well over a thousand volunteers, many recent converts to Republicanism and many with limited strategic vision. Still by and large the Brigade staff managed to hold the three battalions together.

In Belfast the Provos began with the dozen or so members of the Northern Command and expanded to several hundred volunteers by the end of the first year and over a thousand early in 1971. In a real sense Belfast was always a Republican city as far as the Nationalist population was concerned; but Derry, on the other hand, had been Nationalist: Hugh McAteer from Belfast was IRA C/S and Eddie McAteer from Derry was head of the Nationalist Party. As a result the Derry Provo unit had started from scratch, created by two or three lads looking for guns and who followed Seán Keenan's lead in not looking to Goulding in Dublin. Derry with the Creggan housing estate and the Bogside, radicalized by the civil rights campaign, proved fertile ground for recruiting, but in competition with the Officials. In Belfast, the Officials had remained concentrated in the Markets, Lower Falls, and one or two other places, and their growth had been steady but limited in contrast to the rapid spread of Provo units. In Derry, the Officials did as well as the Provos and in the beginning there was little to choose in tactics or intentions. A great strength for the IRA had been created by the segregated housing pattern that produced Catholic Ghettos, some bright, new housing estates, others warrens of little streets and tiny brick houses. With well defined boundaries they were closed communities of friends and neighbors and an alien presence was noted and reported at once; moreover, the increasingly aggressive searches and sweeps of the British Army after August guaranteed that the neighbors would remain friends, would supply an urban safe-base for the Active Service Units recruited from the area. Elsewhere in the North most Active Service Units remained with the Officials so that the Provos had to start with a core of older men like J. B. O'Hagen or Kevin Mallon from the 'forties and 'fifties and build anew.[4] Thus for a considerable length of time there was little evidence of the Provos outside the Catholic concentrations in Derry and Belfast, but GHQ in Dublin had great hopes that the traditional Republican countryside in the North would produce a new crop of volunteers.

As usual all this activity went on largely out of sight, while the more public maneuvers of the politicians attracted the main interest, North and South. The Dublin events, beginning with the unprecedented two-day Dáil debate on the sacking of Haughey and Blaney in May and continuing through the revelations of the arms trial in October, focused attention on the problems of Fianna Fáil and in particular on Lynch's gradual abrogation of his uncomfortable Republican heritage. In the North O'Neill, having outlived his time — the flurry of liberalism out of which so much chaos had come—departed in March for the House of Lords. The new man, James Chichester-Clark, was not the hard man—William Craig—that the Orange ultras had wanted; on the other hand he was not Brian Faulkner who most in Stormont and out feared as too clever by half. The atmosphere had changed considerably, however, for O'Neill's old Westminster seat was won by Ian Paisley, hardly a victory for moderation or an omen for the quiet life.

Relatively speaking, events appeared on the surface to be quiet—no screaming mobs or sectarian murders. But this was only *relatively* so, for increasingly the British Army's peacekeeping procedures were chipping away its image of neutrality. This was in part simply because the British Army's minimum response—in military terms—to minor disorder had a disproportionate impact on the Nationalist population in the immediate area. In April 1970, for example, the British Army responded to a Catholic crowd in Ballymurphy stoning an Orange parade, by then a set ritual, with Saracens (armored cars) and CS gas—a "moderate" military response by only 70 Royal Scots in the face of 400 rioters. At this time the Provos were also attempting to maintain order in Ballymurphy—a dim prospect given their limited strength and the impact of CS gas. The British Army did not understand then and often did not later the potential fallout of their firm response to disorder—CS gas did more for the Provos than all the legends of heroes and all the patriot graves. Yet few in London cared to pay very much attention to minor Irish events: the crisis level was way down and those in power had other priorities.

Wilson's government faced a general election with considerable confidence. Ireland would not be an issue. Actually many in the Labour Party felt that the time had come to take severe measures in Northern Ireland. Home Secretary James Callaghan, in fact, was nearly convinced that Stormont had outlived its time, that direct rule or new institutions were the answer. The expected Labour victory at the polls would permit the Cabinet to take a firm line in Ireland before the balloon went up again. The June 18 results, however, returned Ted Heath and the Conservatives, long time allies of the Unionist Party who had no inclination to take severe measures. Heath put Reginald Maudling in as Home Secretary instead of his Shadow Minster Quintin Hogg. As a result, Maudling, who tended to approach most problems with reserve and in some cases indolence if no clear course appeared and who knew little of Ireland, was inclined by wont and policy to let matters drift. Irish events often appear to drift from bad to worse; and with no guidance from London, this proved to be the case. On June 27, there were Protestant-Catholic riots on the edge of Ardoyne and three Protestants were killed. Widespread riots followed at all the raw boundary edges of the two communities, and 276 people were injured. That night the Protestants attacked St. Matthew's Church in the isolated Short Strand, and the IRA defenders shot and killed four. Billy McKee, C/O of the Belfast Brigade, was seriously wounded in the exchange of fire. To the Catholics the British Army had first permitted the Orange parade that sparked the riots and then failed to defend the Catholics in the Short Strand. The British commander Lt.-General Sir Ian Freeland by then recognized that permitting the parade along the Ardoyne route had been a disaster but insisted that the Army had been too finely stretched to get to St. Matthew's until too late. Freeland felt that something had to be done, more troops sent in to Northern Ireland or a political initiative or something. Maudling flew over still devoid of experience or ideas and, as so many others before him, left appalled—"What a bloody awful country"[5]—but still without ideas.

Nothing of significance was done. There was no firm word out of Maudling or London. Drift was the order of the day and the British Army left to its own devices. In July the long slide to chaos began—by accident, of course, but still as a result of British Army policy. On July 3, with the Catholic population still bitter over the events of the weekend, the British security forces carried out a successful arms raid on a temporary official IRA dump in the Lower Falls. Not unexpectedly there was an escalating confrontation in the maze of narrow streets. The British, met by a crowd, stayed put—standard operating procedure—and were soon cut off and harassed by a growing mob. Reinforcements in turn were surrounded by larger crowds. British radio communications broke down. No one knew what was going on. CS gas was used. Barricades went up. The British began to cordon off the Lower Falls. The Official IRA unit decided to take on the "Brits". Snipers opened up on the Black Watch and the Life Guards when they moved beyond the cordon. More CS was used. Firing became general. Freeland imposed a curfew that lasted thirty-five hours until Sunday morning. During that time the British pushed arms searches throughout the Lower Falls—and left, given the past record, with a considerable haul (28 rifles, 2 carbines, 52 pistols, and 24 shot guns). Then the British drove two delighted Unionist Ministers, William Long and John Brooke, about the "pacified" Falls. After that the Lower Falls and most of Nationalist Belfast were alienated. IRA recruiting soared.

Yet, on the surface things still appeared to be much the same. There were still the odd riot, unexpected confrontations, incidents, arrests, searches, threats, and atrocity stories; but there was no political movement. Without public pressure from London, Chichester-Clark could only go so far against his Stormont backbench ultras. The reforms that he did manage had little impact on the Bogside or the Falls. And the Protestant population felt reform to be irrelevant. The result was that the Army was left to cope with limited guidance from London and a frail "ally" in Stormont. All the while the hidden decay of legitimate authority continued.

In large part that authority was represented in Catholic eyes by the British Army as the only visible force of law and order. The British Army had been left to maintain order—an order that seemed as usual warped in favor of the Protestants—by means quite different than those of the police. The British Army saw or was permitted to see a prime mission in the active prevention of renewed disorder—a mission that led to searches and seizures, interrogations of random suspects, CS gas and Saracens. To a degree the long familiarity of the professional British soldier with insurrection encouraged a professional military response to provocation in Ulster, and it was more difficult to identify with the Irish-Catholic provocateurs than the Loyalist-Protestant ones; besides, there were twice as many of the latter. The very tactical skill of the British response led to an escalation of provocation. Instead of seeking a means to disengage, the British fashioned a more effective presence. The IRA Active Service Units increasingly met provocation with provocation. The keen tactics of the British thus encouraged the IRA to move from a defensive to an offensive campaign. By employing against the IRA the "appropriate" tactics to counter an urban guerrilla campaign, the British Army largely transformed the rocks and riots of 1969 and 1970 into a very real if low-intensity war[6] the following year, with snipers, car-bombs, shootouts in housing estates, and battles on the border.

The underlying reason that the British Army was largely responsible for its own undoing as the disinterested guardian of order lay in London. Guerrilla war is much too important politically to be left to the tactics of generals, most of whom on past experience were quite aware that there could only be a political victory in any case. And in London until very late in the game, the British Cabinet, Labour until 1970 and subsequently Tory, did simply that. No one seemed willing to think seriously about the Irish problem that offered so few political benefits for any British politician. Thus the Army had been sent into the North in August 1969 and left largely to its own devices. At least Callaghan as Home Minister had monitored events if not affected them. Maudling did not seem interested. After the weekend of July 3-5, the British Army had largely lost all immediate hope of Catholic support, had become the "enemy"—as dangerous as the "Prods" perhaps—but had not become a target. Neither IRA had the men nor the inclination to take on the British Army, but the possibility of another campaign began to appear less farfetched in certain Provo minds.

The events of 1970 had increasingly rebounded to Provo advantage. Their posture as defender seemed to the Catholic population to fit the objective conditions better than the Officials' radical agitation. The Provos made no secret that they intended to depend mainly on the gun and pursue a military policy—defensive to be sure. The old members of the 'forties and 'fifties knew the language of the tribe and the new volunteers the needs of the present. Perhaps the Officials' tactics of mass confrontation were effective at little cost, but in the heel of the hunt many in the North preferred to trust the gun and the Provos rather than themselves.

During January 1971, the last Provo efforts to maintain the peace in cooperation with local British officers, not a popular posture as far as Belfast Brigade Staff was concerned in any case, collapsed. There were riots at the Ballymurphy estate. As usual there was a hard and heavy British Army response to the stone throwing. In all 700 troops carried another house-to-house search that quelled the riots, alienated the community, and resulted in more casualties, including one soldier who had been shot. The gun had been introduced for the first time by the Provos against the Army. Chichester-Clark was appalled by the scope of the rioting—the British Army did not really seem to be trying; furthermore, London did not seem to be willing to send more troops. His ultras wanted action and without it his position would be untenable. On January 27, William Craig, leader of the hard-liners, related in Stormont that the IRA and the British Army were cooperating. The Orangemen were outraged and Chichester-Clark's position undermined further.

The slide toward open war continued with serious rioting in the Clonard on February 3 and 4. Five British soldiers were hit with a single burst of machine-gun fire and three others by snipers. On February 6, Gunner Robert Curtis, twenty, of the 94th Locating Regiment in the Royal Artillery was shot dead in the New Lodge Road—the first British soldier killed. The following morning Chichester-Clark announced on television that "Northern Ireland is at war with the Irish Republican Army Provisionals". And it evolved into a most curious war of sniping and demonstrations, open confrontations, ritual riots, assassinations, and murder from the ditch. In one form or another the British Army had been through it all before from Palestine to Aden and now once more in the United Kingdom.

On February 9, the Republicans buried two men shot the night of February 6 with the full panoply of IRA ritual—black berets, Tricolor, and a volley over the grave—to the horror of the Orangemen watching on television. They even saw *their* British Army saluting the procession. Three women in black berets were arrested, which in turn led to an incident at the Magistrates' Court on February 26 and more rioting in the Ardoyne. Two RUC men were killed. Week after week there were incidents, shootings, reports of arson, armed robberies, and increasingly, bombs in stores and pubs, IRA sniping, and false alarms. There were intercommunal riots between Catholics and Protestants and repeated confrontations between Catholic crowds and the British Army. As civic order decayed many seized the opportunity to seek vengeance for all manner of past slights or present injuries that in no way related to political matters. On March 10, three Scottish soldiers were kidnapped and shot in the back of the head on a country lane outside Belfast by persons unknown—both IRAs denied responsibility. It proved to be the last straw for Chichester-Clark. He could not get the London Cabinet to give him the troops he demanded—1,300 were to come instead of 3,000—nor maintain his fragile hold on the hardliners. On March 19, he resigned.

Brian Faulkner, Stormont's last hope, came in at last as Prime Minister offering reform with one hand and appointments to the ultra-Orangemen with the other. And the Provos bombs began to rock the province: 37 in April, 47 in May, 50 in June.[7] Long before this the decision had been made in London that some form of internment would have to be introduced. The British Army had not been that keen, for they suspected that Faulkner and the Orangemen saw internment as a *deus ex machina* that would "punish" their foes, i.e. the Catholic community. A massive sweep of *them* would once more put the Fenians in their proper place. Such a symbolic sweep, however, would do the security forces little good unless many of the internees were in fact dangerous. Actually a bungled sweep, even if it gave comfort to the Loyalists, might bring the Catholics to the point of open rebellion. Yet even the British commanders admitted something had to be done. Bombs were going off once or twice a day. Sniping was continuous. Military movement in many of the Catholic areas was, if not impossible, very difficult without a massive buildup and the use of armored vehicles. Between April and August, the sniping and return fire killed four British soldiers and wounded 29. Over 100 civilians had been injured by bombs. People were avoiding downtown areas, fearful of the risks. No one came into the center of Belfast unless necessary. Tourists were a thing of the past. Civil order had collapsed and civilian morale might follow.

There was very little room left for any political maneuvers. The polarization of the two religious communities had become almost total, all the fabled bridges had been bombed out. The nationalist leaders who had formed the Social Democratic Labour Party (SDLP) in August 1970 increasingly found their voices lost in the noise of the bombs. In July the SDLP, with Gerry Fitt absent, delivered an ultimatum to the British that there must be an inquiry into the shooting of two Derry civilians. The SDLP felt it must retain some credibility in the community, but instead further isolated itself. The British could find no means to compromise with the ultimatum and the junior Minister for Defense, Lord Balniel, announced that there would be no inquiry. The SDLP withdrew from Stormont and largely from the picture for the time being. The only dialogue was between the British and the bombers.

Provo operations grew more daring and more spectacular. On July 16, a four-man IRA team disguised in white coats raided the Royal Victoria Hospital in Belfast and made off with a wounded volunteer. On July 17, a bomb destroyed the *Daily Mirror* printing plant in Dunmurry—a £2,000,000 operation. And, as the Provos pointed out, the British government had to pay compensation for bomb damage, so that the campaign not only destroyed the "artificial economy" of the Six Counties but made London foot the bill. On July 19, Faulkner insisted that the time for internment had come. This would permit him even-handedly to cancel the dangerously provocative Apprentice Boys forth-coming parade in Derry, as the British wanted, at the same time that internment was introduced. Internment, of course, was not to be even-handed but limited to Republicans and agitators, i.e., Catholics. For the British Army the problem was knowing whom to sweep. The RUC had long lists, thousands of names, culled from long files and long memories. The old-time Republicans were known as were the leaders of the civil rights campaign, many of whom were Officials; but most of the new volunteers of the past two years were unknown. Thus the British Army's constantly changing lists included sympathizers and suspects, the known hard core, and for good measure several of the civil rights people. Essentially the more distant the potential suspect from the active IRA, the more likely he was to be swept up. Most of the real IRA was unknown or on the run, having left behind family, friends, and supporters. To complicate matters for the British there had been no practice in mass arrests so that a few try-out swoops had to be made in late July and early August. These dry runs coupled with an ample flow of hints, guesses, and threats alerted everyone. The security forces recognized the problem and so informed London.

The British Cabinet did understand the Army's problem but did not recognize that the Protestants wanted a "victory", a public humiliation of the disloyal rather than a rigorous police operation. Neither the Army, the Cabinet, nor the Protestants recognized the real danger that such a humiliation might entail—not one more riot but a real rebellion. When internment came on the night of Monday, August 9, it was a disaster as a police measure, alienating many of the still neutral Catholic middle class, in no way damaging the structure of the Officials or the Provos, and to an increasingly fascinated world revealing the sectarian nature of justice—British justice supposedly—in Northern Ireland. As a symbolic victory for the Loyalists it was an equal disaster. Their good advice had led Northern Ireland into open rebellion and chaos and general disrepute. It was quite impossible to pretend that internment had in any way been effective. When Brigadier Marston Tickell met with the press on August 13 to explain how the IRA had been "vir-tually defeated", his analysis and British credibility was being de-stroyed a few streets away. There Joe Cahill, who had succeeded Billy McKee in March as C/O of Belfast, also held a press conference to underline the limitations of internment except as a vindictive weapon

of a frustrated government. Cahill then moved south to Dublin as QMG
and Seamus Twomey, another 'forties man, took over as C/O and pushed
a full-fledged Provo campaign. Internment did not crush the Provos but
unleashed them.

In August there were over one hundred bomb explosions throughout
Northern Ireland, many of them massive. Rifle fire was general. Thirty-
five people were killed. In Derry the Creggan and Bogside became no-go
areas, protected by IRA barricades beyond the reach of not just the RUC
but even the British Army. Free Derry was Republican territory,
patrolled by the IRA, a secure base to launch guerrilla operations. The
same was largely true in the Catholic ghettos of Belfast. Soon the mass
of the Nationalist population struck against the state, refusing to pay
rent and rates. And day in and day out, the shooting and bombs continued. There were booby-traps, hoaxes, sniping in the city, and
eventually operations in the countryside, land mines and ambushes. The
level of Provo activity soon reached that of 1920–1921. Britain once again
at the end of Empire had another revolt against the Crown to add to
the litany of the past, this time close enough so that the audiences in
Liverpool and Leeds could each evening watch on the telly their own
local Vietnam across the Irish Sea.

The news from Ireland began to raise both moral and pragmatic
questions in Britain. With the stories of British brutality—doors smashed,
suspects manhandled, wives insulted—came a belief that many of those
seized were largely innocent, and the glee of the Protestants surely must
have created a guerrilla-sea for the IRA fish if all the experts were correct. At a single stroke internment had produced another generation of
martyrs—the Men Behind the Wire—and destroyed, even in many
British eyes, any remaining legitimacy in the political institutions of
Stormont. Still by and large the British were content to back their
Army—the lads had an impossible job—and to express distaste for both
Irish tribes, Protestant and Catholic.

In Ulster there had been ample examples of British brutality in dealing with the Catholic population before internment, but henceforth
they would become commonplace. More doors were smashed in, women
threatened, more curses and insults. These were not, military spokesmen assured the press, frequent events and not a result of policy, and
really not so strange, given the British soldiers shot in the back or lured
to their deaths by women and children. For the Nationalists such official
assurances aroused little but scorn. In the Bogside or Falls innocent
neighbors had been dragged off, unlucky pedestrians manhandled, suspects beaten, friends insulted and threatened, and the innocent shot or
gassed. In Britain the politicians and population might feel the British

Army was making the best of a bad job but there was no such feeling in Derry and Belfast.

As stories drifted out of the internment prisons, it became clear that individual initiative was an unsatisfactory explanation of the conduct of the British Army during internment roundups. Suspects were routinely beaten. Some had even been thrown blindfolded and screaming from helicopters they thought were high over Belfast instead of three feet off the ground. All this *could* have been the result of "mistakes" made in action situations, although few Catholics thought so; but soon it became clear that men had been questioned at Palace Army Barracks, Holywood, Co. Down, by British soldiers using "deep interrogation". Suspects were forced to stand in awkward positions for hours, disoriented by strange noises while their heads were covered with bags, threatened and abused —and this for days on end in quite cold blood. The charges eventually produced on November 10 an official British government report prepared under the direction of Sir Edmund Compton. For the Irish it was a monument of British hypocrisy, for not only did Compton believe what the British Army told him but he also denied that there had been brutality because the British forces involved had not "enjoyed" their work—an essential component of brutality according to Sir Edmund.

For the Provos no greater asset could have been found than the British resort to brutality, for it wedded the Catholic population to the campaign and in part reduced the complaints that Provo shooting and bombing operations were endangering innocent civilians. The result was an escalating campaign in no way limited by the losses of internment, a campaign that the British Army could not contain without reinforcements or resort to measures that even a Compton report could not cover. The Provo units outside Belfast and Derry had at last been placed on a war footing and the incidents began to build up throughout the province. At the same time a series of cross-border operations were begun so that between September and November the British Army was fired on 243 times. In response on October 13, the British began cratering the nearly 200 unapproved roads that crossed the 270-mile border—an act that alienated the local population and guaranteed further support. Thus everywhere the British looked during the autumn of 1971 Provo operations were escalating. In early December, 30 almost simultaneous bombing operations rocked Northern Ireland—two hundred Active Service volunteers had been involved, once again making a mockery of British Army claims that the Provos had shot their bolt. There had been nothing like the autumn of 1971 since the glory days of the Tan War.

The Provos were riding the crest. Even Ian Paisley began to mention that if the Irish Constitution of 1937 with its references to the special position of the Roman Catholic Church and its prohibition of divorce and contraception were changed then Northern Portestants might look on Dublin with different eyes. In London Harold Wilson was making noises as if to indicate that the Ulster experiment had come to an end after fifty years. On December 15, Reginald Maudling while in Belfast foresaw a situation where the IRA would "not be defeated, not completely eliminated, but have their violence reduced to an acceptable level".[8] So 1971 ended with what appeared to be a concession by the British Home Minister that the Provo campaign could not be defeated but perhaps only contained.

For Ireland January 1972 proved to be the cruelest month of the Provo campaign. On Sunday, January 30, civil rights groups held a banned meeting in the Bogside. Instead of simply containing the demonstration, the British Army, against the advice of the Derry RUC, decided on an arrest operation. The result was that British paratroopers apparently without provocation fired into the crowd. Thirteen civilians were killed and sixteen wounded—Bloody Sunday. The British Army contended that they fired back at the IRA. Most of those present including the foreign press crews denied any "gun battle". Since most of those injured or killed were young men, it appeared as if the "Paras" had simply opened up on potential IRA men to get their own back. For most of the Nationalist population, there was not even any belief in a spontaneous massacre: the Paras had intended to intimidate the people of Derry. The British Army had acted out of malice. The outcry, not simply in Ireland and Britain, was so great that an investigation under the Lord Chief Justice of England, Lord Widgery, was launched. Despite a display of credulity quite equal to that of Sir Edmund Compton, Widgery could not escape the conclusion that all thirteen men killed had been innocent —no gunmen or bombers—although this did not make the British Army guilty, only mistaken.

Long before the Widgery report further alienated Irish opinion, the island was in the grip of hysteria. The impact of Bloody Sunday in Dublin was profound, for often during the deteriorating Northern situation the South had seemed only marginally interested—the Six Counties as far removed and alien as the Congo or Cyprus. By the evening of January 30, all this seemed transformed. Dublin was gripped by emotion, people gathered in clumps and broke apart, waiters huddled in dining room corners, the city was alive with rumor and soon with crowds. On the night of February 2, a mob burned down the British embassy in Merrion Square. In the North both the Provos and the Officials promised vengeance, and sniping escalated. Again the foreign press poured into

Ireland to film the gutted townhouse in Dublin and the guerrilla war to the north. And the campaign did continue with a vengeance in the North; but as in the past the patriotic emotion of Dublin proved a momentary affair, akin to pub patriotism. Once the Embassy had been burnt and honor done, there was no rise of popular pressure on Lynch to take action. Dublin slipped back into the old ways.

Within a relatively brief period the great wave of sympathy for the Irish cause was dissipated elsewhere as well. The Officials carried out a retaliatory raid on the Paras' regimental home at Aldershot in England; but the bomb killed a Catholic priest, albeit an officer, and several women cleaners. Condemnation was general. The same was true as a result of an Official assassination attempt on Stormont Minister John Taylor that left him wounded but alive. After a bomb went off in the Abercorn Restaurant in Belfast, killing two civilians and injuring 136, some cruelly, Bloody Sunday had almost become a historical event. In the South it was apparent that Lynch was simply waiting for the Provos to blunder before moving in to take harsher measures to prevent the South from becoming involved in the widening violence. On January 27, three days before Bloody Sunday, there had been a gun battle on the border at Dungooly that had lasted several hours with thousands of shots exchanged between the Provos and the British Army. The Dublin government most assuredly did not want a border war but had to wait until the emotion of January and February had further ebbed before acting. In the meantime, the Provo bombs continued. On March 20, six more civilians were killed in a huge explosion of Lower Donegal Street in Belfast. It did not matter that the Provos insisted warnings were always sent. Innocent civilians were being killed and maimed. And the whole spectrum of Irish political opinion insisted the bombing was irrevocably alienating the Protestant population. In a sense the campaign was too explosive, insufficiently focused, and without a viable political purpose.

If a general Provo strategy could be discovered, the intent of the bombing and sniping appeared to be directed toward making the North ungovernable, costing the British government and the British Army more than the "connection" was worth, and so forcing concessions. Yet, no real attempt had been made to strike key utilities, vital industries, or transportation links. There had been no selected assassination nor startling raids. Most of the targets were soft and while the number of operations was, indeed, quite large the major damage seemed to be civilian nerves. British Army casualties were, given all, low, and it was cheaper to keep a regiment in Ulster than on the Rhine. Britain had few very important industrial or strategic targets in the North and the Provos apparently had no intention of carrying the campaign to the other side of the Irish Sea. And even if the Provos *did* make the Six Counties largely ungovernable—then what? As the Officials continued to point out, a military campaign—a terror campaign really—without a political corollary was a mindless and deadly exercise. What did the Provos want that the British could realistically grant?

The necessity of a political option, although a lesser priority, had not been entirely neglected by the Provos. The major effort had been to organize four Provincial Assemblies—Ulster would have nine counties, not six, thus equalizing the two communities—but this appeared to observers to be an exercise in a vacuum. Many Republicans, particularly those deeply involved in the technicalities of the campaign, were inclined to see all in the terms of the armed struggle, imagining in moments of enthusiasm that force alone would do. Neither the activities of Sinn Féin nor the efforts to build world sympathy seemed particularly relevant to some Active Service people with the British at the bottom of their lane. The Army Council had accepted that more bombs alone would not do the job. On March 10, despite some grumbling, a three-day truce had been announced. Almost complete peace reigned in the North, ending speculation that there was no central Provo control. On March 13, the leader of Her Majesty's Opposition, Harold Wilson, arrived in Dublin for talks with the Irish Cabinet. The talks with the Irish government were brief, but those with members of the Provos held secretly in Dublin lasted for four hours. Wilson left the impression that a satisfactory end to the Provos' struggle was in sight. He also left an outraged Irish government which had, as Dave O'Connell gleefully pointed out, been used as a cover for the meeting with the Provos. The Provos were now in the big time politically. At a minimum they had veto power and at best they had bombed themselves ahead of Lynch in the queue to the bargaining table. And the bombs continued in the North, the Lower Donegal Street explosion on the very heels of the Wilson visit.

The Protestant response to the bombing had for a time been confused by the continued optimism first of Chichester-Clark and then Faulkner that the IRA was on the run. The British Army, too, repeatedly reported scoops of weapons, captures of very important IRA officers, the wounding and killing of gunmen, and light at the end of the tunnel. When no light appeared—internment had not done the trick, the bombs continued, and all the while both London and Faulkner kept talking about reforms—a rising wave of Protestant militancy swept through the North. The hard men wanted the British Army to smash into the no-go zones, an end to "reforms", and a return to coercion. Their demands

ore apart the old Unionist establishment already weakened by defec-
tions from the Right and soul searching on the Left. On February 9,
William Craig announced the formation of the Protestant Vanguard.
Besides Craig, the leadership included the Rev. Martin Smyth, Grand
Master of the Orange Order for Belfast, Billy Hull of the Loyalist
Association of Workers (LAW), and Captain Austin Ardill, former
Stormont MP for Carrick. All opposed further reform and any British
effort to sell Ulster's birthright in the name of expediency. On March
18, 60,000 demonstrated at a Vanguard rally, and it was clear that a
large Protestant parliamentary force was in the making, a force with
intimate ties to the RUC and many members in the newly formed gun
clubs, a force based on former B Specials and ex-servicemen. Faulkner,
unable to placate his backbenchers, unable to compete with the forces
of No Surrender led by Craig, and unable to persuade the British to
give him the military support he needed, had run out of time. In London the Cabinet had at last lost patience. Something had to be done
and the obvious was for London to take over security entirely. Faulkner
could stay, if he wanted to be a facade for direct control. He did not,
could not. He flew back to Belfast after a final meeting on March 23
knowing that the end had come.

On March 24, the British government announced that Stormont was
prorogued for a year—there would be direct rule from London. Instead
of the languid Maudling, Heath apponted William Whitelaw as the
Secretary of State in charge of Irish affairs. The advocates of the Provos
claimed that they had bombed Stormont out of existence, for it appeared
that, no matter what, the old Ulster establishment and its institutions had
gone. The leaders of the civil rights campaign claimed credit—as did all
and sundry except, of course, the Protestants who were in a state of shock
despite all the signs during 1972 that London had intended to introduce
severe measures. Many of the Provos, however, felt the struggle was just
beginning. In Navan, Mac Stiofáin announced that the campaign of
course would continue, for the IRA demands had not been met.
There was instant horror among the self-proclaimed friends and advisors
of the Provos as well as general disappointment in more conventional
quarters. All felt that a wee pause might not be amiss, most knew that
Stormont was finished, many felt more bombing would simply cost
lives and further destroy the fragile stability of the North and could
produce a civil war. Mac Stiofáin, however, had responded in the traditional Republican manner—concessions be damned, we want our
country. And there would have been problems with any sudden new
truce. The earlier three-day affair had cost the Provos dearly, particu-
arly in Belfast where many Active Service people had been picked

up. Once the campaign had stopped it might well be impossible to begin again, morale would decay, support would evaporate, men on the run would be a burden. Then, too, there was no sign that the British Army would ease up on harassment or release prisoners. Besides there were many in the Provos who insisted on going ahead, who saw no point in lessening their military capacity to make an unnecessary political point.

Many astute observers felt that the point was very necessary, that the Provos must show a far greater flexibility than repeated recourse to the bomb. This was particularly true of the Officials who made much of the political naïveté of the Provos—Mac Stiofáin as The Man-Without-Ideas. As the Provos could and did point out, the Official's own military acts tended to undermine their self-acclaimed political wisdom—first Barnhill, an old man murdered; then Aldershot, women and a priest; the botched Taylor assassination; and then, the last straw, the murder of a young British soldier, a local Catholic home on leave in Derry, who his neighbors knew as a decent lad not a "traitor". In part, in large part, as a result of the fallout from their ruthless and inept military operations and in part in fear of a Protestant backlash, the Officials announced a ceasefire on May 29. The Provos thus felt that the Officials' "flexibility" was a result of military incompetence, that the threat of a Protestant backlash was a long-lived strawman, that they were still on the crest of the wave.

There were, however, other disquieting signs besides the calls for a truce from various sources in the North. On May 10, the Irish Republic had voted on a referendum to join the Common Market. The proposition had been hotly opposed by all Republicans. And the results for all Republicans had been an electoral disaster: 83% of the voters had supported entry. The voters of Fianna Fáil and Fine Gael followed the party line and the negative voters were approximately equal to Labour's share of the previous general election. In point of fact, a case could be made that the Republicans had no effect, except perhaps to produce more votes in favor. In the North the Provos might have bombed Stormont down, but in the South their campaign had been a dud. Lynch now had not only a mandate to go into Europe with Tricolor flying but also a mandate to use a firmer hand against the IRA. The government brought in a strict Prison Bill and Special Courts. On May 31, Rory Brady was arrested. The Provo GHQ went on the run, although Joe Cahill was soon arrested. To the Southern establishment events after the British imposition of direct rule had seemed to erode the Provos political position and the worst might be over.

In the North, the British security forces could hardly be that sanguine.

The various movements for peace seemed to gain ground briefly then sputter out in recriminations. And always there was the incident that checked any move toward stability. The British troops in the Markets area ran into the popular Official leader Joe McCann. Unarmed he was "shot trying to escape"—murdered, according to the rumor spread immediately through the Falls. On April 19, after a highly emotional funeral, the crowd was addressed by Cathal Goulding, swearing vengeance on British imperialism. For a time it appeared the Officials would go over to the offensive. And the Provos had never let up. Beginning in March with a huge explosion in Shipquay Street in Derry, the Provos had introduced the carbomb, a device that soon produced empty city centers pocked with smoldering rubble, vast no-parking zones, and a further decay in civilian morale. In Protestant areas, Tartan Gangs, half political, half criminal, moved out of the slums into a position as defender of their own no-go areas. Sectarian shooting became widespread, and some suspected more organized. The Ulster Defense Association began open drilling in May. The Officials' ceasefire on May 29 had no visible effect on the Protestants. And the bombing continued, three or four explosions a day. Even in the South Lynch's policy of suppression faltered—after a hunger strike both Cahill and Brady were released and there were signs that persecution of Republicans might produce violence. There seemed to be no way out of the spiral of violence, a spiral that by June everyone feared might lead to civil war, a war that might spread to the South.

The SDLP attempted to bring the British and the bombers to the bargaining table. As long as internment lasted, the leadership of the SDLP felt they could take part in no formal negotiations. In any case, as Gerry Fitt had pointed out, if the SDLP had talked to anyone they would have represented no one. Now in the decaying situation John Hume in particular sought means to get the Provos talking. During June intricate and subtle negotiations were carried out between the SDLP and Whitelaw's people and simultaneously with the Provos. By June 17, London was sufficiently serious to permit the release of the Provo leader Gerry Adams from prison to take part in any future discussions. It was by then clear that, barring accidents, the Provos were going to get to a bargaining table. On June 20 and 22, O'Connell and Adams met twice with Whitelaw's negotiators and arranged for a truce during which the Brish Army would end harassment and de-escalate in sensitive areas. If the truce lasted a reasonable time, there would be a Provo-Whitelaw meeting. O'Connell called through to Dublin and Mac Stiofáin agreed. Word was released that afternoon, Thursday, that the Provos would suspend operations the following Monday at mid-

night. During the last four days there was no letup in the campaign—
four British soldiers and a RUC man were killed. Monday at midnight,
however, an eerie quiet fell over Ulster. The quiet was soon broken by
rising Protestant protests that the British Army seemed unwilling to
contain and, more ominously, by the continuing murders—sixteen between June 27 and July 9. But the truce held and out of sight the Provos
were preparing for the meeting with Whitelaw.

The British Cabinet accepted Whitelaw's analysis that a Provo truce
could be achieved at little real cost and that the longer it lasted the
more difficult would become an IRA return to open violence. Heath
knew the dangers of talking to the bombers but was willing to cover for
Whitelaw. The Provos felt that a dialogue was desirable even if a
return to the campaign was inevitable. The key demand was that the
future of Ireland was to be determined by the whole people of Ireland,
eliminating the Ulster Protestant veto ceded by Westminster in the
Government of Ireland Act 1949. And of course they would insist on a
date for British withdrawal. There was in the summer of 1972 little
chance that Whitehall or Heath wanted to consider even the faint
prospect of any all-Ireland decision or immediate withdrawal, but a
discussion of British difficulties, the restraints on the Cabinet, the potential Protestant reaction might introduce a sense of reality in Provo
considerations. So far their approach had appeared to be a combination of niggling tactics and slogans devoid of any grasp of the com-
plexity of the problem. Even if the Provos held to the slogans, if the
whole affair collapsed around Whitelaw, which given the nature of the
Provos was a distinct possibility, there were other advantages to be
gained. Word could be, would be, leaked to Dublin; and Jack Lynch,
outflanked by the bombers, might be forced to take stronger action.
Lynch was as eager to take stronger action as the British, but London
persisted in feeling that he was difficult. London took longer than most
to realize that not only did many in the Irish Republic not want a united
Ireland in any form but that they would pursue policies dedicated to
preventing such an unpleasant eventuality. In any case, talking could not
hurt too much and Whitelaw indicated the time had come.

On Friday, July 7, the Provo delegation, Mac Stiofáin, O'Connell,
Twomey, Martin McGuinness, C/O of Derry, Gerry Adams, Ivor Bell
from Belfast, and Myles Shevlin from Sinn Féin (Kevin Street), arrived
by courtesy of the RAF at a house in Chelsea to meet Whitelaw and
three members of his ministerial team. The Provos had at last arrived at
the bargaining table. Mac Stiofáin made the Provos' point, stressing
the key demand for an all-Ireland decision. Whitelaw's insistence on the
validity of the Government of Ireland Act was brushed aside and his

concern about the Protestant reaction was not considered a serious matter. In the first case what Westminster had done it could undo, and in the second the old Orange Card was frayed with use. The Provos wanted a relatively swift response to their prepared list of demands. Some of the military demands on the list relating to the North were less sweeping, certainly possible to negotiate. Both sides agreed there would be another meeting in a week when the British would respond to the Provos' list. On this note the meeting broke up. Negotiations had begun, however faint the chance to accommodate the purity of the Army Council's demands with the reality of the British position. And the truce was running.

Two days later on July 9, a forceable rehousing attempt by Catholics in Lenadoon Avenue in Belfast brought a confrontation with the British Army. The Catholics apparently wanted the British Army to back off as they had recently done for the Protestants in a similar situation. The British Army, unaware of the implications of their refusal, had decided on a show of force. Neither Seamus Twomey on the spot nor Dave O'Connell in Dublin could get through to authorities sufficiently knowledgeable to call off the Army. O'Connell did get Whitelaw on the telephone but the situation on Lenadoon Avenue continued to deteriorate and there was no subsequent word from London. The Saracens went in, then rubber bullets and a water cannon and CS gas, and at last real bullets. That was the end of the truce. The Army Council in Dublin assumed that all bets were off, and to gain some benefit from their negotiations revealed on July 10 that they had talked to Whitehall in London.

Not only was the truce over, but there was no hope of patching it up. Whitehall had been caught out, talking with terrorists. It was an occupation he could not renew. For the time being there was to be no more negotiation, only force met with force as the IRA campaign entered still another phase.

NOTES

1. During his time in prison for the Felsted raid, John Stephenson taught himself Irish and emerged as Seán Stephenson at first and finally as Seán Mac Stiofáin the SeánMac of the Provos.
2. Both Republican movements organized a whole new set of clubs and committees both in England and in America—and often wherever there were exiled Irish but the great success story was that of the

Provisionals. In America Jack McCarthy, John McGowan, and Michael Flannery put together the Irish Northern Aid Committee and collected huge sums for Republican purposes. There were more covert channels for financing arms purchases and equally large sums of money involved. Five Irish-Americans, in fact, ended in prison for refusing to answer grand jury questions concerning arms shipments—and isolated far from New York in a Fort Worth prison they still refused to answer.

3. Dave O'Connell, Moira McGuire as translator, who subsequently defected from the Movement, kept one step ahead of a variety of police forces on the continent when one large scale attempt collapsed. It would appear that in several cases the arms source was, in fact, British intelligence or agents thereof.

4. For border operations see the appropriate section in P. Michael O'Sullivan, *Patriot Graves, Resistance in Ireland*, Chicago, 1972.

5. *Sunday Times* Insight Team, *Ulster*, Harmondsworth (Middlesex), 1972, p. 213.

6. *Cf.* Frank Kitson, *Low Intensity Operation, Subversion, Insurgency & Peacekeeping*, Harrisburg (Pa.) 1971. Kitson saw service in Kenya, Malaya, Oman, Cyprus, and Northern Ireland.

7. Despite the number of bombing operations, the Provos' technique left much to be desired. Not only was the technical level of the various devices a generation out of date but also the volunteers' experience and training was limited. The inevitable result was a series of premature explosions that killed and maimed over a score of volunteers. Safety precautions were ignored in the name of expediency or out of ignorance—and the toll was worse than inflicted by the British Army during the height of bombing operation.

8. *Ulster*, p. 309.

CHAPTER XX

The Bloody Watershed, 1972–1974

The inability of the IRA to maintain the truce, a matter of luck, bad communications, differing priorities, and Whitelaw's failure to intervene, reduced the Provos' options. The revelation of the talks, a grievous lapse, meant that it would be some time, if ever, before the Provos returned to British bargaining table. Yet anyone with exposure to Irish Republicans realized that no one else could talk *for* them, certainly not Blaney and Co. or the SDLP or the self-appointed. Now the British government was also unable to talk *to* them once Whitehall and the Cabinet had been caught out. British policy was to make talk unnecessary. On July 24, Whitehall announced that the first aim was to destroy the IRA. In Commons during the debate on Northern Ireland two weeks after the collapse of the truce, Whitelaw assured Captain Willie Orr, leader of the Unionists, that no one would again sit down with representatives of the Provisional IRA. The Provos' response was to redouble their campaign efforts. The bombing and sniping began again. On July 21, alone, there were 21 explosions in Belfast that killed 11 and injured 130 people. On July 27, 4,000 more British troops arrived. It became clear that at last the British Army intended to break up the no-go zones in Belfast and Derry. When the troops moved in—Operation Motorman—at our A.M. Monday morning, July 31, they found no opposition. The IRA had withdrawn to safe houses or across the border.

The British now began a dual policy: talk to anyone but the IRA and simultaneously attempt to reduce the level of violence in Ulster to tolerable proportions. It proved easier to talk than to wind down the Provos. It was becoming increasingly obvious that in the South, faint protests aside, Lynch wanted nothing but the quiet life. No responsible group supported the IRA campaign, and the hard-liners had little influence. Kevin Boland's effort to start a *real* Republican Party, Aontacht Eireann launched June 1971, had floundered. Blaney was still popular in his district but isolated, and Haughey was creeping back into Fianna Fáil. Any British initiative that was not an open concession to the Orange ultras would probably be greeted with relief in Dublin. In the North, the SDLP wanted to talk if the British would just be willing to make the odd concession—internment was still a difficult corner for the SDLP leaders to turn. There were even some individuals drifting toward the

middle—the Northern Labour Party or the Alliance Party—who were
eager to talk. The respectable Unionist, of course, would listen and the
radical Protestants would talk, but it was doubtful if the British would
listen. Vanguard and Craig wanted no concessions and the SDLP wanted
more. So everyone talked about talking.

Irish Foreign Minister Dr. Patrick Hillery met Whitelaw on August 9
and the SDLP on August 7. London announced there were to be all-party
talks in September. Heath and Lynch met in Munich during the Olym-
pics. The SDLP had talks with the government in Dublin. There were
extensive clandestine contacts. In September the all-party conference, as
predicted, produced nothing—the major factions did not show up. All
the negotiations produced a sense of momentum but little had changed
for the better in the North. The bombs continued to go off in Derry
and Belfast, although bombing operations were more difficult to launch
without the no-go zones. Sniping continued as the Provos tried to reduce
civilian casualties. And, of course, there were the searches and sweeps,
the interrogations and arrests, the arms found and the IRA officer
captured, the British soldiers killed and wounded, and increasingly
there was the rising toll of sectarian murders. By the end of September
343 people had been killed during 1972 and there seemed to be no
end in sight. The British diplomatic efforts had led nowhere; and
despite the optimism of the British Army, the violence continued. The
Provo Army Council was relatively content with events.

The Provisional Army Council in the autumn of 1972 overestimated
their assets and undervalued their opponents' cards. Basically the Northern campaign was consuming assets—men and equipment and opportunities—that were difficult to replace. While it was true that some sort
of campaign could be continued almost indefinitely, the British Army
could to a degree reduce the campaign level once the no-go zones had
come down. Unless the IRA could find new means to escalate—new
weapons, new tactics, or a new combat zone—or unless the British Army
blundered—a new Bloody Sunday—the military odds were on the side
of the British, particularly if the IRA's popular support eroded.
And as the campaign dragged on, the Nationalist population in the
North would eventually weary and settle for a bit of peace and quiet,
decent reforms, and an end to murder; fewer would be willing to sacrifice for a united Ireland tomorrow when they could have peace with
justice today. Repeatedly there had been pressure for a truce. Few
would want or dare, however, to deny the IRA and depend for security
solely on the British Army or the RUC; but there was and would be a
general desire that the IRA go over to the defensive. Revolutionaries,
of course, acting in the name of the people have never been willing

to permit the nation's liberation to depend on a popular vote. Still there was bound to be less support and more opposition to the Provos' military activities at the very time when escalation was needed to force the British back to the bargaining table. That escalation would be made even more difficult by the growing confidence of Lynch's government in the South. The Army Council recognized the drift of Lynch but again not how severe the repression would be or extent of the difficulties it might cause. Essentially the Provos seemed to be planning for better days instead of worse.

On October 6, the police closed the Kevin Street office of Sinn Féin. On October 28, a bomb was found in Dublin's Connolly Station and firebombs exploded in four Dublin hotels—the fear that violence might come south of the border was very real. On November 1, there was a cross-border raid, this time into Donegal by the Ulster Defense Association who promised more to come if the Irish government did not curb the IRA. Lynch's cabinet was by November more than willing to curb the Provos. On October 30, the British government issued a Green Paper suggesting the shape of an eventual solution. The Irish government, pleased with the vague mention of an Irish dimension, expressed mild approval. Potential Orange opposition was placated with the publication on November 1 of a plebiscite bill that would permit the Protestants to exercise their veto over a united Ireland.[1] On November 16, Heath came to Ireland to warn that there would be no Orange unilateral declaration of independence *a la* Rhodesia, a favorite strategem of the ultras that had a certain emotional appeal but little basis in reality. Thus by mid-November things seemed to be quickening politically in the North. The lines of an accommodation were being drawn largely in London with Dublin's consent. The Provos' campaign seemed to be running down. In Dublin at the Sinn Féin Ard-Fheis at the end of October, there had been no sign of moderation. Mac Stiofáin had insisted that the British must accept the Provo conditions—an all-Ireland solution, withdrawal of the British Army, and amnesty for all prisoners and detainees. None of the politicians in London, Belfast, or Dublin paid much heed.

The British were apparently securely wedded to the plebiscite concept—no secession without majority consent—and confident that the Army was getting on top of the IRA. In Dublin, the Irish government too sensed that the Provos had run out of momentum. The time had come to close them down. On November 19, Mac Stiofáin was arrested. He was charged two days later and it became clear he was on a hunger and thirst strike. Without liquids he could live for only another week before his outside limits would be reached. By the time he was sentenced on November 25, all the old Irish revolutionary memories had once more come into play. The drama of his life and death struggle awoke romantic Ireland. Carried from the Court he shouted "I will be dead in six days, live with that". Those that had been only barely interested in Northern events since Bloody Sunday suddenly became emotionally involved in Mac Stiofáin's fate. There were prayers and vigils. The demonstrations began. The foreign correspondents began once more to arrive in Dublin, and in distant places Ireland was once more hard news. Dublin seemed gripped in an emotional hysteria as the hours crept by. The government, however, had set its course and was willing to live with it.

On November 22, a draconian amendment to the Offenses Against the State Bill had been introduced in the Dáil. This would permit conviction of a suspect solely on the testimony of a police officer, i.e., his belief alone that a man was a member of an illegal organization. There was violent opposition to the amendment from both Labour and Fine Gael in the name of civil rights and a call at least for moderating amendments. Fianna Fáil held firm. As the debate continued it appeared that the government's Offenses against the State (Amendment) bill would fail. It was obvious that Fianna Fáil could then go to the country on a Law and Order platform. From past experience Fianna Fáil knew that, emotional as it might be, a hunger strike would not make any difference in a general election and the civil rights position of Fine Gael and Labour would win them no votes. Lynch could hardly lose either—he got his bill or an increased majority.

Outside the protest meetings had grown larger. After a rally at the GPO, 7,000 demonstrators marched on the Mater Hospital where Mac Stiofáin was held. In the turmoil, an IRA team, two disguised as priests, attempted to spring Mac Stiofáin. The attempt collapsed and five IRA volunteers were arrested. On November 27, Mac Stiofáin was moved to the Curragh, back in use for Republican prisoners. It was the ninth day and time was running out. In the North the Active Service Units responded with an unexpected series of rocket attacks on British posts and patrols. The simultaneous use of the Russian-made RPG-7 rocket launcher would have been even more devastating if the volunteers had been more experienced. But the point was made—the campaign was far from over with or without Mac Stiofáin. The Army Council had already appointed Seamus Twomey, C/O of Belfast, as the new C/S. Finally on November 28 at the request of Father MacManus, who feared open fighting in the South if Mac Stiofáin died, the hunger-and-thirst strike ended when he took a sip of water with the Host. Although Mac Stiofáin continued his hunger strike, it was clear that he would live.[2] In the North IRA attacks continued. In the South, the Dáil debate did too.

There no longer seemed any way to keep the country from a general election that neither Labour nor Fine Gael wanted but neither could avoid without destroying their credibility. The crucial vote would come on December 1 and, it was assumed, then dissolution. Then came two huge bomb explosions in the center of Dublin, literally within hours of the final vote. The city was horrified: 2 men were killed and 127 other people injured. Two hours after the second bomb detonated behind Clerys in Sackville Place, Fine Gael withdrew the crucial amendment with considerable haste and in many cases unhidden glee. Now, in the very knick, there was a decent reason for such a government measure. The bill promptly passed 69 to 22 in an atmosphere reported as euphoric. It was clear, of course, even before the swift denials by both the Officials and Provos, that the only people the bombs did not help in some way were Irish Republicans, excluding the casualties who were soon forgotten in the excitement of the Dáil events. Lynch had his bill and the authorization to come down on the Provos with the boot. Labour and Fine Gael did not have to face a general election. The British were assured that stringent pressure would soon be exerted on IRA activities in the South. Everywhere there would be more room for the politicians to maneuver as the Provos were shifted off stage center.

During December, the Southern police arrested many of the more prominent members of Sinn Féin (Kevin Street) including Rory Brady, those members of the Provos from the South that did not find a safe haven, and many of the Northerners on the run like Martin McGuinness of Derry who had thought the South would be a safe haven. By the end of the year, there was once more evidence that the campaign had begun to run down hill. In the four months before Operation Motorman, the British reported 500 explosions and 5,940 shooting incidents and in the four months following 393 explosions and 2,833 shooting incidents. The British claimed as well that 500 persons had been arrested and charged with serious offenses and some 200 Provisional IRA officers had been arrested. The Provo Army Council was now on the run and a number of very useful people had been arrested in the South. Yet during December despite the pressure in the North and South, there had been 506 shooting incidents and 48 explosions along with the rocket attacks. If the British considered the campaign winding down, then at the December rate the tolerable level of violence that Maudling had mentioned the previous December was as far off as ever.

Irish political maneuvers continued, violence or no violence. In February Lynch called for a surprise general election, hoping to take advantage of a variety of immediate economic and political pluses and catch the potential Fine Gael–Labour alliance by surprise. The smart money was on Lynch with an increased majority. The Fine Gael–Labour coalition largely ignored the North and ran on a variety of bread and butter issues. And Fianna Fáil's long tenure in office and overconfidence began to tell. On February 28, in a very narrow squeak, the Coalition won.[3] After years in power Fianna Fáil had used up its welcome. Liam Cosgrave took over as Taoiseach. For Republicans it had been a case of throw the rascals in, for Cosgrove, if possible, had less sympathy with their aims and methods than Lynch. The only glimmer of comedy relief was that the Labour spokesman on the North and a most articulate critic of Republican postures and programs, Conor Cruise O'Brien, became Minister of Posts and Telegraphs, not that this would stop his assaults on Republican dignity. The next week on March 8 in the North, the plebiscite on the future of the Six Counties produced the expected results. Protestant-Unionist districts voted to continue the British connection and Catholic-Nationalist districts did not vote. The only unexpected election day event was the detonation of car bombs, this time in front of symbolic targets in London, Old Bailey and Great Scotland Yard. One man died soon after the explosion and 200 people were injured. The bombing operation, authorized by the Army Council, had not come as a surprise to British intelligence which arrested most of those involved before they could make their way back to Ireland. Once again politics and bombs seemed intimately connected in Six County politics.[4]

The British attempt to push on ahead and ignore the level of violence was to a degree aided by the growing concern with the increase in sectarian murder. During 1972 there had been 121 "assassinations"—81 Catholics and 40 Protestants—most killed solely because they could be identified as a member of the enemy faith. Increasingly the backlash that the Provos had for so long labeled "myth" appeared too real. The British hoped that the cycle of murders would concentrate the minds of the alienated Catholic population. The key to any political thaw was the long promised White Paper that described the various institutions that would replace Stormont. The response, as might have been expected, was mixed but with the exception of the Provos all Northern factions indicated grudging interest. Some indication of the Provos' vision of the future came on March 28 when an attempt to run five tons of arms and ammunition, donated to the anti-imperialist struggle by Colonel Qaddafi of Libya, into the South aborted. The gunrunner *Claudia* with Joe Cahill aboard was picked up in Irish territorial waters—another coup for British intelligence.[5]

In the North, British security forces did not do as well. The major task in April and May was to pacify the hard-core areas, cripple the Provo hold on the ghettos so that the June elections to the new provincial assembly could take place. Despite repeated contention to the contrary by various military spokesmen that the Provos had been severely damaged, neither Belfast nor Derry could be called pacified. In fact by mid-April, the very effort to wind down the Provos had escalated civilian opposition to the British Army. In the Ardoyne the Paras had, according to the locals, taken to shooting suspected IRA men on sight. And as always there were incidents, gunmen shot who turned out to be boys or innocent, British soldiers hit by snipers, landmines on country lanes, and still the bombs. The new British operations launched with such confidence might well prove more effective than similar drives in the past by the Provo Army Council was not so convinced. Dave O'Connell had slipped into Belfast on Easter Sunday to deliver the oration at the Republican plot. There once more he expressed confidence that the campaign would lead to a successful conclusion.

Increasingly on a military level, the going became more difficult for the Provos. This by no means indicated a sudden return to tranquility, for even during the first six months of 1973 Provo operations had expended 8,000 pounds of explosives. Indeed, repeated rocket and mortar attacks on British positions and camps added a new dimension to the campaign. Still, the elimination of the no-go zones, the ceaseless arrests and detentions, the general desire of the Catholic population in the North for a bit of quiet, and the growing repression in the South limited activities. Each arrest of a key figure had to be made good under difficult conditions with worsening communications. When Gerry Adams, who had replaced Seamus Twomey as C/O of Belfast, was lifted while visiting his wife, the Belfast Brigade took a week or so to reorganize. Operations along the border of Monaghan had been severely hampered with the loss of J. B. O'Hagan and Kevin Mallon, both arrested in the South. In fact in the South, the most visible Republicans continued to be arrested even when their activities appeared quite legitimate. Eamon Thomas, editor of *An Phoblacht,* was arrested and on August 3 sentenced to fifteen months for being a member of the IRA. Still, in the North, the Active Service Units managed to detonate 167 bombs during July and August. The sniping, cross-border raids, ambushes on the lanes and bombs in the towns continued on into autumn. By then a more ominous, if not unexpected, development had occurred.

On August 18, fire bombs were found in Harrod's department store in London. On August 20, carrier-bag bombs damaged shops in Hampstead and more fire bombs were found in Liberty's store on Regent Street. Book bombs and more fire bombs followed. On August 24, two people were injured in an explosion in the London Stock Exchange.

The series of small but vicious little explosions continued and on August 27 extended to Washington where a secretary lost a hand when a letter bomb exploded in the British Embassy. During September the bombs became larger and casualties more serious. On September 12, five people were injured in a larger explosion in Chelsea and that was essentially the end of the "campaign". While there was serious concern in London and considerable publicity, a few incidents elsewhere and extensive security measures, there were several strange factors. First, the Provos in Dublin appeared to dither on accepting or denying responsibility. Second, a "campaign" of such minimal proportions with such ineffectual match box devices served only to alert British security forces and alienate the British public with no Republican returns. Despite past incompetence on the part of IRA bombers, this time there were many Republicans convinced that the bombing was the responsibility of British security. While hardly likely, a series of spectacular disclosures concerning British agents in Ireland gave some credence to the charge. It appeared that the British might well have been implicated in robberies, explosions, and shootings in the South, all timed for maximum British purpose. In the North the activities of British security agents in extralegal operations had long been accepted even by many of the skeptical. Be that as it might, the rash of bombs in Britain had done the Provos little good. What might well concern British security was Seán Mac Stiofáin's suggestion that if the Provos so chose Britain could be well and truly bombed. Certainly for several years British security had taken exceptional pains to limit Republican activity and to penetrate the Irish community in Britain to forestall just such an eventuality.

As had always been the case with Republican campaigns, a significant role was played in the prisons, schools for the future, pressure groups for the present—and too often site of schism. The few but spectacular escapes from the Maidenstone prison ship or out of Long Kesh had made the boredom of the new generation of felons easier to bear. In the South prison pressure was exerted in order to achieve political treatment, a confrontation with authority that had a long and painful history. Despite the evidence of the past, the hunger strike remained the chosen weapon. The eight volunteers involved in the March bombings in London, sentenced to life prison terms, immediately went on a hunger strike in Winchester prison to force transfer to Northern Ireland prisons and political treatment. In Dublin the sixty Republicans in Mountjoy had on October 3 won sufficient concessions to permit the end of their hunger strike. Generally, however, the hunger strike continued to offer more dangers than advantages. Of all the prison activities, as usual, the escape had the greatest appeal, and the Provos managed perhaps the most spectacular of all prison breaks in Irish Republican history, injecting new life into what appeared a faltering purpose. In Dublin a film producer with an American accent hired a helicopter for some filming in County Louth. When the helicopter arrived on location on October 31, an IRA unit appeared, the American "producer" disappeared, and the pilot received new orders. The helicopter flew into Dublin and dropped down into the exercise yard of Mountjoy to the amazement of all. The stunned guards, unarmed and unprepared—was this a ministerial visit?—could do nothing but watch as Seamus Twomey, Kevin Mallon, and J. B. O'Hagen clambered aboard to the cheers of the Provo prisoners. The helicopter then disappeared over the wall, flitted to the outskirts of Dublin, and landed. The pilot could only report that the Provos had been met and driven off. Neither the road blocks nor the intense security manhunt produced any clues. Twomey re-emerged to give one of those interviews that so frustrated Irish security men to *Der Spiegel,* indicating that the Provos were preparing to go on the offensive. More important, Republican prisoners everywhere—and there were nearly fourteen hundred— felt that their turn to flit might come next and in any case they had not been forgotten.

On their part, the British could feel that however spectacular a helicopter escape might be and disturbing the continued violence in the North, the Provos had become increasingly irrelevant to the major direction of Irish events. The elections in June for the new Assembly had indicated that very little middle ground existed, which should have surprised no one; but despite the limited success of the Alliance Party, the splintering of Unionism, and the doubts of the SDLP, there still appeared to be an opportunity to form an executive of those opposed to the men of violence. After June, for months every effort was exerted by Whitelaw and the British to persuade the moderate Unionists clustered around Brian Faulkner and the representatives of the SDLP to share power in a coalition government. Both had to placate the suspicious. Craig and Paisley adamantly opposed the Assembly and power-sharing and Faulkner. So did many Unionists. On November 20, Faulkner won only a ten vote margin in the 750-man Unionist party council. The SDLP with internment still in force, police reform outstanding, and only vague hints as to the ultimate composition of the proposed Council of Ireland feared contamination by association with their old enemy Faulkner. Prime Minister Heath had come to Northern Ireland in an attempt to fashion the coalition by using a carrot and stick strategy. He expressed impatience and indicated Britain might tire of the problem. Then in Dublin after a long conference with Cosgrave he appeared to reverse his position and indicated that total integration with Britain be a real possibility. He appeared to be threatening everyone with what they wanted — evacuation or integration. Simultaneously Dublin urged the SDLP to seek an accommodation. For a variety of reasons on the evening of November 21, the Faulkner Unionists, despite their ten vote margin, the SDLP representatives, despite their doubts, and the Alliance Party, despite their limited representation, agreed to form a coalition executive. The militant Unionists were outraged, promising to continue the struggle, to oppose with political means or in some cases bombs the new Assembly and most of all the proposed Council of Ireland — the Irish dimension agreed to at the four-day tripartite talks at Sunningdale, in December. Even before Sunningdale, the Provos had hit back at the "politicians". IRA units blew up tracks and a bridge on the Belfast-Derry railroad, set off a mine near Omagh that wounded two soldiers and a civilian, and ambushed and wounded a militiaman in Strabane. On the evening of November 21, a Provo unit machine gunned the house of SDLP leader Austin Currie, long anathema to Republicans. Further action against collaborators was threatened. On November 24, three police and army posts were attacked in Derry and two soldiers killed near Bogside. There was a bomb attack on an army post near the Divis Flats, Belfast, and a hooded body left in the markets area. As usual the middle ground in Ulster appeared to erode almost before it had become visible to the optimistic eye.

In fact, polarization had apparently grown during 1973 with the rise of Unionist militancy. The old wild men — the Craigs, John Taylors, and Paisleys — had unexpected and violent competition from new groups. Some like the Red Hand Commando Group appeared to be little more than murder gangs intent on random assassination and bombings without prior warnings. Others like the Ulster Freedom Fighters and the Ulster Citizens Army had more pretensions if they remained equally obscure. Their militant rivals claimed that both were pro-Communist, probably in touch with the Official IRA, which in the Protestant North is to be in league with the devil. Despite this the Ulster Freedom Fighters expressed loyalty to the ideals of Craig and Paisley and, of course, opposition to any Council of Ireland. Their opposition took the form of bombing Catholic churches and pubs with the threat of more to come. There continued, sanctioned or not, a campaign of murder, cross-border assassinations and bombing, and attacks on Catholic districts. At the same time, Protestant politics became complex, cut through by personalities and competing cliques, increasingly subject to recourse to violence. There was serious concern among the politically minded that some groups were being exploited for private gain and crime hidden under Orange oratory. The most visible evidence of the rifts and jealousies surfaced on Sunday, September 16, when the body of Tommy Herron, former vice-chairman of the Ulster Defence Association, was found in a ditch in Drumbo, County Antrim. In a flurry of accusations that included the British security forces, his associates pointedly had not suggested the IRA as a potential culprit. Differences aside — whether the wild men of the Shankill or the more urbane colleagues of Craig — the militants with substantial emotional and political assets felt that the fragile exercise in power-sharing devised by Whitelaw and the British to be a distasteful but temporary experiment. At the end of 1973, they, like the Provos, had no intention of putting the gun on the shelf.

On Tuesday, January 1, the new year began with the first meeting of the Northern Ireland Executive under Brian Faulkner. In the New Year's Honour's List William Whitelaw, former Secretary of State for Northern Ireland, was made a Companion of Honour. On the following day one of the first spin-offs of Sunningdale occurred when the Anglo-Irish Law Enforcement Commission announced its first meeting would take place on January 16. In an interview in the Belfast *Sunday News* on January 6, the often erratic Loyalist Desmond Boal called for a federal solution to the Irish problem. The politicans were back in business after still another year dominated by the gunmen. Much of this movement was little more than illusion. Those in the middle of the Ulster road were still vulnerable to speeding fanatics and the crush of old loyalties. On January 4, the Ulster Unionist Council had supported a motion rejecting the Council of Ireland contained in the Sunningdale Agreement by a vote of 454 to 374. Thus Faulkner had been rejected by his own and announced his resignation on January 7. He would have to put together a "new" Unionist Party dedicated to power sharing and Sunningdale. With his forces still in disarray, he was stunned a month later when Prime Minister Heath called a surprise General Election for February 28. Loyalist opposition to his policies was extensive, apparently growing, and not limited to the para-militaries and the Paisleyites. Although he had kept all but two of his fellow Assembly members, Unionist sentiment outside had hardened — power sharing and the Council of Ireland were an anathema to most Loyalists.

Despite general satisfaction after Sunningdale in Dublin, there, too, were the unrepentent like Kevin Boland, leader of his small splinter party Aontacht Eireann, who started action in the High Court in Dublin because he felt the Sunningdale Agreement violated the Irish

Constitution's claim to the entire island. Of course, both the Provisional and Official Republican movements hated the new direction nearly as much as the Loyalists. For the Officials it was a middle-class manoeuvre to exploit the workers and for the Provisionals one more betrayal by Irish politicans desperate for a piece of the action. The Officials, maintaining their unilateral truce, did nothing but agitate. The Provos while welcoming Boal's federalism idea simply kept up the military pressure of their campaign. *Their* 1974 had begun with bombs in Belfast, County Fermanagh, at Portadown, County Armagh, and with two explosions in Birmingham. *Their* New Year's message was that "We look forward with confidence to 1974 as a year in which the British rule in Ireland shall be destroyed and the curse of alien power banished from our land for all time."[6]

The Provo bombing campaign in England continued with the usual inexplicable variety of targets. On January 5, bombs exploded in Madame Tussaud's wax museum and at the Earl's Court boat show. There were, too, more relevant sites — on the following day a thirty-pound bomb was found outside the London home of General Sir Cecil Blacker, Adjutant General of the British Army. On February 4, a bomb exploded in the boot of a coach carrying service personnel on the M4 Motorway from Manchester to Catterick Camp killing eleven people: eight soldiers, two children and a woman. In Ulster there was no evidence of a slackening of the campaign, more bombs, more sniping in the countryside, more robberies and blast-bombs and incendiary devices. During January, a novel operation occurred when three armed men and a woman of an increasingly independent Active Service Unit hijacked a commercial helicopter in County Donegal and forced the pilot to fly them over the Strabane RUC station where they dropped two milk-churn bombs. Neither detonated. On other fronts four prisoners in England, including the two Price sisters serving life plus twenty years for the March 1973 London car bombings, were on a prolonged hunger strike and being force-fed. In Dublin on January 30, the Provos phoned in a series of bomb hoaxes to draw attention to the hunger strikers.

On the following day, the random assassinations by Protestant paramilitaries continued when the Ulster Freedom Fighters shot and killed two Catholic electricity workers and wounded three others at Rush Park, Newtownabbey, County Antrim. The Provisional IRA in Dublin had just released a statement welcoming a recent Ulster Volunteer Force statement calling for an end to the killings and accusing the British of sponsoring a killer squad. The problem during 1972-1973 for the Provos, often approached by them almost sub-

minally, was that the more effective they were against the security
orces the more likely were the threatened Loyalists to respond with
ectarian assassinations. While the Provos could protect their own
olunteers and the Catholics deep in the ghettos or in certain closed
arish lands, they could not protect every Catholic, especially the
solated. Thus the contacts with the UVF and various other militant
roups in various places and at various times by both the Officials and
rovos sought – largely without success – to find a mutuality of
nterests opposed to the British presence. Some Loyalists might be
ttracted to the idea but there seemed ample gunmen left at the end
f the lane to continue the killings, and all these "pro-British" killers
ould not be SAS squads.[7]

The Protestant backlash was not the only Provo problem for the
ecurity forces had their successes as well. The Belfast Brigade that
ad been able to function despite excessive pressure – first Cahill
ad left for Dublin to become Quartermaster General and then his
uccessor Twomey to become Chief of Staff after MacStiofáin's
rrest – but in July 1973, C/O Gerry Adams had been lifted and
nterned. On February 24, his replacement Ivor Bell was arrested
nly to escape on April 15 and be arrested again on April 28. The
ew C/O Seán Convery lasted only until March 8 and was picked up
long with Frank Fitzsimmons of the 1st Battalion. In turn C/O
ernard Hughes was arrested on May 10 with Denis Loughlin. It
as a bad spring in Belfast for the Provos but still the Brigade con-
nued operations despite the shifts at the top. On March 7, a five-
undred-pound bomb in a hijacked van was detonated in front of
he former Grand Central Hotel used as a command post for the
irst Royal Horse Artillery. Then, three weeks later, on March 28, a
econd van with a six-hundred-pound bomb exploded in the same
lace causing £750,000 damage and devastating the street. The Provos
ow employed proxy lorry-bombs, forcing a driver to take the bomb
o the target and then to warn the authorities thus keeping IRA
olunteers out of the reach of the security forces. Bombing in
elfast city centre had grown more difficult.

While in Ireland the Provos could manage to live with arrests and
etentions, the new techniques and tactics of the security forces in
he North, and the growing hard line in the South, the English bomb-
ng campaign from the first had been more difficult. First, the British
olice had excellent intelligence, going back decades, on any overt
ympathisers. It was often difficult for the Provos to recruit and use
ew people from the Irish community so that Active Service Units
ere sent over from Ireland, often to make their own way with

limited local help. Any bombing operation met serious obstacles. An
Irish accent was noted in non-Irish districts; hiring a car, much less
buying an alarm clock, was a risk. Odd movements, strange hours
unexplained appearance plus bad luck and carelessness — what the
British police call the Paddy Factor — put the campaign in regular
jeopardy. What the Provos had going for them was the assurance of
new volunteer replacements who knew and accepted the risks that
they might run. The British could and did arrest most of the active
service people involved — and some not involved except in the eyes
of the police and courts. And yet, Paddy factor or not, the Army
Council could turn on and off the bombing. Even the small bombs
and failures had an accumulated effect.

In March, for example, Peter McMullen, who had bombed his
paratrooper barracks and deserted just before Bloody Sunday in
Derry, was sent over to contact one of the most effective volunteers,
Marian Coyle, twenty-six, from Derry. His targer was Claro Barracks,
a Royal Engineer depot, in Ripon, Yorkshire. Along with another
volunteer, on Tuesday evening, March 26, he placed two small bombs,
one was left in a brown leather executive brief case in a barrack corri
dor close to sleeping soldiers and another in a dark brown suitcase
nearby. The bombs were timed with two inexpensive Japanese Coral
brand alarm clocks that cost £3.15 and £2.45. The two were seen
leaving but still managed to slip away. When the bombs detonated
only the manageress of the canteen was injured — the Paddy factor.
By then that unit of the Provos was living on borrowed time, partly
because the British police were closing in and partly because the
members were increasingly involved in operations divorced from Army
Council direction. And this, like arrests, was another perpetual Provo
difficulty.

At various times certain units simply went their own way and made
their own rules. The most notoriously independent fiefdom within
the Provos was "the Republic of South Armagh"; but there were, a
well, other units, particularly in Belfast, that had acted and would
act as they saw fit, seeking revenge for sectarian murders with tit-for-
tat killings or launching special operations. In December 1973, for
example, with the four English prisoners on hunger strike being force
fed, a small group of volunteers in Andersonstown, frustrated and
angry, decided to do *something*. On December 27, almost on the spur
of the moment and without any authorization from battalion, much
less brigade, they kidnapped the German manager of Grundig,
Thomas Niedermayer. Once hustled into a safe-house, he almost
immediately collapsed with a fatal heart attack. Belfast and Dublin

had a dead man on their hands and decided to dispose of his body permanently and maintain silence — which they did despite impassioned pleas from his wife. Some stunts were less embarrassing and more closely related to Provo policy — like the helicopter bombing of the Strabane RUC station. Others caused unwanted trouble and deep embarrassment — on March 11, in the Republic, Fine Gael Senator Billy Fox, a Protestant from Monaghan, was shot and killed — by mistake but no less dead. Tit-for-tat killings or unauthorized attacks on the Officials, provoked or not, were violations of policy but difficult to prevent. Almost impossible to control were the real "independents" — often former volunteers. The most notable group that emerged in 1974 combined Eddie Gallagher's Active Service Unit, Marian Coyle and some of her English associates, including McMullen and one novel recruit — Dr. Bridget Rose Dugdale. Her name first surfaced publicly on a warrant issued on February 23 in Manchester Magistrate's Court on charges of conspiring to smuggle arms and explosives to Ulster. She was also suspected by the British army in Northern Ireland of the Strabane helicopter bombing. And she was a strange recruit — daughter of an English millionaire, at thirty-three, too old to be a rebel without a cause, she adopted the Provos and in time Eddie Gallagher, a hard man who increasingly went his own way, using the unProvo talents of Dugdale. On April 26, nineteen paintings, including a Goya, a Rubens, two Gainsboroughs and a Vermeer, valued at eight million pounds, were stolen by armed men and a woman from the home of Sir Alfred and Lady Beit near Blessington, County Wicklow. The first the Provos knew about it was the unexpected appearance of the paintings in a safehouse. Dugdale and Gallagher were on the loose, again. On May 4, in Glandor, County Cork, Gardai found all nineteen paintings in a house rented by Dugdale. She was detained under Section 30 of the Offences Against the State Act and the following day charged with the robbery and the helicopter attack. Pregnant with Gallagher's child, she was sentenced on June 25 to nine years for the art theft pleading "proudly and incorruptibly guilty".[8] By then, authorities north and south had some idea as to the size and membership of Gallagher's group, whom they suspected of involvement in actions ranging from straightforward murder of members of the Ulster Defence Regiment to the kidnapping of Lord and Lady Donoughmore on June 4.[9] They also suspected that the former Provos had been expelled, which was, indeed, the case, although in some cases contacts remained. Certainly, the Army Council was relieved to have the group go its own violent way.

In the meantime, problems or no, Dugdale or not, the Provos kept up the military pressure, partly because it was congenial, despite the risks from the Loyalist paramilitary backlash; but in the main because if Ulster was ungovernable by the new Northern Ireland Executive, it was not unreasonable to assume that the British would sooner or later withdraw. For exactly opposite reasons the Loyalist militants were determined that the new initiatives and institutions must fail and the old days return or, at least, direct British rule continue. And the results of the Westminster elections on February 28, revealed substantial 'No Surrender' support: eleven of the anti-Assembly United Ulster Unionist Council were elected with just over fifty percent of the vote. The only pro-Assembly seat was Gerry Fitt's in West Belfast. If the various Republican votes were included the anti-Assembly candidates took 58.8 percent. As usual Republicans did not fare well at the ballot box although Albert Price, the Price sisters' father, did show some strength in West Belfast (5,662 votes) but not even enough to keep Fitt out (19,554 votes). The true Loyalist felt that the Assembly had lost its mandate. The power-sharers were determined to carry on: despite the vote, despite the background music of bombs and sniping, despite the rising Loyalist militancy fanned by the familiar names of Unionism — the vitriolic Orange orators and the paramilitary gunmen.

The new Labour government of Prime Minister Harold Wilson fully supported the Northern Ireland Executive. Merlyn Rees replaced Francis Pym as Secretary of State for Northern Ireland and Stanley Orme was appointed Minister of State. On April 4, Rees in the House of Commons expressed that full support. He also gave an indication of the background to such political initiatives in that "in the year between April, 1973 and April 1, 1974, security forces searched over 4 million cars and removed from terrorists' hands nearly 1,600 weapons and over 30 tons of explosives; 19 tons found in made-up bombs. In the same period of a year, 1,292 terrorists had been charged with criminal offences, almost all of a serious nature, ranging from murder to armed robbery".[10] The advent of the Labour government brought no lessening of Provo pressure and, if anything, engendered a greater determination on the part of the militant Loyalists to bring down the Executive, if the members voted to accept the Sunningdale Agreements. The dissent and division — and the pressure on the Executive — was such that the Secretary of State for Defence Roy Mason on April 24, warned that pressure was mounting to pull the troops out unless the warring factions could hammer out a solution. The next day Wilson assured everyone that the troops would stay.

The warring factions, of course, showed no signs of hammering out a solution. The bombs and shooting incidents continued. The public squabbling and private plotting continued. On May 11, as the time for an Assembly vote on Sunningdale grew closer, the Executive Committee of the Ulster Workers' Council (UWC) threatened a province-wide, full-scale "constitutional stoppage" — a general strike.

On Tuesday, May 14, at six in the evening, the Assembly voted forty-four to twenty-eight in favour of Faulkner's amendment supporting Sunningdale. The UWC announced that the strike was on, a strike controlled not by the noted of the Unionist establishment — Craig or West or even Paisley — but by little known workers. The next day power cuts began and the BBC reported widespread intimidations. Slowly, sporadically, the Province closed down. The UWC offered to maintain essential services. The security forces urged people to report intimidation but appeared unwilling to break the strike by force — a strike that, despite statements to the contrary, seemed to be picking up support. Craig said the British must realize that they couldn't impose a government. On the following day, Friday May 17, the paramilitaries made sure that the Irish Republic realized that all were vulnerable. Without warning at five-thirty in the evening, during the Dublin rush-hour, three car bombs exploded killing twenty-two persons and injuring over a hundred, three mortally. Ninety minutes later, in Monaghan town, another bomb detonated outside a public house in North Road and killed five more people and injured several others, one fatally. It was the bloodiest day in the Troubles. No one claimed responsibility. All the responsible condemned the act with revulsion, even some of the Loyalist paramilitaries. And the strike went on. The police announced they were helpless to end intimidation. Petrol was in short supply. Postal and telephone services were disrupted. There were serious power cuts. On May 19, Rees declared a State of Emergency in the province. The UWC continued to cut down on the power supply. Sammy Smith of the Ulster Army Council demanded that Rees meet the UWC. Barricades went up, were removed, went up again. By May 21, power cuts in Belfast lasted for twelve hours and there were long queues for milk and food. Reinforcements had brought the total number of British troops up to 16,500; but it had become apparent that there was no will in London to attempt to break the strike by resort to force, or to attempt to take over the power system — only the workers knew how to run the plants. On May 24, at noon, at Chequers, Wilson met with Faulkner, Fitt and the leader of the Alliance Party, Oliver Napier. They agreed the Assembly provided the only basis for peace, order and good government. There would be no negotiations on constitutional matters. At ten-fifteen the following evening, Wilson on a BBC television and radio broadcast in a vitriolic speech castigated the strike leaders as thugs and bullies. "Who do these people think they are?" he asked calling them spongers on the British public.

Neither Wilson's venom nor appeals by all sorts of respectable and understanding politicians for right reason had any effect. The UWC would not surrender, would if necessary turn off all power and close down the province. Despite the frantic manoeuvring of the politicians within the Assembly to hold firm, Faulkner's back benchers accepted the inevitable. They urged him to ask the British government to talk with the UWC. At a vote at 12.30 p.m., on Tuesday, May 28, with the SDLP members of the Executive abstaining, it was decided that the Secretary of State Merlyn Rees should be informed that the Executive wished to see negotiations between the Government and the UWC. Faulkner met almost immediately with Rees who said that the Government would not negotiate under duress. Faulkner and the Unionist members resigned. Rees immediately issued a statement indicating that "there is now no statutory basis for the Northern Ireland Executive". Power-sharing was dead. Sunningdale was dead. The UWC had won and the general strike was called off.[11] Eventually in July the British would issue a White Paper calling for elections to a constitutional convention so that the people of Northern Ireland could play "a crucial part in determining their own future. No political structure can endure without their support" — a fact that the UWC had made abundantly clear in May.

During the dramatic two weeks of the general strike, the Provos had per force to stand idly by. Both the Officials and Provos helped provide essential services in Nationalist areas of Belfast and the background noise of bombs and snipings of the Provos continued, strike or no. For the Provos the strike was "Fascist" made possible by collusion in Dublin and the toleration of the British, especially the army. In fact most of the "lessons" learned in most quarters simply reinforced long-held prejudices. So after May 28, the Provos went back to bombing and publicizing the condition of the hunger strikers in England, the Price sisters, now very weak, Frank Stagg and Michael Gaughan. On May 18, the force-feeding of the Price sisters had ended after 167 days. Home Secretary Roy Jenkins on June 1 felt that he "must not be forced into a decision". Two days later Gaughan, twenty-four, died in Parkhurst prison, Isle of Wight on the sixty-fifth day of his hunger strike — officially of pneumonia. There were rovo rallies and parades. On June 8, the Provo British Command taff ordered Frank Stagg to end his strike and the two Price sisters nded their 206 day strike as a result of the clarification of Jenkins' une 1 statement, i.e., a deal was implied if not announced. The next ay, Sunday, June 9, a crowd of ten thousand heard Dave O'Connell ive the funeral oration for Gaughan at Ballina, County Mayo. The ampaign continued both in Ulster and in England where on June 17 a bomb detonated in Westminster and a month later on July 17 a atchel bomb went off in the Tower. On Sunday, August 18, came ome good prison news: in broad daylight nineteen Provo prisoners lasted their way through two doors at Portlaoise and escaped. Among hem were Kevin Mallon, several volunteers from the border and outh Armagh, and Eddie Gallagher, who had come in on Thursday nd left on Sunday. Despite an intensive, wide-spread police and army earch, none were recaptured and sixteen were still free at the end of he year.

In the North the Provo campaign continued – business as usual. On August 23, the Provos shot and killed Detective Inspector Peter Flanagan, head of the Special Branch in Omagh. On September 16, n Belfast the Provos shot and killed Judge Rory Conaghan and Magistrate Martin McBirney. One unanticipated result was that the Loyalist paramilitaries returned to sectarian murder. Enthusiastic bout the UWC strike, there had been a shift toward politics. The UDA and Ulster Freedom Fighters had called for a ceasefire on une 23. The Ulster Volunteer Force, newly legalised, announced he creation of a Volunteer Political Party. On August 10, the Red Hand Commandos had declared a ceasefire. After the assassination of he two judges, however, for many paramilitaries it was murder as usual. For the Provos it was bombing as usual: on October 5, five people were killed and fifty-four wounded when two no-warning bombs exploded in pubs in Guildford, Surrey. The bombs were aimed at off duty soldiers: two of the dead were servicemen and wo were servicewomen, only one was civilian. On the same day only thirty people took part in a march in Derry to commemorate he anniversary of the civil rights march of October 1968. Those days were long gone. By 1974 even the death and wounding of security orces, the murder of innocents, the bombs and the explosions, had to be particularly spectacular or unsavoury to make the foreign papers much less those in Dublin. The Troubles just went on and on with no light at the end of the tunnel. On October 10, one more Westminster General Election nearly repeated the results of February, except the normally anti-Unionist seat in Fermanagh and South

Tyrone went to Frank Maguire as an independent. The anti-Assembly UUUC received 407,778 votes to the Faulkner Unionist Party's 20,454. There was no room in the middle of the road — even the Officials' Republican Clubs beat that total with 21,633 votes. All the election did was once more, if need be, underline the polarization of the Province, boding little good for the Convention elections scheduled for May 1, 1975. Until then it was bombing as usual, riots on schedule, hunger strikes and murder as a matter of course.

It was true that the grim figures for fatalities and woundings, bombings and robberies, explosives discovered and arrests made, were all down from the previous year's total, but the sum was still appalling and there was always room for novel violence. On Tuesday evening, October 13, after months of growing tension in Long Kesh — now the Maze Prison to the British — the Republican prisoners attacked prison officers and set fire to most of the huts in the camp. Soldiers were brought in to beat the prisoners back to order. Helicopters flew over the cages sprayin CS gas into the compounds. The flames could be seen for miles. On the next day Republican women in Armagh Prison seized the Governor and three prison officers and held them in an attic. There was a prison riot at Crumlin Road in Belfast. Troops and police surrounded the prison. That evening prisoners at Magilligan in County Derry set fire to their huts. On Thursday five hundred more troops were flown into Ulster bringing the total to 15,600. The Northern Ireland Office claimed that twenty-nine prisoners, twenty-three soldiers and fourteen prison officers had been injured in the Maze. The Provos had already claimed one hundred Republicans had been injured. On Thursday the women in Armagh gave up their hostages. Then it was back to murdering and bombing as usual. The Queen's Speech at the opening of Parliament on October 29 suggested that the Convention would find a solution that included power sharing. For the militant Loyalists, still euphoric about the general strike, and the paramiltary groups, once again involved in random murder, power sharing remained an anathema, a non-starter. Once again the men of violence drowned out the politicians.

The Provos again made it clear that England as well as Ulster would suffer — Dave O'Connell in a recorded interview on ITV said that the Provos would strike at economic, military, political and judicial targets. At 8.15 p.m. on Thursday, November 21, bombs exploded in two public houses in the centre of Birmingham killing 19 people outright and injuring 182. A warning had been phoned to the *Birmingham Post and Mail* a few minutes before the explosions but too late to alert the authorities. Five men from Northern Ireland living in Birmingham were arrested a few hour later. No one took responsibility for the bombing. A wave of revulsion and anti-Irish feeling swept through England. Wilson the next day said that it would be wrong for anyone to take the law into his own hands. In the Commons Roy Jenkins announced that emergency legislation to combat terrorism would be introduced the next week. In Dublin all those in and out of the government condemned the bombing as did all the SDLP leaders in the North. The Provisional IRA issued a statement saying that it was not the policy of the IRA to bomb non-military targets without giving adequate warning and disclaimed the responsibility for the Birmingham bombing. Malachy McGurran of the Officials' Republican Clubs said that the bombings were the "worst chapter to date in the bombing campaign".

In fact, when the Official Sinn Féin Ard-Fheis met in Dublin on December 1, all were convinced that they were well out of the bombing business. The old ways — the rigid IRA structures, abstentionism and Green nationalism — were long gone and the sole property of the "Fascist" Provos. Increasingly, the movement had stressed ideological purity, moving in orthodox ways, creeping closer to the few Irish Communists. Marxism-Leninism, Russian variant, seemed the order of the day. Opposition to the shift within the movement had centred around Seamus Costello who felt that the Nationalist issue could not be ignored or approached solely with imported ideological tools and that to eschew the gun entirely was foolish. Costello had started out in the 'fifties campaign as a hard gunman uninterested in and unaware of politics. Like so many of his erstwhile colleagues in the IRA, he had become converted to agitation and organization and abhorred the break-away Provos. Then as the Officials moved on into discourse and ideological orthodoxy, he had become convinced that there was a place for the gun — two years late the Provos thought. A compelling orator, dramatic, charismatic, a good organiser, he was still not trusted by many of his colleagues. His views increasingly alien to the new direction, his private turf in Bray out of reach of the centre, he was considered too ambitious by half. In May 1974, he was suspended for six months. In July, unrepentant, he was expelled. By December the Officials knew that he was about to create one more Republican movement composed of former uncompromising Officials particularly in Belfast and Derry but scattered about the Republic as well. As was the case with the Provos in 1970, the Officials in 1974 felt their "loss" would be good riddance — only those who failed to understand the reality of the Northern situation would not realize that activists need not be gunmen. So, as expected the Ard Fheis voted to end abstentionism; if elected, candidates would take seats in the Northern Ireland Convention, at Westminster and in local councils. President MacGiolla blamed the Provos and Loyalists like Craig for increasing the strength of Fascism in Northern Ireland. Essentially, by the end of 1974, the Officials were getting out of the secret army business. There would still be armed volunteers in the North for defensive purposes but Dublin wanted no part of any military campaign that would further divide the working class for bourgeoise benefit. Let Costello go that route with his new Irish Republican Socialist Party (IRSP), formed on December 8, if he wanted, but the Officials were moving leftward into orthodoxy, toward a new Sinn Féin — the Workers Party, more Worker than Sinn Féin. At the March 1979 Ard Fheis, Goulding reminded the delegates that it had taken fifty years to turn the movement into a political party. A committee was formed to consider dropping the name Sinn Féin altogether.

In the meantime violent matters proceeded apace. At Westminster The Prevention of Terrorism (Temporary Provisions) Bill swiftly became law, proscribing the IRA, empowering the Home Secretary to expel terrorists from Britain or prevent their entry and giving the police wide powers to arrest suspects without charge and hold them for up to seven days. Merlyn Rees noted, again, that British withdrawal would simply lead to civil war in Northern Ireland. Nothing had apparently changed. The bombing and sniping went on. Yet, beneath the surface, a most curious initiative was under way. A Northern Irish Protestant clergyman the Reverend William Arlow, who served on the staff of the Irish Council of Churches, had recently taken a group of Protestant clergymen to meet with a party of Catholics in Holland. On the plane home, a Catholic of Republican sentiments suggested that he try to arrange the same thing for the Provisionals. He made contacts with Maire Drumm and the prospect was pursued first in Belfast and then with the Provo Army Council. Ultimately a meeting was arranged at a small hotel at Feakle, County Clare, on December 10.

When the clegymen arrived, they discovered that the Provos were taking the matter very seriously indeed. Present on their side of the table were Rory Brady, Maire Drumm, Seamus Loughren, Billy McKee, Dave O'Connell, Seamus Twomey, Kevin Mallon and J. B. O'Hagan — the heart of the Provo movement. The Provos knew that Arlow was informally in touch with Sir Frank Cooper, Permanent Secretary and policy maker at the Northern Ireland Office at Stormont. The meeting proved a chance to by-pass "the politicians" and open direct negotiations with the British Government. Then, "just as some points were emerging which we thought gave hope that some accommodation could be reached in the future,"[12] the Special Branch arrived on the scene alerted by the Northern Irish registration plates on the clergymen's cars. The Provos on the run disappeared and the meeting was over. But a beginning had been made. The clergymen had learned among other things that the Provos were planning a bombing campaign in England for early 1975. As it was, during December, bombs were still going off all over England: Bath, Bristol, Aldershot and in London at Piccadilly, South Kensington, Soho, Tottenham Court Road and Oxford Street. Despite the abrupt end of the meeting discreet negotiations on a Christmas ceasefire opened through intermediaries. At Stormont there was real interest as well. James Allen, an enigmatic Foreign Office official, had begun to explore the politcal landscape even before Feakle. Then the news of the Feakle meeting came on December 11. Speculation over a ceasefire became rife. On December 14, a spokesman at Kevin Street insisted such reports were pure speculation. The reports continued. So did the discreet negotiations.

The Provisional's major demands were: the withdrawal of British troops to barracks, an immediate end to internment, and acknowledgment of the right of the Irish people to control their destiny – but also no ceasefire while internment lasted and while the British army continued to occupy Republican areas of the North. At the public urging of many and the private possibilities suggested by Arlow, the Army Council decided to declare a Christmas ceasefire from midnight, Sunday, December 22 to January 2, 1975. It would be a popular gesture, would not be long enough to cause any disruption of planned operations, and would seemingly lead to direct negotiations with the British authorities. There had been signs out of Belfast. On December 15, the Price sisters were moved from Brixton to better quarters at Durham – and within three months to Armagh. On December 18, Arlow with his colleagues flew to London to meet with Rees and Cooper with a new Army Council message. On the next day he flew to Dublin to meet with the Provisionals. On Friday December 20, the Army Council announced the impending suspension of operations. Rees announced that "No specific undertakings will be given. The Government has received from the Churchmen what it understands to be the Provisional IRA's proposals for a permanent ceasefire. I must make it clear that no proposals have been discussed or considered by the Government."[13] He did indicate that a genuine and sustained cessation of violence over a period would create a new situation. While truthful this was less than frank. The Provos knew that the ceasefire almost certainly would lead to secret negotiations. For their part the British with as yet no formal contact with the terrorists, there was much to be gained: a ceasefire that could be extended — it was to be hoped with minimal concession and a slow shift to an acceptable level of violence. The worst that could happen was an IRA return to the military campaign and the revelation of the talks. So there was to be a ceasefire. Three hours before midnight, December 22, and the beginning of the ceasefire, a bomb was thrown at the London home of Edward Heath in Wilson Street, Belgravia, blowing out the windows on the first floor balcony.

Even when the Provos stood down, others pursued their usual course so the violence did not cease. There were robberies, sectarian murders and sniping attacks. Meanwhile there were feverish attempts by intermediaries to extend the ceasefire. The Provos wanted no harrassment by the army and a substantial release of internees as indication of good faith. The British wanted to make as few visible concessions as possible but still secure an extension of the ceasefire. In Belfast some detainees were released and others paroled and the promise of more to come. On December 31, Rees indicated that "if a genuine and sustained cessation of violence" occurred the Government "would not be found wanting in its response."[14] The Army Council, of course, wanted some response before the ceasefire became too sustained. Still given the events of the year — 216 deaths in Northern Ireland, the Birmingham bombs, the Dublin and Monaghan bombs, the sectarian murders, the prison riots and the collapse of the Executive — there was real hope of movement toward an accommodation of some sort.

In a sense, from the Provo's brief unilateral truce in March 1972, proving their control over the Northern units, until the December ceasefire, there had been a long bloody watershed, every initiative that ignored the Provos collapsed — as did every formula that denied the militant aspirations of the Loyalists. The problem had been that there was no solution. At the least, the very least, in 1975 everyone could hope for something — for conventional politics, for a Convention formula, for concessions or compromises, for all or nothing. Alack, too many of the most dearly held aspirations of one side denied those of the other. The Provos had not changed their minds, nor had the Protestant paramilitaries nor apparently the British mandarins at Stormont and Westminster. Still, a ceasefire was an improvement over bombs on the underground.

NOTES

1. The plebiscite as a symbolic exercise would have been more useful earlier on; but since Heath had refused to permit a referendum on Britain's entry into the Common Market, he could not allow Ulster to display loyalty until the European issue had been settled.
2. Mac Stiofáin was released the following April.
3. Blaney retained his seat outside Fianna Fáil and Haughey, returned again, appeared once more to be in the party's good graces.
4. An interesting summation of Irish events can be found in the *Sunday Times*, March 11, March 18, 1973.
5. The *Claudia*, leased from a West German firm, starting from Cyrpus apparently wandered around the Mediterranean and out into the Atlantic constantly under the watchful eye of the British. It appears that the arms were loaded in Libya. Without being too specific Qaddafi subsequently noted that he was helping the IRA.
6. Richard Deutsch and Vivien Magowan, *Northern Ireland 1968-1974. A Chronology of Events*, vol. 3, 1974, Belfast, Blackstaff Press, 1975, p. 1. These volumes, truly a labour of love, are some of the most useful works for the study of the Northern Troubles and are based on the equally useful *Fortnight* magazine.
7. The SAS, Special Air Service, was the British army's special forces, that made use of seconded officers and men and dealt in various counterinsurgency tactics — they often wore civilian clothing, used no-issue weapons (similar to those of the Provos so "errors" could be blamed on the IRA) and engaged in a variety of dirty tricks. Other than the SAS there had been as well considerable evidence of British involvement in provocation from bank robbery to attempted assassination and unofficial involvement by individual soldiers with the Loyalist paramilitaries. Clearly, the IRA would have preferred to put the blame for *all* sectarian murder on the British.
8. *Chronology, 1974*, p. 107. On November 27, Dugdale was sentenced to nine years on charges relating to the helicopter bombing of the Strabane RUC station. In Limerick prison on December 12, she gave birth to a son, Ruairi.
9. Apparently the kidnappers thought they had seized an important English politician. When it became clear that this was not the case, the two were released in Dublin. Supplied with a descrip-

tion of two of the men involved, the police published photographic identikit portraits — thus making clear the identity to the knowledgeable inside and outside the Provos.

10. *Chronology, 1974,* p. 37.
11. The most detailed account of the strike can be found in Robert Fisk's *The Point of No Return: The Strike Which Broke the British in Ulster* (London, Andre Deutsch, 1975). For many conservatives it was an appalling omen of what could spread to Great Britain from Ulster — besides bombs and gunmen.
12. *Irish Times,* June 9, 1978.
13. *Chronology, 1974,* p. 178.
14. *Ibid.,* p. 182.

Chapter XXI

The Campaign of Attrition Since 1974

On January 1, 1975, the Provisional IRA announced a two week extension of their Christmas ceasefire to the delight of practically everyone, except a few hard men. Negotiations with the British government, however, remained very much in doubt. On January 3, Arlow announced that the Feakle group would no longer be involved. Rees dispatched an invitation to the six major Northern political parties to discuss the ceasefire situation; but on January 9, he rejected proposals that intermediaries take the place of the churchmen as well as any direct or indirect negotiations with the Provos. Rees could not really have anticipated getting something — a continued ceasefire — for nothing. On January 16, the IRA Army Council announced that the truce would end at midnight for eight reasons — (1) no response to the peace proposals (2) increased British army activity (3) only three prisoners released in contrast to sixty-five in 1974 (4) James Moyne had died in the Maze without medical treatment (5) the anti-prisoner campaigns in the various jails (6) no compassionate parole at Christmas (7) John Green had been killed in County Monaghan by a "British execution squad" (8) Kevin Mallon had been arrested in Dublin. It was a curious list, big issues and small, and some beyond British control. So the campaign began again — a British soldier in Belfast was hit and wounded two hours after the expiration of the ceasefire, but it was only a manoeuvre not the end to negotiation.

On January 19, Arlow drove James Drumm and Francis Card to a meeting with James Allan and a younger official, Michael Oatly, both of the British Foreign and Commonwealth Office at a suburban house in North Down. "The atmosphere was stiff and starch and we expected the talks to break down, but once they began talking things improved."[1] This increasingly curious exercise in secret diplomacy would continue at various venues and with a differing cast for much of the year with mixed results. The British wanted a ceasefire to ease the Convention elections and take the pressure off the security forces, yet they did not like talking with terrorists — even if they thought they could politicize the hard men. As well they could not venture too many concessions without outraging their potential Northern

political, power-sharing allies not to mention the Loyalist paramilitaries. On their part the Provos felt that they had the campaign
in hand, that some form of British withdrawal was on the way — or
why else were they talking. On January 22, there was a second Provo-
Northern Ireland Office meeting.

The IRA Army Council knew quite well their major card. On
January 21, there were bombs in Belfast. The British expressed doubt
that the IRA could control the English bombing units. Then on
January 27, six bombs exploded in London and Manchester, twenty-
six were injured — after that — no explosions. The Provos had indicated to the British negotiators that they could turn the bombs on or
off, that just talk, silky generalizations, possible options, detailed
summaries of political difficulties, half-suggestions, all the tools of
elegant discourse, would not do. The Provos wanted something
and something they got. On February 9, the IRA Army Council
announced an indefinite ceasefire from six the following afternoon
following discussions with British officials. The next day the fourteen thousand British soldiers in the Province were ordered to adopt a
low profile. On January 11, Rees announced the establishment of
seven or eight incident centres to monitor the ceasefire. Run by the
Provisional Sinn Féin these would play a crucial local role; in fact,
the by-passed politicians felt that local control had been turned over
to the Provos. What the Provos did not get was a public declaration
of the British intention of withdrawing. What they *thought* they had
was a private agreement that at present could not be made public.
What — apparently — the British officials involved had done was to
fashion this Provo impression in such a way that they could deny any
such intention. They knew quite well, however, what the Provos believed. So from February 10, there was a Provo ceasefire. Deaths and
injuries on both sides dropped dramatically, but Northern Ireland
was by no means at peace. The killing continued but seldom touched
the Provos or the security forces.

On February 6, Charles Harding-Smith of the West Belfast Brigade
of the UDA was shot — the second attempt on his life within a
month but by no means a novel means of settling jurisdictional disputes within the paramilitary organizations. Basically, there were
two major types of paramilitary groupings: (1) those that were a
militia-in-waiting ready for any doomsday situation (rather like the
old B Specials) with a few active service units (2) those shifting,
turbulent groups of gunmen and bombers, usually welded into a
single safe neighbourhood or parish land, who killed "them" — the
guilty, guilty of being Catholic. At this stage, neither military titles,

elaborate paper structure, "ideological" papers or even overt political parties greatly disguised the fact that these paramilitaries were vigilantes. They had seized their main chance for power and profit when order collapsed. So that during 1975, they contineed bombing Catholic pubs, shooting the "guilty" and at times each other. From time to time they issued a political position paper. Their feuds and their campaign of assassination ticked up the Province's butcher's bill — much less then the previous year but still hardly a satisfactory level of violence.

It was not simply the Loyalists who kept the Province in turmoil during the Provo ceasefire. When Costello's Belfast IRSP members had left the Officials, some had taken their weapons with them to supply the armoury of the new Irish National Liberation Army (INLA). While the Officials did not mind the resignations, they did mind losing their weapons. All splits are bitter and this more so than most — the IRSP seem to hate the Officials — the Stickies — even more than the Provos did.[2] It was hardly a surprise when Hugh Ferguson of the IRSP was shot dead by the Officials on February 20, setting off a round of shootings, assassination attempts and knee capping that lasted until late May, despite various arranged and proclaimed settlements. One of the first victims was one of the most prominent Officials in Ireland, Seán Garland, National Organiser of Official Sinn Féin, and a central figure at Gardiner Place headquarters. He and his wife Theresa stepped from his car late on Saturday night, March 1, and stood in front of his sixth-storey flat at Balcurris Road, Ballymun. Two hooded gunmen emerged from a nearby cul-de-sac and opened fire. Garland was shot six times — in the arms, legs and stomach and badly injured. The two gunmen leaped into a light blue Cortina with a white roof and drove off. No one took credit for the shooting. Just two days before a bomb had exploded beside a pub on Leeson Street in Belfast with Cathal Goulding and Michael Ryan inside. The Officials blamed the "Costello-McAliskey group"[3] although the Ulster Volunteer Force soon claimed credit. After the attack on Garland, the incidents in Belfast continued, tapered off, and broke out again. On Monday, April 28, Billy McMillen, the Officials' long-time Belfast commander, was sitting with his wife of nine weeks in a yellow van outside a hardware shop on Falls Road at the corner of Spinner Street. Unknown gunmen opened up with four shots, hitting him in the chest three times and smashing the driver's side window. He collapsed, dying, out of the van door. The IRSP denied responsibility. No one believed them. On May 7, Costello was driving at 12.10 a.m. from a hotel to a house in Lismore Park, Waterford, after a meeting.

In his rearview mirror he noticed a motorcycle following him. The motorcycle hung back for about a mile and then moved up. There were two men, one with a sub-machine gun. Costello floored the accelerator just as the gunman began firing. Out of twenty shots, ten hit the car. Neither Costello nor the three others in the car were hurt. Soon the radical revolutionaries of the Official IRA and the IRSP were in the curious position of needing police protection to move about the Republic. Although the feud ended, internecine Republican shooting was by no means over — on June 10, Larry White of Saoirse Eire, a splinter of Saor Eire, was shot dead in Cork city. And all during this period only three members of the British security forces were killed — and not by the Provos or the feuding Republicans.

For the Provos, beyond the ceasefire negotiations, business continued as usual — hunger strikes, prison escapes, arms slipped into the country and organisers out. One of the more dramatic events was an attempt to break into Portlaoise prison with a "juggernaut" — a specially armoured lorry — that broke down when the driver got lost and the prison's auxiliary generator went on and the searchlights revealed the juggernaut. Unlike the August 1974 escape, this time an IRA prisoner was shot and killed.[4] For the most part, however, the ceasefire meant no casualties for the British and the IRA, and politics as usual for the Northern parties. In the May 1 Convention elections the anti-power sharing Loyalists won forty-seven of seventy-eight seats. Faulkner's Unionists won only five and Faulkner himself scraped in on the ninth count in South Down. There was no serious hope of a "power-sharing" constitution although the Convention struggled on until autumn, seeking some magic formula to accommodate the unreconcilable. Without interest in formulas, the Provos had become uneasy as the weeks went by without a British declaration of intent to withdraw. Instead there were optimistic statements about the Convention's prospects and private evasions to Provo queries. On May 10, the Derry Provos shot and killed an RUC constable but insisted that they would still observe the ceasefire. It became the pattern of the summer: private demands for an intent to withdraw, public threats that the ceasefire might end, scattered violent incidents. And all the time the sectarian murders continued. One of the most violent incidents came on Friday, August 1, when a group of UVF men stopped a van carrying the Miami Show Band back from a dance. The five band members were lined up and machine gunned, three were killed and two wounded. Then in an effort to bomb the van, two UVF members were killed in a premature explosion. During the next two months there were further no warning pub bombs and random assassinations.'

Then, on September 28, a bomb exploded in Caterham in Surrey. The following day a bomb blast in Oxford Street injured seven people. The Provos had decided on a renewed English campaign. On August 29, a Provo bomb on Kensington Church Street killed a bomb disposal expert. On September 2, despite a twenty-three minute warning, a bomb placed in the London Hilton by a four-man Active Service Unit detonated and killed two and injured seven. Rees was still convinced that a political solution would come out of the Convention — no one else was. The Provos still had some hope that a declaration of withdrawal would come out of the bombs. At least in the months since the truce, the British had lost only four soldiers and the RUC one constable, which was a net gain at minimum for London.

As expected the Convention collapsed, the Provo bomb offensive in England was stepped up: the Portman Hotel was attacked with one killed, the Green Park tube stop with one killed, bombs were placed in restaurants and under cars. In October the intensive bombing spread to the North, especially Belfast. The Loyalists responded violently — on October 2, eleven people were killed in paramilitary violence. The most spectacular drama of the month, however, was in the South with the kidnapping of Dr. Tiede Herrema, the manager of Ferenka Ltd. in Limerick by Eddie Gallagher and Marian Coyle. He was held first for several days at a safe house and then moved to a Council House in Monasterevin: Gallagher demanded that the government release Dugdale, Mallon and James Hyland from prison. The government refused. On October 21, police discovered the Monasterevin house. The area was immediately cordoned off and the police prepared to sit out the siege. Then began a long exercise in hostage-bargaining that the police assumed, as had been the case elsewhere, would ultimately result in the surrender of the kidnappers and the release of the hostage. Gallagher and Coyle held out until November 7 — a seventeen-day siege — before giving up and releasing Dr. Herrema. The Provos had assured everyone that they had absolutely nothing to do with the kidnapping. They in fact had at the end of October other and more pressing problems. After what the Belfast Brigade felt was a series of provocations by the Officials, on October 29, the Provos struck back violently killing one man and wounding at least fifteen others. One more Republican feud was under way. There again was the cycle of shootings — Seamus Mac-Osguir O/C of the Provo New Lodge Incident Centre was shot and killed and by the time an accommodation had been reached eleven people had been killed and fifty wounded. The Provos turned back to bombing. Rees had announced the end of the Incident Centres.

The paramilitary Loyalists continued their killings. In South Armagh the IRA killed three British soldiers in a border observation post. In London, on November 27, Ross McWhirter, co-author of *The Guinness Book of Records*, who had campaigned for the introduction of the death penalty for terrorists and offered a £100,000 reward for information to 'Beat the Bombers', was shot dead at his home in Middlesex. Two days later the UDA bombed Dublin Airport killing one man and injuring five. The Dublin government was engaged in the passage of a Criminal Law Bill in response to subversion of all varieties. In the North internment was to end — a cosmetic change — and so was political status for prisoners convicted after March 1, 1976. The year was ending in lost hopes and a Provos bomb campaign with a weight of explosives estimated at one ton a month.

In November and December, there were seventy-two explosions, sixteen attacks on police stations, ninety shooting attacks on security forces with six soldiers, three UDR men and three RUC men killed. The British had one notable success when on Saturday night, December 6, four IRA members of a London Active Service unit were trapped in a small flat in Balcombe Street with two hostages. Scotland Yard's terrorist squad set up a siege and waited them out. They were wanted on thirty-eight charges including the death of Ross McWhirter, Professor Gordon Hamilton-Fairley (killed when a bomb detonated under the car of Hugh Fraser, a Conservative M.P.) and Captain Roger Goad, a bomb disposal expert. The siege lasted 138 hours until December 12. Elsewhere the violence continued with no warning, paramilitary bombs used in the "war against the IRA" that rarely killed anyone in the IRA. The Provo war went on in South Armagh — the British sent in the 2nd Battalion of the Ulster Defence Regiment without noticeable effect. Unlike 1974, and the Provo Christmas ceasefire, there was no hallmark ending 1975. The Provos kept up the bombing even though they had not formally ended the ceasefire. Some might feel the end of internment and the British stand on the necessity of power-sharing was all that could be expected immediately, but for the Provos the pressure to continue the bombing offensive was far greater. The British were politically bankrupt. They had tried everthing in the North but a royal visit. They would sooner or later have to give a declaration of intention to withdraw. What real choice had they?

As had been the case before, the most noticeable spin off of the Provos military campaign was the escalation of sectarian killings. On January 4, five Catholics were killed in two attacks in South Armagh. On January 5, ten Bessbrook Protestant workmen were lined up by their mini-bus near Whitecross and killed in retaliation. If the Republic of South Armagh could not protect their own, they could respond in kind — regardless of what the Army Council intended. For the Loyalist paramilitaries it was a brutal lesson that their people were equally vulnerable if tit-for-tat murder became an IRA policy. And tit-for-tat murders were definitely *not* policy — the Army Council wanted a military campaign not the massacre of the innocent. In fact various Provos at various times contemplated initiatives to the Loyalist paramilitaries. After all both groups disliked the British, both were working class; but in January 1976, their differences still seemed too great. So the Provos concentrated on their new offensive. For the first two months of 1976, there were 129 explosions, 21 attacks on police stations with one soldier, two UDR men and six RUC killed. The British Army recorded 176 shooting attacks and estimated the weight of explosives at two tons a month. The campaign accelerated once again after the death of hunger striker Frank Stagg in Wakefield Prison on February 12.

The events in the South following Stagg's death were a bizarre example of the increasingly tough policy followed by the Coalition government towards the Provos. On Thursday, February 19, the plane carrying the body was diverted from Dublin to Shannon where the casket was rushed to Hollymount cemetary and buried by the police rather than allow the Provos to inter him in the Republican plot at Ballina as he had requested. On February 22, Sunday, there was a memorial service at Ballina with Joe Cahill as orator and ten thousand in the audience. Ultimately, Stagg was reburied secretly in the Republican plot but for the time being the government had won. Accused of prison brutality, body snatching, and police violence, the Coalition spokesman showed no inclination to withdraw from confrontation. They were the elected representatives of the people, not the Provos. The Coalition spokesman on the North, Conor Cruise O'Brien, increasingly cast doubt on the desirability of any foreseeable Irish unity and scathingly attacked Provo pretensions. And the Provos were not the only target of the government.

On March 31, 1976, at Sallins in County Kildare, the Cork-Dublin trains was robbed of registered packets worth £221,000. The police immediately began sweeping up members of the IRSP throughout the country. The first, arrested a few hours after the robbery, was Osgur Breatnach, editor of the party's *Starry Plough* newspaper. Soon forty IRSP people were in jail where they would claim they were clubbed and beaten — certainly the evidence was such to convince many outside the Republican movement that this was so. The case against the

IRSP dragged on and eventually a number of men were convicted, setting off a long civil rights campaign to free the IRSP people. Even at the time informed sources indicated that the Sallins robbery had been a sanctioned operation by the Provos — who for security reasons would not then accept responsibility.

Certainly, as the years passed, some of the enthusiasm of the Irish diaspora for the Provos had waned although there was still considerable financial support coming into Ireland. American money was the greatest and the most visible manifestation of diaspora concern. In the United States the key organisation was Northern Aid — Noraid — with branches all over the country. As a charitable organisation dispatching funds for widows, orphans and dependents as well as refugees from the North, their books almost literally were audited by the FBI. The American government and many observers were convinced that the money was going directly to the IRA to be used for guns. Actually, during a campaign the wellbeing of dependents is a far more important priority of the Army Council than imported guns. In any case Noraid funding was a matter of public record: in a three year, six months pattern from July 1974 to July 1977 the sums were $121,821; $126,355; $114,267; $115,448; $89,159; $80,201; $81,262 and $84,017. There were also — clearly — additional funds going directly to the finance officer at GHQ to be used as the Provos saw fit. Probably this sum was not much less than the open Noraid figures. Coupled with various contributions and assessments elsewhere and the continuing returns from expropriation operations, i.e. armed theft, the Provos, even as the campaign dragged on, were not hurting for funds. In fact they would continue to have no serious fiscal problems although everyone could always use more.

So the campaign continued. Belfast airport was mortared, a five hundred pound bomb went off near Bessbroke, middle class homes on Malone Road in Belfast were bombed. On April 8, the first prison official in the North was shot dead in Tyrone as a "legitimate target." The sectarian killings went on. The Provos blew up the Derry Guildhall again. The Europa Hotel in Belfast was bombed for the twenty-ninth time. The business houses of Portrush were destroyed by ten bombs. Nothing had changed. Still the Provos had not formally announced the end of their ceasefire. Whatever faint hope of renewed negotiations that might have existed disappeared in July in Dublin.

On the morning of July 21, 1976, Ambassador Christopher Ewart-Biggs prepared to drive from his residence in the Dublin suburb of Sandyford into the Embassy in Merrion Square with Brian Cubbon, the Permanent Under-Secretary of the Northern Ireland Office, who was down from Belfast conferring. Ewart-Biggs was new to Dublin and a most striking choice. He had lost his right eye in the Battle of Alamein and wore a black-tinted monocle and looked and sounded like an eccentric squire. He had written thrillers banned by the Irish censors, been threatened by the OAS during the Algerian troubles, and served in posts from the Middle East to Paris. Ireland was his first ambassadorial posting and many thought this indicated that the British Foreign Office wanted to upgrade Dublin by appointing a substantive instead of a social ambassador. Although the Irish newspapers tended to characterise him as a cross between Bertie Wooster and Colonel Blimp, his colleagues thought he was an exemplary taskmaster, a keen negotiator, and an enlightened friend. It soon became clear in Dublin — a very small city — that he was exceptionally well-briefed about Irish matters; so much so that the more suspicious, including the perpetually suspicious Republicans, felt his brief was more than diplomatic. The presence of Cubbon from Belfast certainly indicated that the new ambassador was going to be more than a social cipher.

After breakfast Ewart-Biggs and Cubbon came outside, on a sunny, summer day, and got into the 4.2 litre Jaguar. The ambassador on the left side of the back seat, Cubbon on the right. In the front Judith Cooke, Cubbon's private secretary, sat on the left of the driver Brian O'Driscoll. The Jaguar turned left out of the grounds of Glencairn onto the Murphystown Road followed by an escort car of the Irish Special Branch. A few hundred yards from the residence, the Jaguar passed over a culvert stuffed with over two hundred pounds of commercial gelignite. The road-mine was triggered by an electric detonator operated from bushes one hundred and fifty yards away. There was a tremendous roar and a bright flash. The Jaguar was tossed up into the air, flipped over, and crashed back into the smoking crater. The left side hit first crushing Judith Cooke and Ewart-Biggs. She died instantly with a fractured skull and broken ribs. He, with his neck broken and sternum smashed, was dying by the time the detectives from the escort car could reach the crater. Most of the force of the explosion had gone out the sides of the culvert but there had been enough lifting power to toss the Jaguar over on the left side — O'Driscoll and Cubbon were injured but would recover.

Two men carrying FN rifles were seen leaving the area. A hugh
police and army sweep through the area found a few clues that led
nowhere. For weeks an intensive hunt for the killers continued without results. No one claimed responsibility for the murder and as time
passed police were assigned to other duties. Much of the horror and
outrage of the Dublin government, of the British, of all those appalled
by the long, violent agony of the North, slowly eroded. Everyone, of
course, knew who was responsible — the IRA; if not the Provisional
Army Council or some "Army Council", then IRA people acting independently. In September in Belfast, unidentified Provo spokesmen
accepted responsibility. In Dublin the police bungled the investigation, leading to a scandal over misrepresented finger prints and a
cover-up. No one ever discovered the identity of the two men with
FN rifles. The Provos went back to bombing and shooting, the sectarian killings went on. Indignation faded. Again nothing seemed
changed. Then in August for the first time in years, there appeared
to be real change and, as was the case with the Loyalist general strike,
the result of the actions of unknowns.

At three in the afternoon of Tuesday, August 10, Mrs. Anne
Maguire with her three children, Joanna, eight, John, two and a half,
and Andrew, six weeks, were taking a walk in Belfast along Finaghy
Road North. A few yards behind was Mrs. Maguire's sister Mrs. Pat
O'Connor with her children. There were shots and a sky-blue Ford
appeared at full speed pursued by two British army jeeps. Just beside
the Maguire family the Ford swerved, leaped the curb, and crashed
into them. Andrew and Joanna were killed instantly. John died the
following day. Mrs. Maguire was seriously injured. The car had been
driven by Danny Lennon of the Provos who had run a British army
check point. The British claimed they had seen a rifle and opened
fire. Lennon was killed, dying at the wheel, and his companion
wounded. It might have been one more horrible by-product of the
campaign, an unavoidable accident or urban guerilla war; however, at
six on the local BBC affiliate television station, the children's aunt
Mairead Corrigan dissolved into tears before the camera. The interview was broadcast twice more that evening. Another Belfast woman
Betty Williams decided that something must be done. She began asking her neighbours "Do you want peace?" She and Mairead Corrigan
began circulating a petition. The response was immediate, widespread and enormous. Without plans or programmes they had begun
the Peace Movement and with the arrival of Ciaran McKeown, a
Belfast journalist, they unleashed a wave of emotion that swept over
much of Ireland and then abroad. The key immediate tactic was

essentially an old Ulster habit — the March. The three quickly drew up a March schedule that built on the first spontaneous demonstrations in Belfast. There were to be marches in all Ulster cities and in England. Culminating the first phase of the peace campaign would be December rallies at Drogheda on the Boyne Bridge of Peace and in London at Trafalgar Square — and in the process a provocative walk through Republican territory to Falls Park.

It appeared that the Republicans were the most vulnerable to the peace campaign. They were blamed for the Maguire deaths. No one seemed interested in their demand for peace with justice or their insistence that the British presence engendered violence. No one in the Peace Movement seemed unduly concerned about the Protestant paramilitaries only about IRA violence and Catholic-Protestant reconcilation. Soon there were huge marching crowds singing *When Irish Eyes are Smiling*, public embraces between the two faiths, a spreading elation that the sectarian lines had been broken. All they wanted they said was for the IRA to go away. When Mairead Corrigan was asked by a German television reporter if she favoured power-sharing she replied, "Sorry, we never talk politics."[5] It was their strength and their weakness.

The politicans, of course, had considerable doubts about the Peace People. What did they want? Where would they go? Not hard enough on the IRA said Paisley, misguided said Paddy Devlin. They marched on despite Provo harrassment. They became the media event of the year. And they appeared to present a very serious challenge to the Provos' base. At the very beginning Rees had announced that "They have shown the way. It requires courage to speak out, to accuse, ... The terrorists can only be beaten with the co-operation of the entire population."[6] For the Provos, the Peace People were wittingly or unwittingly agents of the Crown, a media godsend for bankrupt British policy, and a clear and present threat to their already eroding support. The North was exhausted by the Troubles which had lasted longer than World War II. The more cynical and astute doubted that, even in the short run, the Peace Movement was going to "solve" the various Ulster problems, certainly not by marching without politics. The euphoria would pass and did. Action on a community level would face entrenched competition and the erosion of enthusiasm — and this came to pass. There would be internal troubles, uncertain directions, and eventually the residue of the Movement would become one more piece in Ulster's bloody game. And this proved the case. The high point was really the last great rally. The media hung on however.[7] There would be other moments — Corrigan and Williams meeting the Queen for twenty minutes on her yacht during the Jubilee visit to the North — proving the Provos' contention and suspicions — and the 1977 Nobel Peace Prize for the two. In the autumn of 1976, however, the Peace Movement marked a year otherwise without hope and presented the Provos with a challenge, unexpected and without precedent.

The normal challenges and difficulties, North and South, presented less problem. There were the usual prison escapes — five men bombed their way out of the basement in the Special Criminal Court in Dublin. There was a resort to more extreme emergency legislation by the Coalition government that ultimately resulted in the resignation of President Cearbhall O Dalaigh because his conduct had been challenged by a Coalition minister. The Emergency Powers Bill, however, was on the books, authorizing severe restrictions in civil liberties which no one sensibly expected to force an end to the Provo campaign. In the North the removal of special category (political) status for eleven convicted IRA volunteers had by November engendered a strike — men refusing to wear prison clothing and remaining nude wrapped in a blanket on H-Block at the Maze. It appeared that the end of detention meant only that such force would be used during interrogations that confessions could be used to convict and the prisoners then treated as common criminals. For the time being no one but Republicans seemed very concerned about the claims of torture and the conditions of the men on the blanket but increasingly it would be a dominant Provo theme and ultimately an embarrassment to Britain. Yet, the British government refused to back down, even when the prisoners went on a dirty strike refusing to clear their cells or use their toilets. "Their own fault", said Roy Mason, who had replaced Rees as Secretary of State for Northern Ireland in 1976. Any suggestions to the contrary produced outraged indignation.

As the Provo campaign continued the greatest loss came on Thursday, October 28 in Belfast. It came unexpectedly at the hands of the paramilitaries. For years the Loyalist gunmen's problem with the IRA had been access. With their Northern accents they could not easily wander about in the Republic where the Provos might be more vulnerable. They could and did plant no-warning bombs in the Republic. The last wave of hotel devices had detonated in July. In the North the problem was even more difficult. In Belfast the gradual division into Catholic and Protestant areas and the close Catholic and Protestant working class ghettos meant that strangers, even strangers in a car, had real difficulty in penetrating either the little lanes of the old neighbourhoods or the new housing estates. The

British army had great difficulty and the challenge was quite beyond the paramilitaries. They stuck to random murder knowing many of their specific enemies by name but unable to reach them. Some of these enemies were members of the Belfast Brigade or visiting Army Council members, others belonged to the Provisional Sinn Féin party.

In Belfast the most prominent member of Sinn Féin — the Vice President of the national party, one of the most articulate and vituperative orators in a city that had made rabble rousing an art, was Maire Drumm. In October 1976, at fifty-six, she and her family had been life-long Repulicans and had paid the price. Her husband Jimmy had spent much of his life in prison, by 1976 more than any other living Irish Republican, and most of the time without charge. Their twenty-year old daughter Maire Theresa had been jailed in November 1975 for eight years for possession of a loaded revolver. Mrs. Drumm had been convicted in July 1971 of encouraging people to join the IRA — in court she had shouted "I will not accept bail. God Save Ireland".[8] The previous August she had threatened that it might be necessary to take Belfast down stone by stone. She was charged with illegal marching and spent more time in prison. A Loyalist leader charged that her release was a disgrace. Then on October 3, 1976, she entered the Catholic Mater Hospital for cataract treatment. On October 18, her husband Jimmy read her resignation as a candidate for Vice-President to the annual conference of Sinn Féin held in Dublin. She gave her health as the reason but promised to return to the "thick of the fray" when her health permitted. After nearly a month at the Mater, she planned to sign out on October 30 and move to a nursing home in the Irish Republic.

The Mater Hospital is in North Belfast between the Republican New Lodge district and a Protestant area. There was minimal security — at her home in Glassmullan Gardens, Andersonstown, deep in IRA territory, there was a British army post behind wire and a corrugated iron wall. At night a spot-light lit up visitors to the Drumm house and always there was a careful British sentry to take down car numbers. Resented in the Republican stronghold of Andersonstown, the British post still had long been a deterrent for those who might have her on their short list. At the Mater — where her presence had been mentioned in the Belfast newspapers — there was neither the IRA nor the British. On the evening of October 28, 1976, two young men entered the hospital during visiting hours between 7.00 and 7.30 p.m. and apparently disappeared. At 10.30 p.m., a dark blue Ford Escort pulled up and parked opposite the main hospital gate. Inside the Mater Mrs. Drumm was standing at a small six-bed side ward,

next to Ward 38 on the second floor. Two young men in white coats
pushed into Ward 38. One drew a revolver and without a word shot
her in the chest three times. She collapsed on the floor. The two
turned and disappeared out of the ward. The Ford Escort soon drove
off. Mrs. Drumm crawled several yards across the floor and then collapsed again. Ten minutes later in the operating room she died. There
was heavy activity by security forces. Searches and check points were
maintained. The gunmen were not found. No one ever took credit
for the murder. A spokesman for Ian Paisley's party said "that she
died the same death meted out repeatedly to many hundreds of
Ulster people by the Provisional IRA, whose so called cause she so
uncomprisingly espoused, will be seen by many as a poetic irony.
She was indeed a victim of her own hatred."[9] Both the IRA and the
British security forces suspected that she was the victim of the UVF
and one of the very few Republicans in the North that could be assigned to the paramilitaries. The other prominent assassination victim in the North in 1976 had been the paramilitary leader Sammy
Smyth killed by his own UDA.

At year's end, the toll for 1976 was 295 up from 243 in 1975.
Security forces lost fifty-two (contrasted to thirty-two in 1975) plus
three prison guards: British Army 14, RUC 13, RUC Reserve 10, and
Ulster Defence Regiment 15. The total deaths since the beginning of
the Troubles stood at 1,686, less than road fatalities but still appalling.
Yet the British seemed content with a passive role until there was
sufficient agreement between the factions — an apparently improbable
event. Mason insisted that "We've had a good year in 1976."[10] The
RUC had new techniques that zeroed in on the terrorist leaders. There
was promise for the future. There was to be no compromise on the
end of special category status in the prisons. And for the time being
Mason did not "want to step into that whirlpool of politics . . ."[11]
In point of fact, without Mason's knowledge, that most improbable
event — negotiations between the most extreme factions — had been
initiated. By the end of the year, the Provos and the Ulster Loyalist
Central Co-ordination Committee had met and delegated two political
lawyers to act for them. They were Desmond Boal, the independent
Loyalist, who had suggested a federal Ireland, and Seán Mac Bride,
the former Chief of Staff of the IRA, Clann na Poblachta leader and
foreign minister in the Inter-Party government in Dublin, whose
reputation had been enhanced by his Nobel Peace Prize and his work
for the United Nations to find a solution in South-West Africa. Both
the Provos and the ULCCC were attracted by a negotiated settlement
not involving third parties and without recourse to the Northern

politicians. Both had substantive doubts but at least 1977 would begin with some real hope other than the continuing euphoria of the Peace Movement.

The Boal-Mac Bride talks continued for several months gradually fashioning an acceptable ULCCC-Provisional agreement. According to the *Sunday Times'* account, there would be a joint request for British withdrawal presented to London as a fact that would later be blessed by the Dublin government. The European Convention on Human Rights would be used to protect the Catholics in the North and the Protestants in the whole island. There would, then, be a mix of Northern independence and a loose federation with the South. The first step would be a joint and total ceasefire, then the presentation of the document. At that point, April, negotiations faltered.[12] Everyone had doubts of varying degrees. There was considerable lack of trust, considerable fear of an uncertain political future — and several new factors. While all this was going on off centre stage, little else seemed changed. Although the Peace Movement too had faltered, the bombers had not. Eight bombs had started the year off in London but at least there appeared to be a discernible decline in the weight of explosives being used by the IRA. The rings of security in the centre of cities had made car and lorry bombs more difficult to plant. The English bombing tapered off — by conscious decision according to Provo sources, but ending nevertheless. Increasingly, in fact, it appeared as if the Provos were hurting. Certainly Mason had some real room for optimism. Perhaps an acceptable level of violence was around the corner. One key would be the prospect of allotting the primary security task on to the RUC. On January 12, an agreement between the General Officer Commanding and the RUC Chief Constable shifted the final authority to the RUC. Thereafter the weekly security meetings were held at police headquarters. On their part the Provos shifted targets in February and began shooting businessmen: Jeffrey Agate, manager of a Du Pont synthetic fibre plant in Derry, was shot and killed, Sir William McKinney, owner of a laundry business, escaped an attempt, Alistair McManus, head of a chain of shoe stores, was shot and wounded — next a manager of a shirt factory, a financier, a co-owner of a furniture and drapery company, the director of a chain of betting shops. And then the IRA gunmen returned to their old ways and familiar targets.

While Mason and the security people might feel that the Provo strength was ebbing, others did not. Ian Paisley and some of the more militant Loyalists felt London was not doing enough, direct rule had brought no wondrous reduction of violence and there was no hint of a new devolution of power to the Province. The only "initiative" was the arrival in March of Princess Anne to visit Northern Ireland as president of Save the Children Fund — and the second and great royal visit promised by the Queen in August to celebrate her Silver Jubilee. Others might point to fewer IRA incidents, or even the firm policy at the Dublin Coalition government, typified by the batoning of IRA supporters demonstrating outside Portlaoise prison in favour of the twenty hunger strikers — but not Paisley. Even more remarkable had been a St. Patrick's Day statement on March 17, by four prominent Irish-American politicians — Senator Patrick Moynihan, Speaker of the House Tipp O'Neill, Governor Hugh Carey of New York and Senator Ted Kennedy — condemning the men of violence — the IRA — and asking Americans not to support them. This was not even considered a straw in the wind by Paisley. The IRA was still shooting and bombing. No matter that power-sharing appeared dead — the Province was not secure. And once again during April there was another outbreak of Republican feuding between the Provos and the Officials, but Paisley was correct in that the IRA campaign was still on. On April 19, a bomb was defused near the site where Enoch Powell was to speak at Lisburn.

Paisley announced that another general strike would begin on Monday May 2. He wanted an end to direct rule and a return to a provincial government without power-sharing — i.e., the good old days with harsh measures against the Provos. Unlike the successful and then unknown Ulster Workers Council that had led the fifteen-day 1974 general strike, everyone knew Paisley and many Loyalists neither trusted him nor were willing to sacrifice for his latest display. In 1974 the Ulster Workers Council had a specific demand and was targeted on specific Unionist politicians. In May 1977, Paisley was asking for harsher methods against the Provos when it was becoming clear that the existing methods were working. And he wanted a return to Stormont when it was increasingly clear that this had long been a non-starter. This time as well the authorities had been exposed to one general strike, and, with Mason in place, had no intention of being intimidated. The RUC proved quite enthusiastic about batoning strikers, ending intimidation, and putting the boot in. More troops had been flown in, bringing the total on Monday to 15,500. While the strike had the support of most of the paramilitaries, UDA, UVF, and the Red Hand Commandos, it soon became apparent that it would not be a re-run of 1974. Paisley kept up the pretence for a few days and then caved in. The Loyalist paramilitaries were devastated: one of the reasons that the Boal-Mac Bride agreement remained in limbo. On May 29, the UVF called a cease-fire. Mason was delighted. He had the Protestant ultras in disarray and the Provos on the run.

The difference between the bombing in 1976 and in 1977 was considerable. By July 20, 1977, there had been only 3,280 pounds of explosives found contrasted to 21,708 in 1976 and an estimated 7,500 used in explosions contrasted to 55,000 pounds — ten car-bombs to eighty-two, twenty-seven ambush devices to sixty-seven. But it was still early for Mason to rejoice. Large areas of the countryside were still unsafe for security forces. The Provos had stepped up the campaign particularly against the RUC, promising another long hot summer and, secret Boal-Mac Bride talks or no, the sectarian killing went on. Still and all, security matters *were* better.

About the only disturbing news for Mason had come from the South where as early as an October 1975 by-election, the opposition Fianna Fail party had taken a Brits-out line. In January Lynch had called for a British withdrawal and a united Ireland. In May the Fine Gael Taoiseach Liam Cosgrave called a general election for June 16. The Coalition stressed law and order, a government of determination. On June 16, Lynch and Fianna Fail swept into office in one of Ireland's greatest election landslides: Fianna Fail eighty-four seats, Fine Gael forty-three (down from fifty-four) and Labour sixteen (down from nineteen). The Coalition Spokesman on the North Conor Cruise O'Brien lost his seat as did the Provos' *bête noire* — Minister for Justice, Patrick Cooney, blamed for Portlaoise prison conditions. While the Provos were, or course, delighted, they knew all too well that in the past Fianna Fial had been as harsh on the IRA as the Coalition, Elsewhere, however, it appeared that just as they were faltering, the Provos had been given a boost by the Brits-out stance of Lynch.

It soon became apparent that, in fact, the Provos needed all the help they could get. With 32,000 police and troops on full alert during Operation Monarch, on Wednesday, August 10, Queen Elizabeth II arrived on board the royal yacht *Britannia*. The Provos had promised to make the visit a memorable one. On the first day there was a demonstration and riot in Belfast with no casualties. One British soldier was wounded by a sniper in the Falls Road. The next day the Queen attended a garden party at the New Ulster University, Coleraine. After she left, a small bomb exploded in a flower-bed. That was it. The *Britannia* sailed off. Charges were brought against 172 for disorderly behaviour. Mason was delighted. Much of the Catholic population was considerably less pleased. No one had mentioned power-sharing and the visit had largely been to Loyalist

Ulster. Even the Peace Movement complained about the behaviour of British troops in the Turf Lodge. Yet Mason felt that the corner had been turned.

Certainly it was proving a long difficult year for all variants of Republicans. There had been renewed Official-Provo feuding in July. Then on October 5, Seamus Costello was shot and killed near his parked car on Northbrook Avenue off the North Circular Road in Dublin. There were various eye-witness accounts but the assassin simply raced off on foot and disappeared — perhaps into a greyish-brown car, perhaps not. No one knew who was responsible — a Belfast Official recently returned from abroad still bitter at the old killings in the Belfast feuds, or someone within the IRSP, or a Loyalist? The police never discovered the killer's identity. There were five thousand at the funeral in Bray, many prominent Provisionals appeared, but no Officials. Although Miriam Daly took over leadership of the IRSP, it became apparent that the movement had been struck a nearly mortal blow. Still Daly and the others hung on publicizing the case of the accused train robbers, publishing the *Starry Plough,* and in the North keeping the armed units of the INLA intact.

For the Provos it was a long, bleak autumn with the Army Council trying to maintain momentum while reorganizing the Belfast Brigade. The low point came on December 2 with a double blow in Dublin. The police, in strength, on the way to arrest Seamus McCollum of Martello Terrace, Sandycove, discovered, perhaps fortuitously, perhaps not, a car containing Seamus Twomey who, except for a brief interregnum under Eamonn Doherty, had been Chief of Staff since MacStiofáin's arrest in 1972. Along with Twomey, who ended up back in Mountjoy, the police collected an extensive collection of papers including the outline of the Belfast reorganization scheme. Twomey's loss was disconcerting but not crucial. Basically, the Provos had been directed by a relatively consistent group of men, circulating in and out of prison, representing three generations of the Republican movement, and after 1972 dominated by Northerners. Twomey would be replaced by an old Belfast colleague, Billy McKee with Martin McGuinness of Derry as Director of Operations. McKee represented the men of the forties — Joe Cahill, Twomey, Jake McCabe (killed in an explosion in a bomb factory in Dublin), and Charlie McGlade, Seán Keenan, and Jimmy Drumm in Sinn Féin; McGuinness, the new volunteers after 1969 — Ivor Bell, Gerry Adams, Martin Meehan, Francis McGuigan and others. From the fifties had come Mac Stiofáin, the Brady brothers, Dave O'Connell, Kevin Mallon — and some overlapped the forties and fifties, J. B. O'Hagan and John

Joe McGirl. A few in the inner circle of the IRA or Sinn Féin had dropped out or been eased out, but the central core remained, attracting as the years ground on more of the new men, those not as well known to the police or for that matter the newspapers. Thus Twomey's arrest did not result in any great transformation of the control of the IRA — Mac Stiofáin's arrest had greater ramifications since he had run a one-man show. In fact, in 1977, the big change came in tightening up the Belfast Brigade, closing down the large military units and replacing them with small independent cells. Actually much of the "military" structure — including ranks — had been pro forma, pleasing only to the more conservative secret army men. The new structure was intended to improve both security and operational capacity. It did not, however, correct the problem of deploying close friends from a single neighbourhood. In the case of the IRA in Belfast, where the Provos resembled a cross between a street-gang and a secret Jesuitical society, the very strength of operating on home turf among neighbours had often meant isolation from other IRA units (the Turf Lodge Provos not only knew little of South Armagh — much less Dublin — but also often cared little for Andersonstown). Each unit had a special concern with the well-being of their own. This, the 1977 reorganisation, could not greatly alter although with mutually served time in the Maze the extreme parochialism had eroded except in the countryside.

Coupled with Twomey's loss was the collapse of McCollum's mission. He had been the front man in one more Provo attempt to bring a large arms shipment into the country. A fifty-five year old "Englishman" from Liverpool, he had served a six-year sentence in 1954 for possession of a suitcase filled with explosives, got out and gone to Ireland only to be interned at the Curragh in 1958. On release he stayed in Ireland a few years, returned to Liverpool and finally in 1977 surfaced in Dublin using the name of a dead Dublin man, John O'Neill, to acquire a clean passport, and the name of Robin Kingsley to establish the Progress Electro Company. The major purpose of Progress Electro was to ship two transformers to Nicosia, Cyprus for repairs. There the two three-ton transformers were to be gutted and filled with arms, a very considerable shipment: 7 rocket-launchers, 29 French-made sub-machineguns, 2 Bren guns, 29 Machine-pistols, 29 Kalashnikov assault rifles, 18 boxes of six hand grenades, 11,000 rounds of SLR ammunition, 36 kg. of 9 mm ammunition, 60 rockets, 168 lb. sticks of TNT, 264 lbs of TNT in 44 lb blocks and plastic explosive in 1 ¼ and 5 ½ lbs packs. The shipment had been arranged between the IRA and members of the Palestinian Al Fatah fedayeen organization, initially through contact in Europe. The Provos had long had ties with the Palestinians and some volunteers had done training in fedayeen bases in Lebanon (who on the Falls Road had a suntan before cheap flights to Spain was a first clue). For the Provos — and most assuredly for the fedayeen — the prime difficulty was the existence of a highly effective Israeli intelligence net in the area. Cyprus for years had been seething with spies, agents, arms salesmen, pilots-for-hire, gunmen and assassins. And for years the Israelis had penetrated Al Fatah. Thus by the time the two transformers were loaded on the *Tower Stream* for Antwerp, the Israelis had passed along the word, several words, to several potentially interested intelligence services, for although it was known, perhaps only to the Israelis at first, that the eventual destination was Progress Electro, Middle Abbey Street, Dublin, arms shipments have been known to wander. Thus the Belgians immediately seized the transformers off the *Tower Stream* and the Irish police on December 2 arrested McCollum.

The Provos' difficulties in acquiring a large arms shipment in a world stacked with weapons had long ago been relegated to an almost secondary concern. Not that there had not been attempts on the continent that had failed, or from the Middle East that in the case of the *Claudia* failed — the RPG-7 rockets of 1972 did not. The reason was that for most explosives the Provos could make do with legal purchases and stolen material. Some things were moved in illicitly — in particular the huge New York City Water Tunnel under construction from 1970 to 1975 probably required ten percent more dynamite than a careful engineer would have anticipated. Once the appropriate chemicals were to hand, the Provos had developed a considerable spectrum of bombs: radio controlled detonators with three-year lifetimes, light controlled detonators, gravity switches, two-stage timers, and home-made napalm. Not only bombs were constructed, but lacking heavy weapons from foreign sources, the Provos also constructed their own mortar-rocket devices. Placed on the back of a lorry the mortar could be remotely controlled and launch eight to a dozen cylinders with a 20 lb warhead and a 155 lb total weight. As for more conventional weapons — rifles and pistols — if not a glut, there was not shortage.

The major flow of weaponry was from the United States into Ireland, usually in relatively small shipments. Rifles could be broken down and mailed or inserted in the coffins of Irish-Americans destined for a grave in the parish or in the early days stuffed in golf-bags or expressed luggage. In the United States only fully automatic weapons could not legally and easily be acquired. So at first, volunteers had rushed to the gun stores and bought up surplus semi-automatic army rifles, especially the M-1. Eventually there was a bit more order and cunning, but often the purchaser's enthusiasm for acquisition betrayed the destination. Several gentlemen with Irish accents purchasing dozens of rifles at one time usually led to the dealers calling the FBI or the Treasury's Alcohol, Tobacco and Firearms Division.[13] Some agents infiltrated the Irish-American groups; but given the ease of purchase, it was surprising that there were as many arrests. Typical was a federal charge in December 1977 that five Phildelphia men had shipped 300 rifles, largely M-1s and Enfields, along with 140,000 rounds of ammunition, and had conspired to acquire rocket launchers, mortars and machineguns. Three, Daniel Duffy, 42, an automobile salesman, Neil Byrne, 42, a grocery clerk, and Daniel Cahalane, 51, a general contractor, were arrested while the other two were back in Ireland — one was Vincent Conlon of the fifties campaign. Thus, the fact that the IRA had to depend on salesmen and clerks instead of international bankers and import-export dealers did not prove to be an insuperable barrier. Besides, while all secret armies want more, the Provos could only absorb so many weapons and the Active Service Units could use even fewer.

The greatest single arms coup by the Provos proved to be the discovery that two civilian versions of the American Army's M-16 automatic assault rifle could be purchased freely in many states as a hunting rifle. There were in fact two versions, Colt Ar-15 (a semi-automatic M-16) and the Ar-180 (which uses a quite different system of dual operating rods like the FN or the British SLR) which also has the virtue of a folding stock — "Fits inside a Corn Flake Box it does."[14] Until 1973 the Armalite Corporation of Costa Mesa, California, had the weapon manufactured under licence in Japan and after that by Stirling Armament Co. Ltd. of Great Britain.[15] The weapon, besides the collapsible stock of the Ar-180, has several ideal characteristics for an urban guerilla in Ulster. First it is single-shot or semi-automatic eliminating blockages and wasted ammunition. It has a very high muzzle velocity (3250 feet per second) and a flat trajectory, but most important the .233 calibre bullet could puncture both British army body armour and the sides of armoured personnel carriers. The bullet, as well, created a tumble shock wave and produced extensive wounds. Gradually, as the Armalities came into Ireland, the M-1 and the old Enfield were replaced — as were the stolen and acquired NATO FN and British SLR when possible. The result was that basically the Provos were better armed for their business than the

British army for theirs. Equally significant by the end of 1977, the Provos were far more elegantly armed than the Loyalist paramilitaries or the militias-in-being, both dependent upon ageing Enfields, old Stens and shotguns — increasingly a pike-in-the-thatch arsenal. This meant that in any Doomsday situation, the Loyalist paramilitaries — much less rioting civilians — were not going to be able to sweep through the Nationalist areas. No one was going to rush up the Falls Road into the face of machinegun fire. And at the end of December in Derry, the Provos revealed one of their new M-60 machineguns stolen from an American armoury in Massachusetts.

So if the events of December 2 were Provo low point by the beginning of 1978 the tides had again shifted. A senior British officer was soon to acknowledge that "Provo morale, equipment, intelligence and strength are all OK from their point of view. They are pacing the war."[16] Certainly, despite the Provo's 1977 troubles, the year's losses to the security forces had been about the same as the previous year: fourteen RUC killed to twenty-three, fourteen UDR to fifteen, fifteen army to fourteen. It was the civilian casualties that had plummeted from 243 to 67 — largely through a decline in sectarian murder and fewer accidental deaths at the hands of the bombers and snipers. It was about the only cheerful news for the long suffering Ulster population. The Peace Movement had faltered. The secret Boal-MacBride talks had produced nothing. Mason's own plan unveiled in the autumn had by the end of the year been folded up and stowed away. Westminster seemed to have little interest in further initiatives. Lynch in Dublin appeared content with speeches and his majority. So 1978 dragged on, not the year of the truce or the Peace People or even the Queen's visit, just another long bloody year.

The worst moment came in February when an IRA napalm-bomb went off on the wall of La Mons House too soon after the warning had been phoned. Twelve Protestants were killed and even within the Republican movement there was bitterness that La Mons House should have been chosen as a target and one more warning bungled. The security forces had one or two other good days. In March the RUC announced the capture of Seán Patrick Hughes after a gun-battle with paratroopers that left one soldier mortally wounded and one seriously so. The RUC claimed he was responsible for the booby-trap bomb deaths of at least twelve policemen and soldiers in the previous two years. On April 27, in a sweep, 330 RUC backed by the British army lifted fifteen Sinn Féin leaders. Unfortunately for the RUC the courts eventually decided that membership in a recognized political party was not illicit and they were released including Gerry Adams. By April the security forces had lost four RUC constables, four UDR men and four soldiers killed — and twenty-one civilians had been killed.

The greatest Provo political effort was on behalf of the prisoners in the Maze fighting for special status, and for suspects tortured during interrogation. In March at the Maze, the IRA prisoners had gone on the dirty protest and conditions in the cells grew increasingly unpleasant. The British blamed the prisoners. On August 1, Dr. Tomás O Fiaich, Roman Catholic Primate of All Ireland, described the conditions as "inhuman". All segments of British opinion seemed incensed at this intervention. The Northern Ireland Office was "most surprised" and blamed "these criminals". Even more embarrassing had been the Amnesty International report revealed in the *Irish Times* in June listing seventy-eight allegations of RUC mistreatment. The evidence was piling up that indicated the RUC had been employing the seven-day period to brutalise the suspects thereby acquiring confessions used in the special courts to convict the "terrorists" who were then dispatched to prison as common "criminals". Such brutality was difficult to prove to the law's satisfaction since most of those who claimed to be brutalized had suffered at the hands of the police — the law — and assumed not unreasonably that protest would lead to further brutality. To the disinterested, however, the interrogation practices appeared so blatant and so widespread that responsibility could hardly be limited to a few overly enthusiastic RUC constables. The British did appoint the Bennet Commission to investigate the Amnesty International charges, but for months there was no sign of progress. Then, in the following year in March, a Protestant police surgeon (at the Castlereagh police station), Dr. Robert Irwin, in a taped interview on ITV's 'Weekend World' claimed that between 150 and 160 suspects had been maimed by the police. The Northern Ireland Office quickly set up a tour of the Maze for journalists — Britain's most modern prison. And the Bennet Report was released on March 16: alack, it admitted that there had been some mistreatment.

There were some in Britain, exhausted by the long war of attrition, that felt the time to withdraw might be in sight. Some were the militant Troops Out movement, some were those exhausted and nauseated by the endless Troubles. One voice, however, came as a major surprise when in August, 1978, the *Daily Mirror* in a leading article called for withdrawal. The Provos were delighted. Those responsible for the Province were outraged. Major-General Richard Trant, Commander Land Forces in Northern Ireland, told a party of defence correspondents that the army should stay on active service in Ulster for the foreseeable future. So the *Daily Mirror* furore settled down and the Provo's campaign continued. Even the British army spokesman agreed that they could not close it down or bring order to the Province. They noted the Provos had plenty of weapons, more than they needed. There had been one million pounds stolen in the Irish Republic over the course of the year. The most dramatic robbery was half a million pounds taken from a security van near Newcastle West, County Limerick, in June, that involved ten masked men, Armalite rifles, disguised vehicles, two-way radios, roadblocks and hijacked vehicles as well as sophisticated steel-cutting equipment. While no one claimed the Newcastle West theft, the British army and most observers suspected that much of the money stolen in the Republic ended up in the hands of the IRA GHQ finance officer or in the coffers of local Northern units acting independently. So there was money to go with the Armalites. Belfast had been reorganised and was back in business and the hard core rural areas like South Armagh remained cowboy country. In Belfast in the Nationalist districts, the Provos had built up a whole economic and social infrastructure: drinking clubs built on city property, serving untaxed whiskey, fleets of black cabs, social services, housing bureaus, a ghost working force at some businesses collecting wages or unemployment benefits. While certain areas in Belfast, like the Ardoyne, had never been adequately police patrolled even in the quietest times, now most of the Nationalist areas were RUC danger zones. Sniping and ambushes were common-place and the toll of British casualties consistent. Thus 1978 ended, as it had begun, with bombs. On December 14, nineteen bombs went off across the province. On December 17, there were seven blasts in five British cities. The next day three car bombs went off in London. Two days later there was a wave of Northern Ireland hotel bombings — nine blasts. The next day three soldiers were shot and killed in the middle of the main street of Crossmaglen in South Armagh. The Ulster total for the year came to 755 shooting incidents, 455 explosions, 21 army dead, 10 RUC and 50 civilians. Again the decline in civilian deaths — twelve occured at Le Mons House alone — was the only good news.

One of the increasingly noticeable facets of the IRA-British Army struggle was the use of SAS men and undercover agents by the British. On January 25, 1979, two agents who interrupted an IRA bombing operation near Maghera were shot, one was seriously wounded. Five undercover agents had been killed by the IRA in the past few months — the greatest debacle had occurred some while before, soon after the SAS operation had intensified, when RUC police opened up on several civilians carrying what appeared to be Armalite rifles (and hence a Provo Active Service Unit) and the SAS not unreasonably fired back producing a number of RUC and SAS casualties and an effort at better liaison. The SAS had also been responsible for the death of a number of young men who turned out to have been innocent; in fact, in 1979, two SAS men were actually charged with the killing of sixteen-year old John Boyle at a stake out. They were tried — and acquitted. Elsewhere the campaign continued in the old ways — in London, in January, two bombs in rented cars exploded and a big gas storage tank was blown up south-east of the city. The big news from London, however, came when Prime Minister James Callaghan's shaky minority government lost a vote of confidence by one vote. There would be a May 3 election. Before then, in March, the Northern Ireland Unionists had been demanding major concessions to keep Callaghan in power. Now with a general election coming up, there might be some movement on Irish matters. The Provos certainly intended that the candidates did not forget Ulster, for it had been obvious for some time that hardly anyone in Britain wanted to be reminded of the Troubles — charges of torture or mistreatment of prisoners had simply made everyone angry. In fact when Governor Carey of New York complained about this and urged that new initiatives were needed, everyone was again angry at an ignorant and biased Irish-American interfering in a British election campaign. In any case the Irish element, in March and April, was not a discussion of issues but a succession of violent events — more "senseless" killing.[17]

On March 22, the British ambassador to the Netherlands, Sir Richard Sykes was shot and killed — along with his footman — beside his Rolls Royce parked outside his home. The two gunmen simply walked off. No organization claimed credit although IRA spokesmen in Belfast indicated that the Provisionals might have been responsible. Sir Richard did have an 'Irish' connection. He had been in charge of the investigation of the assassination of Ewart-Biggs in July 1976. Even more shocking, on March 30, Airey M. S. Neave, the Conservative's spokesman on Northern Ireland with a reputation of being uncompromising on the British presence, was assassinated when a bomb went off under the seat of his car just beyond the underground parking garage at Westminster. Although the Provos had warned the British government that before the general election "you had better state that you have decided not to stay in Ireland",[18] the Irish National Liberation Army of the IRSP claimed responsibility. After that the killing was limited to Ulster where the Provos intensified their efforts.

On April 5, two soldiers were killed in Andersonstown. On April 12, one soldier was killed and one wounded in an attack on an armoured car in Ballymurphy. On April 17, a prison official was shot and killed in front of his wife while holding the hand of his three-year old child — a "legitimate" target. The next day in Bessbrook a one-thousand-pound lorry-bomb was detonated as two RUC patrol cars drove alongside. Four RUC constables were killed and two others injured as well as eleven civilians. On April 19, a woman prison official was shot and killed outside Armagh jail and three others injured. In Belfast a British Cadet Force officer was shot and killed and another wounded — nine members of the security forces were killed in eight days. Extensive British roundups of suspected Republican sympathizers on April 28 had little effect. Yet, by polling day, the only politicians who concerned themselves with the Irish issues were Americans. The voting in the Province was, as always, predictable - Fitt and Maguire won and the extreme Unionists picked up two more seats. The Conservative victory, however, was sufficient that the Unionists were in no position to extort concessions. On the other hand, Margaret Thatcher had given no indication that Ulster was high on her priority list or that her position would greatly differ from that of Callaghan. As far as could be discerned, this meant that the new government, like the old, would soldier on, insisting that the feuding Irish could not be abandoned to themselves and no political institutions could be imposed or suggested until the feuding ended. In the Euro-election in June the electorate polarized as always — Paisley received more votes than all other Loyalist candidates. As for the Provos, their campaign could not be wound down by the security forces nor for the time being greatly escalated. In fact, in May *An Phoblacht* published a British Ministry of Defence document that had been in the Army Council's hands since the beginning of the year that largely agreed with their own more optimistic analysis of the direction of the campaign. And other than the military option, there was always the possibility of a deal with the paramilitaries. There was still the possibility of a surge of British sentiment for withdrawal. And like the British, in the meantime the Provo would soldier on down the road to the ultimate republic.

For a few, generation after generation, what Pearse and Connolly began in the name of Tone on April 24, 1916, is an unfinished legacy — but a clearly defined responsibility. As long as the British border cuts across the Republic of 1916, as long as Ireland and its people are neither free of exploitation nor Gaelic in tongue and heart, then men will turn to the task as defined by Tone no matter how bleak the prospects: to do less would be to betray the past and deny the future. Each year in June the responsibility to that legacy is made manifest. At the graveyard in Bodenstown before the tomb of Tone under the shadow of the ruined, ivy-covered church, they rededicate themselves. Earlier in the day, the ministerial Mercedes and tailored colonels have descended in a ceremonial flurry leaving an official wreath or two. Hours later another army rises in an empty field by the village of Sallins and behind the tricolour to the wail of pipes marches on Bodenstown. Here, briefly, along a country road materializes the Republican Army, illegal, covert, an army without banners of victory, without uniforms and in most years without prospects. Under the trees amid the gravestones, the little old men from the hills, the children with sweets, the odd uneasy policeman, the hard lads from Falls Road in Belfast and the felons of yesteryear listen once more to the magic words of faith and hear once again the faint whispers of hope. For some — the tired, the cynical — the ritual is barren but inviolate. For others this is but the annual reunion of their failed generation. For a few it is the one shining moment in a year flawed by exhaustion and futility. In the barren years, the ranks were thinner, the young men fewer, the victory more distant; but still there were — and are — men to march down the road as they have for generations, marching to the music of the past toward a call for the future. For a brief hour they stand, red-necked and rumpled, men of no property, under the distant wind of history, listening to the old litany. And they believe, as many of their fathers did and some of their children will, that an Ireland divided shall never be at peace. Then they go home to Dublin and Tyrone and Liverpool and Limerick and the sweet wrappers are blown away and the grass grows uncut over the graves for another year and elsewhere out of sight the secret army of the Republic marches and counter-marches to martial pipes audible only to the faithful.

NOTES

1. *Irish Times*, June 9, 1978.
2. The term Stickies or Sticks came from the Official Republican innovation of putting gum on the back of the Easter Lily commemoration badge while the Provos stuck to the conventional pin.
3. One of the founders of the IRSP was Bernadette Devlin who had married and became Bernadette McAliskey. She later resigned.
4. The most recent escape death had occurred when a large group had tunnelled out of the Maze but emerged within sight of a British patrol. The Provos claimed there was no need for that death either.
5. Richard Deutsch, *Mairead Corrigan — Betty Williams*, Woodbury (New York), Barron's 1977, p. 89.
6. *Ibid.*, p. 6.
7. The phenomenon was worldwide and funds poured in from abroad; in fact, the Peace Movement maintained its momentum abroad far longer than it did in Ireland.
8. *Irish Times*, October 29, 1976.
9. *Ibid.*, October 30, 1976.
10. *Ibid.*, December 22, 1976.
11. *Ibid.*
12. *The Sunday Times*, June 25, 1978.
13. For example in 1974 two men were arrested with seventy Colt ARs loaded in a rented van in Woodside, Queens. The weapons had been purchased in a Maryland gunshop and the authorities immediately notified.
14. Correspondence Charles Libby (Richland, Washington), September 17, 1975.
15. In effect this means that the British Sterling Company has been responsible for the construction of the IRA's favourite weapon.
16. *The Sunday Times*, June 25, 1978.
17. On the assassination of Ambassador Ewart-Biggs in 1976, the British Prime Minister had asked "when will this senseless killing stop?" (v. *Irish Times*, December 14, 1976). Whatever else the murder might have been neither it nor most of the other killings in Ireland had been senseless.
18. *New York Times*, March 31, 1979.

Sources

It is no real exaggeration to contend that there are little or no readily available written records, primary or secondary, for a study of the IRA. There were, of course, IRA records but most are lost, strayed, seized or classified. There are, of course, reports, memoranda, and records, not to mention the documentary evidence accumulated for prosecution, in the files of the Irish, Northern Ireland, and British governments; but what has not been destroyed, has not and will not be in the foreseeable future open to scholars. All that is left is the memory of men, fallible, contradictory, touched by pride, and capable of gross omission. That *only* the collective memory of the IRA remains as a source for historians or that nothing of worth is available for the period after 1923 is not fair but it is close enough to the mark that a book similar to this would have been possible if it were dependent solely on the results of the interviews. Fortunately, that was not the case and the following bibliographical sources give some indication of the ground covered in an effort to piece together the detailed but fragmented information acquired in my travels about Ireland. The period from 1916 to 1923 has been skimmed over since much of the conventional material is well known and a thorough bibliography would simply double, pointlessly, the size of this book.

INTERVIEWS

As noted almost the entire structure of this book rests on the results of a long series of interviews, conversations, and recollections supplied, at times unwittingly, by well over a hundred individuals. I have spent an estimated 1,400 hours in more-or-less formal interviews and at least that in conversations, carefully guiding the discussion from sheep prices or the All-Ireland Final into Republican politics. Yet, despite the time and effort squandered anyone who is familiar with the Republican Movement will note that many vital names are missing and that, in fact, a completely different list of names might be produced which could have been the basis for an even better book. This is all too true, but, alas, not all Republicans for personal or political reasons wanted to be bothered by some strange "writer". Many were most kind and explained in letter or by telephone the reasons for their reluctance to co-operate—for example, Tomás MacCurtain, Maurice Twomey, Robert and Mae Russell, Liam Burke, Dave O'Connell among others. Others were willing to talk only in most general terms and may feel ill-used to be included in the list at all. Some I could only speak to briefly and never managed a meeting or only heard them speak in public — for example, Leo Collins, Joseph Doyle, Liam Gleeson, Mick Kelly, Vincent McDowell, Donal Murphy, J. A. M. Murphy, Máirtín Ó Cadhain, Seán Stephenson. Some I missed altogether, simply by reason of the restrictions of time and space, by bad luck or, I suspected at the time, as a result of Celtic malice. In any case, those listed in the first group are those to whom I have talked in most general terms, or most briefly, or often only listened to their views on the present state of Irish Republicanism. Those listed in the third group were contacted or recontacted concerning events between 1970 and 1974 (MIT edition).

I

In almost all cases I have eliminated titles, however justly deserved; and the places given are interview sites not residences.

Kevin Agnew (Belfast)
John Brennan (Co. Leitrim)
Jerry Campbell (Belfast)
Denny Carmichael (Dublin)
Máirín de Búrca (Dublin)
Frank de Rossa (Dublin)
James Devereux (Limerick)
Christopher Dolan (Belfast)
John Donovan (Cork)
Joe Doyle (Bray, Co. Wicklow)
Patrick Fleming (Dublin)
John E. Greeves (Belfast)
Patrick Kennedy (Dundalk)
Seán Keogh (Doon, E. Limerick)
Tommy Kilroy (Carrick-on-Shannon)

Walter Lynch (Dublin)
Dermot McAteer (Pomeroy, Co. Tyrone)
Máire MacGiolla (Dublin)
Frank McGlade (Belfast)
Paddy McGlynn (Dublin)
Joe McKearney (Belfast)
Seamus McLoughlin (Dublin)
Desmond O'Hagan (Belfast)
Michael A. O'Kelly (Dublin)
Liam Ryan (Doon, E. Limerick)
Paddy Ryan (Doon, E. Limerick)
Fintan Smith (Dublin)
Michael Traynor (Dublin)

II

Seán Ashe (Rathmore, Co. Dublin)
Tom Barry (Cork)
Richard Behal (Kilkenny)
Ernest Blythe (Dublin)
Gerald Boland (Dublin)

Eamon Boyce (Dublin)
Robert Bradshaw (Dublin)
Jack Brady (Dublin)
Rory Brady (Roscommon)
Dan Bryan (Dublin)

Manus Canning (New York City, U.S.A.)

Joe Christle (Dublin)

Brian Clark (Dublin)

James Clark (Dublin)

Joe Clarke (Dublin)

Joe Collins (Dublin)

Maire Comerford (Dublin)

Andy Cooney (Westminster, Md., U.S.A.)

Kenneth Cordner (Belfast)

Seamus Costello (Dublin)

Tony Coughlan (Dublin)

William Craig (Belfast)

James Crofton (London, U.K.)

Seán Cronin (New York City, U.S.A.)

Tom Cullimore (Wexford)

George Dearle (Dublin)

Laurence de Lacy (Enniscorthy)

Eamon de Valera (Dublin)

Seán Dowling (Dublin)

James Doyle (Dublin)

Frank Driver (Ballymore Eustace, Co. Kildare)

Seán Dunne (Dublin)

Kathleen Farrell (Dublin)

Sgt. Ferguson (Belfast)

Peter Finegan (New York City, U.S.A.)

Gerald Fitt (Belfast)

Michael Fitzpatrick (Dublin/New York City, U.S.A.)

Dennis Foley (Dublin)

James Gallagher (Dublin)

Seán Garland (Dublin)

George Gilmore (Dublin)

Cathal Goulding (Dublin)

Laurence Grogan (Dublin)

Charles Harkin (Dublin)

Seán Harrington (Dublin)

Stephen Hayes (Enniscorthy)

Myles Heffernan (Dublin)

Seán Hennessy (Dublin)

Joseph A. Hughes (New York City, U.S.A.)

Sheila Humphries (Mrs. D. O'Donoghue) (Dublin)

Noel Kavanagh (Dublin)

John Kelly (Belfast)

Pearse Kelly (Dublin)

Sir Arthur Kennedy (Belfast)

R. J. Kerr (Belfast)

James J. Killeen (Dublin)

Gery Lawless (Dublin)

Con Lehane (Dublin)

Seán Lemass (Dublin)

Jack Lynch (Cork)

Hugh McAteer (Belfast)

Michael McCarthy (Cork)

Liam MacGabhann (Dublin)

Tomás MacGiolla (Dublin)

John Joe McGirl (Ballinamore, Co. Leitrim)

Charles McGlade (Dublin)

Liam McGuinness (Dublin)

Malachy McGurran (Dublin)

Mark McLaughlin (Dundalk)

Terry McLaughlin (Dublin)

Maurice McNamara (Doon, E. Limerick)

Tom Maguire (Cong, Co. Galway)

Tomás Malone (Seán Forde) (Nenagh, Co. Tipperary)

Gearóid Mangan (Dublin)

Tony Meade (Dublin)

W. Mehare (Belfast)

Tom Mitchell (Dublin)

Peter Mohan (Dublin)

Frank Morris (Convoy, Co. Donegal)

Tom Morris (Dublin)

W. R. Morrow (Dublin)

Patrick Mulcahy (Limerick)

Carmel Murphy (Dublin)
Charles Murphy (Dublin)
Patrick Murphy (Co. Kilkenny/ Dublin)
Joseph Nolan (Dublin)
Nuala Nolan (Dublin)
Patrick Nolan (Dublin)
James O'Beirne (Dublin)
Seán Ó Cionnaith (Dublin)
Laurence O'Connor (Wexford)
Peadar O'Donnell (Dublin)
Florence O'Donoghue (Cork)
Seamus O'Donovan (Dublin)
J. B. O'Hagan (Lurgan, Co. Armagh)
Tarlach Ó h-Uid (Dublin)
George Mahony (Cork)
Terence O'Neill (Belfast)
Paddy O'Regan (Dublin)

Gerald O'Reilly (New York City, U.S.A.)
Seamus Ó Tuathail (Dublin)
John Reynolds (Co. Leitrim)
Liam Rice (Belfast)
Al Ryan (Kilkenny)
James Ryan (Dublin)
Mick Ryan (Dublin)
Tony Ruane (Dublin)
Nicos Sampson (Nicosia, Cyprus)
James Sherlock (Skerries, Co. Dublin)
Myles Shevlin (Dublin)
Petros Stylianou (Nicosia, Cyprus)
Eamon Thomas (Dublin)
Eamon Timoney (New York, U.S.A.)
Harry White (Dublin)

III

Rory Brady (Dublin, Roscommon)
Seán Brady (Dublin)
Vincent Brown (New York)
Dan Bryan (Dublin)
Joe Cahill (Dublin)
Manus Canning (New York)
Denny Carmichael (Dublin)
Joe Clark (Dublin)
Seán Convery (Dublin)
Maurice Conway (Dublin, Donegal)
Seán Cooney (New York)
Seán Cronin (New York)
Seán Daly (Dublin)
Frank Driver (Dublin)
Maire Drumm (Belfast)
Paddy Duffy (Dublin)
Patrick Dwyer (St. Mullins, Co. Carlow)
Roger Fisher (Belfast, Boston)

Walter Lynch (Dublin)
Bob McCann (New York)
Tomás MacGiolla (Dublin)
Seán Mac Stiofáin (Dublin, Navan)
Charles McGlade (Dublin)
Francis McGuigan
Maira McGuire (Dublin)
Martin McGuinness (Derry)
Clan McGuinness (Derry)
Malachy McGurran (Dublin)
Mark McLaughlin (Dundalk)
Peter McMullan (Dublin)
Tony Meade (Dublin)
Martin Meehan (Derry)
Tom Mitchell (Dublin)
Charles Murphy (Dublin)
Dave O'Connell (Dublin)
Donald O'Connor (Dublin)
Rita O'Hare (Dublin)

Michael Flannery (New York)
Seán Garland (Dublin)
Tom Gill (Dublin)
Cathal Goulding (Dublin)
Jimmy Grahame (Dublin)
Fulvio Grimaldi (Dublin)
Seán Henderson (Belfast)
Seán Hopkins (New York)
Seán Og Keenan (Derry)
John Kelly (Dublin)
Patrick Kennedy (Dublin)
Gerry Lalor (Dublin)
Stein Larsen (Dublin)
Des Long (Dublin)

Owen O Murchu (Dublin)
Seamus O Tuathail (Dublin)
Richard Rose (Dublin, Glasgow)
Mick Ryan (Dublin)
Packy Ryan (Dublin)
Tony Ruane (Dublin)
Myles Shevlin (Dublin)
Oliver Snoddy (Dublin)
Liam Sutcliffe (New York)
Anthony Taylor (Dublin)
Eamon Thomas (Dublin)
Eamon Timoney (New York)
Seamus Twomey (Belfast)
Desmond Williams (Dublin)

Not listed by name are members of Active Service Units in Belfast and Derry, staff members Belfast, Derry and Dublin, volunteers from Dublin, and members of GHQ Staff of the Provisional IRA, members of Cumann na mBan (Kevin Street) Derry, and various Republican (Kevin Street) organizers in the Six Counties.

MANUSCRIPT

Because of the conspiratorial, covert nature of the IRA, the regular collecting, ordering, and filing of documents has been out of the question. As little as possible was written and much was destroyed as soon as possible. Since a mimeograph is as vital to a revolutionary movement as a gun and every army, no matter how secret, creeps ahead through forests of written orders, admonitions, and rebukes, there were at any given time heaps of IRA documentation in personal possession, in official and unofficial dumps, and in transient headquarters. Over the years dumps have been lost or forgotten, police swoops have forced sudden bonfires, and usually there were more IRA documents in the Castle or RUC headquarters than in the nominal possession of the IRA. It is quite likely that a considerable number, perhaps the overwhelming mass, of the documents held as evidence by the police have long since been destroyed. Even Sinn Féin, always legal in the South, has only the most recent records while the records of the Second Dáil have disappeared entirely. While a complete set of IRA records would be useful, much had to be left unsaid and much was written by a few men not always representative of the leadership as a whole; in any case, no such records exist. Those that were available from one source or another are merely representative of their time and with one or two periods too scanty to be of use except as collaborating evidence. In general the distribution of the IRA documents has been listed below but not even an effort to include the material in the notes has been made:

Oglaigh na h-Éireann, General Headquarters Documents (typed copies or originals C/S A/G)

July 1922–March 1923	(approximately 200 pages)
1923–1932	(approximately 50 pages)
1932–1938	scattered
1938–1968	scattered
Ibid., Northern Command Documents 1939–1943	very scattered
Ibid., General Army Orders 1925–1962	
Ibid., Training Manuals, Battle Camp Schedules 1950–1956	selections
Ibid., Special Communiques, Manifestoes, etc.	

The grand total of unpublished material is in the neighbourhood of 450 typed pages. The IRA has, of course, published its *Constitution* and in 1934 the economic and social programme not to mention an endless list of Manifestoes or Irish Republican Publicity Bureau statements.

All archival sources in both Ireland and Northern Ireland for this period remain closed. There is some fear in the South at least that in the fullness of official time when access is given by the Ministry of Justice little will be left. In 1933 Colonel David Neligan during a court case admitted to burning some 18,000 items on the eve of Fianna Fáil's assumption of office. Rumour, and Dublin bubbles with rumour, has it that when Clan na Poblachta participated in the government in 1948 the files suffered additional depletion. In any case there is a reasonable tendency to destroy old paper, particularly long out-of-date Sinn Féin trash or thirty-year-old IRA documents, which had probably left very little for the future historians. Simply because of the confusion as to public and private papers, access to a limited selection from the Ministries of Defence, Justice, and External Affairs was possible for the period 1923–1932. The most valuable were the Defence reports on the state of the country, 1922–1923, and Justice reports on surveillance of revolutionary organizations, 1924–1932.

Besides the normal *manuscripts*, I have had access to several collections of clippings, correspondence, photographs and printed matter: Charles Harkin (Ireland, 1932–1935), Gerald O'Reilly (Frank Ryan), Liam Ryan (Packy Ryan), and the extensive but until recently disorganized clipping files of the *United Irishman*. Certain correspondence has been of assistance, particularly with Joe Collins, Seán Cronin, Eamon Timoney, Colonel Dan Bryan, Major Florence O'Donoghue, P. A. Calleary, TD, Richard P. Gogan, TD, and Stephen Hayes. I have also made use of three typed manuscripts: an untitled analysis of the Irish Left, 1931–1938, by Leonard Larkin, Captain Liam Walsh's "General Eoin O'Duffy, His Life and Battles" (1946?), and Eamon Mac Tiománaí and Seamus Ramsaigh, "The Campaign of the Fifties, Notes and Observations on the Campaign in the North, with Especial Reference to Republican Activities in Derry" (1967), an especially valuable source.

DOCUMENTS

In the Republic of Ireland, the United Kingdom, and Northern Ireland, the records of the Dáil and Parliament debates, annually bound, are, of course, available; but after that relevant documentation relating to the IRA is quite sparse. Dáil Éireann did publish *Official Correspondence Relating to the Peace Negotiations, June–September, 1921*, Dublin, October 1921, but other preoccupations eliminated further publications. The Irish Free State published reports of some interest:

> *Correspondence of Mr. Eamon de Valera and Others*, Dublin, 1922.
> *The Army Gazette* (Monthly).
> *Report of the Army Enquiry Committee*, Dublin, June 1924.
> *Coughlan Shooting Inquiry, Report of Tribunal of Inquiry*, Dublin, 1928.
> *Two Documents "A" and "B" Found by the Police on 10th April, 1928, During the Course of a Search of the Premises, 27 Dawnson Street*, Dublin, 1930.
> *Report of the Sworn Inquiry Held at Kilrush, County Clare*, Dublin, 1932.

Since the United States government operates under only a twenty-five-year waiting period, the *Foreign Relations of the United States* from time to time has something of Irish interest as do *Documents on German Foreign Policy, 1918–1945*, Series D, vols. VIII and IX; and the reports of debates within the United Nations and various other international organizations can be scanned for the residue of the Anti-Partition Campaign. The only very relevant publication for the modern IRA is that of the Council of Europe: European Court of Human Rights, Series B: *Pleadings, Oral Arguments, Documents 1960–1961, "Lawless" Case*, Strasbourg (1961?). *Cf.* ibid., Series A: *Judgments and Decisions 1960–1961, "Lawless" Case (Preliminary Objections and Questions of Procedure) Judgment of 14th November 1960*, Strasbourg, 1961, and *ibid.*, Series A: *Judgments and Decisions 1960–1961, "Lawless" Case, Judgment of 7th April 1961*, Strasbourg, 1961.

NEWSPAPERS AND PERIODICALS

Although newspapers, particularly Republican, are of considerable value for the study of the IRA, there are two drawbacks: first, often as a matter of policy, particularly during the Second World War, very little about the IRA appears; second, reliance on the Republican press for information concerning the IRA is often less than helpful since all divisions over policy and personality are argued out of print if at all possible. Finally, the Republican "press" is often ephemeral, banned for a year or so, disappearing under one name and appearing under another, and in the North living, often illegally, from issue to issue. No library in Ireland has, catalogued at least, even a reasonably full collection of the Republican mosquito press although the National Library in Dublin does what it can. Particularly for the earlier period, there are collections of clippings and miscellaneous material in the National Library and in the New York Public Library. With a few exceptions I have included only post-Treaty newspapers.

There are several periodicals, like the old *Bell* and the new *Hibernia,*that are quite useful in general terms. For both newspapers and periodicals listed the place of publication is Dublin unless otherwise specified.

Anti-Imperialist, 1926
Anti-Militia News (Cumann na mBan: Dublin), 1939
Banba, 1921–1922
Belfast Telegraph
The Blueshirt (Army Comrades Association/National Corporative Party), 1933, 1934–1935)
Catholic Mind
Citizen (Labour Party), 1949
Cork Examiner
An Cosantoir (Irish Army Magazine)
Cumann na mBan
Daily Bulletin (1922–1923?)
Daily Sheet (Sinn Féin Headquarters), 1923–1924
Derry Journal
Dublin Courier, 1934
Dublin Evening Herald
Dublin Evening Press
Dublin News (Republican Publicity Bureau), 1929
Easter Week, April 1938
Éire (Glasgow: 1923)
The Fenian, 1923
Fermanagh Times
Fianna (Fianna Éireann), 1935–1936
Fianna Fáil Bulletin, 1934–1941
Fine Gael Digest, 1950–1956
The Flame, 1922

Forum (Fine Gael), 1944–1950
The Freeman (Cumann na nGaedheal), 1927–1928
The Gael (Sydney, Australia)
Gaelic American (N.Y.C.)
The Garda Review
Gléas (Fianna Fáil), 1952–
Glór Uladh (Belfast) 1955–1956
Ireland Today
Iris an Airm (Irish Army Bulletin)
Irish Bulletin (Second Dáil), 1919–1921
Irish Democrat, 1937–1938
Irish Democrat (London), 1944–1968
Irish Echo (New York City)
Irish Freedom, 1939–1944
Irish Freedom (Belfast), 1951
Irish Independent
Irish Jurist, 1935–1948
Irish Militant (London), 1966–
Irish News (Belfast)
Irish People, 1944–1948
Irish People, 1936
Irish Press
Irish Republic, 1939–1941
Irish Republican Bulletin (N.Y.C.), 1961
Irish Republican Bulletin (Sinn Féin), 1966
Irish Socialist, 1961
Irish Statesman, 1923–1930
Irish Times
Irishman (Labour Party), 1927–1930
Irish Workers' Voice, 1933
Irish World and Gaelic American (New York City)
The Kerryman (Tralee)
Kilkenny People
Labour News (Labour Party), 1936–1938, 1965–
Manchester Guardian
Nation (Fianna Fáil), 1926–1932
New York Times
Northern Herald (Co. Down)
Northern Worker (Republican Congress in Northern Ireland)
Northman (Donegal)
An tOglágh (IRA), 1918– (irregular)
An Phoblacht (IRA), 1925–1937 (irregular), 1970–
An Phoblacht (Cork), 1966–1968
Prison Bars (Women's Prisoners Defence League), 1937–1938
Red Hand (Belfast: Communist Party of Ireland)
Republican (Universities Republican Club), 1936
Republican Bulletin, 1922–1923
Republican Congress, 1934–1936
Republican Educational Bulletin (Sinn Féin), 1966
Republican File (IRA), 1935

Republican News (Belfast: IRA), 1942–1943
Republican Review, 1938–1939
Resistance (Ulster)
Resurgence, 1946
Resurgent Ulster (Belfast), 1953–1954
Saoirse na h-Éireann (Cumanna na mBan/Mna na Poblachta), 1929–1937
Sean Oglaigh (National Association of Old IRA), 1937
Sentry, An Fear Faire (National Association of Old IRA), 1939
Sinn Féin (New York City), 1920–1921
Sinn Féin, 1923–1925
An Solas (London: Irish Workers Group), 1965–1966
Spearhead, Voice of Republican Youth (Ulster), 1967
Star (Cumann na nGaedheal), 1929–1931
Sunday Independent
Sunday Press
Times (London)
An Teachtaire (Sinn Féin), 1966–
Tírgréa (Ulster), 1963
Torch (Labour Party), 1939–1944
Tuairisc (Wolfe Tone Society), 1965–
Ulsterman (United Ireland in Northern Ireland), 1965–1966
United Ireland (Fine Gael), 1933–1934
United Irishman (Fine Gael), 1932–1933
United Irishman 1948–
Unity (Belfast: Communist Party), 1962–
Voice of Labour (Labour Party), 1917–1927
Voice of the Nation (Defence of the Nation League), 1967
War News (Poblacht na h-Éireann), 1922–1923
War News (IRA), 1939–1940
War News (Belfast IRA), 1939–1941 and scattered later
Watchword (Labour Party), 1930–1932
Weekly Bulletin (Northern Ireland Publicity Service)
Wild Geese (London)
Wolfe Tone Annual, 1932–1962
Wolfe Tone Weekly, 1937–1939
Workers' Bulletin, 1939
Workers' Republic, 1921
Workers' Republic, 1938
Workers' Republic (formerly *An Solas*), 1967–

PUBLISHED SOURCES

Although Ireland has been well served by historians for the period before
1916, except for interest in the April Rising and the Tan War much of the
last fifty years has remained a blank slate, pocked with the odd volume but
largely left open to rumour, myth, and partisan ignorance. Ireland must

urely be the only fifty-year-old nation without a single conventional history—there is just no standard history of contemporary Ireland; in fact, until 1966 (Timothy Patrick Coogan, *Ireland Since the Rising*, New York, 1966) there had been no attempt of any sort to cover the period even with a broad brush. Before 1916, however, there are excellent studies of broad scope: J. C. Beckett, *A Short History of Ireland*, London, 1952; Edmund Curtis, *A History of Ireland*, London, 1936; *The New Course of Irish History*, New York, 1967, edited by T. W. Moody and F. X. Martin; and P. S. O'Hegarty, *A History of Ireland Under the Union, 1801–1922*, London, 1952. There is no full study of the Irish Republican tradition but around the hallowed dates, 1798, 1848, 1867, or names, Tone, Emmet, Lalor, or movements, United Irishmen, Young Irelanders, Fenians, there are clusters of volumes, memoirs, histories, letters, and journals. The place to begin is with *The Autobiography of Theobald Wolfe Tone* (2 vols; edited by R. Barry O'Brien, Dublin, Cork and Belfast, n.d.), and after that there are the limited but germane writings of Lalor, and the more famous Mitchel, or Davitt or the Fenians, particularly John Devoy's *Recollections of an Irish Rebel*, New York, 1929, and the various jail journals and exile reports from Australia and America. One particularly relevant recent volume is Hereward Senior's *Orangeism in Ireland and Britain*, London, 1966; but between the Rising of '98 and the rush toward the Rising of '16, there is a massive literature, which will go unchronicled here. For the period immediately before the 1916 Rising, Pearse is worth while (*Political Writings*, Dublin, 1958), James Connolly is vital (*Socialism and Nationalism*, Dublin, 1948; *Labour and Easter Week*, Dublin, 1949; *The Workers' Republic*, Dublin, 1951; and *Labour in Ireland*, Dublin, n.d.); *see also* C. Desmond Greaves, *The Life and Times of James Connolly*, London, 1961 . Although James Larkin's career is not central to the Republican movement, any more than Connolly's might have seemed before April 1916, Emmet Larkin's *James Larkin, Irish Labour Leader, 1876–1947*, London, 1965, is a most important and revealing study.

For the 1916 Rising, an extended and often amorphous body of literature exists, bloated in each succeeding year by additional journalistic endeavours, further biographies of varying merits on the Sixteen and an occasional real addition. Just before the full onset of the fiftieth anniversary spate of books, Pádraig O Snodaigh's excellent volume on the 1913–1916 Revolutionary movements had a bibliography listing over 350 published items, many multi-volumed or serial; while after the publishing freshet, Francis X. Martin has taken 120 pages in *Studia Hibernia 1967* to analyse the state of recent 1916 studies and the value of the new contributions (*cf.* O Snodaigh in the August 1968 *Cómhar*). Despite all of this activity there is not yet a single authoritative study (*cf.* Desmond Ryan,

The Rising: the Complete Story of Easter Week, Dublin, 1949, and Max Caulfield, *The Easter Rebellion*); and with the British court martial records under a 100-year ban and the interviews of the Irish survivors taken by the Irish government closed off for fifty, the definitive record is unlikely to be forthcoming very soon. Of the new books several are anthologies, including again the results of the Thomas Davis lectures; but perhaps the three most interesting have been Leon Ó Broin's *Dublin Castle and the 1916 Rising*, Dublin, 1966; Breandán Mac Giolla Choille (editor), *Intelligence Notes 1913–1916*, Dublin, 1966; and A. T. Q. Steward, *The Ulster Crisis*, London, 1967. Some excellent short pamphlets also appeared, among them:

> John M. Heuston, OP, *Headquarters Battalion, Easter Week 1916*, Dublin, 1966.
> John de Courcy Ireland, *The Sea and the Easter Rising*, Dublin, 1966.
> Pádraig O Snodaigh, *Ua Rathghaille*, Dublin, 1966.

Two older books are Diarmuid Lynch's (edited by Florence O'Donoghue) *The I.R.B. and the 1916 Rising*, Cork, 1957, and James Stephens' *The Insurrection in Dublin*, Dublin, 1966 (first edition, 1916) which gives the feel of Dublin during April week.

There are really only two volumes attempting to cover the period 1916–1923 for any but commercial purposes. Edgar Holt's *Protest in Arms, The Irish Troubles 1916–1923*, New York, 1961, is based largely on secondary sources, and marred by a rather astigmatic English view of Irish events; nevertheless, it tells an accurate, plain tale of events straight through. The other massive work is Dorothy Macardle's justly famous *The Irish Republic*, New York, 1965, which is heavy on political history and although scrupulously accurate remains the gospel according to Fianna Fáil. The ubiquitous, always interesting Thomas Davis volume, *The Irish Struggle 1916–1926*, London, 1966, edited by Desmond Williams, despite the title contains only a few selections of material after the Treaty. D. J. Goodspeed's "Ireland (1916–1921)" in *Challenge and Response—Studies in International Conflict* is brief but analytical.

If there is no single satisfactory source for 1916–1923, the sum total of the material for such a work is impressive. At some time, in some place, practically inevitably, a study of the Irish Troubles appears: in training pamphlets for the Irgun Zvai Leumi in Palestine in 1946, in French(Yann Morvan Goblet, *L'Irlande dans la crise universelle (1914–1920)*, Paris, 1921), or Italian (Nicola Pascazie, *La rivoluzione d'Irelande e l'Impero Britanice*, Rome, 1934), even the Special Operations Research Office (Washington, D.C.) included Ireland in *Peak Organized Strength of Guerrilla and Government Forces*, admittedly along with Nagaland. Although there are ample and excellent works by or about English participants, by far the most interesting and profitable have been written by the

Irish involved. The *Kerryman* in Tralee has produced a series of anthologies:

Dublin's Fighting Story, 1913–1921, Tralee, n.d.
Kerry's Fighting Story, 1916–1921, Tralee, n.d.
Limerick's Fighting Story, 1913–1921, Tralee, n.d.
Rebel Cork's Fighting Story, 1916–1921, Tralee, n.d.
With the IRA in the Fight for Freedom, 1919 to the Truce, Tralee, n.d.

The best memoirs are by now almost classics in Ireland and include at the top, Ernie O'Malley, *On Another Man's Wound*, London, 1936, Tom Barry, *Guerrilla Days in Ireland*, Dublin, 1949, and Dan Breen, *My Fight for Irish Freedom*, Dublin, 1929. There are several biographies of varying degrees of merit: Florence O'Donoghue's *No Other Law, The Story of Liam Lynch and the Irish Republican Army, 1916–1923*, Dublin, 1954, is excellent; Desmond Ryan's *Seán Treacy and the Third Tipperary Brigade I.R.A.*, Tralee, 1945, is solid. Michael Collins' biographies need up-dating (Piaras Beaslaí, 1926, Frank O'Connor, 1937, even Rex Taylor, 1958; *see* Batt O'Connor, *With Michael Collins in the Fight for Irish Independence*, London, 1929). Studies on the Anglo-Irish war leave much to be desired: Richard Bennett, *The Black and Tans*, London, 1959; James Gleeson, *Bloody Sunday*, London, 1962; and somewhat better Rex Taylor's *Assassination, The Death of Sir Henry Wilson and the Tragedy of Ireland*, London, 1961. Essentially, there has been little solid narrative military history and even less tactical or strategical analysis.

On the political side of the fence much of the work has been biographical although there are exceptions: Frank Pakenham, *Peace by Ordeal*, London, 1962 (*cf.* Frank Gallagher, *The Anglo-Irish Treaty*, London, 1965), the older but solid P. S. O'Hegarty, *The Victory of Sinn Féin*, Dublin, 1924, and Dorothy Macardle. De Valera has been poorly served by his biographies, left between eulogy and spite. Seán Ó'Faoláin's *De Valera*, London, 1939, is surely the most readable but hardly kind. A fine work if not exactly a major Republican source is Ó'Faoláin's own biography, *Vive Moi*, Besten, 1964. During 1968 and 1969, T. P. Ó Néill and P. Ó Fiannachta will fill in a considerable number of the lacunae in Irish political history with the publication of a two-volume authorized biography of de Valera. Lesser, older, but still interesting works on the Republican side are Robert Brennan's *Allegiance*, Dublin, 1950, and Robert Briscoe's (with Alden Hatch) *For the Life of Me*, London, 1958. On the pre-Treaty side, two substantial works are Pádraic Colum's *Arthur Griffith*, Dublin, 1959, and Terence de Vere White's *Kevin O'Higgins*, Tralee, 1966. A most impressive biography of Griffith by Seán Ó Lúing is available only in Irish. Fortunately many of these volumes extend beyond "The Troubles" for after the Treaty Irish history increasingly becomes a matter of oral tradition or limited description of political institutions.

Once the Treaty is signed historical interest, if not personal involvement, ends almost abruptly. There is only a single book on the civil war as a whole, Eoin Neeson, *The Civil War in Ireland, 1921–1923*, Cork, 1966, although O'Donoghue's *No Other Law* is still the prime work. Calton Younger's very solid *Civil War* (London, 1968) starts earlier and extends later. Some of the works on the Tan War lap over into the Civil War and there are a few specific minor sources: Dorothy Macardle, *The Tragedies of Kerry*, Dublin, 1924, and a splendid prison memoir by Peadar O'Donnell, *The Gates Flew Open*, Cork, 1966. Other than the newspapers, filled with inaccurate propaganda and managed news, the only source suddenly becomes human memory and nowhere is this more true than the history of the IRA after the spring of 1923. As a result even the plain tale of Irish events is difficult to follow.

The only works that tend to carry the story to the present are the various biographies. The political sections, though obviously biased, in Donal O'Sullivan's *The Irish Free State and its Senate*, London, 1940, are the only reliable narrative during the 1930s. *The Years of the Great Test 1926– 1939* (edited by Francis MacManus), Cork, 1967, are Thomas Davis Lectures with even less basis in original scholarly research than usual although after 1925 anything is welcome. One area of particular interest to the Republican Movement which has attracted interest is the whole question of partition:

Denis P. Barritt and Charles F. Carter, *The Northern Ireland Problem, A Study in Group Relations*, London, 1962.
William A. Carson, *Ulster and the Irish Republic*, Belfast, n.d.
Frank Gallagher, *The Indivisible Island, The Story of the Partition of Ireland*, London, 1957.
Denis Gwynn, *History of Partition*, 1950.
Benedict Kiely, *Counties of Contention, A Study of the Origins and Implications of the Partition of Ireland*, Cork, 1945.
Labhrás Ó Nualláin, *Ireland Finances of Partition*, Dublin, 1952.
Michael Sheehy, *Divided We Stand*, London, 1955.

Not to mention studies by the Anti-Partition League, counter-blows from Northern Ireland in pamphlet form, and the more restrained analysis in Tuairim pamphlets out of Dublin (*see* Norman Gibson, *Partition Today, A Northern Viewpoint* (Tuairim 2 Pamphlet), Dublin, 1958). A very fine, short study of contemporary Ireland and one of the very few to analyse rather than describe is Ehard Rumpf's *Nationalismus und Sozialismus in Irland*, Hain, 1959. In other areas of politics, particularly the descriptions of the two Irish governments, there is a great deal of work not always too recent nor too germane to the IRA. See J. L. McCracken, *Representative Government in Ireland, Dáil Éireann, 1919–1948*, London, 1958; Nicholas Mansergh, *The Government of Northern Ireland*, London, 1936; and W. W. Moss, *Political Parties in the Irish Free State*, New York, 1933. There was also a rash of books explaining the new Ireland. North and/or South, or Irish neutrality, or often Irish character as well as solid material on Ireland and the Commonwealth which are of minimal value for a study of the IRA.

Remarkably, given the paucity of secondary material for the period, there are two very different, very solid "IRA" works: Peadar O'Donnell's recollections of the Land Annuity campaign in *There Will be Another Day*, Dublin, 1963, and Enno Stephan's *Spies in Ireland*, London, 1963, which makes apparently accurate sense out of a most tricky and difficult affair—German espionage in Ireland, 1939–1944. Two books which by title alone should be of great help, Seán O'Callaghan's *The Jackboot in Ireland*, London, 1958, on the same subject as Stephan's book, and *The Easter Lily, The Story of the I.R.A.*, London, 1956; however, they are romantic fictions, disguised as history. As one reviewer said of the *Easter Lily*, "A worthless book that cannot be recommended on any grounds" (*Irish Independent*, April 6, 1957). He was being kind. Another book on the IRA, Tarlach Ó h-Uid's *Ar Thóir Mo Shealbha* will be largely worthless outside Irish Ireland. The only attempt to write fairly on the IRA as a whole is Coogan's chapter in *Ireland Since the Rising*, but his dramatic and well-written account is marred by extensive errors, which will undoubtedly be corrected in his recently published account of the IRA and Republican Movement. Much of the remaining literature slips down, in size at least, toward the pamphlet level:

Óglaigh, Óglaigh na h-Éireann, Dublin, 1932.
J. McGarrity (Seán Cronin), *Resistance, The Story of the Struggle in British-Occupied Ireland*, Dublin, 1957.
Saor Éire (Organization of Workers and Working Farmers), *Indictment of Capitalism and Parliamentary Parities in Ireland*, Dublin, 1931.
Irish Communist Organization, *The Irish Republican Congress (1934)*, London, n.d.
George Gilmore, *The Irish Republican Congress*, New York, 1935.
Joseph H. Fowler, *Bombs and Their Reverberations With a Consideration Upon Recent Sentences*, London, 1939.
Letitia Fairfield, *The Trial of Peter Barnes*, London, 1953.
Gerald O'Reilly, *They Are Innocent! The Story of the Irish Republican Prisoners*, New York City (1947?).

Some of the pamphlets, broadsheets, flyers, and throw-aways are more the stuff of history than anything else and much of this kind of material contains little novel. Sinn Féin, Cumann na mBan, the IRA, usually as the

Irish Republican Publicity Bureau, not to mention Saor Éire, the Republican Congress, and the rest have at one time or another published a massive flood of interchangeable or easily forgotten or most transient materials. A few pieces such as the Athlone Manifesto or eulogies to martyrs are either basically valuable as documents or else contain some nugget not found elsewhere. Some highly detailed articles by Seamus Ó Mongáin on the IRA in the 1930s and 1940s have appeared in the *United Irishman* during 1968 and 1969, a good step above previous series but still not analytical history. The major Irish political parties, as well as the new white hopes, published much, but with rare, rare exceptions there is little real reference to the IRA. In recent years a series of political profiles first in the *Irish Times* but in time in the *Irish Press* and *Irish Independent* have provided a half-way house to a real political history of modern Ireland. Again the history of the IRA is largely in the memories of men, often men who are not prone to discussion or analysis, who kept the Army's business to themselves and preferred to know as little as possible. Unlike the Fenians, the men of the IRA since 1921 have largely avoided print—with the few exceptions who prove the rule. Consequently at best only a shallow survey of the IRA would be possible if all that remained as evidence was the available published sources: therefore, much of this bibliographical note has only marginal reference to the silent history of the IRA, much of which will undoubtedly remain silent.

After 1969 and the new Northern Troubles, few were silent on Irish matters. Within a few years more was published on the North than had been published on the entire period after 1921. Much of this was instant analysis or narrow polemic and almost all was part of the problem rather than disinterested investigation. See J. Bowyer Bell, "The Chroniclers of Violence in Northern Ireland: The First Wave Interpreted," *The Review of Politics*, vol. 34, no. 2, April 1972, pp. 147-157, and published in *Éire-Ireland*, vol. 7, no. 1, Spring 1972, pp. 28-38. The crisis engendered not only a hasty flood of analysis but a veritable flood of newspapers, broadsheets, flyers, programs, pamphlets, and position papers churned out by those involved (see for example the Officials' *The Starry Plough* from Derry or the Provos' *Republican News* in Belfast). Much of this ephemera has apparently already been lost—with the bombs going off few have time to amass files. There was even a new entry in America with *The Irish People* (New York) somewhat less fleeting than most of the Irish-American publications. The British government kept pace with events in a series of White Papers (or Green as the case might be). And there were memoires and autobiographical exercises ranging from Bernadette Devlin's *The Price of My Soul*, New

York, 1969 through Maria McGuire, *To Take Arms, My Year with the IRA Provisionals,* New York, 1973, to Terence O'Neill's *Autobiography,* London, 1972. Two largely personal examinations of the North are fascinating although for different reasons: Owen Dudley Edwards, *The Sins of Our Fathers: Roots of Conflict in Northern Ireland,* Dublin, 1970, and Conor Cruise O'Brien, *States of Ireland,* New York 1972. And there is not yet even a plain tale of events, for either prejudice enters or events outrun the printing press. The best of the mixed lot is Liam de Paor's *Divided Ulster,* Hardmondsworth, 1970; and for more recent events there is Henry Kelly, *How Stormont Fell,* Dublin, 1972, the *Sunday Times* Insight Team, *Ulster,* Harmondsworth, 1972, and Andrew Boyd, *Brian Faulkner and the Crisis of Ulster Unionism,* Tralee (Co. Kerry), 1972.

There have been several recent contributions to the background of the crisis:

D. G. Boyce, *Englishmen and Irish Troubles, 1918-1922,* Cambridge, 1972
P. Berresford Ellis, *A History of the Irish Working Class,* London, 1972
Robert Kee, *The Green Flag, A History of Irish Nationalism*
Maurice Manning, *The Blueshirts,* Dublin, 1970
John H. Whyte, *Church and State in Modern Ireland, 1923-1970,* Dublin, 1971

The only new work specifically on the Republican Movement is Seán Cronin's *The McGarrity Papers,* Tralee (Co. Kerry), 1972. There have also been several academic works focused on recent Ulster events. The most significant and useful is Richard Rose's *Governing without Consensus, An Irish Perspective,* Boston, 1971, based on extensive polling. See also Ian Budge and Cornelius O'Leary, *Belfast: Approach to Crisis, A Study of Belfast Politics 1613-1970,* New York, 1972, and Rosemary Harris, *Prejudice and Toleration in Ulster: A Study of Neighbours and 'Strangers' in a Border Community,* Towtowa (New Jersey), 1972, and R. S. P. Elliott and John Hickie, *Ulster: a Case Study in Conflict Theory,* London, 1971.

Despite some highly informed gossip and a great deal of sound information, much that has gone on in the Secret Army in the past few years remains secret. There is hope that when Vincent Brown produces his work on the Provos there will be additional light, but at the moment the men on the run have little time for introspective revelation.

Addenda

Although tapering off of late, the enormous spate of books on the Troubles continued after 1972. Some indication of the scope and worth of the material can be found in my "The Chroniclers of Violence in Northern Ireland Revisited: The Analysis of Tragedy", *The Review of Politics,* vol. 36, no. 4, October 1974, pp. 521-543, and in "The Chroniclers of Violence in Northern Ireland: A Tragedy in Endless Acts", *Ibid.,* vol. 38, no. 4, October 1976, pp. 510-533. There has not, however, been a work specifically on the Provisional movement — as Vincent Brown's project aborted — although none of the new and trendy works on the terrorist phenomena throughout the world appear complete without a chapter on the IRA. For the serious, a real contribution has been made by Irish Microfilms Ltd. who preserved on film an enormous collection of material mostly from the Linenhall Library in Belfast: the haphazard press reports, partly papers, pamphlets and broadsheets. For those who prefer a bit more distillation, the three chronologies of events by Richard Deutsch and Vivien Magowan published by the Blackstaff Press are vital. There is, however, to date no single authoritative work on the Ulster Troubles — first because events keep out-running the final chapter and more recently because even the journalists have wearied of the endless tragedy. Still there are ample scripts for the interested. Some detail a single event (the successful Loyalist general strike) or the history of a party (the People's Democracy) all, as always, offer solutions and suggestions. There are popular biographies, dissertations in sociology, memoirs and privately printed exposures. There are some good books and many awful ones, thousands of articles, endless chapters. In all of this, there is not definitive survey of the inside of the Provisionals, although most interesting material has appeared in the London *Sunday Times, Hibernia* and *Fortnight,* as well as in newspaper accounts of various trials.

The problem for the inquisitive is that a secret army in the midst of an armed campaign prefers to remain secret. Thus, even more than in the years before the present Troubles, the only reliable sources are people — and people often reticent to talk at length. Still, over the years I have shuffled in and out of Ireland, regularly talking to a wide variety of people, and often discovering that the more I knew the less I could print. There does not seem to be any academic purpose in listing again those who appear elsewhere, or even others previously missed but now traced down. Outside Ireland, I have run across many of the concerned — often in odd places. Thus, I have been able to speak with Seán McBride in a Boston television studio, with Peter McMullen in a San Francisco jail cell, with Sir Robert Mark of the Metropolitan Police in a Philadelphia hotel, with Paul O'Dwyer in a courthouse and with a variety of transient Republicans in New York. All this research by osmosis has entailed hundreds of people and thousands of hours with results not always readily apparent in the text, but there appears to be no other approach to a secretive army.

INDEX